Christian Counselling
and
Occultism

Christian Counselling and Occultism

The Counselling of the Psychically Disturbed and Those Oppressed through Involvement in Occultism.

A Practical, Theological and Systematic Investigation in the Light of Present Day Psychological and Medical Knowledge.

by

KURT E. KOCH, Th. D.

KREGEL PUBLICATIONS
Grand Rapids, Michigan 49501

Christian Counselling and Occultism is a translation
of the Fifteenth Edition of the German title
SEELSORGE UND OKKULTISMUS published by
Ev. Verlag, 7501 Berghausen/Bd., West
Germany in 1972.

First edition 1972
First American edition.................1973
Reprinted 1978, 1981, 1985

Library of Congress Catalog Card Number 65-23118
ISBN 0-8254-3010-0

Printed in the United States of America

Contents

Foreword by V. Raymond Edman · · · · · · · 9
Preface to the Twenty-first edition . · · · · · · 11

I. Prolegomena

INTRODUCTION TO THE PRINCIPLES
OF INVESTIGATION OF OCCULT PHENOMENA · · 21

THE FORMAL STRUCTURE OF THE STUDY · · · · 25

ON THE PUBLICATION OF CASE HISTORIES
IN THIS BOOK · · · · · · · · · · · · · 30

**II. Pastoral Cases from the Field of Occultism
Considered with a View to the Aim of our Study**

THE SYSTEM FOLLOWED IN THE PRESENTATION
OF THE EXAMPLES · · · · · · · · · · · 34

AN INSIGHT INTO THE SPIRITUAL DISTRESS
ASSOCIATED WITH OCCULT OCCURRENCES · · · 37
1. Extra-sensory Perception (ESP) · · · · · · · 37
   Spiritism · · · · · · · · · · · · · · 37
   a) Apparition of the dead · · · · · · · · 37
   b) Glass moving (Ouijaboard) · · · · · · 39
   c) Table lifting · · · · · · · · · · · 41
   d) Speaking in trance · · · · · · · · · 47
   e) Automatic writing · · · · · · · · · 50

   Hyperaesthesia · · · · · · · · · · · 52
   a) Visionary dreams · · · · · · · · · 52
   b) Telepathy · · · · · · · · · · · · 56
   c) Clairvoyance · · · · · · · · · · · 60
   d) Clairsentience · · · · · · · · · · · 72

Divination 79
a) Card-laying 81
b) Chiromancy, or Palmistry 84
c) Astrology 91
d) Rod and Pendulum 98

2. Extra-sensory Influence (ESI) 113
a) Amateur hypnosis 113
b) Healing magnetism 121
c) Magic charming 125
d) Remote influence (mental suggestion) 142
e) Black and white magic 145
f) Blood pacts 152
g) Fetishism 157
h) Incubi and succubae 162

3. Extra-sensory Apparitions 164
a) Materialization 165
b) Spooks 173

SUMMARY OF THE FREQUENCY RATIOS OBSERVED
IN CONNEXION WITH OCCULT CASES 184

1. Effects on those who exercise Occult Influence 184
a) The end of active occultists 185
b) The curse on the family and descendants 186
c) The development of mediumistic abilities 186

2. Effects on those Subjected to Occult Influence 187

3. Effects at the Place of Action or Dwelling of Occult Practitioners 189

4. Effects on the Counsellor 189

5. Indirect Effects on the Observer of Occult Manifestations . . 191
a) The attitude of protest 191
b) The confusion of opinion due to ignorance, minimization,
and magic with a Christian façade 192

III. A Critical Assessment of the Cases

AN ATTEMPT AT METHODICAL ELIMINATION OF THE
CAUSES OF ERROR IN COLLECTING THE MATERIAL . 195

OCCULT SUBJECTION IN THE LIGHT OF PSYCHIATRY 200

1. Conformity 201
   a) Hallucinations 201
   b) Depressions 202
   c) Compulsive thoughts and delusions 202
   d) Paroxysmal conditions 203
2. Divergence from Psychiatric Patterns 204
3. Contrast with Psychiatric Patterns 206

OCCULT PHENOMENA IN THE LIGHT OF PSYCHOLOGY 207

1. Schmeïng's Study of Folklore, as it applies to "Second Sight" 208
2. Oesterreichs's Studies on Possession 216
3. The Work of M. and W. Prince on the Split Personality . . 221

THE RESULTS OF PSYCHICAL RESEARCH 226

1. The Objectivity of Occult Phenomena 226
   a) The researches of Schrenck-Notzing 226
   b) The experiments of Rhine 227
2. The Dominance of the Subconscious Factors 228
3. Caution against Over-hasty Demon Theories 230
4. The Border Zone of Inexplicable Phenomena 232
   a) Rational explaining away of the phenomena 232
   b) Theories of clairvoyance, as an illustration of the uncertainty
      of rational explanations 233
   c) The theory of the unexplorable residue 241
5. Indication of Transcendence 243
   a) Unreal transcendence 243
   b) Neutral transcendence 244
   c) Biblical transcendence 245
   d) The theory of extra-sensory centres of action 257

OCCULT PHENOMENA IN THE LIGHT OF THE BIBLE . 267

1. The Evidence of the Old Testament 268
   a) Spiritism 268
   b) Divination 268
   c) Magic 269
   d) The place of these phenomena in the theology of the
      Old Testament 269

2. The Evidence of the New Testament 270
   a) The mission of Jesus and the opposition to it 270
   b) The New Testament aspect of the demonic 271
   c) The double character of the "sign" 272
3. Synopsis of the Evidence and Its Evaluation for our Study . . 272

ON THE DIAGNOSIS OF MENTAL DISORDERS DUE TO
OCCULT INVOLVEMENT 275

IV. The Way of Liberation from Occult Subjection

THE CONTRIBUTION OF THE PSYCHOLOGICAL
BORDER SCIENCES 280

1. Definition and Distinction of the Individual Fields . . . 280
2. The Trans-psychological Reality of Christian Counselling . . 285
3. The Medical and Theological Aspects of Liberation from Occult
   Subjection 291

SPIRITUAL GUIDANCE IN THE LIGHT OF THE
NEW TESTAMENT 293

1. The Foundations for Pastoral Care of those Occultly Subjected 294
2. Personal Qualifications for Pastoral Care of those Occultly
   Subjected 296
   a) The spiritual life of the counsellor 296
   b) The equipment of the counsellor 300
   c) The personal attitude of the counsellor 303
3. Pastoral Guidance of Those Occultly Subjected 305
   a) The differential diagnosis of mental disorders . . . 306
   b) Confession 308
   c) Renunciation of the devil 312
   d) Absolution 315
   e) The spiritual struggle 319
   f) The resistance of the liberated 325

WHAT PERSPECTIVES MAY BE GAINED FOR THOSE
WHO MINISTER TO THE OCCULTLY SUBJECTED? . . 333

1. The Urgent Need for Special Pastoral Help for the Subjected 333
2. The Necessity of a Clear Diagnosis 335
3. The Relation of Law and Gospel 335
4. Christ, the End of the Demons 338

Foreword

One of the least known aspects of the Christian life, and therefore among the least understood, is that of spiritual warfare. Most Christians are quite familiar with basic factors such as regeneration, newness of life in Christ, the Spirit filled life, the fruit of the Spirit, and witnessing for Christ; but it seems that relatively few are familiar with the mortal combat between light and darkness, between God and Satan. In this book, *Christian Counselling and Occultism,* Dr. Kurt E. Koch makes a significant contribution.

The Bible abounds in references to spiritual warfare. There is an Enemy, variously described as "the prince of this world," "the god of this world," Satan, the Adversary, the Accuser of the brethren, and the like. We are warned not to be ignorant of his devices. Satan and his hosts are dreadfully real. From the Bible account it seems that these are highly organized in various ranks: principalities, powers, rulers of the darkness of this world, spiritual wickedness in high places (Ephesians 6:12). The Christian is provided with armour, which when used in its entirety enables him to stand against "the wiles of the devil." The manifestation of demonic forces is not readily believed by some and is wholly ignored by others, yet there are such manifestations as mediums, levitations, automatic writing, voices, clairvoyance, card-laying, palmistry, astrology, magic, both black and white, books such as the falsely called sixth and seventh books of Moses, fetishes, demon possession and the like.

Out of his wide pastoral and evangelistic ministry, Dr. Koch presents the facts on satanic warfare against the people of God. With objectivity he faces the possibility of natural explanations given by psychologists and psychiatrists, and shows their insufficiency in many areas. He is deeply taught in the Scriptures and knows by experience the adequacy of the Christian's armour: the girdle of truth, the breastplate of righteousness, the shoes of the Gospel, the shield of faith, the helmet of salvation, the sword of the Spirit, and in particular, the weapon of all-prayer in the Spirit.

Dr. Koch's ministry has been largely confined to the Continent of Europe, but he has lectured also extensively in other parts of the world, particularly in North America. His ministry has proved to be very informative and enlightening to many Christians. While this volume is designed primarily to help pastors and Christian workers in their counselling and ministry to those who are oppressed or possessed by demonic powers, it will prove to be very helpful to every earnest believer in Christ. Dr. Koch has lectured in such evangelical centers as Fuller Theological Seminary, Mount Hermon Bible Conference, Moody Bible Institute, and Wheaton College. Invitations have also come to him from Westmont College, Biola in Los Angeles, Trinity College, and Waterloo University. In the same way the doors of large churches such as Calvary Baptist Church in New York, the Church of the Open Door, the First Presbyterian Church of Hollywood and others have been opened to the author's ministry.

Dr. Koch has also lectured and promoted lively discussions at numerous universities all over the world, as for example in Buenos Aires, Johannesburg, Brisbane and Sidney in Australia, Tokio, Seoul, Manila, Palmerston in New Zealand, Madras, Bangkok, and European towns such as London, Manchester, Berlin, Zürich, Paris, Cologne, Munich and Heidelberg etc.

These invitations indicate the very acuteness of the problem of occultism among Christians in the world today.

I have been personally greatly helped and instructed by the ministry of the author.

V. Raymond Edman

Chancellor
Wheaton College
Wheaton, Illinois

Preface to the Twenty-First Edition

The number of editions this book has passed through is an indication of how acute the problem of occultism and the Christian faith is today.

Current events are reaching a feverish pitch. The red apocalyptic rider is sweeping through the earth. Governments stand aghast at the political chaos appearing in the world.

The explosion of the world's population gives mankind at most only another hundred years. World-wide famine is already looming on the horizon.

With its pollution of the atmosphere and the seas, the human race will soon have signed its own death warrant.

From the moral standpoint a similar picture pervades. While drugs and pot are breaking like a wave over the youth of today, a spread of sexual licentiousness is robbing man of all his self-control.

Evil spiritual forces under the guise of spiritism, occultism, demonism and Satanism are increasing steadily and seeking to enslave mankind.

Is there then still hope?

The crying need of our time is for charismatic counselling

There is much talk today in Christian circles concerning charismata or spiritual gifts. A number of charismatic movements have in fact sprung up. Although the question as to whether they are really genuine or only pseudo movements of God's Spirit cannot be dealt with here, the book will at least attempt to supply some of the answers. At present, however, I would like to refer to just one problem, that of possession.

During the Second World War a young woman working as a telephone operator became intimately involved with a German S. S. officer. As the tide of war began to turn against Hitler, the officer became obsessed with the idea of subscribing himself to the devil with his own blood. This he finally did together with the girl. Some time after this he committed suicide, but the girl, surviving the war, took up a job again working in a telephone exchange. At a mission which was subsequently held in her town the young woman decided to become a Christian. Immediately a terrific battle began to take place within her. On visiting the evangelist he asked her if they might pray together. As he started to pray, however, she fell on the floor unconscious, almost as if in a spiritistic trance. It was then that a male voice began to call out of her, "Leave her alone! Leave her alone! She belongs to me."

The evangelist addressed the voice, "In the name of Jesus tell me who you are!"

"I'm an S.S. officer", the voice replied. "She has subscribed herself to the devil and so she must come to where I am. We belong together."

With that her counsellor commanded the powers to come out of her in the name of Jesus.

If the woman had visited a psychiatrist, in spite of his qualifications he would have been quite unable to help her. More than likely he would have diagnosed her complaint as some form of hysteria. Psychiatrists usually deny the very existence of possession, thus aligning themselves with non-Christian psychologists and modern liberal theologians. Such phenomena are banished by most people to the realm of mental illness; a terrible mistake to make.

The New Testament both recognises and clearly distinguishes between ordinary physical illness and possession. In Matt. 4:24 we read, "And they brought to him all the sick, those afflicted with various diseases and pains, demoniacs, epileptics and paralytics, and he healed them all." Similarly Mark writes in Mk. 1:32—34, "They brought to him all who were sick or possessed with demons... And he healed many who were sick with various diseases, and cast out many demons."

The symptoms of mental illness and possession are clearly distinguishable. In my book "Occult Bondage and Deliverance" I have listed eight characteristics of possession. I will merely refer here briefly to two of these: the clairvoyant powers of the one possessed, and the transference of demons from people to animals.

Clairvoyance is mentioned in Mk. 1:24 for example. Jesus had only just started out on his public ministry and as yet even his disciples had not recognised that he was the Messiah. The possessed person, however, recognised at once that he was the Son of God.

The transference of demons to animals is recorded in Mk. 5:13. Bultmann has described this account as a "terrible story" since he could attach no meaning to it whatsoever. A phenomenon of this nature is completely unintelligible from the psychiatric point of view, even though it is admitted today that animals can suffer from various kinds of neuroses.

Rationalists are therefore unable to differentiate between mental illness and possession for they lack the spiritual antennae needed for this task. Instead, one must turn to the charismatically gifted Christian counsellor, but, let it be said, a psychiatric training is nevertheless of immense value to such a counsellor.

It must be pointed out that there is an equally erroneous extreme to which certain people run. While the medical profession on the whole denies the existence of demon possession, certain primitive religious groups attribute almost everything which they cannot understand to the devil. For example, there are some who maintain that all a man's bad traits are the result of demon activity and that the demons must be exorcized before deliverance from sin can take place. Such people, therefore, seek in their religious eccentricity to drive out demons of pride, demons of anger, demons of fear, demons of immorality and the like. The immediate result, however, on the person they are seeking to help is to leave in a state far worse than the first.

It is imperative to seek a sound balance between these two extremes of on the one hand denying the very existence of the demonic and on the other hand of demonising everything.

The present wave of drug addiction cries out for charismatic authority

A senior police officer told me in Seattle that research has shown that in 1971 some 70 % of the town's youth are affected by drugs. Since 1960 when there was not a single registered drug addict in the town, the number of addicts has multiplied at an almost unbelievable rate. Is there any hope for these victims of narcotics?

Through my frequent visits to the United States I have met numerous young people both desiring and seeking deliverance from drugs. The following are two examples.

A young man tried to get help from the organisation called 'Teen Challenge'. At first it seemed as if he had really found deliverance from his addiction. He had been prayed over with the laying on of hands and had received the so-called gift of speaking in tongues. Immediately he had been freed from his drug addiction. For the following four months he had revelled in this new experience, but then he had lost his gift of tongues and slipped back into his old ways. He had therefore not been really delivered — it had only been a form of transference, and this in the long run is never a genuine help.

The second example concerns a young man named Daniel whom I met in Pennsylvania. He had left home earlier in life and lived among some Hippies with a girl he had picked up. In order to obtain the drugs that he wanted he had resorted to begging and stealing. Yet he found no real satisfaction in life. He would have willingly given up his way of life if only the drugs had not had such a hold on him. But at this time One who was stronger than drugs stepped into his life. One night Daniel had been picked up by a young Christian friend. Round about midnight they had found themselves held up in a traffic jam resulting from an accident. While they were waiting the Christian told him the story of Nicodemas and how he had come to Jesus one night. Turning to Daniel he asked, "Do you want to meet him tonight too? Why not stop living in the dark and come to Jesus now?"

God's hour had come. Daniel confessed his sins there and then and found forgiveness through Christ.

But his problems were not yet at an end. When he had told his girl friend of his conversion she left him at once. He next decided to return home, but on meeting his parents and informing them that he had become a Christian they too refused to have anything to do with him and turned him out of the house. "You dragged our name through the mud by living like a tramp so now you can go and look after yourself", they retorted.

For Daniel, the start of his Christian life was not easy. However, when he approached his sister she allowed him to stay with her instead. His next task was to find a job, and this he did and was soon supporting himself.

To avoid isolation he started also to look for a group of Christians with whom he could meet. Finding a sound biblically based church he joined it, and soon the one time Hippie at the pastor's request was engaged in the work amongst the youth, a job he is still doing today. It was when I visited the church in order to hold a series of meetings there that I met Daniel and heard his story. His faith had stood the test. There had been no backsliding, no returning to his previous ways.

Daniel's deliverance was no 'transference' as in the first example. There are both genuine and pseudo forms of deliverance, and to distinguish between them one needs the gift of discernment — the Holy Spirit who leads into all truth.

Psychically and emotionally disturbed people need charismatic guidance

During this century a number of movements have arisen which are basically psychical in nature, almost like psychical epidemics. Psychologically speaking this fact is quite understandable. Following a period of dry rationalism the pendulum often swings to the opposite extreme. Confusion only arises when these psychical movements are described with scriptural adjectives and regarded as movements of God's Spirit. Let me illustrate what I mean by this.

One of my friends, the Christian psychologist M. Chabrerie of Strassbourg, found himself in 1940 at a teachers' seminary in Perigueux in the

South of France. While he was there God sent a revival amongst the students.

When this happened, quite without warning a woman, a member of a rather fanatical religious sect, appeared on the scene. Declaring herself to be a 'prophetess' she went on to tell new converts, "Conversion is not enough. God wants to give you more. Let me lay hands on you and pray for you that you may receive the gift on the Holy Spirit and speak in tongues as in the Acts of the Apostles."

The young student teachers were faced with a difficult problem. "Is she right or is she not? The New Testament doesn't seem to mention a case of the Holy Spirit being given through a woman laying her hands on people. Didn't we receive the Holy Spirit at our conversion? Isn't it only through the Holy Spirit that a person can call Jesus Lord?"

About two thirds of the teachers rejected the woman' offer. The remaining ten or twelve, however, allowed her to lay hands on them in order to receive the Holy Spirit. In this way they received the gift of speaking in tongues.

This took place in 1940. Later Professor Chabrerie was able to recount the interesting sequel to the story. "Of all the students who received the gift of tongues from the woman," he said, "not one of them is still living the Christian life today. True, they revelled in their experience at first, but later they backslid into the world. On the other hand, the students who resisted the woman's claims are all still actively engaged in Christian work."

Such an outcome of the so-called reception of the Holy Spirit occurs not so infrequently as some people would like to imagine. A parallel example can be quoted from Japan.

About ten years ago a group of eighteen missionaries drawn from various missionary societies decided to hold a week of prayer together at the town of Toyama in Japan. Their aim, an aim I could have subscribed to myself, was to be re-equipped by the Holy Spirit for the tasks He had given them to do.

As the week progressed, however, a certain tendency towards extremism started to creep into their prayers. Basing their requests on the verse, "The Kingdom of Heaven suffers violence, and men of violence take it by force", the missionaries began to demand that God should bless them. Instead of submitting themselves to the power of the Holy Spirit they wanted the Holy Spirit within their own power.

Well, what was the outcome of this time of seeking the Lord? After a few days the missionaries suddenly found themselves speaking in 'new tongues'. They were overjoyed. This was the renewal they had been seeking.

Returning to their congregations they began to preach their new experience, urging the people to seek for 'more', especially for the gift of tongues which, they said, was the sign that they had been baptised in the Holy Spirit.

The Japanese Christians were utterly perplexed, and a number of them began to oppose the new teaching the missionaries were trying to introduce. Cutting a long but tragic story short, 15 of the missionaries later not only lost their experience but also forsook their missionary calling and returned to secular occupations. Another of the men, the missionary from whom I had first heard the story, died within the next two years, while the remaining two missionaries were only able to continue with their work after they had renounced their Toyama experience. Thus, out of a total of 18 Christians who received the gift of speaking in tongues, 15 made shipwreck of their faith, one died and the two remaining only continued with their missionary activities after they had renounced their 'baptism of the Holy Spirit'.

We must never confuse a psychical upheaval with a revival based on the Word of God. Yet having said all this the truth concerning the genuine gifts of the Spirit as mentioned in 1 Cor. 12 remains untouched. We are not striving here against the Holy Spirit but rather against the psychical or sometimes demonic counterparts of the devil.

Our chief aim as Christians is that our bodies become the temples of the Holy Spirit and that Christ should live in our hearts by faith. It is He who should be the decisive power at work within us, and our task is, as Paul wrote in Eph. 5:18, to "be being filled with the Holy Spirit."

Mediumistic faculties must not be confused with charismatic gifts

The problem of distinguishing between mediumistic and charismatic gifts is fraught with many difficulties. Mediumistic gifts are in fact the devil's counterparts to the gifts of the Holy Spirit. It is as if Satan has invented a counterfeit for every charismatic gift of the Spirit, although this statement must be regarded from the spiritual rather than the scientific point of view.

Mediumistic gifts can either be inherited, transferred, or acquired through dabbling with the occult. These powers cannot be regarded as neutral forces of nature stemming from the subconscious, but rather the direct result of either one's own or one's ancestors' sins of sorcery. Yet having said this, a narrow band of harmless neutral mediumism does actually exist as the present book seeks to point out.

People are often quite unconscious of their mediumistic abilities all their lives, or at least for the major part of them. The question arises, therefore, as to what effect conversion has on these gifts or faculties.

Many inexperienced or dogmatic Christian workers maintain that a person's mediumistic powers automatically disappear when he or she becomes a Christian. However, my own experience, which stretches back now for over 40 years, I have found that in as many as 50% of cases mediumistic gifts survive conversion. This is a source of great danger to a person's Christian life. If one subsequently discovers, therefore, that one is in possession of mediumistic powers, one is duty bound to ask God to remove them and to replace them with the gifts of the Holy Spirit.

This confusion results in many tragic errors being made, and it can be quite catastrophic when a person with mediumistic powers only discovers them after he or she has become a Christian then mistakes them for genuine gifts of the Holy Spirit. One can think of several well-known Christian workers where this has actually been the case.

For example, a well-known evangelist at the World Congress on Evangelism at Berlin described how he had been in possession of his gift of healing since childhood. This in itself was proof that his gift was mediumistic and not charismatic.

There is a fundamental difference: charismatic or spiritual gifts are received after conversion; natural or mediumistic gifts are either inherited or acquired through dabbling in sorcery. Gifts of the Holy Spirit can never be inherited.

There is much confusion abroad today concerning this fact. No end of spiritual healers and so-called prophets are arising from within the extremist religious groups claiming that their mediumistic powers are gifts of the Holy Spirit. Many of their followers are in this way being led into serious error. To build one's faith on albeit disguised mediumistic powers is not to be guided by the Holy Spirit but rather to be led by the spirit of error, extremism and fanaticism. Yet thousands and thousands of people are falling into this dangerous trap.

When genuine gifts of the Holy Spirit come face to face with their religiously disguised mediumistic counterparts, however, it is the Holy Spirit who triumphs and not the mediumistic powers. There are some wonderful examples which illustrate this fact.

In Acts 16:16—18, the apostle Paul came face to face with a young clairvoyant at Philippi. The girl was possessed with a spirit of divination and following Paul would cry out, "These men are servants of the Most High God, who proclaim to you the way of salvation." Why was Paul so disturbed? What the girl was saying was indeed true. With a testimony like that she might easily today have risen to the position of a deaconess or even pastor in a church!

The apostle, however, possessed the gift of discernment and so, turning to the girl, he said, "I charge you in the name of Jesus Christ to come out of her you unclean spirit!"

Here we see a confrontation between mediumism and the Holy Spirit. There was no question as to who held the upper hand.

My work has over the years often led me into the very centres of such spiritual conflicts. One of the most notorious healers the Western world has known this century spoke once in a town in Western Germany. Together with some praying friends I decided to attend one of his meetings. As we sat there during the service we began to pray, "Lord Jesus, if this man is working for you then bless his ministry and use him. If, however, he is opposing your work then hinder his ministry tonight."

That evening the man was completely unable to work. In the end he declared to those present, "I can't do anything tonight, there are some counter-forces at work in the meeting tonight."

How could the ministry of a man of God be hindered by the prayers of his fellow Christians? Such prayers should only serve to bless his ministry.

The earlier history of the evangelist I have just mentioned, however, is only too well-known to me. He comes from a markedly mediumistic background which has resulted in the fact that his ministry has been accompanied by a whole array of spiritistic phenomena.

A number of theologians, particularly those without any true counselling experience of their own, would maintain that mediumistic powers can be cleansed and later used in the service of God. This notion, however, must also be strongly opposed. For the apostle Paul there was only one solution: "Come out of her you unclean spirit!" Any gift which carries with it the odour of occultism can never be cleansed for use in the Kingdom of Heaven. The only course open to a person is that of deliverance followed by the receiving of an entirely different type of equipment, namely, the gifts and the power of the Holy Spirit.

The confusion around us today cries out for charismatic counsellors. These counsellors, therefore, must be genuine spiritually gifted Christians and not religiously disguised spiritistic mediums.

The purpose of the present book is to investigate both soberly and factually the whole question of this extremely involved subject. An indication of its success in accomplishing this task is revealed by the fact of the many editions through which the book has passed, as well as by the number of languages into which it has been translated. For those wishing to obtain further copies of both this and other works of the author the following addresses are given:

in German: Ev. Verlag, 7501 Berghausen, West Germany;

in Spanish: CLIE, Moragas Barrett, 113 Tarrasa, Spain;

in French: Institute Biblique 'Emmaus', Lausanne, Switzerland;

in English: Ev. Verlag, 7501 Berghausen, West Germany,
        Kregel Publications, Box 2607, Grand Rapids, Michigan 49501, USA.

Is there then still hope? Such was the question we asked as we began this forward. Yes, there is a lot of hope, hope of genuine deliverance and salvation through the Lord Jesus Christ, the crucified, risen, ascended and returning Lord.

The author

No created spirit can penetrate
the innermost parts of nature
— *Nikolai*

The natural man does not receive
the gifts of the Spirit of God
— I Cor. 2, 14

The Spirit searches everything
— I Cor. 2, 10

The spiritual man judges all things
— I Cor. 2, 15

PART I

Prolegomena

Chapter One

INTRODUCTION TO THE PRINCIPLES OF INVESTIGATION OF OCCULT PHENOMENA

"Our age is to an outstanding measure an age which has lost its security". In these words Prof. Köberle has summed up his diagnosis of the time in which we live.[1] This loss of security in human existence, due at it is to the sinister aspects of present day world politics, to the economic problems, to unemployment, to the problems of population, food shortage, marriage crises, race, inequality of opportunity, and so on, is the background and fertile hotbed for neuroses of every kind. Experts are actually speaking of a plague of neuroses, a mental epidemic. This epidemic of neuroses has assumed such proportions that in the journal of the German Gesellschaft für Psychotherapie und Tiefenpsychologie, whose president is Prof. von Weizsäcker of Heidelberg, it is stated that there is a shortage of four thousand psychotherapists in Germany, since one specialist with psychotherapeutic training is needed per 10,000 head of the population.[2]

[1] cf. Adolf Köberle, "Glaube oder Aberglaube" in *"Schrift und Bekenntnis"*, Furche-Verlag 1950, pp. 106f.
[2] Programmschrift der deutschen Gesellschaft für Psychotherapie und Tiefenpsychologie: "Psychosomatische Medizin" by Dr. Dr. med. Bitter, Ärzte-Verlag, Giessen.

This epidemic of neuroses, with which the psychotherapist is faced, has its counterpart on the pastoral level in the *flood of psychological disturbances* which has swelled up in the post-war years, and in many observed instances stands in a noteworthy frequency ratio to the increase in occult practices. "Insecure" man seeks in every way to escape from his haunting uncertainty about the fate of his loved ones, about his health, or the threat of the future, or his job, and consequently he takes recourse to advice and help from occult manipulations. The frequency ratio between psychological disturbance and occult activity will be investigated in this study.

As we approach this problem, we must first clarify two basic principles of our investigation. These are the material *investigation principle*, in short the material principle; and the formal *principle of classification*, in short the formal principle. With regard to our use of these terms, we request that they be understood independently of similar formulations in the fields of philosophy, psychology, and, above all, theology. The material principle of our study has reference to the exact investigation of the nature of occult phenomena, carried out with the help of every scientific means. The formal principle has reference to the form in which the occult practice is applied, to its basic premise, and to its spiritual plane. The psychical researcher, the psychologist and the doctor will be almost exclusively interested in the material principle, i. e. the question of the scientific elucidation of the phenomena within the framework of anthropology and natural science. The theologian and pastor, however, will also be interested in the formal principle i. e. the classification of the phenomena in theology and the history of ideas. To illustrate with a practical example: the question that concerns the psychologist is whether or not a series of so-called occult phenomena can be explained as "dissociation artifacts"[3], as artificially produced disintegration phenomena. The pastor, besides being concerned with this, will also, for instance, be interested in the question of the difference between magic conjuration in a tridemonic name or in the name of the Holy Trinity, and neutral conjuration by means of hetero- or auto-suggestion. He will be especially interested in the question of the spiritual significance of magic conjuration practice.

Of importance is the *relation* of the two principles of research to each other. We cannot answer the question of which has the greater significance, since both the scientist and the theologian will be biased in their evaluation, and no existential question can be answered from a neutral

---

[3] cf. Hans Bender, "Psychische Automatismen. Zur Experimentalpsychologie des Unterbewußten und der außersinnlichen Wahrnehmung". Inaugural address at Freiburg, 1936, Verlag J. A. Barth, Leipzig, p. V.

standpoint. From the theological point of view we must state the following:

1. An exact medical and psychological investigation of so-called occult phenomena is an indispensable pre-supposition for the theologian's assessment.

2. When faced with unsolved problems, there is no justification for recourse to the supernatural as long as we can offer valid possibilities of rational explanation. God has given us an intellect and expects us to use it. In addition to the gift of reason He has told us in Gen. 1,28 to have dominion over the earth and to explore all its domains. Over-hasty recourse to occult explanations is a flight into the magical and a departure from the will of the Creator, a repudiation of the senses and mental powers He has entrusted to us.

3. Theology has nothing to fear from exact scientific research into occult phenomena in the field of para-psychology. Her own task of defining the relation of occult phenomena to God remains untouched by the information which science can uncover in this realm. The problems of the formal principle lie on an entirely different, higher plane, than the problems of the material principle.

4. On the contrary, theology has much to gain from exact scientific work in this field. The more scientific research discloses of the occult, the sooner, it may be hoped, will pastoral counselling be delivered from the narrow, legalistic attitude sometimes adopted towards those who confess to being involved in these matters.

5. Science should not, for its part, close its mind to new aspects of reality in an attitude of a priori negativism, when all possibilities of a rational explanation have been explored.

In order to formulate the relation between the material principle and the formal principle in our explanation of occult phenomena, in other words the relation between the principles of strict scientific research and those of the theological, ideological and spiritual viewpoint and criteria, we may use the concept of *different layers*. This term does not mean, as in medicine[4], the interrelation of the mental and organic processes, the co-ordination of psychological and organic components in a disease-pattern, but here refers rather to the different dimensional levels at which the problem is being considered. At the base is the scientific research, which classifies into various scientific categories; the superstructure is the theo-

---

[4] German "Überlagerung": cf. Prof. Viktor von Weizsäcker, "Fälle und Probleme", in Anthropologische Vorlesungen in der med. Klinik, Enke-Verlag, Stuttgart, 1947, p. 29.

logical analysis, the ethical and religious evaluation. The separation of the two fields is, however, not possible without diminishing the results of the research, since both sides represent aspects of truth. The doctor, the psychologist and the psychical researcher on their part, and the philosopher and the theologian on theirs, do well to co-operate. Perhaps the achievement of such an effort of co-operation would fulfil, at least in one area, the wish of Professor von Weizsäcker. In his anthropological lectures he writes:[5]

"In the 16th and 17th centuries, science broke loose from theology and the Church. In the 18th and 19th centuries, science and medicine separated themselves from philosophy. These are the ruptures of reason to which I refer... We hope to learn that psychology can provide help in repairing these ruptures of reason, and in reconciling the alienated brothers."

Having now set forth our two basic principles, we must in a few words indicate the starting point and the character of the investigation. The present study was born out of practical experience. Experience is the mother, theory the child, of this treatise. Such a foundation is basically the route which leads to every branch of knowledge except for theology, which, since it starts out from revelation, is founded upon a transcendent reality. What we call science had its primary origin in the contemplation of the cosmos. It is, therefore, in the last analysis only a derivative of the empirical world, an abstraction and logical classification of that which, in creation and historical development, is recognized as conforming to laws.

This foundation in practical experience gives rise to two requirements:

1. The factual data which pastoral experience reveals in the sphere of occult phenomena must be studied dispassionately and with care for its objective truth content.

2. We must guard the empirical data from two extremes: firstly a priori negativism, and secondly, an inordinate belief in occultism. This is the warning of Prof. Bender (loc. cit.[3], p. VI). In similar vein is the treatment of this matter by Hans Driesch in his introduction to para-psychology.[6] He erects two fronts: first, against the gullibility which takes the easy way out and accepts even what cannot be checked as genuine; second, against those rigid dogmatists who, in their traditional opposition to all that is metaphysical, categorially deny the possibility of new discoveries being made. We might also add to these two groups

---

[5] loc. cit. p. 42—43.
[6] cf. Hans Driesch, "Parapsychologie. Die Wissenschaft von den 'okkulten' Erscheinungen. Methodik und Theorie", Bruckmann-Verlag, München, 1932, p. 4.

the gullibility of some Christian groups, who, in a gross oversimplification of the problem, attribute to the devil everything they do not understand.

These two principles of research, with their clarification of the limits of competence and their caution against a priori assertions of a rationalistic, occultist, or religious nature, will help us to avoid uninformed statements, tragic misinterpretations and unjustified assumptions in the course of our study.

Chapter Two

THE FORMAL STRUCTURE OF THE STUDY

1. As stated above, the *impulse* behind the study of the present theme arose from practical experience. Fifteen years of evangelistic ministry at home and abroad have given me a startling insight into mental disorders, some of which belonged to the field of the medical specialist, but which in many cases involved occult practices. For years I have recorded and collected the most severe and unusual instances of such disorders. The "pressing spiritual problem"[7] of those seeking help led me to select from this mass of material some six hundred cases of occult subjection, and to submit them to critical scrutiny and evaluation. The impulse for this undertaking was strengthened by the encouragement of a number of colleagues, who were often at a complete loss in treating those who were involved in occult participation.

2. The *purpose* of this study is to represent a special concern of practical theology: the giving of help to those who are psychologically disturbed as a result of occult activity. My experience in counselling those with this sort of problem reveals that this particular kind of counselling does not consist merely in extending words of encouragement, sympathy and comfort; rather it is a matter of really freeing those occultly subjected from the shackles of mental constriction and the compulsion of inexplicable forces.

To state our aim still more clearly we must say that we are not concerned solely with the restoration to health of those who are mentally ill, as are the methods of modern medicine[8], but we are concerned to lead the afflicted person to the great liberator, Jesus Christ.[9]

---

[7] C. G. Jung, "Die Beziehungen der Psychotherapie zur Seelsorge", Rascher Verlag, Zürich, 1948, p. 5.

[8] Dr. med. Lechler, "Seelische Erkrankungen und ihre Heilung", Steinkopf Verlag, Stuttgart, 1940, p. 99.

[9] A. Maeder, "Wege zur seelischen Heilung", Rascher Verlag, Zürich, 1948, pp. 23-24.

3. The *problem* of our study is threefold:

(a) Firstly, we must establish that this so-called occult subjection exists.

(b) Further, we must discuss the still much-debated relation between occult subjection and mental illness.

(c) Finally, there is the very urgent problem, whether those occultly subjected can be helped decisively by the pastor, or whether the pastor must confess himself powerless before such a task, and hand every mentally disturbed person over to the specialist.

4. Out of this group of problems, we may summarize the various *tasks* of our study:

(a) By means of a large number of examples from pastoral experience, we must give an insight into occult subjection, so as to show the *consequences* of participation in occult activities.

(b) We cannot evade an investigation into the *causes* of occult subjection, for without a clear knowledge of the roots of mental disorders no help or cure is possible. Just as the pre-requisite of any medical treatment is a penetrating and accurate diagnosis,[10] so it is indispensable for the Christian counsellor to consider the background of mental disorders in relation to occult activity."[11]

(c) Then, further, we must seek a way of liberation from occult subjection. That is the specific pastoral concern at the centre of all the other, lesser tasks we have to pursue.

5. The *method* of treating these problems has already been indicated. First, we shall set out from the human side, from pastoral experience, and then we shall list the results of practical observation. This procedure is the way of induction, i. e. from the specific instances a general principle is constructed. If we wanted to explain the method in terms of medicine, we would say:

(a) By comparison of many background histories, the typical symptoms and laws are worked out — we may call this the *pathognomy* of mental disorders arising because of occult subjection.

(b) At the same time it is possible, by this comparison of many case-histories, to draw conclusions as to the ultimate causes of these parti-

[10] Th. Brugsch, "Lehrbuch der inneren Medizin", Verlag Urban und Schwarzenberg, Berlin, Vienna, 1941, vol. 2, p. 1454.

[11] C. G. Jung makes the following accusation against pastors: "In general the pastor lacks the knowledge which would enable him to penetrate into the psychological background of illnesses", (loc. cit [1] p. 14).

cular mental conditions. In other words, a clear picture is gained of the *pathogenesis* of occult subjection. The ultimate dark background of these mental complications becomes evident.

(c) For the man who takes the New Testament as his guide, there will now arise out of the confused picture of the origin of these mental conditions a clear point of approach for the pastoral treatment of occult subjection. From the position gained by the empirical method, we shall seek a pastoral *therapy* for the occultly subjected.

6. The *arrangement* of our study is according to the various fields to be investigated. In the first part, the pastoral problem of occult subjection is shown by means of 120 examples drawn from pastoral experience. In the second part, the contributions of bordering sciences are adduced, in order to carry out a critical examination of these cases. Above all, the particular mental conditions which the evangelist comes to recognize as resulting from occult subjection, must be confronted with the cross-fire of medical scientific criticism. With regard to these mental disorders, we must determine the relation between medical and theological research. In clarifying knotty problems we may make additional use of the guidance afforded by the contributions of psychological and psychical research. After taking these bordering sciences into account, the theological position must then be determined for the evaluation of mental disturbances of occult origin. The third part is devoted to the question of actual pastoral ministry. Here we concern ourselves with the means of liberation from occult subjection. Here we must rightly evaluate firstly the contribution of psychotherapy, before the New Testament findings are introduced. Finally, we present the particular contribution of Christian pastoral counselling.

7. The *title* of the book arises from the pastoral question which is our concern. Almost everywhere, but especially in South Germany, Switzerland and Austria, the evangelist meets in his personal counselling many cases of mental disorders, which are often connected with occult subjection. It is from this abundance of special pastoral problems that we draw our sub-title: "The counselling of the psychically disturbed and those oppressed through involvement in occultism". We must carefully define four terms in this subtitle, in order to avoid misunderstanding.

(a) When we speak of *"counselling"* or *"pastoral care"*[12a], we are not referring to any form of medical treatment, like a psychotherapeutic

12a German "seelsorgerliche Behandlung".

consultation[12b], but to pastoral care conducted on New Testament principles.

(b) The meaning of the expression "*occult*" is the subject of some debate. Hans Driesch opposes the use of the term in the foreword of his book "Parapsychologie. Die Wissenschaft von den 'okkulten' Erscheinungen. Methodik und Theorie". He writes: "With the mystic, irrational tendencies of the present day, para-psychology has no connection. Para-psychology is a science fully as much as chemistry and geology are sciences... Its work is entirely rational... Para-psychology stands in the service of genuine enlightenment... Therefore we should leave off calling it 'occultism'".

Recent researchers, however, in spite of this protest from a professional source, have continued to use the term. Thus Tischner, in his book "Ergebnisse okkulter Forschung", Holmsten with "Okkultismus", Baerwald in his publication "Okkultismus und Spiritismus", and many other writers.

The term "occult" is moreover not unequivocal. That which the uninitiated and the psychologically unschooled would regard without hesitation as occult, can still be rationally understood and explained by the depth-analyst.

In our use of the term "occult" in this study we intend, despite the ambiguity of the concept, to designate thereby the border-zone of sense experience, i. e. those phenomena which on a rational plane we can hardly believe, manifestations which reach over into the metaphysical and metapsychical sphere, relationships between the sensory and the supersensual realm.

(c) The third term which we must define somewhat is "*involvement*" with occult things. The term "involvement" includes both active experimentation with occult practices, and passive reception of occult influence. Both active and passive participation, involvement whether as subject or object in the occult realm, create the condition of occult subjection, with the pastoral care of which we are here concerned.

(d) Finally, we must deal with the terms "mental distress" and "mental sickness". The term "*psychical*" or "*psychological*"[13a] (sometimes "spiritual") has two distinct meanings in this book. First there is the purely

---

12b Dr. med. Gerhard Kloos, "Grundriss der Psychiatrie und Neurologie", Müller und Steinicke, Munich, 1951, p. 452, 2a: "a deep consultation ('opening up one's heart' or 'confession') in connexion with psychotherapeutic treatment".

13a German "seelisch". Since we have no word in English which covers both the religious and medical connotations of the German "Seele" (='soul'), I have had to use several different words in the translation. — translator.

technical sense, the inner nature of man: the mental as opposed to the physical.[13b] Further, the term "mental illness" also includes the religious problem of being sick in one's relationship to God. The sickness in this sense is not, as above, a purely natural biological fact, but a disturbance in man's basic relation to his Creator.[14] Hence by mental illness, psychological disturbance, or mental disorder, we shall mean a disturbance on the psycho-somatic level as well as on the religious.

In considering our *main title*, two groups of questions must be borne in mind. Now that we have defined the scope of our sub-title, we must deal with the two subjects mentioned in the main title. There are two main realms involved here, two branches of knowledge whose problems overlap in this study. Summing them up in brief, we may state them thus: Christian counselling, as a discipline of practical theology; and occultism, as a practical discipline of scientific psychical research. In our title, "Christian counselling and occultism", these two spheres of interest are named in relation to one another.

8. The Christocentric *premise* of our study. The title we have suggested does justice on the formal level to our legitimate concern for scientific clarification and definition. It is, however, a formulation scarcely adequate for the ultimate pastoral goal of our treatise, namely the indication of a way of liberation from occult subjection. Further, we dare not overlook the fact that in the last few years talk about occult and demonic things has become a malady of our time; indeed, it has become a craze. The psychiatrist would perhaps even speak of a psychic epidemic.[15] Thirdly, there is theological ground for questioning the propriety of such an interest. It is not the task of the pastor to let himself drift in the channels of present-day currents of thought, and to try for instance to plumb the breadths and depths of demonic dominion. According to Acts 20,24, the pastor is not called to prove the existence of the demons — nor, of course, to deny it — but he is entrusted with the ministry of the word of God.

In view of this, it should be a theological impossibility to publish informative literature under such titles as "Under the Spell of the Devil",[16]

13b cf. Ed. Thurneysen, "Die Lehre von der Seelsorge", Kaiser Verlag, Munich, 1948, p. 180.

14 cf. Thurneysen, loc. cit. 13b p. 194.

15 Against this sickness of our times, all this talk about the occult and the demonic, Lic. Dr. Würtenberg speaks out in the "Deutsches Pfarrblatt" of 15. 3. 49: "We can indeed no longer deny the uncanny, mysterious and disturbing elements of reality, but by bringing them together under the concept of demonism, we seldom allow them to retain their numinous character, their real existence, their nature as antithesis to God. An thus this talk of demonism has taken on a somewhat undefined espect".

16 Ernst Modersohn, "Im Banne des Teufels", Verlag Harfe, Bad Blankenburg, 1930.

or "Powers of Darkness".[17] This much speaking about demons can lead, in people who are emotionally unstable, to an induced demonic subjection.[18] The New Testament therefore gives us only a positive premise, not a negative one, with regard to this enigmatic realm of occultism: the statement that Christ in this labyrinth of unsolved questions once again has the last word. Christ is the "end of the demons".[19] This fact is clearly testified in the language of the early church, which speaks only of *one* Kyrios, the Lord Jesus Christ.[20]

In our study it must be made clear from the outset that the message of the Gospel is the premise for every assertion about the domain of occultism. The proclamation that Christ is the Victor over all mysterious forces and dark powers is the dominant focus and Christocentric premise of this study.

Chapter Three

ON THE PUBLICATION OF CASE HISTORIES IN THIS BOOK

There are disclosed in the course of this study, as already mentioned, some 120 pastoral cases, which are critically examined and evaluated in the light of the question which concerns us. The reporting of these cases follows the method used for publishing psychotherapeutic treatments.[21] In respect of the publication of these case-histories, whether they come from the pastor's or the psychotherapist's files, we must at this point mention the very grave doubts which some feel in the light of the duty of secrecy applying both to pastors and to doctors.

Before we can discuss these scruples, we must deal with a few basic questions regarding this pastoral and medical obligation of secrecy.

1. From early times the Church has imposed upon its ministers the duty of preserving silence about the matters confided to them in the course of pastoral care. This regulation is not merely a commandment of the Church,

---

[17] Ernst Seitz, "Mächte der Finsternis", Verlag der Plakatmission, Stuttgart-Waiblingen. Though the titles of these two books are objectionable, this is by no means true of their contents.

[18] cf. Lechler, loc. cit. [8] p. 98: "Much talking about demons can bring about all sorts of neurotic conditions".

[19] Walter Hoffmann, "Christus, das Ende der Dämonen", Verlag Wilhelm Freese, Berlin.

[20] Compare the places in the Acts of the Apostles, where *kyrios* stands in association with the name Jesus or Christ: 1, 21; 2, 36; 7, 58; 9, 28; 10, 36; 11, 17; 11, 20; 15, 11; 15, 26; 16, 31; 19, 5; 19, 10; 19, 13; 19, 17; 20, 21; 20, 24; 20, 35; 21, 13; 28, 31.

[21] For example in the books of the well-known doctors Bovet, Maeder, Tournier, Lechler and others.

but is the basic, indispensable condition for every pastoral interview, even though the New Testament knows of no "secret of the confessional", and only presupposes it indirectly.

In the Middle Ages the seal of the confessional was already made obligatory for the clergy in the Canon Law, and was upheld by the state. In more recent codes of law, this seal is likewise sanctioned by the recognition of the right of the clergy to refuse to give witness. In Germany this is provided for in § 53:1 of the Penal Code and § 383:4 of the Civil Code.

This obligation to pastoral secrecy finds its limit, however, where for conscience' sake the minister is duty bound to prevent existent or planned evil. A confessor can, on the ground of his acquired knowledge, become an accessory to the crime, if he keeps silence, when a situation would make it his duty to break his silence. This situation is provided for in § 139 of the German Penal Code. This regulation states that "anyone who receives trustworthy information, at a time when the crime could be prevented, of any plan to commit high treason, betrayal of country, forgery, murder, robbery, kidnapping, or crime endangering the community, is responsible for telling, at the proper time, the authorities or the person endangered by the crime".[22]

2. In a similar way the doctor is bound to secrecy by a kind of honour-code of professional ethics which extends back to 400 years before Christ, to Hippocrates. This medical obligation of silence is laid down in the German Reichsärzteordnung, §13. Just as in the case of the clergy, the state provides in §53:3 of the Penal Code and §38:5 of the Civil Code the right of the doctor to refuse to give witness. Further, §76 of the Penal Code and §408 of the Civil Code add the corresponding right to refuse professional advice. And, in §300 of the Penal Law Book, the unauthorized disclosure of private secrets confided to a doctor is made a punishable offence. However, the provision regarding the doctor's obligation to secrecy is extensively undermined by the National Safety Ordinance of July 17th 1911, and by the many obligations to disclose confidential material which have been imposed.

Hence there has arisen for the medical profession, through the unclarified points of law regarding duties of silence, disclosure and information, a great deal of uncertainty and an unhealthy conflict of duty.[23]

3. After this basic clarification, we must face the question whether examples of pastoral counselling or case reports of psychotherapeutic

---

[22] cf. Church Law, by D. Dr. Friedrich, p. 41.
[23] cf. Prof. Dr. Eberhardt Schmidt, "Brennende Fragen des ärztlichen Berufsgeheimnisses", published by the Deutscher Bund für Bürgerrechte, Isar Verlag, Munich, 1951.

treatments may be made public without violating the duty of the pastor and the doctor to maintain secrecy.

Indeed, many evangelists are accused of colouring up their messages with numerous pastoral experiences, thereby destroying the confidence of the audience in the speaker. Undoubtedly many evangelists do run the risk of breaking confidences, in their natural desire to use the riches of their wide pastoral experience in order to add colour to their proclamation. Often more tact and discretion would not impoverish the total effect of their preaching. Our psychotherapists find themselves in a similar situation, and sometimes they report their case histories in a dangerous manner.[24a]

In view of these doubts, we thus face the important question whether or not the publication of the cases in this book is a breach of pastoral confidence. In defending ourselves against such a charge, we may note the following points:

(a) In striking and difficult cases, permission to publish was first obtained from the person concerned.

(b) All the cases reported omit mention of names of people and places. When typical details might reveal the identity of the person, they are carefully omitted.

(c) No conclusions can be drawn about the whereabouts of the people concerned by reference to the residence of the author, since the cases are drawn from evangelistic work in Germany, Switzerland and Austria.

(d) Further, hardly any occult cases involve matters which would affect people's reputations. The work is usually a matter of giving pastoral advice to those spiritually[24b] disturbed or ill. If occult conjurers are exposed in the examples, it can only be for the good.

(e) Besides the arguments above, which are all confined to the area of technical and literary precautionary measures, we must add a word of justification for this public disclosure. A field so unusual as that of the pastoral care of victims of occultism, which has not yet been systematically explored, must be tackled for once for the sake of the many Christian workers who are quite ignorant of it, in order at least that the pastor can no longer pass by this urgent task without thought. When such a service of enlightenment and education is involved, when it is a matter of helping these grievously afflicted people, then publication is not only permitted, it becomes a duty. It is in this sense that

24a cf. Maeder, loc. cit. 9, p. 119.
24b German "seelisch", cf. 13a.

the well-known doctor, Prof. Frh. von Weizsäcker, at a convention of ministers and doctors at Herrenalb in the summer of 1951, made the remark, "Under some circumstances it is a duty to be indiscreet" — namely when it is required for the sake of helping the afflicted. In his "Studien zur Pathogenese", Weizsäcker urges a further point. He writes on page 4: "Every piece of medical casuistry is open to abuse. But in my opinion the blame in every instance should be laid on the one who commits the abuse, i. e. on the one who uses the information he has to injure others. In this sense a reader would be morally and, I believe, legally guilty who, after he had identified the person referred to here, went on to mention his name to others and so perhaps to bring harm to that person."

The way, then, is to some extent clear. It remains a problem, when a personal conversation with a pastor is torn out of its setting in the encounter of two persons and made public property. Hence the objection to publishing the sample cases in this book cannot be completely removed. The pressing need, however, of this pastoral ministry outweighs the gravity of the objections raised.

PART II

Pastoral Cases from the Field of Occultism Considered with a View to the Aim of our Study

Chapter One

THE SYSTEM FOLLOWED IN THE PRESENTATION OF THE EXAMPLES

1. The field of occult phenomena is so diverse that it is necessary to classify them under unifying aspects. The simplest scheme would be an alphabetical enumeration of the more than twenty branches of the subject. But in such a classification, related fields would be torn apart. A second possibility would be a classification according to para-psychological aspects, such as the analysis of Tischner:[25a]

(a) Para-psychical manifestations
(b) Para-physiological manifestations
(c) Para-physical manifestations   .

This classification does not, however, do justice to the pastoral concern of this study. We must find a way that will facilitate the treatment of the particular problem we have set ourselves. We shall come a step further if we ask what are the problems involved in the occult phenomena. Occult occurrences involve essentially two provinces: knowledge, and power. These are the two basic principles of the first temptation (Gen. 3, 5): eritis sicut deus — "you will be like God, knowing good and evil". Freely translated, this says, "you will be mighty, like God, and possess knowledge". The first temptation thus has a double content: the raising of man to power and to ultimate knowledge of things, both in a way opposed to God. Applied to the occult realm, this means: man frees himself from his ties to the Creator; he aspires to break the bounds di-

---

[25a] Rudolf Tischner, "Ergebnisse okkulter Forschung", Deutsche Verlagsanstalt, Stuttgart, 1950, List of contents.

vinely set and to penetrate secret and future things. Here we are confronted with extrasensory perception. The secret background of this striving for occult knowledge is the passion for power. Man desires to hold his own against God and man, and to gain the upper hand in the power struggle. This striving manifests itself in the occult sphere as a method of overcoming one's partner or adversary. Here we are dealing with psychological and — as still remains to be proved or disproved — with demonic influence. There is, of course, a further group of occult phenomena which cannot be classified under either of these two heads. To this group belong above all spook[25b] manifestations, which can also occasionally be observed by those wholly uninvolved. This group can be put under the heading of extra-sensory apparitions. Thus after a short reflection we have distinguished three main areas:

(a) Extra-sensory perception
(b) Extra-sensory influence
(c) Extra-sensory apparitions

2. Before we go on to the presentation of the pastoral cases, a word of explanation must be given regarding the procedure followed in dealing with the people concerned. A pastoral interview with a person spiritually disturbed usually follows the following pattern. First, the person seeking help tells of his problems. He can report everything that moves him and troubles his soul. The counsellor must learn the art of listening. To fill out the picture, he may put in the occasional question. From what the person has told him, the pastor can now begin to form an overall impression of his personality. Further, some first conclusions may be drawn about the nature of the mental disturbance involved, by the observation of certain physical characteristics, e. g. protrusion of the eyes in Basedow's disease, yellow pigmentation of the eyeballs in jaundice, the characteristic fold in the upper eyelid in depression, so-called symptoms of degeneration, etc. This report by the sufferer is followed by a cautious attempt to work out a case-history of the disease. First there will be the personal anamnesis: previous sicknesses, organic complaints, neuroses, etc. In the case of women, any abnormal psychological reaction to menstruation, pregnancy, or change of life is also of significance. In the case of men, notice should be taken of emotional instability associated with precocious puberty, alcoholism, nicotine addiction, sexual perversions, male change of life, etc. After this personal anamnesis comes the family anamnesis

[25b] German "Spuk", used in this book to refer to *objective* phenomena of an occult nature.

concerning psychoses, hereditary diseases, causes of death, cases of suicide among the relatives and ancestors.

Having established the medical findings, an anamnesis of occult connexions is conducted, concerned with participation in spiritist séances, visits to magic charmers, fortune-tellers, card-layers, pendulum practitioners, etc. Not only personal occult experiences, but also those of the person's forebears, are important. At this point, however, it must already be made clear that if it appears from the anamnesis that the causes of the mental disturbance are medical, the person being counselled should by all means be comforted from God's word, but he must be referred to a medical specialist for the actual treatment. For this reason we shall in this study not consider medical cases, but adduce them only for critical comparison.

A schematic representation of an example of pastoral counselling therefore looks like this:

Present condition

(a) The person's report of his troubles

(b) Observation of bodily symptoms by the counsellor

Prehistory of diseases

(a) Personal anamnesis

(b) Family anamnesis

Anamnesis of occult involvement

(a) Personal occult experiences

(b) Occult experiences of forebears

Explanatory note on the numbering of the examples

All examples taken from pastoral experience will be prefixed with the abbreviation *Ex*[26], and all those taken from literature will be prefixed with the abbreviation *Lit.*[27]

We may now begin the study of the various pastoral cases.

---

[26] Ex = example: so Ex 1, Ex 2, Ex 3, etc.

[27] Lit = literature: Lit 1, Lit 2, Lit 3, etc. are examples drawn from literature by way of comparison.

Chapter Two

AN INSIGHT INTO THE SPIRITUAL DISTRESS ASSOCIATED OCCULT OCCURRENCES

1. Extra-sensory Perception (ESP)

Spiritism

The first area which we shall illustrate with examples from pastoral experience will be spiritism. We are not here concerned to go into the origin and history of spiritism. On that subject many experts have written basic studies already. The presentation which follows is guided, as above stated, by a practical concern in pastoral work, viz. to show the consequences of involvement in occult activity. The clear definition of Tischner[28] brings us to the heart of the matter. "Spiritism", he says, "is a spiritual activity, grounded in the belief that people can by means of certain persons, the 'mediums', make contact with the deceased and so acquire revelations from the beyond." Here we see also the ruling motive for participation in spiritist sessions. Many people desire to learn something about the beyond, or to make contact with their deceased relatives or friends. How the realization of this goal is sought in individual cases, we may indicate by reference to five kinds of spiritist practice.

(a) *Apparition of the dead*

Ex 1 During an evangelistic campaign, a woman of seventy came for counselling. She was a faithful churchgoer, and for forty years had been a member of a lively fellowship. Others testified that she had proved herself as a Christian. She complained of depression, suicidal thoughts, no desire for prayer and bible study. She added that she had never had these problems before, not even after the death of her husband. Thoughts forced themselves upon her of which she was ashamed. Constitutionally she was a solid, healthy farmers's wife. Only her somewhat troubled face led one to suspect emotional conflicts. First I made sure she was not suffering from any old-age infirmities such as arterio-sclerosis[29], or from any other organic or nervous disorder. Receiving a negative answer, I made further enquiry regarding hereditary diseases, and the causes of death in her parents. Here too I found no particular clues.

---

[28] cf. Tischner, loc. cit. [25], p. 167.
[29] cf. Brugsch, loc. cit. [10], vol. 1, p. 615, "Arteriosclerosis is a general term for degenerative changes in the arterial system, which occur especially in advanced age, but also sometimes in youth, with a proceeding loss of elasticity".

The interview now proceeded to the anamnesis of occult involvement. On being questioned about this, the woman replied that she didn't know what that meant. After I had explained, however, a typical report of an occult experience emerged, belonging to the realm of spiritism. She told me that her husband had been a drunkard and an unchristian man. Because she nonetheless loved him, she had after his death become much exercised about his eternal state. In prayer she had often besought God that He might grant her to see her husband in a dream. Then one day a strange woman told her that she could fulfil her desire. She could call on her in the evening. The old woman did so. After she had performed what seemed to be several sacred rites, one wall of the room became brightly lit. In the circle of light appeared the deceased man[30], with a terrible expression on his face, seated on a billy-goat, riding towards her. The woman was terrified, and from that moment renounced the desire ever to see her husband again.[31] Asked whether her depression had set in before or after this experience, she affirmed that soon after this very unusual event thoughts of suicide and resistance to God's word set in. Of special importance here is the fact that the stranger who brought about the apparition of the dead is the notorious leader of a spiritist group. She and her destructive practices have been known to the author for some twenty-two years.

We shall not fully evaluate this example at this point. We shall merely indicate the problems here involved. Four questions will here chiefly interest the *doctor*. Do the emotional disturbances of this woman have as their cause an organic disorder? Or is this a reactive psychogenic depression[32], with the dreadful experience with the spiritist as its initial stimulus? Could the apparition of the dead not have been simply an hallucination?

[30] Dr. Karl Schmeïng reports in his book "Das zweite Gesicht in Niederdeutschland. Wesen und Wahrheitsgehalt", ("Second Sight in North Germany: Its Nature and Truth Content"), p. 156ff. examples 30—33, a number of typical apparitions of the dead. (Verlag Ambrosius Barth, Leipzig, 1937).

[31] This example is similar to the materialization phenomena of the great mediums. Reports of the materialization of entire persons are found in the well-known collection of studies "Die physikalischen Phänomene der großen Medien", edited by Dr. med. A. Frh. von Schrenck-Notzing, Union Deutsche Verlagsgesellschaft, Stuttgart 1926. The medium Einer Nielsen produced a materialization of an entire woman's form (p. 252). The strong medium Eusapia Paladino showed a series of magnificent materializations of complete forms such as Lambroso's mother, Gellano's child and mother, Venzano's lady friend, etc. (p. 100). Here we can also adduce the materialization phenomena of the medium Eva C. several times there appeared next to the medium the materialized form of a man, as shown in illustrations 127, 135, 136, 137 of the book by Schrenck-Notzing ("Materialisationsphänomene. Ein Beitrag zur Erforschung der mediumistischen Teleplastie", Verlag Reinhardt, München, 1914).

[32] cf. Kloos, loc. cit. [12], p. 423.

Is the coincidence of the mental disorder with the apparition real or imaginary?

The *psychical researcher*, on the other hand, will be mainly interested in three questions. Should the hypothesis of deception be applied to the apparition of the dead? Is this phenomenon the result of hypnosis or suggestion? Is this perhaps even a case where the spiritistic hypothesis is valid?

The *pastor*, besides being interested in the medical and para-psychological aspects, will be interested in the consequences of the occult practice and the way in which pastoral help can be given.

With this group of various questions, we must in this case firmly grasp the fact that the old woman, having found no success in prayer, obtained the help of a spiritist without realizing that "of the spirits which she called, she would nevermore be rid". As a consequence of this occult experience, there followed disturbances in her emotional life and her religious attitude. The other problems which arise in this case will be separately treated in a later chapter.

(b) *Glass moving*

Ex 2 At a Bible conference a Christian worker with university training related the following experience. His desire to investigate spiritualistic phenomena led him to take part in séances. The members of the circle sat round a table upon which a large alphabet was spread out. The letters were covered with a sheet of glass, on which a liqueur-glass stood. After the séance had been opened with a philosophicalcum-religious prayer, a spirit was invoked. Those present then directed questions to the invisibly present spirit, which were answered by the liqueur-glass dancing over the alphabet and coming to rest on single letters. When the letters were written down in order, they gave the answer to the questions.

The narrator of the experience first of all took pains to determine what was the source of energy behind the individual movements of the glass, but his investigation, carried out at many séances, produced no result. Finally he found himself faced with the alternative of adopting the hypothesis either of actual spirits, or the much more readily understandable phenomenon of telekinesis.

The participation in these spiritist sessions, which was undertaken only in the interests of studying occult phenomena, had serious consequences for the experimenter. His interest in God's word faded away. When he had to conduct a service on Sundays, remarkable spiritual struggles took place within him. When he went up to the altar or the pulpit, he always had to overcome a dreadful inner resistance. These struggles intensified to such an extent that at last he had no other way out than to hand in his resignation to the consistory, which they reluctantly accepted.

From the *medical* point of view, there was in the case of this Christian worker no explanation for his emotional disturbances. He was seldom ill. There was no nervous or mental disorder. After his release from the pastorate, he entered another profession, which he has continued to pursue without hindrance, up to the present time.

From the *para-psychological* point of view, four questions press upon us. Were the participants under hypnosis while observing the dancing glass?[33] Were the observers victims of a trick? Is the spirit theory valid here, or can the procedure be explained animistically, as psychokinesis? The explanation of the psychologist Prof. Bender, in his book "Psychische Automatismen", is in this direction. He speaks (p. 8) of the communal intellectual effort of a group, and of the dependence of automatic productions, of a collective personality in the sense of a "polypsychism".

For the *pastor* the enigmatic course of this energy is only of secondary interest. In the first place he is concerned rather with the effects of this occult activity on the spiritual disposition of the experimenter. He is concerned with his total disinterest in the word of God, and with the unaccountable struggles which occurred whenever the man set about his task of ministry in the church.

Ex 3   A second kind of glass movement[34] introduces a new element into the discussion. A young lady practised in private the art of glass-moving on a circular sheet of glass supplied with letters. By this means she claimed to be able to supply information on decisions and questions of every kind. She developed this private practice from experience she had gained at spiritist séances. The remarkable thing in this case was that the young woman was of the opinion that she could invoke from the beyond even great personalities like Luther, or even Paul and Christ. She used to open her glass-moving sessions with prayer, and was convinced of the religious character of her practice. In the village she was known as a faithful churchgoer and regarded as a godly woman. Occasionally she gave advice to her acquaintances and friends as well by means of her magic pane. Her usual habit on such occasions was to say, "Just a moment, I'll ask the Saviour."

This spiritist was granted only a short span of life. In the bloom of life she was unexpectedly taken sick. She sensed her approaching end and

[33] Dr. Christian Bruhn defends such a hypothesis in his book "Gelehrte in Hypnose", Hamburg, 1926. This book occasioned a rejoinder from Schrenck-Notzing in the final chapter of the collection on the great mediums (loc. cit. [31], p. 275).
[34] cf. Tischner, loc. cit. [25a], p. 46.

remarked that the Saviour would come to take her. A neighbour who was present in the room when she died told me about the last moments of her life. As she was dying she suddenly cried out in her agony, "Now the Saviour is taking me." She glanced expectantly toward the window. The focus of her eyes betrayed the approach of someone invisible. In a flash her expression changed to a grimace of terror, and with a fearful cry she departed. According to the report of the eye-witness, it was as if at the moment of dying this woman awoke from a delusion to a horrible reality.

From the *pastor's* point of view there are elements here which repeat themselves in many occult cases. The woman carried on a spiritist practice under the cloak of Christianity. Presumably she was even persuaded herself of the Christian character of her activity. Only at the gate of eternity was this veil of pious delusion rent.

The *doctor* would object that the sudden change of facial expression and the dreadful cry must not be referred to religious attitude or occult activity, but to her agony, to the last exertion of her bodily functions. *Psychical research* is not interested in the ethical evaluation of occult phenomena. It would here be interested merely in the experiment of glass-moving: is this a question of the phenomenon of cryptomnesia or hyper-mnesia[35], of clairvoyance, of "contact with spirits", or some other form of extra-sensory perception, apart from the fact that there are also many instances of gross swindling and financial exploitation.

Even though in this case too not all the problems can be considered at this point, we must note two findings which emerge. Firstly, the spiritistic activity took place under a veil of piety; secondly, the practitioner experienced a very difficult and terrible death struggle, a symptom which has emerged in every case of occult practice within my knowledge. We must observe that Professor Bender, a specialist in the field of glass-moving, expressly warns against this psychic automatism. (loc.cit. [3], p. V).

(c) *Table lifting*

Occult literature is full of examples of table lifting. This form of spiritistic practice has found many severe critics and many convinced champions. Among the documents of critical rejection are the researches of the medical doctor Gullat-Wellenburg[36], who with a flash photograph has shown how the medium Kathleen Goligher lifts a little table by means of a rod held between her knees. Some of the best proofs of authenticity are provided by the sessions of the physicist, Prof. Zöllner, with the American

---

[35] cf. Tischner, loc. cit. [25], p. 28.
[36] Max Dessoir, "Der Okkultismus in Urkunden": "Der physikalische Mediumismus" by Dr. med. Gulat-Wellenburg, Ullstein Verlag, Berlin, 1925, Plate III, no. 13, p. 288.

spiritist Dr. Slade.[37] Slade's levitations and apport phenomena aroused great amazement and could not, despite the most stringent checks and controls, be unmasked as a swindle or explained rationally.

As with all the examples in this study, we are not here concerned to investigate the phenomenon of levitation, but only to point out the mental disturbances which occur as a result of the occult activities.

Ex 4 A cultured lady of good Christian family told me in an interview of the following experience. One day she received from the headmaster of the municipal school an invitation to a social evening. Innocently she accepted the invitation. She found a group of some seven people together at the headmaster's house. After dinner the host proposed an entertaining party-game. The guests were required to form a chain with their fingers stretched out, and to hold their hands about six inches above the table. Having done this, the seated group of people waited expectantly for what was coming next. The master then announced: "Someone here is a non-conductor". So one person was set apart, taking his seat away from the group, and allowed to watch the others. After the removal of the "non-conductor" from the chain, the participants felt a tingling sensation in their fingers, as if a slight current of electricity was passing through the chain of hands. Now there was nothing to obstruct the experiment. The participants were informed that a dead person would be invoked, who would answer their questions. The presence of the dead person was revealed by tapping signals. Now the question and answer game began. Finally one of those present requested that the spirit tap out his name to him. Immediately the answer came. Thereupon one of the people in the group cried, "I knew him! he hanged himself twenty years ago!"

So the evening was spent playing this unusual party-game. The lady who related this experience returned home that night with remarkable impressions. Before she retired, she took up her bible, as had been her custom for many years, to read God's word and to pray. At that moment she felt a violent resistance to the bible, and an inexplicable pressure on her throat, so that she could bring no word of prayer to her lips. Turning her head to one side she saw two white forms with a demonic look, standing at the head of her bed. She let out a cry of terror, upon which her sister immediately hurried in to her. Her fear was so great that her sister had to stay and sleep in her room with the light on. These attacks lasted many nights. Not until six months later had the effects of that

[37] a. "Das große Geheimnis", ed. Enno Nielsen, Ebenhausen, Münich, 1923, p. 216; b. "Okkultismus", by Georg Holmsten, Deutsche Buchvertriebs- und Verlags-Gesellschaft, Berlin, 1950, p. 241.

evening's séance subsided, so that she could again read her bible and pray as before.

Upon enquiry it appeared that neither in the life of the lady herself nor in that of her forebears were there any medical peculiarities which would explain the acute psychological disturbances mentioned in her report.

Firstly, let us hear what the *doctor* would have to say about this case. The throat pressure will perhaps be explained by attributing it to nightmare.[38] There is a possibility, too, of angina pectoris, with its pressure and cramp-like pains, which can extend from the middle of the sternum to the left side of the throat and the angles of the jaw.[39] Another possibility is the shortness of breath in an acute attack of bronchial or cardiac asthma. Further, there are also the feelings of suffocation, of an emotional kind, found in some forms of hyperthyroidism, such as exophthalmic goitre, and idiopathic myxoedema.[40] Paroxysmal tachycardia[41] is also accompanied by painful feelings around the upper chest and throat, coupled with strong emotional agitation. The depressive symptom of a feeling of suffocation is found quite distinctly in the form of the precardial anxiety of patients with poor circulation. Beyond the diagnoses of medicine, the *psychiatrist* has a great number of possible explanations for the apparition of the two white figures, as an hallucination caused by emotional excitement or various medical conditions. We shall give attention to this again in a later section.

The *psychologist* would perhaps view the resistance towards the bible felt by the lady as a guilt reaction, since, according to Christian conceptions, participation in occult practices is disapproved. This particular lady is well-known for her clear Christian position. In the vision of the two strange forms, the psychologist will probably see the personified projection of a restless and accusing conscience. Nightmares and visions are easily understood on a basis of strong psychological stimuli.

The *psycho-analyst* would perhaps explain the appearance of the two forms which she saw as a visual reflex of an unassimilated psychological experience. He would point out that this vision represents the healthy reaction of the subconscious, which thereby resolves a threatening con-

---

[38] "Medizinische Terminologie", by Dr. Herbert Volkmann (Berlin 1942) gives an interesting definition of nightmare (German "Alpdrücken"): "(alp = Elf, ghostly being); feeling of anxiety on going to sleep, or during sleep, as if the chest were being compressed by a beast or monster." In medicine the nightmare is known as a pathological form of sleep occurring with neurosis, cf. Brugsch, loc. cit. [10], vol. II, p. 1343.

[39] Brugsch I, loc. cit. [10], p. 619.

[40] Brugsch I, loc. cit. [10], p. 107, 118.

[41] Brugsch I, loc. cit. [10], p. 558.

flict, which would unfailingly have arisen if the emotional shock of the spiritistic session had been forced back unassimilated into the subconscious, and had remained there as a constant motive for later collisions between the subconscious and the conscious mind. A simpler explanation would be that in the case of the two white forms we have an illusion, arising in the form of active productions of the subconscious as a result of post-hypnotic reaction.[42] When here and elsewhere in this book we speak of the "subconscious", we must note that in the more recent school of Freud, Adler and Jung the term "the unconscious" has become predominant. The older school of Moll, Dessoir and Janet employed the term "the subconscious". In our study we shall preserve the terminology of the older school.

Psychical research is concerned to investigate, besides the phenomenon of levitation, the question of the so-called "conductor" or "non-conductor", of the weak circulating "current".[43] Do we have here a case of hypnosis by the headmaster, or is there actually such a thing as human magnetism, which can be passed on by its bearer to various sensitive conductors? Or is this conductivity nothing other than mediumistic ability? These questions will be discussed in the section on healing magnetism. Here in passing we merely note that the phenomenon of a "current" pulsing through a chain of hands seldom occurs in séances.

The *pastor* has, though well aware of the medical and psychological questions that arise here, some important points of his own to make. The problem whether levitation of the table and the tapping signals are the result of deception, or psychokinesis, or a spiritistic phenomenon, is to him in the first place a matter of little concern, when he is faced with the empirical evidence of a distressing mental disorder. Since the lady who reported this experience was up to the time of the fateful séance in good health both physically and mentally, and also regained her mental stability six months after the incident and since then — now eighteen years — has never lost it again, the pastor easily arrives at the conclusion that the mental disturbances were produced by the spiritist séance. For

[42] cf. Prof. Dr. med. Brauchle, "Von der Macht des Unbewußten", Reclam, Stuttgart, 1949, p. 10.

[43] The direct production of an electric current is known as one of the physical phenomena of the medium Stanislawa Tomczyk. cf. "Die physikalischen Phänomene der großen Medien", loc. cit. [31], p. 175. Further, I have myself come across a medium who emitted a low-voltage current from her extended fingers. Later we shall consider what phenomenon is involved here. Prof. Dr. med. Brauchle reports a similar phenomenon as an effect of healing by magnetizers. He writes: "Some patients assert that at this moment they have a sensation similar to that which occurs when a small electric current flows through the body". Alfred Brauchle, "Hypnose und Autosuggestion", Reclam, Stuttgart, 1949, p. 7.

the pastor such experiences, especially since there are hundreds of similar cases, are sufficient ground for issuing a warning against any participation in spiritist séances. Further, the strong resistance to the word of God and to prayer which accompanies every case, insofar as the subject was a convinced Christian, certainly indicates something more than a purely psychological condition.

A further example will illustrate the effects of table-lifting, and another element of spiritist practice.

Ex 5 A home-help in her thirties came for an interview. She complained of various emotional disturbances such as depression, boredom, suicidal thoughts, and blasphemous thoughts against God and Christ. She had fits of rage and a tendency to mania. When she heard people praying, she felt like running away, or would block her ears and close her eyes. In the presence of faithful Christians she was disgusted by everything and felt a repugnance to the word of God. She felt an urge to break and tear up everything around her.

Externally she was well off. She lived abroad with her employer in comfortable circumstances. She had the opportunity of a promising marriage, but did not know whether or not she ought to burden a partner with her depressive state. My first question, whether the emotional conflicts had been brought on by the question of marriage, she answered negatively. A few questions about previous ailments disclosed nothing more than a few colds. She had not reached the change of life. Next came the anamnesis of occult involvement. Her first reaction to my question about occult activity was one of ignorance. There was nothing to do but to go with her through the whole catalogue of occult activities. She was surprised when I mentioned table-lifting. She admitted that she had done this for years, and saw nothing harmful in it. Her mistress had often taken her to a club where table-lifting was practised amid solemn ceremonies. One day, as she faced a very weighty decision, it entered her mind to have a try at table-lifting in private. According to her report, the experiment took place in the following way. The girl set a little parlour table in front of her, and used the same solemn phrase which she had heard at the club. But she could not remember the second phrase. The little table remained motionless. She flung out a curse, "If you won't move in God's name, then move in the devil's name!" Thereupon the table began to tap. This was for this girl the beginning of years of habitual table-lifting. In answer to further questions, it became once again clearly established that for years she had practised table-lifting in private; that she did not use her table for giving advice to other people, but that in every important question and decision she consulted it. To answer "yes" it would incline itself towards her; for "no", it would sway sideways. She never darkened her room during this practice.

The *psychical researcher* will be interested in this private practice of table-lifting. The hypothesis of deception is excluded, since the woman never admitted other persons to her experiments. The most that could be suggested along these lines is that she did not tell the truth in the interview. But this too is excluded in the present case, since the woman came for consultation only because of her emotional distress, and not with some purpose of making herself appear important by her success in occult experiments. The real question is: what was the energy behind the levitation of the table? Did this lady by means of psychokinesis rap out the answer of her subconscious mind? Does this phenomenon belong to the class of "motor automatisms" which are merely "standpipes of the subconscious"?[44] Or did she stand completely under the remote control of the leader of the spiritist club where she had experienced table lifting? Are we here faced with the problem of mental suggestion?[45] Or are perhaps the spiritists right when they speak of their power over "operators" from the beyond?[46]

Whichever hypothesis may be used to explain this phenomenon of table-lifting, of one thing the pastor who has been faced with a number of such instances is convinced — that active or passive participation in spiritistic experiments produces disruptions and disorders in the mental structure of the participant, and hardens the religious disposition in an anti-Christian direction. This last assertion will evoke much contradiction from spiritists, and we must therefore return to it in a later section.

Lit 1   While on the subject of table-lifting, we may add an illustration from literature, since in spiritist practice not only levitation (the simple lifting) of the table and tapping are known, but the moving away, jumping and flying of the table have also been observed.

Martensen Larsen[47] reports an experience of the physicist Barrett, who was very sceptical about the phenomenon of telekinesis. We should attach more significance therefore to the fact that his doubts were overcome by a series of experiences. The physicist described one of these in the following words:

"I had the opportunity to hold a ... séance ... The room was brightly illuminated, and after various tapping sounds had spelled out a message,

---

44 cf. Tischner, loc. cit. 25, p. 41f.

45 Tischner adduces on p. 66 of his book an informative example of this.

46 cf. Max Dessoir, loc. cit. 36, vol. I, p. 279.

47 Martensen Larsen, "Das Blendwerk des Spiritismus und die Rätsel der Seele", Agentur des Rauhen Hauses, 1924, p. 20.

a small table came, with no one touching it, hopping across the floor towards me, until it completely closed me in in my armchair. There were no threads or leads, or other means of accounting for these movements of the table."

Lit 2 The ultimate extreme of this phenomenon of table-lifting is reached in the verbal reports of researchers and missionaries from Tibet,[48] who unanimously testify that many priests of the Tashi Lama possess enormous occult abilities and can make small tables fly through the air for a distance of a hundred feet. The so-called red-hooded monks are masters par excellence of telekinesis, levitation, materialization and black magic. It is not possible to check these fantastic reports by researchers from Tibet. The only argument for their probability and truthfulness is that these reports fit in with the general attitude to life in Tibet. For according to travelling researchers and missionaries, Tibet is of all countries and peoples of the world the greatest stronghold of occultism.

Even though in these examples from literature and from the study of cultures we cannot conduct a psychological or personal pastoral investigation, we can still gain some light on our subject from the example of Tibet. The fact is that Tibet has resisted Christian missionary work longer than has any other land. Up to very recent times missionaries were killed there; very probably this was the fate of the Indian missionary Sadhu Sundar Singh. Not until 1934 did Christian refugees from China carry the gospel into Tibet. And only in 1946 did Tibet receive the bible — the translation of Yoseb Gergan — in her own native language. Hence from the aspect of the history of religion we have here the interesting insight that occult activity and the advance of the Christian mission stand in inverse proportion to one another. Admittedly the hypothesis of a universal inverse ratio is not established by one example. But this example fits well into the pattern which emerges from other examples. Above all, this thesis is corroborated by reports of missionaries from India and China.

(d) *Speaking in trance*[49a]

By the phenomenon of speaking in trance we mean a somnambulant condition into which mediums are brought by auto- or hetero-hypnosis. Spiritists maintain that by the help of speaking mediums they can obtain messages from the deceased. To show the consequences of this speaking in trance we shall cite three examples from pastoral experience.

---

[48] cf. Enno Nielsen, loc. cit. [37], p. 141.
[49a] cf. Tischner, loc. cit. [25a], p. 47.

Ex 6 A bicycle shop was broken into and many accessories were stolen. The owner reported the burglary to the police. In addition he asked the leader of a spiritist group to hold a séance in the shop, in order to have the thieves described by a speaking medium with the help of the "spirits". The séance was held, six people attending. The medium described the criminal, and so suspicion centred strongly on a labourer who was in debt. This séance did not lead to a full exposure of the guilty person, since two relations of the suspected man were present at it.

Quite apart from the dubious and highly questionable nature of such a method of detection, this séance had remarkable consequences from the *pastoral* angle. Two Christians who took part in the séance, a man and a woman, came to the pastor for consultation. They complained, just as in all the other examples, of depression, and boredom, and also of spook apparitions.[49b] We shall not here unfold the whole complex of problems in this case, since it is similar to those of the preceding cases. We must however note that here a new element, the observation of spook apparitions, appears.

Ex 7 A pastor told me of the following experience at a deathbed. The leader of a Christian fellowship group lay dying. The man, who enjoyed public respect, was suffering a terrible death struggle. In the house and in the garden there was a rumbling, rattling and banging going on as if hell had been let loose. The village pastor, who was called in to support the victim of this attack, commented after he had died, "There you can see that even believing people can go through terrible trials on their death-beds". It is not my purpose to dispute the truth of this remark and opinion of the pastor. However for the sake of completeness it must be added that I have known for twenty years that spiritist séances with a speaking medium were held in the house of this leader of a Christian fellowship group. The local pastor who was called in had no knowledge of this fact.

In the problems it raises, this example belongs to the same group as *Ex 4*. The *psycho-analyst* will explain the mobilization of these unusual forces in the hour of agony, viz. crashing, scratching, scraping, clatter, rumbling, hissing, by the theory that at the moment of extinction of the conscious mind the powers of the subconscious are set free and perhaps withdraw to a separate existence. But in the framework of our present study, we must here answer with a question: why according to pastoral experience do such splits often occur with people who have engaged in occult practices or who stand in the occult tradition of their forebears?

49b cf. 25b.

The *psychical researcher* will view the "poltergeists" at the hour of death under the category of para-physical apparitions. "From certain people" an "energy-material" emanates, which "is guided by the mind and produces purposive achievements".[50] Something is put forth from the psyche that previously existed in the psyche.

In contrast to psychical research, which is concerned with the phenomena and with experiments, the *pastor* sees as being of prime importance the person who needs help. Here the pastor will ask, "Who are these 'certain people' who experience such a revolution and dissociation of their mental powers?" An answer will be forthcoming in the course of our study. It has however already been suggested in the form of a question, in connexion with this example. In the present case we must further mention the pastoral observation that the preaching of the fellowship leader concerned was unacceptable to many, and not felt to be challenging. The cause of this was not a lack of natural ability, but his occult involvement. Spiritism and Christianity stand opposed like fire and water. Spiritism immunizes against the Holy Spirit. Therefore evangelical churches reject spiritism as a witness for the survival of the soul. This surprises psychical researchers, who hold that spiritism is the trump card for Catholic and Protestant churches alike.[51]

Ex 8   An example which is very informative for the purposes of our study, an example supported by the complementary reports of three persons who are all well known to me, will make some further aspects clear. On the second floor of a house regular spiritist séances were held with a speaking medium. The neighbour on the first floor, a Christian woman, soon became aware of this activity. On the evening concerned she always had such an uncanny feeling. The next time this spiritist group met, this woman knelt down in her room and prayed that God might command the men to stop. While she persevered in prayer, she heard tumult in the room above her. Chairs were overturned and a man rushed downstairs. She saw him mount his motor-cycle and race away. After some thirty minutes he returned with a pillion rider. As reported later by members of the séance, the medium had ceased from her speaking in trance while the woman was praying, and had remained in a state of deep unconsciousness. The leading spiritist was not able to rouse her from the trance. Therefore he rode into the neighbouring village to fetch a second spiritist leader. With combined energies they succeeded in bringing the medium back to consciousness.

---

50 Tischner, loc. cit. 25a, p. 165.
51 cf. Tischner, loc. cit. 25a, p. 187.

To fill out the record we add a report of the fate of the organizer of these séances. At the peak of his strength, when he was forty years old, he contracted a severe illness and died in great torment. A few days before his death he cried aloud in his pain, so that the neighbours heard his cries. I received further insight into this group from the leading spiritist himself. After the death of his wife, he was so upset that for some time his mind was open to the word of God, and he desired to begin a new life. During these days he confirmed[52] that his wife, whom he often employed as a medium, became blind through his practices.[53] He knew of the demonic nature of his activity. For days he struggled, with pastoral help, to break out of his spiritist maze. But he was bound as by iron chains, and soon fell back into his earlier way of life.

To study this example on the level of psychoanalysis and psychical research sheds little light on the occurrence. We shall only elucidate the *pastoral* aspect. Plainly, the Christian is able, by prayer and faith, to oppose occult activities. That is a matter of experience in Christian work. The dreadful end of this spiritist organizer is not the result of a naive or mystical approach, which paints everything in black and white, but is an experience constantly observed. The present example fits into the pattern of *Ex 3* and *Ex 7* in this respect. The fact of the medium turning blind is a not uncommon happening in occult practice, for in pastoral consultation with those occultly subjected, this always comes to light from time to time. The fruitless struggle for a spiritual break-through with spiritists reveals that occult activity creates a spiritual bondage. Persons with such an involvement can only with great difficulty make a decision for Christ.

(e) *Automatic writing*

Persons gifted with mediumistic powers are able either in a waking state or in a trance, excluding conscious reflection, to write down sentences, words, or letters, which are assumed by spiritists to be messages from the beyond, but are regarded by many psychical researchers as motor automatisms.[54]. Since I have no clear example from my own pastoral work, I shall borrow one from literature. Tischner, who as a psychical researcher investigates only the occult phenomena, without taking any interest in the pastoral aspect, adduced in his book which appeared in

---

[52] This report is no breach of a confidence.

[53]'Blinding as a functional disturbance (as opposed to an organic disorder) is observed: (a) in hypnosis, cf. Brauchle, loc.cit. [43], p. 41; (b) in hysteria, cf. Kloos, loc.cit. [12], p. 442; (c) in occult activity. I can furnish examples of this from pastoral experience.

[54] cf. Tischner, loc. cit. [25a], p. 41.

1950 some examples which are of great importance for the pastoral counsellor. We shall adduce one of these here. He writes:[55]

Lit 3 "We must warn people against abandoning themselves unreservedly to this fascinating business (sc. of automatic writing). It is best to receive advice from a specialist, who will urge that from the very outset the affair be conducted with moderation, and not to yield to every wish or urge; otherwise it can reach a point where one is no longer master over his own body, but its servant, indeed slave, who must obey if he would not meet the very unpleasant results of refusal. I once had the experience with a lady who did a great deal of automatic writing, that she felt the urge to do so in a coffee house, and when her husband said, 'No, no, you can't do that here!', her hand suddenly began to rap loudly on the marble table, so that it drew the attention of the people around and we had to leave the room in haste."

Thus Tischner himself bears witness to the fact that by such occult activity a person is in danger of losing control of himself. Here a specialist, who has no religious interest, must in his own capacity as a scientist confirm the view of the Christian counsellor that occult activity breaks up the integrality of a person's psychological make-up. Occult activity is like a built up charge of energy, which explodes the stability of a person's psychological constitution. Tischner's observation is corroborated by the psychiatrist Albert Moll. Moll writes:

"The dangers to health accompanying occultism are essentially different. I refer to the fact that even in connexion with automatic writing, when practised and cultivated by sick persons, severe personality splits are observed. I too have seen cases of this kind, in which what was at first a very faint personality split was so aggravated by automatic writing, that finally a real disease of the personality set in... I have repeatedly seen strong morbid influences as a consequence." (Ein Leben als Arz der Seele, p. 113.)

The *psycho-analyst* likewise gains "water for the mill" from Tischner's report. This spontaneous occurrence is for him a demonstration how the usually latent relations between the subconscious and the conscious mind can become visible. By repression of the consciousness, the subconscious produces not only sensory but also motor effects. Occult activity is thus the cyclotron which accelerates and intensifies the energy of the subconscious.

After the presentation of these five kinds of spiritist practice, we ought now to go on to the most interesting area, the phenomenon of materi-

[55] Tischner, loc. cit. [25a], p. 42f.

alization. This area, however, will come under discussion in connexion with black magic, since in pastoral experience many examples of materialization appear which show active influence upon certain people, and consequently come under the heading of extra-sensory influence. Furthermore, we should point out here that the question of mediumistic activity and the phenomenon of poltergeists will be raised again in other connexions.

In this first section, which investigates the pastoral problem of spiritistic phenomena, we have only been concerned to indicate a group of questions which the pastor encounters in individual interviews with those who are spiritually distressed.

Hyperaesthesia

Excessive sensibility is a phenomenon to which recent psychologists and psychical researchers have given extensive attention. In particular, Richard Baerwald[56] has investigated this problem in his books "Die intellektuellen Phänomene" and "Okkultismus, Spiritismus und unterbewußte Seelenzustände". Recently the American researcher Rhine[57] deals with extra-sensory perception in his book "The Reach of the Mind". These researchers refer hyperaesthesia to a heightened capacity of perception, present in a person from the start. In pastoral care we are interested not only in the psychological and para-psychological questions, but especially in the picture presented by the spiritual condition of a person having hypersensory gifts. The examples which have come my way in pastoral counselling will be discussed under four headings.

(a) *Visionary dreams*

The opinions of medical science vary on the importance to be attached to dreams. Many psychologists and doctors see in the dreams of adults only a sum of disharmonious images and confused fragments of events. Others on the contrary — a number of psychotherapists and depth-analysts — see in dreams valuable bridges on the way to decoding the subconscious processes of the mental life. This school sees in the adult's dream a combination of "day residues"[58] and "childhood wishes". By "day residues" they mean the impressions, worrying experiences, unresolved conflicts, unsatisfied urges, which have been carried over from waking

---

[56] Richard Baerwald, "Die intellektuellen Phänomene", Berlin, 1925; "Okkultismus, Spiritismus und unterbewußte Seelenzustände", Leipzig, 1929.

[57] J. B. Rhine, "The Reach of the Mind", Penguin Books, 1954.

[58] cf. Prof. Dr. Brauchle, "Psychoanalyse und Individualpsychologie", Reclam Stuttgart, 1949, p. 17f.

experience to the sleeping state. By "childhood wishes" are meant those unsatisfied libidos and egoistic desires which appear in the development of a child. According to this school of thought the "day residues" and "childhood wishes" are the latent background of the conscious content of the dream.

In connexion with the approach of this study, the problem of dream interpretation recedes in importance, giving way to the question of dealing with a pastoral situation. Is there a specific relationship, with attaching problems, between hyperaesthesia and the psychological make-up of a person? To illustrate this question we shall adduce some examples of predictive dreams.

Ex 9 A Swiss girl related in an interview how one night in a dream she saw a great fire. She could clearly recall many details of the place where the fire occurred. After the night of the actual fire, the press brought out picture-reports of the conflagration, which corresponded in fine detail with the observations made in the dream. The girl's home and the site of the fire were 120 miles apart.

The *psychical researcher* is interested in the question of how this extra-sensory communication of an actual event takes place. The customary explanation, that a telepathic process is involved, is still debatable. The girl did not know anyone living at the place of the fire, who could be regarded as the sender of the message. Unless our psychical researcher, therefore, can obtain proof that some unknown observer, experiencing the event at the distant place, served as a general thought transmitter, whose "waves" were picked up by "receivers" with telepathic powers, the explanation remains unproved.

The *pastor* is concerned with the question whether the girl experienced any psychological disturbances in connexion with the dream. Our present case presents no findings in this respect.

Ex 10 A Christian woman learned in a dream one day that a relative living 150 miles away had become sick. She noticed in the dream how the fingers of the patient were strangely bent. Some time later she learned that the relative had been told by his doctor that the was suffering from Dupuytren's Contracture.[59]

The *psychical researcher* will explain this dream as telepathy. Even so the process of telepathy remains a mystery.

---

[59] Dupuytren's Contracture = contraction of the finger in a curved position (fibrous contraction of the Palmar Fascia).

From the *medical* point of view it must be noticed that this woman had suffered for years from a psychoneurosis, in the form of a recurring reactive depression.[60]

In the pastoral situation there are several special points to be noted. The woman had engaged from her youth in superstitious dream interpretations. With advancing years her visionary dreams and telepathic capabilities increased. This proves that the capacity for extra-sensory perception can be developed. In her religious life, the characteristic results of occult participation discussed in the section on spiritism were absent.

Ex 11 We shall now give an example which shows up visionary dreams in another light. A young man known to me from his childhood was taken to hospital for surgery. In the night after the operation, he suddenly cried out so loudly, that the other patients in his ward awoke. He groaned loudly and cried repeatedly, "I don't want to die!" In the morning another patient in the ward asked him the reason for his cries. The young man said he had dreamed that four black men wanted to lay him in a coffin. After his vehement resistance, a white figure suddenly appeared, who revealed to him that he still had another six months to live. He should come to his senses and be converted. Upon this the four sinister men had disappeared.

So ends the report of the young man himself. The sequel is reported by his sister. The incision healed up quite surprisingly fast. The weird dream experience bore fruit. The young man was given grace to begin a new life in the fear of God. After six months the operation had to be repeated. The chief surgeon said to the patient, "You will certainly recover again. There are no complications to fear." The patient contradicted him, and said, "I am going to die tonight." The doctor simply laughed at him. But in the night the patient called for his believing father-in-law, who came and prayed with him. In the same night the man died, exactly six months after the dream warning.[61, 62]

The *psychologist* will regard this dream as the product of two components: fear of death, and a guilty conscience. The threatening condition of the illness nurtured the fear of death, which was symbolized by the coffin. The conscience, aroused in view of the uncertain outcome of the

---

[60] cf. Kloos, loc. cit. [12], p. 440, "reactive depression = psychogenic, motivated depression brought on by distressing experiences".

[61] 'I have already reported this predictive dream in my little book "Der Höhenflug", Kurt Reith Verlag, 2nd., edn. 1951, p. 92.

[62] Holmsten describes in his book (loc. cit. [37], p. 78) a double dream of a similar character. His example shows that the predictive dream is not the efficient cause of the event which follows it. The objection that it is a case of autosuggestion is here untenable.

operation, recalled the dark things of his past life, symbolized by the four dark figures. The fear of punishment at God's judgment led to a review of his relationship to God, symbolized by the white figure. Thus the working methods of psychology can easily work back from the manifest content of the dream to the latent background of dream-material.

More difficulty is experienced in explaining the religious conversion of the young man, and the fulfilment of the dream after six months, if psychological criteria alone are used. If the psychologist can explain the conversion after the dream as the result of fear, he cannot avoid resorting to forced exegesis in explaining the dream's fulfiment. Pushing psychology to its very limit, a psychoanalyst could at the most hit on the idea of attributing his death to autosuggestion, adding the explanation that the man had for half a year been going round with the idea that he must die six months after the dream. There are indeed plenty of cases known of death resulting from suggestion.[63]

The pastor will, in spite of the scientific nature of such a psychological explanation, have strong objections to raise. With this solution of the dream problem by the psychoanalytical method, we are on the right way to ending up with the theory of Sigmund Freud and explaining all the content of the Christian faith as a function of the subconscious. The Christian knows that besides the immanent relationships of the mental life, there are also transcendent events. The pastor recognizes, besides the conversions known in the area of psychotherapy, which have their root in the Socratic "gnothi sauton" ("know thyself"), the "anakainosis tou biou" ("renewal of life")[64] mentioned in the New Testament. From long experience of observing and counselling those who seek his help, he is able to distinguish psychological conversion from renewal of life, just as a doctor can distinguish an organic disease from a neurosis affecting an organ. In the case here under discussion, we cannot by means of psychological categories do justice to the man's dream experience and his

---

[63] cf. Holmsten, loc. cit. [37], p. 23. Dr. Karl Schmeïng also holds such a view (loc. cit. [30]). He writes on p. 140: "The seer himself by his prevision sets the alarmclock of his life to a definite hour". Further, the work of Prof. Österreich, which is so significant in the study of the phenomenon of possession, reports cases of death by autosuggestion. The best-known example of this is the death madness, or thanatomania, found among the Australian aborigines. "If a savage believes that he has been struck by remote influence, he will lay himself down and die purely as a result of a psychological affect". cf. T. K. Österreich, "Die Besessenheit", Verlag Wendt & Klauwell, Langensalza, 1921, pp. 233f.

[64] Anakainōsis: cf. Theologisches Wörterbuch zum Neuen Testament, ed. Gerhard Kittel, 3rd. edn. p. 455. The two NT references to anakainosis show the character of this renewal: subject of the renewal is the Holy Spirit, object the "nous" (EVV: "mind") — Rom. 12, 2; Tit. 3, 5.

spiritual renewal. The short period of six months revealed a deep and basic change, so that other members of the family were also blessed and spurred on to Christian discipleship by his example.

These three examples, to which many more could be added, show that such spontaneous experiences leave no trace of occult subjection in the life of the soul.

(b) *Telepathy*

By telepathy is meant the "acquisition of knowledge... without the use of the senses".[65] We distinguish thought-sending, thought-reading, mixed telepathy (in which telepathy is mixed with clairvoyance), triangular telepathy (in which sender, mediator, and receiver work together), and psychometric telepathy, in which "persons with mediumistic gifts can by means of some object make paranormal disclosures about its owner".[66] As with all para-psychological phenomena, what interests us here is not the telepathic experiments, but rather the persons who have telepathic abilities. If we are to classify them here from the pastoral point of view, the spontaneous occurrences must be distinguished from telepathic experiments. We shall begin with a series of spontaneous experiences.

Ex 12   A Protestant pastor during the war suddenly saw his son, who was fighting on the Eastern front, lying in his own blood. Immediately the father had the feeling that something had happened to his son. After three weeks news came of his death. The day and hour of his death coincided with those of the vision.

Ex 13   A Catholic priest one night saw his father, who told him that he had just died. The priest glanced at his watch and noted the time. The next day a telegram arrived announcing the death. The hour of his death coincided with the nocturnal vision.

Ex 14   A missionary deaconess was deep in prayer in her room. The door opened and in came her brother, who was at the time fighting on the Western front. The sister called to him, "Hermann! are you on leave?" At this question the figure vanished. Some time later she received news of his death. The day and hour coincided with the vision.[67]

Ex 15   A Protestant pastor went out to pursue his duties. After he had been on his way for ten minutes, he was suddenly seized by a great unrest.

[65] cf. Rhine, loc. cit. [51], p. 24.
[66] cf. Tischner, loc. cit. [25a], p. 76.
[67] Dr. Schmeïng, in his book (loc. cit. [30], p. 146ff.), a number of examples similar to those adduced in *Ex 13—Ex 15*.

He turned and hurried back home. There, to his great alarm, he saw that his five-year-old son was clambering about on the roof of the tall house. The boy wanted to play chimney-sweep. Fortunately the father could rescue his child from this precarious position.

Ex 16 An unusual and very pronounced form of telepathy was reported to me at an interview in Switzerland. The wife of a Christian worker lived in a suburb of a large town. A Christian friend of hers often used to do her shopping for her in town, without asking her beforehand what she needed. Every time she was surprised how he brought all the food and other things which she had thought of while busy in her kitchen.[68] This man and this woman both have mediumistic gifts. They gave other evidence of extra-sensory abilities.

Lit 4 A typical historical example is found in Jung-Stilling's "Geisterkunde".[69] King August II of Poland was a friend of King Friedrich Wilhelm I of Prussia, and his field-marshal von Grumbkow. On February 1st. 1733, at three o'clock in the morning, von Grumbkow suddenly saw, in the glow of his night-light, the form of King August coming into his bedroom and pulling aside the curtains round his bed. King August said to the astonished Grumbkow: "Mon cher Grumbkow! Je viens de mourir ce moment à Varsovie."[70] The field-marshal wrote down the happening at once and provided for immediate notification of the Prussian King. Forty-six hours later a courier arrived from Warsaw reporting the death of the Polish King. The nocturnal experience and the hour of his death coincided exactly.

To make a summary examination of the five examples just cited, we may put *Ex 12 — Ex 14* under the heading of thought transmission. The dying people in their hour of death thought of their dear ones and sent their last regards. *Ex 15* could at a pinch be called an example of thought-reading. The father grasped the precarious situation of his child. *Ex 16* is an example of co-operative thought-sending and thought-reading.

In the classification of these examples we must not forget that this nomenclature in no way characterizes the essence of the phenomena, still less explains them. The psycho-technical process of extra-sensory thought-

---

[68] Dr. Schmeïng (loc. cit. [30], p. 78) reports a similar occurrence. By purely silent volition, a woman induced her housemaid to do certain tasks, without issuing any verbal instructions. The girl carried out the tasks suggested to her, without realizing that she was under a psychological influence. Later she reported only that she always felt a certain unrest and tension.

[69] cf. Heinrich Jung-Stilling, "Theorie der Geisterkunde", Zeitbücherverlag Nuremberg 1921, vol. II p. 50.

[70] "My dear Grumbkow! I have just this moment died in Warsaw".

transmission has to this day remained undiscovered. There have been a number of hypotheses, none of which, however, has gained general acceptance. As the main ones we may mention the wave and atom theory of Democritus (460 B.C.); the theory of emanation of rays from the brain (Kotik, "Die Emanation der psychophysischen Energie", Wiesbaden, 1908); the brain-wave theory of the physicist Crookes (d. 1919, noted for the invention of the Crookes tube); the theory of psychic energy of the chemist Ostwald (d. 1932, Leipzig); the electronic transmission theory of the psychiatrist Forel (d. 1931); the theory of the electrical oscillation of the body (Prof. Rohracher of the psychological institute of Vienna University).[71] As an admittedly inadequate illustration of the phenomenon of telepathy within the family circle we may use radio technique. The carrier wave of the emotional bond between the members of a family is modulated by their mutual love. We must however again emphasize that this is merely an illustration.

From the *pastoral* viewpoint, these spontaneous occurrences are without any findings as far as the theme of our study is concerned. This is not so with deliberately conducted telepathic experimentation. Prolonged attempts in this field can provoke psychological disturbances, as the following example will show.

Ex 17   A twenty-year-old girl was engaged to a sailor. Every evening she was with her young friend in her thoughts, for she was very strongly attached to him. One night she awoke in terrible anxiety about her fiancé. She besought God graciously to protect him in the perils of the sea. Some time later she received a letter in which her fiancé told how they had weathered a dreadful storm in the North Sea, which they had not expected to ride out. At the very height of the storm, he had grasped her photograph, and had had her vividly in mind.

This was the beginning of an animated telepathic exchange for these young people. They were in the course of time able to communicate their thoughts to each other by telepathy. There arose, notwithstanding the great distance between them,[72] a powerful emotional tie as a result of which the girl felt, to a pathological degree, everything that happened to the young man. If he became ill, so did she by remote communication. If he experienced pain, so did she. When he took medicines, she had the

[71] Treatments of these theories of telepathy are to be found in: a) Dessoir, loc. cit. [36], p. 6; b) Rhine, loc. cit. [51], p. 25; c) Tischner, loc. cit. [25a], pp. 199f., 128; d) Zeitschrift für Arbeit und Besinnung, 15. 12. 50, No. 24, p. 558.

[72] Tischner reports (loc. cit. [25a], p. 73) well functioning telepathic experiments which took place over a distance of 500 miles.

same experiences of taste and smell.[73] Although at first this transference of the emotional experiences of her fiancé was a pleasure to the young girl, the telepathic union gradually became a burden, causing her great distress. Out of the originally amusing game there developed a psychic enslavement, in fact a kind of possession, from which the girl could no longer protect herself. She consulted a psychiatrist, who tried to help her by hypnotism. After the treatment the girl told me that this had brought her out of the frying-pan into the fire. She had indeed been liberated from the psychic union and the telepathic exchanges with her fiancé, but now she was under the influence of the specialist, of whom she found herself continually compelled to think, although she had no interest in him.

The *psychical researcher* will be interested in the unusual phenomenon of the transference of experiences of smell, taste, pain and joy. First, this case confirms the often observed fact that telepathy functions most easily between people who deeply love each other. Prof. Bender adds corroboration to this. He writes (loc.cit. [3], p. 52): "Here it is well known that affective relationships create especially favourable conditions." Driesch, too, holds the view that material obtained from two persons who harmonize with each other is usually richer than that gained by experiment. One can in fact speak of a remote operation of love,[74] of a psychic connexion between lovers. The mode of transmission remains, however, a mystery. Further, this example is proof of the fact that in telepathy the distance between the partners makes no difference. Whether the young couple were separated by 100 or 1000 kilometres, the reception functioned with equal intensity. According to the laws of high frequency signalling, this is a technically incomprehensible process.

Perhaps we may be allowed a slight *digression* here. The telepathic receiver need never, as would his "colleague" at the wireless set, signal to the man at the other end: "I'm receiving you strength 1 — can you boost your power?" By this comparison between psychical and technical communications, we can plainly see that in the phenomenon of telepathy we are faced with a miracle of creation. That which man with his complicated technical apparatus of transmitter and receiver, and by using great quantities of energy, does only poorly, two adapted persons can accomplish without effort. Does this not demonstrate again how the creations of God's laboratory far excel the technical achievements of man's workshop?

[73] Telepathic transmission of the experiences of taste and pain are mentioned also by the researcher Rhine (loc. cit. [57], p. 16). Further, Dr. Schmeïng (loc. cit. [30], p. 152) reports a case of telepathic transference of disease.

[74] cf. Holmsten, loc. cit. [37], p. 145.

Besides the above example, there is a quantity of good parallels available in psychical literature. One of the best is mentioned by Tischner (p.73). Dr. von Wasielewski practised telepathic exchanges with a young woman over the whole distance from Thuringia to the Riviera (over 600 miles). The tests which were carried out can be regarded as having been fully successful.

The *doctor* will first of all be detained by the fact that through hypnosis by a psychiatrist the young lady was freed from telepathic bondage to her fiancé, but from then on became emotionally bound to the doctor. In an analytic treatment by a psychiatrist it is a normal transition stage for the patient (depending on his sex) to fall in love with, or to be moved with hatred against, the doctor concerned. This process is known in psychiatry as transference. This transference, which at first puts the doctor in a position to deal with the patient's various complexes, must disappear at the end of the treatment. With the process of hypnosis we have a similar procedure. When one mental tie has been dissolved by suggestion, a new one must not be allowed to arise in its place. That would not be a cure, but merely a psychological transference. If the psychiatrist has been successful in abreacting this transference, the effect of the hypnotic treatment probably indicates a psychological complication in the patient. The possibility of a psychosis, perhaps a schizophrenic condition in the course of which, for instance, smell and taste hallucinations occur, is ruled out in the case above, since the patient had been examined by a psychiatrist in this respect, without any positive findings. To work out a conclusive medical diagnosis is outside the scope of this study. Besides, this is a task for the specialist.

The *pastor* is, in connexion with this example, satisfied in establishing that continued experimentation with telepathy can throw the experimenter off his mental balance. This is evidenced by this girl, who through years of practice attained a mediumistic ability for telepathy. This has been further confirmed to me by a specialist who experimented for eighteen months in this field and observed the unfavourable effects on his own emotional life.

(c) *Clairvoyance*

"By clairvoyance we mean the extra-sensory perception of objective facts, of which no one has knowledge, without the use of any of the known senses."[75] This is how Tischner characterizes the peculiar gift of some people to grasp with clear vision, in spontaneous experiences, things hidden in the past (Retroskopie), the present (Kryptoskopie, Teleskopie),

---

[75] Tischner's definition, loc. cit. 25a, p. 86.

and the future (secular or religious prophecy). As hitherto in this study, the actual phenomenon of clairvoyance interests us only secondarily; the person of the clairvoyant is our primary concern. Not the psychical problem, but the pastoral problem, is at the focus of our consideration. In pastoral experience, clairvoyant phenomena emerge in three forms. We have spontaneous occurrences on the religious level, the secular level, and the occult level.

Dr. Schmeïng in his book[76] groups all phenomena of clairvoyance, regardless of their character, under the heading of eidetic. From a pastoral point of view this grouping is impossible, since the psychological effects of these clairvoyant phenomena are completely different. A few examples will make this clear.

Ex 18   One of my friends was walking along an important street of a great city. Suddenly, in the midst of the crowd, his surroundings faded completely out of his sight and consciousness. Instead, he saw himself in an unfamiliar cemetery. Before him he saw a large funeral going on, with a clergyman, an open grave, a coffin, and himself standing at the graveside. After the clergyman's address, which were about his dead friend, he himself, at the request of the family, read a passage from the bible and spoke for a few minutes upon it.

This was a vision in full daylight, in a busy street, surrounded by passers-by. How long his normal consciousness was suspended, he did not know. He only looked anxiously about him, concerned whether the passers-by had noticed his loss of consciousness. He could not determine anything of the sort. During the vision he must have moved automatically, with his eyes open, like a sleep-walker. That same day came the solution to the mystery. He received a telegram reporting a friend's death, with a request from the parents that he speak at the grave of their son. My friend travelled there and found at the grave just the situation he had seen two days before, 100 miles away in the great city, in a clairvoyant vision: the congregation arranged in the same way, the same order of wreaths, the same order of service.[77] Naturally he spoke on the bible passage that had been indicated to him in the prophetic vision. To forestall any false conclusions, we must say that my friend had no idea of the illness of his acquaintance, and had never before set foot in that cemetery. Moreover he is a convinced Christian and a well-known worker in God's kingdom.

[76] cf. Schmeïng, loc. cit. [30].
[77] In Schmeïng's book the example of the prevision of funerals is frequently mentioned, cf. p. 5.

The *psychical researcher* will, in connexion with this incident, first of all have something to say about two questions. The sickness and death of the acquaintance could have been conveyed by telepathy. The sending of the telegram perhaps released some psychic impulse. The layout of the cemetery could possibly have been transmitted by the relatives of the deceased man as a telepathic image. That is as far as these basic categories take us. The concept of telepathy does not suffice to account for the exact prediction of the position of the congregation, the pastor, the pall-bearers, and the nature and composition of the wreaths. Here then we have the phenomenon of temporal prevision. In the second phase of the discussion we therefore have this phenomenon of clairvoyance, telaesthesia. We are not here concerned to deal with the various hypotheses used to explain telaesthesia. It suffices to mention them. Hans Driesch[78] supposes that the "world subject", or the higher vision of the departed, could be drawn on. E. von Hartmann speaks of a "telephone connexion in the Absolute". The psychologist Dr. Karl Schmeïng speaks of a sensitive, teleological depth perception. He thinks that the subconscious mind of man can, by instinctively sure sensitivity, develop and round off into a total picture the most tenuous contact points by "flash thinking" or "shortcircuit thinking".[79] With the remark that in the case of this prevision we are generally dealing with an assessment of possibilities and consequences, he tries by excluding metaphysical and metapsychical possibilities to emphasize the purely subjective character of these phenomena. Despite his strictly down-to-earth approach, Dr. Schmeïng admits that there is an unexplained residue, an unfathomed and perhaps unfathomable factor which remains.[80] This concession of an impenetrable residue satisfies the theologian. This conclusion is the starting point for theological reflection on the phenomenon of clairvoyance. For the theologian it is plain from the present example that the eidetic theory does not do justice to all the facts, e. g. the clear prevision of meaningful detail. Here the prevision of the whole scene, the arrangement of the wreaths, the position of the pall-bearers and the clergyman, mourners, etc., could not have been produced by a "combination at the first glance" or by a "mental snapshot",[81] since the special contents of the scene were exactly reproduced in the vision two days beforehand.

For the *pastor* it is plain from the preceding example that in the case of such visionary experiences of a religious nature, no spiritual distur-

---

[78] cf. Driesch, loc. cit. 6, p. 144.
[79] cf. Schmeïng, loc. cit. 30, pp. 143f.
[80] cf. Schmeïng, loc. cit. 30, pp. 144, 191.
[81] cf. Schmeïng, loc. cit. 30, p. 143.

bances arise, except perhaps the temptation to spiritual pride. Schmeïng writes in connexion with this, "In general those seers whose visions bear a religious character have a feeling of being favoured and elected, which under some circumstances can assume enormous proportions without being actually justified."[82] This development, however, lies on the ethical level, with which we are not here concerned.

In passing, let us say quite explicitly, in order to avoid misunderstanding, that not every clairvoyant phenomenon that has a religious content automatically stems from religious, Christian roots. There are innumerable clairvoyant phenomena with a religious tendency which arise from occult or eidetic origins. In fact, according to the material at my disposal, they present a numerical ratio of about fifty to one; i.e. for every one genuine Christian vision, there are perhaps fifty or more occult or eidetic-based apparitions. This is a remarkable fact of experience in pastoral work, which testifies that our present day with its countless visions of Mary, of Christ, or of saints, is not experiencing a great activity of the Holy Spirit, but is undergoing an occult, if not actually demonic, invasion. This pastoral observation is confirmed at least by the main premise of the psychologist Schmeïng. He writes, "It is evident that a great number of religious visions can be referred to eidetic or synaesthetic substrata."[83] Here the psychologist is giving valuable help to the pastor in his battle with the miracle craze, and with a mysticism rooted in eidetic and magic.

Compared with clairvoyant phenomena of a religious nature, the non-religious prevision experience is much commoner. This phenomenon is often nothing more than a matter of vague forecasts, but often such secular prophecy surprises by its great accuracy and minute fulfilment. In general we can probably say that in the popular mind the many misses are not weighed up against the few bulls-eyes. For this reason, far too much importance is attributed to the prevision experience. On the other hand, these non-religious prophecies are often so ambiguous that a fulfilment can almost always be read into them whatever happens. A few illustrations will elucidate the character of these visions of past and future events.

Ex 19 In 1934, a man published in a circular, which came into my hands in the same year, a number of clairvoyant and divinatory experiences. He wrote in visionary style that the German army would overrun Poland and France at a breath-taking pace. Five and six years later these "forecasts" came true.

---

82 cf. Schmeïng, loc. cit. 30, p. 162.
83 cf. Schmeïng, loc. cit. 30, p. 161.

In his explanation of this example of telaesthesia, Dr. Schmeïng may be right. Perhaps this prophesier had sensitive political intuition, which he developed in a "flash thought". Certainly there is no necessity for assuming that extrasensory perception is involved here.

Lit 5 Still more interesting is a case from literature.[84] An army captain in Germany had a prevision in 1914. He saw the development of World War I correctly. In particular, he saw the collapse of Germany in 1918 and the abdication of the Kaiser, four years before this took place. The most important part of his vision is the sentence: "Russia awakes and struggles with America for the possession of the future." Since the book in which this prophecy appears came out in 1923, this political prediction is not a *vaticinium ex eventu*. Moreover the written record of the vision was read by Prince Friedrich Wilhelm in 1915. Incidentally, we may read a similar prophecy in the "Atlas der deutschen Volkskunde".[85]

Lit 6 Besides these spontaneous experiences, which do not always cause mental disturbances, there are cases of people with "second sight" who often submit their faculty to testing. Well known is the German poet and Swiss mayor, Heinrich Zschokke, who could often read the life of a stranger as if he were reading from a book. In his case only retrospective vision is involved, and this can be explained as telepathy.[86]

Among those who have this faculty of "second sight" there are some who consider their gift interesting and regard it as a kind of blessing, not suffering under it at all. But there are others — and the picture gained in pastoral experience suggests that these are the majority — whose nervous system suffers gravely as a result. Dr. Schmeïng reports, for instance, the case of a farmer who as recently as 1933 gave a considerable sum of money to be relieved of the faculty of previsions concerning deaths.[87]

When the experiences of clairvoyants are examined from the *psychological* and *psychical* viewpoints, then this phenomenon can be explained (apart from the "impenetrable residue") in terms of telepathy and eidetic. From the *pastoral* viewpoint, the occasional, spontaneous occurrences are mostly without psychological after-effects. It is only the typical representatives of "second sight" who often experience after their visions a physical weakness and nervous exhaustion. In the cases where eidetic is coupled with magic practices — a very prevalent phenomenon — severe

84 cf. Nielsen, loc. cit. [37], p. 312.
85 cf. Schmeïng, loc. cit. [30], p. 122.
86 cf. Nielsen, loc. cit. [37], p. 37.
87 cf. Schmeïng, loc. cit. [30], p. 101.

mental disturbances result. This naturally leads us on to discuss the phenomenon of clairvoyance with *occult* roots. There follow a few instances
from pastoral experience.

Ex 20   A typical case of the coupling of eidetic and magic appears in
the occult practice of a well-know shepherd. In a series of pastoral interviews I came to know of this man as a clairvoyant, fire-charmer, cattle-
conjurer, disease-charmer, and fortune-teller. His occult gifts have won
him a great following. Since he masks his disastrous occult practices under
a cloak of bible phrases, he is regarded as a godly man. This is always the
culmination of these dark arts, when gullible people are deceived by this
Christian facade.

An example will introduce us to the practice of this man.

In the pasture this shepherd suddenly saw in accurate detail the farm
of one of the villagers in flames. The prevision was so vivid and so impressive that the shepherd told the owner of the farm concerned, "Within
four years your house will be destroyed by fire, but if you want to put
out a charm against the fire, give me an old shirt and I will charm the fire
away in it." The owner of the farm laughed about the vision and the
offer of magic protection. He declined the offer. Four years later the
property did actually catch fire, and the police were unable to in-
criminate the shepherd. For it was certainly a possibility that he would
try to establish his reputation as a seer by an act of arson. Schmeïng also
reports such exploitation of previsions. Thus a property owner once
burned down his own farm as a "fulfilment" of a prevision, in order to
improve his own financial situation.[88]

The *psychical researcher* will recognize two phenomena in this incident.
First, telaesthesia, i.e. the vision of the imminent fire, and secondly the
offer of magic protection. Here we touch on the field of so-called white
magic, which will be treated later.

The *psychologist* Schmeïng sees here one of the typical eidetic cases.
He shows in his book how such previsions of fire provide opportunities
for fire-charming, and the so-called "removal" of it into a pond, tree or
stone. He finds in the field of his own investigations many examples of
"fire-stones", "fire-trees" and "fire-lakes".[89] This "removal" is supposed
to protect against fire the object endangered by the vision.

From my pastoral work I am acquainted with stories similar to those
reported by Schmeïng in his book. In the South German area men do not
use trees or stones as charms, but rather a worn out shirt belonging to the
person threatened by the vision. The charmer wears this shirt or buries

88 cf. Schmeïng, loc. cit. 30, pp. 8f.
89 cf. Schmeïng, loc. cit. 30, p. 9.

it in the ground. Also used as charms are "fire letters", which are laid on the top beams of the house.

From the *pastoral* viewpoint I have gained some important information about the above-mentioned shepherd. For 15 years I have repeatedly had people coming to me for help, who had received occult advice or treatment from him. In particular we may note the following points, as being important for our study.

Ex 21 A woman who was charmed by this shepherd had serious emotional disturbances from that day on. She felt as if she were being chased by furies. Never before in her life had she had such experiences.

Ex 22 A young man was charmed by the shepherd and as a result actually healed of an organic disease. However from that time on he had manic fits, blasphemous thoughts against God and Christ, and abnormal sexual degeneration.

Ex 23 A family let the shepherd help them in the investigation of a theft, and also had him conjure their cattle. From the day on which they received this occult advice and help, the occupants observed peculiar spook apparitions in their house.

The list of this shepherd's activities could be continued. In all the cases with which I have become acquainted in pastoral interviews with those concerned over the last 15 years, the occult treatments of this shepherd have produced very serious emotional disturbances. The most remarkable thing about the occult practice of this man is that some of the persons treated by him suddenly became clairvoyant themselves and saw certain spook apparitions. Psychologically this is readily explained by the fact that the shepherd with his occult healing methods addresses himself to the subconscious of the patient, and thus arouses and mobilizes the powers of the subconscious.

There appears here the phenomenon, often to be observed in counselling those occultly involved, that those conjured themselves become clairvoyant. We are dealing in the case of this kind of occultly conditioned clairvoyance not with a metaphysical process, but with an activation and manifestation of the previously latent powers of the subconscious. This mobilization of the subconscious powers by an act of conjuration has a weakening, disturbing and depressing influence on the emotional life of the person concerned. Indeed, in many cases there even arises a dissociation, which is manifested in the form of spook apparitions.

The fact of the combination of eidetic and magic, which is almost always to be observed in pastoral counselling, will now be documented by a really classic case.

Ex 24 A man, constitutionally of Nordic type, tall, fair, blue-eyed, austere and reserved, for years experienced retrospective visions. On the street, in broad daylight, he would suddenly check his stride and become completely absent in spirit; his face would pale, his facial expression become immobilized, and there he would see a funeral procession coming down the street. Often the people would be wearing modern clothes, but sometimes they were in costumes of the 18th. and 19th. centuries. The cars and vehicles would drive through the processions, without their moving aside. The figures cast no shadows. They were not fixed images like photographs, but were moving, lifelike forms. If the visionary were called by name in the moment of his trance, his cataleptic state vanished and he could report his vision. These visions of the past and future were always a nerve-racking experience, which left him in a state of mental and physical exhaustion.

Besides these visions of funeral processions, he often saw ghosts of individuals. Then too he would lapse into immobility, and would see, for example, an acquaintance who had died years before. If he addressed the ghost, it would disappear. Sometimes he would see these ghosts busy at some occupation typical of them during their lifetime. Thus he might observe a former stingy farmer counting the wood pile in front of his house, just as he had always done when alive, to guard against theft. Most of these visions did not occur at dusk, but in broad daylight.

As one of his most interesting experiences, we narrate the following, which we have express permission to publish. One morning the visionary was standing at his place of work. The door opened, and a former fellow-soldier stepped in. The visionary greeted him cordially. When, however, the man he had addressed stood there with ashen face and made no answer, the seer started, and recalled that he had fallen in battle 22 years before. Then the ghost actually began to speak, and said to him: "You are partly to blame that I am with the unsaved in a place of torment: you could have warned me. So that my wife may not share my fate, go to her and say that she must repent. Otherwise she too will come to the place of torment". With this demand, the ghost vanished. The seer was now aware that this was one of his usual visions, only of an exceptionally clear quality. Thereupon he went to the local pastor and asked him what he should do about this demand. The pastor advised him to carry out the task. The woman was deeply moved by this appearance of her husband. She reviewed her life, and from that time onward became a diligent reader of the bible and a faithful attender at church services.

The evaluation of this example will yield much valuable material within the framework of our study. Therefore we shall make a rather more thorough examination of this story. The basis for this discussion is a thorough investigation into four generations of the family's history.

Since we have already given a short sketch of the physical constitution of the man, we give now the *medical* anamnesis. From the time of his youth, this visionary had not suffered from any organic or nervous disease. With advancing years he had varying rheumatic ailments. From a psychological standpoint, we can establish a certain tendency to depressions. In his youth he inclined to melancholia and suicidal thoughts. The feeling of ennui vanished when he turned to Christianity. The depressive condition did not have its root in any demonstrable psychoneurosis, organic neurosis or organic disease, but in an occult involvement, as we shall see presently.

From a biochemical point of view there is no ground for the development of "second sight", since the soil of his area is very alkaline and the water hence alkaline also.[90] As for the psychological characteristics of his racial type, we have already noted that his external constitution represents a Nordic type. The Nordic race is thought, because of its scotiogenic retardation of development (i.e. the slowing up of development due to lack of sunlight), to be especially predisposed to "second sight". It can be shown that for 300 years, however, the ancestors of this seer have lived in South Germany.

The occult anamnesis is in this case very revealing. The grandmother of this seer had, with the help of the "6th. and 7th. Book of Moses",[91] conjured cattle, charmed illnesses, practised black and white magic, and the like. This woman infected her family with magic influence for four generations. Children, grandchildren and great grandchildren all struggled with ennui, suicidal thoughts, unusual gifts of clairvoyance, and the capacity of "second sight". Further, this family is characterized by warped character and the retroversion of all their emotional relationships. The offspring of this family are on the whole reclusive, egocentric, uncongenial, insensitive and hard-natured.

Taking the apparition of the soldier with his request under critical scrutiny, we may first consider the evaluation of the *psychical researcher*. The advocate of spiritism will see in the appearance of the deceased warcomrade a proof of the spiritist hypothesis. This assumption is, however, not necessary. As long as some rational explanation is possible, we need not have recourse to the supernatural. The animistic explanation suffices

90 cf. Schmeïng, loc. cit. 30, p. 125.

91 The 6th and 7th Book of Moses has nothing to do with the biblical books of Moses. This title is a pseudonym for a collection of magic enchantments. The foreword states that the book was discovered in 1522 and published by Peter Michel, the last Carthusian monk at Erfurt. In 1950 the ruinous book was again published by the Planetverlag.

completely in this case. With this visionary, repressed feelings of guilt in his subconscious, experienced with regard to his dead comrade, may suddenly by means of hypermnesia, which functions as the familiar "stand-pipe of the subconscious",[92] have come back into his consciousness. This guilt-complex, arising from the subconscious, supplies the brain with an impulse, which sets in motion energy running outwards from the brain. This backward flow of energy produces something visible, audible, tangible and susceptible of taste and smell. Thus we have here a reversal of the respective sense experiences. This so-called reversibility theory was developed by L. Staudemeier, who was professor of chemistry at the College of Philosophy and Theology at Freising.[93] Even without this theory it is known that persons with vivid powers of imagination, such as painters, artists, sculptors, suddenly see before them, in authentic material form, the ideas which they have conceived intuitively. Then they only need to copy the "materialization" of their own ideas. This capacity to project to the outside a mental conception, and to see it again in objective form, was arributed to the poet Otto Ludwig, the author Gustav Frenssen, the English painter William Blake, and others.[94]

This genuine case of "second sight" will be of even greater interest to the *psychologist*. The experiences of this visionary bear the real marks of eidetic. The theory of so-called eidetic vision was developed by Prof. Jaensch (University of Marburg).[95a] By eidetic is meant the faculty of seeing before one as an after-image what one has seen already. To clarify this with a simple illustration: anyone who after staring at an object for one minute, and then averting his eyes or switching off the light, can see the object before him as an after-image, has eidetic vision. Eidetic vision is a normal phenomenon with many young people, but the faculty seldom appears in adults. Dr. Schmeïng has tried, by building on the research findings of Jaensch, to prove that prevision also, i.e. clairvoyant phenomena and second sight,[95b] are of an eidetic nature. He distinguishes, as Jaensch does, between a Basedowoid B-type and a Tetanoid T-type. The B-type is marked by large, shining eyes; he is lively, outgoing, conversational, confiding. He is the well-integrated type, with good harmonization of all his physical and mental functions. This B-type projects moving, lively, true-to-life "after-images", which he can also revive at will long afterward. Hence the B-type can reproduce things seen once

---

92 cf. Tischner, loc. cit. 25a, p. 42.

93 cf. L. Staudenmeier, "Die Magie als experimentelle Naturwissenschaft", Leipzig, 2nd edn. 1922.

94 cf. Schmeïng, loc. cit. 30, pp. 44f.

95a cf. E. R. Jaensch, "Die Eidetik", 3rd edn. Leipzig, 1933.

95b German: "the visions of the 'Spökenkieker' ".

in his life, project them out from himself, and see them again true to form, mobile and three-dimensional.

The T-type is marked by dull, deep-set eyes and a hard-bitten facial expression. His movements are stiff, angular and awkward. He is reserved, distrustful, timid, insecure, uncongenial. He is not integrated, and has poor co-ordination of his physical and mental functions. His eidetic images are immobile, stiff, flat like photographs, and appear only in complementary colours. The visions are felt to be annoying and depressing, and come upon the visionary involuntarily, without or against his will, and without any previous mental attunement.

These two types seldom appear in an unmixed form. Young people and occasionally artists belong predominantly to the B-type. Adult visionaries are usually T-types. The visionary whose experiences we are here discussing likewise belongs to the stiff, depressive T-type, with however a touch of the B-type, in that his visions produce lively images that are true to life. Moreover with this seer we find typical features of eidetic: the trance in the moment of vision, the spontaneity of the visions during working hours, in broad daylight, the release from the cataleptic trance when his name was called, the feeling of depression after the experience, the characteristic observations of ghosts engaged in a typical activity. Dr. Schmeïng[96] reports similar stories of two ghost appearances. In one an old man returned regularly and took a book from the shelf. In another, a miller counted at night the sacks in his mill. The dead man's sons saw this apparition and were not troubled by it.

A special mark of the intensity of the seer's vision in our present example is the conversation with the deceased war comrade. Here we have a good example of the backward flow of energy in the visual and auditory fields. The seer sees and hears that which his own subconscious stages before him. A person with eidetic vision thus has the faculty of projecting outside himself complexes from his subconscious mind, and then experiencing the projection in clear and definite sensation, passively without the use of his will. In this way we can however explain only the phenomenon of retrospective visions. Rational and psychological explanation of non-relgous prophecy presents considerably greater difficulties. Dr. Schmeïng, we recall, had to resort here to the already familiar compromise of the impenetrable residue.

The *pastor* has a valuable contribution to make in the case of the seer. Significant, just as in *Ex 21*, is the occult origin of the "second sight". The grandmother of the seer practised magic. Her descendants, involved in similar occult activity, developed more and more clearly the phe-

---

[96] cf. Schmeïng, loc. cit. [30], p. 155.

nomenon of "second sight". With the daughter there was as yet no definitely eidetic stamp, but she did have other marks of occult involvement. The grandson was a seer. However, he only experienced visions of the past, and no predictive visions. One of the great grand-daughters had previsions. Once she saw in advance the death of her own child, which occurred soon afterwards. Another great grandson also had a strong eidetic predisposition, which however he strongly resisted. Our present case is one of the many examples which show how magic conjuration will result in clairvoyance and eidetic in following generations. Dr. Schmeïng has related in his book many examples where "second sight" is coupled with the practice of charming, without his having seen any deeper connexion in this combination.

The second question which interests the pastor is: was the advice of the clergyman correct? Presumably the clergyman let himself be misled by the religious content of the vision into counselling the seer to carry out the request of the ghost. The psychotherapist will perhaps under some circumstances approve of the clergyman's advice, seeing here an opportunity of dissolving the guilt complex. For psychotherapy is of course always concerned with the uncovering, disentanglement and dissolution of complexes. In spite of this, I should like to challenge the decision on three grounds. First, the New Testament rejects the idea that the dead are sent as messengers of God. A similar request by the rich man in Luke 16 met with the answer: "They have Moses and the prophets; let them hear them".[97] Thus the N.T. rejects messages from the dead, on the ground that the living have the word of God.[98] That is where they can learn God's will. Secondly, I am against the obeying of such requests because I know from many similar examples what such mysterious happenings can lead to. The first request is sensible; the second less sensible; the third is ill-advised; the fourth is nonsensical and absurd. Thus the requests continue to come until the unfortunate seer is in the grip of a compulsion neurosis, and is forced to carry out the most absurd commands. I have followed the development of such complusions from their outset, and am of the opinion that such requests are to be refused from the beginning, however much they be in accord with a known religious truth. My third ground for declining such a request is the fact that a Christian does not need the command of a ghost in order to be freed from his sense of guilt. For this the bible has an entirely different way, the way to Jesus Christ.

97 cf. the parable of the rich man and Lazarus, Luke 16, 19—31.

98 Jung-Stilling likewise rejects the carrying out of requests by phantoms. cf. Heinrich Jung-Stilling, "Theorie der Geisterkunde", Zeitbücherverlag, Nuremberg 1921, vol. II p. 65.

The third question which concerns the pastor in this case is whether the seer desires to be delivered from his visions, always accompanied as they are by a certain feeling of depression and nervous exhaustion. It is a well-known fact that the gift of "second sight" increases or decreases, according to whether the seer yields himself to his aptitude or resists it. Moreover, it is also continually observed that with advancing age the gift gradually disappears. Nonetheless there are seers who retain their gift to a great age. Schmeïng tells of a visionary who was eighty-six years old.[99]

In our example it happened that the visions of the seer persistently increased, although he resisted them and told them to no one. Only his own wife, and in this one instance the local pastor, knew of his gift. The visions were a terrible nuisance to the man. Not only did he see funeral processions on the street; at every house and corner, in the trees, fields and meadows, wherever he stood or walked, he saw spirits of the departed. The result was that he developed an anxiety state. In this condition he came to me for an interview. After both he and his wife had found the way to Christ in a succession of interviews, I asked him whether he really desired liberation from his clairvoyant ability. On receiving an affirmative answer, I pointed him to Matthew 18, 19; "If two of you shall agree on earth about anything they ask, it will be done for them by my Father in heaven". We joined together with his wife in prayer that God might deliver him from the gift of spirit visions, since his nervous system was suffering severely because of them. Our prayer was answered. Since that united prayer in 1938, the man has never again had any more visions. And so he was finally delivered from his clairvoyant gift, which was certainly not a gift of grace, but the curse resulting from the conjuration practised by his family.[100]

(d) *Clairsentience*

A further case of hyperaesthesia is clairsentience. In the examples which have become known to me in pastoral experience, we are dealing with an irrational diagnosis of illness. Several types have come to light in the course of my pastoral work. A few examples will introduce the complex of problems.

Ex 25 A man in an East German university town before the war became well-known for his amazing accuracy in diagnosing ailments. In his diagnosis he used no medical helps such as percussion, stethoscope,

---

99 cf. Schmeïng, loc. cit. 30, p. 155.

100 Jung-Stilling reports a similar pastoral experience: cf. loc. cit. 98, p. 74: "This black spirit was later removed by the prayers of the preacher. It appears no more".

analysis of urine and faeces, blood-count, X-rays, cardiograms, etc., but merely laid his hand on that of the patient, concentrated on him, and then pronounced his diagnosis, which agreed in all cases which were checked with the diagnosis of the university clinic. Sometimes doctors tried to deceive him, in order to test his ability. They were not successful.

Ex 26   Another para-psychological method of diagnosis is the discovery of diseases by "crystal gazing". I know of a Black Forest farmer who advises his patients in this manner. In contrast to *Ex 25*, this clairvoyant's diagnosis is not always successful.

Ex 27   For twenty years I have known of the disastrous practice of two brothers, who, without touching their patients, are able by simple concentration to diagnose with great accuracy and then prescribe homoeopathic remedies.

Ex 28   A fourth kind of diagnosis became known to me from the practice of rod and pendulum manipulators. Often I have had this process of rod or pendulum diagnosis explained to me by a practitioner. The rod or pendulum is held against the body of the patient. When it is held over the affected organ, the rod or pendulum moves.

Ex 29   A fifth kind of para-psychological diagnosis is the use of the pendulum to select medicines. Here the practitioner makes no diagnosis of the ailment; he is only concerned with finding the correct medicine. A man known to me, a respected practitioner, who is at the same time a spiritist, healer, magnetizer, and so practises a whole series of occult functions, possesses a square medicine cabinet with 225 compartments, arranged 15 by 15, with medicines. Above the compartments hangs a pendulum. The patient sets the pendulum swinging with his hand. The pendulum then points out which medicine is needed for his ailment.[101]

Ex 30   A sixth kind of diagnosis is the use of a pendulum over charts of the human body and of the individual organs. While the practitioner's left hand rests on the hand of the patient, his right hand operates the pendulum. The pendulum circles over the ailing organ. This procedure corresponds in principle to the use of a pendulum with a photograph, which we shall discuss later.[102]

[101] Glahn reports a similar pendulum practice carried on by the Catholic priest Dr. Adolf Pientka in Lewin. In a sample box there are a great number of medicines in little tubes. The priest touches the various medicines with his left hand. With his right he holds the pendulum. The movement of the pendulum indicates the correct medicine. cf. Glahn, "Pendellehre", Uranus Verlag, Memmingen, 1936, vol. V, p. 147.

[102] cf. Volkmann, loc. cit. [38], § 87.

From the *para-psychological* point of view, several phenomena arise here which do not all fall under the heading of clairsentience. They are merely grouped together here because they all concentrate on the diagnosis of disease.

Ex 25 is undoubtedly a remarkable phenomenon. Are we dealing, in this example of clairsentience, with a psychometric process analogous to psychometric clairvoyance,[103] since the practitioner first establishes a contact by touching the hand of the patient, and then feels his way into the diseased condition? Or does the hypothesis of Baerwald apply here, that in every form of psychometry we are dealing with telepathy in "disguise"?[104] We shall not yet offer an answer to this, but merely indicate the problem.

Diagnosis by crystal gazing brings us on to a different level. Tischner treats this phenomenon as a sensory automatism. He calls the products of crystal gazing meaningless fantasies. He admits however that genuinely super-normal facts do sometimes come to light in this manner as well.[105] Beyond the customary explanation of it as a "stand-pipe of the subconscious", he has nothing to add regarding this phenomenon.

Ex 27 leads us a step further in our investigation. In my pastoral work these two brothers have caused me much trouble. Both of these clairsentients have been consulted for many years by thousands of patients. What lies behind the accurate diagnosis of these medically unschooled brothers? Although we may make some progress towards explaining it by putting it down to quackery, or a general, highly-developed gift of empathy, or an above-average understanding of people, we cannot attain a full explanation in this way. According to my observations in many pastoral cases, we may regard this clairsentience as a mediumistic gift in these untrained healers. The clairsentient is able, just as is the medium, to tap the subconscious of the person present. The next problem which arises from this explanation is the question whether a person's disease can be read out of his subconscious anyway.

To find an answer, we shall first hear the view of a *medical* expert, Prof. Brauchle.[106] Man is in his mental structure a unity with three levels, consisting of the conscious, the subconscious and the organic unconscious. To the consciousness, i.e. the peak of this power pyramid, belongs above all the power of volitional activity. The consciousness has no direct in-

---

[103] cf. Tischner, loc. cit. 25a, p. 92.
[104] cf. Tischner, loc. cit. 25a, p. 125.
[105] cf. Tischner, loc. cit. 25a, p. 46.
[106] cf. Brauchle, loc. cit. 43, pp. 62f.; op. cit. 42, p. 10.

fluence on the subconscious or organic unconscious. The subconscious is a mental power store. It is characterized above all by its activity as the motor of the imagination. The deepest level, the oldest power and base of the power pyramid, is the organic unconscious. This term includes all the involuntary body functions, such as the heart-beat, the gland-activity, the vascular functions, metabolism, secretion and decontamination.

"Just as there is a mutual exchange between the conscious and the subconscious in the sense that forgotten or repressed experiences are preserved in the subconscious, and memories and recollections are made available to the consciousness, so there are also mutual relations between the mental subconscious and the organic unconscious".[107] This relation between the subconscious and the organic unconscious becomes visible in suggestion. If, for instance, in hypnosis a stigma is suggested, then there is present in the subconscious only the idea of the wound. The organic unconscious then takes up this impulse of the subconscious and effects, through changes of the blood supply to a certain area of the skin, the bleeding wound, as a secondary effect of the suggestion. This secondary effect is possible as a result of both hetero- and auto-suggestion. (If at this point we may be allowed to make an observation in parenthesis, it is that stigmata as a religious phenomenon are to be understood entirely in medical terms, and not as miracles of God.) Brauchle's theory of the relations between the separate levels of the power pyramid is a key of the first importance for the understanding of mental disturbances, and especially for the pastoral treatment of those occultly subjected. It gives us further evidence that rational ideas can, by way of the subconscious, release organic reactions. This assertion, which has been proved experimentally for many years in hypnosis, and has recently undergone a more thorough scientific investigation in the pscho-somatic school, enables us in the framework of this study to understand the amateur practice of suggestion, as it is practised by a host of unqualified conjurers. This practice of conjuring will be discussed in a later chapter.

Here in this section we are concerned with the question whether a clairsentient with mediumistic gifts can make a reliable diagnosis of an ailment. This question can only be answered affirmatively if, apart from the psychical problem of mediumistic gifts, proof can be provided that the organic unconscious also mediates impulses back to the subconscious. The first question, viz. whether the subconscious reacts on the organic unconscious, has been answered affirmatively by medical science. The second question, whether the organic unconscious acts upon the subconscious, has also been affirmed by medical science, insofar as in a num-

[107] cf Brauchle, op. cit. [42], p. 10.

ber of mental disorders the cause may be traced to organic changes.[108] Medicine thereby acknowledges both forward and backward working relations within the power pyramid. We can illustrate this process by two medical examples. First we note a case of organic disturbances due to psychogenic causes. In cases of purposive hysterical reaction, disturbances of motor function can lead to psychogenic paralysis.[109] These hysterical paralyses lack, of course, changes of tonus or reflex, fibrillation and atrophy. Through prolonged inactivity, however, an atrophy will set in in the paralysed members.[110] An example from pastoral experience will illustrate this process.

Ex 31   In the first World War, a soldier had the experience of being buried under a small quantity of earth, from which he was soon released. The desire to be classed "unfit for combat" and to be given a pension brought on a "pension neurosis",[111] with the symptom of paralysis in one leg. He attained both his wishes. After the war his leg speedily improved. Nonetheless, each time he went to the doctor he limped considerably worse than the time before. The paralysis must not disappear, for then he would lose his pension. Today his leg, after thirty-five years of disuse, shows clear indications of atrophy.

Thus there appears here the forward movement of the wish for a pension, through the subconscious to the organic unconscious. The wish is transmitted from the apex of the pyramid down to the base. The final result is an emaciated, deteriorated leg.

Examples of the reverse process are common enough in internal medicine. Let us adduce one example as an illustration.[112] Among the vascular ailments there is a form of cerebral sclerosis which manifests itself chiefly in mental disturbances. Among the emotional symptoms melancholia must in particular be mentioned. Here we have an organically conditioned vascular disease, which through the organic unconscious and the subconscious arouses mental disturbances which are registered in the consciousness as an emotional disorder. Here we have a mental impulse from the base of the power pyramid to its apex.

---

[108] As examples we may mention that emotional disorders like melancholia, bad temper, sadness, depressions, can have various organic causes, e.g. organic diseases like jaundice; disturbance of the endocrine glands like oxophthalmic goitre and idiopathic myxoedema; heart diseases like cardiac asthma, paroxysmal tachycardia, weakness of the heart muscle, etc.

[109] cf. Kloos, loc. cit. 12, p. 442.

[110] cf. Kloos, loc. cit. 12, p. 56.

[111] cf. Kloos, loc. cit. 12, p. 447.

[112] cf. Brugsch, loc. cit. 10, vol. I, p. 621.

These descending and ascending interrelations in the mental pyramid accordingly form a circuit of psycho-organic correspondence *(circulus relationis psychoorganicae)*. Here we have a key to the understanding of the phenomena of clairsentience and conjuration. Conjuration, which involves an active exertion of influence upon this circuit, will be discussed in the section on extra-sensory influence. Clairsentience, which is the passive tapping of this circuit, is the subject of our present discussion. The clairsentient takes up, by means of his mediumistic sensitivity, the impulses which arise from the affected organ, through the organic unconscious, to the subconscious. Medically, the *circulus relationis psychoorganicae* is the presupposition for this tapping process. It remains now, as far as the phenomenon of clairsentience is concerned, only to explain the psychical process of tapping in.

In psychical research we are acquainted with the tapping of the consciousness in the phenomenon of telepathy, which is recognized by scientists. We further know the tapping of the subconscious in the phenomenon of mediumship, which in the last 80 years has been confirmed by hundreds of thousands of experiments carried out by trained experts and competent laymen. In the pastoral care of those occultly subjected, the fact of mediumship is discerned in many cases.

In view of these experiments, we can perhaps understand the phenomenon of clairsentience in *Ex 26* and *Ex 27* as a mediumistic tapping of the subconscious of the patient. Probably the phenomenon of rhabdomancy and pendulum diagnosis in *Ex 28* lies on the same plane. The impulses which are tapped from the subconscious of the patient are merely converted, in the subconscious of the pendulum diagnostician, as a motor automatism[113] into movements of the rod or pendulum. *Ex 29* comes very near to irresponsible charlatanry. If we wanted to read a psychical phenomenon into *Ex 29* we should need to link a series of metaphysical processes, like mediumistic tapping, psychokinesis or suggestion, and a clairvoyant ability to select the right medicine. This conglomeration of magical processes is, even for the psychical researcher, still beyond the range of reasonable discussion. *Ex 30* again lies on the level of quackery. We have not in this section touched on spiritistic clairsentience, in which not only the astral dissociation effect of clairsentience, but allegedly also information from the deceased, is sought, in order to give the right diagnosis and to prescribe the correct medicine.

If we are asked to make an empirical judgement regarding the degree of accuracy in the diagnosis, then we must say that the diagnosis is only medically accurate in the case of a strong mediumistic aptitude in the

113 cf. Tischner, op. cit. 25a, p. 44.

clairsentient. The less sensitivity there is present, the less reliable will be the diagnosis, even to the point of a complete chaos of gross errors. In our series of examples of clairsentients, experience shows that only *Ex 25* was a reliable diagnostician. *Ex 27* also produced for years some astonishing diagnoses. All the other examples fall away rapidly in the matter of accuracy. Since clairsentience is not built up on exact medical science, but is dependent for its accuracy on the degree of mediumistic sensitivity, it must be rejected from the medical point of view. These occult methods of healing are not defensible from the standpoint of public health. It always remains a mystery why the officials of public health allow so much liberty to occult workers of nature cures, magnetizers, healers, pendulum diagnosticians, wonder-doctors, etc. We urgently need a revision of the laws dealing with healing practitioners.

From the *pastoral viewpoint* the whole series from *Ex 25* to *Ex 30* almost always present the same psychological consequences: melancholia, boredom, anxiety, aversion to God's word, inhibition in prayer, inability to make a spiritual decision — in one word, a freezing of mental and spiritual functions. An example of a pastoral interview will emphasize this.

Ex 32   During a Bible Week, a 19-year-old girl came to me for an interview. She complained of melancholia, joylessness, unusual visitations during the night, as if someone were trying to strangle her. She had no desire for prayer, and although she was a follower of Christ, she felt nausea at any religious activity. She did not understand herself, since she had on the one hand a desire to follow Christ, and on the other a revulsion against doing so.

A medical anamnesis disclosed nothing of note. The girl, apart from her emotional disturbances, was in good health. There was neither organic nor neurotic disorder. Neither had she had any unsettling experiences, such as a disappointment in love. The melancholia had begun while she was still going to school. Parents, brothers and sisters were all well. No other member of the family had had such an ailment; she was the sole case in the family.

After the medical anamnesis we conducted an anamnesis of occult involvements. Many questions in this direction disclosed nothing. Finally we hit on a decisive point. As a schoolgirl she had suffered from lack of appetite. Because of this her mother took her several times to see a "wonder-doctor", who sought the source of the ailment by means of a pendulum. The girl remembered that since that treatment her melancholia had set in.

This example is only one out of a large collection in this field. Pastoral experience shows that with all the healing methods of these unqualified healers, in which the subconscious of the patient is actively influenced or passively tapped, decisive changes in the mental condition of the patient take place. An emotional torpor results, which not only shows itself in melancholic states, but above all paralyses the ability to make decisions in small matters of daily life, and in the spiritual sphere scarcely allows any decision of faith to take place. The mass of examples and observations which have been collected through the years paint a shocking picture of the spiritual devastations which result from the activity of occult healers in every branch of this disastrous profession.

Divination

By divination is meant the art of soothsaying in its widest sense, i.e. the unveiling of hidden things in the past, present and future. The difference between this and clairvoyance lies in the fact that the retrospective and predictive visions of the clairvoyant are spontaneous experiences, which come over the seer without any preparation or mental volition on his part. The diviner, on the other hand, makes use of certain omens and means — arrows (the Babylonians and Persians), livers,[114] goblets (the Egyptians), entrails (the Greeks and Romans), runic letters (the Germani), rock crystals, snow crystals, marbles, mirrors, cards and palm lines (the enlightened Europeans), hazel-twigs, pendulums, etc. — to achieve his prophecy. Divination appears in every epoch of human history.

From the O.T. we know of the Canaanite charmers, wizards, augurs, necromancers, dowsers etc.[115] From the same source we also learn something of the Babylonian practice, already mentioned, of inspecting livers and arrows,[116] and also of the Egyptian custom of cup-divining.[117] The Bible also gives us much material regarding the pagan roots of astrology. It was the Babylonians who held, as a basic ingredient of their faith, the unity of the macrocosm and the microcosm, and who taught that a man's fate was greatly dependent on the constellation of the star groups at the time of his birth. The O.T. consistently rejects this worship of the stars.[118]

---

114 There is a clay model of a sheep's liver from Babylon (from ca. 2000 B. C.). On it can be seen socalled magic lines squares and perforations. Probably it was used for giving instruction.

115 cf. Deut. 18, 10—12; Hos. 4, 12.

116 cf. Ezek. 21, 21.

117 cf. Gen. 44, 5.

118 cf. Isa, 47, 12f.

From the Greek world we know of Cassandra of Pytho, and the oracle at Delphi. Paul met a sooth-sayer at Philippi.[119] The Etruscans and the Romans had their *haruspices*, who divined on the basis of entrails from the sacrificial beasts. Also the fraternity of water-diviners, or dowsers, was to be found at Rome. They were called *aquileges* (water-readers). Juturna, nymph of the watersprings, was represented with a hazel-twig in her hand. A digest of Roman soothsaying is provided by the Sibylline Books, which extensively define the sacrificial cultus.

Of the Scythians we know that they exposed perjury by the use of a wand. Strabo knows of female soothsayers among the Cimbrians. The Germani also had their soothsayers, e.g. Veleda and Thorbjörg, whom Roman writers mention.[120] The Germanic tribes also practised rune divination with their letter staves.

This line of magic runs through all the millenia to the present day. In the last two centuries the history of missions has yielded valuable material on this question. On all the mission fields Christianity has had to struggle with the heathen arts of divination. In Africa it was the witch-doctor, in Tibet the red-hooded monks with their occult practices, among the Malays it was the Pawang and among the pigmy peoples of Malaya the Poyang. In China there existed besides the idol-priests the stronger cult of geomancers with their system of Fung-shui.[121] In East Siberia there were the Shamans, among the Eskimo the Angekok, among the American Indians the tribal or magic priests. These all presented a strong occult and magic resistance to the advance of Christianity.

In enlightened Europe divination is, in spite of rationalism and the blossoming of science, very prevalent. The daily and weekly papers satisfy the superstition of all classes of society with their astrological forecasts. Card-layers, fortune-tellers, palmists, tea-leaf-diviners, crystal gazers, etc. pursue a flourishing trade.[122] Information about the fate of missing persons is given by means of a pendulum held over a photograph. Superstitious dependence on omens and fetishes such as lucky mascots, horseshoes, four-leaf clovers, lucky pigs, chimney-sweeps, black ravens,

---

[119] cf. Acts 16, 16—18.

[120] cf. Tacitus, Germania 8; Caesar, de bello Gallico I. 50.

[121] Fung-shui means "wind, water". This expression is a term for a superstitious system of sooth-saying in China.

[122] cf. Hans Lilje, "Sonntagsblatt" of 10. 10. 48: "In America $ 125 million are spent every year on fortune-telling, according to a report made at the opening of an exhibition about superstition in New York. In Berlin some 1000 people gain their livelihood by fortune-telling, palmistry, horoscope casting, and similar mysterious arts. Church leaders estimate that in Germany there are more fortune tellers with "supernatural" powers than clergy in both confessions."

owl-calls, the number 13, etc., reveals that departure from the Christian faith ends in magic enslavement and occult subjection. What effect this magic propensity of modern man has upon his soul is a serious problem of pastoral work, to which we are seeking to find an answer in the course of this study. As the first section we shall deal with in this field, we take cartomancy.

(a) *Card-laying*

A few examples from pastoral experience will show the mental effects of both passive and active involvement in card-laying.

Ex 33   A young woman came for an interview during a Bible Week, and related the following experience. She had grown up in a pietistic family. At sixteen she moved into a town to take up a job in domestic service. On her free Sunday afternoon she was taken by a friend into a neighbouring town to see a woman who was a card reader. It was the first visit to this woman for both of the girls. The fortune-teller laid cards for both of them, and explained to the one who came to me, "In eight days your father will be dead". The girl laughed aloud and said, "My father is in perfect health. I don't believe you". The girls returned to the place where they were living. In the evening the girl who was telling me this took up her bible, as she had always done at home, to read it and to pray. Immediately she had a feeling of anxiety, and a gripping pain about her throat. She could neither read the bible nor pray. At the same time she heard a sound of whirring, rushing and flitting around her bed. In her fear she kept the light on. These peculiar spook manifestations recurred every evening. The peak of her tension came on the eighth day, when she received a telegram from home, calling her to come home as her father had died. He had been stricken by a heart attack in the midst of his work, and snatched away from life. Shaken, she hurried home, thinking, "The card-layer was right after all". From the day of her father's death further manifestations began. Every night her deceased father appeared in a dream and asked her accusingly: "Why did you bring this upon me by consulting the card layer?" For six months the dreams recurred. She confessed her sin and claimed Christ's promise to forgive and free her. Afterwards she was again able to read the Bible and to pray.

First we may let the *doctor* have his say. He will have little to say about this incident. The girl was healthy. Nor did her family reveal any emotional disorders or mental illness. The psychiatrist will of course explain the spook manifestations as hallucinations, although there was no medical reason for them. A shock neurosis alone — if we are to understand that one developed as a result of the obituary telegram — can certainly lead to delusions at the moment of shock; but these never last very long.

The *psychologist*, with his knowledge of the hidden mental processes of the subconscious, will explain the spook manifestations by reference to the two components of fear and guilt, conditioned by the girl's Christian upbringing. A similar solution to the problem of the father's appearance in a dream will be offered by the *dream analyst*. For, of course, in her youth the girl must have been often told by her father, "A Christian does not involve herself in occult matters". The transgression of this command was intensified by her fear of her father and the consciousness of sin committed, until it became a guilt complex, which was abreacted in a waking or sleeping dream.

The *psychical researcher* will be less interested in the psychological effects than in the phenomenon of cartomancy. Was the exact prediction of the death a coincidence? There can be no thought here of telepathic tapping, for the girl knew nothing but the image of a perfectly healthy father. The theory of teleological depth-vision, of a concentration of thought on the final result, is just as untenable. Nor does the hypothesis that the father died as a result of auto-suggestion fit here, since the girl had not written to her parents about the forbidden visit. Here we certainly have a case involving the unexplained residue.

From the *pastoral* standpoint these psychological disturbances again fit into the pattern already suggested. The Christian incurs damage in psychological as well as in spiritual respects by passive occult treatment or influences. This will be confirmed by some further examples.

Ex 34 A young lady desired to know at the beginning of the war whether her fiancé would return home from the field. She went to a card layer, who told her that her wish would be granted. He did in fact return home safe and sound. But from the day of her visit to the fortune-teller, the girl suffered from moods of depression, and ennui. After her fiancé had returned, she one day cut her wrist and elbow veins. Fortunately her life was saved.

From the medical point of view this example offers nothing in response to the usual questions we have mentioned. The girl came from a healthy, solid, Christian family. Nor is there anything of particular interest from the psychical point of view. On the pastoral level we have here the same typical pattern of occult involvement and its effects.

Ex 35 A young woman whose husband was missing on the Eastern front went to a card layer to find out whether he was still alive. The fortune-teller replied, "Your husband is dead". The wife waited three months, and again visited a card layer to find out about the uncertain fate of her husband. Again the answer was, "Your husband will not return". She went home in despair, and turning on the gas killed herself and her two children. The next day the husband returned from a Russian prison-camp, and found the dead bodies of his three loved ones.

This is a shocking example from the post-war period, which on the one hand shows the unreliability of cartomancy, and on the other the urgent need for statutory prohibition of this dark art.

From the *pastoral* point of view we see here once more the curse of occult activity. The young wife did not gain accurate information from the fortune-teller, but the inspiration for a triple murder.

Ex 36 After these examples of passive participation in occult practice, we now see an example of the active practice of cartomancy. A man who engaged in fortune-telling and card laying began to suffer severe depressions, as a result of which he one day threw himself under a train. His wife and daughter, for whom he often laid cards, both show tendencies to melancholia.

For the *pastor* these psychological effects of divination are always appearing, in the form of suicidal thoughts, blasphemous thoughts about the Trinity, a sense of impending insanity, fits of rage, complete loss of concentration, attacks of mania, and suicide. I have been told repeatedly in pastoral interviews that the visits to card layers resulted from ignorance or curiosity. They were not believed or taken seriously at all. In reply to such arguments, I generally use a parable to illustrate what my experience has shown me: "Whether it is out of ignorance or curiosity, whether as a joke or in all seriousness, when I release the catch of a hand grenade, the result is always the same!"

A new element in our discussion will be introduced by an example from the experience of the Swiss evangelist Schwendimann.[123]

Lit 7 An eighteen-year-old girl had her fortune told concerning her love affairs. The fortune teller declared, "You will not live past your twentieth birthday". The girl lived for two years in fear of her predicted early death. At the approach of her twentieth birthday a dreadful suspense arose within her. The date predicted passed without any special occurrence. But the girl had not survived the emotional trial. The next day she had to be sent to a mental hospital, where she died two years later.

Psychologically this case is perfectly straight-forward. Through the fortune-teller this girl fell under a suggestion spell, and obeying this unconscious pressure she contributed to the fulfilment of the forecast.

---

123 cf. Hans Schwendimann, "Gegen die Not des Aberglaubens", Heft 2, "Wahrsagerei und ihre Folgen", Kommissionsverlag, Ev. Buchhandlung, St. Gallen, pp. 4f.

Here we see entering in what Schmeïng too has expounded in his study.[124a] The recipient of a forecast or divination is, by his willingness to believe the forecast, setting his own terminal date. There follows a reversal of cause and effect. The fortune-teller does not actually know of the impending death, but by her influence upon the psyche she contributes to the outcome. Seen from a legal point of view, many cases of fortune-telling ought to be brought to the bar of justice, just like actual murder.

From the *pastoral* point of view, we see here the curse of fortune-telling, which would be more accurately described as lie-telling.[124b] The lie believed becomes a reality. The word of Jesus is here fulfilled in reverse: "According to your faith be it done to you".[125] The so-called unveiling of the future by diviners reveals itself as no more than a frightful psychological pressure, to which many are not equal, especially as most of the divinations are unmasked as arbitrary products of the imagination or as subconscious desires latent in the seeker, which have been tapped by the mediumistic gifts of the fortune-teller. It is very remarkable that an experienced warden of a mental hospital reports that 60 % of mental disorders of all kinds — to be taken with a pinch of salt — originate in some kind of connexion with fortune-telling and divination.[126] Since the pretended unveiling of the future by magical practices has such consequences, we judge that the veiling of the future is part of the great wisdom and mercy of Him who has hung an impenetrable veil over it.

(b) *Chiromancy, or Palmistry*

The Romans said, "Ex ungue leonem", i.e. "you can recognize the lion by its claws". Graphology and palmistry take their cue from this proverb. The *graphologist* concurs with the Roman and says, "you can recognize the man by his paw". This sentence undoubtedly has its element of truth. In recent times character study and medicine have accepted the thesis that man presents a harmonious unity in his spiritual and mental functions and in his organic, bodily parts. Every segment of his body bears in form and function the impress of man's unified personality — his gait, his bearing, his manner of speech, his imitations, his facial expressions, his handwriting, his temperament, etc. Hence we cannot reject outright a graphology which is conducted with moderation and purpose according to these psychological and medical points of view. The hand of man is

---

124a cf. Schmeïng, loc. cit. [30], p. 140.
124b The German for fortune-telling is "Wahrsagerei" lit. "truth-telling".
125 cf. Matt. 9, 29.
126 cf. Schwendimann, op. cit. [123], p. 4.

such a distinct, characteristic instrument, that from its structure conclusions about the person can be drawn. There are sensitive, artistic hands; firm, strong-willed hands; weak, sentimental hands; lax and apathetic hands; sensual and perverse hands. All these give an immediate clue to the student of human character. From this viewpoint it is easy to understand why law courts and large firms ask for and evaluate the findings of graphologists.

Though we acknowledge the rational and scientific basis of graphology, it must be stated that this scientific basis is often abandoned. Just as with many specialized branches of psychology, — we shall see this again in our critical analysis of eidetic — there is here too such a thing as a combination of graphology and magic. Magazines carry advertisements inviting people to send a sample of their handwriting, together with an advance payment of 50p and their date of birth, and offering a character analysis and a forecast of the person's future. Here we see a mixture of true character analysis and fortune-telling.

We are brought a step further when we come to chiromancy, which no longer has anything to do with graphology. Here we have fortune-telling by study of the hands. The hand is divided into areas and lines. There is a lunar mountain, the Venus belt, the Martian plain, and areas for spirit, fortune, success, fame, imagination, will and sensuousness. Further, there are four lines which dominate the surface of the palm: the head line, the heart line, the profession line and the life line. From these indications palmists claim to divine and foretell the future. A few examples will show the kind of results which this chiromantic practice presents for the pastor.

Ex 37 A friend of mine who is an art dealer told me in an interview of the following experience. After a business deal he travelled with a certain client from Switzerland to Milan, to sell a lot of diamonds worth £6000. The client wished to negotiate the sale. After a two-day stop in Milan, the client tried by every means to persuade the dealer to make a trip to Venice, under the pretext that the buyer had gone there. The dealer had a suspicious feeling and declined to go on the trip.

The next day the diamonds were suddenly stolen. The owner immediately notified the police. Meanwhile he also sought out a fortune-teller in Milan, to get information about the theft. The fortune-teller, who practised card laying as well as palmistry, notified him that on the previous day he was to have been killed in a city with much water. Further, she said, he would recover the diamonds that day. They lay under a vehicle in the cathedral square. But he should fetch them that day: the next day would be too late. After this amazing oracle, the dealer returned to his hotel. Two detectives had arrived there to investigate the case. After a phone call, the client showed up at the hotel late in the evening, and was at once taken into custody. When cross-examined, the prisoner admitted to complicity in the theft. The same night, with the help of the prisoner, the diamonds were recovered from their unusual hiding place. They were precisely where the fortune-teller had said.

As appeared from the subsequent trial, the questionable client belonged to an international smuggling gang. This gang most probably had in mind not only this theft but also the elimination of the wealthy art dealer in Venice. On a gondola ride in the night one blow on the head would have sufficed to enable the unconscious man to "disappear" in the silent waters.

That is the report, confirmed from a first-hand source, of an event which transpired in 1935. But the contact with the fortune-teller had meanwhile a remarkable sequel. For several weeks the art dealer was plagued by vivid dreams. As he was falling asleep, he always saw a hideous dog, which tried to catch him by the throat and would cause painful pressure on his chest. Then he continually saw in a dream a stone whizzing through the room towards him, which first took the form of a snake's head and then of a sneering devil's grimace. After a considerable time these terror-dreams subsided.

Five years later, the dealer experienced a first conversion to Christianity. He began to pray and to read the bible. But now new attacks began. Every time he prayed, he had the feeling that a gruesome form was standing behind him, trying to hinder him from praying. This struggle lasted a long time. Finally he lapsed back into worldliness.

Several years passed, and then during a gospel campaign the dealer once again turned to Christ. He came for several pastoral interviews, in the course of which he made a decision for Christ. In connexion with this new experience, there were again all manner of mental disturbances and obstructions to overcome. It now seems probable that the dealer will persevere in his new resolve, for he has spoken openly to his friends of his new life. It is with his express permission that this story is made public.

From the *medical* viewpoint this example need not be evaluated, since the art dealer has never in his life been seriously ill. The *psychologist* and the dream analyst will connect the terror-dreams with the temporary loss of the diamonds and with the threat on his life suggested by the fortune-teller. A detailed analysis would proceed as follows: the black dog is the usual symbol of an evil conscience; the diamonds had namely been smuggled across the border by the client who accompanied the art dealer, and this troubled the art dealer. The flying stone symbolizes the diamonds, which in those days in Milan filled his mind and thoughts. The snake's head represents the dishonest negotiator, who tried to entice the dealer into a trap. The leering devil's face is again the negotiator, who later proved to be a smuggler and a thief. The progressive changes from stone to snake's head and then to devil's face show the growing distrust of the dealer, who experienced how the originally innocent-seeming jewel-jobber gradually was exposed as an illegal contrabandist, smuggler, deceiver and finally thief. The originally honest client changed by degrees into a wily rogue bent on throwing a noose round the dealer's neck and pulling it tight. The mounting threat appears in the dream as a collocation of the three successive symbols coming to attack him. The recurrence of the similar dreams shows the intensity with which this theft affair was experienced.

The *para-psychological* problem raised by this case is not so simple as the dream analysis. How did the palmist know the whereabouts of the hidden diamonds? The usual explanations fall down here, such as knowledge of human nature, empathy, telepathy, tapping of the subconscious, etc., since the dealer himself did not know of the hiding-place and the thief was not present at the interview. Connivance of the fortune-teller with the thief is out of the question. Besides, the woman had indicated the hiding-place six hours before the diamonds were put there, since they were not deposited until 11 p.m., as appeared in the cross-examination of this thief. Hence this is a case of clairvoyance with prevision. The study of the palm was merely an act of mediumistic concentration or mental dissociation on the part of the palmist, if this is what was involved. Never can the future hiding-place of stolen diamonds be read from the palm-lines of the person who has been robbed. The other piece of advice, namely to secure the diamonds on the same day, is common sense. For it is the custom of thieves to get their booty out of their pursuers' reach as quickly as possible. If we do not wish in this case to have recourse to the familiar unknown residue, we shall be compelled to adopt the hypothesis of Driesch,[127] i.e. the tapping of a higher intelligence. When, however, Driesch calls this higher intelligence the World Subject, this is for the theologian an impossible concept. God does not allow us to see Him in the cards, or to tap in on His plans. Higher intelligences that can be tapped by man can, according to the bible, only be of a God-opposing nature.

The *pastoral* aspect of this case again shows the typical outworkings of occult activities. Just as in all the other examples, the following symptoms of occult subjection appear: resistance to God's word, the feeling of the physical, spacial proximity of a sinister power, difficulty in making a decision for Christ, the lapse back into the former way of life, the im-

---

[127] cf. Driesch, op. cit. [6], p. 123.

mediate appearance of mental disturbances and troubles upon decision to turn to Christ. These constantly occurring and typical consequences make possible certain conclusions about the nature of chiromancy.

Another example will illustrate this again.

Ex 38   The cashier of a business corporation drew out of the chief cash office a sum of over £16,000, which he was to pay out to the tobacco planters of two villages. The money lay for only one night in his home, but during that night it was stolen. The robbed man was utterly desperate, since he was responsible for the security of the money to the extent of all his personal assets. He was advised to obtain the advice of two fortune-tellers. The fortune-tellers arrived and attempted, by feeling the empty cash-box, to reveal the thief by a process of psychometry. At their first visit, this method did not completely succeed. They repeated the visit on the next moonlit night. They stood in the moonlight,[128] put themselves into a trance, and could now give such accurate disclosures that the police were able to take immediate steps to apprehend the criminal. The great sum of money was still almost intact.

Some years later the robbed man revealed in a confidential interview that he would never do such a thing again. He said that the mental disturbances which he endured afterwards were indescribable. He would rather forfeit all his possessions.

From the *medical* point of view, there are no questions to be asked here, since until the time of the theft the cashier was a farmer in good physical and mental health. As in many of the other cases which we have adduced, the psychiatrist would only be able to present the following argument. If in many cases mental disturbances can be proved to follow occult activities, it is possible that there was some kind of constitutional emotional disorder existing recessively in the person concerned, which was activated by the shock of an upsetting experience. Apart from the fact that in many cases this argument is invalid, it is plain here that the occult activity could be at least a triggering factor. We shall speak later about the coincidence of psychological disturbance with the beginning of occult activity or subjection.

From the *para-psychological* point of view, we are again faced with the problem of how the two fortune-tellers were able to identify the thief. Since the usual explanations here fail, we must in this case discuss the phenomenon of the "excursion of psychic powers". The problem of the splitting of the mental powers is known in psychiatry by the terms

---

[128] This is the process of selenomancy, or moon divination.

depersonalization or transitivism[129]; in psychology as dissociation or disintegrated personality[130]; in psychical research as excursion, bilocation or wraith[131]; in spiritism under the concepts of astral bodies and somnambulism.[132] There are people who as a result of a disease such as schizophrenia experience depersonalization. People with mediumistic abilities can induce this condition by undergoing hetero- or auto-hypnosis. In this state of detachment they become, as they allege and also prove, clairvoyant over great distances. An example will illustrate.[133]

Lit 8 "Professor Durville and Colonel de Rochas succeeded in an experiment with several of their mediums, whom they beforehand put into a deep hypnotic state, in making their spirit depart temporarily from their bodies, so that only a tenuous tie still bound the absent spirit to its body, and the latter mostly sank into a deep lethargy". One of these mediums then describes his detached condition in the following words. "After observing myself for some time, I looked at the bystanders. They were all transparent. Then I looked at my surroundings, but instead of seeing impenetrable furniture and walls, I saw nothing but transparent things: everything was like glass. I also saw the homes of our neighbours and the people in them, as if we lived in a house of crystal. Then it entered my mind to go out into the open a little. Without losing sight of my body, I was caught up from one end of Paris and taken to the other, just as fast as one can shift one's thoughts from one place to another. I saw the houses, the people, the cars, but they were all transparent, like glass."

Now this experience could undoubtedly be explained as an effect of hypnosis. Therewith its authenticity would be denied. But when such an excursion enables spacially distant objective facts to be learned, as in *Ex 38*, we have proof of the authenticity of the detachment. Spiritists know of numberless cases of the detachment of the so-called astral or fluidic body. To them the detection of thieves as in *Ex 38* is common practice. He who regards the excursion of psychic powers as an unacceptable thesis, must again content himself with an unexplainable residue.

On the *pastoral* level we have only the noteworthy remark of the robbed cashier, that he would rather forfeit all his possessions than ever again apply for help from a fortune-teller.

---

129 cf. Eugen Bleuler, "Lehrbuch der Psychiatrie", Springer Verlag, Heidelberg, 1949, p. 78; Kloos, op. cit. 12, pp. 164, 408, 419, 430.
130 cf. Bender, op. cit. 3, "psychische Abspaltung".
131 cf. Driesch, op. cit. 6, p. 117.
132 cf. Hinrich Olhaver, "Die Toten leben", Karl Röhrig Verlag, Munich, 1949, p. 193.
133 cf. Weyer, "Ist die Wünschelrute ein Mittel oder ein Zaubermittel?" Selbstverlag, Bergholz-Rehbrücken, p. 4.

The significance of passive occult involvement as a triggering cause for psychological disturbances becomes apparent in the experience of a certain pastor.

Ex 39   A refugee couple came to a pastor to apply for marriage. On departing the girl suddenly grasped the clergyman's hand and said, "Oh, pastor, how interesting!" She proceeded, unsolicited, to read his palm. As the pastor assured me later, all her comments about his past were accurate, and all her predictions were fulfilled in the course of subsequent years. This unwanted experience with a palmist brought the pastor all manner of trouble. He told me that for years he was hindered by it in his pastoral work. It had simply cast a psychological and spiritual spell upon him, which hindered his work.

From a *psychical* aspect this example fits into the framework of the others. The retrospective vision of the palmist could possibly be explained by the previous acquisition by the girl of information about the pastor. With the help of what she had divined (= learned) about the past, she had built up her predictions. Then, for the fulfilment of these predictions, the pastor was subject to suggestion. If this explanation does not apply, then her retrospective vision must again be regarded as a tapping of the conscious or subconscious mind. The phenomenon of rightly grasping future events by prevision remains an unexplainable residue, if we cannot show the fulfilment to be the result of suggestion. Tischner also came to the same conclusion when he said:[134] "If we do not want to ascend to the loftiest metaphysical heights and invoke the World Subject,[135] or spirits, as an explanation, then there is much here which is very unclear".

On the plane of our *pastoral* enquiry, this example shows that divination received involuntarily has the same psychological consequences as the deliberate seeking of advice from a fortune-teller. We must qualify this by noting from a psychological standpoint that in the effects here reported the element of fear may have played a role. Knowledge of the psychological consequences of occult activities can bear fruit in corresponding effects in an anxious person.

Another feature of chiromantic practice comes to light in the last example that I shall give in this field.

Ex 40   A robbed farmer sought help from a shepherd who had a flourishing "trade" as conjurer, clairvoyant and diviner. He was not disappointed: the shepherd was able to give valid information about the

---

134 cf. Tischner, op. cit. 25a, p. 126.
135 ibid., p. 127.

thief. But from the time of the occult interview this farmer's family always had spook phenomena in their home. In the course of a Bible Week they came to seek my advice.

Psychical research can here without much difficulty lay bare the connexion between divination and spook apparitions. Conjurers always influence the subconscious actively and passively. The tapped subconscious shows in many instances the phenomenon of dissociation. Detached powers can, according to Prof. Bender, lead a separate existence and produce acoustic, visual and kinetic manifestations.

The psychological consequences of the preceding example became apparent to me in my *pastoral* work. The whole family came to me often for advice. They cursed the diviner who had brought such distress and unrest into their home. When each of them made a decision to live under the Lordship of Christ, they were delivered from these after-effects.

Here we must close this series of examples of palmistry, although I have experienced a great mass of them. If we would summarize our various observations in the field of divination, we can distinguish two methods: the inductive method, and mediumistic intuition.[136] The inductive method evaluates the omens and signs used in divining practice and constructs from these its prognostications. By this method only fantasies, ambiguous predictions, hazy images of generalities and unreliable nonsense etc. can be produced. We shall not concern ourselves with this kind of divination. All the examples offered here belong to the field of mediumistic intuition. The diviners of this class use cards, palm-reading, rod, pendulum etc., merely as means of getting into the consciousness or subconscious of the person who consults them. This method represents an invasion into the psychological structure of man, and by tapping the mental power circuit of the conscious and subconscious mind forms a triggering cause for psychological disturbances and insanity.

(c) *Astrology*

At present two forms of astrology are distinguished, true astrology and zodiacal horoscopy, or astrological prognostication. Those seeking information about the first form should read Rosenberg's "Zeichen am Himmel", Anrich's "Gross Göttlich Ordnung", Fankhauser's "Das wahre Gesicht der Astrologie", Schmitz' "Der Geist der Astrologie", the books of Dacqué, and others. Dacqué calls astrology the expression of the spiritual reality of the cosmos. Köberle said at Tutzing in 1951 that the eternal God of the universe has woven light-beams out of the cosmic

---

[136] Schellhammer makes a similar distinction. By intuition, however, he means something different from that to which we refer in this study. cf. Schellhammer, "Wahrsagen und Weissagen", Anker Verlag, Munich, 1950, p. 9.

power-fields into the fabric of our existence. Dorothee Hoch wrote in 1952 in the church newspaper of the Reformed Church of Switzerland (Kirchenblatt), that man and the cosmos are indeed bound to each other, and that the "powers" do not vanish when they are de-mythologized. Of decisive importance is her conclusion that the struggle against modern superstition must be conducted on another level than that of pronouncing these powers to be non-existent.

Here we are near to New Testament thinking. Paul knows of powers (stoicheia, daimonia, archai, exousiai, dynameis: Eph. 6, 12; Col. 1, 16), which rule in the air. This does not imply an identification of Paul's conception with the cosmic "powers" of astrology. We only indicate that arguments of greater weight regarding astrology are to be adduced from biblical thought than from the ideology of the Enlightenment, which with its negation of the reality of magic totally distorts the concern of astrology. From the New Testament standpoint we must say concerning this form of astrology that we indeed know of the existence of cosmic authorities and powers. Man as a microcosm is involved in the macrocosm, as an individual embedded in the great rhythm of the cosmos. We only know that we as Christians are not enslaved to the host of heaven. We do not serve a *kyrios ouranios*, but the *kyrios hyperouranios*, Jesus Christ, who has triumphed over the powers (Col. 2, 15). Hence we do not deny the existence of these powers, but affirm it, not forgetting their dethronement by Christ.

In this investigation we are concerned only with the common form of astrology, zodiacal horoscopy or astrological prognostication. Moreover, we are interested only in the pastoral side of the phenomenon, the psychological consequences of bondage to horoscopy. In order better to understand this pastoral problem, we shall briefly, in broad strokes, indicate the complex of questions associated with this decadent form of astrology. The problem may be considered under the following main headings: cosmic, historical, pagan-religious, scientific, psychical, psychological, pastoral and cultural.

As noted above, we may freely admit that there are *cosmic* relations between the constellations of heavenly bodies and the earth. Without sunlight, no biological process would be possible on the earth. Further, we know that the conjunction and opposition of the constellation of sun, moon and earth cause spring and neap tides. It is generally known that the tides are caused by the attraction of the moon and the sun. Further, there is a connexion between the growth of sun-spots and an increase in the nervous irritability of man. The sensibility of the somnambulist to the full moon also belongs to this group of phenomena. Noctambulism[137] is however more probably a symptom of neuropathy. Again the female menstrual period is said to be related to the lunar cycle. All these in-dications point to an interaction between the heavenly bodies and earth.

The *historical* question is concerned with the historical roots and development of astrology. Although the actual origins of astrology are lost in the mists of remote antiquity, we do know that Chaldean and Babylonian priests of the third millenium B.C. developed the astro-logical system. The heart of this star worship consisted in two theses: the conformity of macrocosm and microcosm, and the identification of the stars with active deities. This pagan star-worship made its way from Babylon to the Egyptians, the Indians, the Chinese, and at the time of the decline of the Roman empire, to Rome also. In the middle ages astrology was accepted to some extent by Thomas Aquinas, and at the beginning of modern history by Melanchthon and Kepler. It was opposed by Savonarola and Pico della Mirandola. Luther called it a shabby art and a violation of the First Commandment. In the present day there is to be observed a widespread publication of astrological material in daily papers and magazines. Worthy of honourable mention is the decision of the Swedish publishers to print no astrological weekly forecasts in their papers.

The *pagan-religious* problem consists in the above-mentioned identi-fication of the stars with divine powers. According to this view, the earth is the centre of the universe. Around her the planets travel in seven spheres as the regents of heaven. Their colour and the velocity of their revolutions determine the temperament and the influence of these planet deities. The second pillar in the astrological system is formed by the twelve zodiacal signs of the ecliptic. According to the Latin hexameter they are called: "Sunt aries, taurus, gemini, cancer, leo, virgo, libraque, scorpius, arcitenens, caper, amphora, pisces". The signs of the zodiac are the twelve astrological departments which at given times are ruled by the travelling planet gods. Decisive for the interpretation of the peculiar characteristics of each planet is the theory of Aspects. The influence of the planet gods is dependent upon the angle of incidence of the planets' rays with respect to each other, as they fall on the earth. Trigon (120°) and Sextile (60°) are favourable configurations. Opposition (180°) are unfavourable configurations.

In the third place there are the so-called directions for the reading of fortunes. Every day after the birth is supposed to correspond to a year.

---

[137] cf. Bleuler, op.cit. [129], p. 63; Kloos, op.cit. [12], p. 437; Brugsch, op.cit. [10], vol. II, p. 1343.

When, e.g., Venus, the star of love, enters after twenty-five days the department of Taurus, the bull (the symbol of fertility), the person born in the sign of Venus will be lucky in love at the age of 25. Anyone who has mastered all these principles of astrological interpretation can, with the help of the Ephemeris (astronomical almanac), read his own fate.

The *scientific* problem is concerned with a critical examination of the astronomical principles of astrology. Here we must have the opinion of the scientist, because only he is competent to make an accurate differentiation between astronomy and astrology. Of the multitude of differences, even the layman can understand a few:

1. The astrological have become questionable since the discovery of three further planets, Uranus, Neptune and Pluto.

2. Through the replacement of the Ptolemaic system by the Copernican, the main conception underlying astrology, namely the geocentric principle, has collapsed.

3. In 26,000 years the earth's axis describes a cone, and thereby causes the precession of the Vernal Equinox. As a result the signs of the zodiac have been shifted out of harmony with the old astrological calendars.

4. The signs of the zodiac are merely symbols projected on to the sky-dome. They are arbitrary groupings, and what is more, they actually belong to different constellations. In 50,000 years, for instance, the constellation of the Great Bear will no longer have its present form. The planets certainly do not rule the signs of the zodiac, since even from the point of view of distance they could not possibly be connected with them.

5. The most weighty factor is the astronomer's objection that no constellation in the sky ever recurs. Hence astrological interpretations lack every basis of comparison. Hence solstitial horoscopy rests on presuppositions which are scientifically untenable.

The total unreliability of astrological prognostication further becomes evident from the methods of interpretation, which mark astrology as a *psychical* phenomenon. One group of astrologists will compute the horoscope according to the zodiac group which, at the hour of birth, is in the ascendant; others observe the star pattern which has reached the zenith, directly overhead; still others take the date of conception as the basis of their computation. Some are strict determinists. They regard the whole course of life as under an iron law of predestination. Others speak of influences, inclinations, possibilities, tendencies, against which man can struggle. The character of astrological fortune-telling and prognostication becomes completely exposed in the phrases commonly used in horoscopes, such as: "as a rule", "it could be", "you may feel", "you find", "in general", "usually", "it will be best", "on occasion", "changes", "at times", "often", "somehow".[138] Where there is no basis of scientific law, and the ambiguity of the predictions leaves all manner of possibilities open, the most we can expect is fortune-telling dressed up in scientific language. In zodiacal horoscopy we are dealing with nothing more than astromancy, which as a psychical phenomenon belongs to the field of divination.

Rather suspicious are the results of astromancy from the *psychological* point of view. This faith in the stars leads, through the theory of an astral influence on fate, to the motto "Fatum est". At the moment of birth the future fate is firmly fixed by the configuration of the stars. Thus there results a certain deterministic attitude, in which there is little room left for the free play of responsibility. Against the background of this determinism conditioned by the stars, there will result one of two different kinds of psychological development, according to the predisposition of the person concerned, if there is a corresponding emotional instability, a melancholic, fatalistic type will emerge, sinking into a lethargic escape from responsibility, and apathy. Otherwise a eudemonistic type will emerge, who does not in the first place inquire about duty, but is governed by utilitarian motives. Very worthy of note is the observation that astrological horoscopes are chiefly concerned only with professional success, happiness in love, avoidance of set-backs, etc. On the psychological level, therefore, astromancy leads people to one of two extremes which by-pass the real demands of life's struggle.

A further psychological result of astromancy is the faith in the horoscope, a problem frequently encountered in pastoral counselling. The person who seeks advice from an astrologer comes with a certain degree of readiness to believe the horoscope. This predisposition leads to an auto-suggestion to order his life according to the horoscope, and thus to contribute to its fulfilment. The first fulfilment enjoyed on the path of suggestion inclines the seeker to have a more comprehensive horoscope cast, which, on the second round of this vicious circle of suggestive influence, again enjoys fulfilment. The final outcome of this horoscope subjection is an astrological compulsion state, where one can no longer escape from the blind alley of entanglement.

Then this person comes to the pastor with his servile fear, his loss of freedom, his dread of making decisions, his depressions. How such a

---

[138] cf. Schwendimann, op. cit. [123], Heft 3, p. 36.

bondage to the horoscope can result in serious affliction will appear from an example.

Ex 41 A Christian teacher in a children's home of a Home Mission read an astrological weekly column for many years. In her mind she applied herself to these prognostications, and in the course of time she found that many of them were fulfilled in her life. Gradually she developed a faith in the horoscope.

Finally, when she was faced with an important decision, she obtained an exact horoscope. Later she repeated this astrological consultation. She fell more and more under an astrological compulsion, which finally brought her to me for a pastoral interview. She complained of a dread of living, inability to make decisions, moods of melancholia, etc.

A medical anamnesis brought little light to bear on her psychological disturbances. The only point of significance was that her mother also believed in astrology and was melancholic. When it came to an anamnesis of occult incolvement, we discovered a faith in the horoscope which exercised a decisive suggestive power. She practically refused to be convinced of the damaging influence of astromancy upon her emotional life. Finally, after a second interview, she was persuaded to give up her engagement in astrology. We shall deal with the question of liberation from the power of occult enslavement in a later chapter.

Without doubt we must here give attention to the *medical* expert, who would point to the probable endogenous causes of the melancholia in this woman, seeing that her mother was affected by the same emotional disorder. Hence it cannot in this example be proved that astrology was the exogenous cause of the psychological trouble. But even though we cannot quite demonstrate that astrology was the efficient cause, we must consider the suggestive influence of this faith in the horoscope as at least the immediate or aggravating cause.

To avoid prejudiced judgements, we must add that only those severely affected by faith in horoscopy come to the attention of the pastor. The more stable devotees, especially those of the eudemonistic type, feel quite equal to life and usually need no pastoral help.

From the *cultural* viewpoint, astromancy is a remarkable phenomenon. In the first place it is, because of its financial exploitation of the gullible, a social evil; and secondly it is a criterion of the degree of health of any culture. On the first point we add an example.

Ex 42 The editor of a large daily reported that one day he did not receive the weekly astrological forecast until it was too late. In order not to annoy his readers, he simply went to his old files and inserted in the appropriate column a horoscope from long before. Not one of the

100,000 readers noticed the "deception". The editor decided that since this had worked so well, he might as well spare himself the astrologer's weekly fee. So for three months he filled the column with old horoscopes. At last a reader wrote in, remarking that the horoscope must be wrong. In order to avoid a scandal, he began once more to send for fresh astrological horoscopes.

This story speaks for itself. Dailies and weeklies are compelled to include a weekly astrological forecast in order to keep their subscribers, i.e. for financial reasons. Ignorance and gullibility are an economic factor here, to which even enlightened and intelligent people have to bow.

Secondly, there is a more serious factor. In times of great catastrophes, of political and racial upheavals, and of cultural decline, the great flood-crest of the dark stream of the occult rises ominously. The history of the Roman Empire shows this, for example. In a healthy cultural epoch, Cato and Cicero carried on opposition to astrology. When, on the other hand, the first emperors, Augustus and Tiberius, employed astrologers, the germs of decay were already to be seen in the fabric of the Roman Empire. The rising flood of astrology is always a yardstick for the cultural state of the people. For this reason Dr. Stucker, former Director of the Urania Observatory in Zürich, has characterized astrology as a sign of decadence not to be lightly regarded.[139a] The frightful increase of astromancy in our present day is an ominous warning sign concerning the condition of our culture.[139b]

Addendum to the American Edition

Perhaps the character of horoscopy can best be presented by an illustration which shocked the free world in November 1963. On Nov. 22nd. 1963 President Kennedy was assassinated. I as a German may state here that the eyes of all Germany were politically directed towards this leader. He was our friend and his political programme was an active factor in our hope for a re-united Germany.

In connexion with the tragic end of this great man, many conflicting horoscopes were compared and discussed. Permit me to adduce the three most outstanding prophecies, so that each may judge what he is to think of this astrology.

In September 1963 there appeared in a magazine in South Germany the horoscope of Kennedy, with the indication that this statesman would shortly die. No one took this pronouncement seriously. Then, when eight

139a cf. Schwendimann, op. cit. 123, Heft 3, p. 15.
139b Köberle, "Die Seele des Christentums", pp. 81, 101.

weeks later the prognostication was fulfilled, the magazine circulated around several factories in Heilbronn. Men were surprised at the prediction and asked themselves whether this could be a mere coincidence.

No less attention was drawn before the death of Kennedy to another horoscope, which announced that in the next election Kennedy would again be elected President.

But this is still not enough. A religious weekly magazine came out a few days after the assassination with a horoscope declaring that Kennedy would have to retire from office in the summer of 1964 because of illness. This issue of the weekly was already in process of distribution when the shocking report of his death came over the air. This issue of the magazine, with its false prediction, could no longer be recalled in time.

Thus we have three exact predictions by our horoscope casters about the same event. And there, at the same time, we have the key to understanding why many horoscopes are apparently accurate.

Regarding great men of world history, many predictions about the future are spread abroad. When 500 astrologers make their predictions, there will always be some among them who to some extent approach the truth. The successful prognosticators are then publicly proclaimed, whereas the 490 false predictions are passed over in silence.

But surely the whole ludicrous nature of horoscope practice is exposed by the above examples. This still does not mean that the whole horoscope epidemic is nothing but humbug. It is not all swindle and superstition; but it is all a great danger for the spiritual life and for the genuine Christian walk of faith.

(d) *Rod and Pendulum*

In our introduction to divination we have already noted that in the ancient world there are traces of the use of rod and pendulum. Of the Chinese emperor Yu of the H-Sia dynasty (2205 B.C.) tradition reports that he used the magic rod.[140] Israel was exposed to the danger of adopting rhabdomancy from the Canaanite people.[141] The Greeks and Romans, the Scythians and the Germani, had their rod divination, or water diviners with hazel twigs, as already mentioned. Ammianus Marcellus reports that the Greek philosophers Patricius and Hilarius used a pendulum to find the name of the future Caesar from an alphabetic tablet. Their prognostications cost them their heads. In the middle ages the rod and pendulum were used to locate ore-veins and wells. The

---

[140] cf. Schwendimann, op. cit. [123], Heft 7, p. 5; Glahn, op. cit. [101], vol. I, p. 4.
[141] cf. Hos. 4, 12.

dowsers belonged to the official staff of the mines, until their great incompetence was revealed and their help declined. In our present day nearly everything is sought by means of the rod and the pendulum — from the physical features of the earth's crust to the fate of the deceased by means of a photograph. There is one element which we must keep clearly in view in this historical sketch. Historically the employment of rod and pendulum has its roots in pagan soothsaying.[142] The Mosaic and prophetic religion of Israel consequently carried on a vigorous battle against the adoption of these pagan divining practices.

Here we must add a word of explanation regarding the combination of rod and pendulum. The observation that rod dowsers usually have success with the pendulum and that pendulum manipulators can also use the rod has led to a *union* of the two branches.[143] Whereas in 1913, when an international society of dowsers was founded, the art of the pendulum was still regarded as a separate field,[144] these two branches have, since October 2nd. 1948, been united in a guild of rod and pendulum practice.[145] It must be admitted that this organization concerned with "radiaesthesia" — a term coined in 1930 by Abbé Bouly — is struggling to clarify its position. They desire to co-operate with geologists, hydrologists, municipal water authorities and well constructers; at the same time they want a clear distinction to be made between their activities and superstitious practices, fantasies, muddled nature-philosophy, charlatanry and everything occult.[146] The relation between geology and radiaesthesia was defined as follows by the geologist Prof. Dr. J. Walther (Halle): "The geologist is the anatomist of the earth; the dowser is the internal surgeon, who feels his way into the interior of the earth".[147] Despite the efforts of the radiaesthetes, tensions have already often arisen with geologists. Moreover, as will appear, their second resolve has never been achieved either.

In order to understand the essence of radiaesthesia we must first, now that we have considered the history and organization of the practice, clarify the *physical* basis of rod-divining. First we may make some remarks about the earth's magnetic field. A little test will introduce us to the subject.

---

[142] Is it for this reason that the use of rod and pendulum is so little known in the young American nation?

[143] cf. Glahn, op. cit. [101], vol. I, p. 29.

[144] ibid. vol. II, p. 8.

[145] cf. Zeitschrift für Geosophie, Heroldverlag, Dr. Fr. Wetzel & Co., Munich, 1949, No. 1, p. 6.

[146] ibid., pp. 8, 16.

[147] ibid., p. 8.

Scatter some iron filings on a sheet of paper. Now hold a horseshoe magnet under the paper, and the filings will arrange themselves according to the magnetic field of the magnet. If you now hold an iron rod under the paper, near the magnet, the lines of force will be distorted. The iron rod forms a disturbing pole.

Similar observations apply to the earth's magnetic field. The earth is a magnet and thus has a field of magnetic forces. The magnetic north pole lies in the Boothia Felix peninsula (70° N, 96³/₄° W). The magnetic south pole lies in the Antarctic Ocean (72¹/₂° S, 155° E). This magnetic field of the earth is not a homogeneous field, but it is distorted and shifted, compressed and scattered by many centres of disturbance. These fields of disturbance were of great importance for navigation in World War II. As a member of the flying personnel, I was conversant with such navigational questions. Since the effects of these fields of disturbance correspond to the so-called "attraction belts" of radiaesthesia, we shall briefly explain their significance here. The war-time security laws no longer, of course, apply.

In submarine warfare, a magnetic method of detection by aircraft was developed. The principle was that the disturbance centres in the earth's magnetic field caused by the steel of the submarines could be computed by measuring instruments. Even greater was the importance of these disturbance centres in the automatic navigation of aircraft. The compass course plotted by the master compass of the aircraft is a combination of many factors: true course, air speed, wind drift, magnetic variation and aberration. In our discussion we are concerned only with the magnetic declination. To avoid misunderstanding, we must here define our terms. In the old Luftwaffe a different term was used to that used in physics. In physics the angle between true north and magnetic north is called declination. In the air force this angle was called the magnetic variation. During the war, maps were issued for the air force in which lines were drawn connecting all the places with the same variation. These are called isogonic lines.[148] These isogonic lines are drawn not only according to the angle between true north and magnetic north, but they are subject to many deflections due to oreveins, salt-layers, oil-masses, subterranean streams, geological faults, etc. We have here practical confirmation that the main principle of the little test mentioned above is repeated on a large scale in nature: physical features of the earth's crust distort the earth's magnetic field.

[148] The first isogonic chart for maritime navigation originated with the English astronomer Halley (1700).

Science is today in a position to measure these distortions, concentrations and dispersions. The magnometric band of Gauss is of some use for the measuring of unknown magnetic fields and centres of disturbance. It is inadequate, however, for differentiated measurements. A better instrument, developed by means of many practical tests, is the geophysical meter of Stehle-Futterknecht.[149] An instrument which has received much mention and praise is the gerameter, to the perfection of which a number of engineers and other scientists have contributed.[150] A simple but useful measuring instrument is the double compass. Here two compasses are placed one on top of the other. Since like poles repel one another, the two needles are forced apart. The stronger the earth's magnetic field, the narrower the angle. The more the angle exceeds the norm, the stronger the field of disturbance. The best measuring instrument at present is the proton-resonance magnetometer, which is wellnigh perfect in operation.

These fields of disturbance can be established not only by their influence on the earth's magnetic field, but also according to the laws of electrostatics. Just a few remarks on this will suffice. Between the air and the earth there is a continuous interchange of electrical energy. All points of equal voltage are called "levels of potential"[151] or equipotential surfaces. If there are no centres of disturbance, then the equipotential surfaces of this aerial electrical field are, provided the ground is level, parallel with the earth's surface. These equipotential surfaces undergo distortions through irregularities in the surface of the earth and through various good conductors in or above the ground. By many tests it has been established that where disturbance-fields are present, there are lower readings of potential difference, and further that near these fields the air has a higher conductance. Thus again we have proof in nature of a fact which can be readily shown by a little experiment with a conductor, an electrometer and a disturbing body.

It has often been proved by practical experiments with dowsers that the fields of disturbance which have been ascertained by means of measuring instruments cause reactions in sensitive dowsers. Thus the hypothesis of radiaesthesia seems established, viz. that "earth-rays" — a misleading term — produce rod and pendulum reactions.[152]

---

149 cf. Glahn, op. cit. 101, vol. I, p. 26.
150 cf. loc. cit. 145, p. 41.
151 cf. Kleiber/Nath, "Physik" § 36: "Niveauflächen im elektrischen Feld", p. 84.
152 Rod manipulators maintain that physical processes and conditions of the earth's crust exercise an influence on the human body. By this they mean not only the impulse given to the rod, but also effects injurious to health. Radiaesthetes persistently maintain that the prevalence of cancer and thyroid diseases, and also regularly recurring

For the *pastoral* purpose of our study, only the following questions are of interest:

1. Are genuine results obtained with the rod and pendulum about features of the earth's crust?

2. What is the means of transmission from the physical field of disturbance to the sensitive dowser? Is this a natural gift or a mediumistic ability?

3. Do psychological disturbances set in with dowsers or people who seek their help?

In order to deal with these questions we shall select a few examples from the mass of material available. It is well-known that probably the majority of geologists are opposed to the rod phenomenon. I too would sooner side with geology than with this debated art of rod-dabbling. But for all that, it cannot be denied that good dowsers have amazing success in finding springs of water. An example will show this.

Ex 43 A village burgomaster well known to me desired to have a new well dug in his parish. A university professor, the director of a geological institute, was engaged as an expert. At the same time the burgomaster sent for a well-known water diviner, who was able not only to give the situation of the spring, but even the depth and the force, with great accuracy. The professor, who had several times written

---

cattle diseases of the same type in the same stall are to be ascribed to certain influences from the earth. These assertions have been tested repeatedly by various scientists. Prof. Lang of the Kaiser Wilhelm Institute in Munich conducted researches in many parishes in South and Middle Germany, and came to the conclusion that in the areas where goitres are infrequent there are never any radio-active emanations from the earth, while they are more frequent in areas where goitres are common. A further study of this sort was carried out by the regional society for cancer control in Baden. 120 socalled cancer houses were investigated. Besides experienced doctors, they also engaged some well-known dowsers. The result was that in all cases the rod reacted. Prof. Dr. med. Dr. phil. Kurt Saller of Munich University also writes in his book "Diagnostik und Therapie" that in many places there are goitre and cancer houses, where radio-active emanations or other disturbing influences in the earth favour the ailment concerned. The fraternity of rod and pendulum manipulators have developed protective devices against these injurious "earthrays", which are supposed to avert these disturbing influences. Naturally there has often been heated controversy over these devices. Prof. Med.-Rat Dr. med. Arnold Mannlicher writes in the magazine "Pendelforschung", 1938, No. 1 (Verlag Gesundes Leben, Rudolfstadt): "On the basis of many different and painstaking investigations I have come to the firmly grounded conclusion that this matter of protection is not only no humbug, but that it has for the maintenance of public health a quite fundamental significance".

pointed articles against water divining, was much irked when he heard of the engagement of the dowser. The findings of the two rival experts were completely at variance. The professor pronounced the findings of the diviner wrong, and indicated another place for testdrilling. But the site indicated by the dowser was more economical for the burgomaster and his council. So they decided to accept the dowser's suggestion. They dug, following his advice, to a depth of seven meters (twenty three feet). No water came. Again they called the diviner. He stood on the floor of the shaft. The rod was well-nigh wrenched from his hand. "Another half a meter", he said confidently. They dug deeper. His words proved right. So much water gushed up that the diggers had hurriedly to clamber out of the angular shaft. The village had thereby found for itself an abiding water source. The happy water diviner even experienced a triumphant vindication! For one day the professor drove through the village in his car and learned that not his indications but the dowser's had been crowned with success.

The thesis that rod findings are simply deception can be refuted by a couple of further examples.

Ex 44 One of my friends was a missionary in China. On the mission field he constantly battled against the dowsing practices of the geomancers who roved the land looking for springs and building sites. He took this to be a swindle on the part of the idol priests. One day a geomancer asked him to try it himself, he consented to the request. The result was surprising. The rod struck forcibly. He himself could have taken up the profession of dowsing. I am aware that religious opponents of rod divination would perhaps put this missionary's experience down to suggestion or hypnosis, or even demonic influence. But that would not be doing justice to the rod phenomenon.

Ex 45 A dowser explored a garden for a spring. Afterwards the owner, who was a doctor, took the rod into his own hand. It struck at the same spot. A second professional man tried the experiment, with the same positive result. Both had been up to this time wholly indifferent to rod-divining. They were amazed that the supposed humbug really worked. I witnessed this search as a bystander.

These are only three examples from a long list. For four years I had the opportunity to watch the activities of a very sensitive rod-practitioner and to study them critically. In these four years I can only report that he made one mistake, among a great number of successes. Once I had the work of this man tested by another dowser, without either of them being able to consult the other. The results were identical. Even though the geologist must always be granted the primary place in the task of disclosing the physical condition of the earth's surface, we should allow any inflexible bias to keep us from admitting the success of the dowser. Noteworthy is the fact that I have not found, on this physical level of dowsing, any examples of resultant psychological disturbance in my pastoral experience. But the picture changes when we look into the further problems.

Before we do this, we must for the sake of completeness make mention, in the form of a short *excursus*, of the position of other authorities regarding the "physical" application of the rod. We have already said many geologists reject the phenomenon of rod divining. Noteworthy is also the disagreement of evangelists on this subject. A great number of them regard dowsing in search of water as a gift of nature. This is the purport of a letter I received from one of the best known of German evangelists. Some years ago he informed me, in reply to a question on my part, that his house is protected against earth-rays. Further, I have discovered that various Christian institutions have had their buildings thus shielded. Thus they evidently regard the discovery of "earth-rays" and the protection of their houses against them as not at all harmful, and indeed very salutary. Opposed to this is the opinion of other ministers of the gospel. At a conference of Swiss evangelists in September 1952, which I had the privilege of attending, we heard the leading men there, Pastor Eichin, head of the Zeller institutions, chief engineer Suter of Zürich, and others speaking out against water divining with the rod and the practice of shielding against earth-rays. They see in the rod reactions in every case something demonic, and they also know of psychological disturbances caused by the use of the rod in searching for water. This disagreement of scientists and experts among Christian workers shows that even the simplest use of the rod to search for water is to this day under debate, and lies open to further research and clarification.

To come closer to the second problem, namely the manner of transmission, we must discuss the *psychological* presuppositions of radiaesthesia. The outside observer will at first find it very simple to explain the psychological content of radiaesthesia, since the specialists among the dowsers and pendulum manipulators have themselves declared the psychological presuppositions behind it.

The first thing that becomes clear upon critical examination of the rod phenomenon is the fact that the physical explanation only does justice to half of the reaction. This appears from the fact that in France the rod strikes upward and in Germany downward. Furthermore, many diviners simply study maps for water sources. It should be plain to every scientific thinker that printer's ink, paint tincture and map paper do not mediate any of the physical impulses of the corresponding area of ground. Hence the physical phenomenon only constitutes half of the process of the rod reaction. The second, and indeed the most difficult part, will have to be explained by the pendulum scientist, the psychologist and the psychical researcher.

When Dr. Glahn's extensive treatise on the pendulum is studied from this viewpoint, we gain some valuable insights. He writes (vol. I, p. 32): "One thing is certain: the motive force of the pendulum is supplied by the manipulator himself. Continued use of the pendulum drains the body of considerable strength, and tires it greatly. Only persons of good health should manipulate the pendulum. Sick people are warned to use the greatest moderation!" Similar statements are found in vol. I, p. 71. To the question what mobilizes the bodily power for the final reaction of the rod, radiaesthetes give two different answers:

1. There is a mental innervation from the conscious mind (a kind of decision of the will), which causes the rod to react. Thus rod and pendulum follow the decision made by the holder. This kind of reaction is regarded as unauthentic.

2. A second mobilizing factor becomes evident in the reflex phenomenon of the rod reaction. According to the psychological theory of the dowsing expert Dr. med. Schreiber,[153] the body of the manipulator forms an oscillating circuit with the rod. This oscillation is the carrier of an innervation drawn from the environment, and is influenced in its function by this innervation. The rod reaction follows as a reflex. Hence only the reflex rod reaction is a genuine one.

Dr. Schreiber summarizes the distinction between mental innervation and the reflex action in the following formula: "The reaction must not emanate *from* the conscious mind: it must come *to* the conscious mind of the manipulator".

If we ask further which receiving station of the human body takes up the innervation coming from the environment, one school[154] of rod specialists answers by pointing to the subconscious. This would make genuine rod reactions "stand-pipes of the subconscious" (Prof. Bender). Thus the subconscious would be no more than a psycho-physiological junction point[155] for the innervation coming in from the environment, and the rod or pendulum only the enlarging indicators of the imperceptible muscle movements controlled by the subconscious. Here we have

153 cf. op. cit. 145, p. 34.
154 ibid. p. 15.
155 cf. Tischner, op. cit. 25a, p. 138.

come somewhat nearer to answering the question of the means of transference, even though this process is still a mystery to many, since true
rod reaction only appears in a few people.

This brings us to another phenomenon of radiaesthesia. Only the
organism of the "sensitive" person, as we have seen, reacts to received
impulses. The gift of dowsing is a matter of disposition. Its friends call
it a gift of nature; psychical researchers sometimes speak of mediumship;
one theologian has called it a charisma; its enemies call it a swindle. So
now we have a choice, but no clarity. By what mark of differentiation
can we here uncover the core of truth? The simple word of Scripture
can be of definite help to us here: "By their fruits you will know them"
(Matthew 7, 16). What are the fruits of sensitivity to be found in connexion with radiaesthesia? While on the physical level ore and water
sources are sought — a process which we can go half way to understanding and explaining — on the psychic level radiaesthesia develops
phenomena which are of para-psychological character. We have given
an example above. Water, oil and ore are sought by means of the rod
and pendulum over a map. Let us now enter further into the problem
with an example of a different kind.

Ex 46 A clergyman who has grown grey in long years of service
has the faculty of telling the sex of the bodies in graves by means of
the rod. He approaches the grave from behind the stone and always
produces 100 % accurate results. It may be objected that if the accompanying observer stands in front of the tombstone, the phenomenon
can be explained as telepathy. The observer who is reading the inscription could be tapped by the radiaesthete. But this arrangement is pur-
posely avoided. And so we are here faced with a form of clairvoyance.
In this instance I consulted an outstanding doctor, who had for years
been chief consultant at a large hospital. This doctor is a friend of the
clergyman. He thought that perhaps the clergyman received an impulse
from the hormones of the deceased; for it is well known that certain
materials (e.g. arsenic) can be traced for many years in the bones of the
deceased. But since he is able with his rod to state the sex of people
who died a hundred years or more previously, this hormone theory can
hardly hold water, if it is really to be taken seriously at all.

Perhaps the words of a French researcher are here relevant:[156] "Le
radiésthésiste est un voyant qui s'ignore" ("the radiaesthete is a clairvoyant who does not know it").

Such occurrences as this example shows can be adduced in great
numbers. The pendulum expert Dr. Glahn writes in Vol. VI, p. 108,

[156] cf. loc. cit. [145], p. 15.

of his "Pendellehre": "We can discover by the pendulum any substance that has grown. We can also interrogate the subconscious about processes which lie in the past. But we cannot determine happenings which lie in the future". Hence the pendulum manipulator is given the broadest scope for his activities in the past and present. From Glahn's pendulum books I have noted the following objects of pendulum practice: stones, types of wood, plants, eggs, colours, animal diseases, human illnesses, vocational advice, crime detection, suitable books, foods, seeds, blood tests, sexual relations, medicines, poisons, jewels, metals, fertilizers, age of works of art, photographs, and many other things. The pendulum gives information about anything if one concentrates on the object. The scientific radiaesthetes classify such phenomena under the headings of clairvoyance, telepathy, cryptomnesia, etc. and name them teleradiaesthesia, referring such use of the rod and pendulum to the province of psychical research.[157] Since such admissions are made by exponents of radiaesthesia itself, we need not produce the evidence in this study.

As a slight indication that rod and pendulum practice really belongs to para-psychology, we again refer to Glahn's volumes. In these specialist books pendulum practice is mentioned in connection with the phenomena of psychometry, telaesthesia, telepathy, divination, fetishism, astrology and spiritism. The labyrinth of occult methods becomes visible at many points.[158] Glahn calls himself an astrologer. He also openly admits his somnambulistic and mediumistic gifts.

With the practical results on the psychic level, a clear light is thrown upon the character of the dowser's abilities. Although on the physical level the sensitivity may perhaps still be regarded as a gift of nature, on the psychic level this sensitivity has developed into a purely mediumistic function. This affirmation agrees in its religious-historical aspect with its origin in pagan divination; in the para-psychological aspect, with other paranormal aptitudes; and from the pastoral viewpoint in its resultant psychological disturbances.

In the *pastoral* field there are on the psychic level many examples of consulting a pendulum in connexion with a photograph, and of pendulum diagnosis. In the post-war era this photograph divination attained amazing proportions, because of the many prisoners of war and missing persons. Wives and mothers went to the pendulum manipulators in

---

[157] ibid.
[158] cf. Glahn, op. cit. [101], vol. I, p. 37 astrology, p. 38 mediumship, clairvoyance, p. 78 mental suggestion, selenomancy, p. 79 astral body, aura, p. 80 clairsentience; vol. IV, p. 75 reincarnation, p. 97 horoscopy, p. 108 mental dissociation, telepathy, psychometry, p. 111 black magic; vol. V, p. 14 telediagnosis; vol. VI, p. 76 amulets, p. 97 fetishism, p. 112 spiritism.

droves to learn whether their dear ones, imprisoned or missing, were still alive. In one town I was told by an elder of the church that some 200 women had had photographs divined. Apart from the fact that such pendulum divination is a transgression of the first commandment, such nonsense could be dismissed as superstitious humbug, especially since many of the "answers" were false, were it not for the fact that these pitiable women frequently end up with a psychological disturbance. In this process of photograph divination, the subconscious of the person seeking help is somehow addressed and tapped. But where the subconscious is the object of occult influence, psychological disturbances follow. That is a fact of pastoral experience. This empirical finding is still clearer in the case of pendulum diagnosis. In *Ex 28* we have already shown the possibility of a pendulum diagnosis on the basis of the circuit of psycho-organic correspondence.

In the present section we shall show another method of pendulum diagnosis which is defended by radiaesthetes. Dr. Leprince has developed a neurotometer, which indicates the more intensive current of electricity in the human body at areas of inflammation. A second instrument constructed by the same researcher, called a radiobiometer, makes it possible to study the local variations in the electrical field surrounding every organism, which is due to the living activity of that organism, which is exactly what the rod and pendulum do.[159] Thus in the opinion of this researcher the principle of rod and pendulum diagnosis rests upon the location of fields of disturbance of the body electricity, resulting from diseases in its members. According to this view, pendulum diagnosis would be merely a matter of electrostatic measurement. If the use of this method of diagnosis can be justified by scientific and medical proof, then no objection will be held against it. Up to the present, however, there are two factors which speak against these methods. The pendulum manipulator can only discover these fields of disturbance by means of his mediumistic sensitivity, and not without addressing the subconscious, as the psychological effects show. And meanwhile we have not even mentioned the hard fact that a great number of these diagnoses are quite wrong from a medical point of view. The psychological disturbances which arise after pendulum diagnosis and pendulum therapy come to light in pastoral counselling. From this end effect we may draw conclusions as to the efficient cause. Actually we have in pendulum diagnoses only a shifting of the trouble on to another level. The electrical field of disturbance is found, but at the same time a psychological field of disturbance is brought into being. The results of pendulum diagnosis

[159] cf. loc. cit. [145], p. 14.

can be seen in *Ex 32*. We could mention a whole collection of similar cases. On the ground of the forms of psychological trouble which have come to light in my pastoral experience, I reject pendulum diagnosis, regardless of whether the pendulum is manipulated by a doctor, a pastor, an engineer or a charlatan. And with this kind of diagnosis it makes no difference whether the instrument is a pendulum, or a door key, a ring or a medal, a prayer book or a bible wrapped up over a cross, as is often the case. The process remains the same, whether a secular or religious sign is employed. These symbols merely demonstrate the magical, pagan, irreligious background of pendulum divination.

The danger and evil of the rod and pendulum practice become most obvious in the *spiritistic* level of radiaesthesia. Here we mean the use of the rod and pendulum in spiritist practice. In pendulum literature the relation of the pendulum art to spiritism often becomes apparent.[160] This is shown to its fullest extent by the pendulum expert Glahn. He distinguishes three kinds of pendulum: the magnetic pendulum, the psychic pendulum and the spiritual pendulum. In Vol. VI of his "Pendellehre" he treats at length the spiritistic use of the pendulum. In this phenomenon we have a process which is similar to glass-moving. A dead person is invoked. The conversation is carried out by means of an alphabet table. The pendulum selects letters, which when arranged in order, spell out the answer of the deceased. What results such a spiritistic pendulum conversation can have, we may see in an example cited by Glahn.[161]

Lit 9 We record a letter from a lady pendulum manipulator to the pendulum expert Glahn: "I wrote and told you that I have experimented with the pendulum... my deceased grandmother informed me that a serious danger threatened my son-in-law from a car accident. This recurred several times, until one morning the pendulum moved in a most solemn manner, and very carefully, as when in life someone desires to prepare a person for some dreadful news in a most sparing manner, I was given to hear, 'Remain at home today, for some bad news is coming this very day. Erich has gone out with the Prince... in a large car to Upper Silesia... the crash has just taken place... Erich is unconscious ... he has passed away...'

"And then... there was not a word of truth in it! I endured two days of most dreadful anguish. I didn't dare to phone or send a telegram, lest I should be disobedient through lack of faith. And I tortured

160 cf. Schwendimann, op. cit. 123, Heft 7, p. 40.
161 cf. Glahn, op. cit. 101, vol. VI, pp. 118f.

myself with terrible self-accusations on various grounds, so that the next morning there was a grey streak in my hair.

"Then, when no report came, I consulted the pendulum once more. Suddenly I had a most ridiculous feeling — you old crank, you can say what you will! But the pendulum! — it raced over the table, and I was cursed for my insolence, until I said indignantly, "If they curse like that in the beyond, they are no better than we human beings..."

"However, since that time I can no longer think clearly about divine things. That is for me the most serious consequence of the folly. Whenever I hear or speak of God or Christ, in short of that which in Highest and Holiest, or occupy my mind with them, a base, vulgar tone enters in, sometimes loud and sometimes soft. I cannot get rid of it, no matter how much I fight against it. There surely must be some way in which to suppress these abominable voices... If I were not a person with perfectly sound nerves (as my doctor confirms) you might well believe that I was not quite normal." In a later letter, this same lady stated further, "I now use the pendulum only for food research and for purely scientific purposes, where it can surely do no harm... I hope that I can be rid of these whisperings (i.e. those mentioned in the first letter — Author) completely soon. Whenever these voices try to enter in, I always repeat some sentence from the new mysticism of Curtis, e.g. "My inmost life is holiness and grace"; "In me is all-embracing love"; "I am controlled by wisdom, beauty, goodness, righteousness, etc...."

No pendulum manipulator could better show us the psychological consequences of spiritistic pendulum practice. This case recorded by a specialist on the pendulum outweighs a whole list of examples from the pastor.

From a medical point of view the phenomena of blasphemous thoughts, voices, and distressing auditory hallucinations are well known. In this connexion I refer to the two fine works of Dr. Lechler, "Psychopathie", and "Seelische Erkrankungen und ihre Heilung".[162] Lechler shows that a high degree of sensibility can under certain circumstances result in the hearing of inner voices. Convulsions, restlessness, compulsive thoughts and the hearing of voices are often the signs of a depressive or sensitive psychopathic disposition. Impure thoughts and blasphemous thoughts also appear sometimes with a compulsion neurosis. In grave cases, the hearing of voices also occurs as a symptom of schizophrenia,

---

[162] cf. Dr. Lechler, op. cit. 8, p. 45; Dr. Lechler, "Psychopathie", Neubau Verlag, Munich, 1949, pp. 16, 43.

or of alcoholic or syphilitic delirium. A peculiarity of these voices is that the unpleasant elements predominate.[163]

Although these medical comments on *Lit 9* have to be considered, we have the insistence of this practitioner that an examination by a psychiatrist revealed no disorders. It appears here that not all occult cases which come to the attention of the pastor can be medically diagnosed. The doctor and the pastor must co-operate in the treatment of these cases.

We have now investigated some of the main divisions and problems of divination. Many special areas could not be touched on the limited framework of our study. We may at least name them, using the catalogue of Schwendimann:[164] arithmancy, (from numbers), coffee-grout reading, horoscopy, (star divination), geomancy (dot reading), cartomancy (from cards), crystallomancy (crystalgazing), capnomancy (smoke-reading), catoptromancy (mirror reading), dice-reading, liver-reading, lead-pouring, pyromancy (fire-reading), selenomancy (moon divination), sun divination, sleep reading, tephromancy (ash reading). The firm foundation of pastoral work in this field is that Christ has rescued us from this dragon's tail of occult practices.

Addendum to the Section on Rod and Pendulum

In the span of time between the appearance of the German edition of this study and the American edition, the field and fronts in connexion with this material have been further clarified.

First, this present work has aroused a very lively discussion. The author received many invitations to lecture, not only at European universities, but on all the five continents.

In connexion with this work of lecturing, so much new material has come to light that the complex problem of rod and pendulum has been further elucidated. Thus, for instance, at the academy in Tutzing, near Munich, a convention of European pendulum and rod manipulators was held. At this conference the leading psychical researchers of Europe also took part.

The sixty pendulum manipulators there present gave many examples of their abilities. They distinguished physical and mental divination. They applied the term "physical" to the process which takes place when a diviner goes out to the field to seek a pendulum indication. The process was called "mental" when the diviner merely uses maps to seek the

---

[163] cf. Kloos, op. cit. 12, pp. 136, 171, 401.
[164] cf. Schwendimann, op. cit. 123, Heft 7, p. 47.

resources of the earth. For mental divination the map was said to serve as a psychic bridge, forming contact with the resources. In French parapsychology this bridge is called a *temoin* (witness).

Mental divination is very suitable as a means of making clear the mediumistic character of radiaesthesia. This is best shown by the following experiment, which was demonstrated at the Tutzing Academy.

Ex 46a   A Swiss diviner spread out a map of Japan on the table and sought, with the aid of a pendulum, water and other resources of the earth.

When the outcome was tested, the results proved correct. Yet certainly no one would claim that the map of Japan, which was printed in Switzerland, contained elements of the composition of the earth's crust in Japan. All the materials of this map originated in Switzerland. In this case the map was merely a contact bridge between the diviner and the object being investigated. Since we know of no method in exact science by which the human mind can know, without technical aid, the physical situation some thousands of miles away, we must designate such a method as occult or mediumistic. Prof. Bender of Freiburg University, who was also present at the conference, came to this conclusion.

The occult nature of this pendulum divination appears even more clearly when we come to deal with temporal prevision. After the appearance of the German edition of this book, the author received word from many doctors, pastors, engineers and other university graduates, who had knowledge of pendulum practice through experience. The reports of these people enriched the author's collection of data by many typical and valuable cases. I shall here give one of the most revealing examples.

Ex 46b   A Swiss manufacturer practised pendulum divination over a long period, and developed an uncanny aptitude for the art. He used a circular pane of glass, on which lay an alphabet. If someone put a photograph in the middle of the pane, he could by means of the pendulum disclose complete particulars of the person concerned. If an air crash took place, he could speedily indicate the location of the missing plane. All he needed for his search was a map and a pendulum.

Especially typical for the evaluation of this pendulum practice are the prognostications of the future. When in the spring of 1938 unrest arose in Austria about the Sudetenland, this man consulted his pendulum with the question, "Will this lead to a second world war?" The pendulum answered, "Yes". Then the manufacturer asked about the date and received the correct answer, September 1st. 1939. Thus, 18 months before the actual event, the pendulum indicated the outbreak of World War II.

Everyone is inclined to doubt such a pronouncement. This pendulum manipulator came to a conversion after a dreadful struggle and is today a successful evangelist. He became a friend of the author, and confirms the truth of his report with his good name and person.

There are more such well-attested examples regarding temporal prevision in the author's files. We have here one of the most ticklish problems of all para-psychology. Temporal prevision cannot even by the boldest hypothesis be integrated into the world view of our natural sciences. Insofar as biblical prophecy is not involved — and it certainly is not in the case of pendulum clairvoyance — we are faced with a mediumistic and occult process here.

The expansion of the author's collection of data by means of important additions since the appearance of the German edition has led the author to distance himself further from pendulum activities. Being persuaded by the weight of evidence, he has approached nearer to the conception of the more radical group of critics.

2. *Extra-sensory Influence (ESI)*

In the section on ESP we have dealt with phenomena that do not fit into the hitherto accepted physical view of the universe. It is a fact of experience, which has recently been confirmed by exact scientific research, that there is a relationship of perception and interaction from mind to mind, and from mind to matter,[165] which employs no known physical means. In the section which follows, concerning ESI, we shall present in addition to this first factor of a para-physical act of perception, the factor of an act of para-psychological influence.

As a first phenomenon in this class, we shall discuss the magical misuse of hypnosis performed by amateurs.

(a) *Amateur hypnosis*

We use the term amateur hypnosis advisedly. The medical technique of hypnosis has long since been divested of its magical overtones and earlier suggestive method, and therefore it does not fall under the heading of ESI. To make plain the essence of amateur hypnosis, we shall first contrast it in one respect with medical hypnosis, and then illustrate by examples from pastoral experience.

[165] cf. Rhine, op.cit. [57], p. 93.

The three main types of medical suggestion therapy are waking suggestion, hypnosis and autogenic training. This is the classification used by Prof. Kretschmer, Director of the University Nerve Clinic in Tübingen, at the Tübingen Congress of Psychiatrists of September 10th. 1948. To specify the application methods of suggestion technique, we may cite Prof. Brauchle's[166] distinction: "hetero- or auto-suggestion, waking or sleeping influence, secret or open suggestion". It is not the task of this study to probe further into the medical technique of suggestion. Here we are only concerned to compare it with amateur hypnosis, in order to gain an understanding of the cases which come up in pastoral work. The characteristic mark of medical hypnosis therapy is, as already noted, its liberation from the chaos of magic and the mists of enchantment which still to a great extent surround amateur hypnosis. A very real distinction is, above all, Dr. Kretschmer's complete reconstruction of the hypnotic technique from passive to active participation. In the old hypnotizing technique, the patient received suggestion in a passive attitude. Kretschmer, on the other hand, now seeks to have hypnosis, in its neurophysiological components, applied in a staggered series of reflex-like processes. Here the patient is led to active exercises, while the doctor's part in the therapy consists merely of guidance. The cure is thus not a passive effect of hypnosis, but an achievement of the patient himself, encouraged and directed by an active method of stimulation on the side of the doctor. In this field medical science is years ahead of amateur hypnosis. As a very important distinction, we must mention two elements often observed in pastoral care, namely that charlatans misuse hypnosis in a selfish manner, and that they are not able afterwards to undo the mischief they have wrought. A very prevalent manifestation, which it is our task to investigate here, is the religious and occult embellishment of amateur hypnosis. A series of examples will now introduce us to this strange and confused field of phenomena. They will also show us the psychological consequences.

Ex 47 During an evangelistic campaign, a woman came for an interview. She confessed that she and her friend had come under the influence of a man whose will they were compelled to obey in various respects. This man had such a power over them that, against their wills, or with their wills paralysed, they were compelled to do things which otherwise they abhorred. Sexually they were helpless against him, and they committed acts of theft which they themselves did not understand.

For example, her friend was one day standing in the garden. Suddenly a peculiar urge came over her, and she stepped into another person's

166 cf. Brauchle, op.cit. 44, p. 33.

garden next door and stole some vegetables, though she had a great quantity of the same kind in her own garden. This woman was in good circumstances and had no need whatever to steal; indeed, she detested such deeds. After the theft of the vegetables she clasped her head and asked herself, "Am I out of my mind?"

After several interviews with this woman, an increasingly clear picture of the situation began to form. The man whose will these two women were forced in slavish subjection to fulfil was the possessor of a notorious magic book, the so-called 6th. and 7th. Book of Moses. In connection with this book he practised suggestion and cast spells. When I visited him, the man admitted his occult practices, and after some reluctance he proved willing to surrender the magic book, which was thereupon immediately burned.

With the unveiling of these connexions and the breaking of every association with the conjurer, the woman felt much relieved. However, a hard struggle now ensued, before she was free of the pernicious suggestive influence. True, from the time of her confession she no longer lapsed with regard to the seventh and eighth commandments, but for weeks and months she felt a resistance to God's word, and great difficulties in her life of faith. Moreover she was repeatedly afflicted with bouts of depression.

Because a small group of faithful Christians committed themselves to earnest prayer for the afflicted woman, she made good progress. She herself made repeated use of pastoral guidance, and faithfully attended services and bible studies, and in spite of a certain unwillingness at first, she faithfully read God's word. After a year there was no trace left of her original occult, hypnotic subjection.

From the *medical* point of view this case seems plain enough. This is a classic disease-pattern for a psychopathic person of unstable moods.[167] Marks of these psychopathic reactions are the compulsion to senseless or misguided actions, urges or impulsive actions which come over the patient without his being properly conscious of them. Especially characteristic of this class are kleptomania, sexual aberrations, pyromania, fugues, oniomania, etc. These impulsive aberrations are not only found with some neuroses, the compulsion states, but also in the case of endogenic depressives. Also the conversion of the woman might be considered by the psychiatrist from the aspect of conflict between her amoral impulses and her higher moral aspirations.[168] In accord with this there are in *Ex 47* four outstanding symptoms which make the dia-

---

167 cf. Kloos, op.cit. 12, pp. 126, 429.
168 cf. Bleuler, op.cit. 129, p. 374.

gnosis easy for the psychiatrist: kleptomania, sexual aberrations, depressions, and the sudden change from an amoral state to morality. To complete the diagnosis we note that the woman during her compulsive action had no clouding of consciousness. Moreover, she had no further ailments such as epilepsy, schizophrenia, or brain injury, which might be considered as causes of the compulsive acts.

The *psychical researcher* is confronted in *Ex 47* with the oft-observed phenomenon of remote influence (mental suggestion). The possessor of the 6th. and 7th. Book of Moses was able to influence both women by telepathy, either commanding them or presenting himself to them telepathically. This problem can be classified as "remote telepathic compulsion", but it cannot be explained. In para-psychological literature, the names of Dr. Dusart, Richet, Janet, Giberts and others are well known in connexion with such experiments.

From the *pastoral* standpoint, suggestion at every depth-level, as practised by the occult conjurer, is a phenomenon frequently observed. In *Ex 47* there is first the problem of the part played by suggestion in the well known pattern of psychopathic compulsions. We must note that these compulsive urges began when the woman made the acquaintance of the occultist, and suddenly stopped with the breaking off of the acquaintance. From the time of her first pastoral confession, the aberrations we have mentioned ceased. We may further note that although psychiatry may classify such forms of disorder into a known system, as disturbances of instinct and will,[169] or even as induced insanity,[170] and may speak of endogenic and exogenic causes, yet of the actual cause little is known. The basic origin of such reactions lies for medical science very much in the dark. Although occult influence cannot perhaps at the moment be acknowledged as the efficient cause in the medical world — and this is anyway unnecessary — yet according to the unanimous testimony of many pastoral cases occult influence does indeed constitute an incidental cause, among others. Noteworthy in *Ex 47* is the fact that faith in Christ evidently and finally conquered these misguided impulsive actions. This fact, that psychological disturbances have been cured by turning to Christ is the justification for our study.

Ex 48   A girl whose inner development I was able to observe over a long period of time, suffered from compulsive actions which she performed in an hysterical, twilight state, of which she afterwards knew nothing. She would for instance shake salt into the milk, throw clothes

[169] cf. Kloos, op.cit. 12, p. 124.
[170] cf. Bleuler, op.cit. 129, p. 372.

into the stream, deliberately and violently disturb the furniture, and so on. Remarkable was the good moral disposition of the girl. She was open regarding religious questions. Her psyche did not seem particularly ill. In the course of medical treatment, the doctor found impressions in the subconscious following an induced hypnosis.

From the *medical* standpoint we have the same kind of disorder as in *Ex 47*, except that here the girl also suffered a loss of consciousness. Another element is the establishment of a hypnosis, regarding which neither the girl nor her mother could give an explanation.

In the *psychical* respect this case provides interesting material. The mother of this girl had a similar condition. Searching the family history, we discovered that in the home of this girl the 6th. and 7th. Book of Moses had for many years been used for magic suggestion and conjuration. It is not an absurd idea when we connect the compulsive acts of mother and daughter with this fact. As we shall see in the section regarding conjuration, occult subjection operates into the third and fourth generations. This fact may seem incredible to some psychical researchers. The psychical researcher knows, however, that mediumistic abilities or gifts of dowsing are often hereditary. To the medical expert, the hypothesis of an occult subjection passed on in heredity is a stumbling block, since for him not even the fact that there is such a thing as occult subjection is settled. Thus Bovet, for instance, in his book "Lebendige Seelsorge",[171] shows that the enchantments of many occultists are phenomenologically identical with the acts of compulsive neurotics who have compulsions of a different kind, without any occult flavouring. Only a naive layman could therefore connect the mechanism of compulsion with enchantments. Without doubt an authority such as Bovet, who as a doctor and as a Christian has a decisive word to say on the subject of our study, must be heard. Bovet's examples fit moreover into the line of thought pursued in our study. Certainly in many cases the compulsion neurosis is primary, and the profusion of magic practices the consequence. Still we must here, for the sake of completeness, add that the magic practices mentioned in Bovet's book (p. 56) are merely peripheral practices, which do not constitute the essence of occult subjection. Even in the case of damage "apparently" due to magic, Bovet points to a previously existent psychological constitution of the patient. Here, too, however, the medical reference does not exclude the factor of occult involvement, but rather includes it. It is indeed a fact established by some 600 examples from pastoral experience with those involved in the occult, that prolonged

171 cf. Theodor Bovet, "Lebendige Seelsorge", Katzmann-Verlag, Tübingen, 1951, p. 57.

occult practice creates a corresponding psychological constitution, a susceptibility, an inclination, a breeding-ground for various psychological disorders. In a long series of cases it has been possible to establish that occult subjection is an especially marked psychological constitution lasting through four succeeding generations of the same family.

If then in these cases the symptoms of occult subjection piece together to form one solid pattern, then not only does the law of probability apply,[172] but, just as with every scientific demonstration on an empirical basis, the thesis is established that occult activity is involved as an efficient cause or an incidental cause of the psychological disturbances.

The *pastoral* angle of *Ex 48* must still be examined briefly. After psychiatric help had several times been obtained, the girl came to me for pastoral advice. It goes without saying that counselling by the pastor in such cases must never replace or suppress the specialist's work. Compulsive neurotics always call for specialist treatment. But nevertheless there is a second task, which the pastor must perform. It is important for the patient to gain a trust in Christ, and by God's grace to make a decision for Christ. In the present case *(Ex 48)* the mother and the daughter were willing to be led in this respect. The rest of the family took the same step also, with a great readiness to believe. Thus the entire family became a prayer circle, which daily placed itself under the direction of God's word and engaged in communal prayer. The blessing of God followed. From the day this prayer group was formed, the aberrant, complusive actions which had previously taken place almost daily, came to an end. Not until some two months later did there appear, at intervals of several weeks, a few minor compulsive actions. Whether this was connected with a relaxation of the daily prayer of the circle, or had some medical cause, I am not able to say. In any case, the condition of the patient has improved powerfully since her turning to Christ. She has not come to a total surrender of her life to Christ. That may be part of the reason why she has an occasional relapse.

Ex 49 A thirty-eight-year-old master craftsman, a sensible, down-to-earth man, came for a pastoral interview, in which he admitted to mental disturbances. After some preliminary questions, an unusual life story came to light. His father was a spiritist, astrologer, magnetizer and hypnotist. He conducted experiments with the members of his family, and also wanted to teach his growing children occult practices. The brothers and sisters and the daughter of the man took part. The son — our craftsman — refused these things and inclined more towards

---

[172] cf. Bovet, op.cit. 171, p. 56.

the views of his Christian-minded mother. This refusal angered his father, and as a consequence he made his son the object of his hypnotic experiments. For years he remained unsuccessful, and one day he even expressed anger at the fact that he could not overcome his son. Finally the hypnotist effected a progressive condition of sleep in his son.

Thereupon the son went for treatment to a psychiatrist, who confirmed the hypnotic condition of the patient. There were none of the customary causes of a sleeping condition, like encephalitis lethargica, basal meningitis, i.e. the usual narcoleptic disorders.[173] The sleepiness improved rapidly when the son was withdrawn from the influence of his father. After his return from the psychiatric clinic, his condition again worsened. But soon a change came about in the family through the death of his father.

The son described the remarkable circumstances that accompanied the death of his father. On the day of his death, the son sat with his father and held his hand. Then he felt how, from his father's finger-tips, there issued a light current, or certain magnetic energy. He also saw standing at the head of the bed a scornful, sneering figure, which bent itself over his dying father. Every time the sneering figure bent over, the dying man became short of breath.

Fourteen days after his death, the dead man appeared, accompanied by a black form who called to the son: "Take your life! Your life has no value!" The son felt a chill creep over his body and paralyse his will. Then the black figure called out: "Hang yourself!" Finally the afflicted son was able to recite the verse of Luther's hymn:

> "Were the whole world with devils filled,
> That threaten to undo us,
> We will not fear, for God is near,
> And He will triumph through us!"

At these words the black figure vanished.

The apparitions of his father continued for eighteen months, sometimes with and sometimes without the black figure. These visions appeared either by day, while he was at work, or at night. Once the dead man gave him a command: "Go to Louise (the daughter of the dead man) and tell her that she must desist from her astrology and her other practices. Then she must go to the pastor and make a confession, so that she may be liberated. Otherwise she will come to the same place where

---

[173] cf. Kloos, loc.cit. [12], p. 267.

I am. It is not nice here. If you do not carry out this command, you will have a fatal accident. If you fulfil it, you will be able to tell people the past and the future".

The troubled man once more turned to the psychiatric clinic. There the leading professor told him that he was involved in a posthypnotic reaction, which can often persist for years. After a visit to a pastor, the apparitions ceased. At long intervals minor psychological disturbances would begin again. In one such crisis, he came to me for an interview.

Here we are concerned with the question of how this case is to be understood from the medical, psychical and pastoral points of view. First, the truthfulness of the reporter must be discussed. Is the report true? Is there no deception, no boastful exaggeration, or even total invention? But both the first pastor, whom the patient could no longer consult because he had moved, and I had a good impression of the man. I discussed this with the pastor concerned. The victim of these assaults is a worthy, dependable, religious man, who really stands in the tradition of his praying mother.

The various phenomena which appear in this report, such as visual, acoustic and felt hallucinations, and also the persecution complex and delusions of self-destruction, are well known to *medical* science as symptoms of various psychoses, psychopathies and other disorders. We shall not go into these here, since there are so many different phenomena present.[174] We shall only emphasize the persistent post-hypnotic effects of amateur hypnosis practised over many years, effects which arose to such an extensive degree because a certain psychological constitution, namely an occult subjection, had been formed through the occult practices of the father.

From a *psychical* and psychological point of view, it is not hard to arrive at an understanding of this case. The apparitions of his father and the threat by the black figure are merely the result of the persecution complex, which arose during the lifetime of his father as a result of the latter's hypnotic experiments. The father's command to the sister to stop her occult practices is the Christian conscience of the son. From his godly mother he had often heard about the wickedness of occult activities. So we have here a meeting together of two separate notions present in the subconscious of the person concerned: the father and the mother complexes. They meet in an "outward curve", i.e. in an optically visible form (Schmeïng). The hallucinations of the man had therefore no objective significance, only a subjective one. Of the dubiousness

---

174 cf. Kloos, op.cit. 12: hallucinations, pp. 135, 171; voices, pp. 136, 171, 401; persecution ideas, p. 173; suicidal madness, pp. 126, 145.

of a command from a deceased person we have already spoken. In the threat of a fatal accident and the promise of clairvoyance, we again see the meeting of two factors, fear and curiosity, in the patient, referring to the occult things which were prized by the father and feared by the mother. Thus here also we have a double complex, the mother's fear and the father's curiosity, deposited in the subconscious of the son. Hence these hallucinations are not evidence for the spiritist cause, but are to be explained purely from an animistic point of view.

From the *pastoral* point of view it is significant that the troubled man was able, during these dreadful hallucinations, which were only the mirror of his own inner conflicts, to overcome the distressing apparitions by a word from the bible or a verse from a hymn. It is further worthy of note that after he had sought pastoral help the hallucinations completely ceased and to this day, eight years later, have not returned. Faith in Christ and consequent personal trust in His powerful help proves repeatedly to be a calming and relaxing factor with these psychic disturbances.

We might mention other forms of the abuse of hypnosis by charlatans and experimenting amateurs. There are occasional cases which come to the attention of the pastor of sexual and financial exploitation, although these cases are not frequent. But in this section we were interested only in the dangerous coupling of magic with amateur hypnosis. Where these two spheres merge together in practice, we find in the person involved a latent subjection, which becomes a breeding ground for various psychological disturbances and sometimes their point of origin. Again we urge that it would be in the interest of public health if our health officials would work for a legal measure banning all amateur literature aimed at teaching the art of hypnosis. The pastoral counsellor cannot expose too often the evil of this quackery.

(b) *Healing magnetism*

A further form of ESI is magnetic stroking. As far as its history is concerned, we may note the following facts. In 1771 the French Abbé Lenoble introduced a new method of healing by covering or stroking diseased areas of the body with steel magnets.[175] Hence we could call Lenoble the founder of healing by inanimate magnetism. A step further in this question was taken by Mesmer, who produced the theory of animal magnetism. Mesmer taught that the healthy person could charge himself magnetically from the earth's magnetic field, and then by

[175] cf. Brauchle, op.cit. **43**, p. 5.

stroking sick persons with his hands could exert a curative influence upon them. The views of Lenoble and Mesmer were taken up by the English doctor Braid, who led them into new channels. He declared that not a magnetic, but a mental influence was involved, which he called hypnosis. From this time forward, the two views existed as rivals. Those holding the hypnotic theory say that animal magnetism is only a preliminary stage of hypnotism. The "magnetic fluid" has, they say, proved to be an error.[176]

Over against this opinion are the research findings of the chemist Baron von Reichenbach, who believed he could prove that from many inorganic and organic bodies there emanated a kind of flame, which he called "od", which "sensitives" perceived as light.[177] Reichenbach has many critics among the scientists, but at the same time many adherents in the fraternity of magnetizers and mesmerists, and even among the group of scientists who defend radiaesthesia and para-psychology. In any case, we cannot, in the opinion of some serious scientists, simply dismiss with a wave of the hand the possibility of an emanation of some unknown "phosphorescence", "magnetic fluid", or "magnetic transference", when our knowledge of the physical aspect of this process is so limited. Of late, Prof. Farny of Geneva has found traces of a physiological process which points in the direction of the above mentioned theory. It concerns a kind of "electrical transmission", which has its source in the insensible perspiration proceeding from the main pores of the skin: along with the separation of the fatty acids, there is an emanation of positive and negative ions, having its origin in the blood.[178]

An important contribution to this question has been made by Tischner, by means of approximately 250 tests of separating the faculty of perception.[179]

Lit 10 He put into the hand of a lady under deep hypnosis a glass full of water, and made her separate her "nervous energy" into the water. After five minutes he put the glass on the side, next to similar glasses, and let a third person come in and move the glasses round. Then Tischner stuck a pair of forceps into the glasses. Each time the test person could tell him exactly which glass it was into which her nervous energy had been separated. The conditions under which the test was conducted, which are not all described here, were such that no phenomenon such as

[176] cf. Tischner, op.cit. 25a, p. 35.
[177] cf. ibid., p. 135.
[178] cf. Dr. Wendler, "Physikalische Betrachtungen zu den Fragen der Radiästhesne", Herold-Verlag, Munich, 1950, p. 20.
[179] cf. Tischner, op.cit. 25a, pp. 135f.

telepathy or involuntary muscle movements could be involved. Just what constituted the charge in the glass, Tischner could not say. Only the fact that some substance had been isolated was established.

Lit 11 A similar test was conducted by Olhaver.[180] He "magnetized" four out of six glasses by holding his fingers over them. The process of magnetizing was staggered: one glass was magnetized for 5 minutes, one for 10 minutes, one for 15 minutes, one for 20 minutes, and two not at all. The glasses were numbered on the underside and were re-arranged without the knowledge of the experimenter, so that telepathy was excluded. The medium, Miss Tambke, set the glasses in order and sorted them according to the degree of "magnetism". Such tests constantly prove accurate. Here likewise only the fact of a transference into the glasses is established, not the nature of the "magnetic substance" transferred.

These experiments will now form the presupposition for the treatment of the pastoral problems which arise in connexion with so-called healing magnetism. In pastoral care we are not concerned with magnetic experimentation, but only with the treatment of the psychological disturbances which sometimes result from healing treatment by a magnetizer. An example will now introduce this group of questions.

Ex 50 A woman with a nervous heart disorder had a mesmerist give her magnetic stroking treatment twice a week. The magnetizer ran his spread-out finger-tips along the woman's spinal column from top to bottom, and then made throwing movements with his hands as if he were trying to shake something out of his fingers. The woman sensed a wholesome relaxation as a result of this treatment.

The *doctor* is interested whether the result of this therapy is due to a suggestive influence or an actual magnetic one. For the discussion of this debated question I am not competent.

The *psychical researcher* is in this case interested in knowing with what phenomenon we are faced in healing magnetism. We shall not repeat the points of historical development. The fact that in essence we are not here dealing with suggestion, but with a vital power, appears from the fact of the speedy exhaustion of a magnetizer. Magnetizers repeatedly emphasize that after three or four treatments in one day their magnetic energy is exhausted. Hence they can treat at most four patients per day with success. In the course of the day, however, the expended energy regenerates itself rapidly.

180 cf. Olhaver, op.cit. 132, pp. 65f.

From the *pastoral* viewpoint, many such magnetic treatments are without any harmful effects. Psychological disturbances can only be established when this gift is used by unworthy characters, or when healing magnetism is coupled with magic practices, a phenomenon often to be observed. An example of this kind follows.

Ex 51 A student came for an interview and told me of his spiritual problems. He suffered from depressions, occasional compulsive images, resistance and disgust at the word of God, even though he was a student of theology. When he desired to pray, his throat was clamped shut. He had not suffered from this condition as a child, a schoolboy, or even at the beginning of his university training. A psychiatric examination produced no explanation of his condition. Presumably the student was himself responsible for the fruitlessness of this psychiatric treatment, since he withheld from the doctor an embarrassing fact.

Since the sudden development of depressions and of compulsive images is, in the case of hitherto non-psychotic and non-psychopathic persons, very often a symptom of psychological disturbances conditioned by occultism, we conducted an anamnesis into this area with the young man. Astounding things came to light. The young student had got into a circle of young men where there was a strong magnetizer. This magnetizer often gave proofs to the group of his magnetic power. Anyone who touched his outstretched fingers felt a mild current pulsating through them. Our student came under the influence of this magnetizer and suffered a strong emotional subjection. The subjection became so strong that he could sense the approach of the magnetizer by means of telepathic remote action, (mental suggestion). On one occasion I myself witnessed this foreboding. On the way to a church service the student suddenly said to me, "He is coming again!" We took a seat in the gallery of the church, and although the magnetizer was a complete non-churchgoer and non-Christian, he appeared in the church and passed by us. Once again after this I was witness, in a small group of students, to the remarkably strong magnetic powers of this man. Being induced by the distress of our young student, and spurred on by personal acquaintance with the magnetizer, I was deeply concerned that the student should be freed from the spell of suggestive subjection to the magnetizer. For eight months I met the young student almost twice a week. Finally, through faith in Christ, he was liberated from his enslavement. With this, he was also freed from the depressions, the compulsive images, and his resistance to the word of God and to prayer.

It is a fact of experience in pastoral counselling, that in all cases in which magnetic healing is joined with magic or spiritism, the by now sufficiently familiar consequences appear. Often magnetizers are simply compelled to engage in other occult activities besides their magnetizing, such as conjuration, pendulum manipulation, etc. From the four patients whom a magnetizer can treat with his daily "magnetic supply", he cannot gain enough to live on. If he wants to avoid the reputation of being an unsuccessful practitioner, he must turn to other methods of healing as well. Since many magnetizers and mesmerists therefore use, besides their natural magnetic powers, some occult approach, such as mediumistic magnetism, every treatment by such a healer must be preceded by a thorough investigation of the man's religious disposition.

A theologian, who kindly read the present study through in manuscript, considered this section (b) to be a condemnation of healing magnetism. This misunderstanding can readily be removed. On the ground of the examples available to me, the conclusion seems clear that in the case of healing magnetism, we are dealing in the first place with an ethically neutral power of nature. It all depends upon the presupposition under which it is applied. Modersohn, too, represents this point of view ("Im Banne des Teufels", pp. 66 f.). Basically it is possible to have a God-conformed, God-shaped, productive use of healing magnetism, as many would have it. I personally know cases of definite Christians who have this gift. What troubles Modersohn and also me is the fact that for every one positive case of good use, there are easily ten cases of occult use. Hence Modersohn gives the following warning, "Inform yourself beforehand most carefully, who it is with whom you are dealing. If you do not know exactly whether you are dealing with a really Christian magnetizer, then we must caution decisively against magnetism."

(c) *Magic charming*

The medical expert Prof. Dr. Walter Seitz, of Munich, explained in a lecture: "The psychosomatic approach, i.e. the knowledge of the connexion between the emotional life and the bodily processes, has brought about a great change in medicine. We have again come to recognize that disturbances in the emotional life can often be the cause of very severe bodily ailments". This connection between the psychological and the organic fields has in our study already[181] been cast into the thesis of the circuit of psycho-organic correspondence (circulus relationis psychoorganicae). Through the mental power pyramid ailments from the organic sphere can evoke disturbances of the emotional life by way of the organic unconscious and the subconscious. Naturally this

[181] In the section on clairsentience.

is not to say that this is the only way in which organic ailments can have psychological effects. This ascent from the organic to the emotional is utilized in the para-psychological phenomenon of tapping the subconscious. We have here a passive appeal to the subconscious, in which the mediumistically sensitive person receives impulses from the subconscious of the test person. In addition to this passive appeal — passive only for the test person, but active for the experimenter — there is also an active appeal to the subconscious in the para-psychological phenomenon of conjuration. Here we are faced with the utilization of the descent from the mental to the organic. By way of the subconscious and the organic-unconscious, impulses are worked out in the organic sphere. The psychosomatic school has already drawn this process of conjuration within its field of research.

Ex 52 A doctor well known to me asked a university professor who employs the psycho-somatic approach to suggest an effective remedy against warts. Promptly the answer came, "The only good remedy for them is conjuration".

This medical process of conjuration will not be considered in this study. It is only an example of the fact that as medicine advances it is becoming more and more conscious of the connexion between body and soul.

At this point we shall, in connexion with *Ex 52*, deal in the form of an excursus with the objection of a well-known and recognized authority on psychical problems. He contradicts the statement that the use of occult abilities is a transgression of the first commandment, and that occult practice necessarily causes psychological disturbances. To this we may reply, from the viewpoint of this study, that we are not in this study denying neutral powers of nature. Among the 600 cases I have collected, there are examples of diagnosis with the rod, telepathy, telaesthesia, magnetism etc., which have been without apparent psychological disturbances. *Ex 52* even leaves open the possibility of a neutral medical conjuration. In Part II, ch. 2, 2(e), we shall, in connexion with the work of Diepgen, mention neutral magic also. Besides this, I have records of observations that animals also possess such mysterious natural powers, when, for instance, they react to bands of attraction on the earth's surface or to apparitions which remain invisible to man. In view of these neutral powers, the above-mentioned objection is valid. However, since it has appeared during 15 years of systematic and exact critical observation that in the case of healing magnetism the neutral use is outnumbered by the occult by approximately ten to one, and that in the case of magic the proportion is probably 100 to 1, it is our duty to sound the most urgent note of alarm. For this reason the neutral use of the mysterious powers of nature is in this study merely mentioned in passing, in the same proportion as the problems arising in the case material.

When I use the term "occult" I have therefore given little attention to the neutral factor, in proportion to the importance it has in actual practice. That is, the concept "occult" has in our present study undergone a shift of emphasis in the direction of the non-neutral use of magical powers. This should be remembered in passing judgement upon the conclusions we have reached. The justification for this lies in the following observation: the para-psychologist is mostly interested only in scientific research into occult phenomena, without giving very much attention to the psychological symptoms which accompany them. The pastor has to meet this abuse in the conviction that the living person, as a creature of God, transcends scientific problems.

In this section on magic conjuration, therefore, we are not dealing with neutral medical conjuration, but with magical, God-opposing conjuration as practised by amateurs. On this magical branch of conjuration I have a quite inexhaustible supply of material at my disposal.

Addendum to the American edition

Since the earlier appearance of the German edition, the number of examples I have of magic conjuration has grown enormously. Hundreds of people have come to me for counselling who showed the effects of conjuration in their psychological life after having been subjected to these practices. For this reason I am now inclined to doubt altogether whether there is such a thing as a safe and harmless medical form of conjuration.

Just as the psychologist Dr. Schmeïng came to the conclusion, in his studies regarding "second sight", that there is a belt of magic around the Baltic Sea, so we can say that there is a flood of magical conjuration which washes the Alps. Many evangelistic tours in South Germany, Switzerland and Austria during the last 15 years have resulted in the personal counselling of a great number of people involved in cases of conjuration, which have made it possible to make a study of the processes concerned. In comparison with other occult phenomena, conjuration and divination stand at the head of the list for prevalence. The reason for this lies in the nature of the case. The most common threats to man are occasioned by illness and by the uncertainties of the future. And so occult customs aim at the control of these two dangers. However, before we enter into a basic discussion of the question, we shall introduce it with a few examples.

Ex 53 After an evangelistic meeting a young man came for an interview. He complained of blasphemous thoughts, depressions, violent sexual temptations, violent temper and other disturbances in his inner life. Besides this he suffered from unusual attacks, which he was unable to describe accurately. It was not epilepsy, since he retained full consciousness and did not fall down.

From the *medical* standpoint, an anamnesis produced no particular findings apart from these psychological troubles. None of the ailments associated with fits fitted the bill, such as pycnolepsy,[182] psychogenic (hysterical) fits,[183] genuine epilepsy,[184] tetany spasms,[185] epileptiform attacks in myxoedema,[186] etc. The blasphemous thoughts might point to a psychopathy, being regarded by the psychotherapist as a symptom of compulsion neurosis. I will not contradict these medical judgements. However, it causes me to think very seriously when I consider that all cases of blasphemous thoughts which I have known were connected with occult involvement. Sometimes the occult practices of ancestors are sufficient to cause the children to develop blasphemous thoughts.

From the *psychical researcher's* point of view, this was a typical case of conjuration. The young man had as a child been taken by his father with an organic disease to see a shepherd. The latter had worked a charm over him. His organic disease had vanished, but in its place there arose disturbances to his mind and character.

On the level of *pastoral* care, we shall have to give particular attention to this case at a later stage. We may however at this point say that the young man was psychologically cured by turning to Christ.

Ex 54 A young woman was paralysed. Her mother wanted to force her recovery, and just as with all her children, she had her charmed. She regained her health, but after the conjuration she became afflicted with periodic loss of consciousness and attacks of mania. She had to be taken to a mental home. The other daughters and son, who had also undergone charms, had psychological disturbances too.

The *psychiatrist* may object that we must not here confuse cause and effect. The paralysed woman may have had a psychosis, in the course of which it became necessary to send her to a mental hospital. This objection may be justified. But it is remarkable that in many cases the act of conjuration brings out an endogenic predisposition or hastens

182 cf. Kloos, op.cit. 12, p. 373.
183 ibid., p. 26.
184 ibid., pp. 274, 360.
185 ibid., pp. 91, 371.
186 cf. Brugsch, op.cit. 10, vol. I, p. 117.

a hidden process. Occult influence often shows itself as an incidental or aggravating cause.

Ex 55 At an evangelistic meeting a woman of sixty years appeared, who complained of many kinds of psychological distress, such as depressions and resistance to the word of God, even though with tears she sought the way to Christ and desired to follow Him. For 45 years she had longed for forgiveness of her sins and simply could not believe.

After a *medical* anamnesis, with special attention to the causes of depression, an anamnesis of occult involvement was conducted. The woman related that as a child she had been taken with eye trouble by her father to an old charmer, known as "old Winklere", who succeeded in removing the "evil" in her eye by charming it and blowing it away. Later the child was again put under a charm when she caught cold, with speedy results.

On the *pastoral* level it is worthy of note that the girl, who had at the age of confirmation been seeking and was spiritually awakened, could not believe, even though she desired to follow Christ. Even though we must allow for the fact that depressive persons have special difficulties of faith, we have here again a typical form of occult subjection, which reveals itself in resistance to God's word and prayer, and in an inability to make decisions of faith.

Ex 56 The wife of a missionary reported that as a child she had been to a man to have a severe toothache charmed away. The charmer scratched a cross on his chest with a knife and removed by his own pain the pain of the child. The toothache subsided immediately. Later, on other occasions, recourse was again had to conjuration. The charmed girl developed mediumistic gifts, especially of clairvoyance and telepathy. The clairvoyance, which before her conversion to Christ was applied to secular things, assumed after her conversion a religious content.

Here, from the *para-psychological* point of view, we have the very common phenomenon that the process of conjuration favours the development of mediumistic gifts, especially that of clairvoyance. Remarkable here is the rite of pain transference, which appears in the same manner among primitive people. Here we have a form of homoeopathic magic.

Ex 57 A man went to a conjurer, obtained advice from him, and took his medicaments. His physical trouble vanished, but instead there appeared psychological disturbances and the development of clairvoyance. The son of this man suffered from early youth from melancholia, blashemous thoughts, periodic depressions and attacks of various kinds.

From the *para-psychological* and *pastoral* points of view, some significant phenomena come to light here, such as the development of clairvoyance, the shifting from bodily to psychological trouble, the psychological disturbances in the life of his son. These are all symptoms which belong to the typical pattern of the after-effects of conjuration.

Ex 58 A fifty-year-old manufacturer came for an interview. He suffered periodically, especially on bright, moonlit nights, from depressive states with fits of rage, temper, mania, destructive fury, disgust towards God's word, and suicidal thoughts. After full moon the attacks subsided. Then the man was even open to religious questions, read the word of God and desired to follow Christ.

From a *medical* viewpoint these changing states and reversals of mood could be classified as the experience of alienation in psychoasthenia,[187] as somnambulism, or as depersonalization phenomena in a case of endogenic depression,[188] or schizophrenia.[189] The dissociation of personality leading to ego-alien processes is a form of disorder very familiar to psychiatrists.

From the position of the *para-psychologist,* it is remarkable that the manufacturer was charmed as a child at night by full moon. What connexions are there now between the medical and the para-psychological diagnoses?

One thing is clear: this manufacturer was no schizophrenic or psychoasthenic. It is questionable whether there was an endogenic depression.

In the *pastoral* sphere it is significant that this man, in the course of many interviews, and with the help of an intercessory prayer group, was relieved upon turning to Christ, without any medical care, and has remained free for sixteen years.

Ex 59 A woman with an organic disorder had it charmed, and as a result had a rapid recovery. But from this time on psychological troubles set in, especially disturbances of perception in the form of acoustic hallucinations. She heard and saw spook apparitions, which plagued her for many years. Finally her life ended with an unusually severe death struggle.

Acoustic hallucinations in the form of coherent and incoherent sounds are known in *psychiatry* as symptoms of schizophrenia; alcoholic and syphilitic hallucinosis; during the treatment of malaria; and endogenous depression.[190]. None of these ailments apply in the case of this woman.

187 cf. Kloos, op.cit. 12, p. 430.
188 ibid., p. 419.
189 ibid., p. 408.
190 ibid., p. 171.

From the viewpoint of *psychical research* and of *pastoral* care we must again maintain the sequence of organic cure and psychological disorder. The conjuration process is almost always only a transformation from the organic to the mental sphere.

In the examples of conjuration which follow, we shall find illustrated something we have already noted in a few cases. We shall see clearly the pattern of psychological disturbance continuing through three or four generations of a conjurer's family.

Ex 60   In a pastoral interview concerning his mental disturbances, a man reported the following experience: "There was no doctor in our village. My great grandmother was versed in all kinds of absurd healing crafts, especially in charms. She was the muchsought "village doctor". She was moreover regarded as a pious woman, since in her charms she used the names of the Trinity. Although she had a charm for every disease of man and beast, she was unable to control the psychological sufferings of her own posterity. From her own children down to her great grandchildren, an enormous variety of psychological disorders are to be observed."

Ex 61   A young lady complained in an interview of various emotional problems, such as troubled faith, bad temper, strong sexuality, depressions, etc. The anamnesis of occult relations revealed an interesting picture. Her grandmother was a charmer for many years. Her oldest son, the father of the girl who came to me, was harassed by suicidal thoughts. The second son hanged himself. This first granddaughter had fits of mania. The second granddaughter was the girl who came to me.

With all these examples we are faced with the question: which is primary here, the occult involvement, or some psychopathy or psychosis?

Ex 62   A cattle charmer from the Black Forest used the 6th. and 7th. Book of Moses. He introduced his charms with the names of the three devils. After years of successful healing practice, his own mind became disturbed. He was taken to a mental institution. Two of his children suffered the same fate. The whole family had psychological disturbances for several generations.

Ex 63   A Christian woman related to me in an interview the deep spiritual problems of her family. Her grandfather worked with magic books and conducted occult experiments. Finally he became blind. He burned his magic books and warned his children that they must not continue his occult practices because he had become blind as a result of them. In the following generation an astounding picture of psychological abnormalities presented itself. The son was an alcoholic. The grand-daughter is a clairvoyant. She sees the sky, the house and the streets full of spirits. Five of his grandchildren are mentally abnormal, some with psychopathies, some with psychoses. Only one member of this family of occult subjects found her way to Christ, namely the woman of our example. Since she has to live in the same house as her abnormal relatives, she is exposed to great emotional stress. When in the night her mentally ill niece begins to laugh horribly, she prays together with her Christian husband. Thereupon a banging is heard. Then silence settles in the house once more.

The *psychiatrist* will most probably view these acoustic hallucinations of the only normal person in this sick family as a psychological infection, if he does not diagnose it as induced insanity[191] or a genuine perceptual disturbance. We must emphasize that these spook noises are heard not only by this woman but also by her husband and the other members of the family.

Ex 64   At an evangelistic meeting a farmer's wife sought my advice and help in her spiritual troubles. From her fortieth year she had been melancholic, and had suicidal thoughts and blasphemous thoughts against God and Christ, although this caused her distress. She faithfully attended church services and bible studies in a fellowship group. She often desired to pray, but could not. Her daughter had had the same spiritual disturbances since she was twelve. A question about occult associations revealed the customary pattern. The grandfather, that is the great grandfather of the twelve-year-old girl, was a charmer and acted as "doctor" for his own children. He possessed only one "powerful saying", which always worked, and was passed down in turn from father to eldest son. Alongside his healing charms, the family also read Luther's morning and evening blessing and prayed. The conjuring activity was not regarded as evil in any way. They did not acknowledge a connexion between the occult method of healing and the psychological disturbances in the family.

Ex 65   During a Bible Week, a young man of twenty-one came for an interview. From his youth he had suffered from melancholia, psychogenic dyskinesia (impairment of voluntary motion) such as tremor and tic,[192] intensified sexuality, etc. Medically, the depressive syndrome could be classed as melancholia[193] and the dyskinesia as hysteria.[194] However,

191 ibid., p. 450.
192 ibid., p. 443.
193 ibid., p. 122.
194 ibid., p. 418.

the special forms of the psychological disturbances gave me occasion to carry out an anamnesis of occult relations. Investigations carried out with the help of the young man into the family history brought startling material to light. Into the fourth generation of this family occult activities can be traced. The great grandfather (first family member) was an expert in the field of occult practice. He mastered the art of charming people, animals and plants with the help of the 6th. and 7th. Book of Moses. He also performed telekinesis. Later he disposed of his magic books. This man died in dreadful pain and amid the spread of a penetrating odour. His sister (second family member), who was sceptical about the magic incantations and considered them to be humbug, on some occasions used the magic formulae of the 6th. and 7th. Book of Moses as a joke. During the next weeks she sensed a change in her emotional equilibrium, became insane, suffered manic attacks, heard voices, committed compulsive acts, and ended in a mental institution. In the generation of the grandparents, the magic and psychic activities continued. The grandmother (daughter of the second family member) had fits of manic and destructive fury. She demolished the furniture, and twice she was in the same mental hospital as her mother. Her sister (fourth family member) had visual, acoustic, and tactile hallucinations and a persecution complex. She repeatedly told her grandson to warn people that they should turn to Jesus, because it was dreadful to be tormented by evil spirits. In moments when her consciousness was affected, she would lie down in the street and cry aloud. Another sister of the grandmother (fifth family member) heard voices which predicted her death. This unhappy woman was also taken to a mental hospital. Upon a temporary improvement she was released, and at this point threw herself with her five- and eight-year-old children down a cliff 125 feet high. All three of them were killed.

In the generation of the parents, the same tradition continued. The mother's sister (sixth family member) was a card layer, pendulum manipulator and could work charms on moonlit nights. As a pendulum she used a thick prayer-book, on which her house key was bound over the cross. Her charms were introduced by the names of the Trinity. Among the brothers and sisters the same psychological troubles prevailed. The eldest brother of the person who reported all this was a clairvoyant, a speaking medium, and experienced phenomena of dissociation. He experimented in the field of excursion of the soul, and claimed to have visited China and India in a state of psychic dissociation. Later he was admitted to a mental hospital because of delusions of persecution and probable schizophrenia. The eldest sister of the man who gave the report (eighth family member) had her youngest sister (ninth family member), who was afflicted with with tuberculosis of the lung, charmed at full moon. In her village this procedure of conjuration was known as "Messen gehen" (going to mass). This conjurer had, like several members of this family, illegitimate children. Our young man, as the tenth member of this magic-practising and psychotic family, was afflicted with psychological disorders. It is also worthy of note that not only did these people themselves experience unusual phenomena, but that objective spook apparitions were also seen and heard in the house. After 7 p.m. a noise would begin as if someone were falling down from the ceiling to the stone floor, breaking his skull. Then a footstool would be swung high and thrown with force on to the ground. Other spook apparitions appeared in different generations of this family.

To the *psychiatrist* these cases seem quite straightforward. First of all he will undoubtedly think of hereditary schizophrenia. And he will think of the abundant practice of magic as a symptom and effect of this psychosis.

A discussion of the *para-psychological* phenomena which come up in this report, such as conjuration, telekinesis, clairvoyance, psychic dissociation, etc. is unnecessary, since we shall later give a summary of these magic processes.

From the *pastoral* point of view it is a most important fact that our young man, the offspring of such a sick and psychologically disordered family tree, found his way to Christ after several pastoral interviews, and has since enjoyed complete mental health. This mental recovery is a fulfilment of the words of the apostle Peter: "ransomed from the futile ways inherited from your fathers... with the precious blood of Christ" (I Peter 1, 18).

Ex 66 A young woman came during an evangelistic campaign to have an interview. She complained of spiritual troubles and of ennui. She also had fits which were not, according to the doctor, of an epileptic nature. He called them attacks of anxiety. Since medical treatment brought no relief from her suffering, she desired pastoral advice. An anamnesis of occult relations revealed an unusual background. Her great grandfather had been a conjurer. He hanged himself. The grandfather continued in his father's tradition. He was one day crushed to death by a tipping hay-wagon. His brother was kicked by a horse and died. That man's son was a successful cattle charmer, who was always called in by the farmers. Three-quarters of the stables in the village had been the scene of his charms. His end was terrible. He strangled his wife and then comitted suicide. His sister jumped into the well in front of the house and drowned herself. Our young woman stood in the fourth generation, and she was now suffering from psychological disturbances and anxieties. One murder, two fatal accidents, three suicides — that is the terrible balance-sheet of this family.

From the *medical* point of view it may be noted that in *Ex* 66 we are not dealing with schizophrenics as was perhaps the case with *Ex* 65. These men were vigorous farmers, with both feet on the ground. There was little sign of a depressive condition, unless perhaps we have here the symptom of dissimulation. It is further questionable whether in the diagnosis the pattern of melancholia, as part of a manic-depressive psychosis,[195] is a possibility.

Worthy of special note from the *pastoral* angle is the fact that this young woman turned to Christ and was thereupon freed from attacks for several months. I do not know how she is faring at the present time, since I have lost touch with her. A further religious phenomenon which we have mentioned several times already is the cold resistance to God's word when conjuring activities have been practised to a great extent. The village in which the cattle charmer had worked charms over three-quarters of the cattle was like a brazen fortress against the church, the word of God, and every Christian activity.

After these 14 first-hand examples which come from the "flood of magic which washes the Alps", we shall now investigate the question of the process of conjuration. The first question concerns the *means* of conjuration. Analogous to the rites of black magic and white magic, there are black and white charms. The black charm is introduced by the names of the three devils, and addresses itself to dark powers. The white charm is introduced by the names of the Trinity, and is supposed to put divine powers at the service of man. The magic spell which is used is generally spoken only half aloud, or murmured. The magic spell is occasionally emphasized by a magic action, or connected with a trans-ference or protective charm. Magic actions include the following: stroking, blowing, spitting, sprinkling with "Easter-water",[196] fumigation with the ashes of a burnt snake, toad, bat or bone,[197] and suchlike. Transference spells are supposed to "charm", i.e. transfer, the illness of a man to a dog, a corpse, a stone, etc. With protection charms, there are again both black and white magic practices. One black protective charm consists, for instance, of wearing the heraldic amulet of Lucifer. An example of a white charm is the wearing of an amulet with Psalm 29 written on it. Many amulets of religious content are merely meant to be a magic protective charm, whether they have a bible passage, the

---

[195] ibid., pp. 416f.

[196] Water drawn from a pond at 12 p.m. on Easter night.

[197] Charmers are good at obtaining human bones when graveyards are being re-dug.

image of a saint, or a sacred religious phrase to "christianize" them. The use of the names of the Trinity or of religious symbols is a fatal, beguiling mask and deception, to which many Christians readily fall victim.

That black and white charms are really essentially *equivalent* appears first of all from the similar psychological effects attaching to them. Further, the equivalence of the procedures can easily be seen from a simple theological consideration. The charmer who seeks to force a cure, whether by God's help or that of the devil, stands in relation to these transcendent powers as one who would dispose over them. This is clear from ch. 1 of the well-known charm book, the 6th. and 7th. Book of Moses. Here guidance is given as to how to subject the spirit helper to oneself and to become master of the transcendent powers. Theologically viewed, such a venture is the basic rebellion of man. Man gives orders to the transcendent power; man wants to have God at his disposal. This arrogance is the starting-point of magic, which makes it easy for the theologian to understand the nature of magic conjuration processes.

The next question concerns the *objects* of conjuration. Its most frequent use is for sick persons and for babies which cry in the night. Second come valuable domestic animals which are sick, such as horses and cattle. During my term as a pastor in the Black Forest and on the Baar, I often met with cattle charming. Many farmers feel that a charm is cheaper than veterinary services and gives quicker results. Thirdly plants (fruit trees) are charmed, to make them more productive. Fourthly, natural catastrophes, village fires, forest fires,[198] floods,[199] and volcanic eruptions[200] are also objects of conjuration.

A further question concerns the *instrument* or medium of the conjuration process. When it is a matter of charming sick persons, the influence proceeds via the subconscious of the patient, using, as we have seen, the circuit of psycho-organic correspondence. In this respect charming is a process of suggestion, which in its degree of penetration exceeds hypnosis, as the analysis of several hundred cases proves. What psychical phenomenon lies behind the conjuration of cattle, plants and natural catastrophes, has still received relatively little study. If we accept here a real process and not merely superstition, then we can only mention the phenomenon of psychokinesis, or telekinesis. In any

---

198 In my book "Feuerzeichen in der Nacht", Kurt Reith-Verlag, 2nd. edn. 1952, the story of the charming of a forest fire is reported.

199 Such an incident is known to me.

200 At the eruption of Etna on August 1942, which I witnessed from nearby, a process of this sort was carried out.

event enormous energies would here be needed in order to produce any actual effect. Up to the present we have nothing more than a great number of reported healings of people and animals.

The next question is that of the *effects* of the process of conjuration. The consequences which, after years of observation of cases which have come up for pastoral counselling, appear to be regular results of conjuration can be classified under six headings.

1. Regarding the *character* of the persons concerned, acute and persistent intensification of affects can be seen. Persons who have been magically charmed incline to violent temper, explosive irritability, extreme sensibility, and increased sexuality. The entire emotional life is marked by extremes. Charmed persons become unstable characters who are thrown off balance by trivial emotional stresses, and are subject to intense moods which have the character of affective intractability. We are dealing here with a kind of pre-psychopathic stage, which has no clear-cut boundary, and where the person is in a fluid state, bordering on and leading to psychopathy.

2. From the *pathological* point of view, symptoms develop in the charmed person which the psychiatrist can only partially fit into the pattern of melancholia, such as dejection, gloom, depressions, ennui, suicidal thoughts, etc. The unhindered mental powers do not fit into this pattern of melancholia.

3. From the *religious* aspect we see such symptoms as resistance to God's word and to prayer, immunity to the Holy Spirit, anti-Christian fixation — elements which cannot all simply be put down to the psychological and psychiatric facts of the case. Naturally it is admitted that normal cases of depression, with the accompanying hindrances to thinking and volition, also exert from the religious point of view an adverse influence on faith.

4. In the *para-psychologist's* view the charmed person reveals the development of mediumistic abilities. In a great number of cases clairvoyance appears as a secondary consequence, usually not until the second and third generation of charmers, seldom in the first generation. It is an empirical fact that in many cases where the subconscious of a test person is repeatedly appealed to by magical means, either actively or passively, clairvoyance will develop. From the foregoing examples this is evident in *Exs 1, 4, 20, 24, 33, 37, 40, 49, 56, 57, 59, 63* and *65*. Besides this phenomenon there will be developed in many cases a general mediumistic sensitivity together with the gift of psychic dissociation. The degree of sensitivity corresponds with the intensity of the mobilization of the subconscious.

5. From the aspect of *psycho-analysis*, we see as a consequence of magic conjuration the very unusual phenomenon that the psychological effects continue as far as the third and fourth generations. To elucidate this phenomenon we must first say something about the structure of the subconscious. Prof. Brauchle[201] distinguishes three levels of the subconscious: "The highest level is the personal, individual subconscious, in which childhood recollections, and forgotten, repressed and evaded experiences are stored. The middle level contains the buried elements of family, clan and race history. Family experiences find their way, as the runes of fate, into the hereditary chain and are retained in the following generation... Sometimes the colouring of a mental disorder bears a clear family impress" (Brauchle). The lowest level of the subconscious is the collective subconscious, which all people share in common.

Now we are here concerned with the phenomenon found in *Exx 24, 60, 61, 62, 63, 64, 65, 66*, viz. the inheritance of psychological disorders in the form of a mental constitution or in the form of a clear-cut psychological illness, such as depression. Magic conjuration, when applied intensively, leaves behind, in the middle level of the subconscious, engrams which enter the hereditary chain and constitute a latent breeding ground and efficient cause for psychological disorders in the next generation. This mental constitution will more certainly experience a development in the next generation when there enters, in addition to this latent efficient cause, a further psychological provocation through occult activity in the children, as an incidental cause. Engrams can, through suspension of occult activity in the following generations, fade rapidly and become recessive; on the other hand, in descendants who themselves practice magic, it can be intensified and appear as a dominant trait in the next generation. In this way the development of strong mediums can be explained. When three generations have all actively experimented and practised magic, the fourth will reveal an intense mediumistic sensitivity. Two or three successive generations of charmers will, first of all, as already noted, develop clairvoyance, but then also somnambulance, psychic dissociation, and a generally increased sensitivity for paranormal phenomena. Magic conjuration thus has, according to our findings so far, a primary effect of psychological disturbances, and a secondary effect of the development of mediumistic abilities. The connecting link between these two effects is the process of "opening" the subconscious. The powers of the subconscious are unlocked and mobilized. Since this unlocking process is carried out by laymen who have no scientific training, psychological complications set

201 cf. Brauchle, op.cit. 42, p. 16.

in — to say nothing, for the moment, of the religious factors. It often happens that in the third and fourth generations clairvoyance emerges, without the person concerned being aware of the occult roots in the first and second generations. The secondary effect still exists, even though its origin may have been forgotten in the course of the generations. This fact becomes especially evident in the investigation of Dr. Schmeïng: in his book, "Das zweite Gesicht in Niederdeutschland", he accumulates a great mass of examples which illustrate the connexion between clairvoyance and magic, without his own attention having been drawn particularly to this connexion. In the part of this book where we make a critical analysis of the pastoral cases, we shall again give thorough attention to Schmeïng's book.

6. We have still to consider the effects of this healing process from a *medical* point of view. There are reports of a great number of cures which have resulted in connexion with magical charms. In all the cases which I have observed over a long period of time, it was only a matter of apparent cure. Either the ailment appeared again after a considerable pause, or there was only a shift, a transfer from the organic to the psychological, as mentioned already. The organic ailment, the physical pain, had been forced via the organic unconscious into the subconscious, and there produced strongly charged complexes, which discharged themselves in violent changes of character. The total result of this cure by magic charms is thus a mere shifting of the symptoms, a change from bodily ailment to psychological disturbance. Such a shift of symptoms is known also to the psychotherapist, as a result of suggestive treatment.[202] After this medical reference, we must again take up and further discuss the problems of psycho-analysis involved in magic conjuration.

In the suppression of organic disturbances into the realm of the subconscious, we have a parallel to the suppression of non-assimilated experiences into the subconscious in the opposite direction. In the one case the transfer is ascendent; in the other it is descendent. In both cases a mental trauma results, but with this difference, that the transference from organic to mental gives rise to much more heavily charged complexes than does the opposite transference. The mental energies increase with their distance from the consciousness. The transformation from psychic to organic and vice versa requires greater energy than the transformation from the consciousness to the subconscious and vice versa. Expressed in the terms of psychical research, this means that e.g. telepathy (thought sending and thought reading) requires less energy than

[202] cf. Fritz Künkel, "Die Arbeit am Charakter", Wichern-Verlag, Berlin, 1951, p. 138.

does the process of charming. If we may imagine the circuit of psycho-organic correspondence as a circle, then the consciousness is the zenith, the organic unconscious is the nadir, and the subconscious forms the east and west extremities, since the subconscious is passed twice in the circuit, both in the upward and downward directions. Kinetic activities in the two lower quadrants, i.e. subconscious to organic unconscious and organic unconscious to subconscious, require more intense suggestive power than do activities in the upper quadrants, i.e. consciousness to subconscious and subconscious to consciousness. This fact means that the engrams which result from the processes of the lower quadrants are more intensely stamped and therefore more inherent in the hereditary transmission than are the engrams which are left by the processes of the upper quadrants. Among the parapsychological phenomena, therefore, those cause the most enduring and persistent psychological complications which are limited in their processes to the lower quadrants. As an example we may point not only to the magical conjuration which is the subject of this section, but also to psychic dissociation (excursion of the soul), which plays a special role in the phenomena of materialization.

A further problem is the question of the *principle* of magic conjuration. If we compare magic conjuration with the methods of suggestion, regardless of form, used by doctors, we shall notice two fundamental differences. In the latter the scientifically trained specialist uses suggestion as a healing method; in the former, the layman and the charlatan experiment in a field whose intricacies they do not understand. The results of this are continually brought to the notice of the pastor. The second difference is the complete stripping of all the magic tinsel from the suggestive method of cure — the demythologizing of medicine — and here, in the case of conjuration, the removal of all the magical, religious framework of its suggestive activity, behind which there exists not only a myth but a transcendent reality, as we still hope to show theologically. Thus we have in magical conjuration both a suggestive and a magical component, a double process, which must be investigated by both medicine and theology.

The last question in connexion with magical conjuration touches on two problems of research which we indicated in the prolegomena of this book. Firstly: is there such a thing as so-called occult subjection? Second: What connexion is there between occult subjection and mental illness? From the preceding analysis we may state the following: if by occult subjection we are to understand a new disease-pattern of psychological disorder, the suggestion is from a medical viewpoint to be rejected as a fiction. Practically all the psychological disturbances which appear in our pastoral examples can be classified under some disease-pattern of psychiatry or neurology, if we disregard the theological elements in the picture of mental disturbances. Only with regard to the causes of such disturbances will the pastor question the views of medical science. If medicine enjoys the same rapid development in "nuclear psychology" as science has enjoyed in nuclear physics, then we are due for a series of surprises. What the pastor senses and knows from a comparison of many pastoral cases, namely that mental and organic processes can be controlled by suggestion, today finds its counterpart in the psycho-somatic approach. In this respect medicine is in agreement with pastoral counselling.[203] Medicine is still taking too little notice of the amateur, charlatan, magical forms of suggestion in psychical phenomena, which employ as their medium the subconscious of the occult practitioner or of the person subject to occult influence.

The psychic complications which result from this amateur practice of magical conjuration, we call occult subjection. It would be better if we could, to obviate misunderstanding, avoid this term. But as long as there is no better designation available- which does justice to the medical, parapsychological and theological sides of this fact of pastoral experience, we shall have to put up with this unscientific-sounding term. In order, however, that in future no misunderstandings and no rivalries may exist between theology and medicine we must here expressly state that, with this term "occult subjection", we are dealing with a theological concept. There are, however, a great number of medical questions which arise within the scope of this theological concept, as our preceding study has shown.

The second problem is concerned with the relation between occult subjection and psychological disturbances. The very heart of the matter is the question of cause and effect. Are the psychological disturbances the result of occult activity, or is the maze of magical practices the result of psychological disorder, in for instance an unrestrained psychopath or an addict, in magic dabbling? An authority in the field has brought the problem down to the brief formula: post hoc aut propter hoc? Is it, as Bovet[204] has said, true that we confuse cause and effect when we would see in magic practices a source of mental suffering? Much as I respect Bovet as a writer and as a person, I must nevertheless here definitely oppose this thesis with two considerations: a medical one, and a theological one. The significance of engrams conditioned by suggestive magical charms as the presupposition of a mental constitution justifies the assumption that occult activity, among other things, is causally

203 Bovet, op.cit. 171, p. 57.
204 ibid., p. 56.

involved in the emergence of certain psychological disturbances. That is, to begin with, an empirically established pastoral fact. What we have here expressed, medicine knows both in application and in principle. Depth analysis knows the fact of engrams,[205] and the psychotherapist knows the fact that not only are neurotic disturbances caused and curatively influenced from the subconscious, but also that certain organic disorders can arise and be eliminated there.[206]

From a biblical standpoint, the chief argument against the thesis of Bovet is found in the second and third commandments. Anyone who uses the names of the Trinity to practise white magic charms is trying to dispose over God. He places himself next to and above God, and he cannot escape the judgement expressed in the words: "The Lord will not hold him guiltless who takes his name in vain", and "I the Lord your God am a jealous God, visiting the iniquity of the fathers upon the children to the third and fourth generation of those who hate me".[207] In the field of magic it is obvious what is meant when people are "given up" by God.[208] From this biblical viewpoint magic practices always bring spiritual disturbances in their wake, not in the either-or of *propter hoc aut post hoc,* but in the both-and of *propter hoc et post hoc.*

(d) *Remote influence (mental suggestion)*

In the phenomenon of remote influence we are dealing with a remote transference of mental powers. This phenomenon could be classed for special treatment under the headings of telepathy, hypnosis or magnetism, since the symptoms which appear with remote influence also appear in these other fields. Tischner classifies this form of mental suggestion in a sub-section of telepathy, under the main heading "Pure Telepathy Experiments".[209] In this section he describes the experiments of the French doctor Dusart, who without any previous arrangement put a girl to sleep at a distance and woke her again. In our study we shall consider remote influence in this separate section, since in it the phenomenon of ESI is seen in a special form.

In *Ex 16* we have already shown how a missionary's wife communicated to a friend telepathic requests to buy her grocery supplies. We shall now give further examples, which will introduce us to the problems raised by the question of remote influence.

205 cf. Brauchle, op.cit. 42, p. 16.
206 ibid., p. 51; op.cit. 43, p. 57.
207 cf. Exod. 20, 5 and 7.
208 cf. Rom. 1, 28; Lev. 20, 6 and 27.
209 cf. Tischner, op.cit. 25a, p. 66.

Ex 67 In two evangelistic campaigns in Bern I learned the following from a missionary friend and another witness. In the vicinity of Lake Thun there lives and practises a healer who is in great demand. I am acquainted with his name and the place where he lives. Since, according to Swiss law, charmers and other occult quacks are not allowed to accept fees for their consultations, this conjurer has found other ways of making sure of his livelihood. Anyone who after a consultation does not voluntarily offer to pay his five or ten francs finds himself unable at the station to board the passenger train. This magic conjurer exercises power over his patients by remote influence. The railway officials know of the situation and laughingly tell such passengers, "First take your five francs to . . . then you can get on". So much for the report of two reliable people.

Examples of financial and sexual exploitation by means of suggestion do appear occasionally, but are rather rare. In the viewing of such examples we must naturally eliminate psychotics and psychopaths with their hallucinations of sexual contacts and their delusions of sexual persecution.[210] We are here dealing only with cases in which people otherwise healthy have been abused by suggestion. In *Ex 47* and *Ex 51* we have already met the problem of remote influence.

Ex 68 An unmarried university graduate gained the confidence of an irreproachable and respectable girl in the course of pastoral work. Over a period of time a tender friendship developed, in which erotic feelings arose in the man but not in the girl. Out of this friendship a suggestive influence over the girl was gained by the man. This went to such an extreme that the girl, under the man's influence, yielded herself to him as if in a drunken stupor. Afterwards she clasped her head in complete astonishment. But she could no longer withdraw herself from his suggestive influence. Even during the night she would be called by the man, and would go to his house in a somnambulant state. Upon awaking she would be seized with fear and disgust. She put her problem before an old evangelist, a friend of mine. She had a serious desire to get release from the suggestive power of this man. The evangelist made the following plan with her. He would sit up all night in a chair in the parlour, through which she always went when walking in her sleep. At a very late hour the door actually opened. The girl came through the parlour murmuring, and whispered half aloud to herself, "You are calling me and I must bring the letter". The waiting evangelist called the girl by name. She started, dropped a letter, and awoke. The evan-

---

210 cf. Kloos, op.cit. 12, p. 402.

gelist was able to read the letter, which she had received that same day. In the letter the man requested that the girl keep silent about their relations. He offered to pay her RM. 200 if she would tell nobody. Presumably the man had sensed the danger of this letter as evidence against him, since on the same day he had mentally suggested to the girl that she should come and bring the letter with her.

From the *pastoral* aspect, we may mention that the girl was completely freed from the suggestive enslavement. However, from that day the evangelist for some time experienced strange persecutions. It looks very much as if the practitioner tried to use his power of remote influence to take his revenge on the evangelist.

In the literature regarding occult problems there is in the book of Holmsten[211] an example of sexual enslavement through suggestion. Holmsten further gives an example of the power of thoughts working at a distance by adducing the episode mentioned by K. F. Meyer concerning the remote-controlled bookkeeper.[212a] These kinds of phenomena are in our own day finding their confirmation and parallels in the reports about the leader of an American negro sect, who calls himself Father Divine and is known for his mental suggestion.[212b] When ailing members of the sect send a phone call or telegram to Father Divine, the person is said to be healed at the moment the message is received, by a process of remote mental suggestion or magical conjuration. Apart from press reports, which I cannot check, about this phenomenon, I once had a foreign evangelist as my guest who told me of a personal experience from his own family circle with this sect-leader who practises mental suggestion. Holmsten also gives an example of telephone hypnosis.[213]

The phenomenon of remote influence is not only a fact of pastoral experience, but a fact which has now been proved by the experiments of numerous doctors and psychologists. Prof. Bender in his book "Psychische Automatismen" (p. 43) points out that two Frenchmen, Janet and Gibert, made 22 tests of remote suggestion, of which 16 were completely successful and accurate. And how the mastery of the suggestive powers can be abused in the hands of immoral people has appeared in the examples recorded in this section. It is of some comfort at least that the ability to practise remote suggestion is a very rare phenomenon.

---

211 cf. Holmsten, op.cit. 37b, p. 21.
212a ibid., p. 150.
212b Father Divine has now been dead for several years — *translator.*
213 cf. Holmsten, op.cit. 37b, p. 22.

(e) *Black and white magic*

Prof. Diepgen in his book "Medizin und Kultur",[214] drawing on his knowledge of medieval medicine, gives us the following definition of magic: "Magic is every activity which aims at influencing either the super-sensible or the sensible world, which cannot be classed either as a cultic activity or as a technical operation."[215] According to this definition, magic belongs neither to theology nor to medicine, although in pastoral care and in psychiatry these two sciences must concern themselves with magic. In his book Prof. Diepgen gives us further information regarding magic, classifying it into various types. He writes: "Within this concept, we can, by noting the means employed by magicans, clearly differentiate three sub-classes. First, there is magic with the help of the demons, or of the devil. This is witchcraft, or black magic. Then there is religious magic, which borrows its means from the thought field of the religious outlook, although these means do not belong to the recognized rites (e.g. the therapeutic use of bible texts, special forms of prayer for healing, etc.). Thirdly, there is so-called natural magic, which without any reference to the two factors already mentioned assumes a mysterious relatedness of all things to each other. This relatedness is considered fully natural, although not fully understood, and may transcend the purely material. Natural magic seeks to influence these relationships and so to accomplish magical effects."

For the person who has the pastoral care of those involved in magic, it is a significant fact that magic practice has not changed from the middle ages until the present day. The definition given by Diepgen fits the present situation of magic exactly in all points. In pastoral experience the first and second classes distinguished by Diepgen are those most frequently met. Here we are dealing with types of black and white magic. Black magic introduces its spells and magic actions with the invocation of the devil or the demons. White magic uses, in a magic form, the names of the Trinity, bible phrases, whole psalms and other religious symbols. In pastoral experience we find the following principal spheres of application for black and white magic respectively.

Black magic: persecution spells, vengeance spells, defence spells, healing spells, etc.

White magic: protection spells, defence spells, healing spells, fertility spells, etc.

[214] cf. Paul Diepgen, "Medizin und Kultur", Ferdinand Enke Verlag, Stuttgart, 1938, p. 150.
[215] In this definition Diepgen is indebted to Alfred Lehmann, "Aberglaube und Zauberei von den ältesten Zeiten an bis in die Gegenwart", Stuttgart, 1908.

Persecution and revenge spells appear only in black magic. In this class also we must place the death spells of primitive peoples, e.g. of the Papua in New Guinea. The other magic actions are found in both forms. A few examples will introduce us to the problem, and to the question of pastoral approach.

Ex 69 A woman reported in a pastoral interview that for a time her twelve-year-old boy always began to cry out terribly at the same time every night. Since he showed no complaints during the daytime, the nightly scene struck her as mysterious. She went to a woman occultist, who told her, "Your son is being magically persecuted. You must use a defensive spell. Lay an open pair of scissors on the window-sill when you go to bed, and the persecution spell will be made ineffective." The mother followed this advice. The amazing fact is that the nocturnal crying scences actually stopped.

Medically there is little to say about this incident. We can hardly claim to see here an example of black persecution magic and defensive magic at work. Rather it is a case of some kind of sleep disturbance of the son, e.g. nocturnal screaming, nightmares, sleep-talking, pavor nocturnus, etc.[216]

Pastorally there was here no evidence of psychological harm. Humanly it was culpable of the mother not to consult a doctor; and it was a sin against God to take recourse to magic.

Ex 70 A farmer, who had never in his life had any psychological disturbances, returned home early from being a prisoner of war. His friend, the son of a neighbour, was still missing. His mother was greatly burdened about the fate of her son, and begrudged her neighbour his joy. Out of this understandable human tension the fortunate man who had returned began to develop nightmares. He had the feeling while he was asleep that his neighbour was strangling him. Sometimes he saw her in his dreams, and heard her say, "You will have to kick the bucket yet!" The vexed man sought out an occultist, who explained to him, "You are under magic persecution from your neighbour. I will help you. Go home. The case will be dealt with." The nightmares actually stopped from that time on.

Some time later the man again went to the occultist and explained that he was certainly free from the persecution, but that the neighbour was now after his cattle. They were dying one after another. The conjurer promised to deal with this situation too. He gave him some scraps

[216] cf. Kloos, op.cit. 12, p. 437.

of paper on which was written a magic formula. The man was told to mix these in with the cattle fodder. He did so, and again the astonishing result occurred. The cattle epidemic disappeared.

In the third act of this magical tragedy, the man began to have disturbances, in the course of which he came to seek pastoral advice.

What are we to say about this from the *medical* aspect? The simplest explanation is that the physical and mental constitution of this man had been weakened by the privations of imprisonment in Russia, and therefore could not stand up to the neighbour's spite. These persecution dreams would then be merely a reaction due to internal conflict.[217] The second possible diagnosis is that of an irrational delusion arising in a condition of diminished rationality — here in a dream — which was not corrected later.[218] Bleuler writes of this: "A residual delusion of this kind can be confused, without any great concurrent and corresponding disturbance of intelligence." A third possibility is given by Kloos.[219] He writes: "Magic ideas such as remote influence, telepathy, thought-transference, witchcraft, etc. appear in schizophrenics, but also in healthy superstitious persons."

From the *psychical researcher's* point of view, it is of interest to ask whether any authentic phenomenon occurs in this magic advice. The disappearance of the nightmares after the consultation could be put down to coincidence or to suggestion. Faith in the magic protection perhaps had a suggestive effect on the man. The halting of the cattle epidemic is harder to explain. Suggestion is excluded, and to explain all magic cures of cattle as coincidence is not feasible. Hence the question remains open.

From the *pastoral* point of view, there are two questions which arise in connexion with the advice to be given to the man. First he should be sent with his psychological complications to the doctor, for thorough examination and advice. Secondly, the pastoral counsellor has the task of showing the man the wickedness and danger of resorting to magic. The neighbour, he should remember, could have become unjustly suspected of witchcraft. Further he must show him the way to Christ.

We shall now show by an example how black magic works out in practice.

Ex 71   In a village a large area of orchard was to be sold. There were several people interested in making the purchase. Finally it fell to a

217 ibid., p. 449.
218 cf. Bleuler, op.cit., 129, pp. 53f.
219 cf. Kloos, op.cit. 12, p. 173.

wealthy farmer. One morning however, he was horrified to learn that some thirty young fruit trees on the land he had bought had been sawed down. He notified the police immediately, but they did not succeed in finding the culprit. The man then resorted to a black magic persecution spell. After a pig had been slaughtered, he took the fresh navel and hung it up in the chimney, with a curse formula. Just as the navel gradually roasted away in the smoke, so the unknown perpetrator should die by a prolonged illness. Six months after this spell, one of the men who had been interested in the orchard sale died. The "black magician" is now confident that his revenge has overtaken the offender. For such dark and superstitious customs no explanation is necessary. It is in this way that the belief in and burning of witches, one of the darkest chapters in the history of human culture, originated.

A further example will show us the use of magic protection.

Ex 72   A woman established the infidelity of her husband, who had a girlfriend. In her distress she went to an occultist who practised magic, who confided to her a defence enchantment. The wronged woman took one of her husband's shirts and buried it at full moon, pronouncing a magic formula. In the measure that the shirt mouldered away in the ground, so her husband's love for this girl-friend would dissolve.

The tragedy of such magic practices is the credulity and readiness of those in need to support such mischief instead of seeking help and advice in reasonable ways.

Often black magic is found in connexion with experiments from the 6th. and 7th. Book of Moses. Whether the following example belongs to this class is not quite certain.

Ex 73   A woman in a pastoral interview complained of melancholia, ennui, etc. She said that her child was also afflicted in this way. At night the child would cry out at exactly 12 p.m. At 1 a.m. the voice of the mother-in-law, living fifty miles away would be heard saying "Quiet!" Immediately the child would be silent.

The *medical* question in this case divides itself into two parts. What are the causes of the mother's depressions? and what is the explanation for this punctual crying of the child? An anamnesis on the case permits the conclusion that the mother is the emotionally disordered psychopathic type, although the symptoms are not straightforward. In the case of the child we may think in terms of the sleep disturbances already mentioned, since by day he is thoroughly healthy. There is no explanation for the cause of the acoustic hallucinations of the voice of the mother-in-law. The normal causes of perceptual disturbances do not fit the case of this woman.

From the *psychical researcher's* point of view, it is significant that there are some strong occult connections present. For many years the woman was an active card layer. Her mother-in-law possessed the 6th. and 7th. Book of Moses, and practised magic charms. There is just a possibility that the starting from sleep (pavor nocturnus) of the boy, which always lasted an hour, was stopped by mental suggestion. We only mention this possibility for the reason that in pastoral experience the extremely rare phenomenon of remote influence almost always appears in connexion with conjuration dependent on the 6th. and 7th. Book of Moses. He who knows nothing of the suggestive power of those who experiment with this book will naturally dismiss as absurd this notion, which we only put as a final possibility. Most probably, however, a psychological or medical factor is here involved.

From the *pastoral* viewpoint it is worthy of note that the woman turned to Christ and was visibly delivered of her depressive subjection.

Ex 74 A man in Switzerland was a conjurer and experimenter in the field of black magic. In the house where he conducted his black art, the family, altogether four in number, saw spook apparitions such as a large dog, an old woman, a white man, snakes, etc.

Since these spook apparitions were seen only by the members of the conjurer's family, this must be classed as a subjective experience. It was presumably a disturbance of consciousness with some exogenic cause.[220] Significant is the wearying prevalence of such phenomena in connexion with occult activity.

The examples considered hitherto have all been of a fairly simple nature. There are however in the field of black and white magic sometimes such confusions of events, that it is not worth while to disentangle all the subsidiary phenomena. We will conclude this series with one such example.

Ex 75 At an evangelistic meeting in Switzerland, an emotionally disturbed woman came for an interview. She disclosed a family history that was totally riddled with things of an occult nature. Her grandmother worked charms. She was therefore suspected by her own family of plaguing during the night her son's eleven children. When the nocturnal crying of the children became too much for the parents, they sought out three Solothurn monks, who were reputed to practice white magic. The monks promised help within a short time. Remarkably, the old woman died within three days. The father of the eleven children

220 ibid., p. 171.

— the charmer's son — maintained that he had, at the hour of his mother's death, seen two black women hurrying away from the house. So much for the report of this troubled woman concerning her family. Then she added a personal experience. Her grandmother had taught her as a schoolgirl a conjurer's enchantment, a magic spell which she herself had once effectively employed at the age of twelve. She had walked for three steps behind a certain woman she hated, stepping exactly in her footprints and mumbling a curse against her. The woman would, she had been told, thereupon have to stop. The spell worked. The woman stopped in her tracks. She turned round and said, "You devil's toad, get out of here!" The girl raced away in fear. The woman proceeded on her way.

Here we have an example which contains the phenomenon of black magic on the part of the charmer, and white magic in the protective charm of the Solothurn monks. Believers in the occult swear that these charms work. For our study it suffices to establish that it is always psychologically disordered families which go in for this kind of magic. Very few of these magic practices will stand up to scientific investigation. The few genuine phenomena which remain will now be discussed in principle.

White magic has the same character as black magic, except that it appears in a religious guise. This fact deceives many people. Here is a case of the refined veiling of magic. The apostle Paul asks: "What has Christ in common with Belial?" (II Cor. 6, 15). We have already said that it is a feature of man's basic rebellion that he attempts to make God amenable to his own plans. In fact it also appears in pastoral experience that the psychological results of black and white magic are the same.

We must now discuss a few basic questions as to black and white magic. First we shall again give attention to the means involved in the process of magic. The magic action consists of an invocation (of God or Satan), then a spell, and then sometimes a symbolic action. A transference charm in black magic consists for example of boiling pork in the urine of a sick person and then feeding this, while repeating a healing spell, to a dog. The dog is then supposed to die and the sick person to recover. A healing charm in white magic is for example to eat some walnut leaves inscribed with a bible text, without reading them. A white magic fertility charm is the placing of a woman's hair between two loaves of bread, and feeding this to the cattle.[221] The essence of magic does not

---

[221] These spells are taken from the 6th. and 7th. Book of Moses, and the collection of magic spells of Tennenbronn.

however consist in healing spells, but in the persecution of hated persons and in the repulsion of such attacks from enemies.

Herewith we come to the *distinctive mark* of magic over against the simple magical charming of ailments. Magic charming aims only at cures, fertility, and protection against natural catastrophes, and does not aim at the persecution of or defence against an enemy. Although both black and white magic also include healing and fertility spells, the heart of the issue is *enchantment* and *release*. Dr. Schmeïng has in his book a footnote on this double process of magic.[222] He writes: "States of immobility and torpor are sometimes reported apart from prevision. The spell is dissolved when the person is spoken to. Presumably also the active form of spell, which renders a particular person, such as a thief, immobile on the spot, has here its original source. Perhaps suggestion or hypnosis are also present. A girl told me that she had ridden on her bicycle past a witch, who sat in front of her house peeling potatoes. Suddenly she could ride no further. The bicycle was so hard to move that she had to dismount. This is plainly a case of auto-suggestion. This 'witch' is moreover a perfectly normal person." Here we have mention of a double process of enchantment and release.

The weightiest problem of black and white magic is the question of whether the phenomena are *genuine*. Do we have here throughout only a foolish popular superstition, or is there an unknown power operative behind these phenomena? Is there an energy emanating from the occult experimenter which can be used for attack and defence? Is there a power which can be projected out of man? The occultists swear that there is.[223] Psychical researchers of repute prove it by experiments. For example, the phenomenon of telepathy is today recognized, and even the phenomenon of remote influence is no longer strange to science. Basically hypnosis as applied in medicine is also a transference of energy, or at least a releasing of energy. These points of contact show us that in the field of "nuclear psychology" we are standing only on the threshold of fresh territory. This is also shown by the hundreds of thousands of experiments conducted by Prof. Rhine. According to his researches, conducted with the utmost scientific accuracy, it must be regarded as proved that there exists in man a super-physical factor.[224] The fact that psychokinesis belongs to the normal sphere of the human mind is a revolutionary discovery, which permits us to think that behind the confused chaos of superstitious ideas there may be some slight point of contact with a real

---

[222] cf. Schmeïng, op.cit. [30], p. 113.
[223] cf. Glahn, op.cit. [101], vol. VI, p. 8.
[224] cf. Rhine, op.cit. [57], p. 173.

phenomenon. Even if we must consider 95% or 98% of black and white magic to be superstition, we must therefore still suspend judgement regarding the last little remainder, until the advance of scientific research can at last give us an answer.

Even though the judgement of natural science has to be suspended, theology already has a starting point for the ethical and theological evaluation of these phenomena. To thinking which is biblically orientated, black and white magic is an offence. Premise, content and symbolical form of magic spells stand in extreme opposition to the spirit of God's word. Where God or Satan are made the handymen of human beings, man is playing the part of lord, and we have a rebellion against the ordinances of creation. Where man resorts to material objects like coffin-nails, hearses, coffin-wood, shirts buried in the ground, amulets of every kind, magic at full moon, Easter water, fetishes, women's hair, spittle, urine, burnt bones, animal carcasses, etc., there we have flight from the Creator, there we have idolatry, there we have Belial and not Christ. In this situation, the judgement of natural science on magic plays a subordinate role; for here this phenomenon comes within the field of faith in God, into the domain of theology.

From the *pastoral* standpoint, therefore, we are not in the first place concerned with the question of the genuineness of magical phenomena, nor with the successes and failures of the craft, but with the consequent psychological disturbances and their pastoral treatment. For it is a fact of pastoral experience that where black and white magic are practised we find psychological disturbances in the family. This rule may have exceptions, although I have met with no exceptions in the case of active occultists. Here we are not seeking in the first place to establish which is primary, the psychological disturbance or the magic action; we are only interested in the coincidence of the two phenomena. With this coincidence we must not of course reverse the major and minor terms. That would give us a fallacious conclusion. But psychiatry and theology must discuss and elucidate in the case of this double phenomenon what is cause and what is effect.

(f) *Blood pacts*

One of the most unusual areas of occultism is that of blood-pacts. Before I made the acquaintance of this phenomenon in pastoral work, I regarded it only as an outgrowth of medieval devil worship. In the Legend of Theophilus of Adana, we already find the motif of a pact with the devil.[225] In the era of belief in witches, this motif was a common

---

[225] cf. Religion in Geschichte und Gegenwart, V, p. 1066.

one. In secular story-telling, we find the theme of a pact with the devil in the stories about the knights-errant. The blood pact first became for me a serious problem and object of reflection in connexion with counselling. A few examples will introduce the problem.

Ex 76 A refugee girl who was without country, parents or livelihood drifted, in her emotional distress, into disreputable ways. During the night hours she earned herself a morsel of bitter food. One day she was caught in a police raid, and was committed to the Office of Health and Welfare, which established that she had an infectious skin-disease. She spent a few weeks in detention. In her cell an unusual idea struck her. She took a sheet of paper, cut her finger, and with her blood wrote a pact with the devil. The conditions of this pact were as follows. If the devil would advance her to a respectable life, she for her part would give him her soul. After this period of detention, she was sent to a protestant home for unfortunate girls. There she was treated kindly. But she was uncommunicative, unreceptive to all kindness, and completely resistant to God's word. A small prayer group was formed to intercede for her. This was also without fruit. The girl seemed bound as with iron shackles.

Ex 77 A girl who had a leading position under the Third Reich fell into such despair with the collapse of Germany and the loss of her position, that in her distress she wrote a pact with the devil in her own blood. After this psychological disturbances set in. She had visual hallucinations, seeing all the streets, houses and trees filled with spirits, suffered from attacks of mania, and had spook apparitions of many kinds. In her powers of reason she remained fully normal. Her reports were deliberate and objective. Hysteria was certainly not present. Her troubles drove her to a neurologist. He received the impression that this was more of a case for pastoral help, and after his treatment had proved ineffectual, he referred her to the pastor. Up to the present the young lady has not been relieved.

Ex 78 Now we shall give an example which can scarcely be credited by a person of sound mind. At an evangelistic meeting a man brought forward for interview his cousin, who was mentally ill. Since a strongly occult background was reported to be involved, one of the members of the church council, a faithful Christian, was brought in for spiritual support. Thus in this group there were the pastor, the church elder, the labourer and the occultly subjected man. Since it was dark, the shutters were closed and a light put on. Then the occultly subjected man told of the following experience. In 1935 he desired to marry. Neither he nor his fiancée had the money for the bedroom furniture. In a public house an acquaintance gave him the following advice: "Write a blood pact with the devil and ask for 500 marks; lay the pact on the table at midnight in a darkened room, and call three times, 'Lucifer, come'." The man took the advice. He cut his finger and wrote out a request for 500 marks, guaranteeing to give his own soul in payment. About midnight he called three times, "Lucifer, come!" Suddenly he began to have a most uncanny feeling. He saw two red, glowing eyes above him. Then a pale hand passed over the table. The startled man switched on the light. There lay 500 marks in bank-notes. The written note had vanished. Instead there was a piece of paper on which was written: "Tomorrow at midnight, come to the crossroads above the village". From this moment the man became decidedly restless. He decided not to go to the crossroads. But when the second evening came, he found himself inwardly compelled by a great pressure to go to the crossroads. He went, taking a pistol with him. At the crossroads he saw a horrible figure, half man and half animal. He shot off the whole magazine at the figure, which then disappeared from his sight.

The puzzling part of the whole story for the man himself was that he was able to keep the 500 marks, and that no one ever came to recover the money, with some explanation that he had only played a joke on him. The man bought his bedroom furniture and got married. But he could never find relief from the dreadful unrest which he had felt ever since he had received the money that night. He often had times of feeling as if he were being pursued by furies. His eyes began to flicker, his face became lined, his hair went white. At the age of forty-three, when he made this report, he looked like a man of seventy.

During the report, which lasted for two and a half hours, the four men were periodically startled by raps on the window. The peculiarity of these was that although the shutters were closed the rapping was not a dull sound as of somebody striking the wood, but the sound of tapping on glass. Despite this interview, the troubled man was not relieved of his disturbances.

We shall not discuss all the details of this occurrence. We shall only touch on the main phenomena. Before the experience this man was mentally sound. Even afterwards no psychosis could be established. The receipt of the money could, if necessary, be explained as a bad joke on the part of the man who advised him to make the blood pact. It should however be noted that the friend who gave the advice was also a poor simpleton. The psychologist to whom I went for advice on this case thought that the receiver had perhaps stolen the money somewhere in a somnambulant state. But this seems highly improbable, since the person who was robbed would surely have bestirred himself and reported the theft. The peculiar experience of the fiery eyes, the pale hand, the hideous figure, could have been hallucinations caused by fear. Premature aging and grey hair are a phenomenon well-known to medicine. At the session of the Association of Doctors in Vienna in 1952, for instance, a two-year-old girl was presented to the professional group who showed all the marks of an old woman. Her head was almost bald, she had many wrinkles in he face, the characteristic vein-pattern of old age, the degenerative stoop, etc. The lecturing doctor, Dr. Klöll of the Vienna university clinic, said that in the whole of medical literature only 23 cases of child senescence were known.[226] The rapping which recurred three times during the interview would perhaps have to be regarded as a mass hallucination, or a conversion of energy from a psychic dissociation of the man making the report, that is if we must explain everything fully in rational terms. Thus we could bring the four outstanding phenomena under a rational denominator. These easy explanations do not however suffice in this case. This victim of occult activity had never before in his life experienced hallucinations. The pastor, the elder, who is a sensible businessman, and the patient's cousin, who is a down-to-earth labourer, never had any hallucination either before or after this window-rapping incident. These three men will not accept the view that the rapping was of anything but supernatural origin. It is impossible to give a satisfactory explanation of this story.

Ex 79 At a youth conference a 17-year-old lad came to an evangelistic meeting with a New Testament in his left pocket and, bound in similar format, the 6th. and 7th. Book of Moses in his right. My assistant at this meeting took the 6th. and 7th. Book of Moses from him. We looked through the magic book and found that the lad had bound himself to the devil by putting his signature underneath a picture of Lucifer. We then burned the book. The parents, who did not know that the lad had this magic book, made a typical answer to our inquiry. They said that the lad suffered from strange fits of mania, and possessed in general a strange, dark, restless character. They simply could not make him out.

These four examples have a number of symptoms in common. From the *medical* point of view it is to be noted that none of the four people occultly subjected had any psychological disturbances before they made these blood pacts. After the pact had been made, psychological complications set in, which cannot be put into a known psychopathic or

---

[226] Dr. Klöll, University of Vienna.

psychiatric disease-pattern. In one case here the neurologist gave up the case and conceded the greater competence of the pastor.

From the *pastoral* point of view we have here a phenomenon which goes back thousands of years. Isaiah speaks of those who made a covenant with Sheol (28, 15). Significant in these four cases is the fact that none of these four persons found relief. There are various reasons for this. In pastoral counselling it is an empirical fact that those who are shackled to sins of magic cannot find release without a thorough confession and a conscious renunciation of the devil. Further, it is a prevalent observation that blood-bound occultists can be delivered only with great difficulty. We have here to reckon with a *demonic captivity*. Here a new term makes its appearance in our study.

This term is the subject of much debate, both in medicine and in a particular movement of theology. The questions associated with this concept still await a critical discussion in another chapter. Here we shall only cite the position taken by a man well known in Christian and medical circles. We refer to the psychiatrist Dr. Lechler. In a lecture concerning demonism and psychopathy he writes as follows:[227]

"What then must we regard as the cause of demonic enslavement and of possession? If we enquire closely from such people as bear the marks we have just mentioned, we very often find in their background the use of magic means such as are employed in black magic, viz. acts of charming or being charmed, the sin of fortune telling or visits to fortune tellers and card layers, and participation in spiritist sessions. Black magic is much more prevalent than is ordinarily assumed... When we look into the Bible, we note that it too is well acquainted with enchantment. It is in Acts 19 described as a 'prying art' (here we also find mention of magic books). Together with spiritist activities, magic stands in a class of its own in relation to other sins, when it includes an appeal to Satan's services or even a formal *pact with Satan*. The bible speaks of this too (cf. Isaiah 28, 15—18). For by invoking Satan man yields himself unequivocally to powers of darkness, in that he attempts by magic and the help of Satanic power to gain something that God has forbidden or withheld."

[227] cf. Dr. med. Alfred Lechler, "Dämonie und Psychopathie", Lecture given to the conference of doctors and pastors at Hohe Mark on 7. 5. 49. I would like at this point to express my warm thanks to Dr. Lechler for allowing me to use this paper, and also the other one entitled "Dämonie und Seelenstörung". We may also refer the reader to the various publications of Dr. Lechler: 1) "Seelische Erkrankungen und ihre Heilung", 5th. edn. 1946, Verlag Fehrholz, Baden-Baden; 2) "Seelsorge an Gemütskranken", Spener Verlag, Marburg, 1937; 3) "Psychopathie"- by Drs. Lechler and Mader, Neubau Verlag, Munich 1949.

This explanation from the mouth of a psychiatrist must be seriously considered by every pastor. There is nothing to add from a theological standpoint. Pastoral elucidation of the four examples above is thus unnecessary.

(g) *Fetishism*

Fetishism is a superstitious cult involving fetishes, amulets, talismans. The word goes back to the Portuguese *feitico* (charm), and to the Latin *factitius* (magical, effective).[228] In the history of religions we understand by a fetish an artificial object, which is regarded as being animated, as having powers, and is carried as a protection or revered. Fetishism is the believing attitude assumed towards these powerbearing objects and protective symbols.

The word *amulet* is derived from the Latin *amuletum*[229] and signifies a "means of defence". An amulet is a power-charged object for protection against magic and demonic danger. *Talisman* is derived from the Arabic *tilasmun* and from the Greek *telesma*, and means firstly "completion" or "conservation", and thus also "acquisition charm". As amulets and talismans we must consider all objects and parts of the organic and inorganic world, to which ancient, primitive - or modern - man ascribes inherent powers. The effectiveness of fetishes, amulets and talismans is heightened by inscriptions, especially in the form of magic formulas. It is important for us in the treatment of fetishism today to note that it actually has its roots in pagan magic.

Fetishism is not merely a manifestation of ancient and primitive religions, but is also a phenomenon of present-day superstition. Thus, the honour shown to hairs, feathers, nails, horns, claws, teeth, spiders, scarabs, mascots, laurel, garlic stalks, threads, knots, tassels, bands, flints, spear-heads, etc. in the ancient world and among the primitives has its parallel in the similar deification of objects such as fourleaved clover, lucky coins, toadstools, mascots, horse-shoes, lucky letters, amulets, relics, Easter water, mascots, ships' pets, chimney sweeps, as symbols of luck; and in the fear of owls, ravens, spiders, black cats, old wives, stopping of the clock, the number thirteen, etc. as bad omens. A few examples will illustrate the situation of this modern superstition and fetishism.

Ex 80 When I was a student I occupied a room in the hostel numbered 12a. By checking I discovered that this 12a was a substitute

---

[228] cf. "Religion in Geschichte und Gegenwart" II, p. 567.
[229] ibid. I, p. 315.

for 13. They had rooms 12, 12a and 14 — and this, mind you, in an enlightened university city. But there is more to the story of this room number. Later the man who ran the hostel desired to occupy this room himself. He asked a sign-writer to come and change the number 12a into 13. The painter asked, "What is this room going to be used for?" The man replied, "For my bedroom". The painter refused to change the number, adding, "I don't want to be responsible if something happens to you in this room." Apparently the sign-writer had not gained much light from the rays of Enlightenment proceeding from the local university.

Ex 81 I took the following report from a daily newspaper in January 1950, and cannot of course vouch for its truth personally. The English submarine *Laurentius* was due to put out to sea at 1 p.m. on Friday, 13th January, 1950. The captain postponed the trip until the Saturday morning, since a Friday which was also the 13th day of the month would undoubtedly bring misfortune on the voyage, being a double omen of bad luck. Since however the date scheduled was Friday 13th and not Saturday 14th, the submarine collided with a Swedish ship and immediately sank. The press stated that ninety seamen were lost. Thus here superstition had fatal consequences.

The use of charms for luck and protection against fire, misfortune and war wounds is a field to itself. Fire charms are laid on the beams under the roof. Amulets are supposed to guard against enemy bullets. A silver horse-shoe on the watch-chain or key-ring guards against burglaries and thefts. A saint's medallion buried in the floor of a cattle-shed is supposed to protect against epidemics. A wedding ring which has been stroked with a relic is said to protect the wearer against adultery. A medallion with the image of a saint on it will bless the harvest if buried in the field. And so we could continue ad lib. Perhaps even a cross suspended from a necklace has a magic meaning. Many a Christian worker thinks so. It is evident here that Christianity has become infected with magic influences. According to the New Testament, this intrusion of magic elements turns the Christian faith into a matter of materialism and idolatry. Pastoral experience shows in many cases how this superstition captivates men and subjects them to magical influences. It is not seldom that houses protected by fire charms, and other fetishes and amulets, become haunted.

After noting how all fetishism is rooted in magic, we must now study its mysterious influence on people. An important key to the understanding of this influence is the recognition of the imago content in the subconscious of man.[230] Ignoring for the moment the organic unconscious plane, we may say that the mind of man embraces two areas of function. The conscious mind is marked by rational categories such as analysis, logic and abstraction. The subconscious is ruled by imago forces. Psycho-analysis teaches us that the hidden imago forces of the subconscious are stronger than the conscious volitional purposes. These imagos have enormous power. They direct and influence the concept-world of the consciousness. When we recognize this fact, it becomes quite intelligible that many persons drift into dependence on fetishes. Further, it becomes plain how dangerous it is to transgress the second commandment ("you shall not make for yourself any graven image, or any likeness"), and thus to yield oneself to the imago forces of fetishes, amulets and talismans.

The problem of attachment to images becomes still more serious when to this dependence on the effective power of images there is joined the subscribing of a magical pact with the one who stands behind all magic. Here we are in the unholy sphere of amulet pacts, which is a parallel to blood pacts. We shall give a few examples.

Lit 12 The best example in the field of amulet pacts is probably Samuel Keller's report about Frau Brandstätter.[231] This lady had attacks every morning and evening at 9 o'clock, when a male voice would issue from her. During these spells she was able to tell Pastor Keller things which she could not possibly have known about. In this state she moreover spoke a fluent High German, which she could not speak at other times, since she came from the Crimea. Her character also became completely altered. In her normal state she was humble, modest, and well-behaved, but during the attacks she was rude, unfriendly, fitful and possessed dreadful strength. One day Pastor Keller saw a little leather pouch suspended from her neck. He grasped it, to take it away. At this a man's voice, which had already before now made itself known as the voice of the gipsy Elkimo, cried out: "Don't give up the pouch!" The pastor jerked it off. The attack subsided at once and the woman was completely cured. In the pouch there was a piece of paper with a pact charm. The formula began with a few meaningless phrases in Hebrew. Then there followed in Roman characters: "I am he who holds the seven fevers in his hand, and can send out the seven powers, and if you will hide this and live in my name you will succeed in all things, and I will

230 In this connexion we refer the reader to the important contribution made by Prof. Köberle in "Schrift und Bekenntnis", Furche Verlag, 1950: "Glaube und Aberglaube", pp. 106f.
231 cf. Samuel Keller, "Aus meinem Leben", Walter Loepthien Verlag, Leipzig.

protect you." It ended, as it started, with a few Hebrew words. Frau Brandstätter admitted that a few years before she had bought this amulet from a gipsy. Keller commented on this: "Plainly there was a connexion here between the superstitious use of such magical means and the influence of dark powers".

The problem of these states of possession will be studied critically at a later point. Here, however, we must clearly notice the fact that the woman became well as soon as the pact-charm was removed. A similar case took place in recent years in a well-known Christian mental institution.

Ex 82 A mother consulted many doctors for help for her 12-year-old daughter. None of the treatments given was effective. Finally she turned to a minister of the gospel, from whom she requested help for herself and her daughter. The mother spent many weeks in the institution, without any noticeable improvement in the girl. One day the pastor noticed a little chain around the girl's neck, holding an amulet. He asked the mother to give him this little metal case. The mother at first refused, remarking that she had been strictly commanded not to remove the amulet from the child's neck, since if she did her condition would worsen. The pastor, who was well acquainted with occult practices, became suspicious and explained the truth of the situation to the mother, who then gave him the little case. In it he found a written pact-charm, which he read out to the astonished woman and then destroyed. From that day on the girl's condition improved, and soon she was able to leave the institution fully well.

In these two cases we must note the coincidence in the opposite direction. The psychological disturbances vanished with the destruction of the amulet pact. The frequency ratios are of the same order as those of the temporal concurrence of the origin of psychological disturbance and occult activity.

Also connected with fetishism and amulet pacts is *indirect subscription* due to possession of and keeping of magic books. Among the magic books which circulate among the population are the following: "Tennenbronner Zaubersprüche" (Spells of Tennenbronn); "Romanusbüchlein"; "Der schwarze Rabe" (the black raven); "Heiliger Segen" (holy blessing); "Der wahrhaftige, feurige Drache" (the genuine fiery dragon); "Der wahre, geistliche Schild" (the true spiritual shield); "Das siebenmal versiegelte Buch" (the book with seven seals); "Engelshülfe" (angelic help); "Geheime Kunstschule" (school of secret arts); "Der Gesundbetungspsalter" (the psalter of healing prayers); "Das 6. und 7. Buch Moses" (the 6th. and 7th. book of Moses); "Das 8. bis 13. Buch Moses" (the 8th. to 13th. book of Moses).[232] The most prevalent and most patently ruinous in its effects is the so-called 6th. and 7th. book of Moses. Since in this section we are concerned with indirect subscription, we may illustrate this from the 6th. and 7th. book of Moses.[233] In the sixth chapter of the sixth book, the following pact is made: "The person who possesses this book at any given time Lucifer promises to help, and to carry out all his commands, but only as long as he possesses this book." If the connexions which are here declared to exist between Lucifer and the owner of the book all originate in stupidity and foolish superstition, and if faith in the devil is only the pitiable delusion of an unenlightened age, we can pass over this with a wave of the hand. In a rational age, we no longer need to waste time with such banalities. But it is a remarkable observation of pastoral experience, that in all homes and families in which the 6th. and 7th. Book of Moses is kept, or even used, psychological disturbances of various kinds appear. Among the many examples which have become known to me in the course of pastoral experience, I will select just one.

Ex 83 An elder of the church, who year after year was a faithful attender of church services, was lying on his deathbed. The man, who had always borne himself as a true churchman, relinquished this attitude on his deathbed. He began to curse terribly and to blaspheme God and Christ. He rejected the spiritual words of comfort offered by his relatives, would have nothing to do with the word of God, or with prayer, and died cursing dreadfully. After his death they found among his belongings the 6th. and 7th. Book of Moses.

If we list the possessors of these magic books according to their various attitudes to them, we find that three groups energe. The first group operates under a religious mask. It regards the magic book as a sacred book. In all cases known to me, this mask fell away on the person's deathbed. The second is aware of the reprehensibility of the books. It anxiously keeps secret the possession of such a book. Often no one in the whole family except the possessor knows of the existence of the book. In such a case the book is at death committed to the eldest son, who is then initiated into these mysteries.

The third group has the courage to reveal its dark practices before the presence of eternity. This third group calls the family to the death-

---

232 cf. Schwendimann, "Sympathie - Heilkunst und Zauberei", Ev. Buchhandlung, St. Gallen, pp. 16f.

233 This book was re-published in 1950 by the Planet-Verlag. It is said to have been discovered in 1522 and published by Peter Machel, the last Carthusian monk in Erfurt, cf. 91.

bed, reveals the occult arts, and begs that the magic book be burned. Common to all three is subjection to various psychological disturbances. In the many cases which I have come to know in pastoral work, I have not met one possessor of the 6th. and 7th. Book of Moses who had no psychological complications. In view of these empirical findings, it is not possible to tone down the frequency ratio and simply to write off the phenomenon as belief in demons. It is a remarkable fact of these observed psychological disturbances, that the consequences of direct and indirect subscription are almost identical. There is only a slight difference in degree.

(h) *Incubi and succubae*

We now come to discuss spook phenomena in the form of sexual experiences, which is surely the most repellent area of pastoral work. There are namely some severely troubled people who have nocturnal sexual spook experiences, and are tormented by them. This is not a matter of "wet dreams" or of the sexual hallucinations of schizophrenics, but of experiences in a waking state. In the history of religion this phenomenon is known as *incubi* and *succubae*. These are male and female seducing demons. In the bible there is such a story recorded in Gen. 6, 4. There we read how sons of God united with daughters of men. This would be the phenomenon of angel marriages.

Among the ancient peoples we can point to such conceptions too. The Babylonians and Assyrians had myths of so-called night maidens (*ardat lili*), which continued in Jewish tradition as *lilith*.[234] In the Christian era this motif of demon marriage continued. In the Legend of St. Antony, the devil appears in the form, among others, of an enticing woman. The theme continued in the popular beliefs of the middle ages. In the 6th. and 7th. Book of Moses it is reported (6, 6) how the demons make sexual assaults on people at night in the form of beautiful maidens or young men. In our day the phenomenon is constantly appearing in pastoral interviews. A few examples will illustrate in a striking way the mental distress of those afflicted.

Ex 84   A woman often experiences nocturnal visitations. In a waking state she sees five wild boars charging at her, with intent to violate her. The woman cries loudly for help. Her husband finds it hard to calm her. He does not see the boars; he only hears strange noises.

Ex 85   A friend of mine who was a missionary in China reported similar things among the Chinese. We have here a problem well known

---

[234] cf. "Religion in Geschichte und Gegenwart" II, p. 960.

in the history of missions, that of fox-possession. Girls who are by day perfectly normal psychologically, and go about their work quite regularly, are at night sexually plagued by apparitions. Figures appear with the head of a fox. As soon as the figure draws near, the fox-head changes into the handsome face of a man. These girls suffer dreadfully from these nocturnal visitations. It is worthy of note that girls who turn to Christ are delivered from this. Christian Chinese girls are not subject to this affliction.

Ex 86   A young man of Christian disposition lost his wife. After one and a half years he married again. With the second wife he enjoyed a successful and happy marriage, except that from the time of this second wedding he was plagued at night by spook apparitions. His first wife, now dead, would appear to him in the night in a waking state and try to approach him sexually. He found this apparition a great burden, and came for pastoral help. He confessed his need and determined to follow Christ. He had an urgent desire to be freed from these nightly visitations. The pastor, a widely known home missionary, undertook to intercede for the man. The result was that the intercessor himself experienced peculiar visitations. One night the trouble reached a climax. The praying pastor sensed behind him a strong current, which drew nearer. The afflicted pastor "commanded" in the name of Jesus. The spirit departed. From this night on, the troubled husband was freed from the sexual apparitions of his deceased wife.

These three examples will now require a few words of critical examination. From the *psychiatric* viewpoint we must again emphasize that these are not delusive ideas or sexual hallucinations in psychotic persons. The persons troubled by these sexual visitations are, apart from the nocturnal affliction, mentally healthy people, who for years carry on their normal professions without hindrance, and without their associates perceiving anything different about them.

From the viewpoint of *psycho-analysis* the objection could be raised that these phenomena perhaps express unfulfilled sexual longings or unbroken sexual ties. This would be a new form of the reversibility theory, viz. that unfulfilled desires which have been repressed into the subconscious are again subjectively experienced, by way of the "outward curve", as visual and tactile experiences. That which the afflicted person experiences as an objective happening would only be the experiencing of a projection out of his own subconscious, and thus a purely subjective happening. This would strip the sexual spook apparition of any transcendent significance.

This psychoanalytic explanation contains, however, some decisive gaps. Christian Chinese girls are not subjected to fox-possession, and Chinese who turn to Christ are freed from it. The above-mentioned missionary, a highly educated and experienced counsellor with university training, experienced these assaults during his intercession, until the person for whom he was praying was freed.

The phenomenon of psychological infection, or of the primitive concept of magic transference, does not apply here. In these gaps in the explanation of the analyst we have a strong pointer toward the transcendent character of the sexual spook apparitions above mentioned. Naturally this pointer is not seen in the sexual hallucinations of those mentally ill, or in the sexual dreams of healthy persons which result from unrelieved bodily tensions, or in sexual perversions which are the expression of repressed instincts.

From the *pastoral* point of view it is significant that faith in Jesus Christ puts an end to these sexual spook apparitions. If we may say something about the cause of sexual apparitions which are perhaps of demonic character, then on purely empirical grounds we suspect that perhaps a conjunction of sodomy and occult activity may be at the root. For it is observed again and again by the pastoral counsellor that in Christian marriages where one partner maintains a legalistic, narrow, negative attitude towards sex, the deprived partner sometimes lapses not only into adultery but even into sodomy. If to sodomy there is then added a magic enslavement due to occult subjection, then psychologically and psychically the necessary ingredients for sexual apparitions are present.

A second possibility would be the view that occult subjection is the immediate cause of both phenomena, viz. of intensified, unnatural sexuality as in sodomy, and also of the sexual apparitions; for indeed occult subjection always brings extremes of character and psychological extravagances to the fore. The exact empirical proof of these relations can, however, only be given when more pastoral cases have been collected in this sphere. Until now the findings have the character of surmises, though they certainly fit into the general pattern of occult involvement.

3. *Extra-sensory Apparitions*

In the sections now following we enter the most debated field of psychical research, that of para-physical manifestations. If the sections on ESP and ESI gave examples only of inner processes of man, the phenomena of this new section assume an objective, sensible character. But for this reason they are not the subject of less debate, but rather of more vehement attack than the preceding ones. Two phenomena in particular will be presented here: materialization and spooks.

(a) *Materialization*

The most remarkable area of psychical research is that of the phenomenon of materialization. Prof. Nusser[235] defines this phenomenon as an unaccountable appearance and disappearance of material images. In this definition, however, there is no mention of the fact that such phenomena occur only in connexion with the activities of a medium. More accurate is the definition of Prof. Gruber, in his book about psychical discoveries. He writes: "Telekinesis and materialization are scientific facts. Certain persons have, under special circumstances, the ability, without the help of any known body function, to exercise a moving or shape-altering influence on objects in their environment, and also to create outside their bodies from unknown materials some visible, tangible, more or less highly organized form, sometimes supplied with its own illumination (efflorescent substance), patterned in many cases on parts or the whole of the human body. These materializations appear and disappear suddenly."[236]

In these materializations, we are faced with manifestations of various degrees of teleplastic morphogenesis. The *first* stage is the emission and separation of veil-like, gauze-like, slimy substances of rubbery elasticity from the body cavities of the medium. Schrenck defines this first stage of materialization as follows: "the appearance of elementary matter in the form of white lumps, strips and shreds".[237] Such forms have been photographed with a flash camera (see plates 23—30 in Schrenck-Notzing's exhaustive work).[238] Further, these phenomena are treated in the book of the French writer Mme. Bisson, "Les phénomènes dits de matérialisation".[239]

The *second* stage is the formation of body parts such as outline, arms, legs, head, etc. In many cases deformed or defective body-parts are seen. With some teleplastic forms of this kind a cord- or thread-like

---

235 cf. Holmsten, op.cit. 37, p. 247.

236 "Zeitschrift für Arbeit und Besinnung", 1. 1. 51, pp. 16f. (Quell Verlag, Stuttgart).

237 "Materialisationsphänomene", a contribution to the study of mediumistic teleplastics by Dr. A. Frh. von Schrenck Notzing, Verlag Reinhardt, Munich, 1914, p. 513.

238 loc.cit. 237.

239 Mme. Bisson, "Les phénomènes dits de matérialisation", Paris, 12th. edn. 1921.

connexion is maintained with the medium. In Schrenck's work there is a series of photographs of such teleplasms. Besides these photographs, even wax casts of such materialized members have been made.[240]

The *third* stage is the solidification into complete shadowy forms, which appear as phantoms near the medium. Schrenck's book shows photographs of such phantoms (plates 127, 135, 136). In these three stages we have purely visual materialization phenomena. In the next three stages we move on to active and passive manifestations of energy by the phenomenon.

The *fourth* stage shows a combination of materialization phenomena with telekinesis. The medium is in a position to display energy at a distance by means of an unknown remote power. In this connexion Tischner reports the floating in the air of a bell (p. 149), and a violin (p. 150), and the automatic writing of a typewriter (p. 149). Modern psychical researchers call this output of energy on the part of the teleplasm telekinesis or psychokinesis. Besides the active manifestation of energy, a passive pain experience of the teleplasm has also frequently been observed. Since these pain experiences play a part in many pastoral cases, we shall give further attention to this later.

The *fifth* stage of the materialization is the penetration of matter. Here we have the enigmatic "apports", of which psychical literature has much to say, and also the four dimensional aptitudes of some mediums. "Apport" means the appearance and disappearance of objects in closed rooms and containers. Such phenomena are well known from the experiments conducted by the Leipzig physicist Zöllner with the American doctor Slade.[241] From locked and sealed containers, enclosed coins were brought out, or stones and other objects were seen inexplicably to fall from the ceiling. Such phenomena are very numerous.[242] In this stage we find also the strongly disputed ability of some mediums to penetrate solid material while they are in a trance. We take an example from Larsen's book.[243]

Lit 13   In twelve sessions held with the medium Mme. d'Espérance, it occurred that while the medium sat in the "cabinet", a phantom built itself up on the floor outside the cabinet and finally took shape as a

---

[240] Wax casts are reported in: a) loc.cit. [236], p. 19; b) Holmsten, op.cit. [31], p. 249; c) Schrenck-Notzing, op.cit. [31], pp. 103, 232; d) Walter Schäble, "Der großer Zauber", Schriftenmissionsverlag Gladbeck, 1950, p. 22; e) Bovet, op.cit. [171], p. 48.

[241] cf. Enno Nielsen, op.cit. [31], p. 221.

[242] Reports about spirit stones: a) Schäble, op.cit. [240], p. 29; b) Nielsen, op.cit. [37], p. 218; c) Tischner, op.cit. [25a], p. 156.

[243] Larsen, op.cit. [47], p. 37.

female person, who moved in and out among the participants. She extended her hand to one of these, and while he held the hand dematerialization set in before the eyes of all. The gentleman, a well-known person, called out, "Now the hand is growing smaller and smaller. Now there is nothing left!" Finally there was only a small ball left on the floor, which rolled into the cabinet. Such a strong medium is, however, extremely rare, and is perhaps non-existent at the present time.

The *sixth* stage of materialization probably makes greater demands on the imagination of a person of sound mind than any other phenomenon in the whole field of para-psychology. This is the occasional testimony given to metamorphosis into animal shapes. Tischner reports such phenomena in connexion with the mediums Guzi and Kluski.[244] Further, Dr. Leubuscher records the phenomenon of hyaena-mania[245] among the clay-workers of Abyssinia.

Addendum in the American Edition

In the summer of 1963 I travelled through Tanganyika, and was told that in one district there is a law against metamorphosis into animal forms. Criminals and superstitious persons sometimes confess before the courts to having changed themselves into a lion or leopard and killed a person. Upon such a confession the punishment inflicted is hanging.

The greatest number of testimonies to this strange phenomenon is found in the above-mentioned book[246] of Prof. Österreich on the problem of possession. In this phenomenon of animal metamorphosis there is a distinction to be made between psychological and organic metamorphosis. Such is the opinion of ethnologists, students of religions, missionaries and travelling researchers. On the psychological level we only find empathy into animal individualities. Psychologically abnormal persons think they have changed into an animal, and imitate the animal's sounds or movements. Thus Jerome (d. 420) reports in his biography of St. Paula that she met with possessed people near Samaria who acted like animals (zooanthropy), howled like wolves (lycanthropy), barked like dogs, roared like lions and hissed like snakes.[247]

Further, one author, Dom Calmet, has reported that nuns in a German convent during an epidemic of possession, thought themselves changed

---

244 Cases of animal metamorphosis are mentioned by: a) Tischner, op.cit. 25a, p. 154; b) Schrenck-Notzing, op.cit. 31, p. 234; c) Nielsen, op.cit. 37, p. 16; d) Österreich, op. cit. 63, pp. 143, 158, 186, 239.

245 cf. 77.

246 cf. loc.cit. 63.

247 cf. Österreich, op.cit. 63, p. 158.

into cats and miaowed.[248] There are also cases of possession with the delusion of metamorphosis into dogs (cynanthropy), badgers, foxes, and monkeys, etc.[249] According to the accounts of the two Livingstones, there is a belief in South Africa that some people can change themselves into lions for a time.[250]

Apart from the preliminary, psychological stage of animal metamorphosis, there are also reports of material metamorphosis into corporeal animal forms. Among the pygmies it is believed that magicians can change into various animals and can in this form injure people.[251] This tradition of the pygmies corresponds to the Abyssinian hyaena-mania. The delusion of being changed into animals is found also in schizophrenics.[252] It is not necessary to investigate these reports of animal metamorphosis. They are merely mentioned to make it plain that the mediumistic capers of materialization phenomena, as we know them in spiritist circles, have corresponding parallels in primitive peoples.

These various stages of materialization phenomena will not be investigated here, but are merely indicated by way of reference, for information, without any position being adopted regarding them. There are many hypotheses to explain these puzzling manifestations of physical mediumistic gifts. No doubt much of it can be dismissed as deception, popular superstition or conjuring tricks.[253] But we would not in this way do justice to the genuine phenomena of materialization. Generally speaking, in psychical research five ways of explaining materialization phenomena are prevalent.

The *spiritistic* hypothesis claims that the spirit world employs the od force of mediums to produce teleplastic forms.[254] In the same way also material objects are dissolved at one place and recomposed at another.[255]

The *physicist* Zöllner saw the penetration as evidence of the fourth dimension.[256] According to his view, matter is open to the fourth dimension as a plane is open to the third dimension.

---

[248] ibid., p. 186.
[249] ibid., pp. 217—219.
[250] ibid., p. 143.
[251] ibid., p. 239.
[252] cf. Bleuler, op.cit. [129], p. 78.
[253] In this connexion we should note the controversy between Gulat-Wellenburg and Schrenck-Notzing: Dessoir, loc.cit. [36].
[254] cf. periodical cit. [236], 15. 1. 51, p. 37.
[255] ibid. loc.cit.
[256] cf. Tischner, op.cit. [25a], p. 156.

The discoveries of *nuclear physics* enable us to understand the penetration of matter, since the spaces between the atom's nucleus and the orbiting electrons is much greater than their mass. What we call matter is much more empty space than compact mass, so that penetration does not seem impossible.

Modern *para-psychology* has offered proof, especially through the experiments of Prof. Rhine,[257] that the reach of man's mind and the abilities of his soul are considerably greater than was previously known in science. The cerebro-centric image of man must gradually yield to the psycho-centric. What para-psychology has here discovered is parallel to the physical law of the conversion of energy. Just as two hundred years ago physicists discovered the law of the conversion of potential to kinetic energy, so parapsychology has now established in the case of occult phenomena — especially of telekinesis — the conversion of psychic energy into a physical activity.

Psychology has invalidated the spiritistic explanation of materialization phenomena through the results of psycho-experimental research. Prof. Bender has succeeded in showing that in the case of materialization phenomena we are dealing with dissociation artifacts, artificially induced manifestations of psychic separation. We shall give more particular attention to this in the section on the dominance of the subconscious factors (Pt. III, ch. 4, 2).

The question which Bender, with his psychological explanation, still leaves open, viz. how dissociated psychological factors can be materialized, can be taken further in connexion with a problem of recent nuclear physics. In atomic research we have succeeded in building a number of heavy atoms, which are not known in nature, above and beyond the 92 elements which occur in nature. In this compounding of particles into new atoms, a loss of weight can occur. So we have the interesting phenomenon that the mass of the resultant new atom is less than the sum of the masses of its constituent parts. This lost mass has converted itself into energy. Hence we note here a process whereby mass is immaterialized, or, in psychical language, dematerialized. The reverse process is therefore feasible too, namely, that energy can materialize itself into mass. This process, which means a momentous revolution in physics, can be stated by Einstein's formula ($E = Mc^2$: Energy is equal to Mass times the velocity of light squared). Thereby physics tells us that it is theoretically possible to change mass into energy and energy into mass. Now, applying this to materialization phenomena, we have

[257] cf. Rhine, op.cit. 57.

the thought that psychic energy can be materialized, and matter can be dematerialized into energy. Regarding the manner of these processes, we still know very little. We only see the practical realization for just a few minutes in the materialization phenomena of strong mediums. In the history of religions we also have a few examples of dematerialization. Since it is an interesting phenomenon, we shall give two examples.

Ex 87   A missionary related to me that in Japan pagan priests dematerialize themselves on one mountain peak and rematerialize themselves on another. That would be the phenomenon of rapture in a heathen setting. It is well said that the devil is the ape of God.

Lit 14   Luke the physician reports in Acts 8, 39—40: "The Spirit of the Lord caught up Philip; and the eunuch saw him no more ... but Philip was found at Azotus, and passing on he preached ..." Gaza is twenty-five miles from Azotus. If now, to avoid misunderstanding, we may add a word to these examples, we must point out that the New Testament knows both miracles of God and miracles of Satan (e.g. Mark 13, 22).

Beyond this sketch of the basic phenomena of materialization we must now give a short presentation of one peculiar characteristic of *teleplasm,* since the understanding of certain special pastoral cases is connected with this. This concerns one of the features mentioned in the fourth stage, viz. the pain experience of the teleplasm and consequently of the medium. There are the so-called mediumistic birth-pangs.[258] Both Schrenck-Notzing and the Parisian doctor Dr. Geley, who have both made important tests in the field of materialization phenomena, testify that mediums always express pain while producing teleplastic forms. Still more revealing is the fact that attempts to grasp the emanations of the medium cause the medium to feel pain.[259] The use of force against the teleplasm causes injury to the medium.[260] If, for example, the teleplasm is pricked with a needle, the corresponding prick marks appear on the body of the medium. If the teleplasm is burned with a candle flame, burns and blisters appear on the body of the medium. If the "fluidic" threads which are occasionally seen between the medium and the teleplasm are cut with a pair of scissors, then the medium groans with the resulting pain, and cut wounds even appear on the body of the medium.

[258] cf. Holmsten, op.cit. [37], p. 247; also Schrenck-Notzing, op.cit. [237], pp. 497, 505.
[259] ibid.
[260] cf. periodical cit. [236], 1. 1. 51, p. 19.

It is on the observation of this fact that the use of physical energy against the teleplasm causes injuries to the medium, that the numerous defensive practices popularly used against attack from mediums are based. We shall give a pastoral example of this.

Ex 88 In the course of an evangelistic campaign a woman came for counselling and disclosed a peculiar experience. After her marriage the young bride found that her husband's mother could not detach herself either externally or mentally from her son. The new marriage was thus like a ménage à trois, and was constantly endangered. Nor did the situation improve when the mother moved away from the couple. For many years the man remained under the influence of his mother. He wavered to and fro between mother and wife. The young wife suffered from this situation. To make matters worse, the mother possessed mediumistic abilities. Often when the young wife went to bed at night red disks of light would come in from the hall and approach her bed. After she had been terrified and plagued in this way for many weeks, she sought advice from some spiritists. After questioning her thoroughly they assured her that she could fend off the mediumistic attacks. She must take a leather strap, tie three knots in it, and strike at the disks of light when they appeared. The medium involved, who was causing her this unrest, would have bleeding weals on her body as result of this resistance. The troubled wife followed the advice, with the astounding result that the visitation by the disks of light ceased quite suddenly after this magical resistance, and that the next day the mother-in-law had whipmarks on her body.

In circles where occult activities are practised, there are very many examples of this idea that mediums are able through psychic dissociation to annoy and to persecute people they do not like, and also that they can be fended off by magic. Many of these cases are even more strange than *Ex 88*. One such seemingly absurd example follows.

Ex 89 A farmer's wife with a gaggle of geese found that every day one of the geese died before her eyes in peculiar circumstances. The goose would twist its neck in a spiral, then the neck would be wrung backward and the creature would die. Since the woman knew no remedy, she sought advice from a spiritist. She was told to catch a goose at the moment its neck was being wrung, and to hold it over the open fire. Then the person causing this evidently magic persecution would get heat blisters and cease from his sport. The farmer's wife asserted that this prescription had worked. I am not able to check the truth of her claims.

We shall not enter into an investigation of these examples, which are more than strange, bordering as they do on spook apparitions and black magic. In all of these appearances there is one basic thought, viz. that people can bring about harm by psychic dissociation, by the materialization of psychic energy, but that they in turn can easily be injured while in the state of materialization.

What we have offered in this section, apart from a basic introduction into the various stages of materialization phenomena, are, to be sure, only marginal situations of the materialization phenomena, which are however more prevalent among the people than are "apparitions of the dead" in spiritist sessions. This is the field proper of materialization phenomena. The genuineness of the reincarnation of the deceased, brought on the scene by mediums, has had both its proponents and its opponents among scientists of repute.

Basically there are two opposing theories, namely the spiritistic and the animistic, which are discussed in Pt. III, ch. 4, 5. To give a glimpse into the form which this reincarnation of the deceased takes, we give an example from the book of Olhaver.[261]

Lit 15   A medium, Miss Tambke, made seven deceased persons appear in one séance. First there was a white woman figure, who circulated between the rows of the eighteen persons present and magnetized a sick merchant by the laying on of hands. The man sensed a faint current passing through him. Next came the materialization of a deceased woman, who came and sat on the lap of her husband, who was present. The third appearance was the author Olhaver's father, who kissed his son on the forehead. Fourthly, the daughter of a gentleman present appeared. Finally a six-year-old lad came, who kissed his brother who was present there. After the seventh apparition the energy of the medium was exhausted. She had to be awakened.

Olhaver[262] tries to furnish proof of the reality of these "reincarnations" of seven dead persons. He provides a chart giving their respective heights, ranging from 3ft. 10ins. to 6ft., the different shades and styles of hair, and the shape of their hands. Remarkable also is the fact that those present recognized these apparitions of their own relatives by their voice, expressions and peculiar characteristics. Yet, in spite of this, Olhaver can only persuade those who believe in spiritism. The whole process of reincarnation can be explained with the help of psychology and para-psychology as a series of immanent processes, so

261 cf. Olhaver, op.cit. 132, pp. 115f.
262 ibid., p. 133.

that it is still unnecessary to assume that the dead are disturbed. Basically there are three phenomena involved here: psychic dissociation of the medium in a state of trance; drawing on the subconscious of those present, whose deceased relatives appear; and modification of the dissociated psychic elements by the material drawn from the others. Also, preceding these three stages we would have the whole process of the putting to sleep of the medium, whether by magnetic stroking or by autosuggestion. We shall not discuss theories which suggest that it is a swindle, like that of the masquerade, or the transfiguration of the somnambulant medium, since these are rendered untenable by sufficient precautionary measures.

In order here, in our investigation of the spiritistic phenomena of materialization, to allow full force and objectivity to views we feel bound to reject, it must be granted that in the knowledge that is revealed by the "reincarnated" person there is often an unexplained residue. And moreover this residue can often not be explained by reference to the contents of family, clan, race or collective subconscious.

From the *pastoral* viewpoint we find in the case of the medium and of the participants in séances the same pattern which we see in the families of conjurers: psychological disorders of the most varied kinds, although spiritists and others not concerned with pastoral problems would want to deny this and warn against exaggeration. Especially frequent are permanent dissociation phenomena in two directions. The person who is influenced by spiritism does not only experience processes of dissociation in his own person; in his home surroundings spook phenomena appear, which are judged by Prof. Bender to be dissociated psychic powers with a separate existence. We shall deal with such phenomena in the section on spooks. The deliverance of a person from spiritism, and the turning of such a person to Christ, seldom occurs, since spiritism is itself interwoven with Christian and biblical ideas, and the person involved therefore fails to discern the error of his ways.

(b) *Spooks*

Prof. C. G. Jung declares in his foreword to the work of Dr. F. Moser:[263] "Regarding research into psychical phenomena we are still at the very beginning. We do not even know the whole scope of the field under consideration. Hence the collection of observations and of the most trustworthy data possible is a very meritorious service." Such a collection of cases, taken from pastoral experience, we want to offer

---

263 cf. Dr. Fanny Moser, "Spuk, Irrglaube oder Wahrglaube? Eine Frage der Menschheit", Baden, nr. Zürich, 1950, p. 9.

in this section. Again, it is not our purpose here to investigate spook phenomena, but rather to state the presuppositions of pastoral help. In pursuing this goal it will however be absolutely necessary to seek a scientific explanation of this field, insofar as that is at all possible.

In order to obtain a uniform grouping of the material, we make the following distinctions. With respect to the degree of observation, we can distinguish the subjective and the objective spook. Regarding the site of action and character of the apparition, experts usually distinguish between those bound to places and those bound to persons. Since the distinction subjective-objective is weighted with problems not only of a philosophical but also of a psychological and of a psychical nature, we must attempt a definition here. The problem of objectivity is a question which Kant already found it necessary to discuss. In its earlier sense the concept of the objective has become very shaky as a result of modern nuclear physics. Moreover it appears that in the phenomena of parapsychology the distinction of subjective and objective is often not justified. But in spite of this obstacle we shall retain the distinction in this section in order to view the material given in a practical way. An example will very quickly make our meaning clear.

Ex 90   Prof. Bender of the University of Freiburg reported at a convention of the Evangelical Academy in Tutzing, in 1950, the following case. A student for a long time observed a man pursuing her. The observation could not be made by other people. The pursuer would repeatedly say to the girl, "Take your life!" This visual and auditory "phantom" ceased to appear after the girl had been counselled by a psychiatrist. This subjective spook was the projection to the outside of a persecution complex, i. e. a subjective process which was experienced as an objective happening by way of the "outward curve". Most hallucinations can be explained in this way.

In the examples which now follow we shall not be concerned with such subjective spook experiences. Actually they do not merit the name of "spook" at all. We are here concerned with objective appearances of spooks, observable by any person, excluding the possibility of mass hallucinations by psychic contagion, telepathic thought-transference or object suggestion as a collective delusion. An objective spook must be observable, without these factors, by persons not initiated, by photography, or by animals. First we shall give a few cases of spooks which are bound to some particular location, i. e. site-bound spook phenomena.

Ex 91   A well-known pastor and evangelist told me of a peculiar experience, which he has allowed me to make public. As a young pastor, our reporter was assigned to an irreligious parish. The villagers had little respect for the word of God. Rather, all manner of superstitious customs were carried on. The charmer was esteemed more highly than the vet. The magnetizer had more work to do than the doctor. The village card layer was visited more often than the council house or the parsonage. At first the young pastor did not feel happy in his new field of work. In the parsonage several remarkable things were to be seen,[264] which could not be accounted for rationally. Repeatedly the pastor's wife would say to her husband that there was something uncanny about the house. The husband would brush this off with a laugh: "There is no such thing. It is all humbug and swindle. Either our senses are playing some trick on us, or a special 'friend' of the pastor is playing a practical joke." This thoroughly sober, intelligent man of sharp judgement gave no further attention to the happenings in the parsonage. But one night he was compelled by a remarkable incident to take note of the unusual occurrences. Their baby, which slept in the adjoining room to its parents, suddenly set up a most horrible cry. The young wife hurried through the open door into the adjoining chamber to comfort the child. But she started back in astonishment, and called her husband. Both parents saw how the child had been drawn out of its bedclothes and had been turned round in its cot. On its body there were blood-smeared fingerprints. The man first thought it must be some brazen trick. He carefully checked the window catches and the doors into the corridor, and then searched the whole room with a torch. The child's clothes and nappy were then carefully checked for a cause of the injuries to the child. But the parents could not find the slightest clue to explain this painful occurrence.

The mother settled the child again in its cot and quieted it. Then they went back to bed again. But almost immediately the terrible cries and moans broke out again. The parents together hurried into the room. The baby was again unwrapped, drawn out of the clothes and turned round in the cot. The little body showed new traces of having been violently seized, with the typical marks of a human hand. The couple now had a distinctly uncanny feeling. They took the baby into their bed, and the husband said to his wife, "Something mysterious seems to be going on after all. Come, let us pray." The couple earnestly prayed for God's protection and in faith committed themselves consciously to His care. Then they lay down quietly to rest, and were troubled no more in their sleep.

---

264 Dr. Moser, op.cit. records several cases of spooks in parsonages (pp. 189f, 213f., 236f., 242f.). I also know of a number of haunted parsonages.

Early in the morning there was another surprise. The pastor noticed flames shooting out of the window of the farm-house next door. He hurried over with his wife to lend a hand in dealing with the fire. How surprised they were, when they found everything quiet in the neighbour's house! The appearance of fire had vanished. Shaking their heads, they went home. For a little while all was quiet. Then there was a new alarm. The farmer, deeply disturbed, came to the pastor to tell him that his daughter had an attack of mania, was beating about wildly and had gone out of her mind. The pastor accompanied the troubled man to his home and saw the maniacal girl. Now he was almost convinced that something was wrong with the parsonage and with the farm-house. What it might be, however, he had no idea.

A few months passed by. Everything in the parsonage and in the farm-house was quiet once more, although the farmer's daughter had unfortunately had to be taken to a mental hospital. The pastor had consciously avoided speaking in the village about these strange events. But secretly he continued to search for some explanation of these mysterious happenings. Then one day an old elder of the church shed some light on the problem. The old man told him confidentially that the previous pastor, who had been the village's spiritual guide for almost a lifetime, had for twenty-eight years maintained a spiritist group in the parsonage and experimented in occult things. At first no light dawned in the mind of the young pastor concerning a connexion between these experiments in the field of the occult and the strange events which he had experienced in his house. He was, like so many other people, a man of academic training who did not accept these superstitious things at their face value but regarded them at most as an interesting hocus-pocus. In the course of his ministry, however, and as he was invited to conduct various evangelistic campaigns, he gained an insight into this mysterious realm.[265]

This experience, which is guaranteed by the reporter's truthfulness and soundness of judgement, certainly makes great demands on the rational mind. We thus have here the question of how we should evaluate the occurrences in these two houses. In connexion with this case, the following questions need to be considered:

[265] During a Bible Week in the district of this pastor I gained some shocking insights into the occult activities of that area. Whole generations are afflicted with mental illness, frequent suicides, emotional disorders and psychological disturbances of various kinds, all connected with occult activities. After I had given an address on this subject, I was sought out from morning to late at night for days on end by people who came to confess their spiritistic and magic practices.

Was the pastor's family victim of a gross sense delusion? Was the observation of flames from the farm-house window merely an hallucination? Were the ten blood-smeared finger-marks merely insect bites?

Had the baby only kicked itself loose and twisted round because of the pain of insect bites? Were the flames coming out of the farm-house window perhaps a reflection of the sunrise, or the flickering of a fire in the farmer's grate? The layout of the buildings and rooms makes this suggestion untenable. Or have we here a prevision of fire, such as those often mentioned by Schmïng?[266]

Was there any connexion between the occurrences in the parsonage and the mania of the farmer's daughter? Is there in the sphere of the occult such a thing as transference from one person to another? Do spook activities leap from place to place?

Can people be physically or psychically attacked by powers unknown to us? Is there such a thing as psychic or magic persecution?

Were the occult practices of the old pastor the cause of the strange events in the parsonage?

Do experiments in occult activities leave behind them peculiar effects after the death of the one who practised them?

Are there actually haunted houses?

Must we not dismiss all such apparitions as mere humbug, or is a rational explanation of all these phenomena possible?

Do all occult apparitions involve simply an activation of mental powers present in man, or are there invasions by powers from the beyond? In other words, which is valid, the animistic or the spiritistic hypothesis, or some other view?

Can the disturbances in the parsonage be explained as a dissociation of certain psychic powers, which lead a mysterious separated existence? This would involve the problem of depersonalization or psychic dissociation. The possibility is here excluded, because the young family were emotionally stable, balanced people.

If we are to give these occult apparitions a genuine validity, is there then any safeguard or deliverance in this area?

This whole series of questions will not be dealt with in detail, but is only intended to indicate the difficulties of the situation in which those who would examine spook phenomena find themselves. To the psychologically and para-psychologically trained observer it will be

[266] cf. Schmeïng, op.cit. [30], pp. 63, 91.

clear from such spook experiences that these phenomena cannot be forced into a mould before the forum of rationality.

From the *pastoral* standpoint it is clear that this experience constituted a severe trial for the pastor's family, which they could not readily explain. But out of the welter of questions one thing stands out clearly, that faith in Jesus Christ brought them help in their affliction. In this fact of experienced deliverance from the mysterious occurrences, we have in clear lines a New Testament truth. It is the message which Matthew reports as the words of the Lord (Matt. 28, 18): "All authority in heaven and earth has been given to me". Christ has the final dominion in all the areas of the cosmos. He is Lord over all the power of darkness.

Ex 92   A man well known to me, of above average gifts, was appointed as a private tutor in a castle. Soon after his arrival he learned of the peculiar ghost stories which were connected with the castle. He smiled somewhat benignly at this. One evening the staff of the castle came running together into the court-yard, as they had often done before. The white form, which had often been seen, had appeared again. The caretaker informed the tutor. The tutor took his pistol and went to the scene of the ghost's appearance. A white form, larger than life size, was gradually moving towards the inquisitive crowd of onlookers. There were about ten people present. The tutor stepped forward and demanded that the masked white form should put off his mask. He raised his pistol, and threatened to shoot. Then he sent a warning shot and repeated his threat. The white form did not react. Then he shot, first low, at the legs, and then finally at a distance of fifteen feet he emptied both magazines, altogether fourteen well-aimed shots, into the middle of the figure, which then bowed low and disappeared. Besides the tutor, the whole staff of the castle witnessed this happening. A further witness of other spook phenomena in the castle is a deaconess, who without having any knowledge of the occurrences, came from her mother-house to nurse the dying lord of the castle. The nurse stayed only one night, and the next morning left the castle in fear, without waiting for the nobleman to die. She had experienced terrifying apparitions during the night.

Ex 93   At a gathering of the Evangelical Academy in Herrenalb in autumn 1951 the problem of occultism was raised in the course of a discussion between doctors and pastors. The literary editor of a large weekly paper, who was present, told how his sister, as the lady of a Silesian castle, had often experienced a nocturnal ghost appearance. About midnight a young woman would hurry out of a chamber, up the stairs, disappearing in the corridor above. At first the story did not interest me particularly, since there are plenty of similar stories about female ancestors going around. But suddenly the name of the castle made me prick up my ears: Lubowitz. I recalled a report from the diary of Eichendorff about this castle.[267] Eichendorff was watching, together with a few friends, in front of the ghost chamber. While they chatted about commonplace things, the doors opened and a slender young lady stepped out and hurried lightly up the stairs. A servant who had that day begun service in the castle and did not know about the ghost followed the woman with a light, in order to guide her. Suddenly a piercing cry resounded through the castle. As soon as they recovered from their first shock, Eichendorff and his friends hurried up the stairs. The servant lay dead on the floor, with an expression of horror on his face. Eichendorff had this experience in 1810. The last lady of the castle of Lubowitz left in 1944 at the approach of the Russians. Consequently we have here testimony of a ghost phenomenon which remained unvaried over a period of 134 years.

Ex 94   A young pastor moved into a parsonage. Soon he and his wife discovered that sometimes in the evening a red-haired man stood in one of the rooms, who would vanish when someone entered. Besides this apparition, there were also scraping and sweeping noises to be heard in the hall. This phenomenon was also occasionally observed by visitors. After careful inquiries, it seemed quite probable that the red-haired man was identical with the pastor who had formerly lived in this parsonage, and who, in the judgement of the older people in the village, had lived a very evil life. The young pastor was not content with this analysis. He called some faithful Christians together to the parsonage to join in persevering prayer, with the result that the spook phenomena ceased.

Ex 95   At an evangelistic meeting in Bern I was shown a haunted house which was closed because all the occupants had been plagued by a nocturnal spook. The house has been uninhabited for many years.

Lit 16   Jung-Stilling reports in his "Theorie der Geisterkunde"[268] on a haunted house which for 300 years was continually troubled by a nocturnal ghost. During the night heavy steps were heard on the upper floor, as of someone carrying a sack. Several times also a form appeared wearing a monk's cowl.

A special type of site-bound spook is the so-called stable-ghost, of which I have learned of many cases in the area of the Black Forest.

267 cf. Nielsen, op.cit. 37, p. 28.
268 cf. Jung-Stilling, op.cit. 98, p. 101.

Besides the unnumbered stories current of such stable-ghosts, I also have some examples at first hand.

Ex 96   At an evangelistic meeting I was called into the house of some Christian people. They complained that their cattle were constantly disturbed by nocturnal ghosts. The tails of the horses and cows were plaited at the ends, and the cows were often already milked dry by the morning, even though both the stable doors were locked at night.

When one hears such a story for the first time, one is inclined to regard it as a bad joke by a "good" neighbour. But these experiences are in many cases attested beyond question. Usually such farmer families are ashamed to reveal troubles of this kind. Thus one learns of such spook phenomena only in confidence.

Ex 97   One of my neighbouring pastors in the Black Forest was requested to come one day to a farm. The stables were being disturbed every night. In the morning the tails of the animals would be plaited and the cows milked dry. The farmer had doubly secured both doors of the shed, and even sometimes set a night-watch. He himself also sometimes spent the night in the shed. All was to no avail. The spook persisted. He knew no other answer than to call the pastor, and ask him to pray in the cow-shed and ask for the protection and blessing of God. The pastor was called in several times for this spiritual service, until the intensity of the spook attacks subsided.

These stable-ghosts basically display the following characteristics. A regularly recurring phenomenon is the tying of animals together, the plaiting of their tails, cows which have been milked dry, and blood in the milk. If there is no prankplayer involved, then the first two of these points remain very puzzling. The observation of blood in the milk is easily explained by a vet. There is a whole series of milk disorders which cause unpleasant changes in the milk. One of the most common disorders is blood in the milk, in which a number of little clots appear. Some causes of this are the after-effects of calving, rough milking, injuries, feeding on poisonous plants, such as crow's foot, spruce, pine, yew, etc.

The second factor accounting for the frequent circulation of stories of stable-ghosts is the widespread belief in ghosts among many classes of people. An example which I experienced myself concerns the ghost of Rotenberg.

Ex98   At a certain farm various telekinetic phenomena were observed in the house and yard. Pieces of wood would sail through the air. Utensils rolled away as if thrown by an unseen hand, and so on. Rumours about the new haunted house spread fast. Press reporters moved in; the broadcasting company came to make a recording; people interested in psychical research turned up. There was great excitement. And the result? A boy of thirteen admitted at a hearing before the police and the two local pastors that he had thrown wood and utensils in order to hoax his grandfather. One of the two pastors involved in the enquiry told me of this development after I also had travelled there to get confirmation of the story. Very revealing now is the attitude of the villagers. They do not believe the report of the police and of the pastors. They say, "This admission was forced from the boy at the police hearing. The ghost is real..."

This inclination of ordinary people towards the mystical and magical stands in contrast to rationalism. C. G. Jung says of this phenomenon: "Rationalism stands in a complementary relation to superstition. According to the rules of psychology, the shadow grows with the light, i. e. the more rationalistic the attitude of the conscious mind, the more lively becomes the spook world of the unconscious".[269]

The characteristic phenomenon of the stable-ghost is the cross-connexion between spook phenomena and magic. In all cases of spooks which I have been able to investigate, occult practices lay at the root of the spook phenomena. In *Ex 96* it was established that before the stable began to be haunted the family had consulted a magic charmer and obtained his help. Dr. F. Moser reports[270] concerning a stable-ghost that a popular magician was called in to help and was immediately successful. When a home engages the help of conjurers, it may be assumed that such help has also been solicited in the past. Further instances of this cross-connexion will be given in the examples which follow.

We shall now report some cases which belong to the category of *person-bound* spooks. Both cases have been investigated by me in cooperation with police officers and fellow pastors.

Ex 99 In a highly intelligent family, spook phenomena would often appear about 11 p.m. at night. While all the family was still together, and the grandmother was reading her bible, the doors would open without a gust of wind or a human hand to cause it. Often too after the old lady had retired for the night, human heads would appear at her window, although this was not possible since her bedroom was on the third floor. Also in other respects various spook phenomena were noticeable in the house. The head of the household, who originally was

269 cf. Moser, op.cit. 263, p. 10.
270 ibid., p. 296.

very sceptical about these things, now took to leaping to the door when it opened, to find out the cause. Sometimes men's footsteps were heard in the hall, coming nearer, although the house was locked. Because of these experiences, the man got himself a large watch-dog. The remarkable thing about this dog was that in the case of every human who entered the house, he immediately barked, but upon the appearance of the spook he would whimper and creep away.

When these things were told me in this home, and my opinion asked, I countered with a question as to whether any spiritist séances had been held in the house. The answer was negative. Then I asked further whether any of the members of the family had taken part in séances anywhere else. This question was answered affirmatively by the old lady. She had often in her youth taken part as a little girl in a party game called table-moving. For me this answer was sufficient, since I had often experienced such a connexion between ghosts and occult practices before.

Ex 100 A family that was severely troubled by spooks sought my help. I went to the place and saw the destruction for myself. Shoes, shirts and linen sheets had been thrust into the stove and set alight. Ink was thrown over the smoked meat and into the wine-jar; spirits and water were poured on the beds; weights were thrown into the flour; eggs were smashed in the hen house or stolen; money, house keys, and all kinds of utensils disappeared suddenly without visible reason; wire hoops were cut to pieces, garments torn, etc. In a few months the family suffered several hundred marks' worth of damage.

It was not a simple matter to determine who had caused this damage. Thanks to the confidence and co-operation of the family, it was possible for me to speak with each member of the family separately. The honest, upright character of these solid people speaks for the reliability of their statements. It was, first of all, important to establish whether it was an enemy of the family or a family member who had caused the destruction. The first possibility was excluded, as far as any direct activity was concerned, since the room in which some of the havoc appeared could only be reached through the kitchen. The kitchen, however, was normally occupied by the family. As for the second possibility, suspicion centred on one member of the family. After several interviews, which were continued later, clear symptoms came to light of purposive psychogenic dimness of consciousness,[271] with accompanying erratic actions. I took this member of the family into my own home for a few days

271 cf. Kloos, op.cit. 12, p. 132.

so that I could keep her under observation. My supposition was again confirmed. In my home too there was one occurrence in the woman's room of a destruction similar to that which had occurred in her own home. Visits to relatives had similar results. After all the observations, which discretion forbids me to relate here, it was practically established that this woman was the cause of the destructions. Yet there was one decisive counter-argument, a cogent alibi on the part of this woman.

It became evident, through intentionally casual questioning of individuals in the family, that the havoc also took place when no one was at home, above all when this woman, whom I suspected to be the cause, was not at home. Consequently there was one gap in this story, if we dismiss the parapsychological hypothesis.

From the *pastoral* standpoint this example fits into the pattern of other experiences. The grandfather of this family was a charmer who used the 6th. and 7th. Book of Moses. Three of his children have particularly marked psychotic disorders, which point to the occult tradition. It was significant that after thorough pastoral counselling the family gave itself to daily prayer together. Quite suddenly and noticeably the destructions disappeared, except for a few traces which only lingered for a few months before disappearing entirely.

According to the evidence provided by these cases, we are faced with the psychical question of how these acoustic, visual, tactile and telekinetic phenomena of haunting can be explained. Prof. Tischner[272] is content simply to mention the various theories, such as collective hallucination, influence of the deceased, demonic powers, and finally to admit that we are completely in the dark about these spook phenomena. There is some justification for the view held by Prof. Bender, that[273] spook phenomena always appear in connexion with people who have psychological disorders. When such people are cured, the spook disappears. I have myself come to know examples in my pastoral experience — perhaps *Ex 96*, *Ex 99* and *Ex 100* belong to this category — in which the theory of Bender is possible. In our section on the circuit of psycho-organic correspondence, and in further explanations, at various points, of the significance of the subconscious processes, we have already suggested that all persons whose subconscious has in any way been affected by occult contacts, whether of an active or passive character, experience dissociation symptoms. Starting from this observation Bender's theory is intelligible, viz. that mentally ill people produce dissociated psychic

[272] cf. Tischner, op.cit. 25a, p. 193.
[273] Prof. Bender read a paper on this subject at the conference of the Ev. Academy in Tutzing in 1950.

energies, which have a separated existence and cause the weird happenings which we experience as spooks. In this case Bender's view is
identical with some of the findings of our study, which have been
obtained from a different field, namely from the systematic observation of occult practices.

Nevertheless, it is, according to my observations, only a small number
of cases which can be explained by this theory, a theory which to date
it has not been possible to prove. Of the spook cases listed in the foregoing section, *Ex 91*, *Ex 93*, *Ex 94* and *Lit 16* certainly do not fit this
theory. And, of course, we may *a priori* exclude those cases where
spook appearances have been consistently observed over many decades
or even several centuries. Here psychology and psychical research have,
as things stand at present, simply reached an impasse as far as rational
explanations are concerned.

For our present study we must once more assert that all spook
occurrences, including those not adduced here, which I have had the
opportunity of studying, showed a background of occult practice on the
part of some person who has lived there. On the basis of this fact, spook
phenomena, since they result from occult practices, are to be viewed in
just the same light as other magic activities. In cases of ghosts which
continue to be active for more than a human lifetime, there is strong
ground for assuming a transcendent centre of operation.

We are now in a position to sum up the cases we have studied so far
in the form of a partial conclusion, our first thesis: Evangelists engaged
in home missions find, in the personal counselling of those who come
to them during evangelistic campaigns, numerous cases of occult activity
and subjection, which give evidence of extra-sensory functions and
relations of the human soul.

Chapter Three

SUMMARY OF THE FREQUENCY RATIOS OBSERVED IN CONNEXION WITH OCCULT CASES

1. *Effects on those who exercise Occult Influence*

By this group we mean those occultists who, as spiritist leaders,
mediums, practising diviners and experimenters with magic charms,
carry on an *active* occult practice. The family histories and the end of
these occult workers are, in many cases known to me, so tragic that we
can no longer speak in terms of coincidence.

(a) *The end of active occultists*

In our section on magic charms we have already given many examples of the tragic end of magic charmers. In many instances we see suicide (e. g. *Exs 36, 61, 65, 66, 114*), fatal accidents (e. g. *Ex 66*), psychoses (e. g. *Exs 54, 62, 63, 65*), or horrible death-bed scenes (e. g. *Exs 65, 82*). Besides the instances recorded in this study, there are numerous other examples of this kind well known to me, e. g. the leader of a spiritist group in South Württemberg who hanged himself, and the leader of another group who ended his life in an asylum. Perhaps we should also mention here some examples from literature. The famous medium Dr. Slade[274] suffered two apoplectic fits; a pioneer in the field of psychical research, Crawford, who made experiments with the medium Kathleen Goligher, took his own life in 1920.[275] In the literature of psychical research we continually find reference to such happenings.

Those who are unfamiliar with the inner connexions of psychical phenomena will find it very strange that an association is seen here between the two apoplectic fits of Dr. Slade and his occult practice. We must therefore add a brief word of explanation. According to Dr. Bender, many of the experiments of Dr. Slade, and especially the telekinetic phenomena, can be regarded as effects of dissociation artifacts, or, in other words, as processes of separation. Dissociation processes are also occasionally found in connexion with apoplexy. An interesting case of this is reported by Prof. Weizsäcker (op. cit. [4], p. 142). A woman who suffered an apoplectic fit experienced at the same time a dissociation of consciousness, in the form of temporal discontinuity, an interval of amnesia. We know, moreover, from the researches of the neurologist Prince (op. cit. 332), that the splitting of consciousness can have psychogenic or somatogenic causes. If then in the case of Dr. Slade two attacks of apoplexy followed psychogenic processes of dissociation, we cannot completely rule out certain interrelations between them; for the splitting process gives us the common factor for the connexion between dissociation of consciousness and apoplexy, as it has been observed in both para-psychological and medical fields. A conversation with Prof. von Weizsäcker made this relationship still more plain to me. He told me that he knew a few cases in which psychogenic causes led to a dissoci-

---

[274] In order not to extend this study beyond due proportions, we shall not deal with the phenomenon of "excursion of the soul", or several other bordering themes. Further we find phenomena in a number of sects, which parallel those considered in our study. The occult field is of a wider compass than can be included within the range of this study.

[275] cf. Tischner, op.cit. [25a], p. 158; Nielsen op.cit. [37], p. 216.

ation of consciousness, followed by apoplexy. This confirms my
suggestion.

(b) *The curse on the family and descendants*

In the field of heredity, a coherence persisting into the third and
fourth generations is seen in the case of active occultists. These effects
are thus no less persistent in their hold on succeeding generations than
those of alcoholism, syphilis,[276] and psychoses.[277] In our study we have
already shown in *Exs 24* and *60—66* how psychological disturbances
and mediumistic gifts developed through occult practices extend as far
as the third and fourth generations. An example in outline form will
emphasize this once again.

Ex 101 The grandfather of a line of magic charmers worked with
the 6th. and 7th. Book of Moses. His son continued the tradition. While
the grandfather, apart from some psychological complications which
were beginning to arise, retained full possession of his mental powers,
his son developed compulsions and religious delusions. The grandson
was subject to still more fanatical compulsions than was his father. This
grandson got a church key from the verger of the local church. At midnight he would go and preach in the church. He would also occasionally
come into the main Sunday service, stand at the altar, or in the pulpit,
and preach. In this way, he said, he wanted to overcome the curse which
had come on his family through the possession of the 6th. and 7th. Book
of Moses. A few men would then bring the disturber down from the
pulpit in front of the whole congregation and eject him by force, since
he could not be persuaded to go of his own free will. We cannot
establish any effects in the fourth generation, since this compulsive had
no offspring.

(c) *The development of mediumistic abilities*

In our discussion of the many cases of magic charming, we made
the startling discovery that in the second to fourth generations clairvoyance developed as a secondary effect, after one or more conjurations.
This is evident from *Exs 1, 4, 20, 24, 33, 37, 40, 49, 56, 57, 59, 63, 65,
74.* The development of clairvoyance also tends to appear, especially
in the form of spirit-visions, in the case of blood pacts and amulet
pacts. We saw this in *Ex 24.* The spirit-seer mentioned there had, during

[276] cf. Tischner, op.cit. [25a], p. 153.
[277] An interesting case of congenital syphilis, with blindness, insanity and idiocy is
recorded in my book "Feuerzeichen" (op.cit. [198], pp. 177 f.).

his youth, undertaken a pact with the devil, as he once told me. *Ex 77* and *Ex 78* also give typical examples of this. I have also been told repeatedly by participants in spiritist séances that for years, long after they had ceased from all participation in séances, they still saw spirits and ghostly figures, apparently in accord with the line of Goethe, in the *Sorcerer's Apprentice:* "Die Geister, die ich rief, die werd' ich nun nicht los" — "Of the spirits which I called, I can no more be rid." We have such a case in *Ex 99*.

Besides the development of clairvoyance, there appears in connexion with occult practice also an increase -of mediumistic sensitivity. We have already mentioned that mediumistic gifts will appear in the next generation, where rejected, in a recessive form, but where there is further occult practice will appear as dominant. Mediumship is susceptible of both decline and development. If four generations all actively practice occult arts, then very strong mediums will develop. In the case of a person with a mediumistic predisposition who turns to Christ, the sensitivity may either be retained or vanish. Examples of this are *Ex 24*, where upon conversion to Christ mediumship disappeared, and *Exs 16* and *56*, where the sensitivity was retained and sometimes assumed a religious content. The missionary's wife mentioned in the latter example, who had been charmed while she was a child, had never known the cause of her sensitivity and clairvoyance. That is why she yielded herself to this ability without any scruples. For reasons of discretion we have not revealed the whole story of *Ex 56*. According to the example of Acts 16, 16f., it is better that people who have mediumistic tendencies should pray for deliverance from this ability, especially since the origin of this sensitivity is in the occult realm. Naturally we are not here speaking of spiritual visionary experiences, which have a totally different origin. But religious visionary experiences should be treated with great caution in pastoral counselling, since they can have a mediumistic as well a spiritual character.

2. *Effects on those Subjected to Occult Influence*

Now that we have presented the consequences for people actively engaging in occult practices, we must show the frequency ratio for those *passively* involved. We must emphasize that we are here only concerned with establishing a frequency ratio, and do not intend to offer any kind of compendium of psychiatry *ex occultismo*. In the many pastoral cases with which I have had to deal in the last 15 years, occult subjection has been seen in relation to psychological disturbances which have the following predominant characteristics:

(a) Warping and distortion of character:
    hard, egoistic persons;
    uncongenial, dark natures.

(b) Extreme passions:
    abnormal sexuality;
    violent temper, belligerence;
    tendencies to addiction;
    meanness and kleptomania.

(c) Emotional disturbances:
    compulsive thoughts, melancholia;
    suicidal thoughts, anxiety states.

(d) Possession:
    destructive urges, fits of mania;
    tendency to violent acts and crime;
    inhabitation by demons?

(e) Mental illnesses.

(f) Bigoted attitude against Christ and God:
    conscious atheism;
    simulated piety;
    indifference to God's word and to prayer;
    blasphemous thoughts;
    religious delusions.

(g) Puzzling phenomena in their environment.

For all the above detailed material there are sufficient examples from a total of 600 pastoral cases to justify the frequency ratio given. Only in the case of pure possession are we limited to six or seven examples, and for the fact of inhabitation by demons with the symptom of strange voices issuing from the possessed, I have no example of my own. In these cases we shall have to use examples adduced from literature. In most cases Dr. Lechler's definition of demonic enslavement suffices. Hence we have added a question mark at this point. If we adduce a biblical example, we might mention the Gadarene of Mark 5. Perhaps also Blumhardt's struggle over Gottliebin Dittus lies in this direction.[278]

The question of how far the psychological disorders observed in connexion with occult subjection agree with classic disease patterns of psychiatry will be discussed in Pt. III ch. 2. Point (g) above, concerning the puzzling phenomena in the environment of persons subjected to occultism, again confirms Prof. Bender's theory of the separated existence

---

[278] cf. Kloos, op.cit. [12], pp. 390, 424.

of dissociated psychic powers with telekinetic effects. Many of the adduced indicative marks coincide with the marks of demonic influence enumerated by Lechler in his lecture on demonism and the disturbance of the soul.[279]

3. Effects at the Place of Action or Dwelling of Occult Practitioners

One of the most puzzling manifestations is that of spook phenomena at the scene of action or the home of occultists, while they are still alive and even after their death. As long as the occult practitioner is still alive, the spook phenomena can be understood by Bender's theory of the separated existence of dissociated psychic powers. The persistence of the puzzling phenomena after their death is, however, beyond rational explanation. *Ex 91* and the cases of ghosts, e. g. *Ex 93, Ex 94* and *Lit 16*, come into this category. Here we must resort to a transcendent explanation, unless scientific psychical research should one day supply the key to the mystery.

4. Effects on the Counsellor

We are now concerned with the question whether a Christian who helps a person occultly subjected with advice and prayer can himself become the object of such attacks in the course of this ministry. Dr. Lechler treats this question in the lecture mentioned above, "Dämonie und Seelenstörung",[280] under the heading "The alleged transference of demons". He puts this idea down to the over-anxiety of abnormally impressionable people, who are further strengthened in their opinion by the pastor's prohibition of prayer on behalf of people troubled by demons. For some pastors, as Lechler correctly sees, the confession of grievous sins also has a burdening effect, so that this idea that demonic influence can be transferred easily arises. We have no intention of disputing this declaration by an experienced psychiatrist and Christian counsellor. But none of the examples at my disposal fits into the framework of this statement.

---

[279] cf. Joh. Chr. Blumhardt, "Krankheitsgeschichte der Gottliebin Dittus", Brunnen-Verlag, Basle. This story is debated in medical circles. Prof. von Weizsäcker described it at a convention of the Ev. Academy at Herrenalb as a case of hysteria. Dr. Bovet classes the case among the small remainder which cannot be explained psychologically. (op. cit. [171], p. 53).

[280] cf. Lechler, op. cit. [227], p. 8. This lecture was sent to me by Dr. Lechler after I had written Pt. II, ch. 3, 2. The partial agreement which I found on comparing it with my findings was very encouraging for me in the prosecution of this work.

First, we must say a little more about *Ex 86*. There the pastor experienced a modified transference.[281] This missionary is a man with university training who works in an important position. He is not abnormally impressionable, and is well versed in the theological, psychological and psychical problems of so-called occult transference. The above-mentioned statement does not apply in his case. Two more examples of a similar character follow.

Ex 102   A girl came for a pastoral interview. She had had no direct dealings with occult things, though she was perhaps indirectly affected since she lived in a village completely riddled with occultism. She reported the following family experience. After the defeat of Germany at the end of the second world war, a Nazi postmaster had been dismissed and this girl's sister was appointed to the job. The man who had been dismissed hanged himself. The sister, who did not bear the least blame for his dismissal, was from this time on plagued by anxiety states. In the evening she saw the hanged man following her up the street as a ghost. Under the continuing visions she suffered greatly, grew thin and became mentally ill. At this time the girl who had come to me for pastoral help began to pray much for her sister. Her prayers were answered. Her sister was no longer followed by the ghost. But now she became the object of this persecution. While her sister recovered and put on weight and became stronger again, this girl underwent a similar process as that which her sister had endured. Now she came for pastoral help. I learned two years later that the pastoral guidance had helped her.

For the *psychologist* this case is easy to analyse. The anxiety states of the sister led, through an outward projection, to the visions of the ghost. The intercession favoured the transmission of the psychological disorder. So much for the psychological interpretation. But how are we to explain that the first girl got better while the second became afflicted? One might say that the anxiety states and hence also the visions subsided with time. But experience shows that such visions of ghosts last for years, often decades. Moreover such cases begin to have a suspicious ring about them when they constantly recur. A further case, where the conditions were much more severe, follows.

Ex 103   At an evangelistic campaign in Switzerland, a woman came to me for consultation who was suffering from severe psychological disturbances. She told me the following story. Some years ago her friend

---

281 cf. Lechler, op. cit. 227b, p. 14.

had become ill. The neurologist diagnosed schizophrenia, and arranged for her to go to a mental institution. Our reporter gave herself to earnest prayer on behalf of her friend. She fairly stormed the throne of grace. The result was strange. The schizophrenic's symptoms subsided. She no longer needed to be sent to an institution. But instead the intercessor now became mentally ill. Although she remained quite capable of clear thought, she became subject to violent troubles, so that she too had to consult the neurologist.

The difficulty of this report lies first of all in the fact that a psychiatrist will usually not concede that schizophrenia subsided because of intercessory prayer — if it did, he will say it was not schizophrenia. Further the troubles of the second woman will perhaps be seen as induced insanity.[282] Yet this does not explain all the facts. The remarkable frequency ratio in such cases between the illness of the intercessor and the recovery of the person originally ill, leads us to look for another principle here.

Here we have three cases from a number of other different ones which caution us to reserve in dealing with the question of occult transference. I am aware that these cases are subject to question and attack from the viewpoints of science and medicine. Nor shall we here make any attack on the medical explanation. By adducing *Ex 102* and *Ex 103*, we only mean to say that when a pastor has a multiplication of such cases, he has to contend with the phenomenon of transference, because not all cases can be unequivocally in medical and psychological terms. In any case we must keep this question open for further study. And, moreover, co-operation with the medical specialist is here absolutely essential. Maeder makes an interesting contribution to the problem of psychological infection in his book, "Wege zur seelischen Heilung", under the heading "Über die Ansteckbarkeit seelischer Depressionen" (pp. 59f).

5. *Indirect Effects on the Observer of Occult Manifestations*

(a) *The attitude of protest*

It was one result of the Enlightenment that for a long period little attention was given to the border areas af the human mind. The number of those who hold all psychical phenomena to be humbug and swindle is very great among all classes of society. Schopenhauer calls this a priori attitude of protest the scepticism of ignorance.

---

[282] cf. explained Kloos, op. cit. 12, p. 450.

(b) *The confusion of opinion due to ignorance, minimization, and magic with a Christian façade*

Prof. Thielicke writes in his book, "Fragen des Christentums an die moderne Welt" (p. 199): "If there is one thing we know assuredly, it is this, that the devil does not leave visiting cards". It is the tactic of every temptation always to operate under a bright cover, never to show its real face, but always to carry on its activities in anonymity. Thus Paul says in II Corinthians 11, 14: "Satan disguises himself as an angel of light". Therefore we can understand how such camouflage tactics lead to confusion of thought, and it becomes plain why a right estimate of the significance of occult practices is not easy to arrive at. An example will illustrate this.

Ex 104 In an evangelistic campaign I gave, in a series of ten talks, one talk about the occult field. The local pastor was afterwards rather annoyed at my choice of theme. He said there was no such problem in his congregation, and that in my talk I had drawn their attention for the first time to something that did not really exist. Since I was not quite convinced by what he told me, I spoke to the elders of the church without mentioning my conversation with the pastor. The elders assured me that there was an abundance of occultism in the village. You could safely count on there being 200 church members, they said, who had had the pendulum swung over photographs of their missing loved ones, or had had cards laid for them.

Why did the pastor know nothing of this state of affairs in his church? Presumably because he dismissed it as humbug. His ignorance about this field was the cause of his not being able rightly to counsel the wives of those who were missing.

As well as ignorance, we find minimization.

Ex 105 A 15-year-old girl had tubercular inflammation of the hip-joint. Medical treatment brought no cure. So the mother decided to have her magically charmed. The nurse heard about this and advised her strongly against it. But the mother would not listen. The nurse decided to call in the local pastor to help. The pastor replied to the nurse, "Oh, let the mother go to the charmer. It won't help anyway — it's nothing but humbug." The magic charm was undertaken. The "humbug" promptly worked, and the girl recovered. But alas! at what a price! Healings by magic conjuration are simply a shift of level from the organic to the psychic, and so bring about an illness on a higher level.

When the pastor himself carries on occult practices, the situation is still worse.

Ex 106 A young pastor returned home from war imprisonment in Russia. During his long spell in prison camp, he had learned card reading. At home he now continued this practice. He laid cards not only for his own household, but also for the people of the village. He told them the future, and counselled them on important decisions by means of the cards. People came from neighbouring parishes for this kind of advice.

As well as minimization, we must mention the most serious degree of confusion, namely the Christianizing of magic. For this we have a great mass of revealing data. We will give a few examples in outline form.

Ex 107 An important theologian, whom I otherwise regard very highly, declared that the "Tennenbronner Zaubersprüche" was a godly book. He came to this conclusion because the magic formulas begin with the names of the Trinity.

Ex 108 A pastor known to me went to the magic charmer with his ailment. The result was that psychological disturbances set in. The harmful practice of this particular charmer is known to me from a number of pastoral examples.

Ex 109 I know the director of a large deaconesses' motherhouse who intersperses what she says with superstitious expressions. For example, when she is asked, "How are you?", she will reply, "Very well, thank you, touch wood!" Often she will strike the table three times an say "Toi, toi, toi" ("Toi" is in German an abbreviation for the devil). How can we reconcile Christian office with such superstitions?

Ex 110 At a large conference of pastors a magic conjurer was characterized as a genuine and godly man. I have known his harmful occult practices as a cattle-charmer, sickness-charmer, fire-charmer, clairvoyant and diviner for twenty years. I protested against this praise. Eight days later the pastor of the place where this very conjurer lived told me of a wholly new incident which again substantiated my protest.

Ex 111 A farmer's wife in the Black Forest once said to me, "Pastor, I am engaged in a calling like yours. You begin your services with the Three Highest Names, and I lay my hands on the cattle, pronounce the Three Highest Names, add a powerful spell, and the cattle recover."

Ex 112 In my pastoral work in Switzerland, I often came across stories of three Solothurn monks who practise white magic. Their advice is sought from near and far.

Ex 113 A woman belonging to a fellowship group had an organic ailment for years. Finally she went to a charmer. Organically she was relieved, but after the magic conjuration an emotional disorder set in. She had the persistent urge to injure herself. Stubborn compulsion of thought developed, and finally this poor Christian woman hanged herself.

Ex 114 Prof. Brauchle writes[283] that the cure of warts by suggestion is successfully practised among the people by shepherds and wise women, who use suggestion in disguise. The suggestion in disguise of which Prof. Brauchle speaks is nothing other than magic. I know of many kinds of magical cure for warts. These have nothing in common with the suggestive method of the psycho-somatic school.

If Prof. Brauchle knew what mental changes and conflicts result from magic charming, he as a doctor would not speak with such praise of this occult practice. These shepherds and wise women who practice such magic charms are, along with the conditions of our times, a decisive factor in the origin and growth of the epidemic of neuroses. We have added this example because it shows that both pastors and doctors know very little about the harmful sphere of magic, for otherwise we should not have this minimization and even leading of people astray because of the religious disguise worn by this magic practice.

This is only a small selection of cases which give proof on the one hand of the ignorance caused in this field by rationalism, and on the other of the cunning camouflaging of magic by the use of Christian symbols and customs. On this last point, we can see here a process at work which we know already from the history of Israel. The brazen serpent (Num. 21, 8) was given as a sign of deliverance for Israel, and prefigured the lifting up of Christ on the cross (John 3, 14). But this symbol was emptied of its real content. It became an idol. Hezekiah had to destroy this "Nehushtan", because the people were committing, idolatry with it. And so there are in the field of magic plenty of Christian symbols which have become a "Nehushtan" to the New Testament Church. The time has come for this age-old and yet very up-to-date idol cult to be exposed.

Thesis 2:

In view of the systematically observed frequency ratio between occult involvement and psychological disturbances, we may make a diagnostic evaluation of the data, viz. that to accept as coincidental the concurrence of the two groups of phenomena does not exhaust the deeper connexions which exist between them.

[283] cf. Brauchle, op. cit. [43], pp. 55f.

PART III

A Critical Assessment of the Cases

Chapter One

AN ATTEMPT AT METHODICAL ELIMINATION OF THE CAUSES OF ERROR IN COLLECTING THE MATERIAL

The first task in making a critical assessment of these pastoral cases is to investigate the reliability and authenticity of the material presented. The objective search for truth, with avoidance as much as possible of sources of error, must be a main concern. Hence we shall in the following section look for the sources of error in the statements of those who were interviewed; sources of error on the part of the pastor; and finally sources of error in the method of investigation.

1. We have already shown, in the section regarding our system of presenting the examples, how a counselling session with a person involved in occultism is conducted. In the reports of those counselled, the pastor must constantly make sure whether the person reporting his experiences is sober in his attitude and capable of sound judgement. Has what is being described been observed by others as objective fact, or is it a matter of purely subjective impressions? Is the person inclined to bragging, or loquacious over-statement and exaggeration of what he says? Is his judgement affected perhaps by emotional, nervous or mental disorders? Are his statements fabrications? Are there unverified conclusions, a jump from temporal coincidence to assumed causality? With regard to all these questions we have tried to establish the reliability of the statements, e. g. by checking with a psychiatrist, where one has been consulted in the case,[284] or by asking the questions again in a different way, or repeating the investigation when the person is in a different

---

[284] Naturally the psychiatrist may not violate his professional duty of silence. All that is needed is his statement that the patient is capable of giving correct information.

mood.[285] As an example of this last point we may mention an interview with a pregnant mother.

Ex 115   During pregnancy a young woman had a spook apparition. For several months she experienced the noise of milk-cans being dragged over the floor of the neighbouring dairy as an attack of evil spirits that wanted to rush on her and destroy her. Several pastoral interviews failed to disclose anything significant from either the medical or the psychical point of view, which might have explained the acoustic and tactile experiences of these spook phenomena. There was only the suspicion that physical and emotional changes caused by pregnancy were at the root of this unusual depressive condition accompanied by spook experiences. This supposition proved true. After the child had been born, a new pastoral conversation revealed that all the spook phenomena had disappeared and that her emotional equilibrium was restored exactly as it was before the pregnancy. The noise of the milk-cans no longer bothered her in the least. Here it would have been a fatal pastoral error to have assumed occult roots behind the spook apparitions.

From the psychiatric point of view, this case must be interpreted as illusion. Sense stimuli reach the sense organs, but are interpreted wrongly or inverted. Illusions are encouraged especially through affective states such as expectation, fear or physical exhaustion — in this case through the physical and emotional effects of pregnancy.[286]

2. The sources of error in the pastor himself are no less possible or numerous. For an exact and empirical study and evaluation of such data, we cannot be content with cases which rest on hearsay. That is the great weakness of Schmeïng's study,[287] which though it embraces as many as 5,000 cases, only has a very few cases at first hand. He writes, "Examples from first hand are very scarce". In the case of one prevision, for instance, he was able to establish fourteen different versions. These variant reports cannot be given any more weight than a travel saga, which can only offer a vague basis for an exact study. In distinction from Schmeïng's method, we have in this study used only first-hand material, in order from the first to cut down to a minimum the range

---

[285] Schlink proceeded in the same manner in confirming the truth of the information given. It was a confirmation of the correctness of our procedure to establish post factum that this psychologist and pastor adopted the same method. cf. E. Schlink, "Persönlichkeitsänderung in Bekehrungen und Depressionen": Inaugural Address Marburg, 1929, p. 84.

[286] cf. Dr. K. Jaspersen: "Lehrbuch der Geistes- und Nervenkrankenpflege", Bethel Verlag, 3rd. edn., p. 6.

[287] cf. Weizsäcker, op. cit. 4, pp. 50f.

of possible sources of error. The evidential value of a first-hand experience is rather different from that of a rumour in fourteen versions.

The next possibility of error on the part of the pastor lies in his use of leading questions. Oesterreich in his book[288] gives us an example of demon visions and personality disturbances which resulted from a pastor's suggestion of the idea of demon possession. Suggestive questions that are carefully aimed usually produce the desired results. A further source of error is the self-deception of a pastor who himself has a strong belief in demons. Even exact research is always influenced by the corresponding a priori attitude of the researcher. The Roman proverb is proved right even today: "*Quae volumus ea credimus libenter*. This proverb could well be reworded to say: *Quae credimus ea demonstrare libenter possumus*", i.e. "what we believe we are easily able to prove".

A weighty argument in the critical analysis of pastoral cases is the question whether it is not merely a certain section of those involved in occult things who come to the pastor for help, so that the pastor again becomes the victim of self-deception. We must consider this objection. It is of course a fact that in pastoral work only those cases of occult subjection appear which are accompanied by psychological disturbances. Indeed, these cases are often severe. This is because things have to reach a desperate state before the person concerned overcomes his sense of shame before the pastor. In general mentally ill people find it easier to go to a psychotherapist than to a pastor. Hence the pastor is usually confronted with cases which are by no means mild. This fact can lead to an overemphasis on the connexion between occult subjection and mental-religious disturbances.

The establishing of the actual selection of cases will therefore justify the question whether there are not persons involved in occult activities who experience *no* psychological or spiritual ill-effects as a consequence. Fifteen years of evangelistic experience have given me the following insights on this question:

(a) It is only a small percentage of those occultly subjected who desire pastoral care. The majority of these people know nothing of the causes of their psychological disturbances.

(b) There are in fact some people whose psychological constitution is so stable that it can weather a process of dissociation of their subconscious. At least, so it appears. They do not however escape the religious fact that for their transgression of the second and third commandments they stand under the judgment of God.

288 cf. T. K. Oesterreich, op. cit. 63, p. 95.

(c) Such occult practitioners are also of the opinion that their occult activity has had no effect on them. But the counsellor who takes the trouble to enquire from neighbours, relations, the local pastor, etc. often comes to learn the significant fact that such people at one time were regular or at least frequent attenders at church services, but have gradually become unfaithful to this good habit. The symptom of un-obtrusive resistance is typical of the insidious progress of occult enslave-ment. This silent resistance immediately becomes acute when such a person's conscience is touched and he desires to turn to Christ. Then suddenly the latent subjection appears, and we have the phenomenon that the involved person was himself unware of his own previous con-dition. If this turning to Christ does not take place, the occult sub-jection remains latent and the person concerned never finds out his real condition. That is the condition which the apostle Paul describes with the words "God gave them up to a base mind".[289] Another apostolic word takes the same line: "They are darkened in their mind, alienated from the life of God".[290] When therefore people claim that occult practice has not harmed them, the truth of the claim has not been tested until the conditions have been fulfilled.

3. Sources of error must also be limited as much as possible from the method of evaluating the material. The examples were obtained in the course of pastoral interviews sought by people mentally afflicted. Some pastoral interviews consisted first in a spontaneous disclosure by the person seeking help; then, in a loose form of question and answer; and finally in a careful invesigation using the classified anamnesis already mentioned. To make sure of the reliability of the disclosures, informa-tion was obtained from relatives or friends, and occasionally from a doctor. Above all notes, and especially letters, were evaluated. Thus, in the case of one girl who had come for several interviews without any light being shed on her condition, her bizarre handwriting, typical of schizophrenia, led me to suspect in the first instance a psychosis. In a few cases, where no damage whatever could result either for the pastoral assignment, or for the subject of the test, or for the conductor of the tests, a simple experiment was conducted, although in other cases I would from religious and pastoral considerations reject experimentation.

Ex 116   In the section on rod and pendulum we have already re-ported how a dowser was brought in to check on the results of a colleague, without either of them knowing of the experiment. The

[289] cf. Rom 1, 28.
[290] Eph. 4, 18.

conditions of the test were such that no deception or connivance was possible. The results tallied.

Ex 117 At another time I checked the ability of a pendulum manipulator, who was convinced of the reliability of his practice. Three different lots of six medicines, i. e. 18 medicines in all, were done up in similar white paper packets. The man explained that circular movement of the pendulum would mean that the medicines were beneficial to him; straight movement back and forth would mean not beneficial; and rest would indicate neutrality. The man held his pendulum twice over the eighteen medicines. The result was completely negative. Twice gynergen (for expectant mothers) was indicated as beneficial to him, and the third time the opposite was indicated. So it was with coramin, rheumasan, cibazol, ichthyolan and dextropur. No consistent pattern emerged at all. Thus the test did nothing at all to convince me of the competence of the practitioner. Psychologically, perhaps, the failure of the tests may be put down to the fact that the practitioner — they are usually very sensitive people — could sense my scepticism, and that this unnerved him.

Another methodological consideration is the question whether 600 spontaneous cases of occult subjection are a sufficient ground for the building up of a thesis. When one thinks of the 300,000 or 400,000 experiments of Rhine, or Schmeïng's 5,000 examples, or the extensive material in Oesterreich's work on demon possession, then it may seem rather rash to base an argument on 600 examples. Yet we must not let ourselves be impressed by quantity alone.[291a] A comparison with Schmeïng has already been made. In Rhine's innumerable tests only extremely small energies appear, which when compared with the psychokinetic phenomena of spontaneous occurrences are in about the same proportion as that of a fire-cracker to a demolition bomb. Rhine himself suggests such a comparison. Furthermore, Rhine's experiments cannot be used for purposes of comparison, since he studies psycho-kinetic phenomena in an exact, scientific manner in persons who are not at all involved in occultism. Rhine is thus working in an entirely different area. Of the variegated material of Oesterreich we may say "that the strictly empirical procedure conducted on living persons"[291b] is fully justified over against the descriptive analytical method of Oesterreich, since, in these practical methods with living persons, every possibility is given for an intensive, detailed examination of the psychological processes that

291a Meanwhile I have some thousands, to date nearly 10,000 examples — *addendum in American edition.*
291b cf. Schlink, op. cit. [285], p. 85.

are under consideration. This practical conduct of research differs from experimental methods in the strict sense, such as those of Rhine or Schrenck-Notzing, which are not possible here with the continually changing complexity and variety of experiential situations. And furthermore the strictly experimental method cannot come into consideration here at all, since pastoral care is not the place for experimentation but for giving help. On all of these grounds, the use of the spontaneous occurrences retains its justification, cogency and value, as a basis from which to conduct methodical research. All questions regarding the manner of gathering materials may be summarized, in the words of Schlink,[292] as the method of directed personal observation.

We cannot close this section on possible sources of error without pointing to the necessity of complete truthfulness in the presentation of cases. The backbone of every method is the truthfulness of the data and the readiness of the researcher to submit to objective fact, even when he sees his own theories refuted. Gulat-Wellenburg[293] says on this, in his chapter on method, that "when a goal has become especially prized by someone, and has become dear to his heart; when he has permitted a hope regarding some problem, which he has cherished through long years, to become a part of himself; then everything that would render illusory his hope of attaining his goal is instinctively dismissed. The researcher pursues a theory which he has constructed on a priori grounds; he attempts to support it and prove it by experiments. If the facts which emerge from the experiment contradict his theory, then he sets these facts aside or unconsciously re-interprets them." What we have in section 2 above called the a priori attitude is substantiated in psychological terms by these words of Gulat-Wellenburg. It is for the researcher, in his reporting of the material in this study, likewise a question of truthfulness and conscience not to dress and construct the reported cases according to some preconceived goal of research, but to search objectively for the truth content of the material. The method of our research must be an *ars derivandi* from the simple facts, not an *ars demonstrandi* of fixed opinions on the part of the investigator.

Chapter Two

OCCULT SUBJECTION IN THE LIGHT OF PSYCHIATRY

In the critical assessment of the cases in this book, the judgment of the psychiatrist has an important part to play. The first thing the

---

292 ibid. loc. cit.
293 cf. Gulat-Wellenburg, "Grundlagen des physikalischen Mediumismus", Verlag Ullstein, Berlin, 1925, p. 17 (Documents of Occultism, ed. Max Dessoir).

psychiatrist will tell us is, probably, that for him there is no such thing as occult subjection. For our study this assertion causes no dilemma. We have already explained that by this term we are indicating a theological, pastoral category, although this certainly has, because of the psychological disturbances involved, strong contacts with medical and psychological science. We shall now subject to scrutiny, from a medical, and more particularly psychiatric, viewpoint, those psychological disturbances which are observed in occult involvement.

In this attempt, a few limits must be set, to avoid discussions which would take us outside the range of our study. Firstly, we cannot take into comparison the whole complex of psychological disorders, but only the main symptoms. Further, we can in this comparison only treat that group of questions concerning psychological disorders which is of interest for our study. Thirdly, a person who is not a medical specialist may perhaps be pardoned if he does not present all the findings in the correct professional terminology. The comparison will be centred around three relations: *conformity, divergence,* and *contrast* between the psychological disturbances of occult subjection and the corresponding disease-patterns known to medicine.

1. *Conformity*

Limiting our study as explained above, we shall now take four phenomena for quick comparison: hallucinations, depressions, compulsive thoughts and paroxysmal conditions.

(a) *Hallucinations*

Psychiatry knows the phenomenon of hallucinations as disturbances of sensation and of perception[294] in connexion with the following diseases: hyperthyroidism (e. g. exophthalmic goitre[295]); fever delirium due to infections diseases; head injuries; lesions of the sense organs; toxicoses; cerebral diseases (e. g. encephalitis[296]); intoxication psychoses[297]; schizophrenia,[298] etc.

According to the five senses, hallucinations may be classified as visual, auditory, gustatory, olfactory and tactile.[299] In contrast to illusions, which are merely faulty interpretation and mis-reading of sense perceptions,[300] hallucinations are perceptions without any external stimuli.

294 cf. Bleuler, op. cit. 129, pp. 30f.
295 cf. Brugsch, op. cit. 10, vol. I p. 110.
296 cf. Kloos, op. cit. 12, p. 259.
297 cf. Bleuler, op. cit. 129, p. 36; Kloos op. cit. 12, p. 379.
298 cf. Kloos, op. cit. 12, p. 401.
299 cf. Jaspersen, op. cit. 286, p. 7.
300 cf. Bleuler, op. cit. 129, p. 32.

According to their content Bleuler classifies them as follows: teleological, sexual, kinaesthetic; and further, stimulated, reflex, relaxing and de-inhibiting hallucinations.

As the result of occult involvement we find, according to our summary of the frequency ratios, that magic charmers and those charmed reveal a general clairvoyance; blood pacts and agreements with the devil result in spirit apparitions;[301] frequent participation in séances or consultation of occult diviners is followed by the observation of spook phenomena. The hallucinations in both fields, psychiatric and occult, show great conformity, although the expert will discern a shade of difference in the characteristics.

(b) *Depressions*

Internal medicine and psychiatry know of many diseases which bring depressions in their train: e. g. hyperthyroidism (idiopathic myxo-edema[302]); sometimes jaundice; vascular ailments (arteriosclerosis[303]); heart diseases (cardiac asthma, paroxysmal tachycardia, myocarditis[304]); and organic brain diseases. Depressions may also have psychogenic causes, e. g. in reactive depression due to dissatisfaction with circum-stances,[306] or psychological reactions to puberty, menstruation, preg-nancy and change of life. Pronounced depressions are the typical symptoms of manic-depressive psychoses.[307]

Depressions are observed following every kind of occult activity apart from spontaneous telepathy, predictive dreams, dowsing which is limited to the physical sphere, and one form of clairvoyance. When the pastor discovers depressions, he should first ascertain the medical findings, before he proceeds to an anamnesis of occult involvement.

(c) *Compulsive thoughts and delusions*

The phenomenon of compulsive thoughts and delusions is found with idiopathic myxoedema,[308] with myelo-encephalitis,[309] with toxicoses, head injuries, tumours, with compulsive neuroses,[310] and with psychoses (schizophrenia, manic-depressive psychosis[311]).

---

[301] The spirit-visions of wellknown men of God like Blumhardt, Oberlin, M. Hauser and others probably had spiritual rather than occult roots.

[302] cf. Brugsch, op. cit. [10], vol. I p. 118.

[303] ibid., p. 624.

[304] ibid., pp. 523, 557, 574.

[306] ibid., p. 440.

[307] ibid., p. 416.

[308] cf. Brugsch, op. cit. [10], vol. I p. 117.

[309] ibid., p. 378.

[310] cf. Kloos, op. cit. [12], p. 429.

[311] ibid., pp. 410, 420.

Compulsive images and ideas are recognized by the patient to be untrue. Delusions are incorrigible as long as the condition which gave rise to them persists.[312]

In the pastoral care of people subjected to occultism we find, besides the psychiatric phenomena, compulsive ideas like fear of mistakes, scruples, compulsions to make vows, to conversion, to confession, to reparation, to doubt and, above all, to blasphemy.[313] Dr. Lechler, Dr. Bovet and Prof. Brauchle evaluate the phenomenon of compulsion to blasphemy as a symptom of compulsion neurosis.[314] Dr. Lechler admits, in the case of the blasphemous compulsion of an emotionally stable person, the further possibility of a demonic enslavement.[315]

In the pastoral care of those enslaved by occultism, there appears a frequency ratio of compulsive ideas particularly in active or passive participants in occult activities whose subconscious has been activated and mobilized in a special way. If for a moment we bring to mind the schematic pattern of the circulus relationis psycho-organicae, we may say that compulsive thoughts arise especially as a result of processes which run their course in the two lower quadrants of the circle: subconscious — organic unconscious — subconscious. This can be regarded as an indication that compulsive thoughts arise where the subconscious gives strong impulses to the conscious mind with which the latter cannot cope. It is a remarkable fact that in all the cases of blasphemy against divine things which I have known in pastoral counselling, there was a background of occult activity. Dr. Bovet found frequently in such cases a tendency to masochism.

(d) Paroxysmal conditions

The medical profession knows many forms of fits and paroxysmal conditions, such as genuine epilepsy,[316] psychogenic (hysterical) epilepsy,[317] epileptiform convulsions in idiopathic myxoedema,[318] convulsions due to birth trauma,[319] alterations in the blood calcium (tetany[320]),

[312] cf. Bleuler, op. cit. [129], p. 49.
[313] cf. Lechler, op. cit. [8], pp. 31f.
[314] cf. Bovet, op. cit. [171], p. 159; Brauchle, op. cit. [42], p. 45; Lechler, op. cit. [8], p. 45.
[315] cf. Lechler, op. cit. [272b], p. 12.
[316] cf. Jaspersen, op. cit. [286], p. 40.
[317] cf. Kloos, op. cit. [12], p. 26.
[318] cf. Brugsch, op. cit. [10], vol. I p. 117.
[319] cf. Kloos, op. cit. [12], p. 22.
[320] cf. Brugsch, op. cit. [10], vol I p. 121.

pycnolepsy,[321] a form of chorea,[322] epileptiform convulsions with whooping cough,[323] and with epidemic encephalitis,[324] lapses of consciousness without convulsion or collapse,[325] minor attacks in the form of rudimenary convulsions,[326] etc. We shall give an example of hysterical epilepsy:

Ex 118   A girl well known to me had epileptic fits which arose from the fear that she would have to face life without a husband. The spells only came when there was a young man near who could catch her when she collapsed. The distance was always well calculated. The psychiatrist, whom I knew, saw through these well-planned attacks at once.

In the pastoral care of those occultly subjected we find cataleptic seizure in visionaries, and also fits of mania with destructive compulsions in full consciousness, in the form of uncontrolled affective outbursts of rage. In addition we have the artificially induced dissociation phenomena of occult practitioners. Tischner gives us a good example of this last point.[327] An automatic writer, as mentioned in *Ex 3*, suddenly began in a coffee-house to drum with her fingers on the table, as a signal that she was about to start some automatic writing. This act, which happened at an inconvenient time, shows how the consciousness at this moment of attack could not master the impulses it received from the subconscious. Further, I also once observed a flood of blasphemy from a conjured person at the very moment when a little group was praying for him. The experience with this man had the nature of a psychological surprise attack.

In the comparison of psychological disturbances due to occult subjection with corresponding patterns in ailments known to medicine, there appears in many cases, and especially in cases of depressions and compulsive thoughts, a definite similarity of tendency in the symptoms. This similarity obligates every counsellor, who finds himself faced with victims of occultism, to take pains to procure a medical diagnosis from a specialist, if he himself is not schooled in the basic medical questions in this field.

2. *Divergence from Psychiatric Patterns*

The conformity we have just noted is not unequivocal, even in the case of the four ailments we have discussed, particularly in cases of

---

321 cf. Kloos, op. cit. **12**, p. 373.
322 ibid., p. 263.
323 cf. Brugsch, op. cit. **10**, vol. I p. 353.
324 ibid., p. 378.
325 cf. Kloos, op. cit. **12**, p. 363.
326 ibid., p. 362.
327 cf. Tischner, op. cit. **25a**, p. 43.

hallucination and fits. Distinctive peculiarities are to be observed in the details. The main argument which shows the difference between the psychological disturbances of those occultly subjected and the corresponding psychiatric ailments is the fact that the occult phenomena, with all their consequences, are experienced by persons who are otherwise normal emotionally and mentally. Well-known researchers such as the psychologists Prof. Bender, Dr. Schmeïng and W. Prince repeatedly observe this fact. It is especially in the phenomenon of depersonalization that we can see this fundamental difference readily. In psychiatry depersonalization is a subjective, pathological disturbance of the personality, an experience of alienation which appears in mental illnesses (schizophrenia, melancholia) and in asthenic psychopaths.[328] In parapsychology there are various correlative concepts like psychic disintegration, dissociation, splitting of consciousness, etc. In psychiatry we are dealing here with a disease process; in para-psychology dissociation means an unusual psychic ability in healthy people. In psychiatry the disturbed ego is the object of these processes; in parapsychology the healthy ego is the subject of the dissociation, or in spontaneous cases both subject and object.

Bender in his dissertation[329] takes account of this fact by using the term "dissociation artifacts". He too describes his subjects in this field as being in a clinical sense completely healthy. And he further states that these productions are not a pathological symptom.[330]

Dr. Schmeïng is likewise concerned to distinguish predictive visions from the hallucinations of the schizophrenic. He writes: "Those who see predictive visions are not schizophrenics; they are fully able to cope with reality, and often lead successful and normal lives".[331] Prince, the psychologist, is likewise very concerned to distinguish the dissociation phenomena observed in test-persons from mental illnesses. He writes[332] of a certain medium: "Doris Fischer is a living refutation of the view that mediumship, even though it may involve a kind of splitting of the ego, is in itself pathological". Prof. Oesterreich has since his researches also advocated the view that the dissociation phenomena of schizophrenia and of mediumship are different in nature.[333]

[328] cf. Kloos, op. cit. [12], pp. 164, 408, 419, 430.
[329] cf. Bender, op. cit. [3], p. V.
[330] ibid., pp. 39, 57.
[331] cf. Schmeïng, op. cit. [30], p. 121.
[332] cf. M. and W. Prince, "Die Spaltung der Persönlichkeit", Verlag Kohlhammer, Stuttgart, 1932, pp. 154f.
[333] ibid., p. 252.

The results of the investigations of these three or four psychologists agree with my own observations on this point, that para-psychological phenomena, including their effects, are to be distinguished from psychiatric disease patterns.

3. *Contrast with Psychiatric Patterns*

Psychological disorders with different causes require different diagnosis and therefore different therapy. With this medical platitude we can state the contrast between psychological disturbances conditioned by occultism and parallel disturbances in the psychiatric disease patterns. First, we will demonstrate this contrast in the case of the simple psychiatric phenomenon of induced insanity.[334] The person who has an induced psychological disorder takes over the delusions of a mentally ill person in his proximity. Therapy consists simply in isolating the originally afflicted person from the one with an induced disorder. This isolation usually leads to the rapid cure of the "infected" person. So-called occult transference presents a different problem. We may agree to exclude here what Dr. Lechler has said about the alleged transference of demons.[335] In *Ex 102* and *Ex 103* we have given cases of occult transference. Intercession for the mentally disordered person was the means whereby the intercessor himself became affected, while the patient recovered. In such cases isolation does not help. In *Ex 103* the intercessor was in any case isolated from the patient. Here the contrast is clear. With an induced insanity, there is no recovery of the person who is ill, but there is recovery of the infected one after isolation. In the case of occult transference, the person who is mentally ill may recover, while the infected person remains ill, even after isolation, until competent pastoral advice has been given. It thus becomes plain that from the difference in consequences, different causes may be concluded. This will be confirmed by a further aspect.

In medicine there is an inviolable law: "The gods ordained diagnosis before therapy"[336] No one would think of overthrowing this principle. Yet there are cases of psychological disorders where diagnosis is only possible in the light of the therapy. Mental illnesses are usually more difficult to diagnose than organic diseases. In many disorders which are hard to diagnose, it is permissible to try therapeutic probing. When, for

---

[334] cf. Kloos, op. cit. 12, p. 450.

[335] cf. Lechler, loc. cit. 281.

[336] This is the title of the memorial volume for the late Prof. Dr. Volhard. Verlag Deutsche Hoffmann La Roche AG, Grenzach, Baden.

instance, a cure is achieved by shock or convulsive treatment (insulin, cardiazol, brufalgin, azoman, E.C.T.),[337] then it is not a case of occult subjection or what Lechler calls demonic enslavement. But when, on the contrary, a pastoral interview, with thorough confession, renunciation and a trusting appropriation of salvation, leads to a wonderful liberation, then it was a case of occult subjection. We can thus make a diagnosis from the result of therapy. At the same time there becomes visible a contrast between the two fields. It is worthy of note that Dr. Lechler, the well-known psychiatrist, follows the same procedure in order to differentiate the phenomena of the varying levels.[338]

These briefly sketched relations of conformity, divergence and contrast between psychological disturbances in the field of occultism and in the field of psychiatry make clear the relative independence of the two areas. Since in nearly all cases there is some overlapping of the problems, correct therapy is dependent upon the decision of two specialists, the psychiatrist and the Christian counsellor.

Chapter Three

OCCULT PHENOMENA IN THE LIGHT OF PSYCHOLOGY

In our introduction we have set forth the material principle of this study, which states that we must use every scientific means in our effort to clarify the occult phenomena. In pursuit of this principle we must, having confronted occult involvement with the results of psychiatry, further study the occult manifestations on the level of psychology. We shall do this by making a critical comparison of three main phenomena, as they are viewed by well-known psychologists, with the results of our own investigation. We shall consider the gift of "second sight", as investigated by Dr. Schmeïng,[339] the phenomenon of possession, as investigated by the philosophy professor Oesterreich,[340] and the problem of the split personality, as investigated by the neurologist M. Prince and the psychologist W. Prince.[341]

337 cf. Jaspersen, op. cit. 286, p. 81.
338 cf. Lechler, op. cit. 227a, p. 7.
339 cf. Schmeïng, op. cit. 30.
340 cf. Oesterreich, op. cit. 63.
341 cf. M. and W. Prince, op. cit. 332.

1. *Schmeïng's Study of Folklore, as it applies to "Second Sight"*

In connexion with *Ex 19* and *Ex 25*, we have already spoken of the theory of eidetic developed by Prof. Jaensch.[342] Dr. Schmeïng took up this theory and applied it to an evaluation of the gift of "second sight", which is very widespread in North Germany. First we shall point out in summary form the eidetic theory, and then we shall consider its significance for our study.

(a) Eidetic is a capability inborn in man, whereby objects once registered can be seen again after the light-source is cut off or the object removed, as "after-images" or "intuitive images", in an external optic appearance before one. This kind of eidetic vision is a form of perception generally found in childhood, which normally disappears with the beginning of puberty. This eidetic tendency may be retained to an advanced age in some persons: in artists, highly sensitive people, or in cases of late maturity due to inheritance or environment. Many clairvoyant phenomena can thus be explained on an eidetic basis as after-visions.

The explanation of prevision is more difficult. Schmeïng thinks that people with eidetic gifts have a subconscious intuition, a teleological depth-vision. On the basis of this ability they would then be able, by means of a "mental snapshot",[343] to see as present before them the end of the development in a prevision, through combination of the data at one glance. Those who have previsions usually have a highly developed logical faculty for thinking and empathy. In this explanation of "after vision" and "prevision" Schmeïng insists that they are purely subjective experiences, excluding all metaphysical and metapsychical presuppositions. He admits, however, the existence of an unexplainable residue in the future reference of prevision.

(b) After this brief introductory sketch, we must extricate the positive value of Schmeïng's research. First we must establish that theology has no need to fear the eidetic theory in regard to biblical prophecy. Anti-Christian and atheistic critics will, it is true, adopt the position that it is now even easier for them to bring biblical prophecy and the religious visions of the bible down to a rationalistic common denominator. Thereby every religious vision would be reduced to a natural, subjective occurrence, and unmasked as a delusion. This assault will in no way trouble theology. God has the power, and the habit, of making use of man's spirit, soul and body in His revelations to man. Is the Creator not per-

---

[342] cf. E. R. Jaensch, "Neue Wege der menschlichen Lichtbiologie", Leipzig, 1933.
[343] cf. Schmeïng, op. cit. p. 143.

mitted to use the natural ordinances which He himself has created?[344]
He can make use of eidetic capabilities, too, in order to get through to
man. Schmeïng has by means of his researches unwittingly come upon a
further mode of revelation, if we re-cast and develop further his work
in a theological form.

Schmeïng's research is of much greater significance for pastoral work.
An evangelist is often during Bible Weeks much afflicted by people who
come to him and want to relate their religious dreams and pious visions.
It is, to be sure, a thankless task, but nonetheless an absolutely essential
one, to demolish these pious illusions and to nurture people into a sober
faith in God's word. In this struggle against a false mysticism, against
religious emotionalism, and against spiritual arrogance, Schmeïng has
delivered a scientific blow. He writes:[345] "It is evident that a great
number of religious manifestations can be explained on a basis of eidetic
or synaesthesia." In this category we must place especially those present-
day appearances of Mary, of Christ, of angels and of saints which flood
in like an epidemic. Even to a Christian worker who is not familiar
with the laws of eidetic, these appear to be results of suggestive, psychic,
subconscious happenings. Naturally it must be admitted that in this
present-day psychosis of visions, there is, among all the mass of chaff,
an occasional good kernel of wheat to be found. The Creator has not
forgotten how to speak. The possibility must certainly be taken into
account that the believer can also receive genuine revelations.

(c) The most dangerous feature of Schmeïng's approach, from the
point of view of the theologian, is the harmless coupling together of
eidetic and magic. We must take into account, of course, the fact that
Schmeïng is writing a psychological study of folk-lore. The theological
connexions which are very dominant in the field of his investigations
lie outside the scope of this study. However, this does not make it
undesirable to subject his conclusions to critical examination from a
theological and pastoral point of view. In no less than 63 places in his
study,[346] the phenomenon of eidetic is found in typical conjunction with
magic practices. The characteristic marks of occult involvement appear
in the eidetic material presented by Schmeïng, as we shall now show.

[344] cf. Johannes Rickers, "Profane Prophetie", article in the Deutsches Pfarrerblatt
1950, pp. 389—425.
[345] cf. Schmeïng, op. cit. [30], p. 161.
[346] ibid., pp. VI, 4, 6, 8, 9, 10, 14, 15, 17, 31, 34, 40, 47, 57, 59, 60, 63, 64, 65,
66, 67, 68, 71, 72, 73, 75, 76, 77, 80, 81, 83, 84, 87, 88, 90, 95, 100, 101, 102, 103,
112, 113, 114, 116, 121, 122, 123, 124, 125, 128, 137, 148, 157, 159, 161, 162, 163, 166,
176, 178, 179, 181, 186.

Depressions. Schmeïng reports (p. 4) that the majority of his examples of prevision contain dark, depressive motifs. He also knows of a combination of eidetic tendencies with melancholia (p. 124). It is worth observing that in the North German area prevision is known as Quadkieken (= "woe-seeing") (p. 17). So strong is this one-sided limitation to dark motifs such as fire, death, accidents, wars, catastrophes, etc. (pp. 49, 116), that this is repeatedly emphasized by Schmeïng. Also the fear reactions and depressive feelings which many visionaries experience immediately after their visions fit into this pattern. We must hold fast to these facts, since we know from our own investigation that depressions are primary consequences of occult involvement.

Nightmares. The phenomenon of nightmares, which appears after spiritist séances or conjuration, also appears in people of eidetic vision. Schmeïng reports of his case no. 4: "From his youth he has dreamed vividly, and at full moon he has nightmares" (p. 34). The same diagnosis is found in case 13 (p. 37): "He had nightmares, and once saw the form of a lion above him, and awoke covered in perspiration". A further characteristic is the increase of visions or the experience of psychological disturbances at full moon. In case 12a Schmeïng describes the appearance of a vision in clear moonlight (p. 71). Here we should mention also a quotation from Annette von Droste-Hülshoff: "His gift asserts itself at any time of day, but is most prevalent on moonlit nights." (p. 114). Nightmares and visions on brightly moonlit nights are a primary effect in persons who have been charmed in their childhood against diseases on the night of a full moon. Since these same marks appear in persons with eidetic vision, we again see a bright spotlight thrown on the relation between eidetic and conjuration.

Tapping sounds and voices. The hearing of these is a further symptom belonging to the pattern both of eidetic and of occult subjection. Schmeïng's case 12b (p. 72) "hears voices and rustlings, as when a bale of straw is dragged across the floor". Case 13 "plainly hears the voice of his brother and the song of angels" (p. 73). Case 14 (p. 76) "hears voices and continually has the feeling that Christ is with her". Case 18 (p. 83) heard voices when he was a student. Case 15 (p. 77) "hears knockings and hands rubbing on the wall". Case 28 (p. 148) hears tapping on the door although no one is there.

We have no wish to contradict Schmeïng's theory, according to which acoustic manifestations are to be explained as synaesthesia. But when we have explained the process we have still said nothing of the origin of eidetic and synaesthesia. There is at least a significant parallelism between these acoustic symptoms and the occult effects of magic involvement.

Dreams and light appearances. A further characteristic in the eidetic ladder is the occurrence from early youth of vivid dreams and appearances of light. Of case 4 Schmeïng writes (p. 34): "From his youth he has dreamed vividly". He writes further (p. 88): "From the cases reported we find that the first visions of the seers often occurred in their childhood" (cases 7, 8, 10, 18, 21, 33). The beginning of the appearances is, according to many reports, fixed as early as the age of four years. (p. 90). In case 8 manifestations of light began at the age of 12 (p. 63). Case 18 had seen coloured circles and visions since he was four. At first it seems that these appearances of light, which occur in early childhood, contradict the hypothesis that we have here likewise the effects of occult subjection. But Schmeïng has himself given us material which invalidates this criticism. For in the case just mentioned (no. 4) it is stated that the father of this child was a charmer. He charmed and cured ailments. In such a case it is to be assumed that his own children too would be charmed for any illness they might have. If this point cannot be demonstrated in case 4, the last doubt vanishes when the further development of the eidetic and occult abilities of this visionary is examined. The above-mentioned manifestations of light occurred from the fourth year onward; later, as a student, he had acoustic manifestations; and finally he developed an ability for magnetic healing. The conclusion from effect to cause indicates that this visionary was already charmed as a very small child, perhaps even as a baby. Plainly the eidetic disposition here had its roots in occult activities.

Spook apparitions and ghosts. The observation of these forms the next group of eidetic phenomena. Schmeïng writes (p. 40): "There are some people with eidetic vision who are able to see without stimuli purely imaginative images such as dwarfs, animals, spooks, religious apparitions, etc." Case 17 (p. 81) could for instance observe various kinds of spook phenomena. Case 18, too, (p. 159) had an abundance of apparitions, mostly of a spookish nature. Case 10 had the ability to see the deceased as ghosts (p. 7). The seeing of ghosts is also elsewhere reported by Schmeïng (p. 155). These two phenomena are similarly found in cases of occult subjection. In many pastoral examples of spirit visions there is involved, in the past, an act of magic conjuration.

Mediumistic abilities. The combination of prevision with these forms the next stage of eidetic abilities. The development of healing magnetism in case 18 (p. 84) has been mentioned already. In cases 16 and 18 telepathic abilities also appeared. Very remarkable here is the affinity to spiritist phenomena. One visionary (case 16, p. 80) has the ability upon concentration to summon any person known to her. Thus she could act as a medium in séances. Another visionary (case 10, p. 66) herself says:

"I could have earned a lot of money among the spiritists as a medium". The characteristic relationship between eidetic and spiritist phenomena also becomes plain in Jaensch's study regarding the structure of the world of perception,[347] in which he explains as eidetic the spiritist phenomena known as "oura", "astral bodies", "odic flame", mystical separation etc. Anschütz[348] also "brings into prominence the relation of synaesthetic apparitions to the corresponding occult experiences" (p. 179). Significantly Anschütz found in occult meetings a surprising number of persons subject to synaesthesia (p. 31).

At this point we might investigate whether it would be right to explain spiritist phenomena as eidetic, or to classify eidetic apparitions among occult phenomena. Yet when this question is considered from the higher plane of the theological, pastoral viewpoint, the important question is seen to be not the priority of psychological or psychical research, but the psychological disorders which attach to this phenomenon and their cure. When we see the problem thus, the experience of pastoral care testifies that both phenomena, both eidetic and occult activity, stand on the same level. If we do actually pose the question of priority here, then the analysis of some hundreds of cases indicates that occult involvement is the cause, and eidetic predisposition is the secondary effect.

The phenomenon of the *excursion of the soul* also makes evident the occult roots of eidetic. The visionary of case 10 (p. 68) was of the opinion that the spirit of man can leave the body and go to distant lands. He had in this manner visited his nephew in Algeria and his son in Australia. Another visionary (p. 159) likewise had dissociation manifestations and the condition of being absent from himself, in which the feeling impressed itself upon him that his spirit was sent out and was absent from the body. Schmeïng would refer such a case of excursion to a splitting of the ego (p. 187), to a division of the consciousness. In such a case the subconscious makes itself independent and is active, and the consciousness assumes the role of a passive observer. We must note also in this case that the dissociation occurs in a very prevalent way in magic conjuration and in spiritist practices.

The combination of eidetic with the process of *enchantment,* magic defence and charming is a very important element from the pastoral point of view. It is in this section that Schmeïng has provided the

[347] cf. E. R. Jaensch, "Über den Aufbau der Wahrnehmungswelt", 2 vols. Leipzig, 1931.
[348] cf. Georg Anschütz, "Das Farbe-Tonproblem im physischen Gesamtbereich", Halle, 1929.

greatest quantity of material. Predictive visions are in many cases associated with magic protection. The prevision of fire is charmed by a magic spell or incantation (p. 157) into a stone, tree, or pond (pp. 6—9) as we have already seen. Here we have the practice of "fire-charming". In a similar way there is also a practice of charming, conjuring, or "witching away" diseases (pp. 9, 101). This is in many cases the harmful conjuration practice of many lay healers, mentioned by Schmeïng in case 14 (p. 76). In this belief in charms, the phenomenon of *transference* appears, which often occurs in connexion with occult practice. Such things as imminent fire, sickness, or even the eidetic ability itself, are transferred. The last fact is attested by Schmeïng (p. 101), as already mentioned in another context, in the case of a rich farmer who in 1933 paid a considerable sum of money to be liberated from the gift of prevision. At this point we see the Achilles' heel of the eidetic theory, viz. eidetic in conjunction with that branch of occult practice which has as the most frequent of its psychological consequences the devepolment of clairvoyant gifts — conjuration. The best example of the combination of clairvoyant and conjurer appears in Schmeïng's book (p. 122). The visionary here acted as a prophet of the future and at the same time as a sickness-charmer. People attributed to him great magic powers, and he was feared in the neighbourhood.

The belief in charms also includes the practice followed by people of eidetic ability, of heeding *special signs* and using *fetishes*. The origin of "second sight" is, according to popular belief, dependent on some special hour of birth, such as midnight at the New Year, Easter, or Christmas. Special destinies attach also to posthumous and premature babies, and to those which relapse to second nursing (p. 11). In many areas the phenomenon of "second sight" is combined with divining from cards, coffee and palmistry (p. 14). The boundary between eidetic and superstitious, magical practices is here completely obscured. Eidetic has an even stronger link with magic in predictive charming, which employs fetishes to ward off threatening woes. We may here mention the fire stone in North Germany and the fire letter in South Germany. As a protective fetish (p. 59) black sheets are used also, which are nailed to the boards of the threshing floor as a protection against predicted deaths. All these magical protection customs have one thing in common: "Man seeks means to become master of his fate (p. 10). For this however higher powers must be enlisted by prayer and by magic." The psychologist could not tell the theologian more plainly what kind of spirit it is which lies behind eidetic. When man tries to dispose over higher powers by means of magic, in order so to become the master of his fate, we many clearly discern the basic bent of occult behaviour.

The development of a magical-religious *vision-psychosis* provides strong evidence for the occult nature of eidetic. What we so often see in our pastoral counselling, namely that persons who have been charmed develop clairvoyance, has been reported by Schmeïng, even though he does not recognize the relationships which here obtain. In case 14 (p. 76) he shows how a woman who had often been charmed by an amateur healer experienced religious and acoustic apparitions, and the feeling that Christ was with her. In case 36 we have a report of the appearance of angelic visions. Further, a boy kept seeing Christ with him, even when he was riding his bicycle through the streets (p. 146). Appearances of the devil also take place through eidetic and synaesthesia, as in case 37 (p. 163).

What Schmeïng here adduces from his collection of material are all examples similar to those which become apparent in pastoral counselling as results of occult involvement or occult subjection. The phenomenon is the same — semper idem! Jaensch and Schmeïng have merely chosen a psychological term for the concept, and being unaware of the theological relations have developed the eidetic theory. They were unaware that magic customs are not just an appendage of folklore, but the very sinew of the thing, the root of eidetic.

The *hereditary transmission* of eidetic ability must also be noted. To omit this would be to miss one of the chief arguments for the close relationship of eidetic with the occult. In cases 7—9 we have four visionaries in three generations of the same family (p. 65). In case 10 (p. 66) there is a similar situation. In cases 12 (p. 72), 15 (p. 76), 18 (p. 83), 21 (p. 102), 28 (p. 148), and 40 (p. 176), we again see transmission through several generations. In this category we may also place the case on p. 112 of the "Atlas der deutschen Volkskunde". If eidetic is actually only the secondary effect of magic charming, as is clear from the overwhelming evidence of many pastoral examples, we should not be surprised at the fact of hereditary transmission. For as we have seen in considering the consequences of occult involvement, the engrams produced by conjuration retain their hereditary coherence as far as the fourth generation. Hence here in this case the factor of heredity becomes evidence for a connexion between eidetic and magic conjuration.

Another argument for the occult character of eidetic is the difference between it and *pathological hallucinations*. Schmeïng sharply distinguishes eidetic abilities from the hallucinations known in psychiatry: "We can say at the outset that in eidetic we are dealing not at all with pathological hallucinations, since both eidetic phenomena and prevision appear in thoroughly healthy people" (p. 47). Further, Schmeïng discusses (p. 121) the hallucinatory effects of schizophrenia, and here comes to exactly the same conclusion, that typical visionaries do not suffer from schizophrenia. For these visionaries are not by any means people who are incapable of coping with normal realities. On the contrary, there are people among them with astounding accomplishments (p. 122) and great mental alertness (p. 124). In this matter eidetic again proves to be the partner of occultism. The point of comparison here is the difference from hallucinatory and visionary phenomena of a psychiatric character.

With regard to *functional disturbances* which result from charms, we can again find material in Schmeïng's book. In case 7 (p. 57) we have a report about a visionary who, besides having apparitions of light and dream visions, also had previsions and at the same time worked magic charms against predicted deaths. This man had a daughter who was deaf and dumb, and he himself saw a prevision that he would suddenly die in an apoplectic fit. We would not mention this instance here, if pastoral experience did not show us many cases where in conjurers' families there is a prevalence of deafmutism, strokes, attacks of mania, etc.

In order now to round off the picture which emerges from these arguments, we mention the place of eidetic in the *history of religion*. Schmeïng in fact lets the cat out of the bag when he writes (p. 15): "Near the southern border of the prevision area, visionaries are in danger of conflict with the civil authorities. On the North Frisian Islands, which were Christianized late and have retained many *ancient* (sc. pagan) *beliefs*, this would be most unlikely and would not be understood by the general population". Hence the prevalence of visionary occurrences among the Frisians has its roots in the fact that of all the German tribes the Frisians remained pagan the longest. Here the psychologist concedes in passing that it is against a background of paganism, which in its basic tendencies means magic customs, that we find also the greatest prevalence of eidetic ability.

He corroborates this indirectly a second time when (p. 14) he writes that, strangely enough, in Swabia, the land of the visionary woman of Prevorst, and of the Blumhardts, there are really very few visionaries. Now this fits well into the religious historical pattern of the previous example. Swabia is the land in which strong pietism and a marked loyalty to the church predominate. Where God's word is at home, occultism cannot flourish. There is thus to be seen from the example of the Frisians and the Swabians an inverse ratio between their church life and their eidetic tendencies. From this established fact, for which the psychologist and not the theologian has provided the evidence, we again discern the fact that the eidetic ability has occult roots. What Schmeïng has here noted about the German peoples is widely known in the history of missions. I would only point to the example of Tibet mentioned earlier in *Lit. 2*.

If we now survey all the evidence which Schmeïng provides, there can be no doubt left as to the connexion between eidetic and occult involvement and subjection. In an unbroken series this psychologist produces all the points of contact with magic conjuration. Without intending to do so, or, as a nontheologian, without noticing it, he gives us impressive circumstantial evidence for the thesis, which is confirmed by hundreds of examples from pastoral experience, that eidetic ability is only a primary or secondary effect of magic conjuration. It is a primary effect in the sense that people who were as children charmed in cases of sickness become as adults clairvoyant, i.e. they develop the gift of "second sight". It is a secondary effect in the sense that, in families in which conjuration has been practised for two or three generations, the third or fourth generation displays clairvoyant gifts, i.e. an eidetic ability. Eidetic ability in adults, apart from artistic or intuitive vision, is nothing other than a mediumistic gift of clairvoyance conditioned by occult involvement. This agrees with the mathematical axiom: if two quantities are equal, to a third, they are equal to each other.

From this perspective it is, of course, wholly absurd to propose an investigation of the prophetic and visionary sections of the bible from an eidetic viewpoint. The prophets and apostles were not men of eidetic vision but men of the Holy Spirit. The appearance of the Risen One[349] to 500 men was not the hallucinatory experience of 500 people with eidetic gifts, but an objective happening.

2. *Oesterreichs's Studies on Possession*

The work of Prof. Oesterreich gives us a thorough insight into the characteristics, form and essence, origin and cure of possession.

The outward pattern of the condition of possession is marked by a complete change of personality. The possessed person seems to be dominated by an alien individuality. The *characteristic marks* of this change from primary to secondary personality are: the rapid change of facial expression from friendliness to a dreadful grimace; the sudden change of voice, for instance from a high soprano to a deep bass; the assumption of a new personality, with new contents of consciousness. These three psychological metamorphoses are usually accompanied by powerful motor phenomena. The possessed person has attacks of delirium, wild flailing of the limbs, dislocations, destructive mania, acts of

[349] cf. I Cor. 15.

violence towards other people present. A phenomenon often observed is the fact that even children or delicately built women can offer effective resistance to three or four strong men. From a religious viewpoint it is significant that possessed persons often shout out curses and blasphemy against the Trinity, and express their aversion to the word of God.

As to the subjective state of the possessed person, Prof. Oesterreich distinguishes between the somnambulant and lucid *forms*. The somnambulant form is characterized by loss of primary consciousness in the state of possession. At the moment of the paroxysm a second ego speaks out of the consciousness. The transition from primary to secondary consciousness follows suddenly and immediately. The primary consciousness fades; the gift of memory vanishes. In the religious centuries, this secondary ego was a "demon"; in the 18th. and 19th. centuries, when the belief in demons lost its power, it was "the soul of someone who dies unsaved". The lucid form of possession is marked by the fact that the possessed person does not lose his normal consciousness during the attack. In the midst of the paroxysm the person can observe his own attack without being able to rise above the condition, which seems alien to him. Even during the violent motor compulsions the consciousness sometimes remains fully clear.

Regarding the immediate cause of the state of possession, we can further distinguish two forms: the unplanned, undesired state, and the state that is induced deliberately by magical or suggestive practices. This second form is found with the magic priests of all non-Christian peoples, and with spiritistic mediums.

A further classification of states of possession is gained by borrowing the corresponding terms from French psychology. They distinguish *possession* and *obsession*. *Obsession* is the main concept, and means every kind of compulsive condition that exists, possession included. By *possession* is meant demonic somnambulism, the condition in which the person concerned experiences a second ego as a "demon".

The most difficult problem is the question of the nature of the possessed state. We must here make several aspects prominent. The common denominator to which Oesterreich reduces states of possession is not a split in the subject, nor the genesis of a new subject, but merely a change of functions in the normal subject. Therefore he rejects the notion of an invasion of the normal consciousness by a secondary personality. We have, he thinks, only a variation of the primary consciousness of the personality.

Therewith he rejects at the same time the hypothesis of a deception, as if the state of possession were a matter of play-acting or simulation. Oesterreich says: "In the state of so-called demonic possession there is developed in the psyche of the patient a kind of secondary personality system, which carries on its life in opposition to the will of the individual. The subject loses control over a considerable part of his faculties, and fulfils compulsively the role of a 'demon' with this part of himself."[350] Thus the condition of possession is, in the view of Oesterreich, in its essence not the phenomenon of a possessing spirit, but a compulsive process which the subject pursues against his own will. Hence possessed persons are compulsive neurotics, who are ruled by an intensive psychological process, without accepting this process themselves. If we ask concerning the cause of this compulsive process, then Oesterreich points to the maximal development of the subconscious. According to this view, we must conceive of possession as a co-ordination of this maximally developed, intermittently active, subconscious with the conscious mind. At the moment of paroxysm, there is even a subordination of the consciousness to the subconscious. Thus consciousness and subconsciousness have in their activities exchanged roles. Hence there are here certain reversing processes in the psychic structure of the possessed person. Incidentally we note that this is a parallel an another level to the theory of reversibility in the phenomenon of clairvoyance. The nature of the state of possession has thus been reduced by Oesterreich to an anti-transcendent basis in depth-psychology.

If we are now to take a brief look into the causes and cure of states of possession, we must first take note of a feature of the history of religions. In antiquity, possession did not necessarily take the form of psychological disturbances. Bodily ailments were regarded as a demonic influence. Even today among primitive peoples bodily ailments are considered as demonic possession. The protection spells against diseases are therefore directed at the banishment of evil spirits. Succeeding this primitive level of possession comes the next level of view, among the peoples of higher culture, according to which mental disturbances are considered to be the result of demonic influence. Thus it was in the religious middle ages.

The third, modern stage is the scientific view that there is no such thing as demonic possession, but only dissociation symptoms and compulsive processes. Besides this third stage, there is a fourth small movement, which holds that not all phenomena of this kind are catered for by the psychological and psychiatric explanation of possession as a pathological process of the mind. An important unexplainable residue remains, for which there is as yet no psychological explanation, and which continues to leave the question open as to whether certain happen-

---

[350] cf. Oesterreich op. cit. [63], p. 63.

ings transcend nature. This ladder of religious history shows that the evaluation of possession is dependent on the level of education and religious conceptions. In the age of a very strong belief in demons, the very dread of demons and the belief that one was ruled by them was sufficient to bring about a possession state. Here we have the phenomenon of possession arising from auto-suggestion. To this class of possession, which arises under the pressure of a belief in demons, there also belongs the hetero-suggestive form under the influence of a doctor or a pastor who has become subject to the influence of such conceptions. Oesterreich in this connexion mentions the poet-physician Justinus Kerner (d. 1862), and above all a pastor under whose suggestion of the idea of possession a person who sought his counsel developed visions of demons and disturbances of personality.[351] "This origin of possession in the belief in demons coupled with auto- or hetero-suggestion has this characteristic, that it is always most widespread in classes of little education and culture."[352]

A second possible cause of the state of possession is the phenomenon of psychic infection. It has often been observed in the past that the environment of possessed persons became infected. This would explain the epidemics of possession and the fact that exorcizing priests have themselves become victims.[353] We are acquainted with transmission of psychic disorders, in the phenomenon of induced insanity.[354] There are also elements of imitation in purposive hysterical reactions. Also, in the child's imitative instinct a similar phenomenon appears in a healthy form. Hence there are also states of possession as a kind of imitation neurosis. The realization of this imitation follows so easily because with this faith in demons there is at the same time the belief in the transmission of demonic conditions.

A third possible cause for conditions of possession is, according to Oesterreich, the fact of an a priori predisposition. There can exist on an endogenic basis a dual and self-contradictory disposition, existing concurrently, which can be activated by some experience or impulse, now in this direction and now in that.

The fourth possible cause of possession is a residual obsession in an unstable or gullible person arising because of an hallucination or vivid dream, or a feverish delirium. Such a person will sometimes stubbornly cling on to the idea that an evil spirit has entered into him.[355]

---

351 ibid., p. 95.
352 ibid., p. 96.
353 ibid., pp. 38, 47, 89, 94, 105, 136, 182, 183.
354 cf. Kloos, op. cit. [12], p. 450.
355 cf. Oesterreich, op. cit. [63], p. 90.

Related to the question of the cause of possession is that of cure. In the case of psychological infection psychiatry will recommend isolation from the infector. This is the best guarantee of cure. In the case of possession caused by auto- or hetero-suggestion the suggestion will in general lose its power if it is met with a rational elucidation or a counter-suggestion. Against the belief that one is possessed the opposite belief is energetically directed, namely, that one is no longer possessed. Oesterreich says:[356] "If the artificial dismissal of the possession is successful, it was of a suggestive nature." In this view, exorcism would be the counterpart of possession. In the case of compulsive ailments the therapy is not so easy, and it is difficult in the case of an a priori predisposition. Unusually interesting is the psychological therapy described by Oesterreich[357] of a possessed person who suffered from a burdened conscience because of adultery. In hypnosis the wife was brought to the burdened husband in an hallucination, and she assured him full forgiveness. Thereupon the possessed man recovered. From the theological viewpoint this procedure is very questionable, since the guilt complex was compensated by a hypnotic process, and not righteously reconciled before God and man. The successful attempts at cure of splits of consciousness by the neurologist Morton Prince are well-known. After first making a careful study of his patient, he then produced a fusion of the separated states of consciousness.[358]

After this sketchy survey we must elucidate the *tendency* of Oesterreich's work. He pleads unequivocally that the phenomenon of possession consists of psychological compulsion states. He calls possession an extended compulsion complex.[359] But as a scientist he is careful enough in treating this problem to suspend final judgement. We have an important statement when he says at the end of his work: "Unfortunately our knowledge of the para-psychological conditions is up to now much too limited. There is no other solution than to postpone the answer to these questions until we are better informed than we are today on para-psychological conditions. The purely negative answer, which made it so easy for the rationalist to conduct historical criticism against all these reports, is no longer possible for us today".[360]

Along with this attitude, which does credit to him as an objective researcher, Oesterreich suggests, like scientists of other disciplines, an unexplainable residue. On this aspect he introduces a report by the well-

[356] ibid., p. 96.
[357] ibid., p. 113.
[358] cf. Prince, op. cit. 332.
[359] cf. Oesterreich, op. cit. 63, p. 121.
[360] ibid., p. 386.

known missionary A. Le Roy, who writes:[361] "There are also other forms of possession, before which the greatest sceptic must admit that he is at a loss, when e. g. a possessed person remains floating for several minutes above the earth, or fluently speaks in another language of which she previously did not understand a word." This reference shows that research into the phenomenon of possession is a task which is ever anew being set us. The final line has not been drawn. Rather the door remains open, perhaps for the transcendent nature of these compulsive phenomena.

3. *The Work of M. and W. Prince on the Split Personality*

This collection of one neurological and two psychological contributions offers some illuminating evidence and new avenues of thought for our study. We can essentially select five groups of questions in this work which are of special interest to us here: the nature of the splitting of consciousness; the causes of the splitting; splitting of consciousness and mediumship; psychological effects; and the contrast with psychoses.

(a) M. Prince examines the *nature* of dissociation of consciousness in a neurasthenic student, Miss Beauchamp. After a mental shock a basic change of personality set in, which was so marked that for a time certain areas of knowledge were completely lost, e. g. her knowledge of the French language. The integrality of her psychological structure vanished. Her personality split into three or four separate personalities. After an exhaustive study of the case, M. Prince came to the following conclusions:

"1. Dissociation of the consciousness is a suspension of activity of some brain centres and groups of centres and hence a disruption between the centres.[362]

2. The ego-subconscious can develop into a genuine, independent personality, which can assert itself at the same time as the original personality, or acting alone while the other personalities are asleep.[363]

3. The subconscious is not necessarily to be identified with the hypnotic ego."

With regard to this conclusion we must note that the neurologist established that the subconscious attained to an independent, separate

[361] ibid., p. 142.
[362] cf. Prince, op. cit. [332], p. 26.
[363] ibid., p. 29.

existence, and maintained itself for many years before the reuniting fusion of the various states of consciousness. The psychologist W. Prince arrived at similar conclusions in his study of the nature of the splitting of consciousness. He writes:[364] "In the dissociation of personality there develop two series of recollections, thoughts, taste, and experiences, which are often sharply distinct; facial expressions and voice are different. The secondary personalities are not regarded by psychologists as an invasion by spirit intelligences, even though two psychologists of eminence quite openly take this question into consideration, but they are considered as splits of the consciousness in which the separated or dissociated fragments make themselves independent."

(b) To the question concerning the *cause* of this splitting of the consciousness, we have already suggested an answer. A psychological shock in the case of Miss Beauchamp resulted in a process of dissociation of the primary consciousness. For this M. Prince uses the illustration of a prism. Just as a prism separates the sunlight into the seven colours of the spectrum, so a mental shock produces a multiple splitting of the primary consciousness.[365] In the case of Doris Fischer, W. Prince established three such shocks: at the age of three, by a fall with a hard impact; at the age of seventeen by an emotional experience, the death of her mother; and at the age of eighteen again through a tragic fall. Prince assumed that as a result of the third fall a group of neurons was thrown out of its functional direction by the shock.[366]

In the case of Hanna, we also have to do with a splitting of consciousness due to a fall.[367] Pastor Hanna fell out of a carriage and crashed heavily on his head. After two hours of unconsciousness, Hanna awoke with a split consciousness, which was cured after prolonged treatment. Hanna regained his primary personality.

The case of Meyer is remarkable. He was treated by W. Prince.[368] As a result of a great business failure Meyer lost his primary personality. After a trip he was taken by the police to a hospital, completely insensitive and dumb. He had lost all recollection of his earlier life. Hence there were the phenomena of amnesia, aphasia and aphonia. W. Prince, the psychologist, took a special interest in the man, and after months of treatment restored his speech and other abilities, so that he again became a competent member of society. Meyer never however regained

[364] ibid., p. 173.
[365] ibid., p. 24.
[366] ibid., p. 75.
[367] ibid., p. 173.
[368] ibid., pp. 172f.

his primary consciousness. Everything he experienced before the moment of dissociation was lost, e. g. his name, speech, family connexions, profession, etc. From February 20th. 1914, he lived only as his second personality.

When these cases of Beauchamp, Fischer, Hanna and Meyer are grouped according to the cause of dissociation, we get the following pattern. In cases 1 and 4 it was mental shocks which brought on the dissociation. In case 3 it was a fall which brought about the splitting of consciousness, which was later healed. Case 2 had both kinds of shock, mental and organic-traumatic. In case 1 the recovery was effected by a reintegration of the fragmented thought content. Likewise in cases 2 and 3 a cure was achieved. Case 4 lived continuously in his secondary personality from the time of the shock.

For our study it is of interest that there are various kinds of dissociation, which differ as to cause, degree of dissociation, prospects of cure, and type. For us special importance attaches to psychological causes of dissociation. A psychological impulse can split the psychological unity of a person so that the separated parts live a separated existence, usually in opposition to each other. Here the basic principle of magnetism applies, that like poles repel each other. The process of this dissociation casts a clear light on the origin of psychological disturbances in connexion with occult activity. It has been established as an empirical fact in the case of occult practices, that in all cases where the subconscious of a person under occult influence is addressed, psychological disturbances appear as a consequence. We have here a process parallel to the above phenomena of dissociation. We shall treat this particularly in section (d), but we may make mention of it already in this connexion. In the case of the para-psychological phenomenon of occult influence on, i. e. appeal to, the subconscious, we have basically a phenomenon of dissociation in a light degree. In the phenomenon of excursion of the soul, we have a high degree of dissociation. And in the materialization phenomenon of the medium, we have a double process of dissociation. The medium separates psychic powers from his own personality, and then carries out a light degree of dissociation in the participants in the séance, whose subconscious is tapped. The comparison of occult phenomena with the phenomenon of the splitting of the consciousness is by no means absurd. This appears clearly in the mediumistic ability which develops at the time of or after the dissociation.

(c) We shall investigate this coupling of dissociation of consciousness with *mediumship* in the cases of M. and W. Prince. M. Prince reports concerning Miss Beauchamp that, among a whole mass of dissociation phenomena, numerous psychical phenomena such as automatic writing, crystal gazing, negative hallucinations, etc. appeared.[369] This parallelism of dissociation phenomena and occult phenomena shows that their common denominator is the activation of the subconscious and its development of a separate existence. In the case of Doris Fischer (case 2), W. Prince found this same parallelism. In her case history there are many occult occurrences such as telaesthesia, auditory hyperaesthesia, telepathy, enhanced suggestibility, crystal visions, automatic writing, spiritistic mediumistic gifts with visions of spirits, hallucinations, telekinesis, and the hearing of bangs and knockings which everyone else could hear objectively.[370] Remarkable is the fact that Doris Fischer, in the process of being cured of her main dissociation phenomena, became a spook medium. All people in her presence would hear steps, noises, knockings, and so on. Prince attributes these spook apparitions to a gift of the medium. This would mean that we have here the phenomenon of psychokinesis, i. e. a process similar to the dissociation of the personality. When Prince tells us that Doris Fischer during the cure developed into a medium, then we must insist for our part that in this process only a shift of the dissociation phenomena to another level is here involved, a re-direction of the dissociation energy towards the outside. In the case of Meyer no occult phenomena were observed. Here it was a matter of no more than a few sense illusions in a state of acute hysteria of an extreme kind, occurring just before the change from primary to secondary personality. So it is described by W. Prince.

(d) The range of *psychological consequences* shows the conformity of the different kinds of dissociation in the matter of mental disturbances and traits of character. M. Prince reports of Miss Beauchamp that personality B III destroyed everything[371] that personality B I had constructed. A destructive urge is a frequent secondary effect of occult subjection. Further, as typical results of both dissociation and psychical phenomena, there are suicidal thoughts, rage, hatred of the church and of religion.[372] With Doris Fischer there were similar effects. She had bursts of rage and a destructive urge; religion was nonsense to her.[373] Hence in both cases we see the familiar phenomenon of resistance to divine things. The case of Meyer apparently yields no findings in this respect.

[369] ibid., pp. 3, 15.
[370] ibid., pp. 41, 57, 107, 127, 135, 154.
[371] ibid., p. 9.
[372] ibid., pp. 20f.
[373] ibid., pp. 40, 41, 75.

(e) From the *medical* aspect, the relation of dissociation to psychoses is interesting. For the psychologist W. Prince it is a matter of great concern to present the contrast between the phenomena of dissociation and of mental illness. He writes:[374] "Doris Fischer is a living refutation of the view that mediumship, even though it involves a kind of splitting of the ego, is in itself pathological". Doris Fischer showed only minor signs of mediumistic disposition as long as her dissociated condition was of a wholly abnormal kind. But when she reached the height of physical and mental health, she gave strong mediumistic evidence for her paranormal abilities.

In this striving to dissociate mediumship from the psychoses, Prince has been supported by authorities on psychical problems.[375] Prof. Oesterreich writes regarding this question,[376] "Works on schizophrenia remain (in the bibliography concerning pure cases of dissociation) generally disregarded, since the phenomena related to dissociation which appear in them are obviously of a different nature". On the same lines are the studies of Schmeïng, the psychologist, who came to the conclusion that the phenomenon of "second sight", i. e. of telaesthesia, has nothing in common with the hallucinations of schizophrenics. It is a fact of importance for our study that psychologists and psychical researchers recognize the existence of dissociation phenomena which do not belong in the sphere of psychotic depersonalization symptoms.

If now we draw up a sum total of the three psychological studies, we may note the following points.

Schmeïng shows us the strong association of eidetic and magic. Oesterreich tries to reduce possession to a psychological compulsion state, but leaves unanswered the question regarding the final explanation of those cases which cannot be rationally understood. Prince proves the possibility of a separate existence of the subconscious, and shows the relation of split personality to mediumship. In his search for the cause of the dissociation of the personality, Prince comes to the conclusion that such splits can be brought about by organic-traumatic or emotional shocks. For the special questions raised in our study, these three works provide most useful material. Schmeïng gives indirect proof that magic practices produce psychological changes in people, in the sense of the development of mediumistic gifts or psychological disorders. Oesterreich indirectly proves that in the case of some possession phenomena rationalization can be carried to absurdity. The possibility that such occurr-

[374] ibid., pp. 154f.
[375] ibid., p. 252.
[376] cf. Schmeïng, op. cit. [30], p. 121.

ences are of a transcendent nature can be read between the lines in many places in his work. Prince shows, besides the relationship of dissociation phenomena and mediumship, a fact which is of great importance for us, viz. that dissociation can be brought on by a psychological shock. This is parallel to the frequent pastoral cases of dissociation brought on by magical suggestion by amateurs. In these psychological findings some essential positions of our own study are supported by non-theologians.

Chapter Four

THE RESULTS OF PSYCHICAL RESEARCH

Besides the results of psychology and psychiatry, we must also consider those of psychical research, the scientific branch of occultism, in order to help us to elucidate, define and establish the results of our own studies. First of all, we must establish the objectivity of occult phenomena in the face of ignorance and a priori scepticism.

1. *The Objectivity of Occult Phenomena*

There are two types of psychical research, which differ as to method and as to the subjects used. The one concentrates on experimentation; the other makes systematic observation of spontaneous cases. The one works with test-persons who are fully conscious, and use the highest possible degree of concentration; the other works with mediums in a state of trance. Thus the one employs conscious energies, and the other subconscious energies. We shall give a short discussion of both methods.

(a) *The researches of Schrenck-Notzing*

The counter-arguments arising from a rigid bias against psychical phenomena consist mainly of charges of trickery, deception, self-deception and superstition. Scholars of rank in both sciences and humanities, like Prof. Driesch, Prof. Gruber, Prof. Oesterreich, Prof. Zöllner, and internationally recognized authorities in the field of psychical research like Schrenck-Notzing and Tischner, have therefore undertaken the task of studying these problems with scientific exactness. Their results are in essential agreement. There are para-psychical, para-physiological and paraphysical manifestations. And there are, after the elimination of deliberate and unconscious deceptions and sleight of hand and foot, also genuine manifestations of mediumistic gifts.

Among others, the researches of Schrenck-Notzing with the medium Eva Carrière, produced such results.[377] By two means the objectivity of the materialization phenomena was assured. First a large number of photographs established the existence of products materialized by the medium, from a gauze-like or rubbery substance to the full material-ization of human forms.[378] Still more striking is the result of a micro-scopic investigation.[379] The Schwalm chemical laboratory in Munich analysed what was left after dematerialization, with the following result: cell detritus, with variously formed epithelial cells, with or with-out nuclei. The result of this analysis leaves no doubt that the residuum was organic, i. e. originally living matter, and not inorganic products such as textiles, paper and rubber, which might have been used for an artifical staging of the phenomena. Besides the photographic and micro-scopic checks, paraffin casts[380] and weight measurements[381] were taken, as further evidence for the objectivity of the materialization phenomena. When we here speak of objectivity, this is with the reservation that these objective products are only dissociation artifacts,[382] artificially produced effects of the dissociation of the medium. I am acquainted with the objections which have been raised against Schrenck-Notzing, on the ground that he was deceived by the medium.

(b) *The experiments of Rhine*

It is Rhine's merit that he has rescued psychical research from its sporadic character by bringing the field into the laboratory. He has conducted several hundred thousand systematic tests, with the purpose of studying the reach of the mind.[383] Starting out with the purpose of studying the interrelations of mind and matter, Rhine discovered that the reach of the mind is wider than was formerly assumed. The mind has an inborn capacity to influence matter. There is such a thing as psychokinesis. Thereby Rhine has discovered, in a way differing from other researchers in the field of para-psychology, a basic principle of the relationship between mind and matter, which is capable of illuminating the mysterious darkness of spiritistic processes and magic practices, and of reducing them to the level of immanent occurrences.

[377] cf. Schrenck-Notzing, op. cit. 237.
[378] ibid., pp. 405, 407f.
[379] ibid., p. 449.
[380] cf. op. cit. 240.
[381] cf. Bovet, op. cit. 171, p. 48; Tischner, op. cit. 25a, p. 153.
[382] cf. Bender, op. cit. 3, p. V.
[383] cf. Rhine, op. cit. 57.

That which however distinguishes Rhine from other psychical researchers is the thesis that the best telekinetic accomplishment is achieved where there is a fully integrated consciousness in the subject. This is a new discovery, which contrasts with the view of earlier psychical researchers, that separation phenomena only occur as a result of disintegration or dissociation. Rhine however concedes that his thesis only applies in spontaneous cases.[384] Further we must remember the proportion of the energies which appear in Rhine's tests to those of spontaneous cases. Perhaps we may say that the minute energies of Rhine's tests stand in a similar ratio to the immense energies of spontaneous cases, e. g. in materialization phenomena, as the integrated powers of the consciousness to the disintegrated powers of the subconscious. This comparison forces itself on the observer.

It is the merit of Rhine, as compared with other well-known researchers in this field of science, to have removed from this border area the stain of superstitious quackery. With his exact scientific experiments, psychical research has been brought completely within the realm of genuine scientific work. The objectivity of psychical phenomena can no longer be dismissed with a wave of the hand.

2. *The Dominance of the Subconscious Factors*

In this problem the psychological dissertation of Prof. Bender, "Psychic Automatisms",[385] can be a guide. Bender's treatment is, to be sure, a psychological study, but it touches on so many para-psychological problems that it lays at the same time a foundation for psychical research. Indeed since his first study a second has appeared "On the problem of extra-sensory perception",[386] which goes still further into the basic parapsychological phenomena.

Bender begins with glass-moving, which is practised in some circles as a party-game, and he studies the character of the answers mediated by the glasses. He succeeds in proving, by methods of introspection and observation of behaviour, that in automatic spelling there actually appears a mental feat which is accomplished without the knowledge of the subject. Automatic spelling is a subconscious, dissociated, psychological process. This discovery was a promising start for the experimental psychological study of various psychical phenomena such as

---

[384] cf. Bender, op. cit. 3, p. 56; Rhine etc., "Extra-Sensory Perception after Sixty Years", Henry Holt & Co., New York, 1940, p. 129.

[385] cf. Bender, op. cit. 3.

[386] cf. Bender, "Zum Problem der außersinnlichen Wahrnehmung", Verlag Barth, Leipzig, 1936.

clairvoyance, crystal gazing, extrasensory perception, hypermnesia, cryptomnesia, cryptaesthesia, muscle-reading, depersonalization, possession, remote suggestion, mediumship, excursion, hallucinations, somnambulism etc. In a detailed study he comes to the following conclusions:

(a) Following Gurney's test of the double performance of the consciousness and the subconscious, he establishes the *intelligence* and the independence of the subconscious. Gurney's subject received under hypnosis a mathematical problem, was then immediately awakened, and then had to repeat the anthem "God Save the Queen", omitting every other word. In this way the consciousness was kept fully occupied. At the same time the mathematical problem was unconsciously written down and solved. This simultaneous action of the consciousness and the subconscious provided a brilliant demonstration of the existence and independence of the two levels of consciousness.

(b) In the phenomena of hyperaesthesia and hypermnesia, cryptaesthesia and cryptomnesia, Bender sees, on the basis of his researches, *hyper-functions* of the subconscious. One of the so-called superior capabilities of the subconscious is to register peripheral perceptions, which remain unnoticed, and in response to a suitable stimulus to bring to light again such subliminally received knowledge. The reception of knowledge in a para-normal manner from another subject usually takes place in a state of psychic dissociation.

(c) In the same way Bender sees the origin of the splitting of the personality, which he calls *depersonalization,* as the equivalent of possession in the psychiatric sphere. He writes: "Quite often characteristic traits of the subject appear in the automatic productions — features which are only imperfectly or not at all integrated into the structure of the normal personality, and which therefore appear to the normal ego as being completely foreign or alien. This can go so far that such desires and thoughts are attributed to alien energies and powers, which need not of course be a psychopathic symptoms, and must be distinguished from a compulsive symptom, as this shows itself in psychopathic forms of possession".[387]

(d) The most striking form of dissociation phenomena are the so-called *materialization* phenomena. "Here the dissociated psychic material arises with a claim that it is itself a personality, and assumes an ego-character, so that forthwith a conflict ensues between the two dissociated parts. In extreme cases as many as five fully organized pseudo-person-

[387] cf. Bender, op. cit. 3, p. 39.

alities have been known, which have a complicated relation to each other, the analysis of which requires sharp psychological discernment. The tendency to personality-synthesis of dissociated mental fragments can frequently be observed in the automatic writing or spelling of wholly normal persons. Usually the impulse towards the formation of such personifications lies in the environmental suggestions, in incidental stimuli which are seized upon as cores of crystallization for the most fantastic productions. In spiritist sessions such representations of personalities often claim to be incarnations of the deceased, and they exert themselves to give proof of their identity. In unusual cases such personalities show an astounding fullness of verifiable data, which cannot be acquired by the medium by the normal use of the senses."[388]

These four sections of Bender's material, which we have sketched in brief, show that experimental psychology of the subconscious is an indispensable tool for research into the occult area. It has become plain from Bender's study that the dominance, or superior power, or the subconscious is a general mark of para-psychological manifestations.[389] He has thus proved, on the basis of experiments, what our study has disclosed on the basis of observation of many spontaneous cases.

If now we scrutinize all the examples of this study from the viewpoint of the significance of subconscious factors, we can reduce all occult phenomena, except for the familiar "unexplainable residue", to functions of the subconscious. In practically all occult practices we have active or passive forms of artificial dissociation phenomena, receptive or active functions of the subconscious. Nearly all spiritist phenomena, as well as nearly all the varieties of hyperaesthesia, forms of divination (except for astrology), the various fields of extra-sensory influence (except for blood pacts), fetishism and the phenomena of incubi, and further the field of extra-sensory appearances (apart from site-bound ghosts), can be explained as functions of the subconscious in a state of mental disintegration or dissociation. Thus here the results of systematic, methodical observation of spontaneous cases agree with the results of experimental psychology.

3. *Caution against Over-hasty Demon Theories*

Convinced occultists, spiritists and, sadly, often simple and solid Christians also sometimes accept without question a belief in spirits and demons where this is completely unnecessary. Over against this ex-

---

[388] ibid., pp. 34f.
[389] cf. Bender, op. cit. **3**, p. 41.

cessive belief in transcendent powers, we must seek the objective facts with sobriety and realism. We shall present three arguments which warn us against a premature recourse to the spirit theory.

(a) Various researchers have noticed that certain medicines and drugs will alter the mental and subconscious capabilities of some people of mediumistic disposition. Schmeïng for instance points out that the introduction of calcium causes the gift of "second sight" to fade away.[390] Clairvoyance would in this case be due to a lowering of the blood calcium. Prof. Rhine makes similar observations. He shows that caffein increases the performance of the subject, and sodium amytal reduces it.[391] Such observations were also made in telepathic experiments in the Psychological Institute of the University of Groningen.[392] Perhaps in this field of the psychological influence of drugs we must also place the injection of "truth drugs", as used in some countries. These observations make it clear that the processes are physical and not demonic.

(b) A further argument against the over-hasty adoption of the spirit theory is the therapeutic success of Prince, the neurologist, with his patient Miss Beauchamp. He was able in the course of treatment to identify four or five independent forms of dissociated personality. In the middle ages this case would presumably have been judged as a case of possession, since several different voices issued from this girl. Prince succeeded, after months of study, in fusing the different states of consciousness and so effecting a cure.[393]

(c) A further argument appears from an amusing experience of Prof. Bender in the field of glass moving. During the round of questions put by the players, the glass was asked the meaning of "duzen" (= "to address with the familiar 'du' form of the personal pronoun"). Immediately the glass spelled out a line from Goethe containing the word "Dutzend" (= "dozen").[394a] Here the spirit present evidently made a hearing mistake! No, here we see the group itself spelling out the subconscious collective knowledge of the group, according to the law of polypsychism.[394b] An experience on the same level was related to me by a colleague.

[390] cf. Schmeïng, op. cit. 30, p. 117.
[391] Rhine, op. cit. 57, p. 106; Bender, op. cit. 3, p. 50.
[392] ibid., p. 63.
[393] cf. Prince, op. cit. 332, p. 28.
[394a] "Und wenn dich erst das Dutzend hat - - -"
[394b] cf. Bender, op. cit. 3, p. 2.

Ex 119　An unmarried pastor took part in a game of glass moving.[395] Besides several other male participants, there was a red-haired single Jewess in the group. After they had played at questions and answers for some time, one player posed the tactless question, who would marry the Jewess. Immediately the glass spelled out the name of the single pastor. He declined the suggestion with a laugh, and said that he was already attached to someone else. This time the glass had made a mistake. One could ask ironically whether the spirits were having a try at match-making. No: one of the participants, who wanted to do a good turn for the girl, guided the glass with psychokinetic energy. The planned match with the Jewess never materialized. This example of glassmoving shows the immanent character of the process and shows that the spirit theory is superfluous in such cases.

This whole section may be summarized in one sentence: where there are physical, psychological or subconscious connexions, we need not make use of any questionable theory of spirits in order to explain the phenomena.

4. *The Border Zone of Inexplicable Phenomena*

Prof. Driesch writes in his "Grundprobleme der Psychologie":[396] "Until a few years ago there were still many, and there are today still some, who simply lay down that para-psychological problems cannot exist. These people were apparently there when God created the world, and hence they know what He is capable of doing and what not". The attitude of such rationalists is marked by the postulate of rationalism: there are no parapsychological phenomena. The first kind of attitude to this border zone of extra-sensory appearances is thus one of negation. We shall make a few comments on this.

(a) *Rational explaining away of the phenomena*

One of the most radical exponents of this view is Dr. von Gulat-Wellenburg, who in a collection of studies edited by Dessoir investigates physical mediumship. The volume written by Gulat-Wellenburg betrays an a priori attitude of complete negation regarding psychical phenomena. With great expenditure of effort, but without a convincing knowledge of the subject, he tries to bring all psychical phenomena down to a rational denominator. Where this is impossible, mediums are accused

---

[395] Sadly one is always coming across Christian workers who get involved in such practices. When the psychologist Prof. Bender expressly warns against it in his book (op. cit. 3), the theologian should take heed.

[396] cf. Hans Driesch "Grundproblem der Psychologie", Leipzig, 1926, p. 186.

of deception, and researchers of medieval magic, and the checking of the processes is branded as defective. He takes his stand on the view that scientific evidence of para-psychological phenomena has up to the present been completely unconvincing.[397]

A second way of explaining the phenomena away rationalistically is the suggestion that here the limits of the normal five senses have been extended beyond the measure of what is physically intelligible. We find such a procedure used when Baerwald attributes clairvoyance simply to hyperaesthesia of the senses. Tischner calls this an explaining away of clairvoyance,[398] and he writes of this that to assume such an extraordinary extension of the limits of the physical senses is hardly better than saying that because every few months someone improves the world long-jump record by a fraction of an inch, it follows that there is no limit and that one day men will jump over Lake Constance.[399]

(b) *Theories of clairvoyance, as an illustration of the uncertainty of rational explanations*

The second kind of attitude in the border situation of unexplainable appearances is seen in the effort to uncover the facts of the psychical phenomena. Such methodical investigations are to be seen in many theories in the psychical field. When we here adduce some thirty theories of clairvoyance from the last sixty years, and subject them to appraisal, then we shall see that the main principle should not be that of explaining it away rationalistically at all costs, but the obtaining of the most rational explanation possible.[400] That was the principle of research adopted by William James, one of the pioneers in the problem of occultism. He said, "It is obvious that no mystical explanation ought to be invoked so long as any natural one remains at all plausible".[401]

Some thirty theories of clairvoyance will now introduce us to the characteristics of rational explanation.

The trick. Here the phenomena of clairvoyance are explained as a swindle. An example personally experienced will illustrate.

Ex 120 At a party a clairvoyant wrote a number with six digits on the blackboard. He took paper and pencil, and let a guest write a five-digit number on the sheet. The same was done with three more guests.

---

397 cf. Dessoir, op. cit. 36, p. 489.
398 cf. Bender, op. cit. 3, pp. 46f.
399 cf. Tischner, in "Zeitschrift für Parapsychologie", Leipzig, Mutze, 1926, 1., p. 53.
400 cf. Dr. med. Max Hopp, "Über Hellsehen. Eine kritisch-experimentelle Untersuchung", Inaugural dissertation, Berlin 1916.
401 cf. "Proceedings of the Society for Psychical Research", vol. II Pt. 58, p. 4.

He now let a fifth guest add the series. The sum agreed with the six digits he wrote first. The solution of the riddle? The sheet was prepared beforehand. On the back of the sheet there were a series of numbers, whose sum was worked out beforehand. When the fifth person came up, the paper was turned over surreptitiously.

Another well-known trick is the mirror trick, where the clairvoyant turns his back to the audience and with the help of a hidden mirror can tell the audience all the movements going on behind his back.

Technical clairvoyance. A finely developed device used for studying the embryo inside a bird's egg, called an embryoscope, enables one to read writing through eight sheets of paper.[402] Likewise a letter in a closed envelope can be read if the envelope is moistened with alcohol.[403] Thirdly, there are writing fluids which leave an invisible script, which can be made visible by applying certain fluids such as lemon-juice, milk, or water, or by the application of heat.

The ambiguity of the oracle. The prognostications of many clairvoyants are known for their ambiguity. One can always read a "fulfilment" into the equivocal oracles they give. Such was the case with the oracle at Delphi. The classic example of such ambiguity is the Delphic oracle's prediction at the beginning of the campaign of the Lydian King Croesus against Cyrus of Persia, which ran: "When you cross the Halys, you will destroy a great kingdom". The oracle left open the question whether Croesus would destroy his own or the Persian kingdom, i. e. whether he would win or lose the battle. Basically it said nothing, and everything. That is the art of many a clairvoyant: by skilful wording to leave every possibility open.

Coincidence. In the popular passion for the miraculous and bias in favour of the magical, one bull's-eye compensates for a hundred misses. A hundred false prophecies and clairvoyant failures are passed over in silence, but two or three hits are published far and wide. That is the way of every lottery, and also the way of those interested in occultism.

Combination. Some people have a sharp intuition combined with teleological depth-vision. They intuitively grasp a situation and are able to think through from this starting point to the end of the process by a "combination at first sight", a kind of flash thinking. This clairvoyant gift is nothing but short-circuit thinking, in which the intervening steps of logical thought are passed over by a leap of genius.[404]

[402] cf. Hopp, op. cit. [400], p. 79.
[403] ibid., p. 77.
[404] cf. Schmeïng, op. cit. [30], p. 143.

Muscle-reading. A personal experience will illustrate this phenomenon.

Ex 121 At a social evening a clairvoyant person was looking for a hidden watch. He grasped the hand of one of the people present. The guide helped, by unconscious muscle twitchings, to show the clairvoyant the place where the object was hidden. Usually the entire audience helps by the reaction of their eyes, mimicking expressions, etc., so that the clairvoyant soon fulfils his task. This is not clairvoyance or telepathy, but the phenomenon of "muscle-reading".

Clairvoyance as telepathic transference. Many clairvoyant phenomena can be explained as telepathy. For this reason Dr. Rhine, the researcher,[405] in his tests always took care to make a clear distinction between the two phenomena. Even the experimenter himself must not know the objects which the subject is to find by clairvoyance. Thereby he avoided the telepathic tapping of the experimenter by the subject.

Increase of the eye's sensitivity to light. Du Prel in his psychic studies develops the following theory. There are persons in whom the sensitivity threshold of the normal sense (i. e. of the retina) is shifted, so that they are receptive to finer stimuli.[406] Such people see more than others do.

Biological basis of clairvoyance. Our eye has two systems of receiving and processing light, the system of diurnal vision and the system of twilight vision.[407] The diurnal eye uses the colour-sensitive spot in the middle of the retina. This is the daylight eye. When darkness falls, the eye uses the light-sensitive rods which lie around the centre. The vivid eye is the long-wave "receiver" of the colours red to yellow (400—600 million Mc/s), and picks up a clear image of form, colour and distance. The twilight eye is the short-wave "receiver"[408] of the colours green to violet (600—800 million Mc/s)[409] and only obtains vague images of blue-green tint. In twilight there is a switch from the diurnal vision to twilight vision. Colours, sharp outlines, distances, and cubic and plastic vision ceases, and only cloudy, shadowy, linear and indistinct images of dark colour are received. This is the biological starting point for many stories of spooks and ghosts.[410]

---

405 cf. Rhine, op. cit. 57.
406 cf. DuPrel, "Das Hellsehen", Psychische Studien, 1890.
407 cf. E. R. Jaensch, op. cit. 342.
408 The terms "long wave" and "short-wave" are here only relative, since all light-waves are short.
409 On wave-lengths of colour, cf. Kleiber-Nath, "Physik", Verlag Oldenbourg, Munich, Berlin, 1931, p. 249.
410 cf. Schmeïng, op. cit. 30, p. 22.

Synaesthesia. The senses of man are more or less joined together in their functions, the extent of this being somewhat dependent on disposition. They are in symbiosis. This mutual adaptation is the ground for the stimulation of one sense when another is activated. As an example, when I was at school I had a gifted and well-known art-teacher. For him the magnificent colours of nature were not only a matter of visual effect, but he also experienced these colours acoustically as a musical harmony. The visual stimulus acted synaesthetically as an auditory stimulus. In the same way there are musical people who, upon hearing good music, suddenly see an array of colours. This is so-called "coloured hearing" — *audition colorée.*[411] In physics we have an experiment which illustrates this process of common stimulation. If, for instance, little steel bells are placed on the register of an organ, and the right notes are played, the bells will ring with the corresponding notes from the organ pipes. Here of course we have direct participation of the same kind of energy. But in synaesthesia there is a certain conversion of energy. A direct visual stimulus can be converted indirectly into acoustic energy. Thus we have here a process in which a sense-organ primarily stimulated brings about the secondary stimulation of a second organ. This fact explains how, for instance, visionaries can also hear their visions speak. Because of this synaesthetic union, visual hallucinations can be accompanied simultaneously by auditory hallucinations and vice versa. Thus, when in the twilight the indistinct image of a willow stump becomes, by means of the biological entrance mentioned in the previous paragraph, or by an illusion, a threatening monster! and then, because of a co-ordinated synaesthetic reflex, this monster begins to speak or to growl, the ghost story is complete. Actually it was just a subjective experience.

The reversibility theory. We have already discussed this theory in connexion with *Ex 25.* We have here "a kind of reversed sense-experience, which converts energy led backward from the brain to the eye back into light-waves in the retina, and produces a corresponding visible light-image outside the person of the observer".[412] We thus have a reversal of the process of perception. In the normal process of vision the light stimulus is led by the second cranial nerve (the optic nerve) to the brain (via the optic chiasma), and there reproduced as an image of the object seen. In the reverse process, an impulse from the subconscious stimulates a seeing-process in the optic centre of the brain, which is then projected to the outside and seen again as an external optic appear-

411 ibid., p. 28.
412 ibid., p. 190.

ance.[413] Thus the visionary sees appearances which are really subjective products of his own mind.

The emanation of psycho-physical energy. As early as the middle ages the theory arose that there is a certain radiation, or fluid, emanating from each individual person. Paracelsus (1493—1541), the founder of a new method of healing, took account of this emanation. Two hundred years ago, in accordance with a theory proposed by Stahl (d. 1734), this emanation was given the name of "phlogiston". Mesmer (d. 1815), who developed the theory of animal magnetism, called this magnetic energy emanating from people "fluid". This view of Mesmer was defended by Baron von Reichenbach (1850), who set out to prove[414] that from many organic and inorganic bodies "odic rays" emanated, which "sensitive" persons could perceive as light.

These emanation theories underwent a change at the hands of Kotik (1908), who thought that parallel to man's thought processes there issues a stream of brain-rays.[415] This thesis is defended by many in our own day. The researcher Dr. Manfred Curry of the medical and bioclimatic institute of Riederau[416] has developed instruments with which he hopes to measure the "od". Curry says that in the case of od rays we are dealing with "ultra-ultra-short-waves", which have wavelengths of 0—150 cm.[417] With this theory of emanation we can explain many clairvoyant and telepathic phenomena as a kind of radio signalling on the same wave-length.

The solar plexus. Puységur,[418] a pupil of Mesmer, explained that the solar plexus — a sympathetic nerve-net in the epigastrium behind the stomach — is the seat of the so-called sixth sense. He thought that this solar plexus was a transmitter and receiver for a psychic agent.

The inborn clairvoyant gift of man. The American researcher Rhine[419] has published the results of some 400,000 tests in his book, "The Reach of the Mind". He has succeeded in proving the fact of an inborn clairvoyant gift in man. He defends the normality of the characteristics of "psi" phenomena,[420] and explains that man has beside his normal con-

---

[413] cf. Schmeïng, op. cit. [30], p. 189.

[414] cf. Tischner, op. cit. [25], p. 135; Hopp, op. cit. [400], p. 35.

[415] cf. Kotik, "Die Emanation der psychophysischen Energie", Wiesbaden, 1908.

[416] cf. article "Erd- und Menschenstrahlung" in the Zeitschrift für Radiästhesie, 3rd. year, No. 3.

[417] Report by Dr. Rolf Reissmann in "Weltbild" Jan. 1952, No. 2, p. 17.

[418] cf. Hopp, op. cit. [400], pp. 17, 20.

[419] cf. Rhine, op. cit. [57].

[420] psi = parapsychological, or psychical. cf. Rhine, op. cit. [57], p. 112.

sciousness an introspective window which continually experiences invasion from extra-sensory perceptions.[421] Rhine regards it as shameful that we are better informed about nuclear physics than about nuclear psychology.[422]

Clairvoyance and environment. Clairvoyant phenomena as the result of *upbringing* appear in youth. Tales of ghosts and demons and creepy stories make such an impression on the sensitive soul, vivid fantasy and imagination, that later these ghostly forms appear in both waking and sleeping states.

A second factor in the development of visions is the *landscape*. The broad sweep of heath and moor, the loneliness of forest vales, the remoteness of mountain farms, the link with nature of people little touched by civilization, create a tendency to contemplation and an inclination to see thoughts as plastic images.

A third element which may be noted for the development of telaesthesia is the degree of sunlight on our earth. In contrast to the heliogenic acceleration of development in southern peoples,[423] we may speak of a scotiogenic retardation of development in northern peoples. This retardation is probably the cause of late maturity among these peoples. "Thus a late-maturing type of adult, with retention of youthful characteristics was formed".[424] With this phenomenon we may probably connect the observation of a "magic ring" around the Baltic Sea.

A theory, which is fascinating but hard to prove, for the appearance of second sight in the northern lands is the accumulation of magnetic effulgences in the human soul. Prevision would then be a kind of "Northern Lights" of the soul.[425]

Clairvoyance from nutritional lack. Schmeïng reports in his book[426] that a lack of calcium in drinking water favours eidetic manifestations. Hence regular doses of calcium can decrease clairvoyant abilities.

Another theory is suggested by Prof. Jostes of Münster. He traces the phantom visions back to the buckwheat pancakes baked in oil and hard to digest, which are eaten at the evening meal in Westphalia. He thinks that they lie so heavy on the stomach of the country people, that they have powerful dreams in their sleep, which remain so vividly in their

---

[421] ibid., p. 171.
[422] ibid., p. 189.
[423] cf. Schmeïng, op. cit. [30], p. 118.
[424] ibid.
[425] ibid., p. 117.
[426] ibid., p. 116.

memory that they are taken for visions of the waking hours.[427] The pancake thus attributes the origin of visions to *indigestion*.

Clairvoyance due to inbreeding. A large incidence of prevision has been observed among those who marry their blood-relatives.

Hunger and thirst. These are a very intelligible and probable cause of hallucinations. Researchers who have faced hunger on their travels, and hungry soldiers, have often reported visions of delicious smelling bread loaves. Also the mirage, which is seen by desert travellers, is known not only as an objective fact of atmospheric reflection, but also in the form of subjective hallucinations due to extreme thirst.

Clairvoyance through psychic training. By the contemplative life of the medieval mystics, clairvoyant phenomena were developed as a parallel experience to the mystic union to which they aspired. Many religious visions of the present day have a similar character. On the same principle prevision experiences occur as the result of psychic training among the fakirs and yogi of India.[428]

Hypnotic suggestion as a cause of clairvoyant phenomena is a fact established by experiments. Hallucinations also appear as post-hypnotic effects.

Disease as cause of clairvoyance. Hallucinations and illusions are observed in connexion with the following ailments:

Organic — with fever delirium due to infectious diseases (e. g. typhus, pneumonia[429]);

With functional disturbances of the endocrine glands — e. g. exophthalmic goitre;[430]

On a traumatic basis — with severe head injury, unilateral injury of sense organs,[431] tumours, also with total disorganization of the metabolism through poisoning, critical hunger, or critical thirst.

With brain diseases — e. g. epidemic post-encephalitis,[432] hereditary chronic progressive chorea,[433] cranio-pharyngioma;[434]

[427] ibid., p. 30.
[428] ibid., p. 177; and further cf. Nielsen, op. cit. [37], p. 79.
[429] cf. Brugsch, op. cit. [10], vol. I, p. 302.
[430] ibid., p. 104f.
[431] cf. Bleuler, op. cit. [129], pp. 34f.
[432] cf. Brugsch, op. cit. [10], vol. I, p. 376; Kloos, op. cit. [12], p. 259.
[433] ibid., p. 263.
[434] ibid., p. 269.

With intoxication psychoses — e. g. delirium tremens,[435] alcoholic hallucinations,[436] narcotic addiction,[437] etc.;

With psycho-neuroses — hysterical semi-consciousness;[438] also emotional disorders, e. g. during pregnancy or change of life;[439]

Psychotic — with schizophrenia.[440]

The metaphysical theories of clairvoyance. E. von Hartmann[441] spoke in his book of "telephone connexions in the Absolute". This is his explanation of telepathy and clairvoyance.

Invasion by a higher intelligence is the explanation to which Hans Driesch[442] inclines for telepathic and clairvoyant phenomena. This may be either from the deceased or from the World Subject.

Here also we must place the Frenchman Osty,[443] who represents the view that psychical phenomena find their explanation in the fact that the medium taps the transcendental World Subject.

The spirit theories. Jung-Stilling[444] assumes a connecting member between body and mind, in the form of a light beam or ethereal element. This envelope of light has a natural faculty for presentiment, which is capable of development. Persons with developed organs of intuition can overcome barriers of space, so that they see distant things as if near. Further, they are in the position to establish rapport with the spirit world, and in this way also to lift themselves over the limits of time and thus to see future things as if present.

The spiritist theory of clairvoyance is constructed without a gap.[445] Man is regarded as a double being, consisting of body and astral body. People with mediumistic ability can split off their astral being, establish connexion with the deceased, and appropriate their knowledge. The spiritist calls this process astral separation or somnambulism.

The existence of many theories is on the one hand a symptom of the struggle to find the element of truth in clairvoyance; on the other hand

[435] ibid., pp. 377f.; Bleuler, op. cit. 129, p. 36.

[436] cf. Kloos, op. cit. 12, p. 379.

[437] ibid., p. 383.

[438] ibid., p. 444.

[439] ibid., p. 422.

[440] ibid., p. 401.

[441] cf. Eduard von Hartmann, "Der Spiritismus", 2nd. edn. Leipzig, 1898.

[442] cf. Driesch, op. cit. 6, pp. 126, 138.

[443] cf. Osty et Marcel, "Les pouvoirs inconnues inconnues de l'esprit sur la matière", Paris, 1932.

[444] cf. Jung-Stilling, op. cit. 98.

[445] cf. Olhaver, op. cit. 132, p. 183.

it is an unmistakable symptom of the great factor of uncertainty in all rational attempts at an explanation. We are always running into difficulties when we adopt the old saying that man is the measure of all things both as they are and as they are not. This will become still plainer in the next section.

(c) *The theory of the unexplorable residue*

The impossibility of giving a final rational elucidation of the psi phenomena has led many researchers, who were sufficiently objective, to accept, besides the complex explicable by reason, the existence also of an unexplorable residue. If we may use an illustration to show what we mean by the explorable and the unexplorable areas, we can present them as a mighty bridge, whose broad arch rests on two pillars. The pillar at this end stands on the ground of rationality; the far pillar disappears in the mists hanging over the river.[446] The footing near us can be probed for firmness, depth, and supporting strength, but the footing on the other side cannot be tested by us. The area on this side is open to scientific research, to human logic; the far side is the "meta-area", a "trans-region" which is unaccessible to reason. Many researchers acknowledge the existence of this "meta-area", and integrate the unknown factor into their system.

This becomes evident in the work of the wellknown researcher Dr. Tischner. Repeatedly he finds himself, in dealing with spontaneous experiences, faced with enigmatic facts which cannot be explained by the activation of subconscious energies: e. g. the deciphering of fragments of a cuneiform script by a secret key, the locating of the foundations of an old abbey with the help of a "deceased person", the discovery of a will, telekinetic phenomena,[447] and many similar things. Tischner has in the end no other conclusion to draw than this: "Let us acknowledge our complete ignorance."[448] We cannot expect a franker admission than this from a specialist in para-psychology.

Tischner is not the only psychical researcher to have come to this conclusion. Dr. Moser writes in her book:[449] "A residue remains which is genuine, beyond all delusions...[450] These phenomena exist as objective realities, and are as little to be rationalized away out of nature as is the ring of Saturn".

---

[446] Prof. Heim once used this illustration.
[447] cf. Tischner, op. cit. [25a], pp. 31, 173, 185, 193.
[448] ibid., p. 194.
[449] cf. Moser, op. cit. [263], p. 21.
[450] ibid., p. 342.

The admission of two psychical researchers is followed by the testimony of two psychologists. Dr. Schmeïng writes:[451] "There remains in the future reference of prevision an *unexplained residue*. When the prevision has been through all the seven sieves of the objective research-er, then there still remains an unexplored and perhaps unexplorable factor which withdraws itself from experimentation and from the rational eye". In the same way Prof. Bender concedes in the case of Patience Worth[452] that we are here dealing with a *philological riddle*, when a simple woman without any literary talents or interests is able in a state of trance to produce significant poetical accomplishments in an old English dialect which is no longer spoken.

A further case of a puzzling mediumistic gift, reported by Prof. Oesterreich,[453] may be added to this example of Bender's. A Batak medium, an illiterate woman, could read Old Batak writing in a state of trance. This case also belongs to the unexplainable residue. Dr. Bovet writes:[454] "There remains a *small residue* which cannot be explained by psychology alone, e. g. the history of Gottliebin Dittus, observed by the older Blumhardt".

Nor are the psychical researcher, the psychologist, the philosopher and the doctor alone in introducing the concept of an unexplained or un-explainable residue to help them out: the theologian cannot dispense with this factor either. Harnack writes:[455] "To this day possession often defies scientific analysis, leaving each person free to attribute it to the activity of special, mysterious powers. There are facts in this area which cannot be denied, and which we nevertheless cannot explain". Typical of this fact of "the residue" is a secret report of the Archbishop of Canterbury, Dr. Lang. In it is stated: "Even when every possible ex-planation has been applied, we are still of the opinion that there is always an *unknown factor* remaining. We hold it probable that the assumption that these communications in some cases derive from bodiless spirits is true."[456]

In our attitude towards the border situation of unexplainable phenom-ena, we have looked at three basic views, viz. the unobjective attitude of

[451] cf. Schmeïng, op. cit. [30], p. 144.
[452] cf. Bender, op. cit. [3], p. 30.
[453] cf. Oesterreich, op. cit. [63], p. 265.
[454] cf. Bovet, op. cit. [171], p. 53.
[455] cf. A. Harnack, "Medizinisches aus der ältesten Kirchengeschichte", in "Texte und Untersuchungen zur Geschichte der altchristlichen Literatur", B. VIII, p. 105.
[456] cf. "Zeitschrift für Arbeit und Besinnung", Quell Verlag, Stuttgart, 1. III. 1951, p. 113.

rationalistic "explaining away", the objective stance of scientific research, and the admission of researchers that there remains a residue of unexplainable phenomena. All three groups have in common the conviction that the border zone of unexplainable phenomena is an offence to reason. Reason still stands at the frontier of an unknown territory. The "meta-area" vanishes into a mist. This fact of rational inexplicability has already been assumed by many researchers of every school to be an indication of transcendence. Of this we now come to speak.

5. *Indications of Transcendence*

When in this section we speak of transcendence, we must first make a theological definition in the sense of that of Althaus in his systematic theology.[457] Althaus distinguishes real transcendence from unreal, the true other world from the merely apparent other world. Everything that it traced by the poet, romantic, gnostic, theosophist, magician and medium, in the way of super-sensible, occult and demonic powers, still belongs to this world, and not to that which we understand by revelation. This definition of Althaus is the reservation underlying all the several points in this section. If notwithstanding this we still use the term transcendent, this is because we wish to set over against all the rational methods of explanation which have been produced to date the concept of the absolutely different. In using this term we know also that none of the irrational, metaphysical explanations of psi phenomena "transcend" into the divine sphere. By transcendence we mean only a relative, not an absolute, "beyond". That is the indispensable condition for the interpretation of this whole section.

(a) *Unreal transcendence*

The exponents of spiritism assert that the spirits of the deceased appear when called and show themselves subservient to the medium. We get a good insight into the practice of spiritist activities in the book of Olhaver,[458] which by 1952 had reached a total printing of 1.3 million copies. Olhaver explains various psychical phenomena, such as apports and materialization, as due to the subservience of the spirits. He does not think of these appearances as a bodily, but only as a spiritual presence of the "friends from beyond". The deceased, he thinks, materialize themselves with material borrowed from the medium and those present. Materializations are not perfect facsimiles of the deceased, since

---

457 cf. Paul Althaus, "Die christliche Wahrheit", Bertelsmann Verlag, Gütersloh, 1947, vol. I, p. 26.
458 cf. Olhaver, op. cit. 132.

impressions of the medium and of those present form part of the meta-morphosis.[459] Theories that they are masquerades, or transfigurations of mediums in a somnambulant state, fall down, since all the phantoms have organic defects. Often, too, sudden dematerializations followed before the eyes of those present.

Over against this spiritistic spirit theory stands the animistic ex-planation.[460] This animistic view says that in materialization phenomena we are dealing with the separate existence of psychically dissociated fragments of the medium, which are modified by material drawn from the subconscious of the persons present. That is the almost universal opinion of our psychologists, and agrees with my own findings. Prof. Bender in this respect speaks of a separate existence of dissociated psychic material, which gives itself out to be an incarnation of the deceased.[461] Dr. Schmeïng likewise holds a theory which regards material-ization phenomena as being fully within the bounds of this world. He writes: "Materializations are subjective eidetic phenomena. Therefore we can dispense with metaphysical and meta-psychical presupposit-ions."[462] The words of Wilhelm Wundt, a pioneer in the field of ex-perimental psychology, will conclude this section. He writes:[463] "The greatest spirits of humanity, who willingly appear at the beck and call of unnumbered mediums, have surely become feeble-minded in the course of their journey to the beyond. What they express does not bear their own stamp, but that of the mediums". There we have a short selection of witnesses. Apart from a small unexplored residue, which exists here also, we must surely say that since the knowledge gained by the new psychology, the great mass of materialization phenomena may be regarded as subconscious processes of the mediums. Hence we have generally speaking in spiritism an unreal transcendence.

(b) *Neutral transcendence*

As witnesses for transcendent processes of a neutral character, we may cite Driesch, Osty and von Hartmann. Prof. Driesch discusses in his book[464] three theories: animism, the world subject theory, and monadism.

---

459 ibid., pp. 136f.

460 Prof. Driesch gives the following definition: "A mental, para-psychical theory, which accepts the existence only of the souls of those living, is known as the animistic theory" (op. cit. [6], p. 113). Tischner writes, "The animistic theory draws on telepathy, dissociation of the personality, automatisms, hyper- and cryptomnesia, in fact all the peculiarities, in order to explain (the phenomena) — op. cit. [25a], p. 186.

461 cf. Bender, op. cit. [3], pp. 34f.

462 cf. Schmeïng, op. cit. [30], p. 190.

463 ibid., p. 193.

464 cf. Driesch, op. cit. [6], pp. 123f.

He expresses his own opinion as follows. When alien contents are transferred, animism is excluded. By the world subject theory, he understands the tapping of a "plan-bearing World Subject" by the metagnomist (medium). He is convinced that this World Subject has, firmly
shaped within itself, the life plans of every man. Driesch explains that
this theory does not hold if the metagnomist is able to read trivialities
in the plan of the World Subject. Driesch feels most attracted to the
monad theory. He thinks "that bodiless souls are able, under certain
conditions which are fulfilled by mediums, to enter into a telepathic
exchange of knowledge with those still bound by their bodies, or else
to use the body of the medium directly for expressions such as speaking
and writing".[465] A theory similar to that of Driesch is developed by
Dr. Osty, Head of the "Institut Métapsychique".[466] Like Driesch, Osty
speaks of the *conscience universelle*, which contains within it the past
and future of all men. The medium can make contact with this World
Subject and from it gain hidden knowledge.[467] Thus Hartmann too
speaks of "telephone connexions in the Absolute", in which all the
future is already present.[468]

These three researchers thus have in common the conception of a
secular, non-biblical, neutral transcendence. Theologically this theory of
tapping the World Subject is unthinkable.

(c) *Biblical transcendence*

Now that we have surveyed all the attempts at explanation of the
psi phenomena from the side of psychiatry, psychology, parapsychology
and philosophy, we are coming nearer to the starting point for the
consideration of biblical transcendence. For the moment we shall only
adduce witnesses from non-theologians who testify to biblical transcendence, since the testimony of the bible itself is to follow in a separate
section. We shall hear a psychologist and a doctor, who will give respectively an indirect and a direct pointer to biblical transcendence.
These are Prof. Oesterreich, who held a chair of philosophy in Tübingen,
and the psychiatrist Dr. Lechler.

1. *Indirect testimony.* It is not fully certain how the late Prof.
Oesterreich would have felt about the evaluation of his researches in
a wholly new sense. But the material which he contributed with regard
to the phenomenon of possession may be considered as truly classic, so that

465 ibid., p. 124.
466 cf. Osty, op. cit. 443.
467 cf. Tischner, op. cit. 25a, p. 187.
468 cf. Hartmann, op. cit. 441.

it is suited as no other material in the literature of psychology for the establishing of cross-connexions with biblical transcendence. His material can be our starting point for showing the *status diiudicandi* in the diagnosis of mental suffering. We are concerned with this problem: is possession only a psycho-organic process within man, or are there influences from transcendent centres of operation? We shall investigate Oesterreich's work as it bears on this question.

It often strikes us with this psychologist that, despite his plea for a purely secular approach to possession, he still emphasizes in a remarkable way all the border phenomena which form a transition to the unexplainable residue. We could almost get the impression that besides his open plea that possession be regarded as a condition existing entirely within man, he desires to bring evidence from silence for the transcendence of certain possession phenomena. We shall now set out the typical marks of possession which might cause us to think in terms of a transcendent — although we cannot prove the existence of such. We shall use Oesterreich's material, though we shall arrange it according to the viewpoints and terms of our own study.

The most striking element of the possession phenomena is the *constancy* of its characteristics. Oesterreich points out that the typical distinguishing marks of possession exhibit a constant persistence of unchanging symptoms from New Testament times through the Middle Ages, and down to the present day. He writes:[469] "The descriptions by the New Testament writers bear the stamp of truth, even if they should prove to be partially or even in every case unhistorical. These are typical pictures of conditions correctly reproduced". Whether this constancy is alone attributable to the invariability of human nature and its unchangeable ailments is still very much under debate. This religio-historical factor of possession phenomena is in any case an element that cannot be ignored in the search for the real cause.

A warning signal in the question regarding the transcendence of certain possession phenomena is the oft noted and widely testified immunity of serious, convinced, genuine Christians to infection with possession. Oesterreich writes of this:[470] "Noted systematic theologians are of the opinion that possession never, except in very unusual and passing cases, befell persons who were diligent in striving towards moral and religious perfection... Meynard also writes 'Qu'il est excessivement rare que la possession se manifeste chez les âmes appelées à la contemplation et à l'union intime avec Dieu; c'est plutôt une punition qu'une épreuve

---

[469] cf. Oesterreich, op. cit. **63**, p. 3.
[470] ibid., p. 77.

purifiante'[471]."Oesterreich himself perceives something of this immunity and resistance-power of genuine Christians, for he exclaims: "In doubtful cases of possession one wishes in vain for a man with the power of Jesus' disciples."[472] That is a remarkable admission, coming from the mouth of a psychologist. Proofs for the thesis of immunity are abundant on the mission field. There is a remarkable interrelation between possession and the Christian message. Possessed pagans or ecstatic magician-priests stubbornly resist the Gospel of Christ, and, on the other hand, convinced Christians of the indigenous churches are not subject to the possession epidemics of the primitives. Oesterreich offers a mass of evidence for this, without making a full evaluation of them in this respect. A few examples will illustrate this. On pages 130 and 131 he reports how possessed persons cry out in the presence of missionaries, "I'll have nothing to do with that one!" On p. 136 he notes that Christian natives in East Africa were not subject to possession epidemics. On p. 207 he quotes a missionary report, which states that a Christian woman who had fallen back into heathenism became possessed.

A report reminiscent of the New Testament appears on p. 208. In an epidemic of possession, a Christian village surrounded by pagan communities was spared. The heathen were furious about it. A possessed woman was appointed to bring the pestilence into the Christian village. The Christians heard of the plan and came together for prayer. The possessed person marched into the Christian village at the head of a procession of pagans. Suddenly she stood still, frozen and numb with terror, and screamed: "Look! There he stands, the God Jesus with arms outstretched, protecting his people like a shepherd his lambs. Back! Go back! I can go no further. If I go further, I will die!" When the heathen mob pressed on the possessed woman and beat her, she said to the man who was attacking her, "You have not hit me but them (the Christians)". The man collapsed and when the sun set he was dead. The story made a deep impression on the whole country.

On p. 213 Oesterreich gives the history of a convert. "When a possessed pagan was converted to Christianity, the demon vanished, saying 'This is no place for me'." Warneck also reports the observation that conversion to Christ puts an end to possession. Even a magicianpriest was freed from the evil spirit by going over to Christianity.[473] Oester-

---

[471] "It is extremely rare that possession appears in people who are called to contemplation and intimate union with God; it is a punishment rather than a sanctifying trial".

[472] cf. Oesterreich, op. cit. [63], p. 114.

[473] ibid., p. 268.

reich closes this series of thoughts in his book with the confession:[474]
"Among the primitive peoples, the manifestations of possession everywhere recede when the Christian mission strikes deeper roots".

These observations show the eloquent phenomenon of an inverse
complex of symptoms: the compulsive occurrences of possession and
discipleship of Jesus Christ are mutually exclusive. For the person who
thinks only in rationalistic terms, it is impossible to bring both a medical
and a religious factor down to one common denominator. Oesterreich
indeed tries this mathematical feat, with the proposition that Christianity contains, because of its higher culture, its more mature world view,
greater psychological powers of resistance and a higher sense of security[475] than primitive religion. This escape by means of a comparison
of cultures is however not tenable, for this reason, that in the history
of the church, especially in medieval times, an astounding number of
cases of possession appear. If the medical phenomenon of possession
and the religious phenomenon of the immunity of genuine Christians
is to be reduced to a common denominator, it will have to be on a higher
level, in another dimension. In saying this we are not of course con-
tradicting the connexion often observed and described by psychiatrists
between psychotic ailments and religious delusions. We are not here
speaking of the religious delusions of people who are mentally ill, in
the psychiatric sphere, but of the protection and resistance-power of true
Christians against infection with possession. This wholly different
problem of immunity cannot be invalidated here, as has occasionally
been attempted, by adducing the confusion of medical and religious
symptoms in psychotics. It is also an insufficient explanation of possession phenomena to resolve them on a purely psychological basis. The
inversely proportional relation between the state of possession and
Christian faith cannot be understood by the use of psychological categories alone. No, there is here strong ground for suspecting a transcendent factor behind the problem.

The concept complementary to that of immunity is that of the
resistance of possessed persons to God, God's word, Christ, the Holy
Spirit, and every aspect of the Christian faith. In all the records of the
early church, of the middle ages, and of the mission fields, the key mark
of possession is blasphemy against the Trinity. This characteristic of
possession appears in many examples adduced by Oesterreich. Writing
about a possessed woman in 1830, he says: "Without any special cause,
the woman would suddenly have convulsive spasms. A strange voice

[474] ibid., p. 378.
[475] ibid., p. 268.

spoke out of her and burst out in curses against God. When she wanted to pray, she was forcibly hindered. Her jaws would become distorted. Prayer was interrupted by diabolical laughter."[476] A similar case is the possession of a 24-year-old girl. In the fits of possession a deep male voice spoke out of her and poured out bitter scorn about everything that had to do with religion. In her normal state, the girl was given to earnest prayer.[477] Such conditions of depersonalization are well known in modern psychology and psychiatry as special disease symptoms of schizophrenia, melancholia (endogenic depression) and psychasthenia. The characteristic mark of possession, on the other hand, is the fact that all symptoms of the above-mentioned diseases are lacking. The phenomenon of possession cannot be classified under these standard disease-patterns. The resistance of the possessed person is completely different from the religious delusions of psychotics. Oesterreich's work contains so many examples of this special characteristic of possession, that we cannot cite them all here. Blasphemies and hatred against Christ[478] belong among the constant phenomena of possession. The character of these blasphemies is such that it can only in a small measure be explained as a compulsive process resulting from repressions. Most of these phenomena suggest a reality other than the psychological.

The next phenomenon, the reverse, so to speak, of immunity, is *exorcism*. Oesterreich's presentation leaves many points unclear. Heathen practices of exorcism are not clearly distinguished by him from Christian exorcism, and further, in dealing with Christian exorcism he does not notice the essential difference between an externalized, indeed decidedly de-christianized, rite of exorcism, and an authoritative, spiritual exorcism. For clarification we must make the following distinctions. Heathen exorcism is a magic defence, and belongs to the sphere of occultism. The word of Paul applies here: "What accord has Christ with Belial?"[479] Medieval exorcism lapsed largely into a worldly spectacle, a symptom of a church which had drifted far from the heart of the Gospel. So Oesterreich himself writes:[480] "Even the exorcisms of Nicole de Vervins (1566) were really great spectacles". It is not improper when Oesterreich as a psychologist calls such exorcisms "healing manoeuvres",[481] since indeed thousands of sensation-seekers attended the expulsion rites. "It is reported that in Loudun there were at times 7,000 spectators present."

[476] ibid., pp. 9f.
[477] ibid., p. 19.
[478] ibid., pp. 22, 40, 54, 213.
[479] II Cor. 6, 15.
[480] cf. Oesterreich op. cit. [63], p. 99.
[481] ibid., p. 100.

Apart from these perversions, exorcism in its spiritual essence stands justified by the New Testament as a legitimate means of helping the possessed. *Abusus non tollit usum!* Without grasping the essence of real exorcism, Oesterreich supplies examples of it. On p. 7 he gives a report of Verona (d. 375), who displays the power of Jesus' name in an exorcist conflict. From the history of Chinese missions Oesterreich relays a report which likewise involves a genuine exorcism. Warneck also produces such reports. He writes:[482] "On Sumatra and Nias the Christians have had the courage, when faced with possessed persons, calmly to command in the name of Christ the evil spirit to depart, for it is a matter of course to them that the demon will then leave the unfortunate person. When he has departed, they make no fanfare about the matter. They have firm trust in the mighty Jesus, that He is able to conquer His enemies." Nias is the island which acquired a great name in the history of missions through the great revival of 1916. After this revival, a Christianity like that of the early church prevailed. Hence it is no wonder that genuine exorcisms occurred there. When Oesterreich tries to analyse the success of exorcism in psychological terms, by reference to the firm faith and feeling of security enjoyed by Christians, we must emphasize over against this view of a philosopher and psychologist of religion, that psychology is only one key, by which not all the essential elements of Christianity can be unlocked, nor all those of exorcism.

The next point which must be developed from the work of Oesterreich in the interest of our present study is the *translocation* of the possession complex from possessed persons to their environment. In the well-known epidemics of possession in Morzines (1860), in Verzegnis (1878), in Pledrau (1881), in Jaca, in the women's convent at Zell in Lower Franconia, and further in epidemics among the primitives, possession is seen to transfer itself in the first place by psychological infection, according to the principle of induction and imitation. In this case possession is an imitated experience. We must however point out that psychological infection is not the only form of translocation. The infection of an exorcizing priest is harder to explain. In the epidemic of possession in Loudun, a number of clergy became affected: Fathers Surin, Lactance, Tranquille, Lucas, etc.[483] Also the nun Jeanne des Anges first became properly possessed as a result of exorcism.[484] What relation does this phenomenon of transference to priests and nuns bear to the thesis of immunity? We cannot resort here to the motto, "The

482 ibid., p. 269.
483 ibid., p. 89.
484 ibid., p. 94.

exception proves the rule". On the contrary, two arguments may be adduced — a psychological one, and a religious one. Not every Christian has this psychological and religious power of resistance to infection with possession. When we spoke of a Christian immunity, we were speaking of the powers of resistance in living, genuine, convinced Christians. Moreover, not everyone is a Christian who bears that name. This *skandalon* must be stated and accepted, without any arrogance. Hence the thesis of the immunity of Christians who are well anchored in Christ is here not overthrown, but rather confirmed. *Comprehendat qui comprehendere potest!*

After this presentation of the religious problems, which are important for our study, we shall now give from Oesterreich's work a sketch of the psychological and parapsychological phenomena connected with the possession complex. A chief mark of possession is the *physical alteration* in paroxysm. In our section on the characteristic marks of the change from primary to secondary personality, we have already spoken of these physical changes. Oesterreich gives us abundant material on this phenomenon. He reports how from a possessed girl[485] there issued a deep male voice which spoke in an accent strange to the girl. The extraordinary increase in motorial power of possessed persons is striking. A lad of ten years[486] could scarcely be held by three adults. Two men could barely get control of a possessed girl. This factor corresponds to a similar feature in the New Testament reports. There we read that a possessed person overpowered and wounded seven men.[487] For medicine and psychology it is hard to solve the problem of how a girl's voice can suddenly change to a deep bass, or how women and children can scarcely be controlled by the combined strength of several men.

The next phenomenon of this group, namely the hyperaesthesia which results from possession, poses still greater difficulties of rational explanation. It is a remarkable phenomenon that possessed persons, like the families of magic charmers, develop enhanced intelligence and clairvoyance. As early as the Dialogue of Lucian (b. A. D. 125) it is reported how possessed people in a state of paroxysm suddenly speak strange languages, of which they have no knowledge in their normal state.[488] Oesterreich also says:[489] "Especially frequent are claims by possessed persons to prophetic, clairvoyant and telepathic abilities." Such cases are also known in the history of missions. Dannholz reports from East

---

[485] ibid., p. 367.
[486] ibid., p. 22.
[487] cf. Acts 19, 13f.
[488] cf. Oesterreich op. cit. [63], p. 5.
[489] ibid., p. 379.

Africa[490] that possessed women speak in paroxysm foreign languages, Swahili or English, although they otherwise neither understand nor speak these languages. In the light of depth analysis, such a speech phenomenon could only be attributed to the work of the subconscious insofar as the subconscious had at some time had opportunity to hear the language concerned. But a fluent command of a language in any case supersedes every form of subconscious achievement. As a para-psychological phenomenon the possibility might exist that the possessed person tapped this knowledge from someone present who had mastered the language. But fluent speech has never yet been observed in this para-psychological phenomenon. This speech phenomenon brings us to the extremity of our rational comprehension. Again we find that we can only penetrate further into this mystery by adopting the view that there are transcendent centres of operation. Besides this enhanced intelligence, we note the phenomenon of *clairvoyance*. The connexion of possession with clairvoyance is a noteworthy parallel to the data of the New Testament. The demoniacs who were healed by Jesus were also clairvoyant.[491] They immediately acknowledged Him as the Son of God, who had authority over them.

Oesterreich here again supplies us with much material. A possessed person called with a loud voice to a catechist:[492] "Why do you preach the true religion? I cannot tolerate that you should draw my disciples away from me." "What is your name?" the catechist asked. After some hesitation he answered the catechist: "I am the messenger of Lucifer." "How many are there of you?" The answer came: "There are twenty-two of us." In connexion with such drastic testimonies it is repeatedly noted that possessed persons acquire the gift of visions. We shall give a few examples. "Possessed persons have acquired the gift of clairvoyance. They often make a good business out of fortune-telling."[493] "The possessed woman asserted that his majesty the devil had taken possession of her... she disclosed the future to the bystanders."[494] An Egyptian slave prophesied in a state of possession that his master would be called to the government within three days. In his normal state he knew nothing of this prophecy. When the prophecy was fulfilled three days later, and his master received a government post, the slave was rewarded with freedom.[495] In our section on divination, such fortune-

---

[490] ibid., p. 135.
[491] cf. Mark 5, 7f.
[492] cf. Oesterreich op. cit. [63], p. 214.
[493] ibid., p. 217.
[494] ibid., p. 251.
[495] ibid., p. 255.

telling phenomena were critically examined. The difference between what we are here considering and divination is that diviners give their predictions in full consciousness, while the possessed person only prophesies during the condition of eclipse of the primary consciousness. We shall not enter into the para-psychological problems which arise here. Perhaps the phenomenon of telepathy would be a possible explanation. The emergence of clairvoyance in connexion with possession is a fact which the psychological analysis does not fully account for.

In our study of the effects of possession we have now reached the sphere of para-psychology. What strikes us in the philosopher Oesterreich is the same thing which we saw in the psychologist Schmeïng, namely the *connexion with magic*. With Schmeïng it was a connexion between second sight and magic. Here it is the connexion of possession and magic. Oesterreich gives us (p. 14) an example of how a demon of a possessed person was caused to speak by means of "magnetic magic manipulation". Oesterreich says of this: "These unusual methods of treatment are of great interest for the psychologist, since they show that it is possible by artificial means, with suitable conditions of suggestion or auto-suggestion, to produce an internal division of the mind."[496] Not only for Oesterreich is this discovery of great import: here we may also see a position of our own study clarified by a psychologist. Magic charming produces dissociation manifestations in the person charmed. That is a fact of experience in all areas of para-psychology. Very many phenomena of the dissociation complex, like depersonalization, transitivism, psychic fragmentation, somnambulism, excursion of the soul, bilocation, etc. may be traced — apart from the psychiatric symptoms — to a great extent to this cause. The degree of affinity between possession and magic is therefore very high, since as we know possession belongs to the phenomena of dissociation.

An example of this is the case of Achille.[497] This young man was disposed by heredity to mental illness, as his psychiatrist wrote. After a sexual mishap, the phenomenon of possession appeared in Achille. The family history of Achille is interesting for our study. His father was accused of having made a pact with the devil. As pastoral experience shows, such pacts with the devil are to this day no unusual phenomenon. Thus it again fits the findings of our study, as we saw in the section on magic conjuration that occult activity produces psychological disturbances in one's own life and in that of one's descendants. In the case of Achille, the father's pact with the devil was followed by a state of

496 ibid., p. 95.
497 ibid., p. 105.

dissociation in the life of the son. Hence, there is here too in the field of the phenomenon of possession, a frequency ratio between magic and psychological disorders.

This brings us to the question of the occult consequences of possession. We have already seen that a possessed person develops enhanced intelligence and hyperaesthesia. In this section we are concerned with the whole problem of parapsychological phenomena, which appear in connexion with possession. These connexions are so obvious that Oesterreich has added an appendix to his book called "Para-psychological questions". In connexion with possession a strong mediumship develops, which has numerous subsidiary phenomena. Oesterreich's material makes reference to telepathy, clairvoyance (p. 379), telekinesis (p. 380), para-psychic occurrences (p. 381), ecstasy and magnetism (p. 382), trance, somnambulism (p. 383), etc. Among the reports of Warneck[498] there is an example, which we have already mentioned, of a Batak medium who in a state of possession was suddenly able to read fluently an old Batak writing, although in his normal state he had no such knowledge. Among the effects of possession there also appears the magic charming of illness. The fact of occult effects of possession permits us to draw inferences about the psychological nature and religious character of possession. Pastoral experience and the circuit of psycho-organic correspondence teach us that where mediumistic capacities arise a psychological disintegration connected with accelerated activity and mobilization of the subconscious is in progress. Hence the phenomena of possession takes its place, in the problems it raises, among the other para-psychological phenomena.

One element among the phenomena of possession would still be lacking if Oesterreich did not also supply us with data about depressive states in connexion with possession. Hence the tenth problem in this list is the destruction of mental integrality. The emotional structure of persons mentally sound is marked by functional harmony, by a smooth coordination of all the emotional powers. The essence of depressions is the break-up of psychological unity. It is an empirical fact that occult involvement breaks up the personality structure. The results of this disintegration are sufficiently familiar. It is remarkable that with regard to this disintegration, possession and occult activity have similar effects. A couple of examples can illustrate this. During the epidemic of possession in Loudun, Father Surin became infected,[499] and fell into a peculiar state of depression which lasted many years. The disturbances

---

[498] ibid., p. 266.
[499] ibid., p. 54.

of emotional life, the instability of mood, of possessed persons coincide with similar disturbances in occult subjection, but not by any means with the emotional disturbances of schizophrenics, of manic-depressives, and of psychopaths. In pastoral care the difference appears in the results of treatment.

A further argument for the correspondence of psychological disturbances in depression and in occult involvement is the sudden incidence of increased sexuality. Oesterreich gives some typical examples. St. Antony was plagued by demonic visions of women.[500] This is the phenomenon of succubae, which was so prevalent in the Middle Ages. From the mission field reports of similar mysterious visitations still come in today. Oesterreich also records increased sexuality in the possessed nun Jeanne des Anges, in whom a violent passion flared up for a priest. Psychologically we can understand these phenomena as the effects of repressed sexual stimulation. But these strong effects did not appear until after the dissociation manifestations of possession. Here we have evidence that man loses his mastery over the household of his soul as soon as the unity of his psychological make-up is impaired. From this aspect, too, we can see that possession and the medical side of occult subjection present a phenomenon of psychic disintegration and dissociation symptoms.

This is the ten-fold contribution of Oesterreich's work to our study. The material of Oesterreich is so abundant and so versatile, and the perspectives which it offers are so fruitful, that a major part of the findings of our study can be supported by it. The most important element is the establishment of the fact that amid all the evidence for a greater or lesser degree of immanence in the phenomena of possession, the door remains open for the possible existence of transcendent centres of operation. Theology cannot really demand more than this from the philosopher and the psychologist.

2. *Direct testimony.* Dr. Lechler is one of the few psychiatrists who recognize, besides the psychiatric disease-patterns, psychological disorders which are due to demonic influence. In order that we may not give a one-sided picture of his views in our presentation there, we mention in advance that he emphasizes that psychological disorders of demonic origin occur much less frequently than some pastoral counsellors commonly suppose. In this field great restraint and patient observation are necessary, before we may proceed to this final conclusion. Lechler writes, in the introduction to his lectures,[501] "The doctor of souls, the Christian

---

[500] ibid., p. 80.
[501] cf. Lechler, op. cit. 227b, p. 1.

psychiatrist, has an important contribution to make in this field. But his is not an easy situation. For on the one hand it is impossible for him simply to dismiss demonology as the science of psychiatry does; on the other hand he cannot simply show agreement with the opinions about demons which often prevail in believing circles."

After this statement of his basic position, Dr. Lechler attempts to develop three relationships between "demonology and disturbance of the soul". He distinguishes possession, demonic influence, and deception.[502] On *possession*, he cites three cases from literature: Gottliebin Dittus, Frau Brandstätter, and the case of possession reported by Johannes Seitz.[503] To these Dr. Lechler adds a few cases from his practice, and declares: "Possession is neither an outdated biblical fable, nor a theological intention, but a dreadful reality."[504] He desires to distinguish in all some seven characteristics of possession: double voice, clairvoyance, paroxysms, great bodily strength, resistance to divine things, exorcism during attacks, and complete cure after expulsion. Lechler emphasizes that these marks of the New Testament descriptions agree with the marks of possession in our day. In particular Lechler regards the rapping sounds and the telekinetic phenomena as of demonic origin. Here his view differs from that of Bender.

By *demonic influence* Lechler understands abnormal expressions of the soul as the results of demonic interference. As marks of demonic influence he names: non-receptiveness to everything divine, religious doubt, inability to make a true confession of sin, inability to concentrate on bible reading and prayer, persistent lack of peace, inner unrest, states of anxiety, outbursts of temper, belligerency, blasphemy, depression, suicidal inclinations. In addition there are various addictions: to alcohol, immorality, lying, theft, smoking, narcotics. The marks of demonic influence coincide in part with those of real possession, but there are lacking the symptoms of clairvoyance and of another voice speaking from the subjected person. The third class, that of deception, we shall not deal with here.

In the question regarding the *causes* of possession and of demonic influence, Lechler gives the same answer that has been given by our study: involvement with occult things such as divination, charms, spiritism, fetishism, and so on. Lechler explains however that we may not make a generalization from this fact. He writes: "It depends on the grace of

---

502 id. op. cit. 227a, p. 3.
503 cf. Blumhardt, op. cat. 279; Keller, op. cit. 231, pp. 115f; Seitz, "Erinnerungen und Erfahrungen".
504 cf. Lechler, op. cit. 227b, p. 6.

God whether or not a person incurs damage by engaging in these practices."

We have already spoken briefly (Pt. III ch. 2, 3) of the difference between psychiatric disease-patterns and psychological disturbances due to demonic influence. When Lechler's position is compared with the results of our study, a wide measure of agreement appears, with the exception that in our study we have availed ourselves of the insights of psychology into the field of dissociation (Prof. Bender). Thus we have further broadened the scope of criticism in the evaluation of psychological disturbances.

With regard to theology, the psychiatrist Dr. Lechler has done a great service to Christian counselling, in that he has proved that the phenomena of possession in the New Testament still have their parallels in the same pathological conditions today. This, too, is one of the many counter-arguments against the theology of Bultmann.[505]

(d) *The theory of extra-sensory centres of action*

On the basis of the *material* principle of this study, we have discussed in succession the most important possibilities for explaining the psychological disturbances. Now we come to the question whether we are to be content, as are the other sciences, with an unexplainable residue, or whether we dare take the final step, on the ground of a reflection which includes not only all the rational factors, but also those elements suggested by faith. This question does not arise from idle curiosity or theological considerations, but from the practical necessity of helping those afflicted by occultism. Unless we have a clear diagnosis, no specific therapy will be possible.

[505] Perhaps in the context of this study the question will arise why, in dealing with the problem of demons, we conduct no debate with Bultmann. In answer to this complaint we point out that our present study is of a practical, pastoral, and not of a systematic nature. And further the comment of Prof. Iwand on the theology of Bultmann is here appropriate: "That the end of such a long-travelled road, a road thought to be the only possible one (sc. the road of Liberalism) should be accompanied by great convulsions, which are only just beginning to appear — who could fail to be amazed? But let us not now allow ourselves to be delayed by the rearguard skirmishes which will inevitably break out among these schools of thought which have arrived thus at an impasse. They are debates whose general presuppositions have become outdated" *Stimme der Gemeinde*, no. 6 1951, p. 6. What the N. T. has to say about the demonic is no myth from which the core of truth has to be extricated. Prof. Schlink writes of this in "Studium Generale", 1948, p. 203: "We who would demythologize the bible overlooks the fact that its testimony, as a whole and in its parts, has already been demythologized, when God's word, in the act of revelation, by entering the speech of man broke through man's myths."

If we are to penetrate to the ultimate grounds of the psychological disturbances accompanying occult involvements, as Dr. Lechler has already done, then we shall find ourselves seriously at a loss with the problem of whether there is a possible basis of comparison, a common ground on which we can present a connexion between the sensible and the super-sensible world. We are here in rather the same situation as with the theistic proofs. Can we from our side prove the existence of God? Kant in his "Critique of Pure Reason" denied the cogency of the theistic proofs, since "Reason spreads her wings in vain to rise above the world of sense by the bare power of speculation". Ritschl too rejected all natural knowledge of God, and the traditional proofs. Schlatter, however, in his systematic theology[506] speaks of the inevitability of the God idea. Apart from these philosophical or theological opinions, which we cannot here discuss, it must however be basically admitted that on the question of knowledge of God and the proofs of God's existence we find ourselves on the plane of the "unequal and wholly different".[507]

Similar to this is the situation regarding evil powers, or "nothingness", as Karl Barth describes them.[508] The existence of evil and "nothingness" is, to be sure, demonstrated to us every day, and yet there is no proof for personal or super-personal powers of evil. Reason does not give us direct evidence of their existence, but at most *indications*. When in our critical examination of pastoral cases we make our approach from the rational arguments of medicine, psychiatry, psychology, and para-psychology, then we must, following the basic material principle of our study, content ourselves with these indications. With these metaphysical indications, rational criticism has reached its terminus. Since these metaphysical hints already touch on the field of biblical faith, biblical concepts already play into this border zone of reason, into this forecourt of faith. To this rational tangent, which touches upon the metaphysical sphere, various points pertain. And now we must partially link up with what we have already drawn from the material of Oesterreich. (Pt. III, ch. 4, 5 [c]).

The first indication of metaphysical connexions is the *consistency* of possession phenomena over a period of two thousand years. From the material of Oesterreich, we have already seen the constantly recurring characteristic marks of possession. It is the observation of this psychologist that the phenomena of possession in our day agree with those of

---

[506] cf. Adolf Schlatter, "Das christliche Dogma", Calwer Vereinsbuchhandlung, Stuttgart, 2nd. edn. 1923, pp. 25f.

[507] cf. Althaus, op. cit. [457], vol. II, p. 51.

[508] German: "Das Nichtige" — cf. Karl Barth "Die kirchliche Dogmatik", Evang. Verlag Zollikon, Zürich, vol. III 3, p. 327.

the New Testament. The psychiatrist Dr. Lechler also draws attention to this fact in his lectures.

We must now ask whether this consistency in the marks of possession through thousands of years can be explained by the insights of depth analysis. The Swiss researcher C. G. Jung has pointed out that each person has, over and above the personal contents of his subconscious, also a share in the subconscious of his family, his race and of all humanity. The collective subconscious stores up in itself all the experiential knowledge from the earliest days of man down to the present. Jung thinks that in a moment of special danger or fear we pass anew through the anxieties of thousands of years.

This theory of Jung could partially explain the noted consistency by the perseverance of the human race, if we did not have in the case of possession some phenomena which cannot be explained as contents of the subconscious, such as e. g. prevision into the future by possessed persons and mediums. Prof. Köberle, in his essay on faith and super-stition,[509] also provides evidence that not all the occult phenomena can be explained by the theory of Jung. There is, even on a scientific view, at present no other explanation possible for the fact of this consistency than the continuous existence and activity of supernatural powers through thousands of years.

A second indication of supernatural factors is the arresting regularity of the *coincidence* of the beginning of psychological disturbances with occult involvement. In many cases the point of time at which psychological disturbances arise is shortly after some occult activity. Further, the increasing intensity of psychological conflicts, e. g. in the family of a charmer or of a fortune-teller, is concurrent with an increase in occult involvement. Only in the cases of occult subjection in the second to fourth generations, in connexion with the psychic engrams, does the picture change. We shall now make a short critical investigation into the significance of this coincidence.

Bleuler writes in his textbook of psychiatry,[510] "Errors originate when we take simple coincidence for regular coincidence, and thus for causal connexion (e. g. the sick person recovered because a charm was applied) ..." Such false interpretation of a coincidence can have various causes. Suggestive questions by a counsellor can lead to the belief in a patient who is sick in mind, or unstable and easily influenced, that psychological abnormalities began after occult involvement. In such a case, the coincidence would consist merely in a time point fixed as a

509 cf. Köberle, op. cit., pp. 106f.
510 cf. Bleuler, op. cit. [129], p. 49.

result of suggestion, and thus according to Bleuler an error. There is also the other possibility that the counsellor jumps to a conclusion because of a lack of medical or psychological knowledge, or the attaching of exaggerated importance to the occult problem. If in several cases psychological effects are observed after occult involvement, then on the ground of the frequency ratio he will jump to the conclusion that what has been observed is a regular coincidence, i. e. a rule. The psychiatrist can add yet another example to his list. If in the case of a psychotic there appears after a considerable interval a relapse, which begins a new phase of the illness, and this relapse happens to coincide with an occult involvement, then this is no coincidence conditioned by causality. The ground of the progressive psychological complication was the relapse and not the occult involvement. A regular coincidence deduced from this would be imaginary.

In medicine and in psychology we are warned against jumping to conclusions of any kind. Weizsäcker, for instance, in his "Studien zur Pathogenese",[511] establishes by means of thirteen examples taken from school children a frequency ratio between sexual repression and angina. Although we suspect here the "channelling of the energy of repressed sexual desires into a physical development",[512] Weizsäcker is very cautious about such conclusions. He says that rather than a case of repression, this is a local shift of sexual feelings from the genitals to another region.[513] He summarizes his observations in the statement:[514] "The analysis of these cases must warn us against adopting the slick conclusion that angina has a psychogenic origin in forbidden or mismanaged sex activity." Here a medical expert and psychotherapist tells us the same thing as the psychiatrist mentioned above, Bleuler — namely that frequency ratios must not be magnified into proofs of regular coincidence by jumping to conclusions.

This becomes still more evident in a psychological study conducted by E. Schlink.[515] Dr. Schlink studies by exact empirical methods the frequency ratio between conversion and depression.[516] In an inductive manner the "experience elements" are set out against each other according to certain regularities and laws emerging on the ground of their frequency. In connexion with this method, Schlink warns against over-

---

[511] cf. Viktor von Weizsäcker, "Studien zur Pathogenese", Verlag Thieme Wiesbaden, 2nd. edn. 1946.

[512] ibid., p. 15.

[513] ibid., p. 19.

[514] ibid., p. 23.

[515] cf. Schlink, op. cit. [285].

[516] ibid., p. 91.

hasty attempts at explanation. He says, "The apparent connexion is not always, but in fact very often, a simulation of causality, or, more strongly stated, misleading".[517] Thus this psychologist and theologian sounds a note similar to that of the psychiatrist Bleuler and the doctor Weizsäcker, warning us that the establishment of a frequency ratio must not be assumed to be a proof of causality. This fact can be underlined from the experience of pastoral counselling. Youth counselling, especially at youth weeks and youth conferences, establishes a surprising frequency ratio between puberty and the experience of conversion. This is a parallel to the American observations from which Schlink distances himself. The coincidence between puberty and the experience of conversion, which is so often confirmed, does not lead the counsellor to conclude that puberty is the cause of conversion. But even though this causal connexion is rejected, it is nonetheless true that the inner insecurity, psychological tensions and changing moods of young people at the time of puberty present a psychological constitution on the basis of which the experience of conversion is more readily possible than in the confirmed, settled disposition of the period after puberty. The unstable psychological condition of young people at puberty is not the cause of conversion, but at most it is a state of receptiveness — although this might be disputed on theological grounds — for the true cause, which theology calls the grace of God, or the Holy Spirit.

Notwithstanding all the limitations which we must consider in connexion with the problem of frequency ratios, we shall still find, in the constantly observed regularity of temporal coincidence between psychological disturbances and occult involvement, good grounds for assuming a real relation on the one hand in a causal sense, and in the other just in the sense of a state of receptiveness. To make this clear, we shall return once more to the term "occult subjection", which we have already discussed in the section on magic charms. We said there that the process of conjuration contained both a suggestive and a magical component. The result of the process of suggestion in magic charms is the immediate unlocking and mobilization of the subconscious, and further the production of psychic engrams. This process of deep suggestion in the waking state — not a deep hypnosis — initiates a splitting of psychic in the mental structure of the person influenced. This disintegration of the mental structure is the medical side of the process, to be considered as the efficient cause of the psychological disturbances that follow.

Research into the magical component is the task of the pastor and can never be solely entrusted to psychologists studying folk-lore or

[517] ibid., p. 83.

students of religions. Within our study we have up to now used the term occult subjection as a theological concept. The observation constantly made in pastoral work concerning the coincidence of psychological disturbance with occult involvement compels us to make a closer analysis of this subject. The disruption of psychic unity, with all the accompanying symptoms of mental disorder, including religious disorders, can well be discussed as medical phenomena. Here however the typically religious phenomena are excluded, as will be shown in the chapters which follow. The God-opposing fanaticism which suddenly appears after occult activity indicates a coincidence relation of a parapsychical, transcendent order. This relation is not accessible to medical research, since it lies on a higher plane. This trans-medical character of psycho-religious disturbances, which is a relation empirically established, throws significant light on the question of evaluating magical processes. Notwithstanding the demythologizing attempts of medicine and of the Bultmann school of theology, we find that all attempts at explanation on a secular basis fail at this point. It is evident to the observer in pastoral practice that occult involvement creates a condition of receptiveness for powers of another dimension.

This brings us to the purely religious phenomenon of *resistance*. While the question of coincidence is one that must be studied by both medicine and theology together, here we have a problem which is purely theological. Naturally it must be conceded to the psychiatrist that a number of psychotic conditions are linked with religious delusions. But with resistance, we are not dealing with the religious delusions of those mentally ill, but with an attitude of opposition to God taken up by healthy people who have become involved in occultism. Dr. Lechler as a psychiatrist likewise distinguishes schizophrenia from the phenomenon of possession, exactly as the psychologists Schmeïng and Oesterreich do. But Lechler concedes that the differential diagnosis is difficult, or even impossible, for those unversed in medicine. We shall not enter into this problem again here, since we have already discussed it.

Oesterreich brings some characteristic material on the subject of resistence, as we have already seen in Pt. III, ch. 4. 5 (c). Dr. Lechler presents this phenomenon even more clearly than does Oesterreich. He writes:[518] "Especially indicative of the presence of possession is an opposition to all divine influences. When the possessed person comes in contact with Christians who try to influence him religiously, or to pray with him, we see strong resistant activities, since the demon sets up, a defence against being ejected from his habitation. We see a spirit of

---

[518] cf. Lechler, op. cit. 227b, p. 7.

contradiction against all that is divine, bursts of fury, hitting out at those who are around, and blasphemy. He hates communal prayer; he despises godly people; he flings the bible into a corner. Faith in God, and especially in the propitiatory sacrifice of Christ, is odious to him. The challenge by the counsellor to acknowledge all that troubles him evokes a determined resistance. He appears to be restrained by a mysterious power from disclosing his life to the other person. He cannot express the name 'Jesus', or at any rate only against great resistance."

My own pastoral cases fit into the same pattern as is expressed by Oesterreich and Lechler. The phenomenon of resistance is the most frequent result of all occult activities. We find it with every occult involvement except telepathy, predictive dreams, water-divining with the rod, and clairvoyance as a secondary effect in the second to fourth generations. Resistance is also found in the clairvoyance of the first generation, where it is a primary effect of involvement. A fact which speaks loudly for the metaphysical background of resistance is the outburst of fanatic fury which occurs in the moment of an intercession of which the subject is not aware. An example from Lechler's lectures (a quotation from Johannes Seitz) will illustrate this.

Lit 17 Seitz writes: "Every time we stopped praying, his shrieks would also stop. Then I came upon the idea of waiting until the next evening, and of giving him a room upstairs in the house, instead of on the ground floor. We agreed then to pray as before in the room on the ground floor, but not until he had gone to sleep. We put another young man in the room with him, who was to tell us when he had fallen asleep, so that it would be quite impossible for him to notice that we were praying for him. But when we began to pray, and had been doing so scarcely for a moment, we were forced to hear, as on the previous evening, the most dreadful cries and commotion. We continued in prayer until midnight. Suddenly the cries ceased, but immediately we heard a kind of very loud talking. I slipped up to the door to listen. And what I heard was a cry out of the deepest soul to God. It was an alternation of crying and giving thanks to God, that He had at last delivered him. The next morning he came down with his face beaming, saying, 'Now I am free'."

Our earlier example *Ex 8* fits in with this. There a commotion arose in the spiritist session upstairs while the woman on the first floor was praying. I know of more cases of this kind, some from my own experience. The resistance against divine influences is also a mark of the cases of possession recorded in the New Testament. The possesed person would always begin to cry aloud in the presence of Jesus, and would resist His influence (Matt. 8, 29; Mark 1, 24; 5, 7; Luke 4, 34; 8, 28; 9, 42). The phenomenon of resistance shows itself, like all possession phenomena, as a characteristic which has persisted unchanged for thousands of years.

In the same sphere as resistance we also have the *paroxysm*, i. e. the aggravation of the phenomenon in the form of a fit. According to the New Testament reports there are two forms, viz. the physical alteration, with change of voice and increase of motor activity (Mark 5, 7; Luke 4, 33; 8, 29; Acts 19, 16); and the attacks during exorcism, with loud cries and convulsions (Mark 1, 26; Luke 4, 35, 41; Acts 8, 7). In cases of possession in church history and in the present day, we see a pronounced consistency in these characteristics. Oesterreich reports how a possessed man always had convulsions when he had to pass a church or crucifix. The attack would sometimes occur when the crucifix could not yet be seen by the man. Dr. Lechler likewise tells in his lectures of a girl who at times sensed uncanny powers in her body, so that she had to be held by several people, because she felt the urge to destroy everything. Such cases of destructive fury in connexion with manic attacks are very familiar to me from pastoral experience. Among the examples we have already adduced, we have such phenomena in *Exx 5, 61, 65, 66, 79, 91* and *Lit 12*. I once saw an exceptionally severe case during an exorcism. It is fact corroborated by many that people subjected to occult influence behave quite calmly and normally as long as they do not meet with Christian influences. Dr. Lechler confirms this observation. He writes: "When no religious incursion follows, the possessed person need display no noticeable symptoms. He is usually unobtrusive and friendly.[519] It is in a state of dispute that the occult subjection first becomes evident. The state occurs upon earnest intercession for the subject, or upon his desire to become a Christian, and sometimes also in the agony of standing at the gate of eternity. This rule, which has so often been substantiated, is an eloquent testimony to the existence of a metaphysical background of paroxysm.

A further striking element in the characteristics described is the psychological *disintegration*. The healthy person is characterized in his emotional structure by a harmonious interplay of all functions. This unity can undergo a disintegration, e. g. in the psychiatric phenomenon of depersonalization, in the psychological phenomenon of dissociation, in the para-psychological phenomenon of psychic separation, and in the religious phenomenon of occult subjection. The symptoms of these four phenomena are by no means the same. In pastoral care we are concerned

---

[519] ibid., loc. cit.

with the last named. An example which gives strong evidence for disintegration is *Ex 24*. The visionary in that example was a disintegrated type. That which is characteristic of the religious phenomenon of disintegration in possessed persons is the fact that they are on the one hand desirous of faith in God, and on the other resistant against divine influences. Oesterreich[520] shows an example of this in the possessed priest, Surin, who felt on the one hand a deep peace with God, but was at the same time helpless in the face of the state of possession, in which he felt feelings of hatred towards Christ. He retained consciousness during the attacks. He was torn to and fro between the two conditions, or experienced both simultaneously.

Such inner dissociation is a frequent phenomenon in interviews with people who are under occult subjection. They constantly confess that they do not desire to utter these blasphemies against the divine, these thoughts of hatred towards Christ, but that they cannot overcome them when they rise up within them. The psychiatrist would want to explain this phenomenon as a compulsion neurosis. But the distinction between the psychiatric and the occult spheres has been sufficiently explained already, so that any explanation here would be superfluous. Dr. Lechler, who as a psychiatrist is competent to make this differential diagnosis, likewise records this inner conflict in possessed persons. He writes: "The possessed person is filled with a constant lack of peace, though at the same time he may have a great yearning for inner peace".[521] This disunity of mental state is also a mark of the New Testament cases of possession. The Gadarene of Mark 5 first went to Jesus in his desire to receive help, and not until then did the resistance appear. The dominance of the resisting will is worth noting in this case of split personality.

Hyperaesthesia in the form of temporal prevision is a clear indication of extra-sensory relations. The approximately thirty theories of clairvoyance which we have looked at are unable to explain exact prevision. The explanations of depth analysts, with their reference to subconscious factors, fail in cases where clairvoyants have insight into or mastery of things previously unknown to them, such as fluent speech in a foreign language, etc. Clairvoyance has already been discussed in the section on magic charms (Pt. II, ch. 2,2 (c)), as a primary or secondary effect of the process of conjuration. Both Prof. Oesterreich and Dr. Lechler have pointed out examples of clairvoyance in possessed persons. Among our examples this phenomenon is seen, as already noted, in *Exx 1, 4, 20, 24, 33, 37, 40, 49, 56, 57, 59, 63* and *65*. This list could easily be ex-

---

[520] cf. Oesterreich, op. cit. [63], pp. 37f.
[521] cf. Lechler, op. cit. [227b], p. 7.

panded with many other cases. This phenomenon is anchored in the New Testament, just like the others. There too possessed persons are clairvoyant: they grasp the significance of the Person of Jesus in the present and for the future (Matt 8, 29; Mark 5, 7; Luke 8, 28; cf. Acts 16, 16).

The last feature which we here note as pointing to extra-sensory centres of operation is the *speedy recovery* after exorcism. In pastoral care we can clearly distinguish between persons under occult subjection and e. g. psychopaths or psychotics. Psychological disturbances conditioned by predisposition are very hard to cure, if at all curable, when we speak from a medical viewpoint and not from the biblical. A therapy of such patients in many cases takes months or years. On the other hand people subjected to occultism can, by proper treatment and pastoral care which is empowered from on high, be speedily released and cured. For we are not usually faced with such severe cases as, for example, Gottliebin Dittus, for whom Blumhardt struggled for months (cf.[279]). In the New Testament such speedy cures are often mentioned (Mark 1, 39; 5, 15; Luke 8, 2, 32—39).

To sum up all the characteristics, the narrative of the possessed man at Gadara will suffice, since his case embraces all of them (Mark 5, 1—15):

v. 2:   possession with an unclean spirit
v. 3:   enhanced motorial powers — no one could bind him
v. 4:   paroxysm — he breaks the shackles and strikes himself with stones
v. 6:   disintegration: — desire for and fear of help
v. 7:   resistance: — opposition to Jesus
v. 7:   hyperaesthesia — he recognizes the deity of Jesus and His authority as judge
v. 9:   physical alteration — change of voice
v. 12:   occult transference — entrance into the swine.

To verse 12 we may add an explanation. This phenomenon of transference is not so absurd as many critics perhaps think. Among our examples *Ex 70* lies on the same level. In pastoral interviews confession is often made that, after the spook phenomena by which the person was molested had subsided, the animals in the stables were troubled. The phenomenon of transference from man appears in *Exs 91, 102* and *103*.

With these indications of extra-sensory centres of activity, we have reached the end of the road of reason. The scientific investigation of occult phenomena within the bounds of our material principle is now complete. The findings of this critical examination of the cases gives us our third thesis:

The sciences bordering on the problem of occult subjection, such as psychiatry and psychology, depth analysis and the psychology of religion, para-psychology and philosophy, give the pastor to a great extent the equipment he needs for the rational understanding of the psychological disturbances which are conditioned by occult involvement. In the border zone of the occult phenomena, there is from the scientific point of view an unexplainable residue, with an open question as to the transcendent nature of these processes.

It is now our task to explain the transcendent factor of occult subjection, which cannot be explained using the categories of the material principle of our study. The problem of the theological classification of the occult practices, namely the study of the biblical principles bearing on this question, is now the subject under discussion. We are here concerned to elucidate the upper of the so-called "layers" (cf. Pt. I ch. 1) and to answer the questions which arise in connexion with the *formal principle* of our study.

Chapter Five

OCCULT PHENOMENA IN THE LIGHT OF THE BIBLE

Corresponding to the rational indications of extra-sensory of activity, we have in the bible the mystery of super-personal powers. Since our study is concerned with powers which have a destructive influence on the spiritual life of man, we have in view the powers that fell out of harmony with the Creator, Satan and the demons. Prof. Thielicke writes:[522] "It is not easy to speak of the reality of the demonic powers; for this cannot under any circumstances be a matter of merely putting together some quotations from the bible. As long as we thus proceed merely statistically, we are not facing the reality of the demonic." We do not feel ourselves to be faced with this difficulty, since it is not necessary here first of all to speak of Satan and the demons. The person who works magic is responsible before God for his occult practices, and not before the court of Satan or of the demons. The occultist who carries on and is led astray by sorcery is in the first place answerable to the Creator. For this reason we have until now in our study consciously foregone any development of a theory of demons, in order to explain the occult processes. We shall now study the expressions of the Old Testament and the New Testament as they bear upon the problem which

[522] cf. Helmut Thielicke, "Fragen des Christentums an die moderne Welt", Mohr, Tübingen, 1947, p. 171.

concerns us. It is not our concern here to collect everything in the Old
and New Testaments which has reference to occult phenomena. Anyone
who wants to survey this question can refer to the sections on demons
and magic in the theologies of the Old Testament of Eichrodt, Proksch,
H. Schultz, and further the specialized studies of Jirku ("Die Dämonen
und Ihre Abwehr im A. T."), Duhm ("Die bösen Geister im A. T."), or
Eissfeld ("Jahvename und Zauberwesen"). For the field of the New
Testament, the following can be used for further study: Bauernfeind,
"Die Worte der Dämonen im Markusevangelium"; Müller, "Das Reich
Gottes und die Dämonen"; Karl Barth, "Dogmatik" III, 3: "Das Nich-
tige"; Mager, "Mystik als seelische Wirklichkeit"; Etudes Carmelitaines,
"Satan"; Heitmüller, "Engel und Dämonen" — to name only a few.

Here in ch. 5 we shall investigate only the question of the place of
occult phenomena in the biblical plan, insofar as it is of interest for the
purpose of our study.

1. *The Evidence of the Old Testament*

In the Old Testament struggle went on both in Mosaic and in
prophetic times against a process of syncretism with the religions of
the neighbouring peoples and those of Canaan. The religious leaders or
advisers of Israel are constantly seeking to root out heathen elements
which penetrate. This controversy is a treasure trove of information
about the magical and divinatory practices of Israel's environment.
Specifically we find the following pagan practices rejected and fought
against.

(a) *Spiritism*

Opposition to this appears plainly in Deut. 18, 11—12: "He who
consults the dead (EVV necromancer) is an abomination to the Lord".
The story of the witch of Endor is the subject of much debate (I Sam. 28).
One thing we may hold for certain, however, is that Saul received his
death sentence in visiting this spiritist. The consultation of the dead was
further rejected by the prophets. Isaiah (8, 19) asks: "Should they
consult the dead on behalf of the living?" On the same plane as necrom-
ancy is the consulting of idols. King Ahaziah (II Kings 1, 2f.) in his
illness sent messengers to Ekron, to consult Baal-zebub. By this consultation of an idol he received his death sentence, just as did Saul at Endor.

(b) *Divination*

Divinatory practices are the most prevalent of occult activities in
ancient heathendom. The Old Testament contains many traces of this
fact, e. g. Gen. 44, 5; Lev. 19, 31; 20, 6 and 27; Deut. 18, 10—12;

I Chron. 10, 13; Isa. 44, 25; Jer. 29, 8f; Ezek. 21, 21; Hos. 4, 12; Mic. 3, 6f.; Zech. 10, 2. Throughout these texts we find various forms of divination such as soothsaying by cup, wand, arrows, lots, liver, dreams, the cry of birds, days of ill omen and other signs. Especially noticeable is the worship of stars, astrology (Deut. 17, 2—5; II Kings 17, 16f.; Isa. 47, 9—14). The Torah pronounces the death penalty on those who fall away into heathen practices of divination (Ex 22, 18; Lev. 20, 6; 20, 27; Deut. 17, 5).

(c) *Magic*

In ancient heathendom magic conjurers formed, as they do today among primitive peoples, a separate professional class. Moses had dealings with them in Egypt (Ex. 7, 11, 22; 8, 7). It is the unalterable position of the Torah (Deut. 18, 10f.) and also of the religion of the prophets (Isa. 47, 9 and 12) that this troop of conjurers has no right of existence in Israel. Because of these magicians the wrath of God comes upon His people (Isa. 47, 9).

(d) *The place of these phenomena in the theology of the Old Testament*

The crucial point and locus classicus for the theological understanding of heathen magic in the religion of Israel is Lev. 19, 31: "Do not turn to mediums or wizards; do not seek them out, to be defiled by them. *I am the Lord your God.*" All magic and divinatory practices are viewed in the Old Testament from the standpoint of the first commandment. The Israelite is not, in the first place, dealing with asherah images, or with hobgoblins, or even with demons, but he is called with all his heathenish practices before the bar of God. He must choose whether Yahweh is his Lord or not. He must occupy himself with the reality of God, and not with the existence of spirits or demons. Magic in the Old Testament is therefore not a matter of demons, but a matter which has to do with God. This is clear not only from the first commandment, but also in other connexions.

Among Israel's heathen neighbours, the "name-cultus"[523] played a prominent role. The name of God was kept as much as possible a secret. Thus it was with the Egyptians[524] and with the Romans; perhaps too the altar to the unknown god in Athens has such a background (Acts 17, 23). He who knows the name of God is here held to dispose over magic powers. Hence the essence of this name-cultus is faith in power and in magic. In the Old Testament we seek in vain for instances of the

[523] cf. Walter Eichrodt, "Theologie des A. T.", Pt. I, p. 97.
[524] ibid., loc. cit.

magical use of the divine name.[525] The faith in Yahweh is thus sharply distinguished from the name-magic of the pagan world. In the Old Testament we do not have a contact with God by means of a magic name, but we have a personal converse of man with his Master. That is the sense of the third commandment: "Thou shalt not take the name of the Lord thy God in vain".[526] From the standpoint of the third commandment, with its prohibition of the magical use of the name, and its encouragement of personal communion with God, it is plain that magic poses a basic question about God. The faith of the Israelite is distinguished from that of the heathen by the fact that Israel's conception of God rejects the unknown "it-relation" of heathenism and takes its stand on a personal "thou-relation". For him reality is the "thou" of God, as it arises in the statement of the first commandment: "I am ... thy God". Before this "thou", all other questions, including those of the complex of magic and divination, divide and are decided.

2. *The Evidence of the New Testament*

The occult phenomena which we find reported in the New Testament can only be properly understood in connexion with the great salvation event of the mission of Jesus Christ.

(a) *The mission of Jesus and the opposition to it*

The appearance of Jesus Christ means the dawning of the kingdom of God on earth. This kingdom shows itself in the new reality of salvation: the blind see, the lame walk, the lepers are cleansed, the deaf hear, the dead are raised, and the poor have the Gospel preached to them (Matt. 11, 5); the prisoners are loosed, the oppressed are freed, the year of the Lord's good pleasure has come (Luke 4, 18). Against this reality of the kingdom, the adversary organizes his forces for the counter-attack. He sets all in motion against Christ:[527] the Jewish authorities, the theologians, the priests, the people, His own disciples, the Roman rulers. Whence comes this deadly hostility? The powers of darkness see their kingdom threatened; the Civitas Diaboli is in danger. All their might is therefore summoned up for the counter attack. Against the power (exousia) of God's own Son (Matt. 7, 29) is opposed the

[525] Today however this is normal in white magic.

[526] Eichrodt sees in the expression "qara be šem yahweh", a faint trace of this name-faith, which is removed in the simple expression ".ara 'el qahweh" (op. cit. 523, p. 97, note 4).

[527] cf. Ethelbert Stauffer, "Die Theologie des N. T.", Bertelsmann Verlag, Gütersloh, 1948, p. 103.

exousia of darkness (Luke 22, 53). This opposition is from the start doomed to defeat. Jesus says: "If I by the finger of God cast out devils, then the kingdom of God has come upon you" (Luke 11, 20). By this word of Jesus the place of demonism, of exorcism, of occult involvement and subjection, is clearly stated to be between His first advent and His return.

(b) *The New Testament aspect of the demonic*

The nature of Jesus' mission supplies the answer to our question and to the enigma surrounding the powers of darkness. Karl Heim writes:[528] "The removal of the confusion which has arisen through Satan's rebellion is therefore the ultimate meaning of the mission of Jesus on the earth. If this satanic revolution against God had not taken place, the mission of Christ on earth would not have resulted." Heim sees this conception of the mission of Jesus in the exposition of Paul in I Cor. 15. There it is said that Christ must continue to exercise kingly rule until He has put all enemies as a foot-stool under His feet. Then Christ will have finished His mission, and He can give back to the Father what has been committed to Him. From the extent of the dominion exercised by Christ we are able to deduce a picture of the extent of the satanic rebellion. The authority which Jesus exercises throws light on the power of the adversary. Thus the understanding of the powers of darkness in the New Testament turns upon understanding the Christ; in short, the question of demons is a question of Christ. Thus we have arrived at a result like the one we reached in respect to the data of the Old Testament.

Karl Barth has grasped this point even more clearly. Barth writes in his "Dogmatik":[529] "Whence do we know that nothingness exists, and indeed so really exists, in this exaltation and radicality which is excluded from legitimate inclusion in any world view, that we must be content to be forbidden to have converse with it, as if it were an element of the created world along with other elements? All of this arises directly, clearly and surely from the origin of all Christian knowledge in the knowledge of Christ." Here Barth acknowledges that knowledge regarding nothingness, the satanic, the demonic, is tied up with the question of the knowledge of Christ. Prof. Hahn writes in similar vein (op. cit. [674], p. 7), that demonology must be deduced from Christian facts. In our questions regarding the demonic background of occult phenomena, the question of Christ always stands first of all, in the foreground. Where we overlook this, every idea about the demonic will have a distorted

---

[528] cf. Karl Heim, "Jesus der Weltvollender", Furche Verlag Berlin, 1937, p. 84.
[529] cf. Barth, op. cit. [508], p. 344.

primitive biblicism has given rise to a naive cult of devils and demons. field of vision. We must assert this especially in view of the fact that Just as above, in connexion with the bordering sciences, so here from a theological standpoint, a warning is in place against over-hasty theories of demons.

(c) *The double character of the "sign"*

In the Old Testament the conviction already prevails that the nature of a sign (Heb.'oth) is not unambiguous. The Israelite knew "that anything surprising and fascinating could originate from other powers than God. It could be the work of magicians or other elohim-powers; indeed, God could even permit some dangerous person to succeed in performing a miracle, in order to put His people to the test".[530] In the New Testament the situation is even more precarious. For the word semeion is sometimes used of divine miracles (Mark 16, 17; John 2, 23; 4, 54; 6, 2; 9, 16; 11, 47; Acts 4, 16; etc.), but sometimes also of demonic miracles (Matt. 24, 24; Mark 13, 22; II Thess. 2, 9; Rev. 13, 13; 16, 14; 19, 20). This double meaning of the term shows the difficulty of evaluating signs.[531] Thielicke writes of this:[532] "Satan has the zeal and the expert knowledge of a renegade; hence he can perform miracles as Christ does". We recognize in the ambiguity of the word semeion the imitation of the mission of Jesus in the counter-action of Satan. The sign is in itself no indicator of the origin which inspires it. It requires the word of God as its interpreter and formal principle.

3. *Synopsis of the Evidence and Its Evaluation for our Study*

A summary of the points which we have brought out so far provides us with the following findings in connexion with the formal principle of our study:

(a) The complex of magic and divination in the Old Testament definitely has its roots in the heathenism of Israel's neighbours. The struggle with these heathen intrusions is a problem concerning the true God in the light of the first and third commandments.

(b) On the level of the New Testament, we can only understand occult phenomena in the light of the mission of Jesus Christ. Christ is the King who resists Satan's attempt to seize the authority wielded by God alone. The battle between the kingdom of God and the kingdom

---

530 cf. Eichrodt, op. cit. 523, vol. II, p. 85.

531 In my publication "Interimszeit", Reith Verlag, Wüstenrot, 1949, p. 37, this situation is illustrated.

532 cf. Thielicke, op. cit. 522, p. 191.

of Satan reveals the existence, nature and might of the dark powers, the understanding of which presents one side of the Christ question.

(c) Displays of power from both kingdoms, such as signs and wonders, have, because of their double meaning, no direct value as revelation. The imperative here is: "Test the spirits to see whether they are of God" (I John 4, 1).

We shall include a short excursus here in outline form. In contra-distinction to the *occult* phenomena, the bible has its *charismatic* phenomena:

Extra-sensory perception — in the Holy Spirit
Messages from God's world (Luke 1, 26), in place of spiritism
Prophecy in O. T. and N. T., in place of clairvoyance
Divine promises (Luke 1, 76), in place of divination
Testing of the spirits (I John 4, 1), in place of mediumistic abilities

Extra-sensory influence — in the Holy Spirit
The prayer of faith (James 5, 14), in place of magic
Healing by faith (Matt. 16, 17), in place of conjuration
Outpouring of the Holy Spirit (Acts 2), in place of psychokinesis
Devoted surrender to Christ (Luke 5, 28), in place of blood pacts
Assurance of God's protection (Matt. 28, 20), in place of superstition

Extra-sensory apparitions — in the Holy Spirit
The service of heavenly messengers (Acts 12, 7), in place of spooks
Anchoring of the soul in Christ (Heb. 6, 19), in place of excursion of
    the soul.

(d) Those involved in occult practices who do not come to a decision with regard to the question of God and of Christ stand under judgement, fall under the power of nothingness, of chaos,[533] and end up in dependence on the powers of darkness. The converse is also true: those who accept Christ as Lord stand in the company of the Victor who came to destroy the works of the devil (I John 3, 8).

(e) Magic, occult practices are in our present day a focal point at which the war front between the *civitas Dei* and the *civitas diaboli* becomes visible, a confrontation which is every bit as real today as it was in the time of Jesus. For we are still standing at the dawning of the kingly rule of God, and shall continue to do so until its manifestation before all the world at the Parousia. In occult activities and occult subjection, the last battle between the lordship of God and the power of darkness becomes evident. Here are the bastions, the fortresses in which

---

533 In view of this, Kurt Hennig has given his exposition of the Ten Commandments the right title: "Gehorsam oder Chaos" (Obedience or chaos). Quell Verlag, Stuttgart, 1951.

we can see the concentrated resistance of the enemy, who, in spite of all his violent assaults, is the vanquished one, only able now to engage in a rearguard action. Over against this opponent there is no conditional peace treaty, but only total defeat and subjection; no compromise, but only unconditional capitulation.

At this point we shall insert another short excursus. In view of the perspectives given in this section, it is impossible to accept what Bovet says when he writes:[534] "It is all-important for the pastor to know that there is such a thing (sc. as occult phenomena), demonstrated by all the scientific criticism one could wish for, which shows already certain regular patterns, so that we may hope that in the near future the whole field of occultism may be incorporated into the natural, scientific and Christian world view and enrich it thereby". In the New Testament view, occultism in its magic form is the power of darkness (Luke 22, 53). How then can the power of God's kingdom and the power of darkness be united? What has Christ in common with Belial? (II Cor. 6, 15). How can a compromise be brought about between the Kingdom of God and the kingdom of Satan? Dr. Bovet here misguidedly strikes at the teaching of the New Testament, and that in a book for Christian counsellors, who gladly avail themselves of an expert like Bovet!

It is extremely painful for me to be compelled to be so aggressive on this point against Dr. Bovet, whom on the ground of his other books and personal contacts I regard so highly as a doctor and as a Christian. But truth is above friendship. It would have been less confusing and dangerous if Bovet, instead of speaking of occultism, had at least chosen the term para-psychology, since this scientific branch of occultism has in general little to do with magic. But occultism is always marked by magic, and is shaped by its magical invocation of the Trinity or of the powers of darkness. Magic always means membership in the kingdom of Satan. And membership in the kingdom of darkness can never be harmonized with membership in the body of Christ. Therefore occultism can never be incorporated into the Christian world view, as Dr. Bovet would hope.

The result of our study of the bible to find the theological place of occult phenomena forms our fourth thesis:

Occult phenomena in the Old Testament have their roots in heathen magic. Within the scope of the New Testament, they are to be understood as symptoms of the conflict between the kingdom of the devil and the Kingdom of God. Their implication in this conflict determines their condition of being under judgement, a condition which ends in chaos.

---

[534] cf. Bovet, op. cit. [171], p. 49.

Chapter Six

ON THE DIAGNOSIS OF MENTAL DISORDERS DUE TO OCCULT INVOLVEMENT

We have now applied standards to occult phenomena according to the categories of the material and the formal principles. We have solicited the opinions of the doctor, the psychologist, the psychical researcher, the philosopher and the theologian. We have noted that each of these is versed in a particular aspect of the occult phenomena which is not so well known to the others. The co-operation of these five disciplines makes possible a view of the material in which the sources of error are reduced to a minimum. In now welding the contributions of these five disciplines together into a conclusion which answers the questions we raised in the prolegomena, we must point out that each discipline whose aspect of the occult we have examined has been presented using its own terminology. We have thereby aimed at preserving the distinctness of the concepts, even when these bordering sciences were being introduced almost in a kind of personal union in order to shed light on the problems of occultism.

We shall now again give our attention to the real concern of this study. We are concerned to find a suitable therapy for psychological disturbances of occult origin, in other words a way of overcoming occult subjection. Normally speaking a therapy is only possible when the causes of the disorder are clearly understood. Hence we must once more set forth the concept of *occult subjection,* since all our preliminary studies have been related to this. In the prolegomena we have already remarked that occult subjection is not something like a sum consisting of medical and theological components, but that this concept is divided into different dimensions, existing at different levels. What can the individual disciplines contribute towards the clarification of this concept? We have taken up only one phenomenon from among the various problems, namely that of the *dissociation of consciousness.*

The psycho-somatic school of *medicine* points to the fact that man, in his structure of spirit, soul and body, forms a complete whole, a unity. Prof. Mitscherlich, head of the psycho-somatic seminary in Heidelberg, speaks of a relation of simultaneity[535a] of body and soul. Heyer calls this psychosomatic interrelatedness the "complementarity" of body and soul.[535b] All these terms testify to the close, mutual interrelation between the psychic and the organic. "Every occurrence in man can be understood from the physical as well as the psychological angle." So

535a German: "Simultanverhältnis".
535b German: "Leib-Seele-Komplementarität".

Dr. Scheffen wrote in an article on physical disturbances with mental causes.[535c]

In our present study we have, in view of this fact, worked out the law of the circuit of psycho-organic correspondence on the basis of many individual pastoral observations in the field of occult practices. This means, for example, that organic changes can also be caused by psychological experiences and shocks, and vice versa. As examples of both these facts, we mention the patients of M. and W. Prince. The one patient, Pastor Hanna, suffered a dissociation of consciousness as a result of an organic shock, a fall on the head. The other patient, Mr. Meyer, suffered a dissociation of consciousness resulting from an emotional experience leading to shock. The effect was the same in both cases; the cause was a shock, in the one case due to an organic disturbance, in the other to a mental one.

These insights of medicine have been corroborated and deepened by *psychology*. Prof. Pfahler,[536] proceeding from his ground-work in developmental psychology, came to the conclusion that no "occurrence takes place in the realm of the body without giving rise to a reaction in that of the soul, and none in the mind without a reaction in the body". To come back to the subject of our discussion, Prof. Bender has shown by many experiments that such dissociations can be caused artificially. He it is moreover who warns against a careless handling of such experiments. Thus we here have a further element, namely that psychological disturbances can result as a by-product of such experiments. He writes for instance:[537] "A. Mühl gives us a few safety rules for the practice of automatic writing, which through excessive or uncontrolled use is not free from danger", but has "unsettling effects".

We are led still further into this special field by *para-psychology*, which concerns itself with the whole complex of various kinds of psychic dissociation. By many thousands of experiments and spontaneous incidents, a whole series of phenomena has come to be recognized as resulting from splits in the subconscious. Here too it is sometimes conceded by researchers, e. g. Tischner,[538] that psychological disturbances can arise as secondary effects.

The aspect of secondary effects becomes much clearer in *pastoral counselling*, in which we consciously give special attention to the psychological disturbances which arise in connexion with the artificially in-

---

[535c] cf. Scheffen, op. cit. 541, p. 99.

[536] cf. Gerhard Pfahler, "Der Mensch und seine Vergangenheit", Ernst Klett, Stuttgart, 1950.

[537] cf. Bender, op. cit. 3, p. 38.

[538] cf. Tischner, op. cit. 25a, p. 43.

duced dissociation phenomena — dissociation artifacts, as Bender calls them. Systematic observation by the pastor has this in common with psychology and para-psychology, that in practically all occult phenomena it is found that we are dealing with the effects of subconscious factors. During fifteen years of observation, frequency ratios have become evident between artificially evoked manifestations of dissociation and subsequent psychological disturbances. In all cases in which lay practitioners mobilize and activate the subconscious of themselves or others, traces of this influence were left in the subconscious. This agrees also with the findings of depth analysis, which demonstrates that the subconscious disposes over an enormous faculty for storing impressions, and over great powers of memory.

Thus far pastoral work finds itself on the same level as the aforementioned bordering sciences. The findings of the psycho-somatic school, of depth psychology and of para-psychology receive full confirmation from the side of pastoral experience.

> According to this view, occult subjection is nothing other than an engram caused by the activation of the subconscious through suggestion in a waking state. The ecphory[539a] of this engram produces a series of dissociation phenomena of varying character, analogous to the suggestion which imprinted the engram. This subjection is called occult, because it originated from the magic practices of occultism and has its own characteristic stamp.

So far however we have only explained that element in occult subjection which corresponds with the categories of these sciences. We shall now proceed to the superstructure, the "upper layer", the transcendent element. We obtain indirect indications about this side of subjection from phenomena which cannot be regarded as products of the subconscious. The philosophers and psychologists, Driesch and Oesterreich, are among those who leave open, either directly or indirectly, the possibility of metaphysical factors. Theology however goes much further. From the biblical view we gain a clear interpretation of occult subjection. This subjection is the result of magic practices. Magic is not merely a neutral, ethically acceptable use of the unknown powers of nature and of man, but by its nature as a thing opposed to God it involves membership in the kingdom of the devil. Magic stands in the front line of the opposition to the Kingdom of God. The person who practises magic therefore stands under judgement.

[539a] i.'e. the revival of this memory trace (cf. Drever, "A Dictionary of Psychology", Penguin Books, Rev. edn. 1964, p. 78).

Occult subjection is from a theological point of view nothing other than the fact that the person who abandons his God thereby abandons himself. The man who gives up God is himself given up (Rom. 1, 28). The occultist who desires to bring under his control the Creator, or even the devil, himself becomes a slave. Occult subjection is completed separation from God. Complete separation from God is dissolution, darkness, chaos. The causality which operates in the connexion of magic practice with occult subjection cannot be discerned by the way of understanding, but only by the way of faith. This causality is thus rooted in the ultimate metaphysical correspondence — a thing which can only be spiritually perceived — between sin and disease, and is the proof that the natural man cannot understand spiritual things.

This situation of being under judgement is not merely of future significance, but is effectively operative from the moment of magic activity. Enough examples of this have already been given in this study. We may adduce one more example of the fact that guilt and the sense of sin immediately produce psychological disturbances.

Ex 122 The wife of a prisoner of war took up an adulterous association with another man. She struggled against this relationship, but could not break free. A mental conflict ensued, which asserted itself in an organic way. She developed pains in her throat, with swelling of the glands. She sought help from a doctor and from a pastor. After the return of her husband, she confessed the wrong to him in the pastor's presence. The husband forgave her. The throat pains and the swelling of the glands declined rapidly and did not recur.

Here we have a series of separate stages: guilt — mental conflict — organic disturbance. This sequence is observed very often in the pastoral counselling of occult cases, though nearly always accompanied by the fact that there is no consciousness of guilt in the person involved. In the case of those involved in occultism, the fact appears that the person who breaks with the Creator also breaks with himself. That is the transcendent component in the dissociation manifestations observed in occult involvement. From a theological point of view it is a wholly normal consequence of occult subjection that mental disturbances appear. Where the Kingdom of God is thrown away at one bid, the kingdom of Satan extends. Where the King appointed by God as the Lord of life is rejected, the ruler of this world and his satellites take up their sway. For puny man cannot himself remain in a vacuum between the tension-charged dynamic of the Kingdom of God and the kingdom of the devil. There is no neutrality here.[539]

How then must we conceive of the *integration* of the two-level problem of occult subjection? Must the doctor and the theologian march on along separate paths, or can we expect here the fulfilment of Weizsäcker's wish (Pt. I, ch. 1) for a reconciliation of the alienated brothers through the mediation of psychology? In the question of the treatment of magic — the mother of occult subjection — theology has the prior claim. Medical, psychological, cultural principles, yes, even those of the study of religions, do not penetrate to the heart of the problem. The theologian will naturally accept with gratitude all the scientific help which the other disciplines can offer him. If anyone is disturbed by the multi-lateral nature of the problem, he may listen to the word of a theologian who is also a natural scientist. For Prof. Karl Heim writes:[540] "What goes on in the world is a spiritual battle between divine and anti-divine powers. This battle does not run its course only in the human ego, in the depth of man's spirit, in the hidden inner being where God is alone with the soul and the soul alone with God. No, the physical realm too, indeed the whole realm of nature is involved in this battle. The *physical* and the *ethical* are not two territories separate from and independent of each other. They are two hemispheres of one and the same reality." This sets forth well the unity between the various directions of research. Doctor and theologian are brothers in two hemispheres of one and the same reality.

Thesis 5: We have presented the presupposition for a therapy of psychological disturbances conditioned by occultism. The *pathogenesis* of disturbances due to occult involvement has a secular branch in the ecphory of engrams which have resulted from the activation of the subconscious, and it has a transcendent branch in the condition of the man who stands under judgement because of magic practices. The spiritual background has in its great might priority over the medical and psychological factor. The transcendence of this phenomenon is the bracket which encloses the immanence.

[540] cf. Karl Heim, "Zur Frage der Wunderheilungen", Zeitwende May 1927.

[539] cf. E. Thureysen, op. cit. 13, p. 281.

PART IV

The Way of Liberation from Occult Subjection

In the chapters introducing the troubles of those subjected to occultism and their critical evaluation, we brought in many border sciences, in accordance with our basic statement of the material principle of research. We must travel the same path with regard to the question of therapy. First of all we must now examine the contribution of psychology and psychotherapy, and then we must describe the specifically Christian guidance to be given to people with these particular problems.

Chapter One

THE CONTRIBUTION OF THE PSYCHOLOGICAL BORDER SCIENCES

In order to find a basis for the understanding of therapeutic efforts in this direction, we shall define the border sciences which pertain to this question, in their meaning and in their distinction from one another.

1. *Definition and Distinction of the Individual Fields*

Psychology, psycho-analysis, psychotherapy and pastoral counselling are four special approaches to the treatment of the inner life of man.[541] We can thus bring the four different kinds of procedure which focus on man's psyche under one common denominator.

(a) *Psychology*, as the science of the soul, serves to study the inner nature of man.[542] It attains its goal of research by an exact methodical comprehension of the laws governing the human psyche. The sources of this knowledge are experience, introspection, biographies, systematic

---

[541] cf. Dr. med. Bitter, "Psychotherapie und Seelsorge", an introduction to depth psychology, Gemeinschaft, Arzt und Seelsorger, Stuttgart, p. 163.
[542] cf. Thurneysen, op. cit. [13], p. 174.

observation, studies of the expression of the soul in its cultural creations, psychological experiments, tests, etc. The pastor needs this science, if his words are not to miss the mark. Pastoral counselling without accurate diagnosis is misty and dangerous. In order to know what his message is to be, the pastor needs knowledge of the man to whom it is directed. That is part of the art of pastoral communication. Real entering into the situation of our fellow man is an essential part of the hermeneutics of our message. Hence psychology has its justification as an instrument for acquiring knowledge of people.

Psycho-analysis is a method of study in recent psychology, chiefly connected with the names of Freud, Adler and Jung. It explores the mental powers of man in their dimension of depth.[543] In the view of depth analysts, the mental structure of man is made up of two, or sometimes four levels. The small area of consciousness is undergirded by the great "basement" of the subconscious, or as Jung calls it the unconscious.[544] In the view of those who adopt this approach, man appears as one who is dominated, directed and obsessed by the powers of the subconscious. According to the four-level view, the ego forms the apex of a cone. Next down is the small sphere of consciousness. Third comes the personal unconscious; and fourthly, as the base, the collective unconscious. The view which the pastor takes of depth analysis is like that he takes of the other psychological sciences. He need have no fear of it, nor need he belittle it. On the contrary, the pastor acquires valuable perspectives for his own task from an understanding of the psychological reactions which arise from dreams and childhood experiences, from repressions, from things subliminally received and experienced, from unresolved conflicts, from tensions that have not been released, from erroneous attitudes and habits. It is in fact above all depth psychology that is in a position to point out, in its utter depth and horror, the breach which has come about in man. Many biblical statements are shown up in much greater depth in the light of depth analysis, e. g. Matt. 15, 19: "out of the heart come evil thoughts...", or Rom. 7, 19: "I do not do the good I want".

Psychotherapy is the curative treatment corresponding to psycho-analysis. Marquardt[545] describes psychotherapy as "the discipline which occupies itself with the systematic study, development and methodical application of certain psychological healing methods". It concerns itself

---

[543] cf. Bitter, op. cit. 541, p. 163.
[544] cf. C. G. Jung, "Über die Psychologie des Unbewußten", Rascher Verlag, Zürich.
[545] cf. Dr. Marquardt, OFM, "Psychotherapie vom Standpunkt des kath. Theologen gesehen", WS, loc. cit. 546, 49/4/14.

with man in those disorders which are conditioned by unconscious factors, that is with the whole complex of the various neuroses. According to Prof. Schultz,[546] the neuroses can be classified into the following four groups:

exogenic, alien neuroses, due to injuries received from the environment;

physiogenic, marginal neuroses, due to wrong habits;

psychogenic "layer" neuroses, due to anti-bionomic failure to assimilate the emotional stimuli;

characterogenic depth-neuroses, in which the patient has become neurotically changed down to the deepest level of his personality. Psychotherapy bases its healing methods on the principle that the unlocking of the psychological connexions and the awakening of the consciousness to unconscious conflicts leads to a solution of and release from the trouble. And indeed there are relaxing, releasing, and liberting powers in the mental disclosure and working out of these unassimilated data of experience. Man is called to the truth about himself. This truth will make him free.

With these three special areas of psychological work, carried out on scientific lines, the field of our material principle is again exhausted. *Pastoral counselling* is something of a completely different order from these border sciences. Maeder says:[547] "Psychotherapy is definitely anthropocentric in its attitude: it is concerned only with the man. Pastoral work is theocentric. Its aim therefore is that man shall find peace with God and recognize the fact that he belongs to God". While within the compass of the material principle of our study we have a confrontation of man with himself, in the sphere of the formal principle we have a confrontation of man with God. The concern here is no longer the neurosis of the man and its cure, but the acknowledgement of guilt and its pardon. We have here the same layering and stratification of the problem into various dimensions as we had in the case of occult subjection. If now we are to bring the aim of the four bordering sciences under a single definition, this conceptual definition can be expressed in the words of Dr. Leist: "Man in the condition of his soul, in the depth of his soul, in the sickness of his soul, and — in his guilt, here stands at the focal point of methods of help which aim at illumination and healing".

(b) Now that we have defined their content and nature, we must indicate the *distinction* between these bordering sciences. From our

---

[546] cf. the monthly periodical "Der Weg zur Seele" (abbr. WS), ed. Dr. Dr. Thomas, Vanderhoek und Ruprecht, Göttingen, 1951/11/322.

[547] cf. Maeder, op. cit. 9, p. 246.

knowledge of the various dimensional layers, there arises a principle of sharp separation between pastoral care and the psychological border sciences. We can point out three relationships. First of all pastoral care must result in *no belittling* of the psychological sciences. They have their own scientific right of existence, as every other science has, and they are subject to the permission and indeed the imperative of the biblical command to "subdue the earth" (Gen. 1, 28), just like e. g. physics and chemistry. When the psychological involvements and actualities of human individuality are investigated and examined by these border sciences, man is not thereby affected or encroached upon in his existence before his Creator. The researches on the lower level of the problem do not include the relations in the upper level, but only touch upon them.

In thus drawing a distinction between pastoral care and psychological research, both sides must be warned against blurring and transgressing their bounds. The counsellor may and should make use of the psychological aids, without of course simply turning his counselling into psychology, as for instance the Zürich pastor, Dr. Pfister, who is a disciple of Freud, has done. Prof. Fendt writes in his textbook on pastoralia:[548] "In no case may this involve a substitution of psychology for the dynamic of God's kingdom in word and sacrament. That would be unbelief. Neither may we try to strengthen the dynamic of God's kingdom in word and sacrament by the use of psychological material. That would be half-faith. We are only permitted to remove by psychological means those psychological hindrances which obstruct the external hearing of the word". From the medical side men have likewise expressed themselves on this point. Thus for instance Prof. Schultz writes:[549] "Religious problems are not neurotic problems". The pastor may not by his employment of psychological knowledge degrade pastoral counselling to a psychological technique. Further it is intolerable that he make medical diagnoses and become a psychotherapeutic dilettante and quack. Thurneysen writes[550] in his essay "Seelsorge und Psychotherapie": "Pastors who psychologize, and practise psychotherapy instead of giving Christian counsel — they are almost the worst of all. It leads to catastrophe on two sides. First they miss the mark as far as their proper task of preaching the word is concerned. And then their psychotherapy almost inevitably becomes dangerous dilettantism, which damages not only

---

[548] cf. Leonhardt Fendt, "Grundriß der praktischen Theologie", Mohr, Tübingen, 1949, vol. III, p. 8.

[549] cf. WS, op. cit. [546], 49/1/10.

[550] cf. Thurneysen in "Theologische Existenz heute", Kaiser Verlag, Munich, no. 25 "Seelsorge und Psychotherapie", p. 10.

themselves but also those on whom it is practised. Here we can only issue the warning 'Hands off! Cobbler, stick to your last!'"

What is not proper for the pastor is not proper for the doctor either. If the pastor must constantly give heed to his own task, then this limitation also applies to the doctor. A clean division and clear-cut definition is an urgent need, in the view of Prof. Schultz. He protests against importing metaphysical and religious ideas into psychotherapy.[551] He writes: "There can just as little be a Christian psychotherapy as a Christian surgery. Just as little are there Jewish, Protestant or Catholic neuroses". Neuroses are limited by no confessional boundaries. The blurring of distinctions is just as dangerous from the side of the doctor as it is from that of the pastor. One mistake is the psychologizing of religious values. Thus Freud considered the religious content of faith to be a collective neurosis shared by humanity. Prof. Mitscherlich, head of the psychosomatic seminary at Heidelberg, once called religion an infantile regression. And according to C. G. Jung, "all the divine and religious is merely an element of the human soul, which projects the inner life to the outside. There is no transcendent reality that corresponds to this inner God of religious experience".[552] On the other side, over against these attempts to bring the transcendent down to the level of the secular, we also have the attempts of some Christian psychotherapists to lift psychotherapy to the Christian level. Perhaps we may put Prof. Künkel in this category when he calls psychotherapeutic healing "grace".[553] There is no grace in the sphere of natural science. When Künkel thus borrows from Christian terminology, he ought to explain the fact that he has borrowed, or else he is breaking bounds. As a positive example, we mention Maeder, who during psychotherapeutic treatment of a young man goes on to give religious advice. He explains this in his book,[554] saying expressly: "We are here no longer on the plane of medical psychotherapy, but on that of Christian counselling." In considering the relation of the natural sciences to Christian counselling, we must remember the old principle "suum cuique". Clear-cut boundaries will prevent confusion of concepts, an inept mixing of separate skills, and disastrous quackery. Only a clear distinction of the two tasks will further mutual respect and a healthy basis for fruitful co-operation. Naturally a uniting of these two fields in the work of one person is possible, but then strict attention must be paid to what we have just

[551] cf. WS, op. cit. 546, 51/11/325.
[552] cf. Frh. von Gebsattel, "Christentum und Humanismus", Stuttgart, 1947, pp. 30f.
[553] cf. Fritz Künkel, "Die Arbeit am Character", Wichern Verlag, Berlin, 1951, p. 145.
[554] cf. Maeder, op. cit. 9, p. 137.

said. A good example of this is the book already quoted: "Wege zur seelischen Heilung".

2. *The Trans-psychological Reality of Christian Counselling*

Now that we have seen the external distinction, we go on a comparison of content between the psychological border sciences and Christian counselling. They may be compared in three different ways.

(a) The *superiority* of technical knowledge with respect to secular psychological relations is undoubtedly on the side of these sciences. As mentioned in our opening remarks, Jung writes in his book "Die Beziehungen der Psychotherapie zur Seelsorge"[555] that the pastor usually lacks the knowledge which would qualify him to penetrate into the psychological background of the disorder. In a questionnaire to students, asking how many if they had trouble of this sort would seek help from a doctor and how many from the pastor, 57 % of all the Protestants decided for the doctor, and only 8 % for the pastor. The students gave as ground for their choice the lack of psychological knowledge on the part of pastors.[556] And indeed the psychoanalyst and psychotherapist have the advantage in their ability to penetrate into the depths of the psychological distress of their patients. For the pastor has only something to learn from the psychoanalyst's solidarity and identification with his patient, as he for instance in painstaking work and lengthy detail leads his patient down into the depths and ramifications of his repressions, unassimilated impressions, anxieties, inhibitions, emotional pressures, excessive burdens, distortions, wrong motivations, seclusions, short-circuit reactions, damage due to education and environment, imprisonment of the ego, etc. The factual knowledge which the psychotherapist gathers as the psychological depths are loosened, brought to consciousness, and released is lacked by the pastor. "This lack of factual knowledge in the pastor cannot be substituted by faith".[557] Here we see an urgent call for reform in our theological education.

Marquardt writes:[558] "The student of theology should already be sufficiently instructed in the various forms of neurosis, so that he can at the outset of his pastoral ministry make a swift and accurate judgement as to whether the person seeking his help is psychologically healthy or a neurotic, whether in this case a little pastoral advice will suffice, or

[555] cf. Jung, op. cit. [7], p. 14.
[556] ibid., p. 18.
[557] cf. Dr. Riecker, "Die seelsorgerliche Begegnung", Bertelsmann Verlag, Gütersloh, p. 5.
[558] cf. Marquardt, op. cit. [545], p. 17.

whether a specialist must be brought into the case." Dr. Bitter[559] writes similarly, "A short course in psychoanalysis will facilitate the judgement of the pastor whether a condition is present which calls for the help of a psychotherapeutic specialist or a psychiatrist. It would be very desirable if each large parish had at least one pastor who had taken such a course."

Jung says on this point.[560] "It does not seem that the Protestant pastor of today has sufficient equipment for the staggering psychological demands of our times." Such affirmations, proposals and demands cannot be neglected without injury to the church in a time so pregnant with neuroses as the present one.

(b) The *agreement* of the disciplines over some principles can be seen in the resolution of some of the psychic conflicts at which both the psychiatrist and the pastor aim.

Prof. Schultz writes:[561] "as sharp as the boundaries may theoretically be between Christian counselling and psychotherapy, in the view of all critical representatives of our profession and of theologians with a similarly thorough training, we nonetheless cannot deny the fact that in a definite sector the two fields intersect." We shall give a short statement of the important points of contact.

First of all it is known alike to the psychological disciplines and to pastoral counselling that violation of the elementary laws of life will avenge itself over generations. The individual does not stand in isolation, but he is anchored in a guilt-connexion with his forebears. Our psychologists continue to tell us that the fact taught in the second commandment, that the sins of the fathers are visited to the third and fourth generations of their descendants, is a reality. In this sense Heyer speaks in his book "Vom Kraftfeld der Seele", of man as existing in the field of his ancestors.[562] These findings are parallel to those of our study of the consequences of occult involvement which extend into the third and fourth generations.[563] Man stands in the power-field of his ancestors. That is a theme on which different variations are played by Freud, Jung and others, but also by biologists and pastors.

The next common basis is the knowledge that *unresolved conflicts* lead to a splitting, an inner drifting, a disintegration, a paralysis of mental and organic life, a loss of inner freedom. It is especially the guilt

---

559 cf. Bitter, op. cit. 541, p. 204.
560 cf. Jung, op. cit. 7, p. 17.
561 cf. Schultz, op. cit. 546, 49/1/9.
562 cf. G. R. Heyer, "Vom Kraftfeld der Seele", Stuttgart, 1949.
563 cf. Bitter, op. cit. 541, pp. 122, 127.

complex which has such consequences. Prof. Köberle writes:[564] "Psychotherapy and theology have this directly in common, that both disciplines know clearly that guilt conflicts can cripple and oppress life to a terrible extent. Indeed this condition can result in the outbreak of an organic ailment."

For this reason both psychotherapy and Christian counselling take steps to repair the disintegration. In the language of the psychotherapist, this is known as working up the dissociation which exists. The armour of reticence must be breached. The causes and motives of the inertia and inner divisions, must be laid bare. In the language of the pastor this means conducting a thorough "spot check on the inventory" as in Psalm 32: "When I declared not my sin, my bones wasted away through my groaning all day long ... Therefore I acknowledged my sin to thee, and did not hide my iniquity". Both in psychotherapy and in pastoral care man is called to knowledge of himself, and thereby the goal is sought of "incorporating again the dissociated powers of the personal centre of life. In this way the ego will again get its hand firmly on the rudder of life".[565] The reintegration and healing of psychological disorders has begun when man "again comes to himself", when he is "together with himself again" (Thurneysen). The end result of this goal of psychotherapy again shows up the difference between psychotherapy and Christian counselling, as we shall now briefly indicate.

(c) The *independence* of and the *contrast* between the two fields becomes evident when we consider the ultimate causes of disorder and the final aim of healing. Among the leading lights of psychology and psychotherapy it was Freud who perceived the disabling effects of inhibited or dissociated affects, and who found and developed systematically a method of opening up the soul. He called it psychoanalysis. This psychoanalytical method has done substantial work in the elucidation of conflicts of instinct in the subconscious. But it had three limitations, which Freud was not able to overcome. An example taken from our own pastoral work will illustrate these limitations.

Ex 123 A man of Christian persuasion came for an interview during an evangelistic campaign, and confessed to very serious misconduct in the sphere of sodomy. He explained that he would never have reached such straits if his wife had not for years, ever since their wedding, refused completely to give herself to him. Upon my question whether they both loved each other, he answered affirmatively. There

---

[564] ibid., p. 154.
[565] cf. Thurneysen, op. cit. 550, p. 21.

was little reason for suspecting Lesbian inclinations in his wife. In pursuing theinquiry the reason for this marriage crisis came to light. The wife spoke a great deal about her deceased father. She used only those perfumes which he had liked. She cultivated only his favourite flowers. She ate his favourite foods. She idolized pictures of him. She requested of her husband that he should hold her in his arms, as her father used to hold her when she was little, etc. It was easy to see that the wife adored her father in her husband, and thus was incapable of true married life. The strong attachment to the father had shattered this marriage, which was only a hollow form. The husband, denied his marital rights, fell into sexual perversity as a form of release.

Now the school of depth analysis would, in view of the unfitness of the wife for marriage, regard it as being its essential task to show the two people that the wife's extreme attachment to her father was the cause of her marriage crisis. By the disclosure of this hidden cause, by awaking consciousness of this psychological conflict, the school would expect the trouble to be cured. The identification, on the Socratic principle, of rational explanation and cure is the most potent therapeutic factor which depth psychology can apply. Now Christian counselling is not content with simply making the couple, both man and wife, aware of this false adjustment. The pastor must penetrate behind the disclosed cause, the devotion to the father, and also transcend the secular aim of healing pursued by the psychotherapist. This attachment to the father, which makes the wife unfit for marriage, is not the ultimate cause of the crisis, but is only a symptom of her unfitness for life and for love, arising from the egocentricity of a woman who desires only to be coddled as a child is coddled by her father. This faulty development does not only indicate a faulty upbringing, but also a disturbance of life at the very core and essence of the personality. The problem is not grasped in its depth by psychological categories. In the last analysis we have here problems of faith.

Still more plainly do we see that this vicious circle leads into trans-psychological and trans-biological areas when we more fully analyse the act of psychotherapeutic cure. From the side of psychotherapy it is expected that a rational awakening of awareness about the conflict will bring about healing. What happens if a cure is not effected? These questions are even raised by psychotherapists themselves. Freud speaks in reference to one such case of an "offer of available psychological powers". But whence come these psychological powers? Some psychotherapists say that the soul heals itself. Künkel[566] says that the psycho-

---

[566] cf. Künkel, op. cit. [553], pp. 141f.

therapist is only a midwife. "Our efforts merely remove hindrances. But even when we have removed the hindrances, the healing process is not thereby guaranteed... Healing is the same as grace." Thus, where the psychotherapist has reached the end of his road, he borrows from the sphere which rises above the scope of psychotherapy, from the Christian world of faith. Thus Christian counselling transcends both the starting-point of the psychoanalyst's elucidation of the subconscious and its conflicts, and the goal of psychotherapeutic healing. This is recognized also by the psychotherapist Prof. Schultz, who writes[567] that the religious question lies behind the work of the physician.

Therewith not all has been said. Let us return to our example. We are still far from having dealt with all the questions involved, when we have brought to clear consciousness the wife's attachment to her father, the husband's false adjustment, and the resultant marriage crisis. The woman was in part to blame that the husband, having been cheated of his marriage life for many years, fell into sodomy. Many years ago she had entered into Christian marriage with a promise of fellowship in body, soul and spirit; but she had not fulfilled this obligation. And the man for his part had now made a fatally wrong decision because of the conflict. From the Christian point of view we have here not merely a faulty development and decision on the ethically neutral plane of depth analysis, but also a question of guilt. This brings us to the heart of the problem. Prof. Thielicke, in his book "Fragen des Christentums an die moderne Welt",[568] shows us how the methods of psychiatry operate in an area beyond good and evil. It is not only better technical knowledge that drives secularized man to the psychotherapist rather than to the Christian counsellor, but it is rather the secret knowledge that in the presence of the psychotherapist he can withdraw himself from any kind of divine demand to give an account of himself. This instinct of modern man shows the essential difference between psychotherapy and Christian counselling. The psychotherapist treats his patients as a psychological arena, in which all the entanglements and developments progress according to the laws of causality and motive. The pastor on the other hand desires, if grace prevails, to bring the person he is counselling before the face of God, before Whom the repressed emotions with their consequences are revealed not only as neuroses,[569] but also on the deeper level as guilt associations, which can only be overcome by means of forgiv-

---

[567] cf. Schultz, op. cit. [546], 50/3/18.

[568] cf. Thielicke, op. cit. [522], p. 112.

[569] cf. Thurneysen, op. cit. [13], p. 198: "Neurosis and sin each belong their own order: neurosis is this-worldly and natural, sin other-wordly. Sin is thus something *toto genere* different from neurosis. The two are however related.

eness. The resolution of conflicts, healing and change offered by psychotherapy goes only halfway: despite the work of depth analysis it remains
on the external level, unless it is brought by a creative act of God's
grace into an *anakainosis*, a new birth from above. We do not mean
that there should be a mixing and mutual interpenetration of these two
spheres, but rather that this second event is a continuation of the work
in a higher dimension, where all psychotherapeutic endeavour and aid
is of no avail. Genuine healing of a mentally disordered person, in his
relationship to God, is brought about not by psychotherapeutic transformation, but by forgiveness alone. This fact becomes clear in many
New Testament narratives. Blumhardt affirms, from a long experience
of Christian counselling, that unpardoned guilt is the cause of many
ailments, and that sick conditions are often overcome through the
forgiveness of the guilt.

It is gratifying that many psychotherapists do not hold aloof from
this fact, but become conscious of this problem on a totally different
level. We can easily bring evidence of this from literature. The psychologist Dr. Neumann writes,[570] "A psychology remains on the secular
level, whereas religion, *religio*, is the relation back to the transcendent.
Here psychology points to something which is above itself". A similar
definition is offered by Prof. Gruehn. He distinguishes two sides of
Christian counselling: the psychological, earthly side and the spiritual,
transcendent side.[571] Regarding the meaning of the transcendent side,
C. G. Jung of Zürich makes a noteworthy admission.[572] He says: "Among
all my patients over thirty-five years of age, there is not one whose final
problem is not that of religious attitude. Each one suffers from the loss
of *religio* and is not cured until he has found it." Again, he writes:[573]
"It seems to me as if parallel with the decline of religious life the neuroses have increased noticeably." In opposition to his teacher, Freud, who
would explain all transcendence in terms of processes within man, Jung
admits: "Naturally the doctor is not qualified to speak on the ultimate
questions regarding the soul."[574] The conclusion of Dr. March has the
same perspective: "True Christian counselling is in the last analysis an
event which is operative beyond all consciousness, independent of any
planned pastoral endeavour. Pastoral work so understood stands beyond
all psychotherapy and all discussion. Hence there is also no such thing as

[570] cf. Bitter, op. cit. [541], p. 52.
[571] cf. W. Gruehn, "Seelsorge im Licht der gegenwärtigen Psychologie", 1927, Arzt
und Seelsorger, Heft 7, p. 14.
[572] cf. Bitter, op. cit. [541], p. 61.
[573] cf. Jung, op. cit. [7], p. 19.
[574] ibid., p. 14

a professional counsellor."[575] In a clear definition Prof. Schultz[576] has expressed the difference between psychotherapy and Christian counselling. He writes: "The genuine religious experience remains unassailable by psychological efforts at illumination and analysis." Counsellors are very grateful for the following conclusion in his commendable book "Bionome Psychotherapie"[577]: "The psychotherapeutic experience of change cannot, and does not wish to, displace Christian regeneration, but it often prepares the soil for it, and in the case of deep neuroses it can sometimes be its indispensable presupposition". These are all testimonies for which the pastor is very grateful, since they mean that many doctors have recognized and acknowledged the contrast between, and the respective independence of, pastoral care and psychotherapy. From the pastoral side we must not fail to mention that sometimes the creative power of grace strikes diametrically through all the efforts of the psychotherapist without any previous preparation of the soil and reaches a person in his deepest roots. Prof. Fendt testifies to this in his book on pastoralia:[578] "Often a field untilled by man may be more powerfully grasped by the dynamic of God's kingdom than a field humanly well prepared. However, this does not alter the fact that man has the duty to till each and every field."

3. The Medical and Theological Aspects of Liberation from Occult Subjection

Now that we have indicated the basic relation of psychotherapy to pastoral counselling, we must consider the question of competence in attempting to heal those under occult subjection. We have established in our critical examination of the pastoral cases that occult subjection is a theological problem with a medical exterior. To use a metaphor, it is a spiritual disease centre with a medical outworking. Here we can in passing again note an actual problem complex, a psychosomatic association, the connexion of guilt and disease, which provides a strong link between theology and medicine. Now, in harmony with the above-mentioned need to separate carefully psychotherapy and Christian counselling, we must undertake to treat the medical "sucker" of occult subjection according to medical viewpoints, and to investigate the main problem as a spiritual, pastoral, theological one. In accordance with the definitions we have given of occult subjection, the healing process is seen to have a medical and a theological, pastoral aspect.

[575] cf. March, loc. cit. 546, 50/4/13.
[576] cf. Schultz, loc. cit. 546, 49/1/11.
[577] cf. Schultz, "Bionome Psychotherapie", Thiemel Verlag, Stuttgart, 1951.
[578] cf. Fendt, op. cit. 548, vol. III, p. 8.

The evaluation of many individual cases, systematically observed, reveals by the inductive method that the characteristic of occult subjection viewed from the medical side is an activation of the subconscious by a *deep suggestion in waking state*. First we must give some explanation of this term. The forms of suggestion in waking state, as distinct from hypnosis, are well known to medicine. The term "deep suggestion in waking state" has been employed in our study because suggestive activation of the subconscious in a waking state by means of magic practices releases such overwhelmingly powerful effects that they continue for decades and can, by repetition, persist into the fourth generation. The gift of charmers to exercise suggestion in a waking state is known to medicine.[579].

As already mentioned, Prof. Brauchle speaks of secret suggestion from shepherds and wise women. I am not acquainted with any investigation and explanation in the field of medicine concerning this deep suggestion by means of occult practices. And indeed from a medical point of view there is little to be said about it, since magic conjuration is, in distinction from neutral medical conjuration, a religious phenomenon, in spite of its medical disguise. The magical technique of deep suggestion in waking state is only the outer framework of a religious process. From the medical point of view, a cure of occult subjection would consist of removing this deep suggestion. I am not qualified to describe such a healing process. That remains for a specialist who has at his disposal the scientific techniques of suggestion, but who must also recognize the religious problem as the greater part of the trouble. However, from the viewpoint of the New Testament, I do not believe that an attempt along such purely technical lines to remove a deep suggestion imparted by magic could be successful. Man, who in arrogant pride has taken it upon himself to try and usurp the place of God, is unable to rehabilitate himself after the effects of this revolt against the ultimate ground of the world order. From the Biblical standpoint the above-mentioned attempt at a medical cure for occult subjection is for this reason condemned to failure. It would have to be proved, by the scientific investigation of subconscious engrams caused by the magical use of deep suggestion, that a part of the resultant dissociations or psychic disintegrations could be reintegrated into a unified consciousness. Any such result would be, if proved, only a subsidiary result in the face of the ultimate question raised by the problem, i. e. whether man under judgment can again attain peace with God. To conclude, we may

[579] cf. H. Asmussen, "Die Seelsorge", Kaiser Verlag Munich 1934, 4th. edn. World Council Service N. Y., p. 43.

formulate the attempts at therapy in this field as follows: "Although the genesis of occult subjection in the lower plane of the two-storey problem can be thought of medically as an effect of deep suggestion in waking state, the therapy still belongs to the transcendent upper layer of the problem". This means that it is Christian counselling, grounded on the Bible and carried out on theological lines, which has here the last word.

Thesis 6: The therapy of occult subjection reveals itself in the medical aspect as the problem of dismantling the effects of deep suggestion in the subconscious. This medical concern for healing, however, is only a sub-section of the transcendent complex of occult subjection, and can therefore contribute only a limited, preliminary basis for further pastoral treatment.

Chapter Two

SPIRITUAL GUIDANCE IN THE LIGHT OF THE NEW TESTAMENT

Before we enter upon the discussion of the pastoral problem of this section, we must first briefly define the term "spiritual guidance". Amussen in his book[580] distinguishes between what we have called pastoral counselling *(Seelsorge)* and spiritual guidance *(Seelenführung)* in this way: *Seelsorge* in the strict sense is the proclamation of the word, and *Seelenführung* the whole complex of teaching. He defines this as follows: "*Seelenführung* is the education of the congregation, both conscious and unconscious." Thus in the view of Asmussen *Seelsorge* is the proper task of the pastor, *Seelenführung* an alien task. In this distinction we sense the presupposition that *Seelsorge* only concerns the Gospel, whereas *Seelenführung* concerns itself with matters of the law. A further motive of Asmussen might be his desire to safeguard protestant counselling against all secularization, whether psychological or pedagogic in character.[581] The Gospel must be the exclusive concern of counselling.

Although we must note the weight of Asmussen's objection, we shall nonetheless employ the term "spiritual guidance" in our study, in a sense rather different from that to which Asmussen gives expression in his book. If we here assume the idea that *Seelsorge* is the application of the message of the Gospel to the individual,[582] then "spiritual guidance"

580 ibid.

581 cf. E. Schick, "Der Christ als Seelsorger", Furche Verlag, Berlin, 1936, p. 35.

582 cf. Bovet, op. cit. 171, p. 107; Thurneysen, op. cit. 550, p. 10; Asmussen, op. cit. 579, p. 15.

will in this section indicate only a *method* of application, and not some independent field existing as an *opus alienum* alongside pastoral counselling. To make plain what this means, we may refer to Müller's exposition of the theological, Christological sense of *Seelsorge*.[583] Müller shows that all pastoral care has its original pattern in Christ.

From this view it is understandable that pastoral care has two sides. First there is the service of a signpost, pointing to the objective things of the word, to the indicative of the Gospel; and then there is spiritual guidance, which is the activity of one who is led by the hand of the "One Shepherd", extending his hand to his brother and thus forming a chain. So understood, spiritual guidance is not the work of the pastor, but is rather the fellowship in life and fortune of one sinner with another, as they both place themselves under the guidance of the Shepherd: the one as helper and not as mediator, the other as seeking help, and grasping the free hand of the brother. In modified form this line of thought is found in Müller also. He writes:[584] "The pure image of true pastoral care cannot be found theoretically but only in the venture of discipleship". Spiritual guidance in the sense here indicated exists only on the basis of one's own discipleship under the "One Shepherd".

In the following sections we shall now show how in the pastoral treatment of people under occult subjection the spiritual guidance of those mentally disturbed works out in practice. This presentation is limited exclusively to the problem being considered in our present study. It will not therefore be a kind of compendium of pastoral care in general, but a review, born of experience, of the special care of the occultly subjected. If we wished to classify this task in the categories used by Claus Harms[585] of "Preacher, Priest and Pastor", our task would fit into the latter, since it deals with occasions "in which because of special incidents a particular exhortation is needed or expected."

First of all we shall show the place of such special pastoral work in the history of salvation.

1. *The Foundations for Pastoral Care of those Occultly Subjected*

We shall here presuppose what has been said in Pt. III ch. 5 about occult phenomena in the light of the Bible and especially of the New Testament. The New Testament findings show the background of occult subjection as membership in the kingdom of the devil. The

---

583 cf. A. D. Müller, "Grundriß der praktischen Theologie", Bertelsmann, Gütersloh, 1950, pp. 281f.
584 ibid., p. 285.
585 cf. Claus Harms, "Pastoraltheologie", 1930.

way to freedom therefore takes the form of deliverance from the kingdom of Satan into the Kingdom of God. Thus Christian counselling is concerned with the saving of those subjected by bringing them into the Kingdom of God and preserving them there. Thus Fendt formulates it:[586] "To save people by bringing them into the Kingdom of God (even when the dawn of the kingdom has only just come), and to preserve them therein: that is the basic pattern of Christian pastoral care." Thus pastoral care is only one side of the dynamic of God's Kingdom. The saving and preserving work of the Christian counsellor can only be understood against the background of the dawning of the Kingdom through Christ. Pastoral help for the occultly subjected person means by the grace of God to bring him in from his separation from the Kingdom of God, to snatch him out of the power of darkness, and to help him into membership in the Kingdom of God, in the church, the body of Christ. This view and definition is not peculiar to Fendt. Müller defines similarly:[587] "Pastoral care is the assistance to faith and life, grounded in discipleship of Christ, which seeks to help the individual towards incorporation in the body of Christ." In another connexion he says: "Edification means building a man, who has been born again into the likeness of God, into the structure of the Kingdom of God. So then you are no longer sojourners and strangers, but fellow-citizens with the saints and members of the household of God, built upon the foundation of the apostles and prophets, of which Christ is the corner-stone (Eph. 2, 19)". Trillhaas' formulation also fits in here:[588] "Pastoral care is the care of the body of Christ in His members, or the building up of the body of Christ."

This final definition of the activity of Christian counselling is, however, only concerned with one side of the dynamic of the Kingdom of God. Liberation from the sphere of the dominion of Satan is not only the goal and task of the future: it is already an event completed in the redemptive act of Christ. Christ has come to destroy the bulwarks of darkness (I John 3, 8). The battle has been decided. The victory is won. Liberation from subjection to the kingdom of Satan requires only a *regressus ad perfectum*, a return to the finished work. It has been promised to us in baptism: "Fear not, I have redeemed you, I have called you by your name, you are mine" (Isaiah 43, 1). The pastoral experience of liberation from occult subjection is nothing other than the realization of this call. It is the Lutheran theology which bears witness in a special

[586] cf. Fendt, op. cit. [548], p. 5.
[587] cf. Müller, op. cit. [581], pp. 289, 197.
[588] cf. W. Trillhaas, "Der Dienst der Kirche am Menschen", Kaiser Verlag, Munich 1950, pp. 80, 112.

way to this return to the finished work,[589] and thereby it makes an essential contribution to the understanding of the Gospel and of baptism. When we now in the following sections present the special pastoral task of ministering to those subjected to occultism, this can only be done on the premise that the liberation has already been accomplished before the pastor and the person seeking help ever became conscious of it. Without wanting to lapse into scholastic terminology, we may say that this finished work, as prevenient grace — a term which originated with Augustine and not with Aquinas — supplies a cheering and promising starting-point for the difficult task of ministering to those occultly subjected.

2. *Personal Qualifications for Pastoral Care of those Occultly Subjected*

This formulation might provide an impulse for someone to put forward extremist views. We must therefore at the outset sound a basic note of caution. The working of God's grace does not depend upon our merits and demerits. "Gold is no less gold, even if it is worn by a harlot in her sin and shame."[590] Luther says moreover: "Although an evil priest should administer the sacrament... although a rogue takes or gives the sacrament, he nevertheless takes the true sacrament, that is, Christ's flesh and blood; for it is grounded not in the holiness of man, but upon the word of God".[591] This blanket of divine sovereignty, which embraces all human activity in the work of God's Kingdom, does not at all exclude the duty of internal preparation for pastoral ministry, but includes it. We shall mention here a few qualifications, but we cannot give attention here to all the human qualities needed by a pastor, such as the ability to listen, ability to keep a confidence, the gift of understanding, etc. These points are dealt with sufficiently in the specialized literature on the subject. Here we are concerned with some basic qualifications.

(a) *The spiritual life of the counsellor*

Dr. Riecker writes in his book "Das evangelistische Wort",[592] "The basic presupposition of every spiritual work is the spiritual stature of the worker. The instrument is only then an organ capable of communicating the rich abundance of the Holy Spirit's work in life and character

---

589 cf. E. Schlink, "Theologie der lutherischen Bekenntnisschriften", Verlag Lempp, Munich 1940, pp. 199f.

590 ibid., p. 215.

591 cf. the credal literature of the Lutherian church, ed. Müller, Rufer Verlag, Gütersloh, XII Cat. Maior V Pars, p. 501.

592 cf. Dr. Riecker, "Das evangelistische Wort", Bertelsmann Verlag, Gütersloh, 1935, p. 89.

when he himself is subject to the working of the Spirit, and controlled in his life and actions by the Spirit." The realization that spiritual stature is indispensable for spiritual pastoral work is emphasized by many well-known pastors. Schnepel[593] gives two basic principles in this connexion: That I myself am with Jesus; and that I remain in the personal pastoral care of Jesus". He writes of this: "It is an irrational, mysterious process which brings us into fellowship with Jesus. The Bible calls it regeneration: only he who has himself experienced this second birth knows about this process and has an eye to discern its presence in others. Since all pastoral ministry has this basic event as its goal, only he can perform pastoral ministry who knows the secret of regeneration in personal experience, and knows the hidden communion of man with Christ from daily converse with Him."

Bovet also associates himself with this line of thought in his book.[594] He distinguishes two spiritual processes: *metanoia* (repentance to Christ), and *menein* (abiding in Christ). He writes: "For the aspect of repentance, the expression *metanoia* is especially fitting, since in analogy to metamorphosis, a change of external form, this signifies a change of internal form". Especially worthy of note is that Bovet, who is a doctor and a biologist, here speaks of a change. He writes, "There are still Christians and especially pastors who doubt that human nature can really be changed, and who therefore take a sceptical view of conversion in every form." For the concept of *menein* Bovet refers to John 15 and says: "Abiding in Christ, abiding in His love, and letting His word abide in us — this is really the essence of the Christian life." On the question of fitness for the pastoral calling, Bovet takes the two factors together and says, "The clergyman becomes a pastor not by his theological knowledge but by his Christian faith and life."

Thurneysen expands this theme. He writes,[595] "The pastoral counsellor must himself be rooted in the word and in the church, and live from faith in forgiveness." Here the catch-phrase of Thimme is also to the point:[596] "Caretakers of souls must be men whose own souls have been cared for". The strongest testimony for the personal qualifications needed by the pastor comes from no less an authority than August Vilmar.[597] He writes, "Oh, you must not speak to the sick and the dying

[593] cf. Dannenbaum/Schnepel, "Im Dienst des Christus", Furche Verlag, Berlin, 1939, pp. 42f.

[594] cf. Bovet, op. cit. [171], pp. 99, 101, 107, 109, 164.

[595] cf. Thurneysen, op. cit. [13], p. 298.

[596] cf. L. Thimme, "Unsere Seelsorge". German: "Seelsorger sind Menschen, deren eigene Seele versorgt wurde".

[597] cf. August Vilmar, "Menschenkenntnis und Seelsorge", (essay), 1851.

about strength of soul, and courage, and patience, and the immortality of the soul; you yourself must give them strength, courage, patience and, above all, eternal life. Do you have strength? Then give strength. Do you have courage and patience? Then give courage and patience. Do you have eternal life in you? Then give eternal life." This strictly denominational Lutheran testifies that the pastoral counsellor can only give what he himself has. This agrees with the words of the apostle Peter (Acts 3, 6), "What I have, I give to you. In the name of Jesus Christ of Nazareth arise and walk". This fact is recognized also by psychotherapy. The well-known Berlin psychotherapist Prof. Schultz once said: "One can only lead the patient as far as one has himself advanced." After hearing this series of witnesses, we may now study the situation to which they testify in the light of the New Testament.

Rinderknecht writes:[598] "The pastoral counsellor must be a witness of Christ". In the legal view, only eye and ear witnesses can testify. In the New Testament the spiritual event of being convicted by the reality of Christ's presence, as happened to Paul on the road to Damascus, creates the qualification for bearing testimony. Testimony in the first sense is found in such passages as Acts 2, 32; 3, 15; 4, 20; and I John 1, 3, etc. "That which we have seen and heard we declare unto you". Witnessing in the second sense is described in Acts 22, 15; 26, 16; I Cor. 15, 15. Paul uses the term *martus* of himself. This second use of the term "witness" in the New Testament is the reason why in the New Testament church witness is possible in every age. Wilhelm Brandt points this out in his essay "Die theologische Grundlage des erwecklichen Zeugnisses nach dem Neuen Testament".[599] Thus we must maintain that if the counsellor is to be a witness, then the experience of the Spirit is an indispensable presupposition. Prof. Allwohn says the same in the symposium "Die seelsorgerlich-missionarische Arbeit der Kirche",[600] when he states that the pastor can only bear testimony to, and impart, what he himself has experienced.

We should have mentioned only one part of the pastor's qualification if we went no further than the experience of accepting Christ. No pastor can live from the capital collected in the past. To sit back on the once-for-all experience of Christ means apathy, worldly security, spiritual death. To the Christ-experience must be added daily discipleship, daily dying, daily repentance, daily purification, daily sanctification. He who would exercise pastoral care over others must himself abide in the daily,

---

[598] cf. H. J. Rinderknecht, "Tapfere Seelsorge", Zwingli Verlag, Zürich, 1937, p. 19.
[599] cf. Hans Dannenbaum, "Christus lebt", Furche Verlag, Berlin, 1939, pp. 17f.
[600] cf. Dr. Schadeberg "Die seelsorgerlich-missionarische Arbeit der Kirche", Ungelenk Verlag, Leipzig 1940.

individual care of Christ. Erich Schick, in his chapter on spiritual responsibility and personal sanctification,[601] calls this in his own unique way "dwelling with the eternal fire-glow". To the fact of becoming such a *martus* through encounter with Christ must be added the fact of remaining a *martus*. But this is only possible by abiding in Christ, as Bovet has said.

Being a *martus* involves a further factor as well, namely mission. In secular matters the eye or ear witness may decline to testify. But he who has been touched by the Christ event cannot but be a witness of Christ (Acts 4, 20). He has felt the hand of the Lord who says "I send you..." (Luke 10, 3). He who would withdraw from this mission loses his status as a *martus*. The light that is put under a bushel does not illuminate, but is itself extinguished after the oxygen has been consumed, by the nitrogen which remains — to use a metaphor from the world of physics.

Thus by the use of the term *martus* we have developed three facets, which form the spiritual qualifications for the pastoral ministry. Pietism calls these three facets conversion and rebirth, sanctification, and salvation of other souls. These terms can be characterized by the verbs to become, to remain, and to prove oneself. Reformation theology conceived of this Christian triad as justification, new obedience, and ministry. These terms can be expressed by the three imperatives: Follow Me! Abide in Me! Go forth! The Gospel of John has the following three focal points for this truth: being born again from above (John 3, 3); abiding (John 15); being sent (John 17, 18). In Pauline theology we find, in analogy to this, the terms to be recreated (Col. 3, 10), to be in Christ (II Cor. 5, 17), and to do the work of the Lord (I Cor. 15, 58; 16, 10). This threefold fact must not be conceived of as a series of stages, or a time scheme with step following step. It is a three-sided simultaneous relationship.

By this three-fold truth the spiritual character of the pastoral counsellor is clearly described. It has the testimony of well-know counsellors, it is anchored in the theology of the church, and it is readily gathered from the New Testament. Herewith the thesis is proved that only that pastor can lead troubled persons by God's grace into the fellowship of the Kingdom of God, in whose own life fellowship with Christ has been realized through God's grace. If God is pleased to use those in whom these conditions are not fulfilled — and He does use such, for the Spirit blows where He wills — then this is an expression of His

---

[601] cf. E. Schick, "Heiliger Dienst", Furche, Berlin, 1935, p. 297.

sovereign mercy and of His extraordinary grace. But the New Testament commands us to use the regular way of salvation.

(b) *The equipment of the counsellor*

The craftsman knows his tools, the material he has to work, and has mastered the technique of his trade. We may apply this to the pastor, who should have a specialized knowledge of his work. The counsellor will remain a dilettante if basic knowledge is lacking. Dr. Genrich wrote,[602] "Since any influence which enters man must proceed by way of his soul, the scientific care of souls is impossible without knowledge of the soul's life". In all modern works on pastoralia, great emphasis is placed on the necessity of psychological knowledge. Bovet says in the introduction to his book on pastoralia,[603] "Everyday experience shows that pastoral counselling often fails because the pastor lacks sufficient knowledge of the nature of man, so that his words miss the mark." In another place he writes: "The theologian knows the word of God, but regrettably his psychological and anthropological knowledge is often lacking".

Many hasty and sometimes wholly ineffective diagnoses are the result of a lack of knowledge of the psychological situation. In this sense the neurologist Dr. March writes:[604] "The mistakes of pastoral counsellors originate in lack of knowledge or of modesty in the fields of psychology, medicine and pedagogics". The Catholic psychotherapist von Gebsattel calls it a duty of the pastor to become acquainted with the psychotherapeutic approach (op.cit. [552]). The protestant theologian Müller has accepted this exhortation frequently made by psychotherapists. He writes:[605] "We must once for all frankly confess that the lack of psychological knowledge has severely damaged the reputation and the effectiveness of the church's pastoral ministry." It is therefore a logical conclusion when Prof. Hahn writes, in his proposals for reform in theological training,[606] "A church which trains its theological posterity and therefore has in view the moulding of the whole man for his future office, must not neglect the insights of pedagogics, psychology and sociology, though naturally within the necessary limits". Dr. Hahn emphasizes this concern still more strongly when he writes: "The situation is one of rapid decline in pastoral ministry. In contrast to this, modern man flocks to

---

602 cf. WS op. cit. [546], 52/5/131.

603 cf. Bovet, op. cit. [171], pp. 7, 165.

604 cf. WS, op. cit. [546], 50/4/13.

605 cf. Müller, op. cit. [581], p. 289.

pp. 131f.

606 cf. Hahn, "Reform des Theologiestudiums", Pastoraltheologie 1952, Heft 4,

the psychotherapist. This is not only because the latter sees the complications of man's life on the medical, psychological level, while the people are afraid of the pastor's moral and religious censure. It is rather that the pastor can usually do very little for the man who seeks his help. He neither knows how to diagnose the case psychologically, nor does he know how to make the gospel relevant to a man in this situation. His studies have not prepared him for either."

If we ask in this section what is the necessary equipment of the pastor for his ministry among those occultly subjected, we must reply with the following basic pattern: there is no help without clear diagnosis, and there is no acceptable diagnosis without a thorough knowledge of the causes of occult subjection. This necessary knowledge must, in consonance with the material and with the formal principle of our study, extend to two levels, the secular and the transcendent, the psychological and the spiritual (i. e. in this case the demonic). The demand mentioned above for technical knowledge in view of the psychological factors presents us with a scientific task. This task is accomplished by the study of the specialized literature in the field of medicine, psychiatry, psychology, psychotherapy and para-psychology, and by the collection, critical examination and evaluation of practical cases from daily life and pastoral experience. This acquiring of technical knowledge in the occult field, which must naturally be done from a sufficient personal distance and without any participation in occult experiments, does not imply that the pastor should become a dilettante in medicine and psychology. We are concerned only to make a clear distinction between the necessary tasks. The comprehension of the transcendent factors in occult subjection goes beyond the bounds of a technical knowledge attained by science. We are here moving on to the domain of faith, indeed perhaps into that of spiritual gifts.

The apostle Paul includes among the gifts of the Spirit (I Cor. 12, 7—11) also the charismatic gift of discerning the spirits. And indeed besides the technical knowledge of psychology we need a charisma, if we are to make a causal distinction between the medical and the occult spheres when faced with the entanglements of mental disorder. Besides an exact differential diagnosis, there is an absolute necessity for a charisma in order to discern the point at which we should apply psychological or spiritual help respectively. We may therefore summarize the special equipment needed by the pastor for his ministry to those under occult subjection as *technical knowledge* and *charisma*.

It will be of practical value for pastoral counselling if the relation of the two spheres to each other is defined. Technical knowledge without charisma — generally speaking, the mistake of the sciences bordering on the subject of our study — leads to a denial of occult subjection. Here the catch-words are humbug, swindle, occult credulity, popular superstition, witch-hunting, medieval lack of enlightenment, etc. But charisma without technical knowledge — the condition of many a pastor — can lead to an assumption of demon-possession in the mentally ill, even where no occult subjection is present. Here there is a great danger of reducing all mental disorders which are not understood to a common demonic denominator. A striking example of this is a report of the healing by prayer of a "possessed" person in the magazine "Der Weg zur Seele".[607] Dr. Lechler diagnoses this case as infectious insanity. He cannot see that any evidence has been given of possession. The judgement of this Christian psychiatrist should be given its due weight. For he is not only a specialist in this field, but he is also regarded in Christian circles as a counsellor with charismatic gifts.

A further point of importance in the relation of technical knowledge to charismatic gifts is mutual appreciation. The charismatic pastor is in danger of pride, with the inclination to minimize the technical knowledge gained by the exact sciences. The scientist is in danger of denying the charismatic concern, since without the Holy Spirit he has no organ for the perception of these things. Here we are brought to the heart of the problem under consideration in this present section. At the beginning of our study we have set as guiding mottoes: "No created spirit can penetrate the innermost parts of nature" and "The Spirit searches all things... The natural man does not receive the gifts of the Spirit of God, but the spiritual man judges all things" (I Cor. 2, 10—15). Here the New Testament clearly defines the relation between technical knowledge and charisma. When we discuss occult subjection from this viewpoint, we may say with Müller:[608] "Man as a creature of God is such a deep mystery that only God can know him, and true knowledge of man is simply impossible to unaided reason. Human thought can only elucidate this mystery when it has received the Holy Spirit, who searches all things, even the deep things of God (I Cor. 2, 10)". Although in Pt. IV, ch. 1, 2 we have already spoken of the fact that the superiority in technical knowledge undoubtedly lies on the side of the bordering sciences, yet under this new aspect we shall have to modify this claim to superiority by noting that the essence of man can be more deeply grasped by the spiritual mind than by the intellect. Thus technical knowledge and charisma appear in the following relation to each other: pastoral counselling along New Testament lines is prepared to accord

[607] cf. WS, op. cit. [546], 49/1/15 & 18.
[608] cf. Müller, op. cit. [581], p. 286.

the greatest acknowledgement to every psychological fact which can be conclusively proved. "But this realism, that is open for and prepared to recognize every new discovery, must be on its guard against erasing the difference between the psychological and the Biblical conceptions of man."[609]

In our definition of this relation, this means that the spiritual facts are every bit as superior to the psychological facts as, in the problem of occult subjection the upper, transcendent plane is superior to the secular, subordinate plane. If we may emphasize this by a metaphor, we may quote some words from the biography of Wilhelm Löhe.[610] He wrote: "Knowledge and spiritual knowledge are as different as the picture of man and man himself." Technical knowledge has its importance, which we have no wish to minimize. Nor can lack of technical knowledge be made up for by charisma. But that does not essentially alter the fact that only the Holy Spirit can bring us to the ultimate understanding of man and of his mental disorders. Both factors are indispensable in the pastoral treatment of occult subjection, if we are to avoid a tragic confusion.

When we speak of this absolute necessity, it must not be forgotten that technical knowledge is accessible to human reason. But the charisma of spiritual discernment cannot be attained by our efforts. It is a sovereign gift of divine grace, over which man cannot dispose. No one ever acquired charismatic gifts by theological study — nor, of course, by despising theology. No one has a charismatic gift by virtue of his office, although we must qualify this by saying that God's callings are also His enablings. The charisma is a Spirit-gift which comes from Him who Himself bestows the Spirit. There is only one door which opens the way to this: "Ask, and it shall be given unto you". For this prayer we have the promise of Luke 11, 13: "How much more will the heavenly Father give the Holy Spirit to those who ask Him!" To forestall misunderstanding, we must add that when in this study we speak of the Spirit, we are always expressing a Christological and theological concept. In this study the term "spirit" is not employed as an anthropological concept, as we find it in Paul, alongside the other meaning (I Cor. 7, 34; II Cor. 7, 1).

(c) *The personal attitude of the counsellor*

We have shown that charismatic equipment is the heart of the matter in Christian counselling. This means that Christian counselling cannot

---

[609] ibid., p. 291.
[610] cf. Wilhelm Löhes Leben, Nuremberg 1874.

in its essence be learned. That is the fundamental difference between it and psychotherapeutic treatment. Psychotherapy, with all its methods of healing by covering up and revealing, in all its forms of persuasion, suggestion, hypnosis, autogenic training, occupational therapy, narco-analysis, psychoanalysis, etc., is a technique which can be learned. But pastoral counselling is grace. This is the testimony of Erich Schick,[611] in replying to a pastor who complained of his lack of ability for counselling. He writes: "It is the shocking realization that here theological learning, science, technique, even practical guidance, cannot avail, that pastoral counselling cannot be learned along with other things, but at the most on a foundation of other knowledge." Thurneysen expresses it still more theologically and clearly when he says:[612] "The door of pastoral counselling is a mysteriously closed door, even and indeed especially locked for the theologian who feels himself to be a specialist in the art. This door is not opened from the outside, that is, not by our own ability or resources. It opens only from the inside, and that means as and where God sees fit."

It is especially gratifying that this attitude to Christian counselling is also met with among well-known doctors. Prof. Schultz writes:[613] "Every healing can take place only through grace". The Zürich neurologist Dr. Maeder[614] says it still more clearly: "I have come to the conviction that man cannot save himself; indeed, if you like, that one man cannot ultimately save another. He is so deeply trapped in his separation, that only a humble self-surrender to God, to the personal God, can truly liberate and bring about a change... This decisive change of insight in my life has opened up the approach to another kind of psychological and spiritual help. Besides medical psychotherapy, there is spiritual counselling." The Berlin neurologist Dr. March will complete the picture. In his essay "What really is pastoral counselling?", an essay every minister should read, he writes:[615] "True Christian counselling is in the last analysis an activity which takes place beyond all consciousness, irrespective of any planned pastoral effort. Counselling thus understood stands beyond all psychotherapy and all discussion. Hence there is no such thing as a professional counsellor."

From this insight we may draw some special conclusions about the importance and attitude of the counsellor. Rinderknecht says:[616] "There

---

611 cf. Schick, op. cit. 580, p. 10.
612 cf. Thurneysen, op. cit. 550, p. 9.
613 cf. WS, op. cit. 546, 50/3/17.
614 cf. WS, op. cit. 546, 50/3/1; Maeder, op. cit. 9, pp. 23f.
615 cf. WS, op. cit. 546, 50/4/13.
616 cf. Rinderknecht, op. cit. 598, pp. 33, 40.

are no great Christians; there is only great grace." The pastor does not act out of a professional position, a spiritual reservoir, or a personal power. "The pastor does not sit on the throne of Christian experience, where he can calmly administer counsel and comfort. He stands before God in all his poverty, exactly like the man who seeks his help, and he can do nothing other than pray that God might hearken to the needs which that person brings before him, and that God might entrust him with a word to help the person if it pleases Him." The pastor is at best a midwife. He does not himself bring the child into the world. Or again, he is the gardener who waters and tends the plants. But it is Another who gives the growth. So Bovet describes the meaning of Christian counselling.[617] He is not himself the light-source: at best he holds the burning-glass which focuses the light on to a certain point. Another image is supplied by Schick. He writes,[618] "Anyone who renders spiritual help must play the role in the other man's life of the unknown quantity in an algebraic equation. The unknown must be eliminated". So the pastor, too, must retire into the background after his service is rendered.

Psychotherapy also teaches us this point. It is a basic principle here that all relationships between patient and doctor must be dissolved at the end of the treatment. Thus too in the case of Christian counselling, no human attachments or psychological dependence must remain. The relationship of dependence on a counsellor often constitutes a serious danger and leads to the idolizing of a man and to sectarianism, instead of to fellowship with Christ. The counsellor is of himself not one who knows and has and possesses; he is only an "unprofitable servant" after he has done all (Luke 17, 10). The proper attitude of the counsellor is shown in Matthew 5, 3: "poor in spirit". In this frame of mind he has the promise of Ps. 34, 18: "The Lord is near to the broken-hearted and saves the crushed in spirit". The apparently conflicting teaching of the New Testament, discussed in Pt. IV, ch. 2, 2a and 2c, can be reconciled in the words of the apostle Paul (II Cor. 6, 4 and 10): "In all things we approve ourselves as servants of God, as poor yet making many rich, as having nothing and yet possessing all things".

3. Pastoral Guidance of Those Occultly Subjected

We come now to the discussion of the actual practice, the carrying out of pastoral ministry among those subjected to occult involvement. When now in the following presentation we proceed systematically, this does not and cannot mean that the diversity which is dictated by life's

[617] cf. Bovet, op. cit. 171, p. 167.
[618] cf. Schick, op. cit. 580, p. 21.

situations can be forced into a pattern. A schema can be of help, but it can also mean the formalization and death of counselling. Despite this danger, our presentation will not proceed without the obvious use of a definite method, as it has shaped itself in the course of many pastoral interviews. The knowledge and formulation of definite, recurring laws must, however, be joined with a constant open-mindedness for new ways. The pastor is not a technician, but a listener, an observer, a person who waits, who must follow the footsteps of God's working in the person he is counselling, and who does not set himself up as a forerunner or pace-setter. We shall now assume, as we have in the whole of the foregoing study, that a mentally ill person has come for pastoral counselling. If this person does not himself set the course of the conversation immediately, by a spontaneous or even explosive outburst, in which a confession of guilt breaks forth with primal force from the sick person's heart, then the pastor has first of all the task of diagnosis. We shall discuss this first of all.

(a) *The differential diagnosis of mental disorders*

The central question in the diagnosis of mental disorders is to establish whether the causes are of a purely medical nature, whether an occult subjection is present, or whether the case is a mixed one. In Pt-II, ch. 1, 2 we have already shown, in a schematic presentation, that the question about medical causes is of primary importance with a mental patient. If a valid finding appears, then the patient must be referred to the medical specialist. If the diagnosis discloses a mixed type, that is if both medical and occult causes are demonstrable, then collaboration with a specialist who also acknowledges the religious side of the problem is indicated. Usually, during evangelistic campaigns in Switzerland, I refer people to Dr. Maeder in Zürich and to Dr. Tournier in Geneva; in West Germany I refer them to Dr. Lechler, Dr. Mader and Dr. Spangenberg in "Hohe Mark", and to Dr. March in Berlin, and others. If in the case of a mental disorder there are no medical findings, and an occult subjection is unquestionably present, I omit the help of the medical specialist. Naturally in any doubtful case I refer to a Christian specialist. In no case however is general pastoral counselling of a definitely Christian nature omitted. The special treatment of those occultly subjected is applied only where the evidence is unequivocal. How such an anamnesis is conducted in detail may be shown by means of a briefly summarized example.

Ex 124   After an evangelistic address, which did not touch at all on the occult field, a man came to me for an interview. He explained that he wanted to make a general confession. Exceptional circumstances made time short, so that the interview was not possible until two days later. The man in question came by car from his home town. The discussion began with a spontaneous disclosure by this man, who was a well-known, successful business man, of his mental troubles. He revealed that without any external cause he suffered from emotional depressions. He would confine himself for days in a dark room, take no interest and no pleasure in his work. Everything was overcast by gloom. Food had no appeal to him. In this condition he found it hard to make his business decisions, etc.

Our observations during this interview suggested melancholia. There was the painful, anxious, mimic expression with little movement and the typical folds in the upper eyelids. Other things fitted into the pattern: the decrease of ability to make decisions, the feeling of powerlessness, the occasional sense of sinfulness and poverty even while he was in the best financial situation, the periodic bouts of depression, the "black spectacles" through which he viewed everything — further symptoms to support the diagnosis of melancholia. Noteworthy was the absence of any manic temperament in the intervals, and further the short span of the depressive phase, which lasted about one or two weeks. Between the bouts of depression he pursued his work and was well equal to his business. His openness for religious things was especially marked.

Despite these medical symptoms of periodic melancholia,[619] I had in this case an indefinite feeling that there was some occult relationship here. A question on this point received a negative answer. His forebears were godly people and faithful churchgoers. But I was not convinced, and so I pursued the search into the family background, with the following result. One nephew had a melancholic condition like his own. A sister and an aunt had committed suicide. The grandfather died in a mental home. As a cause, this accumulation of endogenous depression in the family is for the psychiatrist a typical pattern in hereditary manic-depressive psychosis, even though the nature of the hereditary process is not yet clear.[620] This hereditary pattern is no less characteristic in the pastoral treatment of those occultly subjected. In the families of charmers whose history I could trace for three or four generations, we find effects such as death in a mental home, melancholia, suicide, and fatal accidents as a constantly recurring and therefore normal pattern. We cannot here enter further into the causes and priority of the various phenomena. Symptoms of this kind, which appear in well-nigh every family of charmers, always make me prick up my ears. And so I dis-

[619] cf. Bleuler, op. cit. 129, p. 334.
[620] cf. Kloos, op. cit. 12, p. 424.

missed this man after the first interview with a promise from God's word and the intimation that in my view there were among his grandparents occult practitioners and possibly charmers. He again dismissed this as impossible. Two hours later I received a telephone call from him with the surprising disclosure that after he had made immediate inquiries he had established that his grandfather, who died in a mental institution, was a disease- and cattle-charmer.

We cannot here discuss this case further. We had many more interviews, which clarified the situation, showing that the mental disorder of the man was directly or indirectly connected with the occult activity of his forebears. Since we have here a mixed type, the first requirement from the psychiatric point of view is convulsion therapy, and from the pastor's point of view special guidance. This example only shows that the pastor has a difficult task of differential diagnosis, and that equipped with all the scientific helps he must first carefully uncover the causes of ailment before he takes further measures to give help.

(b) *Confession*

Christian counselling does not mean binding a plaster of superficial, pious words over the septic sores.[621] Therefore not only must a diagnosis of the complications be made on the neutral, scientific level, but the wounds must be laid bare and the religious conflicts brought to light, before the healing process can begin. In the sphere of pastoral counselling, this means admission and confession of sin. What is this "confession" in the framework of pastoral help for those enslaved in occultism?

To explain the meaning of confession in the present special connexion, we must distinguish it sharply from consultation in psychotherapeutic treatment. The psycho-analyst seeks to abreact the patient's repressions, inhibitions, subconscious tensions and complexes by bringing to the surface hidden causes and wrong adjustments. Here we have the Socratic principle in action: the relaxing of tension, the assimilation and mastering of the material as the patient learns to understand himself, before the forum of reason. The analytic method is a combination of help from the specialist and self-help. But in the process of confession, the pastor and the confessor stand before God, and it is from Him that they expect and receive their help. Though the two fields have many points of contact, they must be clearly distinguished. This is well expressed by the neurologist Dr. Enke, in an essay on psychotherapy and confession.[622] This clear distinction does not of course mean that a Christian doctor cannot,

---

[621] cf. Rinderknecht, op. cit. 598, p. 11.
[622] cf. WS, op. cit. 546, 49/3/1f.

on the basis of the priesthood of all believers, engage in Christian counselling in addition to his psychotherapeutic treatment.

In here opposing psycho-analysis and confession as understood by the Christian, we must also at this point sound a clear warning of the possible dangers of psycho-analysis, since it has been mentioned so often. I have known Christians with university training to experience dangers for their life of faith as a result of psycho-analysis. A young Christian psychiatrist, for instance, admitted to me that after sessions with a well-known non-Christian psycho-analyst he often had to resist for hours, by means of the word of God and prayer, mysterious forces in his spiritual life. This psychiatrist has since that time been very critical of the analytical method. And, of course, it is psychologically very evident what will result when a psychotherapist of anti-Christian bias analyses the essence of a Christian patient's life. This is also stressed by the Catholic theologian Dr. Marquardt[623] He writes: "Sick Christians are usually directed to non-Christian psychotherapists. But this constitutes a serious danger to their religious position." Worthy of note in this connexion is also what the psychotherapist Dr. Tournier says:[624] "Christian confession leads to the same mental liberations as do the best psychoanalytical treatments."

Having made this clear, we can now turn to the practice of Christian confession. Usually three kinds of confession are distinguished. Acording to Müller[625] these are the confessional interview, private confession, and congregational confession. According to Lackmann[626] they are confession before God alone, or "confession of the heart"; individual confession; and a service of confession. In the pastoral counselling of those involved in occultism, only individual confession or private confession is relevant. In our presentation of the pastoral guidance we are only treating the special problems which arise here. The more general questions are sufficiently treated in the relevant literature. We may here refer especially to the essay of Köberle,[627] to Thurneysen's chapter on confession,[628] to Trillhaas,[629] to Riecker's exposition of the pastoral interview,[630] and further to the other books listed in the bibliography and often quoted in

---

[623] cf. Marquardt, op. cit. 545, p. 20.
[624] cf. Tournier, "Krankheit und Lebensprobleme", Schwabe Verlag, Basel, 1948, p. 239.
[625] cf. Müller, op. cit. 581, p. 331.
[626] cf. Lackmann, Max, "Wie beichten wir?"Rufer Verlag, Gütersloh, 1948, p. 19.
[627] cf. WS, op. cit. 546, 50/6 and 7.
[628] cf. Thurneysen, op. cit. 13, p. 251.
[629] cf. Trillhaas, op. cit. 588, pp. 97f.
[630] cf. Riecker, "Die seelsorgerliche Begegnung", Bertelsmann Verlag 1948, pp. 64f.

the course of this book. It is a gratifying feature within theological circles and the Protestant church that there is much unanimity on the necessity of confession. Here a decisive position of Reformed theology and of the Bible is maintained.

If now we look at Luther's position on confession in the form of an outline, we shall discern five points. At the same time we thus obtain a foundation for our own presentation of this subject, which can in part be developed from Luther's position. For Luther the *necessity* of confession, and in particular of private confession, was beyond question. Luther wrote,[631] "So now we teach what an excellent, precious and comforting thing is confession... And yet I would not let anyone take secret confession from me, and I would not surrender it for all the treasures of the world, for I know what strength and comfort it has given me. I had long since been overcome and strangled by the devil, if confession had not upheld me".[632]

The necessity of confession is maintained also by the Augsburg Confession, Art. XI; Apol. to Augsburg Confession VI; Smalcald Art. VIII.[633]

Secondly, Luther rejected the *obligatory* character of confession: "Regarding confession we have always taught that it must be voluntary".[634] Further we may here mention the reformer's battle against the *legalistic confinement* of confession. The confession of sin must lead to help and comfort, not to the setting up of a new law. Therefore in Smalcald Art. VIII Luther rejects the demand that the confessor must anxiously search his conscience, in order not under any circumstances to forget any sin. He writes: "The confession of sins must be free for each person, to decide what he will or will not tell..." The most painful blow administered to the whole Catholic confessional system was his total reconstruction of the concept of priesthood. From the viewpoint of the general priesthood of all believers, *every Christian can be a priest* and hear his brother's confession. Private confession is no privilege of the ordained priesthood, no reserved territory kept for a spiritual caste. This view is also grounded in Smalcald Art. IV ("De Evangelio"). Luther wrote: "God is boundlessly rich in His grace by the spoken word, by baptism, by the holy sacrament of the altar, and also by mutual converse and consolation of the brethren, Matthew 18, where two or three are gathered, etc." In his resistance to the Catholic system of indul-

---

631 cf. Luther, "Kurze Vermahnung zur Beichte", 1529.
632 cf. Luther, "Sermon von der Beichte", 1523.
633 cf. Müller, op. cit. 591, pp. 41, 185, 321.
634 cf. loc. cit. 629.

gences and the conception of confessional atonement, Luther directed himself against the *work and merit* character of the confessional.

Scriptural support for confession can be found firstly in the following passages: Num. 5, 7; Ps. 32, 5; Prov. 28, 13; Matt. 3, 6; Acts 19, 18; I John 1, 9; James 5, 16. It also appears in Ecclus. 4, 31. We may further adduce David's confession to Nathan (II Sam. 12); the prodigal son (Luke 15); Zacchaeus (Luke 19); the Samaritan woman (John 4); the woman who was a sinner (Luke 7); the criminal on the cross (Luke 23). Actually we need no special proof-texts from Scripture. It lies in the very essence of the Bible that man is called back from his estrangement and sin into fellowship with God. The two essential poles are judgement and grace. In this message the requirement of confession is essentially included.[635] This is how Thurneysen sees it too. If we would express the two ideas of alienation from God and fellowship with God in Johannine terms, we can take light and darkness. Alienation from God is darkness; fellowship with God is light. Confession is nothing other than ceasing from our flight into the darkness, becoming manifest before God, and coming into the light. This significance of confession is seen in I John 1, 7: "If we walk in the light as He is in the light, we have fellowship..." Fellowship with the church and with Christ, membership in the Kingdom of God, comes by way of the process of coming to the light.

This process is of special importance in giving spiritual help to those under occult subjection. Occult activity means in a special way a pact with the kingdom of darkness. That is especially clear in blood pacts and amulet pacts, and with actual, formal invocation of the devil as in magic charming and black magic. For the person under occult subjection, confession consists of recognizing his subjection to the kingdom of darkness and resolving to come to the light. It is an interesting fact, which has been apparent to me in every case of occult subjection, that in cases of occultism confession is indispensable. In general pastoral counselling it is always open to the person concerned to decide whether or not he will make a confession. Indeed we mentioned above how Luther said that confession is totally voluntary and may not be made into a new law. In cases of occult subjection, it is constantly observed that seekers who evade a general confession, including not only occult involvements but the rest of their life as well, do not become free. A confessional interview with one under occult subjection does not lead to deliverance if the seeker's heart and lips are not opened by the grace of God to confession of sin.

[635] cf. Thurneysen, op. cit. 13, p. 253.

Behind this fact there is a two-fold law. First of all, confession is of psychological importance. The confession of guilt has a releasing, unburdening effect. It creates a clear atmosphere. "As long as our sin remains secret, it spreads and expands its power round about. It is therefore most important that it be exposed."[636] So too Trillhaas writes,[637] though from a theological and not from a psychological viewpoint: "Sin is simply that which is secret. It seeks to hide and cover itself, as we see from Adam and Eve after the fall... only he who has recognized this compulsion to secrecy in sin can understand the importance of admitting, disclosing and unveiling sin in confession."

This brings us to the second law. The taking of refuge in secrecy is a characteristic feature of the powers of darkness. Köberle writes:[638] "The demonic tempter always lives of course by the power of the secrecy which exists between him and us. As long as there are certain things kept secret in our life, which no man may know, the crafty enemy will have dominion over our soul. As soon however as the secret is told and betrayed, the power of darkness loses its claim of dominion over us." Hence confession is the notice to quit for the one who claims dominion over us, a counter-action against the kingdom of darkness. Since these dark powers summon all their energies to resist confession, this word of release becomes very difficult for a person to utter. Thurneysen writes of this:[639] "It is a compulsion, something like a demonic spell, which lies upon a person and holds him back from presenting himself to God and committing himself to His grace." Hence confession is an escape from the captivity of the devil's kingdom. This escape is a work of grace. Therefore confession can never be made under compulsion, any more than admission of sin and repentance can be commanded. Compulsion leads only to cramping and distortion of the soul's life. The counsellor can do no more than follow the one and only Pacesetter. We shall not here speak of the concept of penitence, since in every genuine confession there is genuine admission of sin and genuine penitence, the *passiva contritio* which leads to confession.

(c) *Renunciation of the devil*

The terms *abrenuntiare* (Latin) and *apotassesthai* (Greek) indicate a "vow, connected with an ecclesiastical action, or sometimes in private and alone, by which the votary repudiates the devil and his service."

---

[636] cf. Lévy- Bruhl, "Le naturel et la nature dans la mentalité primitive, Paris, 1931, p. 450.
[637] cf. Trillhaas, op. cit. [588], pp. 105f.
[638] cf. Köberle, op. cit. [627], p. 20.
[639] cf. Thurneysen, op. cit. [13], p. 256.

Thus it is formulated in Hauck's Realencyclopädie.[640] The problem of renunciation has been a matter of dispute from earliest times in the history of baptismal practice. Scriptural evidence for renunciation of Satan is usually seen in Matt. 25, 41; John 12, 31; Eph. 6, 11f.; I John 2, 13; 5, 19. The rite of renunciation was justified on the ground that heathen persons receiving baptism had to repudiate the demon-cult of heathenism. The worship of idols is after all called demon-worship in the New Testament (I Cor. 10, 1ff., Rev 9, 20).

This view became fixed in many formulas of renunciation, which we cannot quote here. We refer to Rietschel-Graff's "Lehrbuch der Liturgik".[641] As an example we may mention the formula in Jerome's commentary on Matthew 25—26: "I renounce you, o Devil, your pomp, your blasphemies and your world." In Augustine we already find the godparents being asked at baptism regarding the child, "Abrenuntiat? credit?" (i. e. does he renounce, does he believe?). Here we have the renunciation by infants through the mouth of those who present them.[642] Luther retained renunciation in the liturgy for baptism. The Lutheran service books follow his example. The Württemberg Instruction for Confirmation (1777) includes questions of renunciation. In the newer service books the questions of renunciation appear in two forms. The Lutherans generally have more of the original form: "Do you renounce the devil?" etc. The other books usually have a second form which is somewhat toned down: "Do you renounce evil *(dem Bösen)*?" Some of the provincial churches, e. g. Baden, have no renunciation.

In helping those under occult subjection, renunciation is not a question of the history of doctrine, or of liturgy, but a pastoral question. In the section on confession, we said that occult activity is tantamount to the conclusion of a pact with the dominion of darkness. This pact must be broken, annulled and dissolved by a conscious repudiation on the part of the person subjected, since Christ has already created the objective conditions for this. Although I have until now in my general pastoral counselling wholly omitted renunciation, and shall continue to do so, yet on the ground of my experience in some cases, I no longer completely omit renunciation in cases of occult subjection. It is the concurring pastoral observation of many evangelists that definite renunciation by subjected people leads to a certain liberation. The evangelist Pastor Bruns

[640] cf. "Realencyclopädie für protestantische Theologie und Kirche", ed. D. Hauck, Leipzig 1896.
[641] cf. Rietschel/Graff, "Lehrbuch der Liturgik", Vandenhoek & Ruprecht, Göttingen 1951, pp. 528f., 534f., 573, 583f.
[642] cf. Augustine, "De peccato origins", ch. 40.

uses renunciation for this purpose, making the person say,[643] "I repudiate the devil and all his dark being and works, and I surrender myself to Thee, Triune God, Father, Son and Holy Spirit; and I will be loyal to Thee in faith and obedience until my life's end." Dr. Riecker is of the same opinion.[644] He writes, "Everywhere where magical, occult or enchanting activities are practised, an official confession of liberation from all demonic powers may be necessary, a repudiation of the devil in the words: "I renounce the devil and all his works". The same position is taken up by Dean Hauss, head of the Board of Inland Mission in Baden, as I know from personal conversation.

What is the meaning of renunciation in the pastoral care of those under occult subjection? The renunciation of the devil implies first of all a psychological element. That which until this moment was "in occulto", in secret, now becomes consciously worked off by a firm resolution of the will. Here we see a piece of psychotherapeutic healing method, which can however never penetrate into the depths of this problem. Secondly, in this renunciation of the devil there is a process of demythologization which is the very reverse of Bultmann's. The devil is stripped of his mythical character and is recognized and named as a dreadful reality. No area shows more plainly the untenability of Bultmann's theology than the pastoral care of those under occult subjection. The thesis of Bultmann,[645] that "the belief in spirits and demons is disposed of by the knowledge of the powers and laws of nature", fails to observe the reality of these powers.[645a] Thirdly renunciation is an official declaration before witnesses. Thus it takes on the character of a public repudiation before the "communion of the saints", a severance from the kingdom of darkness. Further, renunciation has the same meaning as it had for heathen catechumens in the ancient church. There disseverance from the demonic idol-cult took place. The repudiation by a person under occult subjection is likewise concerned with his deliverance from the demoncult. For magic is a cult of the devil and demons. The meaning of renunciation is made most clear when we analyse the meaning of the corresponding Greek word *apotassesthai:* to step out of line in battle. He who renounces Satan steps out of the devil's battle line and becomes a foll-

---

[643] cf. Bruns, "Seelsorge ganz praktisch", Verlag Bäuerle, Karlsruhe 1947, p. 16.

[644] cf. Riecker, op. cit. [630], p. 81.

[645] cf. Dr. Bartsch, "Kerygma und Mythos", Reich/Heidrich, Hamburg 1948, p. 20.

[645a] Obviously the problems raised by Bultmann's theology are much more diverse and far-reaching than appears from these remarks. In this study we cannot enter into a discussion of Bultmann. We only wish to remark that in the pastoral care of those under occult subjection we are also concerned with demythologizing, but in a sense completely contrary to that of Bultmann.

ower and soldier of another Lord, Jesus Christ. This thought appears in the ancient church in the pronouncement:[646] renunciation of the devil means *apotage tou Satana* and *syntage tou Christou* (coming out of Satan's battle line and being enrolled in the militia Christi, the army of Jesus Christ). Thus with renunciation we again stand at the centre of the dynamic of the Kingdom of God, which is the foundation of all pastoral activity.

(d) *Absolution*

Along with confession and renunciation comes absolution. Trillhaas takes both of these processes together in his chapter on confession.[647] He writes, "Confession is the personal admission of sin and the promise of forgiveness, on the ground of the authority of Jesus... Confession culminates in absolution." The assurance of forgiveness given by the pastor to the person concerned is especially necessary in private confession, since here usually acknowledgement and confession of sin have assumed a concrete form in a thorough admission and disclosure of details.[648] Absolution has its Biblical anchor first of all in the authority of Christ to forgive sins (Matth. 9, 6); and then, resulting from this, in the power of the keys which Christ gave to His disciples and thereby to the church (Matth. 18, 18—20; John 20, 21—23). The forgiveness of sins is the deepest bed-rock on which the Christian bases his life.[649] It is the most central process in pastoral counselling, the decisive point in the helping of persons who are under occult subjection. Hence we must give special attention to it here.

Absolution is flanked by two errors: legalistic restriction, and premature bestowal. Both errors can lead to tragedy in ministering to the occultly subjected. Thurneysen writes:[650] "That which distinguishes Protestant from Roman Catholic confession is that there are no conditions." Absolution is not bound to the fulfilment of any preliminary or subsequent obligation. Absolution is a central part of the Gospel, which must not be weakened by the law. Here again the principle of unadulterated truth prevails. Riecker writes of this:[651] "In these times that are so poor in spiritual charismata and realized gifts of grace, let us not introduce new requirements and again hedge in the grace which is

---

[646] cf. Rietschel, op. cit. [641], p. 534.
[647] cf. Trillhaas, op. cit. [588], pp. 97f., 107.
[648] cf. Riecker, op. cit. [630], p. 98.
[649] cf. Müller, op. cit. [581], p. 296.
[650] cf. cf. Thurneysen, op. cit. [13], p. 263.
[651] cf. Riecker, op. cit. [630], p. 103.

assured to the penitent." The man who is under occult subjection does not need a new yoke on top of his heavy burden: he needs relief.

In recognizing this truth we must not however ignore the possibility of the other extreme. A thoughtless assurance, a hasty, premature absolution, leads to false confidence and selfdeception. We have here the question of how and by what sign we can recognize the right time to give absolution. Hoch writes of this:[652] "We must ask very seriously how we can know, from the spiritual attitude of the church member, when we really have the right to forgive, and when we must refuse absolution." The refusal of absolution must have behind it the same assurance of God's commissioning as does its bestowal. Thurneysen points in the same direction when he writes:[653] "Merely to pronounce it (sc. the promise of forgiveness) is not enough. For it is just at this point that everything depends on the reception of what is promised from the side of God Himself." This is the problem which is especially involved in ministering to those occultly subjected. We shall now show in a practical way how we must proceed in this special type of pastoral ministry.

After confession, and possibly renunciation, has been made, I read with the person concerned some passages about the forgiveness of sins, such as Isa. 1, 18; 43, 25; 44, 22; Jer. 31, 34; Mic. 7, 18—19; Matt. 9, 21; 26, 28; Luke 7, 48; John 1, 29; Rom. 5, 20; Gal 1, 4; Eph. 1, 7; Col. 1, 14; I Pet. 1, 19; 2, 24; I John 1, 7—9; 2, 2; Heb 1, 3; Rev. 1, 5.

In the course of considering these passages in specific application to the person being counselled, the question is asked, "Can you believe this?" This question about faith does not of course mean that absolution rests upon the faith of the person who has come to seek outside help. If he is expected to contribute everything from his side, then pastoral help has become Law again, and not Gospel. The purpose of putting this question is rather to discover whether there is present this "reception of what is promised from God's side". Just as the ability to make confession is a grace from God, so the ability to believe is grace as well, and a token that the divine absolution has already been granted. When the pastor notes this "ability to believe", there is nothing against pronouncing a word of forgiveness. This simple pastoral situation very rarely occurs in the counselling of those involved in occultism. Sometimes it happens that upon consideration of the promises of forgiveness one can see a very minute spark of faith beginning to glow. Here the pastor may act with confidence. In the human, pastoral "you" of the declaration "Your sins are forgiven you", the "you" of the divine

---

[652] cf. Hoch, "Evangelische Seelsorge", Furche, Berlin, 1937, p. 188.
[653] cf. Thurneysen, op. cit. 13, p. 275.

promise is realized, and the glowing spark grows into a firm faith by means of the promise. In the case of occult subjection, however, the general rule is that those seeking help cannot believe at all. At this point one has simply come to a dead end in dealing with the troubled person. The pastoral interview has for the moment become stranded, since the seeker cannot lay hold on the Gospel and the forgiveness of his sins. This lays upon the pastor the task of meeting this impasse in the process of confession and absolution in the correct manner, and, by God's grace, with spiritual authority. In detail it may be necessary to give attention to the following points.

The first problem will be a medical question. Has this person some emotional disorder, which results in certain inhibitions of will and thought, or decreased powers of resolution and decision? We need not deal now with the medical problem, since we have devoted the section on differential diagnosis to this question. Our next question is that of reflecting whether the person is a generally dull and slow person, who needs the help of a special bridge in order to grasp forgiveness. In such cases the reading of assuring passages in the first person proves helpful. For instance, the seeker may read Isa. 53, 4—7 as follows: "Surely he has borne my griefs... he was wounded for my transgressions... by his wounds I am healed." This kind of help, which was also practised for instance by Pastor Cörper, founder of the Liebenzell Mission, is intended only as a small psychological bridge. But the seeker can be helped by such reading to experience the here and now of the message of forgiveness, the "for me" which is included in the "for us". This kind of help must under no circumstances be allowed to foster an egocentric attitude to faith. This danger does not however in my opinion exist, because a person under occult subjection must after the counselling be incorporated in a special way into the fellowship of Christians.

A further help in getting over this dead end is the reminder that the work of salvation is complete. In this connexion John 19, 30 ("It is finished") may be quoted, and other such texts, alluding to the completion of Christ's work for us. We may also point to the calling which takes place and is completed at baptism. In this case pointing back to baptism corresponds to pointing back to the finished work of Christ. These realities of salvation are realized in our lives by a conscious appropriation and thanksgiving. The word of Luther may be our signpost here:[654] "For if Christ had been given and crucified for us 1,000 times, it would all be in vain if the word of God did not come and distribute it and also bestow it on me, saying: 'This shall be thine, take it and have

[654] cf. Wilhelm Horkel, "Luther heute", Trautmann Verlag, Homburg, 1948, p. 50.

it'." This taking, this acceptance of the finished work, can be brought out in counselling by the following passages: Isa. 55, 1; Luke 11, 10; John 1, 16; 16, 24; Eph. 6, 17; I Tim. 6, 12; Rev. 22, 17. The imperatives such as "come", "take", "eat", "take hold" are in this case not expressions of the law, but of the power of the Gospel.

This process of taking can be clarified to the seeker by borrowing forceful examples from daily life.

I sometimes ask humourously of one who cannot believe, "Can a returnee from prison camp starve at a laden banquet table in his own home?" Yes, if he doesn't help himself. Believing is nothing other than receiving and giving thanks for the finished work of forgiveness, redemption, divine sonship, membership in Christ's body, eternal life, assurance of salvation. Believing is taking hold.

When, in spite of an offer of the Gospel made in a way easy to understand and attractive, the seeker still cannot believe, then we must probe for deeper causes. Perhaps in making his confession he has consciously omitted just those things which were most serious. Perhaps the seeker is only concerned to be rid of his mental vexations, without wanting to follow Christ. Perhaps there are secret commitments with which he is unwilling to break. Köberle write of this:[655] "If the break with sin is not complete, faith will ultimately be lost." Here this means, "Where there is not at least the will to break with sin, no faith can arise." Perhaps the seeker has a false idea of faith, and expects emotional reactions instead of being ready to cast himself simply on God's word. When all these points and others too have been considered with him, we shall have found some further points of contact, which when cleared up will enable us to negotiate the impasse.

If however no specific facts come to light in this direction, and the seeker simply cannot believe, then there is good ground for suspecting the presence of that deep background obstruction which we call *resistance*. The pastoral treatment of this situation will be described in the following section. If the objection be here raised that a long series of detailed probings are here required before absolution is given, we must reply as follows. The practical work of counselling those under occult subjection teaches us that a hasty absolution brings no help, but only fosters new attacks. Furthermore, no word of forgiveness can bring liberation to the subjected as long as the complex of dark entanglements has not been loosed by the word of God. It is quite wrong to speak of a schematic procedure which has been imposed upon the subject. In all the freedom and variety of pastoral ministry to different people, the

---

[655] cf. A. Köberle, "Rechtfertigung und Heiligung", Verlag Dörffling & Franke, Leipzig, 1930, p. 256.

situations above described have proved to be regular features of this special field. We can here proceed only step by step with caution, giving close attention to every small detail. The wish to be of genuine help, the fear of pastoral mistakes, the awareness of our responsibility, and awe and respect for the sanctuary of the brother's soul who seeks our help, demand this caution. Trillhaas[656] writes of this: "He who has no sense of this responsibility should keep his fingers off. We must realize that the special gift of grace (charisma) is needed in order to hear a confession and to accept the authority to forgive." The Gordian knot can only be cut if the Lord Himself with divine power cuts diametrically through all our human and pastoral endeavours and leads the captive to freedom.

(e) *The spiritual struggle*

Resistance is an obvious symptom of occult subjection. Resistance is, as we have just said, often the cause of the impasse in a pastoral interview. When this situation is present, the pastor must concentrate all his powers on the task now before him. Though the term "spiritual struggle" has been chosen for this part of pastoral ministry, this does not mean that the subjected person can be liberated by the battling and struggling of the pastor. The word of Ps. 49, 7 is here relevant: "Truly no man can ransom his brother". Liberation from the bondage of personal, alien powers is only possible through Christ. His Easter triumph is the presupposition for the pastor's struggle for his brother. There are four elements in this stage of pastoral counselling, namely prayer and fasting, intercession by a group of Christians, laying on of hands according to Mark 16, 18, and exorcism.

The pastor's personal effort on behalf of the person who seeks his help has its most beautiful expression in *prayer and fasting,* as a means of assisting the brother who is under attack. Jesus said to His disciples in view of their powerlessness to heal a sick person (Matt. 17, 21): "This kind does not come out except by prayer and fasting". This ministry of help means that the pastor stands as a brother alongside the person seeking help, who is the subject of such severe attacks, and declares himself identified with him in his spiritual distress. This silent service occurs much more often than the Christian public realizes. Schick calls this area of pastoral work one of the central secrets of all spiritual warfare and victory,[657] and the deepest principle of pastoral counselling.[658]

[656] cf. Trillhaas, op. cit. [588], pp. 107f.
[657] cf. Schick, op. cit. [580], p. 39.
[658] cf. Schick, op. cit. [601], p. 291.

Individual work in the special care of persons under occult subjection is often actively supported by a *group of faithful Christians*, who regard themselves as responsible for the person concerned, in support of the pastor. Künkel has emphasized this idea of a circle of helpers in the psychotherapeutic field also: helpers such as a doctor, a physiotherapist, a games instructor, a dietician.[659] What medicine here presents as a special insight is supported in a deeper sense by the passage Matt. 18, 19—20, "Where two or three are gathered in my name, there am I in the midst". In the group of Christians who unite in communal inter-cession for the affected person, Christ becomes manifest in His liber-ating power. What takes place here is part of the realization of the "communion of the saints" spoken of in the third article of the creed; it is an *"actio congregationis sanctorum"*. Luther probably had this special ministry of intercession by a group of Christians in mind when, in the German Missal,[660] he wrote: "Those who would be seriously Christian... ought to subscribe themselves by name, and perchance assemble themselves in a house alone for prayer,... and to practise other Christian works." The ministry of pastoral help is here included and accredited. Hence when modern schools of psychology and medicine speak of the group method and of fellowship as a source of power for the individual, this is an insight which has been acted upon for 2,000 years in Christendom and is of particular importance for the special pastoral help needed by those under occult subjection today. I know cases of people for whom a group of sensible, down-to-earth Christians (not fanatics) united for times of fasting and prayer, and were rewarded by the ex-perience that seriously afflicted people were freed. In biographical litera-ture we occasionally find indications of similar cases. In general pastors do not like talking about this area of experience. When a sensation is made out of such a deliverance, there is "death in the pot" (II Kings 4,40). At this point we must therefore expressly distance ourselves from all the charlatanry and schemings of sectarian and extremist groups.

A further possible way of helping is by *laying on of hands* with prayer. The New Testament knows the laying on of hands in various forms. The disciples before Pentecost received the promise from Christ, "You shall lay your hands upon the sick and they will recover" (Mark 16, 18). After Pentecost the apostles laid their hands on men to impart the Holy Spirit (Acts 8, 18; 9, 17; 19, 6). Moreover charismatic gifts were aroused and

[659] cf. Künkel, "Grundzüge der praktischen Seelenheilkunde", Hippocrates Verlag, Stuttgart & Leipzig, 1935, pp. 149f.
[660] cf. Edition of Luther's Works by Kaiser Verlag, Munich, 1938, vol. 3, p. 244.

given not only by the hands of the apostles (II Tim. 1, 6), but also by the hands of the elders (I Tim. 4, 14). Timothy receives the pastoral advice of Paul to lay hands on no man prematurely (I Tim 5, 22). For our study we would adduce Mark 16, 18, and compare it with James 5, 14. The *arrostos* mentioned in the former passage (= *aeger, imbellis, infirmis, languidus*) is not only a person ill in an organic, physical sense, but also one emotionally discouraged. James 5, 14 suggests a similar condition: *asthenei tis* means "is any powerless, weak especially in physical strength...", but the word can also indicate mental weakness.[661]

From this short exegetical reflection the question arises: may the pastor pray with laying on of hands only for the physically ill, or may he also do so for the mentally ill if requested? A group of evangelists who met in conference in Switzerland in 1952 demanded that pastors refrain in cases of mental ailment when occult roots were present. Basically we must say that the two passages above mentioned leave no room exegetically for such a limitation. Such conclusions might perhaps however be deduced from the practice of Jesus. In the gospels we are struck by the fact that in cases of possession Jesus only commanded (Mat. 17, 18; Mark 5, 8), while He also touched the physically ill (Matt. 8, 15; 9, 29; Mark 7, 33; 8, 23). This fact may give some direction to the pastor in his ministry to those under occult subjection. Of particular force here is the advice of Paul, not to lay hands on anyone prematurely. And yet we must not make this into a new law. When the distress of a grievously afflicted brother grips our heart, and we feel the inner liberty to do so, such service may be rendered. In a few cases I have exercised this ministry with the assistance of two faithful Christians. Riecker also supports this special ministry. He writes in connexion with renunciation:[662] "It is well that this declaration be made with one or more friends present as witnesses. These can unite their prayers with that of the person concerned, and in certain situations lay their hands on him also."

As a guard against misuse, we must say that this (seldom practised) laying on of hands is to be sharply distinguished from any kind of magical healing prayer. It is a thin edge, but a very sharp and decisive one, between charismatic and coercive prayer, between the Holy Spirit and emotional high tension, between the unobtrusive ministry of secret prayer and the deceitful behaviour of wonder doctors. However the proverb *"abusus non tollit usum"* must here once more be maintained.

661 cf. Flügge, op. cit. 546, 50/9/12.
662 cf. Riecker, op. cit. 630, p. 172.

The next stage of help is *exorcism*. Since we are here confronted with the greatest bone of contention in the whole sphere of Christian counselling, we shall give a short history of its development, before we consider its importance in the counselling of those under occult subjection. Descriptions of exorcism, and essays on the history of the concept, will be found in *Religion in Geschichte und Gegenwart*, II, 474f.; Hauck's *Realencyclopädie* vol. 3, 5 p. 695f.; in Bornhäuser;[663] Thurneysen;[664] and above all in Rietschel & Graff.[665] Dr. Lechler[666] has some good illustrative material of psychiatric and spiritual importance. Exorcism in the Christian church has its roots in the expulsions of demons by Jesus, and not in the parallels to be found in the history of religions. The namecult of the sons of Sceva who engaged in exorcism does, however, point to other connexions in religious history (Acts 19, 14). Judaistic exorcists used the name of Jehovah for expelling demons, and in this case they tried to use the name of Jesus. The attempt rebounded, with serious consequences. But Jesus, whose coming proclaims the arrival of the Kingdom of God, drove out the devils (Matt. 12, 27; Mark 1, 27; Luke 4, 36; 11, 19), and gave His disciples the same authority (Matt. 10, 1 & 8; Mark 16, 17). The early church followed this lead and exorcized those who were under the power of alien forces (Gk. *energoumenoi)* or demons. The exercise of this activity was associated with a gift of healing, and those who had this gift were called *exorkistai*, and soon came to form a special class. This kind of exorcism did not take place in the case of candidates for baptism if they were not demon-possessed, but it was always practised with Gentile proselytes.

With the spread of infant baptism, exorcism was carried out on children. Now it underwent a change of meaning, no longer based on Scripture, since it was brought into relation to original sin. In the liturgy of baptism, the practice of exorcism developed with imposition of hands, *insufflatio* and *exsufflatio* (breathing in and out), and the opening of the ears with the command "Effeta" (be opened). In the *Rituale Romanum*, exorcism by water and salt was added. Luther in his handbook on baptism (1523) shortened the exorcism, but retained the Hephata. In the second edition (1526), the following exorcism appears: "I adjure you, you unclean spirit, in the name of the Father and of the Son and of the Holy Spirit, that you come out and depart from this servant of God".

---

[663] cf. D. Bornhäuser "Das Wirken des Christus durch Taten und Worte", Bertelsmann, Gütersloh, p. 49.

[664] cf. Thurneysen, op. cit. 13, pp. 230f.

[665] cf. Rietschel/Graff, op. cit., pp. 512, 526, 543, 556, 561, 573, 593, 605, 608, 617, 621, 872.

[666] cf. Lechler, op. cit. 227.

After the Reformation the upper German territories removed the exorcism from their baptismal liturgy. Pure Lutheran districts in North and Middle Germany retained it. Rationalism then did away with exorcism. From this time on it disappeared from the liturgy. As far as infant baptism is concerned, the opinion represented by the Lutheran systematic theologians Gerhard and Hutter is that exorcism does not belong to the substance of baptism. Spener in his *Theologischen Bedenken* says that the gloss which reads "this may be omitted without sin by whoever so desires" is better than the text. Theologians of recent times reject exorcism as a part of the baptismal liturgy.

Though indeed it is regarded today as theologically established that exorcism has no place in the liturgy of baptism, this does not apply in the pastoral counselling of those under occult subjection. It is one of the findings of this study that, along with widespread magic practices, there exist today people who are demon-possessed or *energoumenoi*, under varying degrees of subjection. In this study the term "occult subjection" has been used to describe this condition, and has been critically examined and firmly established. Up to now in this section we have described three kinds of pastoral help. The final form of help is the *expulsion* of dark powers in the authority given by Christ.

Of this final kind of ministry it must be said that it is the least frequently used method, and is normally employed only in cases of possession. Since cases of pure demon possession form only a tiny percentage of the occult cases, exorcism is not often practised. Moreover it is absolutely essential that this ministry should take place in private. Every tendency towards the sensational is the very opposite of the help which is required. This fact implies a rejection of all externalized displays of exorcism, such as were practised in the medieval church. This limitation also means a rejection of the pseudo-exorcism of some Christian groups, and particularly sectarian movements, in our day. Although we insist on these limitations against the misuse of exorcism, this naturally does not imply that in rejecting abuse we also stifle its proper use, as Bovet does in his book "Lebendige Seelsorge"[667] on pp. 56f. According to the insights developed and presented in this present study, the sections of Bovet's book which deal with occult problems and their treatment give fatal misdirection to servants of God's Kingdom who stand in need of practical guidance.

There are at the present time also some pastors who are subjecting the pastoral use of exorcism to a Biblical evaluation. Erich Schick may be mentioned here, writing as he does on this question in a very general

[667] cf. Bovet, op. cit. 171, p. 56.

way:[668] "In Christianity at home, just as in the foreign fields, the reality and power of supernatural and superhuman powers makes an ever stronger appearance. Hence the pastoral counsellor must be to a considerable extent exorcist and expeller of demons". Thurneysen gives a biblically grounded definition of exorcism:[669] "Behind the captivity of man in sin, the Bible sees an invisible kingdom of evil spirits and powers. Even in these hidden depths, however, God is master in Jesus Christ. Where there is forgiveness of sins, there Satan's kingdom is ended... One little word can fell him. Since the pastor is the bearer of this word, his work must be regarded as the work of casting out demons..."

Among those who practise exorcism we may mention Pastor Bruns. Quoting from Harmanus Obendieck, he says:[670] "What has become of exorcism in the church? Not the formal exorcism of the liturgy, but the spirit-wrought word of power, before which the devil flees and the demons withdraw, and by which in the world of possession the peace of God enters with the liberation wrought by Christ!" It is a great service that Dr. Lechler, as a psychiatrist and as a Christian, has done for all ministers of the gospel by means of his two oft-quoted lectures.[671] In the one on demonology and mental disorder, he presents three cases of possession and shows that they cannot be explained satisfactorily from the psychiatric standpoint. He concludes his differential diagnosis with the words: "That in this situation we were dealing with possession was for me no longer a matter of dispute. Since the condition would not improve, despite thorough pastoral counselling, we proceeded to exorcism. This often resulted in violent struggles of some hours' duration, with blows, screaming, abuse, cursing, especially when the blood of Christ was mentioned. Along with this she showed unusual physical strength. Suddenly she sensed a liberation, and was able immediately to praise and give thanks to God."

With this exorcism the phenomenon of paroxysm appeared, just as in the cases reported in the New Testament. I myself once witnessed a paroxysm in the course of the healing and liberation of a young man who was under occult subjection. It was the conclusion of several pastoral consultations with the man mentioned in *Ex 53*. After the attack the young man suddenly became calm. Although up to this point he had gone on blaspheming, he now began to praise and to give thanks, and therewith he was freed. In other cases there was nothing dramatic.

---

[668] cf. Schick, op. cit. 580, p. 38.
[669] cf. Thurneysen, op. cit. 13, p. 280.
[670] cf. Bruns, op. cit. 643, p. 23.
[671] cf Lechler, op. cit. 227.

In the case of *Ex 65*, I did not think of laying on hands, but was urgently requested to do so by this severely troubled person. In the final pastoral interview it was a deep joy for me to extend this brotherly service to him. The young man was thereupon able to believe that Christ had received him. The forgiveness of sins had become for him an assured fact. There was no longer any need for a direct word of absolution, since Christ had already shown him his forgiveness by a directly accompanying sign. The young man, until this moment torn and depressed, now "went on his way rejoicing".

Regarding the pastoral help of those under occult subjection we may make the following statement about exorcism on the basis of experience:

> In exorcism the pastor engages in a close combat with the powers of darkness. A ministry of deliverance is only possible where there is authoritative, charismatic power. This authority is no human quality, but a decisive break-through of the Holy Spirit in the active faith of the pastor, who is at one mind with Christ (I Cor. 6, 17). The sovereign subject of this liberating ministry is never the pastor, but Christ, whose presence becomes a reality through the Holy Spirit.

(f) *The resistance of the liberated*

The term resistance in this new relation requires explanation. In the phenomenon of occult subjection, resistance presents a mysterious front, a brazen wall against all that is divine. This resistance is sometimes experienced by the afflicted person as an alien power. After deliverance it is absolutely essential that this demonic resistance should undergo transformation into spiritual resistance. The change of front must be diametric, 180°. The occult subject, who was formerly in the devil's milita, now fights as a real deserter in the ranks of Christ, and against his own former camp. It would not be very difficult to choose a different term for this new front of resistance, but we shall retain the same one since we have here a parallel process, except that the starting-point is reversed. If we may quote a scripture passage for the term in this new sense, we may refer to the Latin version of Eph. 6, 13: "propterea accipite armaturam Dei, ut possitis *resistere* in die malo".[672] This word is taken from the section in which Paul is speaking of the dark powers, the evil spirits in the heavenly places, and exhorting the Christian therefore to put on the whole armour of God. This command of the apostle does not represent any empty theory, but a reality of pastoral experience, recognized by faith. The action of resistance is a necessary

---

[672] "Therefore put on the whole armour of God, that you may be able to *resist* in the evil day".

consequence of renunciation and exorcism. This is also clear from the words of Jesus in Matt. 12, 43—45. The evil spirit who went out desires to return, and if he succeeds the state of the man becomes worse than it was before. Stauffer writes of this:[673] "The struggle against the demons of history is a battle with the Hydra. A number of new heads are waiting to sprout forth from the place where one has been severed".

We are now concerned with the question of how the battle of resistance after deliverance is to be conducted. Basically we must begin by realizing that man for his part always stands at a surrendered post. None can wage the battle from his own resources. Further, we establish that the battle has, since Calvary and Easter, been fought and won. The battle thus consists in the fact that man, by his surrender to Christ, is included in Christ's Calvary and Easter work. That is to say, the person in fellowship with Christ experiences the process of dying with Christ and rising again with Him, *mortificatio* and *vivificatio*,[674] the mystery of life in Christ. Paul has presented this fact in Romans 6 and Colossians 2, and relates it to baptism. Prof. Hahn has published a study of these chapters, and has worked out this teaching of identification with Christ.[675] The Christian who has been renewed to a new creation (II Cor. 5, 17) is crucified with Christ (Gal. 2, 19; Rom. 6, 6), has died with Christ (Rom. 6, 8; Col. 2, 20), is buried with Christ (Rom. 6, 4; Col. 2, 12), raised with Christ (Col. 2, 12; Eph. 2, 6), made alive with Christ (Col. 2, 13; Eph. 2, 5), set with Christ in heaven (Eph. 2, 6), and inherits with Christ (Rom. 8, 17).[676] Corresponding to this inward line of identification is the fact that the Christian is also identified in the victory of Christ, who "disarmed the principalities and powers, and made a public show of them, triumphing over them in (the cross)" (Col. 2, 15). The Christian is standing with Christ on victory ground: therefore the resistance of the liberated has from the start a positive note.

Fellowship of life with Christ is the guarantee that the liberated will be preserved in the rear-guard action. The important weapon in this war is the *word of God*. Pastoral experience with people who have been under occult subjection teaches us this particular lesson with instructive clarity: that no storms of emotion can enable us to stand in the battle, but rather building on and trusting in God's word. Paul calls the word of God the sword of the Spirit (Eph. 6, 17), by which the assaulted can withstand in the battle. Rinderknecht calls the word of God the plank

[673] cf. Stauffer, op. cit. 527, p. 106.

[674] cf. Schlink, op. cit. 589, p. 200.

[675] cf. W. J. Hahn, "Das Mitsterben und Mitauferstehen mit Christus bei Paulus", Inaugural address, Bertelsmann, Gütersloh, 1937.

[676] ibid., p. 47.

which bridges every chasm.[677] The pastor therefore has the task of administering the word of God, and the commission of introducing the person he is counselling to this word. In actual practice I often give the person after the interview an introduction to Bible reading. In special cases I write out a simple reading plan, which I read through with the person seeking help. Doing this together encourages the afflicted person to faithful reading. Besides this general introduction to the word, it is important that a person freed from occult subjection should learn to start with how to wield the weapon of God's word in his own personal defence. That is not an individualistic goal, but only an elementary safeguard, to help him resist the powers which once enslaved him. A part of this weaponry is the learning by heart of certain key passages, which the liberated person may use as prayers in times of recurring attacks, e. g. "Thou dost beset me behind and before, and layest thy hand upon me" (Ps. 139, 5); "I will be to her a wall of fire round about, says the Lord, and I will be the glory within her" (Zech. 2, 9). See further Deut. 31, 6; Josh. 1, 9; Ps. 91, 1f; Isa. 41, 10; 43, 1f; Matt. 28, 20; etc. In this battle of resistance, the word of God[678] proves to be a means of realizing and strengthening identification with Christ, and moreover a weapon of defence "which has the effect of liberating one from the dominion of the demons and of this evil age".[679] So Hahn puts it. There are two principal ways of applying the word of God which have proved effective in this defence of the liberated: firstly, the realization by faith of the finished work of redemption and secondly, the command in the name of Jesus, on the basis of His victory. Let me make this still clearer. I read Bible passages with the liberated person, dealing with the blood of Christ as the effectual sign and symbol of redemption:

I Peter 1, 2	... for sprinkling with his blood ...
1, 19	... ransomed with the precious blood ...
I John 1, 7	... The blood of Jesus Christ his Son cleanses us from all sin ...
Hebrews 10, 22	... with our hearts sprinkled clean ...
12, 24	... ye have come to the sprinkled blood ...
Revelation 1, 5	... who has freed us from our sins by his blood ...

Meditation on such passages and the formulation of such words into a prayer has the effect of making present to faith the fact of redemption. Stauffer says in his Theology of the New Testament,[680] "The blood of

677 cf. Rinderknecht, op. cit. 598, p. 37.
678 cf. Hahn, op. cit. 675, p. 123.
679 ibid., p. 127.
680 cf. Stauffer, op. cit. 527, p. 106.

the crucified is the remedy which puts an end to the battle with the Hydra". A prayerful meditation upon such passages brings the liberating and preserving power of the sacrificial death of Christ into our lives. Naturally we must also here carefully observe and maintain a boundary between this and any kind of blood-mysticism or blood-fanaticism. But our fear of fanaticism and sectarianism must not lead us to neglect the sources of power in the word, so that our life of faith dies away. A further means of defence against recurring attacks is the command in the name of Jesus. In general pastoral counselling I do not suggest this form of help to the people I am advising. In cases of severe occult subjection, if the Hydra again raises her head after liberation, then the command "In the name of Jesus Christ I command you, evil powers, to, leave" can be an effective defence. The disciples of Christ used command according to the word of the Master (Mark 16, 17; Matt. 10, 1; Luke 9, 1). Jesus Himself, during His temptation (Matt. 4, 10; 16, 23) commanded His adversary "Depart from me, Satan". Paul defended himself by this means at Philippi (Acts 16, 16—18) against a threat to his ministry. Men such as Blumhardt, Seitz and others (cf. *Ex 86*) strengthened themselves by this means in various pastoral struggles. A person who was originally subject to occult powers, and who has completely surrendered to Christ, should not be denied this means of defence, if he has the inner liberty to employ it. It is of interest that other pastors and evangelists who have to deal with people under occult subjection have come to the same conclusion on the basis of the word of God and of experience. Dean Hauss, head of the Board of Inland Mission in Baden, told me that in connection with his intercession for a married couple who were troubled by occult powers, he himself experienced uncanny visitations during the night. When he commanded in the name of Jesus, the dark power withdrew. Swiss evangelists, who have more to do with those under occult subjection than do German evangelists, reported at a conference in Männedorf that they employ the two ways of applying the word of God, exactly as we have just described them. Thus servants of God engaged in gospel work, who come from different groups and nationalities, have been led in similar ways.

To guard against abuse we must still mention three things. As the history of the sons of Sceva shows (Acts 19, 14—16), there is also an arrogated authority. He who does actually stand in identification and communion with Christ is not in a position to command. Arrogated authority only leads to more intensive danger, since it constitutes a challenge to the evil powers. Now this does not of course imply that the afflicted person must first nervously, anxiously, legalistically probe his own condition before he can command. If he can look to Christ in faith, let him proceed. He who looks back upon himself is always defeated. Repulsion of evil powers is a work of Christ (I John 3, 8), and not a human undertaking. Else man would always be on the losing side. This command issues from the Gospel and not from the Law. It is rooted in Calvary and Easter, not in Sinai. Further, this command must be guarded against any ostentation and hasty repetition. When the person liberated from occult subjection by Christ is no longer in the situation of Matt. 12, 43, then such commanding is no longer necessary. And lastly, we must warn that by the presentation of these special uses of the word of God we do not intend any change of emphasis. When Biblical truths are over-emphasized, then there is a starting point for error. Hence all special suggestions for the care of those under occult subjection must be kept in a healthy tension to other statements of Scripture. In general pastoral counselling, the best results are achieved by the use of the means of grace mentioned in Acts 2, 42, viz. the word of God, fellowship, sacraments, and prayer. These are the means for the realization of identification with Christ. And in the ministry to those under occult subjection, the same basic elements are effective, although in a specialized form of application.

Following upon the word of God, the second support in the battle of resistance, in which the liberated person is engaged, is mentioned in the words just quoted (Acts 2, 42), viz. *fellowship*, the communion of the saints. People who are not interested in going to church often reply to an invitation to attend a service with the catchphrase "Going to church doesn't save you". But this expression betrays an ignorance regarding the organic structure of the body of Jesus Christ. Separated from the body, an individual member will die. A coal taken out of the fire will cease to burn. Isolation from the congregation of Jesus often leads to spiritual death. When the writer to the Hebrews warns us "Forsake not the assembling of yourselves together, as is the manner of some" (Heb. 10, 25), he is by this exhortation proving himself a true pastor of souls. The word of Zinzendorf, who said "I recognize no Christianity without fellowship", finds drastic confirmation in pastoral experience among those afflicted by occultism. The person liberated from occult subjection must stand faithfully in the congregation of the saints, in order there to be connected to the power-current which flows from the Head of the church to all its members. Pastoral experience teaches that for effective resistance by the liberated person normal attendance at church services does not suffice. The Board of the Inland Mission of the Baden Church therefore advocates the formation of small groups of faithful Christians which can act as leaven in large congregations and assume pastoral follow-up work.

I must state, in spite of the hostility of some, that I have several times had the opportunity of observing the pastoral competence of these groups. Once after an evangelistic meeting I commended a woman who was severely troubled by occult powers to such a group for further care. For a whole year this group bore her up in prayer until she was completely freed. Such groups are power houses, from which a person who has been freed from occult involvement can receive strength for the battle of resistance. The little groups thus have their pastoral importance in the battle of deliverance, as above noted, as well as in the battle of resistance. In this connexion something must be said in passing about the follow-up work in this special ministry to those subjected to and freed from occultism. The pastor must not imagine, after pastoral interviews in connexion with a week of evangelistic meetings, that his work is completed. Dr. Lechler says "He who breaks off his care prematurely is like a surgeon who stitches the incision before the impurities have been drained off".[681]

The pastoral follow-up is always the crux of an evangelistic campaign. I usually try to meet this need by noting the names of those who have sought help and referring them to the local pastor. A person who seeks help must of course be incorporated into his local church. Sometimes, however, the disclosure of the seeker's name is not permitted. It is not good for the evangelist to allow a personal congregation of his followers to grow up over a whole area. Here too the thesis of Schick applies, that the evangelist must be the unknown quantity in an algebraic equation, which must be eliminated. In many cases a large correspondence will develop between the people and the evangelist after a campaign. In counselling people with occult problems this cannot always be avoided, since our clergy do not always have the necessary specialized knowledge to give competent counsel to those under occult subjection and those who have been liberated from it. Absolutely no follow-up work can be expected from the pastor who dismisses the whole occult field as humbug and swindle. He who recognizes and sees no fronts here cannot lead in the battle. The best solution is that the seeker, with his own permission and the approval of the local pastor, be incorporated into a small group which maintains contact with the local pastor. Where no such group exists, two or three faithful Christians can sometimes be given responsibility for the person seeking help. Naturally such little cells within the church must not become hot-beds of pharisai-

681 cf. Lechler, WS, op. cit. 546, 51/5/143.

cal arrogance. Such small groups are merely bricks in the total structure of the church, with a special commission towards the person needing help. The formation of bands or cliques does not serve to build up the church, but rather to undermine it. A healthy form of small groups appeared under Blumhardt in Möttlingen, where every evening in forty-four homes family groups met for prayer and study of the word.[682] The *ecclesiola* must stand within the *ecclesia,* and not over against it. Naturally some remarks could be made about the concept of *ecclesia,* but this does not belong to the scope of our study.[683]

The next means of support in the spiritual resistance of the liberated person is the *Lord's Supper.* Emil Brunner calls the sacraments the clamps which the Lord gave to His church, to keep it from collapse.[684] The person freed from occult subjection needs these clamps, which bind him fast to Christ and to His church. As we reflect in passing on the nature of the Lord's Supper, in its pastoral aspect as it applies to the theme of our study, we may follow the perspectives offered by Prof. Hahn.[685] Hahn presents the Lord's Supper as having a three-fold meaning. "In this meal we find first the new, eschatological covenant with God, which is the fulfilment of Old Testament salvation history. This covenant is a reality only in this blood, i. e. in the work of Jesus Christ on the cross. It is the blood of Jesus Christ, shed at Golgotha, on account of which, and in which, the new covenant has its reality. This blood also performs the other task of the Paschal blood: it is a shield against the destroying angel, against the dominion of the demons. He who has a share in this blood is covered against the mighty activity of the demons, though not in a magical manner, but in repeatedly laying claim to the eschatological possibility which is granted in the blood of Christ. As a third element corresponding to the paschal blood, we see the promise for the future which attaches to this blood. This blood is the assurance of participation in the promised land, the parousia."

This presentation could not fit better into the framework of our study. In the Lord's Supper the person liberated from occult subjection is brought into participation in the Christ event. The liberated person experiences by means of visible signs his fellowship with the body and blood of Christ, his incorporation into the church of Christ, the realization of membership in the Kingdom, and thus the strengthening of his spiritual resistance against demonic influences and attacks. The Lord's

---

[682] cf. Riecker, op. cit. [630], p. 144.

[683] cf. Hilbert, "Ecclesiola in ecclesia", Deichert Verlag, Leipzig, 2nd. edn., 1924.

[684] cf. Emil Brunner, "Unser Glaube", Gotthelf Verlag, Bern, 1935, p. 144.

[685] cf. Hahn, op. cit. [675], pp. 135f.

Supper is the focal point of the dynamic of God's Kingdom, in which departure from the *civitas diaboli* and entrance into the *civitas Dei* become a reality for the afflicted and the liberated. Therefore I recommend a frequent attendance at the Lord's Supper for the person who has been liberated from occult subjection. As a marginal note I would suggest that the churches should make the sacrament more available than it has been up to now. In the Baden Church it is for instance at present celebrated only on holy days.

As a further means of strengthening the spiritual resistance of those freed from occult involvement, we must mention the personal *prayer-life,* which makes the plea "Come, Creator Spirit" a daily concern. Just as the essence of demon-possession is the indwelling of the demons, so the essence of being born from above (John 3, 3) is the indwelling of the Holy Spirit (John 14, 23). The realization of identification with Christ, of "being in Christ" (II Cor. 5, 17), is only possible through the Holy Spirit (I Cor. 4, 3). Prof. Allwohn writes in this connexion,[686] "Hence, it must be the goal of the pastoral mission to prepare people for the reception of the Holy Spirit. The objection may here be raised that this goal is too high. Who can and may undertake to impart the Holy Spirit? There is indeed here no possibility from a human point of view. Yet we are to stand in firm faith on the promise that the Father will give the Holy Spirit to those who ask Him (Luke 11, 13; Acts 2, 39)." Spiritual resistance is only possible through the Holy Spirit. The Spirit is bestowed by the divine word and the sacraments.[687]

Summarizing, we may, from the viewpont of pastoral practice, characterize the essence of resistance as follows:

In exorcism a reversal of dominion has been brought about by the impact of the Holy Spirit in the person subjected to and then freed from occultism. Becoming free is followed by remaining free, as a continuous state of standing under the power of Christ, whose reality is experienced in the word of God, in the church, in the Lord's Supper, and in the life of faith and prayer. In the sharp resistance required against the rearguard action of the dark adversary, refuge in the blood of Christ as the sign of the complete victory achieved on the cross, and a command spoken in the name of Jesus, prove themselves to be an effective defence as part of the resistance of the person who has been freed.

After our statement of the special care to be applied to those under occult subjection, we may now state the *7th. thesis:*

---

[686] cf. Allwohn, op. cit., p. 115.
[687] ablative of instrument.

Liberation from occult subjection appears as a special problem of pastoral ministry. The pastoral interview involves the following elements: differential diagnosis, confession, renunciation, absolution, exorcism, and spiritual resistance. Ministry to those affected by occultism can only proceed on a basis of thorough technical knowledge, and — by the grace of God — with charismatic equipment. We point out here that the liberation of those thus subjected is not the fruit of a pastoral struggle, but is an act of Christ. Hence, the liberation of the afflicted person succeeds only through the realization of identification, or fellowship, of the subjected one with Christ.

Chapter Three

WHAT PERSPECTIVES MAY BE GAINED FOR THOSE WHO MINISTER TO THE OCCULTLY SUBJECTED?

According to the guidelines which our study has already yielded, a few marginal questions remain, which were mentioned at the beginning, but now require reconsideration.

1. The Urgent Need for Special Pastoral Help for the Subjected

The first question can be indicated by means of an ironical criticism. Is pastoral care for persons under subjection to occult powers not the "hobby-horse of an extremist who enjoys poking his nose into dark things"? In our prolegomena (Pt. I ch 1), we have already pointed to the flood of mental disorders, which in many cases stand in frequency ratios to occult practices. With regard to these frequency ratios, we shall now give some statistics from the year 1951. In general, it is not a good thing to evaluate statistics of pastoral work. Yet we are driven to make an exception by our desire to help those afflicted by occultism. During evangelistic campaigns with a plan of ten addresses, I usually devote one address to the question of pastoral care for those under occult subjection. This one address usually leads to more interviews than the treatment of the 7th. commandment. A systematic survey yields varying results:[688]

Stuttgart	10 addresses	52 interv.	15 occ.int.	29%
Reutlingen	10 "	60 "	46 "	77%
Village M.	10 "	60 "	40 "	67%
Village L.	10 "	58 "	40 "	69%

[688] interv. = interviews; occ. int. = interviews concerning occult matters.

Bern (centre 1)	8 addresses	12 interv.	8 occ.int.	67%
Bern (centre 2)	2 "	12 "	10 "	83%
Bern (suburb)	8 "	10 "	8 "	80%
Zürich	10 "	72 "	62 "	86%

As an explanation of this survey let us consider one example. In Stuttgart, of the 10 evangelistic addresses I delivered, one was on the subject of occultism. Among 52 private pastoral interviews, there were 15 cases of occultism. This makes 29%. Now what does this statistic, from one year, tell us? In comparison with the statistics of other years, the years since the war always present the same pattern. There is a decrease only in the practice of divining from the photographs of missing persons with the pendulum, since many of those who were missing have given some token of their existence, or have returned home. In our present statistics it appears that the percentage of those occultly subjected in Switzerland is greater than that in Germany. Usually two-thirds or three-quarters of those who come to me to make a personal confession in Switzerland are implicated in occult activities. Swiss evangelists at a conference in Männedorf corroborated this. Pastor Bruns, who is well informed on the problem of occultism, assumes a similar percentage of persons under occult subjection on German territory.[689] "The most striking thing in all this to my mind was that practically two-thirds of the people had some how become enmeshed in such involvements of a demonic or Satanic nature, partly of course for fun, but partly also consciously and with deliberate purpose." Further, the above survey shows us that the percentage in the cities is generally less than that in the villages. The high figure in pietistic Reutlingen is a special case which is hard to explain. He who knows something about the spiritual, historical relations in the Kingdom of God may perhaps understand the remark, "Where God builds His church, the devil builds a chapel next door". Often such special situations are due to a single occult practitioner. This is the situation in two villages often mentioned and visited in Baden. In Switzerland one repeatedly hears in this connexion the name of some particular Alpine valley where magic flourishes. The special cases are thus mostly due to some intelligible pattern. Another question now is the cause of the low percentage rate in the cities as compared with the villages. Here there are several factors to consider. First of all, the city, with its loosening tendency in every direction, is not so bound to the old customs as is the country with its fixed and settled population. Secondly, there is in the city much more of a tendency than in the village to consult a psychiatrist when mental trouble occurs. The

[689] cf. Bruns, op. cit. [643], p. 15.

farming community shies away from the psychiatrist. Then also the villager, who is in general more given to church attendance, more readily seeks an interview with the pastor than does the town-dweller. Thus, we have various data from life, which appear behind the rigid statistical picture. The statistical pattern like many statistics, is only relatively dependable and not absolutely so. But the one thing of which this statistic urgently warns us is the high number of those mentally afflicted because of occult involvement. The reality behind the statistics points to the urgency of special pastoral help.

2. *The Necessity of a Clear Diagnosis*

A question is raised by the objection that some pastors have little dealing with those under occult subjection. This may have various grounds: lack of technical knowledge, not noticing or not taking seriously this problem, little pastoral activity, a priori rejection, etc. The essential point will be the direction of God's leading. In the New Testament there are various gifts and offices. Each Christian has so to speak his own appointed place. Each has his particular assignment, which he must faithfully carry out. He to whom God has given the charisma of discerning the spirits (I Cor. 12, 10) has, along with this gift, the task of familiarizing himself with all the scientific means in the field of differential diagnosis. The complexity of the various mental ailments in connexion with occult involvement makes evident the necessity of a clear diagnosis.

3. *The Relation of Law and Gospel*

One of the most burning questions is that of the place of the Law and the Gospel in the pastoral care of those under occult subjection. Here we have a most decisive touchstone as to whether a pastor is competent to help the occultly subjected person or not. Law and Gospel have each their definite place in the special care of these afflicted persons. In this most difficult area of pastoral ministry, any confusion or mixing will have disastrous effects. The only place where the Law belongs here is in the diagnosis, in which we are concerned with disclosing occult connexions. The aim of proclaiming the Law is to point out to the occult practitioner that whether he be actively or passively involved, he is standing under the judgement of God, because he has by transgressing the first, second and third commandments entered into a pact with powers alien to God. Here we are engaged in the convicting use of the law, by which the person under occult subjection becomes convicted of his sin.[690] But this is definitely the limit of the Law's use in the pastoral counselling of the occultly subjected. In the pastoral interview and confession of these persons, the Gospel must have unlimited sway. To the afflicted person we must administer the word of forgiveness and redemption in the spirit of Eph. 1, 7: "In Jesus we have redemption through His blood, the forgiveness of sins according to the riches of His grace."[691]

There is no place for a "cheerless, pharisaical, legalistic, pushing approach" in pastoral ministry to the man under occult subjection.[692] The person with mental afflictions is usually so crushed, so worn down, that legalistic counselling can only drive him further into despair. All condemnation of the afflicted person, even though he displays the worst of Satanic attachments, is a denial of the Gospel. If during the first part of the interview there has been an honest acknowledgement of his situation under judgement, then there is no room for any further burdening when the promise of forgiveness is given. Where sin has been named, acknowledged, and repented of, only the comfort of the Gospel is in place. The pastoral care of Jesus for the paralytic, for the woman who was a sinner, for Zacchaeus, is our pattern here.[693] Here only one imperative is in place: "Come, all things are ready, take, eat, drink, it is for you".[694] It is in this sense, as an imperative and a help towards accepting the Gospel, that we would have all the above sections (Pt. II, ch. 4, 3 b—f) of our study understood. Luther strongly sets forth the difference between Law and Gospel in his "Sermon on the difference between the law and the gospel".[695] He writes: "This is what it means rightly to define the Law and to distinguish it from the Gospel, namely that that should be called and should be the Law which demands our works. The Gospel, on the other hand, or faith, is the teaching or word of God, which does not demand our works, nor command us to do something, but rather urges us simply to accept and to let ourselves be given the proffered grace of forgiveness of sins and eternal salvation. Here we do nothing, but only receive and let ourselves be given that which is offered

---

[690] The Christian neurologist Dr. Maeder has a policy of proclaiming the unadulterated Gospel to those who are mentally ill, in addition to the medical treatment he gives them.

[691] cf. Jelke, "Kompendium der Dogmatik", p. 335.

[692] cf. Thurneysen, op. cit. [13], p. 274.

[693] cf. Matt. 9; Luke 7; Luke 19.

[694] cf. Dr. Walther, "The right distinction of Law and Gospel", Missouri synod 1946, p. 35.

[695] cf. WA IX, 416f.

us and extended to us by the word, namely that God promises and assures you: this and this I give to you".

The Law shows us what we have perpetrated; the Gospel shows us what God has accomplished. The difference must not be neglected in pastoral counselling. Of this Luther wrote:[696] "Therefore it is highly necessary that this two-fold word be rightly and clearly distinguished. If this is not done, neither Law nor Gospel can be understood."

If now, with a view to the pastoral care of those under occult subjection, we would define the relation of Law and Gospel, then we must state it as follows. He who applies only a pacifying and soothing therapy in counselling the occultly subjected person degrades the meaning of the Law, fails to uncover the depths of the guilt relationship caused by the occult involvement, and thereby also minimizes the Gospel: for where there is no guilt, the Gospel has no real object. In this difficult ministry we cannot do without the Law. If we try to do so, the subjected person will shift his spiritual need on to the level of an emotional disorder which can be medically diagnosed, and so provide himself with a refuge from the hand of God.[697] The Law may not be separated from the Gospel.

The second statement is concerned with maintaining the purity of the Gospel. "No fence may be set up around Golgotha".[698] The Gospel is not a new Law, the fulfilment of which will bring liberation to the man under occult subjection. Here everything depends on God's work in Christ. Every introduction of conditions which must be met beforehand represents a dilution, a mixing, a legalizing of the Gospel. The pastor must have a holy dread of falsifying the Gospel by means of the Law. Not the spiritual struggle of the pastor, nor the spiritual resistance of the person afflicted, brings liberation or preserves a person in the state of deliverance, but Christ alone. If we want a formula to express the relation of the Law and the Gospel, we may use the words applied in the Chalcedonian Definition to the two natures of Christ: *asynchytos, atreptos, adiairetos, achoristos* (unconfused, unchanged, indivisible, inseparable).[699] Law and Gospel cannot be mixed together; neither can they be divided. The dissolution of this unity is a fatal danger in pastoral work. Therefore the ministry of help to those under occult subjection requires the ability to proclaim Law and Gospel in the correct relation to one another.

---

[696] ibid., 412f.

[697] cf. D. Rendtorff, "Worauf Gott mit uns hinaus will", Zeitschriftenverlag, Berlin, p. 35.

[698] cf. Walther, op. cit. [694], p. 36.

[699] cf. Appel, "Kurzgefaßte Kirchengeschichte", Deichert Verlag, Leipzig 1925, p. 50

4. *Christ, the End of the Demons*

Without doubt, in the pastoral care of those under occult subjection, the administration of the Gospel is of supreme importance. It was not the aim of this study to demonstrate the fact of demonic enslavement or possession, but rather to proclaim its conquest and cure. Where the unusual phenomenon of possession, as the extreme manifestation of the evil dominion of the wicked one, actually appears, we must confront it with the glad message of deliverance. This study is not therefore a new "occult book" amid the flood of occult literature, but a book about the liberation from all evil powers through Christ. Since Golgotha and Easter, the power of Satan is a hollow power. In reality all demons have already been conquered in Christ.[700] Christ has broken into the castle of the strong one (Mark 3, 27), and has deprived him of his prey.[701] The Son of God has breached the bulwarks of darkness (I John 3, 8). This fact becomes still more evident when we look more closely at the term "evangelium" (gospel). Friedrich[702] shows that the term evangelium in its secular meaning originated in the language of war, of combat, and is the technical term for the announcement of victory. This basic meaning must be retained in our understanding of the New Testament too. In the conflict between the *civitas Dei* and the *civitas diaboli*, the battle has been won by Christ. The announcement of victory must be applied in counselling those under occult subjection. It tells the afflicted one of participation in the victory, of the breaching of the prison doors of mental suffering. This report of victory spells an end to the tyrannical dominion of Satan, since the Christ of God is the Lord and Saviour of the world.

---

[700] cf. Cullmann, "Christ and Time".
[701] cf. Karl Heim, "Jesus der Herr", Furche, Berlin, 1935, § 9—§ 11, p. 104.
[702] cf. Kittel, "Theologisches Wörterbuch zum N. T." vol. II, p. 719.

BOOKS WRITTEN BY DR. KURT E. KOCH

1. *BETWEEN CHRIST AND SATAN*
   An investigation into occultism which includes chapters on fortune-telling, magic and spiritism, and is based on over 160 examples which have come to light through counselling people.

2. *CHRISTIAN COUNSELLING AND OCCULTISM*
   The counselling of the psychically disturbed and those oppressed through involvement in occultism. A practical, theological and systematic investigation in the light of present day psychological and medical knowledge.

3. *THE COMING ONE*
   The providential emergence of the nation of Israel and the amazing events of the Six Day War illuminated in the light of prophetic Scriptures.

4. *DEMONISM, PAST AND PRESENT*
   Message given to students at more than 100 Universities, Seminaries and Bible Colleges around the world.

5. *THE DEVIL'S ALPHABET*
   A review of 47 forms of superstition, fortune-telling, magic and spiritism.

6. *THE STRIFE OF TONGUES*
   A study of the Tongues Movement including its development, case studies of its effect on people and the answer from Scripture.

7. *DAY X*
   The present world situation reviewed in the light of the nearness of the Lord's second coming.

8. *OCCULT BONDAGE AND DELIVERANCE*
   An introduction into the counselling of people who are under occult bondage and subjection. Part One: Christian Counselling, Part Two: Medical Diagnosis.

9. *REVIVAL FIRES IN CANADA*
   Stories of the Holy Spirit's working in changing individuals and communities as revival fires sweep over Canada.

10. *THE REVIVAL IN INDONESIA*
   Dr. Koch has visited the very centre of the revival area in the Eastern islands of Indonesia several times. He has witnessed there the selfsame things that one finds reported in the Acts of the Apostles.

11. *VICTORY THROUGH PERSECUTION*
   Fascinating stories of changed lives and transformed communities in the battle-scarred land of Korea.

12. *WORLD WITHOUT CHANCE?*
   Out of the present world chaos comes stories of revival fires and the workings of the Spirit of God.

Other Titles to Follow . . .

At Your Christian Bookstore, or
KREGEL PUBLICATIONS, P.O. Box 2607, Grand Rapids, Mich. 49501

Paths in Utopia

Paths in Utopia

by

Martin Buber

Collier Books
Macmillan Publishing Company
New York

Collier Books
Macmillan Publishing Company
866 Third Avenue, New York, NY 10022
Collier Macmillan Canada, Inc.

Library of Congress Cataloguing-in-Publication Data
Buber, Martin, 1878-1965.
    Paths in utopia.
    Translation of: Netivot be-utopyah.
    1. Socialism—History.   2. Communism—History.
3. Cooperation—History.   I. Title.
HX36.B8413   1986   335'.009   85-24248
ISBN 0-02-084190-6

Macmillan books are available at special discounts for bulk purchases
for sales promotions, premiums, fund-raising, or educational use. For
details, contact:

Special Sales Director
Macmillan Publishing Company
866 Third Avenue
New York, NY 10022

First Collier Books Edition 1988

10 9 8 7 6 5 4 3 2 1

Printed in the United States of America

CONTENTS

ACKNOWLEDGMENT   vi

FOREWORD   vii

I.   THE IDEA   1

II.   THE UTOPIAN ELEMENT IN SOCIALISM   7

III.   THE FORERUNNERS   16

IV.   PROUDHON   24

V.   KROPOTKIN   38

VI.   LANDAUER   46

VII.   EXPERIMENTS   58

VIII.   MARX AND THE RENEWAL OF SOCIETY   80

IX.   LENIN AND THE RENEWAL OF SOCIETY   99

X.   IN THE MIDST OF CRISIS   129

EPILOGUE — AN EXPERIMENT THAT DID NOT FAIL   139

INDEX   151

ACKNOWLEDGMENT

THE translator would like to express his most cordial thanks to the author for his great help in the preparation of this volume, both as regards the translation and the correction of proofs. He is also indebted to Mr. Paul Derrick for checking the titles of certain books herein mentioned.

FOREWORD

THE intention underlying this book is to give genetic account of what Marx and the Marxists call "Utopian Socialism", with particular reference to its postulate of a renewal of society through a renewal of its cell-tissue. I am not concerned to survey the development of an idea, but to sketch the picture of an idea in process of development. The fundamental question in the making of such a picture is—as in the making of all pictures—the question of what one has to leave out. Only so much of the massive material seemed to me to be relevant as was essential to a consideration of the idea itself. It is not the false turnings that are important for us, but the single broad highway into which they invariably lead. From the historical process the idea itself rises up before eyes.

There was yet another, if narrower, vista that had to be opened: the one shewing the bold but precarious attempts to bring the idea into reality. Only after that had been done was the ground cleared for a critical exposition of the theoretical and practical relation of Marxism to the idea of structural renewal—a relation which could only be hinted at in an introductory manner at the beginning of the book. At the end, in a kind of epilogue, I had to speak of one particular attempt, the immediate knowledge of which was the occasion for writing this book. I have naturally not described or reported it in detail, only thrown light on its inner connexion with the idea—as an attempt that did not fail.

The chapter preceding the epilogue sums up my own attitude to the idea, which could otherwise only be read between the lines; moreover it was necessary to point out its significance in the present hour of decision.

The book was completed in the spring of 1945; the Hebrew edition appeared in the following year.

MARTIN BUBER.

Jerusalem 1949.

Martin Buber was born in Vienna and studied at the Universities of Vienna, Leipzig, Berlin and Munich. He was professor of religion and ethics at the University of Frankfurt from 1924 to 1933. From 1938 until his retirement in 1951 he was professor of social philosophy at the Hebrew University in Jerusalem. He died in Jerusalem in 1965 at the age of eighty-seven.

One of the most outstanding religious philosophers of our time, Dr. Buber has been active in the Zionist movement and the revival of Hasidic thought. His works include a German translation of the Bible, *For the Sake of Heaven, Good and Evil, I and Thou, Israel and the World, Between Man and Man,* which has already been published as a Beacon Paperback, and numerous other books and articles in the fields of Biblical scholarship, religious existentialism, and comparative religion.

Paths in Utopia

I

THE IDEA

AMONG the sections of the Communist Manifesto which have exerted the most powerful influence on the generations up to our own day is that entitled "Der kritisch-utopistische Sozialismus und Kommunismus" (The Critical-Utopian Socialism and Communism).

Marx and Engels were entrusted by the "League of the Just" with the formulation of a communist credo—an important preliminary to the convocation of a Universal Communist Congress, the "Union of all the Oppressed", planned for 1848. The League Directorate laid down that fundamental expression should also be given in this credo to the "position as regards the socialist and communist parties", i.e. the line of demarcation dividing the League from the affiliated movements, by which were meant above all the Fourierists, "those shallow folk" as they are called in the draft of the credo which the Central Authority presented to the London League Congress. In the draft written by Engels there is as yet no mention of "utopian" socialists or communists; we hear only of people who put forward "superlative systems of reform", "who, on the pretext of reorganizing society, want to bolster up the foundation of existing society and consequently the society itself," and who are therefore described as "bourgeois socialists" to be attacked—a description which, in the final version, applies in particular to Proudhon. The distance between the Engels draft and the final version drawn up substantially by Marx is immense.

The "systems", of which those of Saint-Simon, Fourier and Owen are mentioned (in Marx's original version Cabet, Weitling and even Babeuf are also named as authors of such systems), are all described as the fruit of an epoch in which industry was not yet developed and hence the "proletariat" problem was not yet grasped; instead there appeared those

same systems which could not be other than fictitious, fantastic
and utopian, whose aim was at bottom to abolish that very
class-conflict which was only just beginning to take shape and
from which the "universal transformation of society" would
ultimately proceed. Marx was here formulating afresh what
he had said shortly before in his polemic against Proudhon:
"These theoreticians are Utopians; they are driven to seek
science in their own heads, because things are not yet so far advanced that they need only give an account of what is happening under their eyes and make themselves its instruments." The criticism of existing conditions on which the
systems are built is recognized as valuable explanatory material;
on the other hand all their positive recommendations are condemned to lose all practical value and theoretical justification
in the course of historical development.

We can only assess the political character of this declaration
in the framework of the socialist-communist movement of the
time when we realize that it was directed against the views
which used to reign in the "League of the Just" itself and were
supplanted by Marx's ideas. Marx characterized these views
twelve years after the appearance of the Communist Manifesto
as a "secret doctrine" consisting of a "hodge-podge of Anglo-
French socialism or communism and German philosophy", and
to this he opposed his "scientific insight into the economic
structure of bourgeois society as the only tenable theoretical
basis". The point now, he says, was to show that it "was not
a matter of bringing some utopian system or other into being
but of consciously participating in the historical revolutionary
process of society that was taking place before our eyes". The
polemical or anti-utopian section of the Manifesto thus signifies
an internal political action in the strictest sense: the victorious
conclusion of the struggle which Marx, with Engels at his side,
had waged against the other so-called—or self-styled—communist movements, primarily in the "League of the Just" itself
(which was now christened the "League of Communists").
The concept "utopian" was the last and most pointed shaft
which he shot in this fray.

I have just said: "with Engels at his side." Nevertheless
reference should not be omitted to a number of passages from
the Introduction with which Engels, some two years before the
Manifesto was drafted, had prefaced his translation of a
fragment from the posthumous writings of Fourier. Here, too,

he speaks of those same doctrines which are dismissed as utopian in the Manifesto; here, too, Fourier, Saint-Simon and Owen are quoted; here, too, a distinction is made in their works between the valuable criticism of existing society and the far less relevant "schematization" of a future one; but earlier on he says: "What the French and the English were saying ten, twenty, even forty years ago—and saying very well, very clearly, in very fine language—is at long last, and in fragmentary fashion, becoming known to the Germans, who have been 'hegelizing' it for the past year or at best re-discovering it after the event and bringing it out in a much worse and more abstract form as a wholly new discovery." And Engels adds word for word: "I make no exception even of my own works." The struggle thus touched his own past. Still more important, though, is the following pronouncement: "Fourier constructs the future for himself after having correctly recognized the past and present." This must be weighed against the charges which the Manifesto lays at the door of utopianism. Nor should we forget that the Manifesto was written only ten years after Fourier's death.

What Engels says thirty years after the Manifesto in his book against Dühring about these self-same "three great Utopians", and what passed with a few additions into the influential publication *The Evolution of Socialism from Utopia to Science* a little later, is merely an elaboration of the points already made in the Manifesto. It is immediately striking that once again only the same three men, "the founders of Socialism", are discussed, those very people who were "utopians", "because they could not be anything else at a time when capitalist production was so little developed", people who were compelled "to construct the elements of a new society out of their heads because these elements had not yet become generally visible in the old society". In the thirty years between the Manifesto and the anti-Dühring book had no socialists emerged who, in Engels' opinion, deserved the epithet "utopians" and his notice alike, but who could not be conceded those extenuating circumstances, since in their day the economic conditions were already developed and "the social tasks" no longer "hidden"? To name only one and of course the greatest—Proudhon—one of whose earlier books, *The Economic Contradictions or the Philosophy of Misery*, Marx had attacked in his famous Polemic written before the Manifesto—from Proudhon a series of important works had appeared meanwhile which no scientific theory about the social situation and the social tasks could afford to overlook; did he also (from whose book, albeit attacked by Marx, the Communist Manifesto had at any rate borrowed the concept of the "socialist utopia") belong to the Utopians, but to those who could not be justified? True, in the Manifesto he had been named as an example of the "conservative or bourgeois socialists" and in the Polemic Marx had declared that Proudhon was far inferior to the socialists, "because he has neither sufficient courage nor sufficient insight to raise himself, if only speculatively, above the bourgeois horizon"; and after Proudhon's death he asseverated in a public obituary that even to-day he would have to confirm every word of this judgment, and a year later he explained in a letter that Proudhon had done "immense harm" and, by his "sham-criticism and sham-opposition to the Utopians" had corrupted the younger generation and the workers. But another year later, nine years before writing the anti-Dühring book, Engels states in one of the seven reviews which he published anonymously on the first volume of Marx's *Capital*, that Marx wanted to "provide socialist strivings with the scientific foundation which neither Fourier nor Proudhon nor even Lassalle had been able to give" —from which there clearly emerges the rank he awarded to Proudhon despite everything.

In 1844 Marx and Engels (in their book *The Holy Family*) had found in Proudhon's book on Property a scientific advance which "revolutionizes political economy and makes a science of political economy possible for the first time"; they had further declared that not only did he write in the interests of the proletariat but that he was a proletarian himself and his work "a scientific manifesto of the French proletariat" of historic significance. And as late as May, 1846, in an anonymous essay, Marx had dubbed him "a communist", in a context, moreover, which makes it obvious that Proudhon was still a representative communist in his eyes at the time, some six months before the Polemic was written. What had happened in the meantime to move Marx to so radical an alteration of his judgment? Certainly, Proudhon's "Contradictions" had appeared, but this book in no way represented a decisive modification of Proudhon's views, also the violent diatribe against communist (by which Proudhon means what we would call "collectivist") Utopias is only a more detailed elaboration of his criticism of the "Communauté" which can be read in the first discussion on property, so lauded by Marx, in 1840. However, Proudhon's refusal of Marx's invitation of collaboration had preceded the "Contradictions". The situation becomes clearer for us when we read what Marx wrote to Engels in July, 1870, after the outbreak of war: "The French need a thrashing. If the Prussians win, the centralization of State power will subserve the centralization of the German working-class. German domination would furthermore shift the focus of the Western-European workers' movement from France to Germany, and you have merely to compare the movement in the two countries from 1866 up to now to see that the German working-class is superior both in theory and in organization to the French. Its supremacy over that of the French on the world-stage would at once mean the supremacy of *our* theory over Proudhon's, etc." It is thus in eminent degree a matter of *political* attitude. Hence it must be regarded as consistent that Engels should describe Proudhon soon afterwards in a polemic against him (*On the Housing Question*) as a pure dilettante, facing economics helplessly and without knowledge, one who preaches and laments "where we offer proofs". At the same time Proudhon is clearly labelled a Utopian: the "best world" he constructs is already "crushed in the bud by the foot of onward-marching industrial development".

I have dwelt on this topic at some length because something of importance can best be brought to light in this way. Originally Marx and Engels called those people Utopians whose thinking had preceded the critical development of industry, the proletariat and the class-war, and who therefore could not take this development into account; subsequently the term was levelled indiscriminately at all those who, in the estimation of Marx and Engels, did not in fact take account of it; and of these the late-comers either did not understand how to do so or were unwilling or both. The epithet "Utopian" thereafter became the most potent missile in the fight of Marxism against non-Marxian socialism. It was no longer a question of demonstrating the rightness of one's own opinion in the face of a contrary one; in general one found science and truth absolutely and exclusively in his own position and utopianism and delusion in the rival camp. To be a "Utopian" in our age means: to be out of step with modern economic development, and what modern economic development is we learn of course from Marxism. Of those "pre-historic" Utopians, Saint-Simon, Fourier and Owen, Engels had declared in his *German Peasant War in 1850* that German socialist theory would never forget that it stood on the shoulders of these men, "who despite all their fantasticalness and all their utopianism must be counted among the most significant brains of all time, who anticipated with genius countless truths whose validity we can now prove scientifically". But here again—and this is consistent from the political point of view—consideration is no longer given to the possibility that there are men living to-day, known and unknown, who anticipate truths whose validity will be scientifically proved in the future, truths which contemporary "science"—i.e. the trend of knowledge which not infrequently identifies itself in general with Science—is determined to regard as invalid, exactly as was the case with those "founders of socialism" in their day. They were Utopians as forerunners, these are Utopians as obscurantists. They blazed the trail for Science, these obstruct it. Happily, however, it is sufficient to brand them Utopians to render them innocuous.

Perhaps I may be allowed to cite a small personal experience as an instance of this method of "annihilation by labels". In Whitsun, 1928, there took place in my former home-town of Heppenheim a discussion,[1] attended mainly by delegates from religious socialist circles, on the question of how to nourish anew those spiritual forces of mankind on which the belief in a renewal of society rests. In my speech, in which I laid particular emphasis on the generally neglected and highly concrete questions of decentralization and the status of the worker, I said: "It is of no avail to call 'utopian' what we have not yet tested with our powers." That did not save me from a critical remark on the part of the Chairman, who simply relegated me to the ranks of utopian socialists and left it at that.

But if socialism is to emerge from the blind-alley into which it has strayed, among other things the catchword "Utopian" must be cracked open and examined for its true content.

---

[1] The minutes appeared in Zurich 1929 under the title "Sozialismus aus dem Glauben" (Socialism from Faith).

II

THE UTOPIAN
ELEMENT IN SOCIALISM

WHAT, at first sight, seems common to the Utopias that have passed into the spiritual history of mankind, is the fact that they are pictures, and pictures moreover of something not actually present but only represented. Such pictures are generally called fantasy-pictures, but that tells us little enough. This "fantasy" does not float vaguely in the air, it is not driven hither and thither by the wind of caprice, it centres with architectonic firmness on something primary and original which it is its destiny to build; and this primary thing is a wish. The utopian picture is a picture of what "should be", and the visionary is one who wishes it to be. Therefore some call the Utopias wish-pictures, but that again does not tell us enough. A "wish-picture" makes us think of something that rises out of the depths of the Unconscious and, in the form of a dream, a reverie, a "seizure", overpowers the defenceless soul, or may, at a later stage, even be invoked, called forth, hatched out by the soul itself. In the history of the human spirit the image-creating wish—although it, too, like all image-making is rooted deep down in us—has nothing instinctive about it and nothing of self-gratification. It is bound up with something supra-personal that communes with the soul but is not governed by it. What is at work here is the longing for that *rightness* which, in religious or philosophical vision, is experienced as revelation or idea, and which of its very nature cannot be realized in the individual, but only in human community. The vision of "what should be"—independent though it may sometimes appear of personal will—is yet inseparable from a critical and fundamental relationship to the existing condition of humanity. All suffering under a social order that is senseless prepares the soul for vision, and what the soul re-

ceives in this vision strengthens and deepens its insight into
the perversity of what is perverted. The longing for the
realization of "the seen" fashions the picture.

The vision of rightness in Revelation is realized in the
picture of a perfect time—as messianic eschatology; the vision
of rightness in the Ideal is realized in the picture of a perfect
space—as Utopia. The first necessarily goes beyond the social
and borders on the creational, the cosmic; the second necessarily
remains bounded by the circumference of society, even if the
picture it presents sometimes implies an inner transformation
of man. Eschatology means perfection of creation; Utopia the
unfolding of the possibilities, latent in mankind's communal
life, of a "right" order. Another difference is still more
important. For eschatology the decisive act happens from
above, even when the elemental or prophetic form of it gives
man a significant and active share in the coming redemption;
for Utopia everything is subordinated to conscious human will,
indeed we can characterize it outright as a picture of society
designed as though there were no other factors at work than
conscious human will. But they are neither of them mere cloud
castles: if they seek to stimulate or intensify in the reader or
listener his critical relationship to the present, they also seek
to show him perfection—in the light of the Absolute, but at
the same time as something towards which an active path
leads from the present. And what may seem impossible as
a concept arouses, as an image, the whole might of faith,
ordains purpose and plan. It does this because it is in league
with powers latent in the depths of reality. Eschatology, in
so far as it is prophetic, Utopia, in so far as it is philosophical,
both have the character of realism.

The Age of Enlightenment and its aftermath robbed religious
eschatology in increasing measure of its sphere of action: in
the course of ten generations it has become more and more
difficult for man to believe that at some point in the future an
act from above will redeem the human world, i.e. transform
it from a senseless one into one full of meaning, from dis-
harmony into harmony. This incapacity has become an actual
physical incapacity, in avowedly religious no less than in a-
religious people, save that in the former it is concealed from
consciousness by the fixed nexus of tradition. On the other
hand, the age of technology with its growing social contradictions has influenced Utopia profoundly. Under the

influence of pan-technical trends Utopia too has become wholly technical; conscious human will, its foundation hitherto, is now understood as technics, and society like Nature is to be mastered by technological calculation and construction. Society, however, with its present contradictions poses a question that cannot be dismissed; all thinking and planning for the future must seek the answer to it, and where Utopia is concerned the political and cultural formulations necessarily give way before the task of contriving a "right" order of society. But here social thinking shows its superiority over technical thinking. Utopias which revel in technical fantasias mostly find foothold nowadays only in the feebler species of novel, in which little or none of the imagination that went into the grand Utopias of old can be discovered. Those, on the contrary, which undertake to deliver a blueprint of the perfect social structure, turn into systems. But into these "utopian" social systems there enters all the force of dispossessed Messianism. The social system of modern socialism or communism has, like eschatology, the character of an annunciation or of a proclamation. It is true that Plato was moved by the desire to establish a reality proportioned to the Idea, and it is true that he also sought, to the end of his days and with unflagging passion, for the human tools of its realization; but only with the modern social systems did there arise this fierce interplay of doctrine and action, planning and experiment. For Thomas More it was still possible to mingle serious instruction with incongruous jesting, and, with supercilious irony, to allow a picture of "very absurd" institutions to rub shoulders with such as he "wishes rather than hopes" to see copied. For Fourier that was no longer possible; here everything is practical inference and logical resolve, for the point with him is "to emerge at last from a civilization which, far from being man's social destiny, is only mankind's childhood sickness".

The polemics of Marx and Engels have resulted in the term "utopian" becoming used, both within Marxism and without, for a socialism which appeals to reason, to justice, to the will of man to remedy the maladjustments of society, instead of his merely acquiring an active awareness of what is "dialectically" brewing in the womb of industrialism. All voluntaristic socialism is rated "utopian". Yet it is by no means the case that the socialism diametrically opposed to it—which we may call necessitarian because it professes to demand nothing more than the setting in motion of the necessary evolutionary machinery—is free of utopianism. The utopian elements in it are of another kind and stand in a different context.

I have already indicated that the whole force of dispossessed eschatology was converted into Utopia at the time of the French Revolution. But, as I have intimated, there are two basic forms of eschatology: the prophetic, which at any given moment sees every person addressed by it as endowed, in a degree not to be determined beforehand, with the power to participate by his decisions and deeds in the preparing of Redemption; and the apocalyptic, in which the redemptive process in all its details, its very hour and course, has been fixed from everlasting and for whose accomplishment human beings are only used as tools, though what is immutably fixed may yet be "unveiled" to them, revealed, and they be assigned their function. The first of these forms derives from Israel, the second from ancient Persia. The differences and agreements between the two, their combinations and separations, play an important part in the inner history of Christianity. In the socialist secularization of eschatology they work out separately: the prophetic form in some of the systems of the so-called Utopians, the apocalyptic one above all in Marxism (which is not to say that no prophetic element is operative here—it has only been overpowered by the apocalyptic). With Marx, belief in humanity's road through contradiction to the overcoming of the same, takes the form of Hegelian dialectic, since he makes use of a scientific inquiry into the changing processes of production; but the vision of upheavals past or to come "in the chain of absolute necessity", as Hegel says, does not derive from Hegel. Marx's apocalyptic position is purer and stronger than Hegel's, which lacked any real driving power for the future; Franz Rosenzweig has pointed out, and rightly, that Marx remained truer to Hegel's belief in historical determinism than Hegel himself. "No one else has seen so directly where and how and in what form the last day would dawn on the horizon of history." The point at which, in Marx, the utopian apocalypse breaks out and the whole topic of economics and science is transformed into pure "utopics", is the convulsion of all things *after* the social revolution. The Utopia of the so-called Utopians is pre-revolutionary, the Marxist one post-revolutionary. The "withering away" of the State, "the leap of humanity out of the realm of necessity into the realm of freedom" may be well-founded dialectically, but it is no longer so scientifically. As a Marxist thinker, Paul Tillich, says, these things "can in no way be made intelligible in terms of existing reality", "between reality and expectation there is a gulf", "for this reason Marxism has never, despite its animosity to Utopias, been able to clear itself of the suspicion of a hidden belief in Utopia". Or in the words of another Marxist sociologist, Eduard Heimann: "With men as they are, a withering away of the State is inconceivable. In speculating on a radical and inmost change of human nature, we pass beyond the borders of empirical research and enter the realm of prophetic vision where the true significance and providential destination of man are circumscribed in stammering metaphors." But what is of decisive significance for us is the difference between this Utopianism and that of the non-marxist socialists. We shall have to observe this difference more closely.

When we examine what Marxist criticism calls the utopian element in the non-marxist systems we find that it is by no means simple or uniform. Two distinct elements are to be distinguished. The essence of one is schematic fiction, the essence of the other is organic planning. The first, as we encounter it particularly in Fourier, originates in a kind of abstract imagination which, starting from a theory of the nature of man, his capacities and needs, deduces a social order that shall employ all his capacities and satisfy all his needs. Although in Fourier the theory is supported by a mass of observational material, every observation becomes unreal and untrustworthy as soon as it enters this sphere; and in his social order, which pretends to be social architecture but is in reality formless schematism, all problems (as Fourier himself says) have the same "solution", that is, from real problems in the life of human beings they become artificial problems in the life of instinctive robots—artificial problems which all allow of the same solution because they all proceed from the same mechanistic set-up. Wholly different, indeed of a directly contrary nature, is the second element. Here the dominant purpose is to inaugurate, from an impartial and undogmatic understanding of contemporary man and his condition, a transformation of both, so as to overcome the contradictions which make up the essence of our social order.

Starting with no reservations from the condition of society as it is, this view gazes into the depths of reality with a clarity of vision unclouded by any dogmatic pre-occupation, discerning those still hidden tendencies which, although obscured by more obvious and more powerful forces, are yet moving towards that transformation. It has justly been said that in a positive sense every planning intellect is utopian. But we must add that the planning intellect of the socialist "Utopians" under consideration, proves the positive character of its utopianism by being at every point aware, or at least having an inkling, of the diversity, indeed the contrariety, of the trends discernible in every age; by not failing to discover, despite its insight into the dominant trends, those others which these trends conceal; and by asking whether and to what extent those and those alone are aiming at an order in which the contradictions of existing society will truly be overcome.

Here, then, we have one or two motives which require further explanation and amplification both in themselves and in order to mark them off from Marxism.

In the course of the development of so-called utopian socialism its leading representatives have become more and more persuaded that neither the social problem nor its solution can be reduced to a lowest common denominator, and that every simplification—even the most intellectually important—exerts an unfavourable influence both on knowledge and action. When in 1846, some six months before he started his controversy with Proudhon, Marx invited the latter to collaborate with him in a "correspondence" which should subserve "an exchange of ideas and impartial criticism", and for which—so Marx writes—"as regards France we all believe that we could find no better correspondent than yourself," he received the answer: "Let us, if you wish, look together for the laws of society, the manner in which they are realized, but after we have cleared away all these a priori dogmatisms, let us not, for God's sake, think of tangling people up in doctrines in our turn! Let us not fall into the contradiction of your countryman Martin Luther who, after having overthrown the catholic theology, immediately set about founding a protestant theology of his own amid a great clamour of excommunications and anathemas. . . . Because we stand in the van of a new movement let us not make ourselves the protagonists of a new intolerance, let us not act like apostles of a new religion, even if it be a religion of logic, a religion of reason." Here it is chiefly a question of political means, but from many of Proudhon's utterances it is evident that he saw the ends as well in the light of the same freedom and diversity. And fifty years after that letter Kropotkin summed up the basic view of the ends in a single sentence: the fullest development of individuality "will combine with the highest development of voluntary association in all its aspects, in all possible degrees and for all possible purposes; an association that is always changing, that bears in itself the elements of its own duration, that takes on the forms which best correspond at any given moment to the manifold strivings of all." This is precisely what Proudhon had wanted in the maturity of his thought. It may be contended that the Marxist objective is not essentially different in constitution; but at this point a yawning chasm opens out before us which can only be bridged by that special form of Marxist utopics, a chasm between, on the one side, the transformation to be consummated sometime in the future—no one knows how long after the final victory of the Revolution—and, on the other, the road to the Revolution and beyond it, which road is characterized by a far-reaching centralization that permits no individual features and no individual initiative. Uniformity as a means is to change miraculously into multiplicity as an end; compulsion into freedom. As against this the "utopian" or nonmarxist socialist desires a means commensurate with his ends; he refuses to believe that in our reliance on the future "leap" we have to do now the direct opposite of what we are striving for; he believes rather that we must create here and now the space *now* possible for the thing for which we are striving, so that it may come to fulfilment *then*; he does not believe in the post-revolutionary leap, but he does believe in revolutionary continuity. To put it more precisely: he believes in a continuity within which revolution is only the accomplishment, the setting free and extension of a reality that has already grown to its true possibilities.

Seen from another angle this difference may be clarified still further. When we examine the capitalist society which has given birth to socialism, *as a society*, we see that it is a society inherently poor in structure and growing visibly poorer every day. By the structure of a society is to be understood its social content or community-content: a society can be called structurally rich to the extent that it is built up of genuine societies, that is, local communes and trade communes and their step by step association. What Gierke says of the Co-operative Movement in the Middle Ages is true of every structurally rich society: it is "marked by a tendency to expand and extend the unions, to produce larger associations over and above the smaller association, confederations over and above individual unions, all-embracing confederations over and above particular confederations". At whatever point we examine the structure of such a society we find the cell-tissue "Society" everywhere, i.e. a living and life-giving collaboration, an essentially autonomous consociation of human beings, shaping and re-shaping itself from within. Society is naturally composed not of disparate individuals but of associative units and the associations between them. Under capitalist economy and the State peculiar to it the constitution of society was being continually hollowed out, so that the modern individualizing process finished up as a process of atomization. At the same time the old organic forms retained their outer stability, for the most part, but they became hollow in sense and in spirit—a tissue of decay. Not merely what we generally call the masses but the whole of society is in essence amorphous, unarticulated, poor in structure. Neither do those associations help which spring from the meeting of economic or spiritual interests—the strongest of which is the party: what there is of human intercourse in them is no longer a living thing, and the compensation for the lost community-forms we seek in them can be found in none. In the face of all this, which makes "society" a contradiction in terms, the "utopian" socialists have aspired more and more to a restructuring of society; not, as the Marxist critic thinks, in any romantic attempt to revive the stages of development that are over and done with, but rather in alliance with the decentralist counter-tendencies which can be perceived underlying all economic and social evolution, and in alliance with something that is slowly evolving in the human soul: the most intimate of all resistances—resistance to mass or collective loneliness.

Victor Hugo called Utopia "the truth of to-morrow". Those efforts of the spirit, condemned as inopportune and derided as "utopian socialism", may well be clearing the way for the structure of society-to-be. (There is, of course, no historical process that is necessary in itself and independent of human resolve.) It is obvious that here, too, it is a matter of preserving the community-forms that remain and filling them anew with spirit, and a new spirit. Over the gateway to Marxist centralization stands—for who knows how long?—the inscription in which Engels summed up the tyrannical character of the automatism in a great factory: "Lasciate ogni autonomia voi ch'entrate." Utopian socialism fights for the maximum degree of communal autonomy possible in a "restructured" society.

In that socialist meeting of 1928, I said: "There can be pseudo-realization of socialism, where the real life of man to man is but little changed. The real living together of man with man can only thrive where people have the real things of their common life in common; where they can experience, discuss and administer them together; where real fellowships and real work Guilds exist. We see more or less from the Russian attempt at realization that human relationships remain essentially unchanged when they are geared to a socialist-centralist hegemony which rules the life of individuals and the life of the natural social groups. Needless to say we cannot and do not want to go back to primitive agrarian communism or to the corporate State of the Christian Middle Ages. We must be quite unromantic, and, living wholly in the present, out of the recalcitrant material of our own day in history, fashion a true community."

III

THE FORERUNNERS

I HAVE pointed out that in "utopian" socialism there is an organically constructive and organically purposive or planning element which aims at a re-structuring of society, and moreover not at one that shall come to fruition in an indefinite future after the "withering away" of the proletarian dictator-state, but beginning here and now in the given conditions of the present. If this is correct it should be possible to demonstrate, in the history of utopian socialism, the line of evolution taken by this element.

In the history of utopian socialism three pairs of active thinkers emerge, each pair being bound together in a peculiar way and also to its generation: Saint-Simon and Fourier, Owen and Proudhon, Kropotkin and Gustav Landauer. Through the middle pair there runs the line of cleavage separating the first phase of this socialism—the phase of transition to advanced capitalism—from the second, which accompanies the rise of the latter. In the first each thinker contributes a single constructive thought and these thoughts—at first strange and incompatible with one another—align themselves together, and in the second Proudhon and his successors build up the comprehensive synthesis, the synthetic idea of restructure. Each step occupies its own proper place and is not interchangeable.

A few figures will help to make the relations between the generations clear. Saint-Simon was born twelve years before Fourier and died twelve years before him, and yet both belong to the generation which was born before the French Revolution and perished before 1848—save that the younger, Fourier, belongs by nature and outlook to the eighteenth century and the older, Saint-Simon, to the nineteenth century. Owen was born before the great Revolution, Proudhon at the time of the Napoleonic triumphs; thus they belong congenitally to different generations but, as they both died between 1848 and 1870, death united them once more in a single generation. The same thing is repeated with Kropotkin, who was born before 1848, and Landauer, before 1870: both died soon after the first World War.

Saint-Simon—of whom the founder of sociology as a science, Lorenz von Stein, justly says that he " half understood, half guessed at *society*" (that is, society as such in contradistinction to the State) "for the first time in its full power, in all its elements and contradictions"—makes the first and, for his epoch, the most important contribution. The "puberty-crisis" which mankind had entered meant for him the eventual replacement of the existing régime by "le régime industriel". We can formulate it in this way: the cleavage of the social whole into two essentially different and mutually antagonistic orders is to yield place to a uniform structure. Hitherto society had been under a "government", now it was to come under an "administration", and the administration was not, like the former, to be entrusted to a class opposed to society and made up of "legalists" and "militarists", but to the natural leaders of society itself, the leaders of its production. No longer was one group of rulers to be ousted by another group of rulers, as had happened in all the upheavals known to history; what remains necessary as a police force does not constitute Government in the old sense. "The producers have no wish to be plundered by any one class of parasites rather than by any other. . . . It is clear that the struggle must end by being played out between the whole mass of parasites on the one hand and the mass of producers on the other, in order to decide whether the latter shall continue to be the prey of the former or shall obtain supreme control of society." Saint-Simon's naïve demand of "messieurs" the workers that they should make the entrepreneurs their leaders—a demand which was to weld the active portion of the capitalists and the proletarians into one class—contains, despite its odd air of unreality, the intimation of a future order in which no leadership is required other than that provided by the social functions themselves; in which politics have in fact become what they are in Saint-Simon's definition: "the science of production," i.e. of the pre-conditions most favourable to this. In the nature of things governments cannot implement policies of this sort; "government is a continual source of injury to industry when it meddles in its affairs; it is injurious even where it makes efforts to encourage it." Nothing but an overcoming of government as such can lead society out of the "extreme disorder" in which it languishes; out of the dilemma of a nation which is "essentially industrial" and whose government is "essentially feudal"; out of division into two classes: "one that orders and one that obeys" (the Saint-Simonist Bazard expressed it even more pungently soon after the death of his master, in 1829: "two classes, the exploiters and the exploited"). The present epoch is one of transition not from one sort of régime to another, but from a sham order to a true order, in which "work is the fountain-head of all virtues" and "the State is the confederacy of all workers" (so runs the formula of the Saint-Simonists). This cannot be the affair of a single nation only, for it would be opposed by other nations; the "industrial system" must be established over all Europe and the feudal system, persisting in bourgeois form, annihilated. Saint-Simon calls this "Europeanism". He realizes, however, that altering the relationship between the leaders and the led is not the sole intention, but that the alteration must permeate the whole inner structure of society. The moment when the industrial régime is "ripe" (i.e. when society is ripe for it can be "determined with reasonable exactitude by the fundamental circumstance that, in any given nation, the vast majority of individuals will by then have entered into more or less numerous industrial associations each two or three of which will be interconnected by industrial relationships. This will permit a general system to be built up, since the associations will be led towards a great common goal, as regards which they will be co-ordinated of themselves each according to its function". Here Saint-Simon comes very near to the idea of social re-structuring. What he lacks is the conception of genuine organic social units out of which this re-structuring can be built; the idea of "industrial associations" does not provide what is required. Saint-Simon divined the significance of the small social unit for the rebuilding of society, but did not recognize it for what it was.

It is just this social unit which is the be-all and end-all for Fourier. He thought he had discovered "the secret of associa-tion " and in this he saw—the formula dates from the same time, about 1820, when Saint-Simon gave his "industrial system" its final formulation—"the secret of the union of interests". Charles Gide has rightly pointed out that Fourier was here opposing the legacy of the French Revolution, which had contested the right of association and prohibited trades-unions; and opposing it because it was from the collapse of the cadres of the old corporations that the "anarchic" principle of free competition had derived, which, as Fourier's most important pupil—Considérant—had foretold in his manifesto of 1843 on the principles of socialism (by which the Communist Manifesto appears to have been influenced), would inevitably result in the exact opposite of what its introduction purposed, namely, in the "universal organization of great monopolies in all branches of industry". Fourier countered this with his "association communale sur le terrain de la production et de la consummation" (as Considérant again formulated it in 1848); which is to say the formation of local social units based on joint production and consumption. It is a new form of the "commune rurale", which latter is to be regarded as "l'élément alvéolaire de la société"—a conception not, of course, found in Fourier himself but only in his school that was also influenced by Owen (whom Fourier did not wish to read). Only free and voluntary association, so we are told in 1848, can solve the great organic problem of the future, "the problem of organizing a new order, an order in which individualism will combine spontaneously with 'collectism' " (sic). Only in this way can "the third and last emancipatory phase of history" come about, in which the first having made serfs out of slaves, and the second wage-earners out of serfs (we find this idea in Bazard as far back as 1829), "the abolition of the proletariat, the transformation of wage-earners into companions (associés)" will be accomplished. But one will scan Fourier's own expositions of his system and the drafts of his projects in vain for the concrete expression of his opposing principle. His "phalanstery" has been compared with a large hotel, and in fact it offers many similarities to those typical products of our age which meet the greatest possible part of their requirements with their own production—only that in this case production is managed by the guests themselves, and instead of the minimum conduct regulations as in the notices in hotel-rooms there is a law which regulates the daily round in all its details—a law that has various attractions and leaves one's powers of decision fundamentally untouched but is, in itself, meticulously exact. Although the supreme authority, the "Areopagus", issues no commands, but only gives instructions and each group acts according to its will, nevertheless this will simply "*cannot* deviate from that of the Areopagus, for he is the puissance d'opinion". Many things in this law may strike us as bizarre, but all the same it expresses some important and fruitful ideas, such as the alternation of various activities—a notion that foreshadows Kropotkin's "division of labour in time". On the other hand, and regarded precisely from this standpoint, the phalanstery is a highly unsocialistic institution. The division of labour in the course of a summer day leads the poor Lucas from the stables to the gardeners, from there to the reapers, the vegetable-growers, the manual workers, etc., while the same division of labour leads the rich Mondor from the "industrial parade" to the hunt, from there to fishing, to the library, greenhouses and so on. When we read that the poor have to enjoy a "graduated state of wealth that the rich may be happy", or that "only through the utmost inequality of worldly possessions can this beautiful and magnanimous agreement be reached", i.e. the renunciation by the rich of a great part of their dividends in favour of work and talent—we realize that these units which bear the stamp of a mechanical fantasy have no legitimate claim to be considered as the cells of a new and legitimate order. Their uniformity alone (for despite their appearance of inner diversity they represent, item for item, the same pattern, the same machinery) renders them totally unsuitable for a restructuring of society. Fourier's "universal harmony" which embraces world and society means, in society itself, only a harmony between the individuals living together, not a harmony between the units themselves (although some people may, of course, imagine a "federation of phalanges"). The interconnection between the units has no place in his system, each unit is a world on its own and always the same world; but of the attraction which rules the universe we hear nothing as between these units, they do not fuse together into associations, into higher units, indeed they cannot do so because they are not, like individuals, diversified, they do not complement one another and cannot therefore form a harmony. Fourier's thought has been a powerful incentive to the Co-operative Movement and its labours, in particular to the Consumer Co-operatives; but the constructive thinking of "utopian socialism" has only been able to accept him by transcending his ideas.

Fourier's *chef d'œuvre* appeared in 1822, the *Traité d'Association Domestique Agricole*; Saint-Simon's *Le Système Industriel* in

1821 and 1822; and from 1820 dates Robert Owen's *Report to the County of Lanark*, which appeared in 1821 and was the matured presentation of his "plan". But Fourier's *La Théorie des Quatre Mouvements et des Destinées Générales*, which contains his system in a nutshell, had already appeared in 1808; Saint-Simon's *De la Réorganisation de la Société Européenne* in 1814; Owen's *A New View of Society*—the theoretical foundation of his plans—in 1813 and 1814. If we go still further back in time we come to Saint-Simon's earliest work at the turn of the century, in which the impending crisis of humanity is already announced, and Fourier's article on universal harmony, which may be regarded as the first sketch of his doctrine. At the same time, however, we find Owen engaged in purely practical activity as the leader of the cotton-spinners in New Lanark, in which capacity he brought about some exemplary social innovations. Unlike that of Saint-Simon and Fourier his doctrine proceeds from practice, from experiment and experience. No matter whether he knew of Fourier's theories or not, Owen's teaching is, historically and philosophically speaking, a rejoinder to theirs, the empirical solution of the problem as opposed to the speculative one. The social units on which society is to be built anew can in this case be called organic; they are numerically limited communities based on agriculture and sustained by the "principle of united labour, expenditure and property, and equal privileges", and in which all members are to have "mutual and common interests". Already we see how Owen, as distinct from Fourier, presses forward to the simple pre-requisites for a genuine community where the rule is not necessarily and exclusively common ownership, but rather a binding together and "communizing" of property; not equality of expenditure, but rather equality of rights and opportunities. "Communal life," says Tönnies of the historical forms of "community", i.e. the "true and enduring forms of men's life together", is *"mutual* possession and enjoyment, and possession and enjoyment of *common* property". In other words, it is a common housekeeping in which personal possessions can stand side by side with common ones, save that through the building of a common economy (quite otherwise than in the scheme of Fourier) only a narrow margin is set between differences in personal possessions and that, as a result of mutuality, of mutual give and take, there arises that very condition which is here termed "mutual

possession and enjoyment", i.e. the appropriate participation
of all members in one another. Precisely this conception
underlies Owen's plan. (Later he goes further and reckons
common ownership and co-operative union among the basal
foundations of his projected Colony.) He does not fail to
appreciate that great educational activity is required for its
realization. "Men have not yet been trained in principles that
will permit them to act in union, except to defend themselves
or to destroy others. ... A necessity, however, equally powerful,
will now compel men to be trained to act together to create and
conserve." Owen knew that ultimately it was a matter of
transforming the whole social order, and in particular the
relationship between the rulers and the ruled. "The interest
of those who govern has ever appeared to be, and under the
present systems ever will appear to be, opposed to the interest
of those whom they govern." This must continue "while man
remains individualized", that is, while society refuses to build
itself up out of the real bonds between individuals. The change
will reach completion in each single one of the village communities planned, before it extends from them to the community as a whole. The Committee governing the individual
village will "form a permanent, experienced local government,
never opposed to, but always in closest union with, each
individual governed". Certainly there remain at the outset
the problems of what Owen calls "the connection of the new
establishments with the Government of the country and with
the old society", but from his appellation "the old society"
it is clear that Owen is thinking of the new society as growing
out of the old and renewing it from within. At the same time
various stages in the evolution of the new society will have of
necessity to exist side by side. A characteristic example of this
is given in the Draft of Statutes (inspired by Owen) put forward
by the "Association of All Classes of All Nations", founded in
1835, which, using a term that had only just begun to be
current in this sense, called itself "The Socialists". Of the three
divisions of this association the lower two have only the
function of Consumer Co-operatives; the third and highest, on
the contrary, is to establish a brotherhood and sisterhood which
shall form a single class of producers and consumers differentiated by age alone, "without priests, lawyers, soldiery, buyers and
sellers". This is Utopia, to be sure, but a Utopia of that special kind
without which no amount of "science" can transform society.

The line of development leading from Saint-Simon to Fourier and Owen rests on no sequence in time; the three men whom Engels names as the founders of socialism worked in approximately the same period; one could almost say that it is a development in contemporaneity. Saint-Simon lays down that society should progress from the dual to the unitary, the leadership of the whole should proceed from the social functions themselves, without the political order superimposing itself as an essentially distinct and special class. To this Fourier and Owen reply that this is only possible and permissible in a society based on joint production and consumption, i.e. a society composed of units in which the two are conjoined, hence of smaller communities aiming at a large measure of self-sufficiency. Fourier's answer affirms that each of these units is to be constituted like the present society in respect of property and the claims of the individual, only that the resultant society will be led from contradiction to harmony by the concord of instinct and activity. Owen's answer, on the other hand, affirms that the transformation of society must be accomplished in its total structure as well as in each of its cells: only a just ordering of the individual units can establish a just order in the totality. This is the foundation of socialism.

IV

PROUDHON

"WHEN the contradictions of 'communauté' and democracy,"
Proudhon wrote in a letter of 1844, "once revealed, have
shared the fate of the Utopias of Saint-Simon and Fourier, then
socialism, rising to the level of a science—this socialism which
is neither more nor less than political economy—will seize hold
of society and drive it with irresistible force towards its next
destination.... Socialism has not yet attained to self-consciousness; to-day it calls itself communism." The first sentence
reminds one in many respects of the later formulations of Marx.
Three months before the letter was written Marx had met
Proudhon, who was ten years his senior, in Paris, immediately
to conduct night-long conversations with him.

Little as Proudhon wished to go back to the "utopian"
systems and deeply as he was opposed to their principles, he
nevertheless continued the line of development that began
with them. He continued this line by drawing it afresh, only on
a higher plane where everything anterior to it was taken for
granted. All the same he had a profound fear of himself
adding a new system to the old. "System," he wrote in 1849,
"I have no system, I will have none and I expressly repudiate
the suggestion. The system of humanity, whatever it be, will
only be known when humanity is at an end.... My business
is to find out the way humanity is going and, if I can, prepare
it." The real Proudhon is very far removed from the man Marx
attacks in his polemic and earlier in a letter to a Russian friend,
from the man for whom, as the letter says, "categories and
abstractions are the primary facts", "the motive forces which
make history" and which it is sufficient to alter for alterations
to follow in real life. This "hegelizing" of Proudhon misfires.
No man has questioned more honestly and more pungently
than Proudhon the social reality of his time and sought its
secret. "The economic categories," declared Marx in his

polemic, "are only theoretical expressions for the social
relationships of production," whereas Proudhon, he says, saw
in these relationships only the embodiments of principles; but
the fixed social relationships are produced by human beings
just as are cloth, linen, etc. Proudhon rightly remarks in the
margin of his copy of the polemic: "That is exactly what I'm
saying. Society creates the laws and the raw material of its
experience." In one of his later, and most mature, writings—
Du Principe Fédératif (1863)—he pronounces the same judgment from another angle, when he says of reason that it leads
the movement of history towards freedom but only on condition
that it takes the nature of the forces concerned into account
and respects their laws.

Proudhon's fear of "systems" has its roots in his fundamental
relationship to social reality. He observes society in all its
contrasts and contradictions and will not rest until he has
understood and expressed them. Proudhon was a man who
had the strength and courage to steep himself in contradiction
and bear the strain of it. He did not remain in it in quite the
way that Unamuno thinks, who compares him in this respect
to Pascal; he did, however, remain in it for so long as was
necessary for him to grasp it in all its cruelty, to resolve "the
conflict of elements, the clash of contrasts" fully in his thought.
And sometimes it was *too* long, judged by the shortness of human
life. When Unamuno says of Pascal that his logic was not
dialectics but polemics, this is true also of Proudhon to a certain
extent; but when he goes on to say that Pascal did not seek
any synthesis between thesis and antithesis, it is not in reality
true of Proudhon. He sought no synthesis in the Hegelian
sense, no negation of negation; he sought, as he says in a letter
of 1844, "des resolutions synthétiques de toutes les contradictions", and what he actually means is that he was seeking the
way, the way out of contradiction recognized in all its pitiless-
ness, out of the social "antinomies" (as he says, transferring
the term from Kant's theory of cognition to the sphere of
sociology). For him, thesis and antithesis were categories not
embodying themselves in different historical epochs, but co-
existing; he took over only the formalism of Hegel, but of Hegel
the historian almost nothing. Despite his excursions into history
Proudhon was not an historical thinker; his thought was
social-critical, and that was both his strength and his limitation.
To grasp the contradiction which could, in any given social

reality, in fact be grasped was, for him, the intellectual pre-requisite for the discovery of "the way". That is why he puts tendencies and counter-tendencies side by side and refuses to elevate either of them into an Absolute. "All ideas," he writes in the *Philosophy of Progress* (1851), "are false, i.e. contradictory and irrational, when you grant them an exclusive and absolute meaning, or when you let yourself be swept away by this meaning"; all tendencies towards exclusiveness, towards immobility, tend towards degeneration. And just as no spiritual factors may be regarded as reigning with absolute necessity, neither may material ones be so regarded. Proudhon believes neither in blind providence from below, which con-trives the salvation of mankind out of technical and material changes, nor in a free-ranging human intellect, which contrives systems of absolute validity and enjoins them on mankind. He sees humanity's real way in the deliverance from false faiths in absolutism, from the dominion of fatality. "Man no longer wishes to be mechanized. He strives towards 'defataliza-tion'." Hence the "universal antipathy to all Utopias whose essence is political organization and a social credo", by which Proudhon—in 1858—means Owen, Fourier and the Saint-Simonist Enfantin, and also Auguste Comte.

Proudhon teaches that no historical principle can be ade-quately summed up in any system of ideas; every such principle needs interpretation and may be interpreted well or ill, and the interpretations influence, directly or indirectly, the historical fate of the principle. It must, however, be noted as an addi-tional complication that in no age is any one principle all-powerful. "All principles," writes Proudhon in his posthumous work *Cæsarism and Christianity*, "are contemporaneous in history as they are in reason." It is only that they have different strengths in relation to one another at different epochs. At a time when a principle is struggling for hegemony it is important that it should enter man's consciousness and work on his will in its true essence and not in a distorted form. The "social age" announced with the French Revolution—an age preceded at the outset, naturally, by a period of transition, the "era of Constitutions", just as the Augustan epoch preceded the Christian: both of them working a renewal, but not a renewal that goes to the heart of existence—this social age is characterized by the predominance of the economic principle over those of religion and government. This principle it is that "in the name of socialism is stirring up a new revolution in Europe which, once it has brought about a federative Republic of all the civilized states, will organize the unity and solidarity of the human species over the whole face of the earth". It is important to-day to understand the economic principle in its true nature so as to guard against fatal conflicts between it and a travesty of it which usurps its ideas.

As I have said Proudhon did not merely continue the evolutionary line of "utopian" socialism, he began it again from the beginning, but in such a way that everything anterior to him appeared completely remodelled. More especially he did not set out at the point where Saint-Simon stopped; rather he posed Saint-Simon's demand for an economy based on and conditioned by its groupings, in an altogether new and more comprehensive way that goes much deeper into social reality. Saint-Simon started from the reform of the State, Proudhon from the transformation of society. A genuine reconstruction of society can only begin with a radical alteration of the relationship between the social and the political order. It can no longer be a matter of substituting one political régime for another, but of the emergence, in place of a political régime grafted upon society, of a régime expressive of society itself. "The prime cause of all the disorders that visit society," says Proudhon, "of the oppression of the citizens and the decay of nations, lies in the single and hierarchical centralization of authority. . . . We need to make an end of this monstrous parasitism as soon as possible." We are not told why and since when this need has become so pressing, but we can easily remedy this when we realize two things. First: so long as society was richly structured, so long as it was built up of manifold communities and communal units, all strong in vitality, the State was a wall narrowing one's outlook and restricting one's steps, but within this wall a spontaneous communal life could flourish and grow. But to the extent that the structure grew impoverished the wall became a prison. Second: such a structurally poor society awoke to self-consciousness, to consciousness of its existence as a society in contrast to the State, at the time of the French Revolution, and now it can only expect a structural renewal by limiting all not social organizations to those functions which cannot be accomplished by society itself, —while on the other hand the proper management of affairs grows out of the functioning society and creates its own organs. "The limitation of the State's task is a matter of life and death for freedom, both collective and individual." It is obvious that Proudhon's basic thought is not individualistic. What he opposes to the State is not the individual as such but the individual in organic connection with his group, the group being a voluntary association of individuals. "Since the Reformation and especially since the French Revolution a new spirit has dawned on the world. Freedom has opposed itself to the State, and since the idea of freedom has become universal people have realized that it is not a concern of the individual merely, but rather that it must exist in the group also." In the early writings of Proudhon a sort of individualism still predominates, but already he knows that "through monopoly mankind has taken possession of the globe, and through association it will become its real master". In the course of development, however, individualism beat an increasingly rapid retreat (despite the toleration of individual peasant property) before an attitude in which the problematical relationship between personality and totality was balanced by the largely autonomous group—the local community or commune—living on the strength of its own interior relationships. Although the structural point of view as such is never expressly stated in Proudhon we notice that he comes nearer and nearer to it: his anti-centralism turns more and more to "communalism" and federalism (which indeed, as he says in a letter of 1863, had been boiling in his veins for thirty years), that is, it becomes increasingly structural. Advanced centralization should, he writes in 1860, vanish "once it is replaced by federal institutions and communal customs". What is remarkable here is the connection between the new arrangements to be created—the "institutions", and the community-forms to be retained—the "customs".

Just how powerfully Proudhon felt the amorphous character of present-day society we may learn best, perhaps, from his attitude to the question of universal suffrage. "Universal suffrage," he says in his essay *The Solution of the Social Problem* (1848), "is a kind of atomism by means of which the legislator, seeing that he cannot let the people speak in their essential oneness, invites the citizens to express their opinions per head, *viritim*, just as the Epicurean philosopher explained thought, will and understanding by combinations of atoms." As Proudhon said in his speech to the National Assembly in

1848, universal suffrage needs an "organizing principle". This principle can only rest on the organization of society in groups. "The retention of natural groups," writes Proudhon in 1863, "is of the greatest importance for the exercise of electoral power; it is the essential condition of the vote. Without it there is no originality, no frankness, no clear and unequivocal meaning in the voices. . . . The destruction of natural groups in elections would mean the moral destruction of nationality itself, the negation of the thought of the Revolution." The amorphous basis of elections "aims at nothing less than to abolish political life in towns, communes and departments, and through this destruction of all municipal and regional autonomy to arrest the development of universal suffrage". In such circumstances the body of the nation is but an agglomeration of molecules, "a heap of dust animated from without by a subordinating, centralist idea. In our search for unity, unity itself has been sacrificed". Only as an expression of associated groups will universal suffrage, which is now "the strangling of public conscience, the suicide of the people's sovereignty", become an intelligent, moral and revolutionary force. Provided, of course, that "the various spheres of service are balanced and privilege abolished".

Proudhon by no means fails to recognize that "the real problem to be solved for federalism is not political, but economic". "In order to make the confederation indestructible," he says, "economic right must be declared the foundation of federative right and of all political order." The reform of economic right must follow from the answer to two questions which the workers' Societies have to face: whether labour can be self-financing as regards its undertakings as capital is now, and whether the ownership and control of the undertakings can be collective. "The whole future of the workers," writes Proudhon in a curious book, *The Stockjobber's Handbook* (1853), "depends on the answer to these questions. If the answer is in the affirmative a new world will open out before humanity; if in the negative, then let the proletariat take warning! Let them commend themselves to God and the Church—there is no hope for them this side of the grave." Proudhon's sketch of the affirmative answer is "Mutualism" in its mature form. "Mutuality, reciprocity exists," he writes, "when all the workers in an industry, instead of working for an *entrepreneur* who pays them and keeps their products, work for one another and thus collaborate in the making of a common product whose profits they share amongst themselves. Extend the principle of reciprocity as uniting the work of every group, to the Workers' Societies as units, and you have created a form of civilization which from all points of view—political, economic and æsthetic—is radically different from all earlier civilizations." This is Proudhon's solution to the problem, and he formulates it as follows: "All associated and all free." But in order that this may be so the association must not become a system imposed from above; rather must people associate in Workers' Societies (in the sense of "foci of production") only in so far as—Proudhon writes in 1864—"the demands of production, the cheapness of the product, the needs of consumption and the security of the producers themselves require it". By associating in this manner the workers are only following "la raison des choses" itself, and consequently they "can preserve their freedom in the very heart of the society". Thinking like this it was inevitable that Proudhon should turn in 1848 against the State-financed "social workshops" demanded by Louis Blanc (as later by Lassalle). He sees in them only a new form of centralization. It would mean, he says, a number of large associations "in which labour would be regimented and ultimately enslaved through a State policy of brotherhood, just as it is on the point of being enslaved now through the State policy of capitalism. What would freedom, universal happiness, civilization have gained? Nothing. We would merely have exchanged our chains and the social idea would have made no step forward; we would still be under the same arbitrary power, not to say under the same economic fatalism". Here Proudhon is expressing the view which we find twenty years later in theoretical form in Gierke's great work. "Only free association," says Gierke, "can create communities in which economic freedom persists. For those organisms which spring from individual initiative and from the creative powers of their members enhance the life of each individual member simultaneously with the newly established life of the whole." Communist centralism thus appeared to Proudhon as a variant of absolutism elaborated to a monstrous and ruthless degree of perfection. This "dictatorial, authoritarian, doctrinaire system starts from the axiom that the individual is subordinate, in the very nature of things, to the collectivity; from it alone does right and life come to him; the citizen belongs to the State as the child to his family, he is in its power and possession, and he owes it submission and obedience in all things". Just as we can understand from this standpoint that Marx (in a passage intended for the polemic but not actually incorporated in it) said of Proudhon that he was "incapable of comprehending the revolutionary movement", so it is from this standpoint also that we can understand why Proudhon, in an entry in his diary, described Marx as "the tapeworm of socialism". In the communist system common ownership is to bring about the end of all property, personal as well as parochial and communal; universal association is to absorb all special associations, and collective freedom is to devour all corporative, regional and private freedoms. Proudhon defines the political system of centralist communism, in 1864, in words which are worth pondering: "A compact democracy having the appearance of being founded on the dictatorship of the masses, but in which the masses have no more power than is necessary to ensure a general serfdom in accordance with the following precepts and principles borrowed from the old absolutism: indivisibility of public power, all-consuming centralization, systematic destruction of all individual, corporative and regional thought (regarded as disruptive), inquisitorial police." Proudhon thinks that we are not far removed from pure centralist communism in politics and economics, but he is persuaded that "after a final crisis and at the summons of new principles a movement will begin in the reverse direction".

The book in which these words occur—*The Political Capacity of the Working Classes*—was completed only shortly before Proudhon's death. He attributed especial importance to it as setting forth the "idea of a new democracy" and wrote it, as he says, under the inspiration of the "Manifesto of the Sixty"— the electoral declaration (1861) of a group of workers whose ideas for the most part came very near to Proudhon's own. This manifesto was the fourth in the series of four socialist "Manifestos"; the first being the *Manifeste des Égaux* of Babeuf, the second that of the Fourierist Considérant, the third the "Communist Manifesto"—and it was the first to emerge from the proletariat itself. In his declaration, in which Proudhon hails the "awakening of socialism" in France and the "unveiling of corporate consciousness" in the working-class, he demands *inter alia* the setting up of a *chambre syndicale*, but not one which, as some people had proposed in a "strange confusion of thought" (here Saint-Simon's idea turns up again), was to be composed of workers and work-givers; "what we demand is a Chamber composed exclusively of workers elected by the free vote of all—a Chamber of Labour". This demand bears clear witness of the development of the new social thinking from Saint-Simon to Proudhon.

By advancing from the idea of social reconstruction to the idea of structural renewal, Proudhon took the decisive step. The "industrial constitution" of Saint-Simon does not signify a new structure, but "federalism" does.

Proudhon naturally distinguishes two modes of structure, which interpenetrate: the economic structure as a federation of work-groups, which he calls "agrarian-industrial federation", and the political structure, which rests on the decentralization of power, the division of authority, the guarantee of the maximum degree of autonomy to the communes and regional associations, and the widest possible replacement of bureaucracy by a looser and more direct control of affairs arising from the natural group. Proudhon's "Constitutional Science" can be summed up in three propositions. It is necessary—

1. To form moderately sized and moderately autonomous groups and to unite them by an act of federation;

2. To organize the government in each federated State according to the law of the division of organs. That is to say: inside the Public Authority to divide everything that can be divided, to define everything that can be defined, to allocate among different organs and functionaries everything that has been so divided and defined, to leave nothing undivided, and to surround the Public Authority with all the conditions of publicity and control;

3. Instead of allowing the federated States or the provincial and municipal authorities to merge into a central authority, to limit the competence of the latter to the simple tasks of general initiative, mutual assurance and supervision.

The life of a society finds fulfilment in the combination of persons into groups, of groups into associations. "Just as a number of people by their common exertions give rise to a collective strength which is superior in quality and intensity to the sum of their respective strengths, so a number of work-groups associated in a relationship of mutual exchange will generate a potency of a higher order," which can be regarded specifically as "the social potential". Mutualism—the building up of an economy on reciprocity of service, and federation—the building up of a political order on the brotherhood of groups— are only two aspects of the same structure. "Through the grouping of individual strengths and the interdependence of the groups the whole nation will become a body." And a real brotherhood of man can be constituted from the various peoples, as a federation of federations.

Proudhon treated the problem of decentralization more particularly in his *Theory of Taxation* (1861). He says that he is not unaware of the fact that political centralization offers many advantages, but it is too costly. People regard it as obvious not merely because it flatters their collective vanity but also because "in nations as in children reason seeks unity in all things, simplicity, uniformity, identity and hierarchy as well as size and mass", and this is why centralization—the type of all the ancient kingdoms—became an effective method of discipline. "People like simple ideas and are right to like them. Unfortunately the simplicity they seek is only to be found in elementary things; and the world, society and man are made up of insoluble problems, contrary principles and conflicting forces. Organism means complication, and multiplicity means contradiction, opposition, independence. The centralist system is all very well as regards size, simplicity and construction; it lacks but one thing—the individual no longer belongs to himself in such a system, he cannot feel his worth, his life, and no account is taken of him at all." But the conception of and demand for a public system in which the individual can belong to himself, feel his worth and his life, a system that takes account of him as an individual, does not just float about in the boundless realm of abstraction—it is bound to the facts and tendencies of our social reality. In the modern constitutional State "the various groups need no direction in a great many of their activities; they are quite capable of governing themselves with no other inspiration than conscience and reason". In any State organized in accordance with the principles of modern law there occurs a progressive diminution of directive action—a decentralization. And a corresponding development can be discerned on the economic side. The development of technics in our age (Proudhon had already drawn attention to this in 1855 in his book on the reform of the railways, but it was only long after his death, with the mechanization of communications and the prospective electrification of production, that the matter became topical) tends to make the concentration of population in the big cities unnecessary; "the dispersion of the masses and their redistribution is beginning". The political centre of gravity must gradually shift from the cities to "the new agricultural and industrial groupings".

But Proudhon is by no means of the opinion that the process of decentralization is prospering and maturing in all fields. On the contrary: in the field of politics he sees in the conscious will of man a counter-movement of the gravest import. "A fever of centralization," he writes in 1861, "is sweeping over the world; one would say that men were weary of the vestiges of freedom that yet remain to them and were only longing to be rid of them. . . . Is it the need for authority that is everywhere making itself felt, a disgust with independence, or only an incapacity for self-government?" Only the creative, restructuring powers that reign in the depths of man can avail against this "fever", this grave sickness of the human spirit. The expression of these powers is "the idea" of which Proudhon says at the end of a political treatise in 1863 that it "exists and is in circulation", but that, if it is to be realized, it must "issue from the bowels of the situation".

At that time, when his insight was at its height, Proudhon was far from assuming that this situation was imminent. We know from some of his letters of 1860 how he pictured the immediate future. "We should no longer deceive ourselves," he wrote. "Europe is sick of thought and order; it is entering into the era of brute force and contempt of principles." And in the same letter: "Then the great war of the six great powers will begin." A few months later: "Carnage will come and the enfeeblement that will follow these blood-baths will be terrible. We shall not live to see the work of the new age, we shall fight in the darkness; we must prepare ourselves to endure this life without too much sadness, by doing our duty. Let us help one another, call to one another in the gloom, and practise justice wherever opportunity offers." And finally: "To-day civilization is in the grip of a crisis for which one can only find a single analogy in history—that is the crisis which brought the coming of Christianity. All the traditions are worn out, all the creeds abolished; but the new programme is not yet *ready*, by which I mean that it has not yet entered the consciousness of the masses. Hence what I call *the dissolution*. This is the cruellest moment in the life of societies. . . . I am under no illusions and do not expect to wake up one morning to see the resurrection of freedom in our country, as if by a stroke of magic. . . . No, no; decay, and decay for a period whose end I cannot fix and which will last for not less than one or two generations—is our lot. . . . I shall witness the evil only, I shall die in the midst of the darkness." But the thing is "to do our duty". In the same year he had written to the historian Michelet: "It will only be possible to escape by a complete revolution in our ideas and our hearts. We are working for the revolution, you and I; that will be our honour before posterity, if they remember us." And eight years previously he had replied thus to a friend who had suggested emigration to America: "It is here, I tell you, here under the sabre of Napoleon, under the rod of the Jesuits and the spy-glass of the secret service, that we have to work for the emancipation of mankind. There is no sky more propitious for us, no earth more fruitful."

Like Saint-Simon, though in far greater detail and with far more precision, Proudhon brought the problem of a structural renewal of society to the fore without treating it as such. And just as Saint-Simon failed to face the question of the social units which would serve as the cells of a new society, so Proudhon left it open in all essentials, though he came much closer to it. But in the first case there were contemporaries, and in the second followers, who made this very problem the principal object of their research and planning.

That Proudhon did not study it more intensively has its chief reason in his suspicions of "association" as a State-prescribed uniform panacea for all the ills of society, in the sense proposed by Louis Blanc: "social workshops" in industry as well as in agriculture, established, financed and controlled by the State. It must be noted that Louis Blanc's proposals— if not in intention, at least in character—are socially structural; from the "solidarity of all workers in the same shop" he goes on to the "solidarity of shops in the same industry" and thence to the "solidarity of different industries". Also, he sees the agricultural commune as being built up on the basis of combined production and consumption. "To meet the needs of all," he says in his *Organization of Labour* (1839), "it is necessary to pool the products of the work of all," this is the form in which he sees the immediate possibility of a "more radical and more complete" application of "the system of fraternal association". Proudhon's suspicions were directed, as said, against a new "raison d'État"; hence, against uniformity, against exclusiveness, against compulsion. The co-operative form seemed to him more applicable to industry than to agriculture, where he was concerned for the preservation of the peasantry (note that in all the permutations of his thinking he holds fast to one principle in this connection, that the land lawfully belongs to him who cultivates it) and, when applied to industry, only in those branches whose nature the co-operative form suited, and for certain definite functions. He refuses to equate a new ordering of society with uniformity; order means, for him, the just ordering of multiformity. Eduard Bernstein is quite right when he says that Proudhon denied to the essentially monopolist Co-operative what he conceded to the mutualist one. Proudhon had a profound fear of everything coming "from above", everything imposed on the people and decked out with privileges. In this connection he feared the proliferation of new collective egoisms, for these seemed to him more perilous than individual egoisms. He saw the danger that threatens every Producer Co-operative working for a free market: that it will be seized with the spirit of capitalism, the ruthless exploitation of opportunities and eventualities. His doubts were cogent. They were rooted in his basic view which made justice the criterion of true socialism. (According to him there are two ideas: freedom, and unity or order, and "one must make up one's mind to live with both of them by seeking a balance between them". The principle that permits this is called "justice".) But the structural form of the coming society announced by Proudhon, the form in which the balance of freedom and order is attained and which he calls federalism, required him not merely to concern himself—as he did—with the larger units to be federated (that is, the various nations, but the smaller ones also whose federative combination would in reality alone constitute the "nation". Proudhon did not fulfil this requirement. He could only have fulfilled it had he sought in it and from it the answer to his own doubts, which is to say, only if he had directed his best thought to the problem of how to promote and organize "association" in such a way that the danger inherent in it would be, if not exorcized, at least appreciably diminished. Because he did not do this sufficiently well—important as was the step taken in this direction by his principle of mutualism—we find here no adequate answer to our question: "What are the units which will federate in a new and genuine popular order?", or, more precisely: "How must the units be constituted so that they can federate into a genuine popular order, a new and just social structure?" Thus Proudhon's socialism lacks one essential. For we cannot but doubt whether existing social units, even where the old community-forms remain, can still, being what they are, combine in justice; also whether any new units will ever be capable of it unless this same combination of freedom and order governs and shapes their inception.

V

KROPOTKIN

THIS is where Kropotkin comes in. Born at a time—a hundred years ago—when Proudhon was just beginning his struggle against the inequity of private property, against property as "theft", he consciously takes up Proudhon's legacy so as to amplify and elaborate it. At the same time he simplifies it, though often in a fruitful and stimulating way. He simplifies Proudhon by mitigating the dazzle of contradictory principles, and that is something of a loss; but he also translates him into the language of history, and that is a gain. Kropotkin is no historian; even where he thought historically he is a social geographer, a chronicler of the states and conditions on earth; but he thinks in terms of history.

Kropotkin simplifies Proudhon first of all by setting up in the place of the manifold "social antinomies" the simple antithesis between the principles of the struggle for existence and mutual help. He undertakes to prove this antithesis biologically, ethnologically and historically. Historically he sees these principles (probably influenced very strongly by Kireyewski's picture of historical duality in 1852) crystallizing on the one hand into the coercive State, on the other into the manifold forms of association such as the County Commune, the parish, the guild, the corporation and so on right up to the modern Co-operatives. In an over-elaborate and historically undersubstantiated formulation written in 1894, Kropotkin puts the antithesis thus: "The State is an historical growth that slowly and gradually, at certain epochs in the life and history of all peoples, displaces the free confederations of tribes, communities, tribal groups, villages and producers' guilds and gives minorities terrible support in enslaving the masses—and this historical growth and all that derives from it is the thing we are fighting against." Later (in his book *Modern Science and Anarchy*, a complete French edition of which appeared in 1913) he found a more correct and historically a more justifiable formulation. "All through the history of our civilization," he writes, "two contrary traditions, two trends have faced one another: the Roman tradition and the national tradition; the imperial and the federal; the authoritarian and the libertarian. And once more, on the eve of social revolution, we find these two traditions face to face." Here, probably under the influence of Gierke, who called the two opposing principles domination and free association, there is a hint, bound up with Kropotkin's historical insight, that the universal conflict of the two spiritual forces persists inside the social movement itself: between the centralist and the federalist forms of socialism.

Certainly Kropotkin's conception of the State is too narrow; it is not a question of identifying the centralist State with the State in general. In history there is not merely the State as a clamp that strangles the individuality of small associations; there is also the State as a framework within which they may consolidate; not merely the "great Leviathan" whose authority, according to Hobbes, is based on "terror", but also the great nourishing mother who carefully folds her children, the communities, to her bosom; not merely the *machina machinarum* that turns everything belonging to it into the components of some mechanism, but also the *communitas communitatum*, the union of the communities into community, within which "the proper and autonomous common life of all the members" can unfold. On the other hand, Kropotkin was more or less right when he dated the inception of the modern centralist State—which he confused with the State as such—from the sixteenth century; from the time when "the downfall of the free cities" was sealed "by the abolition of all forms of free contract": the village communities, the Societies of Artisans, the fraternities, the confederacies of the Middle Ages. "With some certainty we may say," writes the legal historian Maitland, "that at the end of the Middle Ages a great change in men's thought about groups of men was taking place." Now "the Absolute State faces the Absolute Individual". In Gierke's words "the sovereign State and the sovereign individual fought to define their natural and lawful spheres of existence; all intermediate associations were degraded to merely legalistic and more or less arbitrary formations and at last completely exterminated". In the end nothing remained but the sovereign State which, in proportion to its mechanization, devoured everything living. Nothing organic could resist "the rigidly centralized directive mechanism which, with its enormous expenditure of human intelligence, could be operated at the touch of a button", as Carl Schmitt, the ingenious interpreter of totalitarianism, calls the Leviathan. Those for whom the important thing is not so much the security of individuals (for which purpose the Leviathan is deemed indispensable) as the preservation of the substance of community, the renewal of communal life in the life of mankind— are bound to fight against every doctrine that would defend centralism. "There is no more dangerous superstition," says the church historian Figgis, "than that political atomism which denies all power to societies as such, but ascribes absolutely unlimited competence over body, soul and spirit to the grandiose unity of the State. It is indeed 'the great Leviathan made up of little men' as in Hobbes' title-page, but we can see no reason to worship the golden image." In so far as Kropotkin did battle not with State-order itself but with the centralist State-apparatus, he has powerful allies in the field of science. In scientific circles it may perhaps be maintained against "pluralism" that the modern State, in so far as it is pluralist rather than totalitarian, has the appearance of a "compromise between social and economic power-groups, an agglomeration of heterogeneous factors, parties, interests, concerns, trades-unions, churches, etc." (Carl Schmitt.) But that says nothing against a socialistic rebuilding of the State as a community of communities, provided that the communities are real communities; for then all the various groups Schmitt mentions would either not exist or be quite different from what they are now, and the fusion of the groups would not be an agglomeration but, in Landauer's words, "a league of leagues". Any element of compulsory order still persisting would only represent the stage of development attained by man at the time; it would no longer represent the exploitation of human immaturity and human contrasts. Contrasts between individuals and between groups will probably never cease, nor indeed should they; they have to be endured; but we can and we must strive towards a state of things where individual conflicts neither extend to large wholes which are not really implicated, nor lend themselves to the establishment of absolute centralist suzerainty.

As in his inadequate distinction between the excessive and the legitimate State, or the superfluous and the necessary State, so in another important respect Kropotkin's view, although perceiving many historical relationships unnoticed by Proudhon, is not realistic enough. He says on one occasion that in his (Kropotkin's) praise of the medieval commune he might perhaps be accused of having forgotten its internal conflicts, but that he had by no means done so. For history showed that "these conflicts were themselves the guarantee of free life in the free city", that the communities grew and were rejuvenated through them. Further, that in contrast to the wars of States, these inter-communal conflicts were concerned with the struggle for and maintenance of the individual's freedom, with the federative principle, the right to unite and to act in unison, and that therefore "the epochs when the conflict was fought out in freedom without the weight of existing authority being thrown into either of the scales, were the epochs of greatest spiritual development". This is substantially right and yet one all-important point has not been sufficiently grasped. The danger of collective egoism, as also that of schism and oppression, is hardly less in an autonomous community than in the nation or party, particularly when the community participates as a co-partner in production. A telling example of this is to be found in the internal development of the "mining communities", that is, the Producer Co-operatives of mine-workers in the German Middle Ages. Max Weber has shown in a scholarly exposition that in the first stage of this there was an increasing expropriation of the owners; that the community became the managing director and shared out the profits while observing as far as practicable the principle of equality; but that a differentiation among the workers themselves thereupon set in. For as a result of increasing demand the new arrivals were no longer accepted into the community, they were "non-union men", hired labour, and the process of disintegration thus initiated continued until purely capitalist "interested parties" permeated the personnel of the mining-community and the union finally became a capitalistic instrument which itself appointed the workers. When we read to-day (for instance in Tawney's book *The Acquisitive Society*) how the workers can "freeze out" the owners from industrial undertakings by making them superfluous through their own control of production; or how they can limit the interest of the owners to such an extent that the latter become mere *rentiers* with no share in the profits and no responsibility—precisely, therefore, what had happened

in the German mines seven hundred years ago—then the
historical warning comes very close to us and commands us to
have a care, to build the checks on collective egoism into the
new order of society. Kropotkin is not blind to this danger; for
instance, he points out (*Mutual Aid*, 1902) that the modern
Co-operative Movement which, originally and in essence, had
the character of mutual aid, has often degenerated into "share-
capital individualism" and fosters "co-operative egoism".

Kropotkin realized very clearly that, as Proudhon had
already indicated, a socialistic community could only be built
on the basis of a double intercommunal bond, namely the
federation of regional communes and trade communes variously
intercrossing and supporting one another. To this he sometimes added as a third principle communal groupings based on
voluntary membership. He sketches a picture of the new
society most vividly in his autobiography (1899), in that
passage where he speaks of the basic views of the anarchist-
communist "Jura-Federation" founded by Bakunin, in which
he played an active part in 1877 and in the years immediately
following. From the documents of the Jura-Federation itself
no comparable formulation is indeed known to us, and it is
to be assumed that Bakunin's ideas, which were never other
than cursorily sketched, becoming in the course of years
intertwined with those of Proudhon, only attained maturity in
Kropotkin's own mind. "We remark in the civilized nations,"
he writes in his autobiography, "the germ of a new social form
which will supplant the old. . . . This society will be composed
of a number of societies banded together for everything that
demands a common effort: federations of producers for all
kinds of production, of Societies for consumption; federations
of such Societies alone and federations of Societies and production groups, finally more extensive groups embracing a
whole country or even several countries and composed of
persons who will work in common for the satisfaction of those
economic, spiritual and artistic needs which are not limited to
a definite territory. All these groups will unite their efforts
through mutual agreement. . . . Personal initiative will be
encouraged and every tendency to uniformity and centralization combated. Moreover this society will not ossify into
fixed and immovable forms, it will transform itself incessantly,
for it will be a living organism continually in development."
No equalization, no final fixation—that is Kropotkin's basic

idea, and it is a healthy one. What is aspired to is, as he says
in 1896, "the fullest development of individuality combined
with the highest development of free association in all its
aspects, in all possible degrees and for all conceivable purposes:
an ever-changing association bearing in itself the elements
of its own duration and taking on the forms which at any
moment best correspond to the manifold endeavours of all."
And he adds with emphasis in 1913: "We conceive the structure
of society to be something that is never finally constituted."

Such a structure means mobilizing the social and political
spontaneity of the nation to the greatest possible degree. This
order, which Kropotkin calls Communism (a term usurped
by that "negation of all freedom" so bitterly attacked by
Proudhon) and which may be called more correctly Federal
Communalism, "cannot be imposed—it could not live unless
the constant, daily collaboration of all supported it. In an atmosphere of officialdom it would suffocate. Consequently it
cannot subsist unless it creates permanent contacts between
everybody for the thousand and one common concerns; it cannot live unless it creates regional and autonomous life in the
smallest of its units—the street, the house-block, the district, the
parish." Socialism "will have to find its own form of political
relationships. . . . In one way or another it will be more 'of the
people'; will have to be closer to the *forum* than parliamentary
government is. It will have to depend less on representation,
more on self-government". We see particularly clearly here
that Kropotkin is ultimately attacking not State-order as such
but only the existing order in all its forms; that his "anarchy",
like Proudhon's, is in reality "anocracy" (ἀκρατία); not
absence of government but absence of domination. "If
I may express myself so," Proudhon had written in a letter of
1864, "anarchy is a form of government or constitution in
which the principle of authority, police institutions, restric-
tive and repressive measures, bureaucracy, taxation, etc., are
reduced to their simplest terms." This is at bottom Kropotkin's
opinion too. As the important words "*less* representation" and
"*more* self-government" show, he also knows that when it comes
to our real will for a "restructuring" of society, it is not a question of manipulating an abstract principle but only of the
direction of realization willed; of the limits of realization possible
in this direction in any given circumstances—the line that
defines what is demanded here and now, becomes attainable.

He knows that tremendous things are willed and how deeply they reach into our hearts: "All the relations between individuals and between the masses have to be corrected"; but he also knows that this can only be done if social spontaneity is roused and shown the direction in which it has to work.

That a decisive transformation of the social order as a whole cannot ensue without revolution is self-evident for Kropotkin. So it was for Proudhon. In the book that Marx attacked as "petty bourgeois" Proudhon knew well enough that the mighty task he set the working-classes—namely to "bring forth from the bowels of the people, from the depths of labour a greater authority, a mightier fact, which will draw capital and the State into its orbit and subdue them"—cannot be fulfilled without revolution. Proudhon saw in revolutions, as he said in a toast to the Revolution of 1848, "the successive declarations of human justice", and the modern State he held to be "counter-revolutionary in nature and in principle". What he contested (in his famous letter to Marx) was that "no reform was possible at present without a *coup de main*" and that "we were obliged to use revolutionary action as a means of social reform". But he divined the tragedy of revolutions and came to feel it more and more deeply in the course of disappointing experiences. Their tragedy is that as regards their *positive* goal they will always result in the exact opposite of what the most honest and passionate revolutionaries strive for, unless and until this has so far taken shape *before* the revolution that the revolutionary act has only to wrest the space for it in which it can develop unimpeded. Two years before his death Proudhon remarks bitterly: "It is the revolutionary struggle that has given us centralization." This view was not unfamiliar to Kropotkin. But he believed that it was sufficient to influence the revolutionary force by education so as to prevent the revolution from ending in a new centralization "every bit as bad or worse", and thus enabling "the people—the peasants and the urban workers—to begin the really constructive work themselves". "The point for us is to *inaugurate* the social revolution through communism." Like Bakunin, Kropotkin misses the all-important fact that, in the social as opposed to the political sphere, revolution is not so much a creative as a delivering force whose function is to set free and authenticate—i.e. that it can only perfect, set free, and lend the stamp of authority to something that has already been foreshadowed in the womb of the pre-revolutionary society; that, as regards social evolution, the hour of revolution is not an hour of begetting but an hour of birth—provided there was a begetting beforehand.

Of course there are in Kropotkin's teaching fundamental elements which point to the significance of pre-revolutionary structure-making. As in his book on mutual aid he traces the vestiges of old community-forms in our society and compares them with examples of existing, more or less amorphous solidarity, so in his book *Fields, Factories and Workshops* (1898, enlarged edition 1912) he makes, on purely economic and industrial-psychological grounds, a weighty contribution to the picture of a new social unit fitted to serve as a cell for the formation of a new society in the midst of the old. As against the progressive over-straining of the principles of division of labour and excessive specialization, he sets the principle of labour-integration and the alliance of intensive agriculture with decentralized industry. He sketches the picture of a village based on field and factory alike, where *the same* people work in the one as in the other alternately without this in any way entailing a technological regress, rather in close association with technical developments and yet in such a way that man enters into his rights as a human being. Kropotkin knows that such an alteration cannot be "completely carried through" in a society like ours, nevertheless he plans not merely for to-morrow but for to-day as well. He stresses the fact that "every socialistic attempt to alter the present relations between capital and labour will come to grief if it disregards the trend towards integration"; but he also stresses that the future he wishes to see "is already possible, already realizable". From there it is only a step to demanding that an immediate beginning be made with the restructuring of society—but that step is decisive.

VI

LANDAUER

LANDAUER'S step beyond Kropotkin consists primarily in his direct insight into the nature of the State. The State is not, as Kropotkin thinks, an institution which can be destroyed by a revolution. "The State is a condition, a certain relationship between human beings, a mode of human behaviour; we destroy it by contracting other relationships, by behaving differently." Men stand to one another to-day in a "statual" relationship, that is, in one which makes the coercive order of the State necessary and is represented by it and in it. Hence this order can only be overcome to the extent that this relationship between men is replaced by another. This other relationship Landauer calls "People". "It is a connexion between people which is actually there; only it has not yet become bond and binding, is not yet a higher organism." To the extent that people, on the basis of the processes of production and circulation, find themselves coming together again as a People and "growing together into an organism with countless organs and members", Socialism, which now lives only in the minds and desires of single, atomized people, will become reality—not in the State "but outside, without the State", and that means *alongside* the State. This "finding themselves together" of people does not, as he says, mean the founding of something new but the actualization and reconstitution of something that has always been present—of Community, which in fact exists alongside the State, albeit buried and laid waste. "One day it will be realized that socialism is not the invention of anything new but the discovery of something actually present, of something that has grown." This being so, the realization of socialism is always possible if a sufficient number of people want it. The realization depends not on the technological state of things, although socialism when realized will of course look differently, begin differently and develop differently according to the state of technics; it depends on people and their spirit. "Socialism is possible and impossible at all times; it is possible when the right people are there to will and do it; it is impossible when people either don't will it or only supposedly will it, but are not capable of doing it."

From this glimpse into the real relationship between State and Community some important things ensue. We see that, practically speaking, it is not a question of the abstract alternative "State or No-State". The Either-Or principle applies primarily to the moments of genuine decision by a person or a group; then, everything intermediate, everything that interposes itself, is impure and unpurifying; it works confusion, obscurity, obstruction. But this same principle becomes an obstruction in its turn if, at any given stage in the execution of the decision reached, it does not permit *less* than the Absolute to take shape and so devalues the measures that are *now* possible. If the State is a relationship which can only be destroyed by entering into another relationship, then we shall always be helping to destroy it to the extent that we do in fact enter into another.

To grasp the subject fully we must go one step further. As Landauer pointed out later, "State" is status—a state, in fact. People living together at a given time and in a given space are only to a certain degree capable, of their own free will, of living together rightly; of their own free will maintaining a right order and conducting their common concerns accordingly. The line which at any time limits this capacity forms the basis of the State at that time; in other words, the degree of incapacity for a voluntary right order determines the degree of legitimate compulsion. Nevertheless the *de facto* extent of the State always exceeds more or less—and mostly very much exceeds—the sort of State that would emerge from the degree of legitimate compulsion. This constant difference (which results in what I call "the excessive State") between the State in principle and the State in fact is explained by the historical circumstance that accumulated power does not abdicate except under necessity. It resists any adaptation to the increasing capacity for voluntary order so long as this increase fails to exert sufficiently vigorous pressure on the power accumulated. The "principial" foundations of the power may have crumbled, but power itself does not crumble unless driven to it. Thus the dead can rule the living. "We see," says Landauer, "how something dead to our spirit

can exercise living power over our body." The task that thus
emerges for the socialists, i.e. for all those intent on a restructuring of society, is to drive the factual base-line of the State back
to the "principial" base-line of socialism. But this is precisely
what will result from the creation and renewal of a real organic
structure, from the union of persons and families into various
communities and of communities into associations. It is this
growth and nothing else that "destroys" the State by dis-
placing it. The part so displaced, of course, will only be that
portion of the State which is superfluous and without foundation
at the time; any action that went beyond this would be
illegitimate and bound to miscarry because, as soon as it had
exceeded its limits it would lack the constructive spirit necessary
for further advance. Here we come up against the same problem
that Proudhon had discovered from another angle: association
without sufficient and sufficiently vital communal spirit does not
set Community up in the place of State—it bears the State in
its own self and it cannot result in anything but State, i.e. power-
politics and expansionism supported by bureaucracy.

But what is also important is that for Landauer the setting up
of society "outside" and "alongside" the State is essentially
"a discovery of something actually present, something that has
grown". In reality a community does exist alongside the State,
"not a sum of isolated individual atoms but an organic cohesion
that only wants to expand and, out of many groups, form a
great arch". But the reality of community must be roused,
must be summoned out of the depths where it lies buried under
the incrustations of the State. This can only happen if the hard
crust that has formed on mankind, if their own inner "statehood" is broken open and the slumbering, immemorial reality
aroused beneath. "Such is the task of the socialists and of the
movements they have started among the peoples: to loosen the
hardening of hearts so that what lies buried may rise to the
surface: so that what truly lives yet now seems dead may
emerge and grow into the light." Men who are renewed in this
way can renew society, and since they know from experience
that there is an immemorial stock of community that has declared itself in them as something new, they will build into the
new structure everything that is left of true community-form.
"It would be madness," Landauer writes in a letter to a woman
who wanted to abolish marriage, "to dream of abolishing the
few forms of union that remain to us! We need *form*, not form-
lessness. We need *tradition*." He who builds, not arbitrarily

and fruitlessly, but legitimately and for the future, acts from
inner kinship with age-old tradition, and this entrusts itself
to him and gives him strength. It will now become clear why
Landauer calls the "other" relationship which men can enter
into instead of the ordinary State-relationship, not by any new
name but simply "People". Such a "People" comprehends also
the innermost reality of "Nationhood"—what remains over
when "Statehood" and politicization have been superseded: a
community of being and a being in manifold community.
"This likeness, this equality in inequality, this peculiar quality
that binds people together, this common spirit, is an actual fact.
Do not overlook it, you free men and socialists; socialism, freedom and justice can only be accomplished between those who
have always been united; socialism cannot be established in the
abstract, but only in a concrete multiplicity that is one with
the harmony of the peoples." The true connexion between
Nation and socialism is discovered here: the closeness of people
to one another in mode of life, language, tradition, memories
of a common fate—all this predisposes to communal living, and
only by building up such a life can the peoples of the earth
constitute themselves anew. "Nothing but the rebirth of all
peoples out of the spirit of regional community can bring
salvation." And Landauer understands "regional community" quite concretely, in the reappearance—if only in a
rudimentary state—of the traditional community-forms and
in the possibility of preserving them, renewing and expanding
them. "The radical reformer will find nothing to reform, now
or at any other time, except what is there. Hence, now and
at all times it is well for the regional community to have its
own boundaries; for part of it to be communal land, for the
other parts to be family property for house, yard, garden and
field." Landauer is counting here on the long memories of
communal units. "There is so much to which we could add
whatever outward forms of life still contain living spirit. There
are village communities with vestiges of ancient communal property, with peasants and labourers who remember the original
boundaries that have been in private possession for centuries;
communal institutions embracing agricultural work and the
handicrafts." To be a socialist means to be livingly related
to the life and spirit of the community; to keep on the alert;
to examine with impartial eye whatever vestiges of this spirit
yet lurk in the depths of our uncommunal age; and, wherever

possible, to bind the newly created forms firmly to the forms that endure. But it also means: to guard against all rigid delineation of ways and methods; to know that in the life of man and human communities the straight line between two points is often the longest; to understand that the real way to socialist reality is revealed not merely in what "I know" and what "I plan", but also in the unknown and unknowable, in the unexpected and the not to be expected; and, so far as we can, to live and act accordingly at all times. "We know absolutely no details," says Landauer in 1907, "about our immediate way; it may lead over Russia, it may lead over India. The only thing we know is that our way does not lead through the movements and struggles of the day, but over things unknown, deeply buried, and sudden."

Landauer said once of Walt Whitman, the poet of heroic democracy whom he translated, that, like Proudhon (with whom in Landauer's opinion he had many spiritual affinities), Whitman united the conservative and the revolutionary spirit—Individualism and Socialism. This can be said of Landauer too. What he has in mind is ultimately a revolutionary conservation: a revolutionary selection of those elements worthy to be conserved and fit for the renovation of the social being.

Only on these assumptions can we understand Landauer as a revolutionary. He was a man from south-western Germany, of the Jewish middle class, but he came much nearer to the proletariat and the proletarian way of life than Marx, also a south-west German of the Jewish middle class. Again and again Marxists have condemned his proposals for a socialist Colony as implying a withdrawal from the world of human exploitation and the ruthless battle against it, to an island where one could passively observe all these tremendous happenings. No reproach has ever been falser. Everything that Landauer thought and planned, said and wrote—even when it had Shakespeare for subject or German mysticism, and especially all designs whatsoever for the building of a socialistic reality—was steeped in a great belief in revolution and the will for it. "Do we want to retreat into happiness?" he wrote in a letter (1911). "Do we want our lives for ourselves? Do we not rather want to do everything possible for the people, and long for the impossible? Do we not want the whole thing—Revolution?" But that long-drawn struggle for freedom which he calls Revolution can only bear fruit when "we are seized by the spirit, not of revolution, but of regeneration"; and the individual revolutions taking place within that long "Revolution" seem to Landauer like a fire-bath of the spirit, just as in the last analysis revolution is itself regeneration. "In the fire, the ecstasy, the brotherliness of these militant movements" says Landauer in his book *The Revolution*, which he wrote in 1907, at my request, "there rises up again and again the image and feeling of positive union through the binding quality, through love—which is power; and without this passing and surpassing regeneration we cannot go on living and must perish." It is important, however, to recognize without illusion that "although Utopia is prodigally beautiful—not so much in *what* it says as in *how* it says it—the end which revolution actually attains is not so very different from what went before". The strength of revolution lies in rebellion and negation; it cannot solve social problems by political means. "When a revolution," Landauer continues, speaking of the French Revolution, "ultimately gets into the terrible situation that this one did, with enemies all round it inside and out, then the forces of negation and destruction that still live on are bound to turn inwards and against themselves; fanaticism and passion turn to distrust and soon to blood-thirstiness, or at least to an indifference to the added terrors of killing; and before long terror by killing becomes the sole possible means for the rulers of the day to keep themselves pro-visionally in power." Thus it happened (as Landauer, his view unchanged, wrote ten years later about the same revolution) that "the most fervent representatives of the revolution thought and believed in their finest hours—no matter to what strange shores they were ultimately flung by the raging waves—that they were leading mankind to a rebirth; but somehow this birth miscarried and they got in each other's way and blamed each other because the revolution had allied itself to war, to violence, to dictatorship and authoritarian oppression—in a word, to politics". Between these two statements Landauer, writing in July, 1914, on the threshold of the first World War, expressed the same critical insight in a particularly topical form. "Let us be under no illusion," he says, "as to the situation in all countries to-day. When it comes to the point, the only thing that these revolutionary agitations have served is the nationalist-capitalist aggrandisement we call imperialism; even when originally tinctured with socialism they were all too easily led

by some Napoleon or Cavour or Bismarck into the mainstream
of politics, because all these insurrections were in fact only
a means of political revolution or nationalist war but could
never be a means of socialist transformation, for the sufficient
reason that the socialists are romantics who always and
inevitably make use of the means of their enemies and neither
practise nor know the means of bringing the new People and
the new humanity to birth." But already in 1907 Landauer,
basing himself on Proudhon, had drawn the obvious conclusion from his views. "It will be recognized sooner or later
that, as the greatest of all socialists—Proudhon—has declared
in incomparable words, albeit forgotten to-day, social revolution bears no resemblance at all to political revolution; that
although it cannot come alive and remain living without
a good deal of the latter it is nevertheless a peaceful structure,
an organizing *of* new spirit *for* new spirit and nothing else."
And further: "Yet it is the case, as Gottfried Keller says,
that the last triumph of freedom will be dry. Political
revolution will clear the ground, literally and in every sense of
the word[1]; but at the same time those institutions will be
preparing in which the confederation of industrial societies
can live, the confederation destined to release the spirit that
lies captive behind the State." This preparation, however, the
real "transformation of society, can only come in love, in work
and in stillness". Hence it is obvious that the spirit that is to
be "released" must already be alive in people to an extent
sufficient for such "preparation", so that they may prepare the
institutions and the revolution as "clearing the ground" for
them. Once again Landauer refers to Proudhon. In the
revolutionary epoch of 1848 Proudhon had told the revolutionaries: "You revolutionaries, if you do *that* you will make
a change indeed." Disappointed, he had other things to do
afterwards than repeat the catchwords of the revolution.
"Everything comes in time," says Landauer, "and every time
after the revolution is a time before the revolution for all those
whose lives have not got bogged in some great moment of the
past." Proudhon went on living, although he bled from more
than one wound; he now asked himself: " '*If* you do that,'
I said—but *why* have you not done it?" He found the answer
and laid it down in all his later works, the answer which

---

[1] "Den Boden frei machen" also means to "free the land", make it available
to the people. The phrase is used in this latter sense in the next paragraph. Trans.

in our language runs: "Because the spirit was not in you."

Again, we are indebted to Landauer rather than to Kropotkin for one vital clarification. If political revolution is to serve social revolution three things are necessary. Firstly: the revolutionaries must be firmly resolved to clear the ground and make the land available[1] as communal property, and thereafter to develop it into a confederation of societies. Secondly: communal property must be so prepared in institutions as to ensure that it can be developed along those lines after the ground has been cleared. Thirdly: such preparations must be conducted in a true spirit of community.

The significance of this third item, the "spirit", for the new society-to-be is something that none of the earlier socialists recognized as profoundly as did Landauer. We must realize what he means by it—always assuming of course that we do not understand spiritual reality merely as the product and reflection of the material world, as mere "consciousness" determined by the social "being" and explicable in terms of economic-technical relationships. It is rather an entity *sui generis* that stands in close relation to the social being, without, however, being explicable at any point in terms of the latter.

"A degree of high culture is reached," says Landauer, "when the various social structures, in themselves exclusive and independent of one another, are all filled with a uniform spirit not inherent in or proceeding from these structures, but reigning over them purely in its own right. In other words: such a degree of culture arises when the unity pervading the various forms of organization and the supra-individual formations is not the external bond of force, but a spirit dwelling in the individuals themselves and pointing beyond earthly and material interests." As an example Landauer cites the Christian Middle Ages (truly the sole epoch in the history of the West comparable in this respect with the great cultures of the Orient). He sees the Middle Ages as characterized not by this or that form of social life, such as the County Commune, the guilds, corporations and trade-confraternities, the city-leagues, nor even by the feudal system, the churches and monasteries and chivalric orders—but by this "totality of independent units which all interpenetrate" to form "a society of societies". What united all the variously differentiated forms and "bound

[1] See footnote, p. 52.

them together at the apex into a higher unity, a pyramid whose point was not power and not invisible in the clouds, was the spirit streaming out of the characters and spirits of individual men and women into all these structures, drawing strength from them and streaming back into the people again". How can we invoke this spirit in a time like ours, "a time of unspirituality and therefore of violence; unspirituality and therefore mighty tension within the spirits of individuals; individualism and therefore atomization, the masses uprooted and drifting like dust; a time without spirit and therefore without truth?" It is "a time of decay, and therefore of transition". But because this *is* so, in such a time and only in such a time will the spirit be conjured to reappear; such conjurations are the revolutions. What, however, makes room for the spirit is the attempt at realization. "Just as the County Communes and numerous other instruments of stratification and unification were there *before* the spirit filled them and made them what they have meant to Christendom; and just as a kind of walking is there before the legs develop, and just as this walking builds and fashions the legs—so it will not be the spirit that sends us on our way, but our way that will bring the spirit to birth in us." But this road leads "those who have perceived how impossible it is to go on living as they are, to join together and put their labour at the service of their needs. In settlements, in Societies—despite all privation". The spirit that animates such people helps them along their common way, and on this way and on it alone can it change into the new spirit of community. "We socialists want to give spirit the character of reality so that, as unitive spirit, it may bring mankind together. We socialists want to render the spirit sensible and corporeal, we want to enable it to do its work, and by these very means we shall spiritualize the senses and our earthly life." But for this to happen the flame of the spirit must be carefully tended in the settlements lest it go out. Only by virtue of living spirit are they a form of realization; without it they become a delusion. "But if the spirit lives in them it may breathe out into the world and suffuse all the seats of co-operation and association which, without it, are but empty shells, gaols rather than goals. We want to bring the Co-operatives, which are socialist form without socialist content, and the trades-unions, which are valour without avail—to Socialism, to great experiments." "Socialism," says Landauer in 1915, "is the attempt to lead man's common life to a bond of common spirit in freedom, that is, to religion." That is probably the only passage where Landauer, who always eschewed all religious symbolism and all open avowals of religion, uses the word "religion" in this positive and binding sense—uses it to express the thing he craves: a bond of common spirit in freedom.

This state of affairs should not wait on our expectations; it should be "attempted" and a beginning be made. In his striving for "common spirit" Landauer knows that there is no room for this without the land, i.e. that it can only have room to the extent that the soil once more supports man's communal life and work. "The struggle of socialism is the struggle for the soil." However, if the great upheaval is to occur in the "conditions of soil-ownership " (as it is called in the twelve Articles of the Socialist League founded by Landauer), "the workers must first create, on the basis of their common spirit—which is the capital of socialism—as much socialist reality, and exemplify it, as is possible at any time in proportion to their numbers and their energy." Here a beginning *can* be made. "Nothing can prevent the united consumers from working for themselves with the aid of mutual credit, from building factories, workshops, houses for themselves, from acquiring land; nothing—if only they have a will and begin." Such is the vision of the community, the archetype of the new society, that floats before Landauer's eyes; the vision of the socialist village. "A socialist village, with workshops and village factories," says Landauer in 1909, continuing Kropotkin's thought, "with fields and meadows and gardens, with livestock large and small, and poultry—you proletarians of the big cities, accustom yourselves to this thought, strange and odd as it may seem at first, for that is the only beginning of true socialism, the only one that is left us." On these seemingly small beginnings (on whether they arise or not), depends the revolution and whether it will find something worth fighting for—something which the hour of revolution itself is unable to create. But whether it finds this something and secures its full development, on this depends in its turn whether socialist fruit will ripen on revolutionary fields apart from the usual political crop.

Although, therefore, there is no beginning, no seed for the future other than what people now living under the rule of capitalism can achieve in their life together, in a common life based on common production and consumption, despite all the weariness, misery and disappointment—yet Landauer is far from regarding these results as the final form of realization. Like Proudhon and Kropotkin he, too, has little faith in hitching the demands of socialism to the dreams, visions, plans and deliberations of men living to-day. He knows well enough "the strange circumstance that this precarious beginning, this 'Socialism of the Few'—the settlement—bears many resemblances to the hard and toilsome communism of a primitive economy". Nevertheless the "essential thing" for him is "to accept this communist-looking state not as an ideal but as a necessity for the sake of socialism, as a first stage—because we are the beginners". From there the road will lead "as quickly as may be" to a society, in outlining which Landauer blends the ideas of Proudhon and Kropotkin: "a society of equalitarian exchange based on regional communities, rural communities which combine agriculture with industry." But even here Landauer does not see the absolute goal, only the immediate objective "so far as we can see into the future". All true socialism is relative. "Communism goes in search of the Absolute and can naturally find no beginning but that of the word. For the only absolute things, detached from all reality, are words."

Socialism can never be anything absolute. It is the continual becoming of human community in mankind, adapted and proportioned to whatever can be willed and done in the conditions given. Rigidity threatens all realization, what lives and glows to-day may be crusted over to-morrow and, become all-powerful, suppress the strivings of the day after. "Everywhere, wherever culture and freedom are to dwell in unison, the various bonds of order must complement one another, and the fixity of the whole must bear in itself the principle of dissolution.... In an age of true culture the order of private property, for instance, will bear in itself, as a revolutionary, dissolvent and re-ordering principle, the institution of *seisachtheia*[1] or Year of the Jubilee." True socialism watches over the forces of renewal. "No final security measures should be taken to establish the millennium or eternity, but only a great balancing of forces, and the resolve periodically to renew the

---

[1] A "shaking off of burdens", the name given to the "disburdening ordinance" of Solon, by which all debts were lowered. Trans.

balance. . . . 'Then may you cause trumpets to be blown throughout the land!' The voice of the spirit is the trumpet. . . . Revolt for constitution; reform and revolution the one rule valid for all time; order through the spirit the one intention—these were the great and holy things in the Mosaic order of society. We need them again, we need redirection and convulsion through the spirit, which has no desire to fix things and institutions in their final forms, but only to declare itself everlastingly. Revolution must become the accessory of our social order, the corner-stone of our constitution."

VII

EXPERIMENTS

WITH the same over-simplification that labelled the early socialists "utopian", people called the two great waves of the Co-operative Movement that agitated the bulk of the working population of England and France in 1830 and 1848, "romantic"—and with no greater justification in so far as this word implies dreaminess and unreality of outlook.   These waves were no less expressions of the deep-seated crises accompanying the mechanization of modern economy than were the political movements proper—Chartism in England and the two Revolutions in France. But, as distinct from the latter, which wanted to alter the whole hierarchy of power, the Co-operative Movements wanted to begin with the creation of social reality, without which no amount of tinkering with legal relationships can ever lead to socialism. They have been accused of rating man's share in the desired transformation too high and the share of circumstance too low; but there is no way of taking the measure of man's potentialities in a given situation that has to be changed, except by demanding the extraordinary. The "heroic" forms of the Co-operative Movement credited their members with a loyalty and readiness for sacrifice which, in the long run at any rate, they were unable to meet; but that does not prove in the least that loyalty and readiness for sacrifice, present though they may be in exceptional periods of political upheaval, cannot be found to a sufficient degree in the daily round of economic life. It is easy to scoff and say that the initiators of the heroic Co-operative Movements "put the ideal man in the place of the real one"; but the "real" man approximates most closely to the "ideal" just when he is expected to fulfil tasks which he is not up to, or thinks he is not up to—not of the individual alone is it true that "he grows to his higher purposes". And finally, it depends on the goal, the consciousness of it and will for it. The heroic epoch of the modern Co-operative looked to the transformation of society, the epoch of technics looks essentially to the economic success of each individual co-operative undertaking. The first has come to grief, but that does not condemn the goal and the way towards it; the second has great successes to record, but they do not look at all like stages on the way to the goal. A champion of the bureaucratized co-operative system expresses himself thus on its origin: "Let us give our fullest admiration to those humble and faithful souls who were guided by the burning torch of social conviction. . . . But let us acknowledge that heroism is not in itself a condition of soul fitted to bring about economic results." True enough; but let us also acknowledge that economic results are not in themselves fitted to bring about a restructuring of human society.

As regards the three chief forms of co-operation (apart from the Credit Co-operatives), to wit, Consumer Co-operatives, Producer Co-operatives, and Full Co-operatives[1] based on the union of production and consumption—let us compare a few dates taken from the two epochs of this movement.

The 1830 epoch: 1827 saw the first English Consumer Co-operative in the modern sense founded under the influence of the ideas of Dr. William King; 1832 the first French Producer Co-operative set up according to the plans of Buchez; in between the experimental "settlements" of Owen and his adherents—the American experiment and the English ones.

The 1848 epoch: first the Consumer Co-operative of the Rochdale weavers, then Louis Blanc's "national workshops" and the like, finally, by way of travesty, the tragi-comic "Icaria" project of Cabet (who was a *real* Utopian in the negative sense, a social constructionist without the slightest understanding of human fundamentals) on the banks of the Mississippi. Of these no more will be said here—as attempts to realize "utopian" Socialism—than is deemed desirable for the purpose of this book.

King and Buchez were both doctors and both, in contrast to Owen—whose war against religion was one of the main tasks of his life—practising Christians, one Protestant, one Catholic. This is not without significance. For Owen socialism was the fruit of reason, for King and Buchez it was the realization of the teachings of Christianity in the domain of public

---

[1] *Vollgenossenschaft* is evidently a term coined by the author. It is here translated literally since no equivalent term is to be found in the English authorities. Trans.

life. Both held, as Buchez says, that the moment had come "to mould the teachings of Christianity into social institutions". This basic religious feeling profoundly influenced the whole outlook of the two men; with King, who was in sympathy with the Quakers and worked together with them, it influenced the very tone of his words—everywhere we feel an unabstract, immediate, upwelling concern for his fellow-men, their life and soul.

King has justly been called in our own day—once he was rescued from oblivion—the first and greatest of the English theoreticians of the Co-operative Movement. But over and above this he had the gift of the simple word, which made plain to everybody the essential nature of the things he spoke of. In the whole literature of the Co-operatives I know nothing that gives such an impression of the "popular" and the "classical" alike as do the twenty-eight numbers of the magazine called *The Co-operator*, which King wrote and brought out between 1828 and 1830 for the instruction of those who were actively spreading his ideas. He had a depth and clarity of social perception like none of his contemporaries, with the exception of the more scientific, but also more abstract, William Thompson. He starts from work as "the root of the tree, to whatever size it may ultimately grow". Work is "in this sense everything". The working classes "have the monopoly of this article". No power on earth can rob them of it, for all power is "nothing more than the power to direct the labour of the working classes". What they lack is capital, that is, disposal of the machines and the possibility of maintaining themselves whilst working them. But "all capital is made out of labour", and it is "nothing in itself". It has to unite with labour in order to be productive. This union is now achieved by capital "buying and selling the labourer like a brute". True union, "the natural alliance", can only be brought about by the working-classes themselves, only they do not know it. Their sole hope of achieving it is to get together, co-operate, make common capital, become independent. King gives passionate expression to the thought already uttered by Thompson before him, of co-operation as the form of production peculiar to labour. "As soon as ever the labourers unite upon a labour principle instead of a capital principle, they will make the dust fly in all directions . . . and it is great odds but this dust will blind some of the masters." If the workers get together they can acquire the tools they need—the machines—and themselves become, in their Co-operatives, the subject of production. But they can also acquire the land. King says clearly that he sees only a beginning in the Consumer Co-operatives, that his goal, like Thompson's, is the Full Co-operative. As soon as they can dispose of sufficient capital the "Society", that is, the Co-operative Society, "may purchase land, live upon it, cultivate it themselves and produce any manufactures they please, and so provide for all their wants of food, clothing, and houses. The Society will then be called a Community." King calls upon the trades-unions to purchase land with their savings and settle their unemployed members on it in communities producing above all for their own needs. These communities will embrace not merely the specific interests and functions of their members but their life as well, in so far as they want and are able to live it in common. But the life-community, even if it can only come to full reality in the Full Co-operative, should already exist potentially in the relations of the members of the Consumer Co-operative to one another. King is thinking not of a bare impersonal solidarity but of a personal relationship, generally latent yet ready at any time to become actual, a "sympathy that would act with new energies, and rise occasionally even to enthusiasm". Hence only members capable of such a relation are admitted. The basic law of co-operative means, for King, the establishment of genuine relations between man and man. "When a man enters a Co-operative Society, he enters upon a new relation with his fellow men; and that relation immediately becomes the subject of every sanction, both moral and religious." It is obvious that this ideal, this "heroic" demand could not be upheld in succeeding years, when membership of the Co-operatives increased with their growing mechanization and bureaucratization; but seen from the standpoint of social re-structure, this is the cause of the inadequacy of these "partial" Co-operatives.

When William King suspended publication of *The Co-operator* in 1830, three hundred Societies had come into being under the influence of his teachings. These for the most part did not live long because of the "spirit of selfishness" reigning in them. as one of the leaders told the Congress of 1832. The crucial stage of the consumer-based Co-operatives did not begin until 1844, when in the grave industrial crisis which had once again descended upon England shortly after the collapse of a strike, a little group of flannel-weavers and representatives of other trades met in the city of Rochdale to ask one another: "What can we do to save ourselves from misery?" There were not a few among them who thought that each man must begin with himself—and indeed that is always right in all circumstances, for without it nothing can ever succeed; only one must know that it is merely a part of what has to be done, albeit an important part. And because they did not know this they proposed to renounce the pleasures of alcohol, and they naturally failed to convince their comrades. (How important none the less the proposal seemed can be seen from the fact that subsequently, in the Statutes of the "Equitable Pioneers of Rochdale", the erection of a Temperance Hotel was mentioned on the agenda of the Society.) And again there were some, members of the Chartist Movement which aimed at altering the Constitution and seizing power, who proposed that they should ally themselves to political action so as to win for Labour its due share in legislation; but the movement had passed its peak and they had learned that although the political struggle was necessary it was not enough. Some of Owen's adherents who were among those assembled declared that there was no hope for them in England any more and that they must emigrate and build a new life for themselves abroad (thinking perhaps of the possibility of new experimental Settlements in America); but that too was rejected, for the predominant feeling was: "doing" means doing *here*, means not fleeing before the crisis but enduring it with what strength one has. This strength was little enough, yet a few of the weavers who were fairly familiar with the teachings of William King pointed out that they could put their strengths together and then perhaps a power would be there with which they could *do* something. So they decided to "co-operate".

The tasks the Society set itself were put very high, without the authors of the statutes being accused of overbold imagination. These tasks were ranged in three stages. The first, the Consumer Co-operative, was regarded as something to be organized at once. The second, the Producer Co-operative, comprising the common building of houses for the members, the common production of wares and the common cultivation of allotments by unemployed comrades, was likewise a prospect for a not far distant future, though not the immediate future.

The third stage, the Co-operative Settlement, was removed still further by the proviso "as soon as practicable": "as soon as practicable this Society shall proceed to arrange the powers of production, distribution, education, and government; or, in other words, to establish a self-supporting Home Colony of united interests or assist other Societies in establishing such Colonies." It is amazing how the practical intuition of the flannel-weavers of Rochdale grasped the three essential fields of co-operation. In the first field, the Consumer Co-operative, their simple and effective methods (among which the distribution of profits among members according to the relative volume of purchases proved to be particularly persuasive) blazed a new trail. In the field of production they made a number of advances with increasing success, particularly in corn-milling but also in the field of spinning and weaving; yet it is characteristic of the whole problem (to be discussed later) of co-operative activity in production that, in the steam spinning-mills constructed by the Equitable Pioneers, only about half the workers were members of the Society, and hence stockholders, and that these immediately put through the principle of rewarding work with payment but of distributing the profit exclusively among the stockholders as "*entrepreneurs* and owners of the business", as the important co-operationist Victor Aimé Huber, who repeatedly visited Rochdale in its early days, remarks in his monograph on the Pioneers. They did not, however, get down to the third, the greatest and decisive task, of realizing the Co-operative Colony based on joint production and consumption.

One element in the Rochdale institution deserves our particular attention. That is the co-operation between the Co-operatives, the working together of several co-operative groups and institutes, which was undertaken by the "Pioneers" themselves and, later, in conjunction with them. "The principle of Federalism," says the Rumanian scholar Mladenatz in his *History of the Co-operative Theories*, obviously basing himself on Proudhon, "derives quite naturally from the idea itself, which is the foundation of the co-operative system. Just as the Co-operative Society unites people for the common satisfaction of certain needs, so the various co-operative cells unite one with another by applying the principle of solidarity for the common exercise of certain functions, particularly those of production and supply." Here we again meet the arch-principle of restructuring, although naturally the consumer associations as such, i.e. Co-operatives which only combine certain interests of people but not the lives of the people themselves, do not appear suited to serve as cells of a new structure.

The modern Consumer Co-operative which has become so great a reality in the economic life of our time derives from the ideas of "utopian" socialism. In William King's plans there is a clearly discernible tendency to reach the great socialist reality through the creation of small socialist realities which keep on expanding and confederating continually. But King recognized at the same time, and with the utmost clarity, the nature of the technological revolution that had started in his day. He recognized the cardinal significance of the machine and approved it; he rejected all assaults on machines as "folly and criminality". But he also recognized that the inventors, who are workers too, destroy themselves and their comrades with their "wonderful inventions", because "by selling these inventions to their masters they work *against* themselves, instead of keeping them in their own hands and working *with* them". For this it is necessary, of course, that the workers should constitute themselves co-operatively in their Societies. "The workmen have ingenuity enough to make all the machinery in the world, but they have not yet had ingenuity enough to make it work *for* them. This ingenuity will not be dormant much longer." Consequently co-operative organization of consumption is, for King, only a step towards the co-operative organization of production, but this in its turn is only a step towards the co-operative building of life as a whole.

In the hundred years since its inception the Consumer Co-operative has conquered a considerable portion of the civilized world, but the hopes that King set on its internal development have not yet been fulfilled. Consumer Societies may in many places, and sometimes to a very great extent, have turned to production for their own needs, and there exists, as Fritz Naphtali rightly stresses, a tendency to penetrate more and more deeply into production and guide it in the direction of "basic" production. But we have hardly come any nearer to an organic alliance of production and consumption in a comprehensive communal form, although we already have notable examples of large Consumer Societies—or groups of the same for individual branches of production—organizing themselves into Producer Co-operatives, or assimilating existing

ones; but that is only technical organization, not the fulfilment of genuine co-operative thought. And just as little has
the confederation of local societies, even where this has occurred
on a large scale, preserved a genuine federative character; in
these cases the small Societies have mostly, as was reported
several decades ago, changed from independent foci of social
solidarity into mere organs of membership, and their stores into
mere branches of the organization as a whole. The technological
advantages of such centralization are obvious; the trouble is
that there was no authority at hand to try to salvage as much
autonomy in the individual Societies as was compatible with
technological requirements, although people did try here and
there—for instance in Switzerland—to counteract the progressive "de-souling" and de-substantiation of the Societies by
planned decentralization. But for the most part the running
of large co-operative institutions has become more and more
like the running of capitalist ones, and the bureaucratic
principle has completely ousted, over a very wide field, the
voluntary principle, once prized as the most precious and
indispensable possession of the Co-operative Movement. This is
especially clear in countries where Consumer Societies have in
increasing measure worked together with the State and the
municipalities, and Charles Gide was certainly not far wrong
when he called to mind the fable of the wolf disguised as a
shepherd and voiced the fear that, instead of making the State
"co-operative", we should only succeed in making the Co-
operative "static". For the spirit of solidarity can in truth only
remain alive to the extent that a living relationship obtains
between human beings. Tönnies thought that in their
transition to communal buying and then to producing
for their own needs the Consumer Societies would "lay the
foundations of an economic organization that would stand in
open opposition to the existing social order", and that *in theory*
"the capitalist world would therefore be lifted off its hinges".
But "theory" can never become reality so long as the life-
forms of capitalism permeate co-operative activity.

Buchez, who came shortly after King and who planned and
inspired the founding of Producer Co-operatives in France, is
likewise a "utopian" socialist at bottom. "The Communist
reform that is everywhere in the air," he writes in his magazine
L'Européen in 1831, "should be implemented by the *association*
of workers." For Buchez—who, although a Catholic, graduated

in the school of Saint-Simon where he was in sympathy with the radical socialist Bazard—production is everything and the organization of consumption not even a stage. In his opinion the Producer Co-operative—by which he, with less understanding of technological developments than King, means manual workers rather than modern industrial workers—leads directly to the socialist order. "The workers of a particular trade unite, put their savings together, raise a loan, produce as they think best, repay the borrowed capital despite great privations, ensure that each man gets equal pay, and leave the profits in the common funds, with the result that the co-operative workshop becomes a little industrial community." *Une petite communauté industrielle*—here Buchez comes close to King's idea that a Society can become a Community, save that he prematurely ascribes this character to the Producer Co-operative as such, whereas King's deeper insight envisaged such a possibility only for the Full Co-operative. Buchez concludes with the simple, all too simple, formula: "Let all the workers do this and the social problem will be solved." He knew well enough that the great problem of ownership of the land was not solved by it in the least, so he devised the makeshift slogan: "The land for the peasants, the workshop for the workers" without appreciating the question of the social reform of agriculture in its true import; the problem of evolving a Full Co-operative, the all-important problem of social re-structure, was hidden from him, though not from King. On the other hand Buchez recognized with astounding acuteness most of the dangers that threaten the socialist character of the Producer Co-operative from within, one above all, the increasing differentiation inside the Co-operative in its initial stages between those comrades who have founded it and the workers who come afterwards—a differentiation which lends the Co-operative, though it plead socialism never so energetically, the incontestable stamp of an appendage to the capitalist order. To eliminate this danger Buchez built two counter-measures into the modified programme he published after his first practical experiences of 1831: firstly the "social capital" accruing at any time from the putting by of a fifth of the profits was to remain the inalienable, indivisible property of the Society, which was itself to be declared indissoluble and was to replenish itself continually by taking on new members; and secondly, the Society might not employ outside workers as wage-earners for longer than one year, after which time it was bound to accept new comrades according to its requirements (in a sample contract published in 1840 in the journal of the Buchezites, *L'Atelier*, the term was reduced to a trial period of three months). To the first of these points Buchez says that, but for this capital the Society "would resemble all the other trade societies; it would be useful only to the founders and harmful to all who had taken no part in the beginning, for in the hands of the former it would ultimately become an instrument of exploitation". As has rightly been said, this programme aimed at the creation of a capital which would finally absorb "the industrial capital of the whole country and thus realize the appropriation of all the means of production through Workers' Co-operatives". Here, too, we find that "utopian" element again; but, which is the more practical in the last analysis: to try to create social reality through social reality, with its rights defended and extended by political means, or to try to create by the magic wand of politics alone? Naturally enough the two rules were only followed very irregularly by the Societies founded under Buchez' influence, and after twenty years the principle of indivisible capital was made so questionable that those who remained true to it had to wage a hard and virtually fruitless fight for it, as for the principle whereby the conditions of property would be changed and capital would come under the rule of work—a principle that had to be upheld if the Co-operative was to benefit the whole of the working-class and not merely "the few fortunate founders who, thanks to it, had become *rentiers* instead of wage-earners". And just about this time, 1852, we read of similar experiences in England in a report of the Society for the Promotion of Working-men's Associations. But from all of them, from the analogous experiences in the Middle Ages as also from similar experiences in the history of the Consumer Societies, there is no other conclusion to be drawn save that the internal problems of the Co-operatives and the dominance of the capitalist principle that still persists in them can be overcome, albeit gradually, only in and through the Full Co-operative.

It is likely that Louis Blanc was influenced by Buchez' thought; but he differs from him on decisive points. At the same time the important thing is not that he demanded, as Lassalle did later for his Worker-Producer Co-operatives, State help for the "social workshops" he wanted to found, since "what the proletariat lacks in order to free itself is tools, and it is the government's job to deliver them". That was, of course, a deep-seated error, indeed a contradiction in terms, since a government representative of a definite State-order cannot very well be urged to call institutions into being which are destined (such was Blanc's express meaning) to abolish that order. It was only logical, therefore, that the anti-socialist majority in the Provisional Government of 1848 should first replace Blanc's plan by a caricature and then play havoc even with this; but as regards the nature of the social reform he planned this demand of Blanc's was not absolutely essential. Far more significant is the fact that Blanc's social programme was itself centralist in thought: he wanted each large industry to constitute itself as a single association by grouping itself round a central workshop. He gave this basically Saint-Simonistic thought a federalist tinge by demanding that the solidarity of all the workers in one workshop should be continued in the solidarity of all the workshops in one branch of industry and finally completed in the solidarity of all the branches of industry; but what he called solidarity was in actual fact more like solidification into centralist management with monopoly status. Well might Blanc be anxious to attack "the cowardly and brutal principle" of competition, as he once called it in the National Assembly, at the root; that is, to prevent collective competition from emerging in the place of individual competition. And this is indeed the chief danger, apart from internal differentiation, that threatens the Producer Co-operative. A good example of the widespread incidence of this danger is afforded by a letter written by one of the leaders of the Christian-Socialist Co-operative movement in England at that time, in which he says of the Producer Co-operatives founded by this movement that they were "actuated by a thoroughly mercenary competitive spirit" and "aimed merely at a more successful competition than is possible under the present system". This danger was recognized by Buchez and his adherents; but they refused to combat it with monopolies which seemed to them even more dangerous, because monopoly meant for them the paralysis, the end of all organic development. According to their proposals competition between the Co-operatives was rather to be organized and regulated by means of a league of the Co-operatives themselves. Here free federation opposes planned amalgamation. But we have to acknowledge that the federalist idea crops up again and again with Blanc and bursts the centralist strait-jacket, particularly of course after the failure of his State plan. He gives a twist to Buchez' plan for reserve funds by intending it to "realize the principle of mutual help and solidarity between the various social workshops". But as soon as he proceeds from the plan for State initiative to the planning of free Co-operatives he sees no other way of reaching this goal except the way of federation, beginning with the Co-operatives already existing; these are to come to an understanding with one another and name a Central Committee which shall organize throughout the country "the most important of all subscriptions—the subscription to abolish the proletariat". Such words are midway between the sublime and the ridiculous; but the call to the proletariat for self-abolition through co-operation implies a certain practical seriousness which is not without significance for the time that followed. And towards the end of 1849 we see Blanc expressing his approval of the *Union des associations fraternelles*, which arose out of the federation of more than a hundred Co-operatives and realized his enemy Proudhon's idea of the *mutualité du travail;* backing himself up, of course, by saying that on the agenda of the Union there was talk of "centralizing business-matters of general interest". Everywhere in Blanc we come across thoughts which belong to the living tradition and context of "utopian" socialism. He sees the Producer Co-operative emerging into the Full Co-operative in the future, just as King saw the Consumer Co-operative merging into it; in which respect, just as the *Union des associations fraternelles* praised by him aimed at establishing, *as a federation*, "agricultural and industrial colonies" on a large scale, so he was aiming at the creation of Communal Home Colonies. His starting-point is the technological necessity for large-scale concerns: "We must inaugurate a system of large-scale concerns for agriculture by linking them up with association and common ownership," and he wants if possible to transplant industry to the country and "wed industrial work to agricultural". Here, too, Kropotkin's idea of a "division of labour in time", of the union of agriculture, industry and handicraft in a modern village-community, is anticipated.

Despite the early suppression of the Co-operative Federations by the Reaction, numerous new Producer Co-operatives came into being in France during the following years; even doctors and chemists united on a co-operative basis (in these cases there could obviously be no question of genuine Producer Co-operatives, since there is no place for communal work here). The enthusiasm for Co-operatives outlasted the Revolution. Even the persecution and dissolution of many of the Co-operatives after the *coup d'état* was unable to check the movement. The real danger threatening them here as in England came from within: their capitalization, their gradual transformation into capitalist or semi-capitalist societies. Forty years after the enthusiastic efforts, beginning about 1850, of the English Christian Socialists to create a wide net of Workers' Producer Co-operatives which "rejected any notion of competition with each other as inconsistent with the true form of society", Beatrice Webb stated that with the exception of a few Co-operatives which had remained more or less true to the ideal of a "brotherhood of workers"—most of which, however, had become questionable at one point or another—all the rest "exhibit an amazing variety of aristocratic, plutocratic and monarchical constitutions".   And fifty years after Louis Blanc there was a thoroughly typical (in this respect) Producer Co-operative in France, that of the spectacle-makers, which, apart from a small number of *associés* and approximately as many *adhérents*, employed ten times as many wage-earners.   Despite this, however, we can find perfect examples of the inner battle for socialism everywhere.   Sometimes there is something tragic about them, but equally something prophetic.   The Producer Co-operative has rightly been called "the child of sorrows and the darling" of all those "who expect the Co-operative Movement to produce something essential for the salvation of mankind"; but it is readily understandable from the facts that a champion of the Consumer Co-operative Societies should call the Producer Co-operatives which work for the open market "thoroughly unsocialistic in spirit and in essence", because "producers, set up by and for themselves, always and in all circumstances have separatist, individualist or cliquish interests".   Apart, however, from the exaggeration inherent in such an assertion, Producer Co-operatives above all should never be "set up by and for themselves". Two great principles should together guard against this: the combination of production and consumption in the Full Co-operative, and Federalism.

The development of the Consumer Co-operative follows the

straight line of numerical progression; a considerable portion of civilized mankind (characteristically enough, outside America) is organized to-day, from the consumption side, on co-operative lines. On the other hand the development of the Producer Co-operatives (I speak here only of the Producer Co-operative in the strict sense, not of the many partial, in the main agricultural associations which aim merely at making production easier or more intensive), can be represented as a zig-zag line which, on the whole, shows hardly any upward trend. New ones are always coming into being, but again and again most of the more vigorous ones pass over into the sphere of capitalism; there is hardly any continuity. The Full Co-operative, however, is in different case; its development, so far as there is one, looks like a cluster of small circles between which there is generally no real connexion. Consumer and Producer Co-operatives were based on an extensive movement which spread to locality after locality; Colonies in the Full Co-operative sense have always had something sporadic, improvised, lacking in finality about them. In contrast to the others they also lacked what Franz Oppenheimer has termed "the power of remote effect". Not but what some of them got themselves talked about; but their power of attraction was individualistic, they did not call new community-cells into being. In the history of Co-operative Colonies, neither in Europe (with the exception of Soviet Russia, where, however, the essential basis of free will and autonomy does not exist) nor with few exceptions in America is there any indication of a federative tendency. Consumer Co-operatives have continually and increasingly federated; Producer Co-operatives in the true sense have done so discontinuously, now on the increase, now on the decrease; communal Colonies in general not at all. Their fate is at odds with their will: originally they did not want to become isolated, but they did become isolated; they wanted to become working models, but they only became interesting experiments; they wanted to be the dynamic and dynamitic beginnings of a social transformation, but each had its end in itself. The cause of this difference between the Consumer and Producer Co-operative on the one hand and Full Co-operative on the other seems to me ultimately to lie in an essential difference of starting-point. The former grew out of given situations which were roughly the same in a whole chain of places and factories, so that from the start there was a germ of reciprocal influence in the experiments undertaken to get the situation in hand, and hence the germ of their federation. In addition the plans that inspired the founding of these Co-operatives did not derive from one all-embracing thought, but from a question addressed, as it were, to the planners by the situation itself. We can accurately follow this process with King and Buchez, because both were federalists at the outset; Buchez even had a federative association in mind for the trades-unions he had proposed. In both cases the plans were directed towards remedying a given state of distress, and they bore a local character in so far as they sought to solve the problems of this emergency at the point where these problems brought themselves to bear. Such plans may be called topical in the precise sense of being locative, inasmuch as they were of their own nature related to definite localities, the very ones in which the problems arose. The identity of the problems in different places led at once to the possibility of federative union, right up to gigantic formations like some associations of Consumer Co-operatives to-day.

It is a fundamentally different story with the generality of "colonial" Full Co-operatives. Here, time after time, with greater or lesser independence of the situation but always without real reference to given localities and their demands, we see the "idea" dictating its decrees, preparing its plans some-where up in the clouds and then bringing them down to earth. No matter how speculative these plans are in origin and there-fore thoroughly schematic as with Fourier; no matter how much they are based on definite experiences and empirical assumptions as with Owen, they will never answer the questions put by a given situation, but will proceed to create new situations irrelevant to the locality and its local problems. This becomes peculiarly evident where Settlements in foreign countries are concerned: emigration is not organized and regulated along socialistic lines, no such thing; rather the impulse to emigrate is associated with a new impulse, namely, the will to have a share in the realization of a social project; and this will is all too frequently coerced into the dogmatism of some organization felt and believed to be the only right one, the only just and true organization, the binding claims of which sometimes stand in opposition to the free play of relationships between members. (Community of sentiment is hardly ever sufficient to establish community of life; for this a deeper and more vital bond is required.) The Settlement that remains faithful to dogma is threatened with paralysis; one that increasingly rebels against it, with fragmentation; and both lack the corrective, modifying power of insight into conditions. Wherever dogma reigns supreme, isolation of the Settlement is the sole result; the exclusiveness of "the only right form" precludes union even with like-minded establishments, for in every single one of them the "faithful" are completely obsessed with the absolute character of their unique achievement. But equally, wherever dogma retreats, the economic and spiritual seclusion of the Settlement, especially in a strange country, succumbs to the same fate—isolation, lack of connective power, ineffectuality. None of these things would be so important if some great educative force, sustained by a vigorous upsurge of life and fate, could assure to the communal will a lasting victory over the residue of egoism that inevitably goes with it, or rather raise this egoism to a higher form. But usually it is only the case that collective egoism, i.e. egoism with a clear conscience, emerges in place of individual egoism; and if the latter always threatens to disintegrate the inner cohesion of the community, the former, which is often tainted with dogmatism, prevents the growth of any real communal education as between one community and another, between the community and the world.

Most of the known experimental Settlements came to grief or petered out—and not, as some think, the communist ones alone. Here we must exempt the individual efforts of various religious sects, efforts whose vitality can only be understood in terms of a particular group's faith and as the partial manifestation of this faith; it is characteristic that the federative form makes its appearance here and here alone, as, for instance, with the Russian sect of the Dukhobors in Canada or the "Hutterite Brothers". It is, therefore, unjust of Kropotkin to trace the collapse of the experimental communist Settlements to the fact that they were "founded on an uprush of religiosity, instead of seeing in the commune simply a mode of consumption and production economically ordered". For it is precisely where a Settlement comes into being as the expression of real religious exaltation, and not merely as a precarious substitute for religion, and where it views its existence as the beginning of God's kingdom—that it usually proves its powers of endurance.

Among the causes which Kropotkin adduces for the collapse of most of the Settlements two are worthy of particular note, though at bottom they are one and the same: isolation from society and isolation from each other. He is in error when he imputes the cause to the smallness of the Commune, thinking, as he says, that in such a Commune its members would acquire a distaste for one another after a few years of living together so closely: for, among the Settlements that have lasted at all, we find small ones as well as large ones. But he is right to demand federation to make up for the smallness of the groups. The fact that federation enables members to pass from one settlement to another (which is of crucial importance for Kropotkin), is in reality only one among its many favourable results; the vital thing is federation itself, the complementing and helping of each group by the others, the stream of communal life flowing between them and gathering strength from each. No less important, however, is the fact that the Settlements stand in some relation, if a varying one, to society at large—not merely because they need a market for their surplus production, not merely because youth, as Kropotkin points out, does not tolerate being cut off, but because the Settlements must, in so far as they do not possess that specifically Messianic faith, influence the surrounding world in order to live at all. Whoever bears a message must be able to express it, not necessarily in words, but necessarily in his being.

To a query coming from Settlement circles Kropotkin once answered with an open letter to all Settlement-minded groups stressing the fact that any commonwealth worthy the name must be founded on the principle of association between independent families that join forces. What he meant was that even the individual group must spring from a union of the smallest communal units, federatively. If the federative movement is to extend beyond the group, space is needed: "The experiment," he says in his book *Modern Science and Anarchy*, "must be made on a definite *territory*." He adds that this territory must comprise both town and country. Once more economic motifs have to be geared to the great social motif; genuine community-life means the full play of all the functions and interaction between them, not restriction and seclusion. But it is not enough, as Kropotkin seems to assume that it is, for a town "to make itself into a commune"; if it confronts the finely articulated federation of villages as an unco-ordinated

and socially amorphous entity, it is bound to exert rather a
negative influence in the long run. It has to co-ordinate itself,
convert itself *as a federation* into societies in order to engage in
really fruitful intercourse with the villages. Already we can see
significant moves in this direction in the "planned economy"
theories of our time, the result, mostly, of technical and
managerial considerations.

From their long and instructive history we can only give
here one characteristic example of the problematical career of
the many experimental Settlements to date—Owen's first
establishment in this kind, the only one that was his own work:
New Harmony in Indiana. He bought the property from the
sect of "Separatists" that had immigrated from Germany; after
twenty years of work they had managed to make it produce
a few blossoms. Members were accepted unselectively; the
important German political economist Friedrich List noted at
the time in his American Diary: "The elements don't seem to be
of the best." In the beginning the Constitution of the new
community was based on complete equality between members,
for which reason it was also called "The Community of
Equality". Two years later, after a number of separate groups
had branched off, an attempt had to be made to transform the
community into an association of little societies. But this and
similar plans for conversion failed. When Owen, returning
from a journey to England, saw the Settlement again after it
had lasted three years, he had to confess that "the attempt to
unite a number of strangers not previously educated for the
purpose, who should live together as a common family, was premature", and that "the habits of the individual system" die
hard. By selling one part of the land in lots and leasing another
in the same way—the experiment cost him a fifth of his fortune
—he replaced the Society by a complex of Settlements run on
private capitalist lines, only giving them this piece of advice by
the way: "To unite their general labour, or to exchange labour
for labour on the terms most beneficial for all, or to do both or
neither, as their feelings and apparent interests may influence
them."

Here we have an example of a Settlement that came to
grief not on dogma—despite his definite plans Owen did not
commit himself on this point—but rather on the lack of any
deep, organic bond between its members.

As an example of the opposite we may cite the development

of Cabet's "Icaria". Undertaken as an attempt to realize a
dilettante but successful Utopian novel, born after terrific
disappointments and privations and, like Owen's Settlement,
the former property of a sect—this time that of the Mormons—
the Settlement, during the half-century from its beginnings
right up to its final ramifications, underwent schism after
schism. First of all there was a schism because Cabet (a tem-
peramental and honestly enthusiastic man, but mediocre)
made a bid for dictatorship in the form of dogmatic planning,
a bid which kindled a civil war of vituperation and fisticuffs.
Of the two groups to which the schism gave rise, the first
crumbled into nothing after Cabet's death; in the second a new
schism sprang up between the "Young" and the "Old", the
"young" championing the dogmatic plan to abolish, for instance, the little gardens that surrounded the houses where the
members could pluck not only flowers but fruit as well. Here
indeed was a deplorable "remnant of individualism". The
affair—after being judicially decided—resulted in the division
of the Settlement, the part that contained buildings put up by
the "Old" with their own hands being allotted to the "Young".
The part remaining to the "Old" lasted another twenty years
and then died of "senile decay". The economic forces were
strong enough to survive, but the power of belief was extinguished. "We were so few and so like the people outside,"
writes a female member, "that it was not worth the effort to
live in the community." The "Young" Settlement was even
shorter-lived. After all kinds of difficulties they moved to
California, but under the new organization the principle of
private ownership took a significant place, so that the Settlement has not unjustly been compared with a joint-stock
company; it soon disbanded itself, the appreciation of land-
values being a determining factor, perhaps. So the career of
Icaria runs in a strange sequence of dogmatism and oppor-
tunism. "We had a furious will to succeed," wrote one of the
members several years later, "but the garment we wore was
too heavy for us and too long, it trailed at times in the mud;
by which I mean to say that the Old Adam in us, or the beast,
inadequately repressed, made a violent appearance." But it was
not the beast at all, it was only the specifically human species of
egoism.

Let us look, finally, at the three chief kinds of "Society"
from the point of view of social restructure.

By far the most powerful of them historically, the Consumer Co-operative Society, is least suited in itself to act as a cell of social reconstruction. It brings people together with only a minimal and highly impersonal part of their total being. This part is not, as might be supposed at first glance, consumption. Common consumption as such has a great power to unite people; and, as we know from ancient times, there is no better symbol of communal life than the banquet. But the Consumer Co-operative is concerned not with consumption proper but with purchases for consumption. Common purchasing as such lays no very significant demands on the individuals participating in it, unless it be in exceptional times when it is a question of common care and responsibility for a common task, as in the "heroic" age of the Co-operative Movement or in the crises since then, when private persons came forward in a spirit of sacrifice to alleviate the distress of the many. Similarly, as soon as common purchasing becomes a business, responsibility for which passes to the employees, it ceases to unite people in any significant sense. The bond becomes so loose and impersonal that there can be no question of communal cells and their association in a complex organic structure, even if the co-operative organization of this or that branch of production is linked up with the Co-operative's warehouses. I find this view expressed with great clarity in a book by the Irish poet George William Russell ("A. E."), *The National Being;* a book written with true patriotism and dealing with the social reconstruction of Ireland. He says: "It is not enough to organize farmers in a district for one purpose only—in a credit society, a dairy society, a fruit society, a bacon factory, or in a co-operative store. All these may be and must be beginnings; but if they do not develop and absorb all rural business into their organization they will have little effect on character. No true social organism will have been created. If people unite as consumers to buy together they only come into contact on this one point; there is no general identity of interest. If co-operative societies are specialized for this purpose or that—as in Great Britain or on the Continent—to a large extent the limitation of objects prevents a true social organism from being formed. The latter has a tremendous effect on human character. The specialized Society only develops economic efficiency. The evolution of humanity beyond its present level depends absolutely on its power to unite and create true social organisms." That precisely is what I understand by an organic re-structuring of society.

The Producer Co-operative is better suited in itself than the Consumer Co-operative to take part in a restructuring of this sort, i.e. to function as the cell of a new structure. Common production of goods implicates people more profoundly than a common acquisition of goods for individual consumption; it embraces much more of their powers and their lifetime. Man as producer is by nature more prepared to get together with his kind in an eminently active way than man as consumer; and is more capable of forming living social units. This is true of the employer, if and in so far as he draws more strength from the association for the discharge of his productive activity than he did and ever could as an individual. But it is particularly true of the employed, because only in and through the association does he draw any strength at all—the question is whether he will become vitally conscious of this opportunity and believe in its practical prospects. But as we have seen, he succumbs very easily, indeed almost with a kind of fatality, to the desire to get others to work for him. If the Consumer Co-operative adapts itself outwardly, in a technical and managerial sense, to the capitalistic pattern, the Producer Co-operative does so inwardly in a structural and psychological sense. At the same time the latter is itself more amenable to a genuine, not merely technical, federation; but just how little the paramount importance— from the point of view of re-structure—of small organic units and their organic-federative growth was recognized (even in those circles most enthusiastic for the regeneration of society by means of Producer Co-operatives), we actually saw two decades ago in the English Guild Socialist Movement. On the one hand the bold step was conceived of converting the State into a dual system: multiform, co-ordinated representation of producers, and uniform, mass-representation of consumers. But on the other hand, there soon manifested itself a Saint-Simonistic tendency aiming at "national" (i.e. embracing a whole branch of industry) guilds for "the regimentation into a single fellow-ship of all those employed in any given industry", which proved much stronger than the tendency to form "local" guilds, i.e. small organic units and their federation. If the principle of organic re-structuring is to become a determining factor the influence of the Full Co-operative will be needed, since in it production and consumption are united and industry is complemented by agriculture. However long it may take the Full Co-operative to become the cell of the new society, it is vitally important for it to start building itself up now as a far-reaching complex of interlocking, magnetic foci. A genuine and lasting reorganization of society from within can only prosper in the union of producers and consumers, each of the two partners being composed of independent and homogeneous co-operative units; a union whose power and vitality for socialism can only be guaranteed by a wealth of Full Co-operatives all working together and, in their functional synthesis, exercising a mediatory and unifying influence.

For this it is necessary, however, that in place of all the isolated experiments (condemned in the nature of things to isolation) that have made their appearance in the course of more than a hundred years of struggle, there should emerge a network of Settlements, territorially based and federatively constructed, without dogmatic rigidity, allowing the most diverse social forms to exist side by side, but always aiming at the new organic whole.

VIII

MARX AND THE RENEWAL
OF SOCIETY

WE have seen that it is the goal of Utopian socialism so-called
to substitute society for State to the greatest degree possible,
moreover a society that is "genuine" and not a State in disguise. The prime conditions for a genuine society can be summed
up as follows: it is not an aggregate of essentially unrelated
individuals, for such an aggregate could only be held together
by a "political", i.e. a coercive principle of government; it must
be built up of little societies on the basis of communal life and of
the associations of these societies; and the mutual relations of
the societies and their associations must be determined to the
greatest possible extent by the social principle—the principle of
inner cohesion, collaboration and mutual stimulation. In other
words: only a structurally rich society can claim the inheritance
of the State. This goal can be attained neither by a change in
the order of government, i.e. those who dispose of the means of
power, alone; nor by a change in the order of ownership, i.e.
those who dispose of the means of production, alone; nor yet by
any laws and institutions governing the forms of social life from
outside, alone—nor by a combination of all these. All these
things are necessary at certain stages of the transformation,
with the restriction, of course, that no coercive order shall
result which would standardize the whole and not tolerate the
emergence of those elements of spontaneity, internal dynamism
and diversity so indispensable to the evolution of a genuine
society. What, however, is essential, so essential that all these
phases should only subserve its full implementation, is the
growth of the genuine society itself, partly from already existing
societies to be renewed in form and meaning, partly from
societies to be built anew. The more such a society is actually
or potentially in being at the time of the changes, the more it

will be possible to realize socialism as an actuality in the changed order, that is, to obviate the danger of the power-principle—be it in political or economic form or both—finding entry again, and of the human relations—the real life of society—remaining, underneath the changed surface of laws and institutions, as hopelessly out of joint and askew as ever they were under the capitalist régime. Those changes in the economic and political order inevitably imply, as regards the realization of socialism, the necessary removal of obstacles, but no more and no less. Without such a change the realization of socialism remains nothing but an idea, an impulse and an isolated experiment; but without the actual re-structuring of society the change of order is only a façade. It is not to be supposed that the change comes first and the re-structuring afterwards; a society in transformation may well create for itself the instruments it needs for its maintenance, for its defence, for the removal of obstacles, but changed power-relations do not of themselves create a new society capable of overcoming the power-principle. "Utopian" socialism regards the various forms of Co-operative Society as being the most important cells for social re-structure; and the more "Utopianism" clarifies its ideas the more patently does the leading rôle seem to fall to the Producer-cum-Consumer Co-operative. The Co-operative is not an end in itself for the "Utopian", not even when a large measure of socialism has been successfully realized within it; the point is rather to produce the substance which will then be released by the new order, established in its own right so as to unify the multifarious cells. Genuine "utopian" socialism can be termed "topical" socialism in a specific sense: it is not without *topographical* character, it seeks to realize itself in a given place and under given conditions, that is, "here and now", and to the greatest degree possible here and now. But it regards the local realization (and this has become increasingly clear as the idea has developed) as nothing but a point of departure, a beginning, something that must be there for the big realization to join itself on to; that must be there if this realization is to fight for its freedom and win universal validity; that must be there if the new society is to arise out of it, out of all its cells and those they make in their likeness.

Let us, at this juncture, put the decisive questions of means and ends to Marx and Marxism.

Right from his earliest socialistic formulations up to the full maturity of his thought Marx conceived the end in a way that comes very close to "utopian" Socialism. As early as in August, 1844, he was writing (in his essay *Critical Glosses*): "Revolution as such—the overthrow of existing power and the dissolution of the old conditions—is a political act. But without Revolution socialism cannot carry on. Socialism needs this political act in so far as it needs destruction and dissolution. But when its organizing activity begins, when its ultimate purpose, its soul emerges, socialism will throw the political husk away." We must read this in conjunction with the following passage written earlier on in the same year (*On the Jewish Question*): "Only when man has recognized and organized his 'forces propres' as *social* forces [it is therefore not necessary, as Rousseau thinks, to change man's nature, to deprive him of his 'forces propres' and give him new ones of a social character] and, consequently, no longer cuts off his social power from himself in the form of political power [i.e. no longer establishes the State as the sphere of organized rule] only then will the emancipation of mankind be achieved." Since Marx is known even in his early days to have regarded politics as obviously nothing but the expression and elaboration of class-rule, politics must accordingly be abolished with the abolition of the latter: the man who is no longer "sundered from his fellow-man and from the community" is no longer a political being. This, however, is not regarded as the first consequence of some post-revolutionary development. Rather, as is clearly stated in both the above passages, Revolution as such, i.e. Revolution in its purely negative, "dissolvent" capacity, is the last political act. As soon as the organizing activity begins on the terrain prepared by the overthrow, as soon as the positive function of socialism starts, the political principle will be superseded by the social. The sphere in which this function is exercised is no longer the sphere of the political rulership of man by man. Marx's dialectical formulation leaves no doubt as to what the sequence of events actually is in his opinion: first the political act of *social* revolution will annihilate not merely the Class State, but the State as a power-formation altogether, whereas the *political* revolution was the very thing that "constituted the state as a public concern, that is, as the real State". On the other hand, "the organizing activity" will begin, i.e. the reconstruction of society, only after the complete overthrow of existing power—whatever organizing activity preceded the Revolution was only organization for the struggle. From this we can see with the greatest clarity what it is that connects Marx with "utopian" socialism: the will to supersede the political principle by the social principle, and what divides him from it: his opinion that this supersession can be effected by exclusively political means—hence by way of sheer suicide, so to speak, on the part of the political principle.

This opinion is rooted deep in Marx's dialectical view of history, which found classical formulation fifteen years later in the preface to his book *A Critique of Political Economy*.

Yet, in the concluding section of his polemic against Proudhon, we encounter what appears to be a not inconsiderable limitation. "The working-class," he says, "will, in the course of its development (dans le cours de son développement), replace the old bourgeois society by an association which will exclude classes and their antagonisms, and there will no longer be any political power in its proper sense (il n'y aura plus de pouvoir politique, proprement dit), since political power is nothing but the official sum (le résumé officiel) of the antagonisms obtaining in bourgeois society." "No political power in its proper sense"—that means: no political power in the sense of an expression and elaboration of class-rule, which is quite self-evident if class-rule really has been abolished. Let us leave aside for the moment the question which obviously never entered into Marx's field of vision, namely, whether in those circumstances the proletariat would really be the "last" class, with whose accession to power class-rule would collapse altogether, that is, whether a new social differentiation would not arise within the victorious proletariat itself, one which, even though the class-designation might not apply, might very well lead to a new system of domination. There still remains, however, the no less momentous question as to the nature and extent of political power in the "improper" sense, that is to say, the political power that no longer rests on class-rule but persists after the classes have been abolished. Might it not be possible for such power to make itself no less felt, indeed more felt, than that based on class-rule, especially so long as it was a matter of "defending the Revolution"—so long, in fact, as humanity as a whole had not abolished class-rule, or even, perhaps, so long as humanity had not adopted the view or the realization of socialism prevailing in that particular State in which the victory of the proletariat had been won? But the thing that concerns us most of all is this: so long, in such a State or States, as this fixed point of view prevails, and prevails with all the technique and instruments of power at the disposal of our age, how can that spontaneity, that free social form-seeking and form-giving, that unfettered power of social experimentation and decision so indispensable to the realization of socialism and the emergence of a socialist form of society—how can they possibly get to work? By omitting to draw a clear line of demarcation between power in its proper and improper senses Marx opens the door to a type of political principle which, in his opinion, does not and cannot exist: a type which is not the expression and elaboration of class-rule, but is rather the expression and elaboration of power-tendencies and power-struggles not characterized by class, on the part of groups and individuals. Political power in the improper sense would accordingly be "the official sum of antagonisms" either within the proletarian class itself or, more precisely, within the nation in which "class-rule has been abolished".

His impressions of the problematical revolution of 1848 served to sharpen Marx's critical attitude to experiments in social re-structure. If the "little experiments, inevitably abortive" had already been censured in the Manifesto, now (in the report *The Class War in France* of 1850) "doctrinaire socialism" was accused of "wishing away the revolutionary conflict of the classes and the need for it by means of petty artifices and gross sentimentalities", and (in the *Eighteenth Brumaire* of 1852) the French proletariat was reprobated for having partly committed itself to "doctrinaire experiments, exchange-banks and workers' associations", and thus to a "movement which, having given up the struggle to overthrow the old world despite all the means at its disposal, prefers to seek its own salvation behind society's back, privately, inside the narrow framework of its existence, and which will thus necessarily come to grief".

Marx's faith in the impending revolution was still unshaken at that time, but his confidence in an impending World Revolution in the full sense of the word began to waver. In 1858 he wrote to Engels: "The difficult question for us is this. On the continent the Revolution is imminent and will immediately assume a socialist form. But will it not necessarily be crushed in this small corner of the earth [meaning the continent of Europe!], seeing that over a far greater area the movement of bourgeois society is still in the ascendant?" His doubts seem to have deepened still more in the following years. On the other hand he became more and more impressed with the significance of the extra-revolutionary political struggle. After another six years this was worked out *inter alia* in the "Inaugural Address to the International Workers' Association". Having praised the Ten-Hour-Law as the "triumph of a principle", he went on to call the rise of the Co-operative Movement "a still greater triumph for the political economy of labour over the political economy of capital". The value of these great social experiments, he said, could not be over-estimated; for the workers, who had set up co-operative factories without any help at all, had thereby proved that wage-labour "is destined to give way to associated labour". The co-operative system, however, if it was to free the masses, needed "developing on a national scale and consequently promoting by national means", hence precisely what Louis Blanc and Lassalle had hoped and striven for. But such a thing would not be conceded by the big landed proprietors and the capitalists of their own free will. "Therefore," he ends, it is "the great duty of the working class" to seize political power. We must give this word "therefore" our full attention. Labour is to win political power in the parliaments in order to sweep the obstacles out of the way of the Co-operative Movement. Marx is here ascribing a central significance to co-operation, and in particular to the Producer Co-operatives. Although it is stressed, as also in Resolutions Marx drew up for the Geneva Congress of 1866, that the Co-operative Movement was not capable of remodelling capitalist society of itself, it is none the less acknowledged as the proper way to remodel it, save that for this to succeed the acquisition of State power by the workers was essential. At this point Marx comes remarkably close to re-structural thinking in practice without accepting it in principle. Worthy of mention in this connection is the fact that he clearly recognizes the danger of the Co-operatives degenerating into ordinary bourgeois joint-stock companies, and even recommends the right remedy: that all the workers employed should receive the same share.

But less than three months before the opening of the Geneva Congress for which he drew up this Resolution, Marx wrote to

Engels about the tendencies expressed by the French in a debate of the General Council of the International: "Proudhonized Stirnerism. Splitting everything up into little 'groupes' or 'communes' and then making a 'company' of them, but not a State." It is here that the undercurrent of State Centralism creeps unmistakably into Marx's ideas if only by implication. The federalism of Proudhon he is attacking has not the slightest wish to split everything up into communes, it only wants to confer relatively extensive autonomy on the existing communes and combine them in units, whose own combination would represent a more organic form of community than the existing State. As against this Marx once more holds fast to the State as such.

But now, another five years later, a revolutionary event exerted a new influence on Marx's views, an event stronger than any preceding it and tending in another direction: the Paris Commune. In one of his most significant writings, the address to the General Council of the International on the civil war in France, he sketched a picture of the growth, activities and aims of the Commune. The historical reliability of this picture has been disputed, but that does not concern us here: the picture is a confession and one that is of great importance for our theme, which is the variations in Marx's views concerning the evolution of a new society.

What distinguished the Commune in Marx's eyes *toto genere* from all earlier endeavours, "its true secret", is that it was "essentially a working-class government". That is to be understood literally: Marx means a government not merely appointed by the working-class but also actually and factually exercised by it. The Commune is "the self-government of the producers". Born of universal suffrage and elected by the Parisians themselves, representation of this kind, consisting as it does of members who can be replaced at any time and who are bound by the definite instructions of their electors—such representation "should not be a parliamentary but a working body, executive and legislative at the same time". The same form of organization was to be provided for every commune in France right down to the smallest village. The provincial communes were to administer their common affairs in the district parliament and the district assemblies in their turn were to send deputies to the national delegation. In place of centralized State-power originating from the era of absolute monarchy, "with its omnipresent organs", there would consequently emerge a largely decentralized community. "The few, but important, functions, still left over for a Central Government were to be transferred to communal, i.e. strictly answerable officials." The decentralization, however, would not be a fragmentation but a reconstitution of national unity on an organic basis, and would mean a reactivating of the nation's forces and therefore of the national organism as a whole. "The communal constitution would have rendered up to the body social all the powers which have hitherto been devoured by the parasitic excrescence of the 'State', which battens on society and inhibits its free movement. By this deed alone it would have brought about the regeneration of France." It is obvious that Marx is speaking here not of certain historical State-forms but of the State in general. By becoming something "self-evident" local self-government renders State-power "superfluous". Never did any "utopian" Socialist express himself more radically on this point.

But the political structure of the Commune is, for Marx, only a prelude to the real and decisive thing—the great social transformation to which, with its plans and its dispositions, it would inevitably have led had it not been destroyed. He sees in the Commune "the finally discovered political form, in whose sign the economic liberation of labour can march forward". The Commune wanted "to make individual property a truth, by converting the means of production, land and capital into the mere tools of free and associated labour", and labour amalgamated in Producer Co-operatives at that. "If Co-operative production," Marx cries, "is not to remain a snare and a delusion, if it is to oust the capitalist system, if the Co-operatives as a whole are to regulate national production according to a common plan and thereby take it under their own control— what else would that be, gentlemen, but Communism, and a Communism that is *possible*?" That is, a communism that proves its possibility in the teeth of the widespread notion of its "impossibility". A federalism of communes and Co-operatives —for that is precisely what this picture sketches—is thus acknowledged by Marx as genuine communism. To be sure, he still sets his face against all "Utopianism". The working-class "has no cut-and-dried Utopias to introduce by a plebiscite". The communal and co-operative system which it wants to build up into a new community and a new society, is not a contrivance of the mind: only out of the reality of the association of old and new generations, the reality that is gradually emerging from the nation itself, out of these things alone can the working-class build its work and its house. "It has no ideals to realize, it has only to set free those elements of the new society which have already developed in the womb of the collapsing bourgeois society." Here we have that notion of "development" again, dating from 1847; but this time it is completely unequivocal and indubitably meant in the sense of a pre-revolutionary prccess, one, moreover, whose nature consists in the formation of small, federable units of men's work and life together, of communes and Co-operatives, in respect to which it is the sole task of the Revolution to set them free, to unite them and endow them with authority. This certainly accords at all points with the famous formula given in the *Critique of Political Economy* twelve years previously, as regards the new and higher conditions of production which, however, will never supplant the old "until the material conditions for their existence have been gestated in the womb of the old society itself". But it is nowhere hinted in the report of the General Council that the Paris Commune miscarried because the gestation had not been completed. And the "elements of the new society" that had developed in the womb of the old, collapsing one—they were for the most part those very Co-operatives which had been formed in France under the influence of "utopian" socialism, just as the political federalism of the communes Marx described had been formed under the influence of Proudhon. It was these Co-operatives that were characterized as "little experiments, inevitably abortive" in the Communist Manifesto; but had the Commune triumphed—and everything in the Report indicates that it could have triumphed but for this or that particular circumstance—then they would have become the cell-substance of the new society.

From this standpoint—i.e. of Marxist *politics of revolution*—statements like the following one by Engels in 1873 can therefore be understood: "Had the autonomists been content to say that the social organization of the future would admit authority only within the bounds unavoidably set by the conditions of production themselves, then we could have agreed with them." As if Proudhon had not time and again emphasized the necessity of constantly setting boundaries between possible decentralization and necessary centralization! Another time

(1874) Engels says—adhering strictly to the formulation Marx gave in the Report of the Commission set up by the Hague Congress in 1872 to examine the activities of the Bakuninists—that all socialists were agreed that the State would wither away as a result of the social Revolution-to-be, and political authority with it; but that the "anti-authoritarians" were wrong to demand "that the political State should be abolished at a blow *before* the social conditions producing it were abolished". "They demand," Engels continues, "that the first act of the social revolution should be the abolition of authority." In actual fact no prudent anti-authoritarian socialist had ever demanded anything but that the revolution should begin by curing the *hypertrophy* of authority, its proliferation, and from then on concentrate on reducing it to proportions that would correspond to the circumstances given at any time. Engels answers the alleged demand as follows: "Have you ever seen a revolution, gentlemen? A revolution is certainly the most authoritarian thing there is." If that means that the revolutionary struggle as such must proceed under far-sighted leadership and strict discipline, so much cannot be doubted; but if it means that in the revolutionary epoch (of which nobody can say when it will end), the whole population is to be limitlessly determined in all branches of its life and thought by one central authoritarian will, then it is inconceivable how such a stage can ever evolve into socialism.

Four years after his paper on the Commune Marx, in a letter sharply criticizing the programme sketched for the Unification Congress of Gotha, set out afresh his misgivings about the Co-operatives, with the obvious political intent of bringing one of the chief points in the programme of the Lassallites into question and thus undermining the possibility of any compromise with them. Certainly Marx was only setting his face against the "establishment of Co-operative Societies with State aid", though allowing Co-operative Production to stand as the socialist goal; but expressions like "specific miracle-cure", "sectarian movement" and even "reactionary workers" in connexion with Buchez' programme are clear enough. Despite that, however, the paragraph dealing with Producer Associations financed out of State Credit was accepted by the Congress.

But nothing affords us a deeper insight into Marx's ambivalent attitude to the question of the internal transformation of society and the conditions for it than his correspondence with Vera Zasulitch in 1881.

The publication of these documents by Ryazanov is therefore particularly valuable, because they acquaint us with Marx's drafts, some of them very detailed, for his answering letter; as published the drafts run to more than 900 lines, with innumerable deletions, emendations, amplifications; the letter itself runs only to about 40.

Vera Zasulitch, "the woman of the moment, the woman with a mission," as Stepniak calls her, had written to Marx from Geneva to ask him, as author of *Capital*, the first volume of which was "enjoying great popularity in Russia" and was also playing a part particularly in discussions on the agrarian question and the Russian village community—to ask him what he thought about the prospects of the village community in the future. It was, she said, "a question of life and death" for the Russian Socialist Party, and on it also depended the personal fate of the revolutionary Socialists. For, either the village communities, once free of the excessive taxes and tributes as well as of the Government's arbitrary dealings, were capable in themselves of developing in a socialist direction, i.e. of gradually organizing the production and distribution of goods on a collective basis, in which case the revolutionary Socialist would have to "devote all his powers to the freeing of the communities and their development"—or else, as many people who called themselves Marxists declared, basing themselves on Marx, the village community was an "archaic form" condemned by history and scientific socialism alike to perdition. In that case the Socialists, who would seek in vain to calculate in how many decades the land would pass out of the hands of the Russian peasants into those of the bourgeoisie and in how many centuries capitalism in Russia might conceivably reach a stage of development similar to that in Western Europe, would have to restrict themselves to propaganda among the urban workers, propaganda which "will continue to pour into the masses of the peasants who, as a result of the dissolution of the village community, will be thrown on to the streets of the great cities in their search for wages". One can see that as a matter of fact it is nothing less than the decision whether or not the work of the Socialists in Russia could have any assured future for the next few generations. Must Russia go the way of Western Europe where, with the rise of Advanced Capitalism, the "archaic" forms of community necessarily dissolve of themselves, and is there no alternative but to prepare a class-conscious core of urban proletariat for the still distant time of industrialization? On the other hand if there exists, by reason of her special agrarian institutions, a special way for Russia, quite apart, as it were, from the general dialectics of history, a way by which to imbue the traditional pattern of communal ownership and production with Socialist spirit; if one could, by developing this pattern from within and obtaining a better position for it externally, create an organic social reality which would ripen into the Revolution, and, liberated by the latter and established in full freedom and right, which would thereupon constitute itself as the backbone of the new society—if all this, then there is indeed a great and immediate constructive-revolutionary task which may lead quite soon, perhaps, to the realization of socialism. The decision as to which of the two was the historical truth was left in Marx's hands.

His exertions to give the right answer are of a thoroughness and scrupulosity worthy of admiration. Already before this he had occupied himself with the same knotty problem, and now he attacked it afresh with especial intensity. Again and again we see him cancelling one formulation of great delicacy and precision only to seek another still more adequate. Although but a series of fragmentary sketches these notes seem to me the most important attempt that has been made to grasp synthetically the theme of the Russian village community.

Owing to the paucity of historical material the village community is still one of the least understood departments of ethnic sociology, within which the Russian type, whose development is extremely poorly documented, forms a perplexing chapter. In accordance with the prevailing scientific opinion of his time, Marx was inclined to attribute a very early origin to it. To-day we are wont to regard it as rather late in origin and as an outcome of Russia's fiscal policy. But this is surely not the final word. Research will, I think (as important works of our own day indicate) establish that Marx was not so wrong as people assume and that the fiscal system did not create new social forms, but made use of old ones. But here we have to concern ourselves not so much with historical inquiry as with an inquiry into the socialist prospects of the village community, as Marx saw them.

Marx declared in his drafts, in connexion with a remark of the

ethnologist Morgan, that the present crisis of capitalism would end
by modern society returning to a higher form of the archaic type
of communal ownership and production, that is, by its going
over to the communist pattern. Hence we were not to let the
word "archaic" alarm us—for in this direction lay the golden
opportunity for the Russian village community. It had a big
advantage over all other archaic communities of the same type:
it alone in Europe had maintained itself on a wide national
scale. It would not, therefore, as had been the fate of communal ownership in Western Europe, disappear with social
progress. Rather, it might "gradually slough off its primitive
characteristics and develop as the direct basis of collective production on a national scale". Marx points out that he had, in
his "Capital", confined the "historical fatality" of the accumulation of capital which progressively expropriates all property
accruing from personal labour, expressly to Western Europe.
Since the land in the hands of the Russian peasants had never
been their private property, such a line of development was
inapplicable to them. Instead, one needed simply to replace the
Government institution of the *Volost*, which "links a fair number
of villages together", by a "peasant assembly elected by the
commune itself and serving as the economic and administrative
organ of their interests". The transition from work in allotments to full co-operative work would easily be accomplished
then, in which connexion Marx stresses the familiarity of the
peasants with the communal work-contracts of the *Artel*[1] as
an added inducement to this. The inevitable economic need
for such a process would make itself felt as soon as the village
community, freed of its burdens and with more land at its
disposal, was in normal circumstances; and as for the necessary
material conditions, Russian society, having lived so long
at the expense of the peasant, surely owed him the requisite
wherewithal for such a transition. It is clear that Marx
is thinking of a change that can actually be accomplished
in the circumstances given. But on the other hand he draws
emphatic attention to a peculiarity of the Russian village community which afflicts it with impotence and makes all historical
initiative impossible for it. By this he means its isolation; it is a
"localized microcosm", and no connexion exists between the
life of one commune and that of the others. In other words,
what Marx is really missing without consciously making use of

[1] Described in the next chapter.

the idea, is the trend towards *federation*. This peculiarity, he says, is not to be found everywhere as the characteristic of this type of community; but "wherever it is found it has given rise to a more or less centralized despotism over the communes". Only by means of a general revolt can the isolation of the Russian village community be broken. Its present state is (for reasons which Marx does not specify) economically untenable; "for the Russian communes to be saved a Russian revolution is needed". But the revolution must come in time and it must "concentrate all its powers on securing the free rise of the village community". Then the latter will soon develop "comme élément régénérateur de la société russe et comme élément de supériorité sur les pays asservis par le régime capitaliste".

In the short letter that Marx actually sent to Vera Zasulitch, a single sentence follows the reference to the relevant passages in his *Capital*. The sentence runs: "The analysis given in my *Capital* offers, therefore, no reasons either for or against the viability of the village commune; however, the special study I have devoted to it and the material for which I have sought in the original sources convince me that the commune is the main-stay of social regeneration in Russia, but that, if it is to function as such, one must first of all eliminate the injurious influences which work upon it from all sides, and then secure for it the normal conditions of spontaneous development."

The basis of the argument is so enormously compressed that even the message it manages to convey can hardly be grasped in its proper significance. Evidently this process of com-pression was inevitable, since in the drafts the pros and cons confronted one another in such a manner as to be irreconcilable in fact if not in appearance. In theory Marx affirmed the possibility of a pre-revolutionary development of the commune in the direction desired, but in practice he made its "salvation" dependent on the timely appearance of the revolution. Here as elsewhere the determining factor is clearly the political element: the fear lest constructive work should sap the strength of the revolutionary impetus. Since, however, the political element in Marx was not offset by any insight into the significance of social re-structure, the pros and cons had ultimately to be replaced by a sentence which could hardly appear to Vera Zasulitch as an answer to her fateful question. Even in his own lifetime Marx, as Tönnies says, was something of an oracle who, on

account of the ambiguity of his answers, was often petitioned
in vain. At any rate Vera Zasulitch, in the answer to her
question as to whether the revolutionary socialist should devote
all his strength to the freeing and developing of the communes,
could have heard no "yes" echoing out of Marx's letter, which
for her was of the highest authority.

Not long afterwards she wrote (in the preface to the Russian
translation of Engels' *Evolution of Socialism from Utopia to Science*,
published in 1884) a few passages on the village community
which draw the conclusion from Marx's oracle: that the gradual
liquidation of communal ownership was inevitable; that
Russia's immediate future belonged to capitalism, but that
the socialist revolution in the West would put a term to
capitalism in the East as well, "and then the remnants of
the institution of communal ownership would render a great
service to Russia". In his Foreword to the Russian translation
(also by Vera Zasulitch) of the Communist Manifesto in 1882,
Engels had given a somewhat different answer to the question
he himself formulated obviously under the influence of Marx.
"Can the Russian village community," he asked, "which is
already an extremely corrupt form of the original communal
ownership of land, pass over *direct* to a higher, communist form
of ownership—or must it first of all go through the process of
liquidation familiar to us in the historical development of the
West?" His answer (as usual, less equivocal and more massive
than Marx's, but also less regardful of the profundity of the
problem) is as follows: "Should the Russian Revolution become
the signal for a workers' revolution in the West, so that both
complement one another, then the Russian communal ownership of to-day might serve as the starting-point for communist
development." Later he seems to have grown more sceptical,
but he avoided (so Gustav Mayer reports) "getting involved in
the internal struggles between those Russian Socialists who
trusted more to the peasants and those who trusted more to
the rise of an industrial proletariat".

As against Eduard Bernstein, who rightly pointed out the
similarity between the programme of the Paris Commune as
reported by Marx and Proudhon's federalism, Lenin declared
emphatically that Marx was a centralist and that his statements
in the *Civil War in France* show "no trace of a deviation from
centralism". Stated in such general terms this view is untenable. When Marx says that the few functions "which will then

remain for centralization" should be handed over to communal
officials, he means without a doubt: decentralize as many State-
functions as possible and change those that must remain
centralized into administrative functions, not, however, only
after some post-revolutionary development lasting an indefinite
time, but *inside* the revolutionary action itself—thus realizing
what, according to Engels' well-known criticism of the draft
to the Erfurt programme, "every French department, every
parish possessed: complete self-administration". Nevertheless,
Lenin was not wrong; Marx always remained a centralist at
heart. For him the communes were essentially political units,
battle-organs of the revolution. Lenin asks, "If the proletariat
were to organize itself absolutely freely into communes, and
were to unite the activities of these communes in a common
front against Capital . . . would that not be . . . proletarian
centralism?" Of course it would, and to this extent Lenin and
not Bernstein is Marx's faithful interpreter. But that is true
merely of the revolution as such, which—in the sense of Marx's
definition of the commune—is not a "development" spread out
over several generations, but a coherent historical *act*, the act
of smashing capitalism and placing the means of production
in the hands of the proletariat. But in the French programme
for the communes each individual commune with its "local
self-government" is by no means a mere cog in the great
apparatus of revolution, or, to put it less mechanically, not
merely an isolated muscle within the revolutionary exertions
of the body politic—on the contrary it is destined to outlast
the upheaval as an independent unit equipped with the
maximum of autonomy. During the act the commune's
particular will merges spontaneously in the great impulse of
the whole, but afterwards it is to acquire its own sphere of
decision and action, so that the really vital functions are
discharged "below" and the general administrative functions
"at the top". Each commune is already invested in principle
with its own proper powers and rights within the revolutionary
process, but it is only after the accomplishment of the common
act that they can come into actuality. Marx accepted these
essential components of the commune-idea but without weighing them up against his own centralism and deciding between
them. That he apparently did not see the profound problem
that this opens out is due to the hegemony of the political
point of view; a hegemony which persisted everywhere for him

as far as concerned the revolution, its preparation and its
effects. Of the three modes of thinking in public matters—the
economic, the social and the political—Marx exercised the
first with methodical mastery, devoted himself with passion to
the third, but—absurd as it may sound in the ears of the
unqualified Marxist—only very seldom did he come into more
intimate contact with the second, and it never became a
deciding factor for him.

To the question of the elements of social re-structure, a fateful
question indeed, Marx and Engels never gave a positive
answer, because they had no inner relation to this idea. Marx
might occasionally allude to "the elements of the new society
which have already developed in the womb of the collapsing
bourgeois society", and which the Revolution had only "to set
free"; but he could not make up his mind to foster these
elements, to promote them and sponsor them. The political
act of revolution remained the one thing worth striving for;
the political preparation for it—at first the direct preparation,
afterwards the parliamentary and trades unionist preparation—
the one task worth doing, and thus the political principle became the supreme determinant; every concrete decision about
the practical attitude to such re-structural elements as were
actually present, in the process of formation or to be constituted anew, was reached only from the standpoint of political
expediency. Naturally, therefore, decisions in favour of a
positive attitude were tepid, uncoordinated and ineffectual,
and finally they were always cancelled out by negative ones.

A characteristic example of the purely political way in which
the spiritual leaders of the movement treated the social structures most important for the re-shaping of society, is afforded
by Engels' attitude to the Co-operatives. In 1869 (in his
preface to the new impression edited by Wilhelm Liebknecht
of the paper on the German Peasant War) he had declared:
"The agricultural day-labourers can only be redeemed from
their misery if the chief object of their work, the land itself, is
converted into communal property and cultivated by Co-operatives of Landworkers for the common good." From this
fundamental premise he seems to draw a perfectly practical
conclusion, when he writes to Liebknecht in 1885 to the effect
that the Social-Democratic party of the German Reichstag
should say to the Government: "Give us guarantees that the
Prussian domains, instead of being leased out to big lease-

holders or peasants incapable of living without day-labour, will be leased to Workers' Co-operatives; that public works will be commissioned to Workers' Co-operatives instead of to capitalists—well and good, we will do the rest. If not, not." All these, Engels adds, are things that can be introduced at a day's notice and got going within a year, and are only blocked by the bourgeoisie and the Government. This sounds like genuine demands to be fought for. But in 1886 Engels is demanding of Bebel that the party should propose socialistic measures such as these on the ground that they would conduce to the overthrow of capitalist production; which, therefore, would be a practical impossibility for that Government as for any other bourgeois Government. Here the tactical-propagandist character of the demands is laid bare: the Co-operative principle is merely made use of, not propounded in all seriousness as something simply to be striven and fought for. The tactical application would not be so bad if only the fundamental thing were put boldly and clearly in words: but that is not the case. I cannot help seeing Lassalle's belief—shortsighted as it was—in the practical possibility of Co-operatives with Government aid, as the more socialistic attitude.

As another example of how the leaders' lack of principle on the subject of re-structure led to the sterility of the movement in this respect, I will again give a characteristic sequence of resolutions passed by the Party held to be the most knowledgeable in Marxist matters—the German Social Democrats—anent their relations to the Co-operative. In the Gotha Unification programme of 1875 (concerning the draft of which Marx had voiced his misgivings as mentioned above) it had been demanded that Producer Co-operatives should be set up for industry and agriculture "of such scope that they would result in the socialist organization of all Labour". This was a clear avowal of the re-structural principle, as appeared to be necessary for union with the Lassallites. But in the Erfurt programme of 1891 nothing more was heard of it—which is not to be explained solely by the failures of the Worker and Producer Co-operatives founded in the meantime, but principally by this same lack of fundamental directive, and at the Berlin Party Congress of 1892 it was decided that the Party "could only approve the founding of Co-operatives in so far as they were designed to enable comrades, on whom disciplinary punishment had been inflicted in the political or trades-union struggle, to live a decent social life, or in so far as they served to facilitate agitation"; for the rest, "the Party was opposed to the founding of Co-operatives". This is refreshingly outspoken. But in the resolution of the Hanover Party Congress in 1899 it was stated that the Party was neutral as regards the founding of Industrial Co-operatives, that it saw in the founding of such Co-operatives a suitable means of educating the working-class to the independent control of their affairs, but that it attributed to the Co-operatives "no decisive significance in the matter of freeing the working-class from the chains of wage-slavery". Yet in Magdeburg in 1910 the Consumer Co-operatives were not merely acknowledged as effectively supporting the class-struggle, it was also declared that Co-operative activity in general was "an effective complement to the political and trades-union struggle to raise the position of the working-class".

This zig-zag line may well serve as a symbol of the tragic mis-development of the Socialist Movement. With all the powerful forces of propaganda and planning it had gathered the proletariat about itself; in the political and economic field it had acted with great aggressive aplomb in attack and defence, but the very thing for which, ultimately, it had made propaganda and planned and fought—the evolution of the new social form —was neither the real object of its thought nor the real goal of its action. What Marx praised the Paris Commune for, the Marxist movement neither wanted nor achieved. It did not look to the lineaments of the new society which were there for all to see; it made no serious effort to promote, influence, direct, co-ordinate and federate the experiments that were in being or about to be; never by consistent work did it of its own accord call any cell-groups and associations of cell-groups of living community into existence. With all its great powers it lent no hand to shaping the new social life for mankind which was to be set free by the Revolution.

IX

LENIN AND THE RENEWAL
OF SOCIETY

JUST as the principle of the renewal of society from within, by a regeneration of its cell-tissue, found no fixed place derivable from the idea itself, in Marx's doctrine, so there was no place for it in the most tremendous attempt of our time to realize this doctrine through the admirable but highly problematical application of conscious human will. In both cases this negative fact can, as we have seen, be justified as regards the pre-revolutionary era by saying that under the reign of capitalism no social regeneration whatsoever, even if only fragmentary, could be accomplished; but as regards the post-revolutionary era it is stated in both cases that it would be "utopian" to outline the appropriate forms of this regeneration. "Utopia," Engels writes in 1872, "arises when, 'from the existing conditions', people undertake to prescribe the form wherein this, that or the other contradiction in existing society will be resolved." "In Marx," says Lenin, "you will find no trace of Utopianism in the sense of inventing the 'new' society and constructing it out of fantasies." But useless as such fantasy-pictures indeed are, it is also of vital importance to let the idea to which one clings dictate the direction towards which one may actively strive. The socialist idea points of necessity, even in Marx and Lenin, to the organic construction of a new society out of little societies inwardly bound together by common life and common work, and their associations. But neither in Marx nor Lenin does the idea give rise to any clear and consistent frame of reference for action. In both cases the decentralist element of re-structure is displaced by the centralist element of revolutionary politics.

In both cases the operative law is that strictly centralist action is necessary to the success of the revolution, and obviously there is no small truth in this; what is wanting is the constant drawing of lines of demarcation between the demands of this action and—without prejudicing it—the possible implementation of a decentralized society; between what the execution of the idea demands and what the idea itself demands; between the claims of revolutionary politics and the rights of an emergent socialist life. The decision always falls—in the theory and directives of the movement with Marx, in the practice of revolution and the reordering of the State and economics with Lenin—essentially in favour of politics, that is, in favour of centralization. A good deal of this can certainly be attributed to the situation itself, to the difficulties which the Socialist movement had to face and the quite special difficulties faced by the Soviet régime; but over and above that a certain conception and a certain tendency subsequently came to the fore which we may find in Marx and Engels and which thereafter devolved upon Lenin and Stalin: the conception of one absolute centre of doctrine and action from which the only valid theses and the only authoritative decrees can issue, this centre being virtually a dictatorship masked by the "dictatorship of the proletariat"—in other words: the tendency to perpetuate centralist revolutionary politics at the cost of the decentralist needs of a nascent socialist community. It was easy for Lenin to give way to this tendency because of the situation itself, which clearly pointed to the fact that the Revolution had not yet reached its end. The contradiction between Marx's demand for the supersession of the political by the social principle on the one hand and the incontestible persistence of it on the other, is disguised and justified by the alleged incompleteness of the revolution; but this does not, of course, take into account the circumstance that for Marx socialism was to slough off its political skin the moment "its organizing activity *begins*". Here there lurks a problem which in its turn is masked by nothing less than the materialistic interpretation of history: according to this view, politics is merely the exemplification and expression of the class-struggle, and with the abolition of the class-state the ground will consequently be cut from under the political principle. The life-and-death struggle of the sole valid doctrine and sole programme of action against all other versions of socialism cannot pass itself off as unpolitical; it must, therefore, brand every other kind of socialism as bogus, as a vestige of bourgeois ideologies; for so long as any other version of socialism exists the Revolution cannot yet be at an end, obviously, and the political principle cannot yet have been superseded by the social, although the organizing activity has already begun. Political power "in the improper sense" can indeed become far more comprehensive, ruthless and "totalitarian" in its centralist pretensions than political power "in its proper sense" ever was. This is not to say that Lenin was a centralist pure and simple: in certain respects he was less so than Marx and in this he was closer to Engels; but in his thought and will the revolutionary-political motif dominated as with Marx and Engels and suppressed the vital social motif which requires decentralized community-living, with the result that this only made itself felt episodically. The upshot of all this was that there was no trace in the new State-order of any agency aiming at the liquidation of State centralism and accumulation of power. How such a liquidation was ever to take place by degrees in the absence of such an agency is inconceivable. Lenin once remarked, in 1918: "What Socialism will be we just don't know. When has any State begun to wither away?" And in history there is indeed no example, however small, to which one could refer. To achieve this for the first time in the world's history one would have needed to set about it with a tremendously vital and idealistic store of decentralizing energy. No such thing happened. That under these circumstances a voluntary renunciation of accumulated power and a voluntary liquidation of centralization would ever take place has not unjustly been characterized (by a Socialist) as a belief in miracles.

The doctrine of the "withering away" of the State after the social revolution was elaborated by Engels from Marx's for the most part very tentative adumbrations. It would not be unprofitable to bring his chief utterances on this subject together in chronological sequence. In 1874 he declared that the State, "as a result of the social revolution of the future, would vanish" because all public functions would simply be changed from political into administrative ones. In 1877 he said more precisely that the proletariat, by converting the means of production into State property, would abolish the State as State and that, moreover, this same seizure of the means of production would "at once be its last independent act as a State", that it would then "fall asleep" or "wither away of itself". In 1882 there follows the eschatological interpretation of this "at once":

there would be the "leap of humanity out of the realm of necessity into the realm of freedom"; nothing could be more out-spoken than this. Now, however, a remarkable retreat ensues. After Marx's death we hear no more of this "at once" from Engels' lips. When he announces in 1884 that the whole machinery of State will be relegated to the Museum of Anti-quities, the date of this singular proceeding is no longer the moment when the means of production have been nationalized, but evidently a much later moment, and evidently the pro-ceedings will be long-drawn, for the authority which under-takes that relegation to the Museum is now "Society, which will organize production anew on the basis of the free and equal association of the producers"—a task only inaugurated, naturally, by the unique act of nationalization. This accords with the formula in the Communist Manifesto about "the course of development", a formula which Engels recalls here; save that there the formula speaks of the concentration of pro-duction "in the hands of associated individuals" as being the result of a development in whose train public power would lose its political character. In 1891 Engels retreats still further, so far indeed that no additional retreat is necessary or even possible. The proletariat, he says, victorious in the struggle for mastery, will not be able to avoid "at once paring down the worst aspects of the State, until a new generation grown up in new, free social conditions is capable of putting aside the whole paraphernalia of State." Engels says this in his Foreword to the new edition of Marx's *Civil War in France*, in which the latter had written twenty years previously that the working-class "will have to go through long struggles, a whole series of historical processes which will completely transform men and circumstances alike". In his Foreword Engels transposes this conception to the post-revolutionary period. But by so doing the cogency of that "at once" is enormously weakened. Not only is it no longer the case that the proletariat will abolish the State as State with the nationalization of the means of pro-duction, but also it will, to begin with and right up to the com-ing of age of the "new generation", merely "pare down" the worst aspects of the State. And yet in that same book Marx had said of the Constitution of the Paris Commune that, had the Commune triumphed, it would have given back to the social body all the powers which hitherto "the parasitic excrescence of the State" had eaten up; consequently he had laid the main stress on the change brought about by the workings of the Commune—hence on the "at once". But now Engels in his Foreword retreats far beyond this. No doubt certain historical experiences were to blame; but that Engels let himself be influenced by them so profoundly is due to the fact that neither with him nor with Marx was there any uniform and consistent ideal aiming at the re-structuring of society or at preparations for the abolition of the State, or any strong and steadfast will for decentralizating action. It was a divided spiritual inheritance into which Lenin entered: socialist revolutionary politics without socialist vitality.

As is well known, Lenin tried to overcome the problematical nature of Engels' doctrine by pointing out with great emphasis that "the abolition" referred to the bourgeois State but that "the withering away" referred to the "remains of the proletarian State system after the Socialist revolution". Further, that since the State as (in Engels' definition) a "special repressive power" was necessary at first for the suppression of the bourgeoisie, it was also essential as the dictatorship of the proletariat, as the centralized organ of its power. That Lenin hit off Marx's (and Engels') intention is indisputable; he rightly quotes the passage in which Marx, in 1852, had characterized this dictatorship as being the transition to a classless society. But for the Marx of 1871 with his enthusiasm for the Commune it was certain that a decentralization would simultaneously be preparing itself in the midst of the centralism necessary for revolutionary action; and when Engels called the nationalization of the means of production an abolition of the State "as State", he meant the all-important process that would be worked out to the full immediately after the completion of the revolutionary act.

Lenin praises Marx for having "not yet, in 1852, put the concrete question as to what should be set up in place of the State machinery after it had been abolished". Lenin goes on to say that it was only the Paris Commune that taught Marx this. But the Paris Commune was the realization of the thoughts of people who had put this question very concretely indeed. Lenin also praises Marx for having "held strictly to the factual basis of historical experience". But the historical experience of the Commune became possible only because in the hearts of passionate revolutionaries there lived the picture of a decentralized, very much "de-Stated" society, which picture they undertook to translate into reality. The spiritual fathers of the Commune had just that ideal aiming at decentralization which Marx and Engels did not have, and the leaders of the Revolution of 1871 tried, albeit with inadequate powers, to begin the realization of that ideal in the midst of the revolution.

As to the problem of action Lenin starts off with a purely dialectical formula: "So long as there is a State there is no freedom. Once there is freedom there will be no more State." Such dialectics obscures the essential task, which is to test day by day what the maximum of freedom is that can and may be realized to-day; to test how much "State" is still necessary to-day, and always to draw the practical conclusions. In all probability there will never—so long as man is what he is—be "freedom" pure and simple, and there will be "State", i.e. compulsion, for just so long; the important thing, however, is the day to day question: no more State than is indispensable, no less freedom than is allowable. And freedom, socially speaking, means above all freedom for community, a community free and independent of State compulsion.

"It is clear," says Lenin, "that there can be no talk of a definite time when the withering away of the State will begin." But it is not at all clear. When Engels declares that, with the seizure of the means of production, the State will in fact become representative of society as a whole and will thereby make itself superfluous, it follows that this is the time when the withering away must begin. If it does not begin then it proves that the withering tendency is not an integral and determining part of the revolutionary action. But in that case a withering away or even a shrinking of the State cannot be expected of the Revolution and its aftermath. Power abdicates only under the stress of counter-power.

"The most pressing and topical question for politics to-day," states Lenin in September, 1917, "is the transformation of all citizens into workers and employees of one big 'syndicate', namely, the State as a whole." "The whole of society," he continues, "will turn into one office and one factory with equal work and equal pay." But this reminds us, does it not, of what Engels said of the tyrannical character of the automatic mechanism of a big factory, that over its portal should stand written: *Lasciate ogni autonomia, voi ch'entrate*. To be sure, Lenin sees this factory discipline only as "a necessary stage in the radical purging of society"; he thinks that it will pass as soon as "everybody has learnt to manage society's production by himself", for from this moment the need for any government whatever will begin to disappear. The possibility that the capacity for managing production is unequally distributed and that equal training may not be able to make up for this natural deficiency, never seems to have entered Lenin's head. The thing that would meet the human situation much more would be the de-politicization of all the functions of management as far as practicable; that is, to deprive these functions of all possibility of degenerating into power-accretions. The point is not that there should be only managers and no managed any more—that is more utopian than any Utopia—but that management should remain management and not become rulership, or more precisely, that it should not appropriate to itself more rulership than the conditions at any time make absolutely necessary (to decide which cannot, of course, be left to the rulers themselves).

Lenin wanted, it is true, one far-reaching change to take place "immediately": immediately after they had wrested political power the workers were to "smash the old apparatus of bureaucracy, raze it to its foundations, leave not one stone upon another", and replace it by a new apparatus composed of these same workers. Time and again Lenin reiterates the word "immediately". Just as the Paris Commune had done, so now such measures shall "immediately" be taken as are necessary to prevent the new apparatus from degenerating into a new bureaucracy, chief among them being the ability to elect and dismiss officials and, in Marx's language, to hold them "strictly answerable". This fundamental transformation is not, in contra-distinction to all the others, to be left to the process of "development", it is supposed to be implicit in the revolutionary action itself as one of its most momentous and decisive acts. A "new, immeasurably higher and incomparably more democratic type of State-apparatus" is to be created "immediately".

On this point, therefore, Lenin held an immediate change in the social structure to be necessary. He realized that in its absence, despite all the formidable interventions, the new institutions, the new laws and new power-relationships, at the heart of the body politic everything would remain as of old. That is why, although he was no adherent of any general decentralist tendency, he was such an emphatic advocate of this demand for immediate change which, as far as the Paris

Commune was concerned, had been an organic part of the decentralist order of society and which can only be fulfilled in a society pressing towards the realization of this order. As an isolated demand it has not been fulfilled in Soviet Russia. Lenin himself is reported to have said with bitterness at a later phase: "We have become a bureaucratic Utopia."

And yet a beginning had been made with structural transformation, not indeed on Lenin's initiative, although he recognized its importance if not all its potential structural qualities—a peculiarly Russian beginning akin to the proposals of the Paris Commune and one that had tremendous possibilities —namely the Soviets. The history of the Soviet régime so far, whatever else it is, has been the history of the destruction of these possibilities.

The first Soviets were born of the 1905 Revolution primarily as "a militant organization for the attainment of certain objectives", as Lenin said at the time; first of all as agencies for strikes, then as representative bodies for the general control of the revolutionary action. They arose spontaneously, as the institutions of the Commune did, not as the outcome of any principles but as the unprepared fruit of a given situation. Lenin emphasized to the anarchists that a Workers' Council was not a parliament and not an organ of self-administration. Ten years later he stated that Workers' Councils and similar institutions must be regarded "as organs of revolt" which could only be of lasting value "in connexion with the revolt". Only in March, 1917, after the Sovietic pattern had been, in Trotsky's words, "almost automatically reborn" in Russia and after the first reports of the victory of the revolution had reached Lenin in Switzerland, did he recognize in the St. Petersburg Soviet "the germ-cell of a workers' government" and in the Councils as a whole the fruit of the experiences of the Paris Commune. By this he still meant, of course, first and foremost "the organization of the revolution", that is to say, of the "second real revolution" or "organized striking-force against the counter-revolution", just as Marx saw in the institutions of the Commune above all the organs of revolutionary action; nevertheless Lenin described the Councils, which he held to be of the same nature as the Commune, as already constituting "the State we need", that is, the State "which the proletariat needs" or which is "the foundation we must continue to build on". What he demanded immediately after his arrival in Russia was, in opposition to the opinion prevailing in the Workers' Council itself, "a republic of Workers', Landworkers' and Peasants' Deputy Councils throughout the country, from top to bottom". In this sense the Soviet that then existed was, in his view, "a step towards Socialism", just as the Paris Commune had been for Marx—but of course only a political, a revolutionary-political step as that also had been for Marx; an institution, namely, in which revolutionary thinking could crystallize, the "revolutionary dictatorship, that is, a power supported from below by the direct initiative of the masses and not by the law, which was dispensed by a centralized State-power"; in other words, "direct usurpation". The devolution of power on the Soviets still meant for Lenin not only no real decentralization but not even the incentive to the formation of anything of the kind, since the political function of the Soviets was not an integral part of a plan for a comprehensive, organic order that should include society as well as its economy. Lenin accepted the Councils as a programme for action but not as a structural idea.

The utterance Lenin made the day after his arrival, at a meeting of the Bolshevist members of the All-Russian Conference of Councils, is characteristic: "We have all clung to the Councils, but we have not grasped them." The Councils, therefore, already had an objective historical significance for him, quite independent of the significance they had for themselves and for their own members. For the Mensheviks and the social revolutionaries the Councils were what they had been for the former in 1905 and what they in fact more or less were at the time of Lenin's arrival in Russia: organs for the control of Government, guarantees of democracy. For Lenin and his adherents among the Bolsheviks they were very much more— they were the Government itself, the "only possible form of revolutionary Government"; they were, indeed, the new emergent State—but no more than that. That the decentralist form of this State *in statu nascendi* did not disturb Lenin is due to the fact that the only thing to make active appearance in the Councils Movement at this purely dynamic phase of the Revolution was the undivided will to revolution.

The model of the Paris Commune was vitally important for Lenin both because Marx had exemplified through it—and through it alone—the essential features of a new State-order and because Lenin's mind, like that of all the leading Russian revolutionaries, had been lastingly influenced by the revolutionary tradition of France as being the "classic" of its kind. The influence of the great French revolution, the habitual measuring of their own revolution by it and the constant comparison of equivalent stages, etc., were themselves sufficient to exercise a negative effect, particularly as regards the bias towards centralism. But Lenin did not apply the model afforded by the Commune to any general understanding of history. The fact that (as Arthur Rosenberg rightly stresses in connexion with Kropotkin and Landauer) whenever, in history, the masses endeavoured to overthrow a feudal or a centralist power-apparatus it always ended in these same Commune-like experiments, was either unknown to him or did not interest him; still less did he grapple with the fact (although he once spoke of the Soviets being "in their social and political character" identical with the State of the Commune) that in all those experiments *social* decentralization was linked up with political decentralization, if in differing degrees. For him, the only decisive lesson of history was the conviction that hitherto humanity had not brought forth a higher and better type of government than the Councils. Therefore the Councils had to "take *the whole* of life into their own hands".

Naturally Lenin did not fail to realize that the Councils were in essence a decentralist organization. "All Russia," he says in April, 1917, "is already overspread by a network of local organs of self-administration." The specific revolutionary measures—abolition of the police, abolition of the standing army, the arming of the whole population—could also be put into effect by local self-government; and that is the whole point. But that these organs could and should come together as a lasting organism based on local and functional decentralization after the accomplishment of this task, is not so much as hinted at by a single word, apparently not even by a thought. The setting up and strengthening of self-administration has no ultimate purpose or object other than a revolutionary-political one: to make a self-administration a reality means "to drive the Revolution forwards". Admittedly in this connexion a social note is also struck, if only in passing: the village Commune— which, it is said, means "complete self-administration" and "the absence of all tutelage from above"—would suit the peasantry very well (that "nine-tenths of the peasantry would be agreeable to it" was, be it noted by the way, a fundamental error). But the reason for this follows at once: "We must be centralists; yet there will be moments when the task will shift to the provinces; we must leave the maximum of initiative to individual localities. . . . Only our party can give the watchwords which will really drive the Revolution forwards." At first glance it does not seem clear how this obligatory centralism can be compatible with the complete self-administration mentioned above; on closer inspection, however, we remark that this compatibility rests on the fact that the guiding point of view is, purely and simply, the revolutionary-political one or even the revolutionary-strategic one: in this case, too, self-administration is only a component of the programme of action and not the practical conclusion drawn from a structural idea. This more than anything else enables us to understand why the programmatic demand for "the absence of all tutelage from above" (a demand not envisaged for any post-revolutionary development, but as something to be secured in the midst of the revolution and destined to drive it forwards) turned so rapidly into its exact opposite. Instead of the watchword, "We must be centralists, yet there will be moments . . .", a genuinely socialist attitude would have put it the other way round: "We must be decentralists, federalists, autonomists, yet there will be moments when our main task will shift to a central authority because revolutionary action requires it; only we must take care not to let these requirements swamp its objective and temporal frame of reference."

For a clearer understanding of the antagonism between centralism and the above-mentioned "moments" we must realize that in the provinces, as Lenin himself emphasized, "communes are being formed at a great rate, particularly in the proletarian centres", so that the revolution was progressing "in the form of local communes". The "watchwords" corresponded to these facts. A watchword corresponding to this description of the situation, such as "Local Communes, complete regional autonomy, independence, no police, no officials, sovereignty of the armed masses of workers and peasants"— such a watchword, appeal as it might to the experience of the Paris Commune, was and remained a revolutionary-political one; that is, it could not, of its own nature, point beyond the revolution to a decentralized social structure; centralism continued to be its fixed basis. We cannot help being profoundly impressed when we read, in the same draft (of May, 1917), from which I have quoted just now, of Lenin's demand that the provinces should be taken as a model and communes formed of the suburbs and metropolitan areas; but once again no other *raison d'être* is granted them except to drive the Revolution forwards and to lay down a broader basis for "the passing of the total power of the State to the Councils". ("We are now in the minority, the masses do not believe us as yet," says Lenin at about the same time.) Lenin is without a doubt one of the greatest revolutionary strategists of all time; but the strategy of revolution became for him, as the politics of revolution became for Marx, the supreme law not only of action but of thinking as well. We might say that precisely this was the cause of his success; it is certain at any rate that this fact—together with a tendency to centralism rooted very deeply in him as in Marx—was to blame for it if this success ·did not ultimately contribute to the success of Socialism.

Nevertheless these words should not be construed to imply that I would charge the Lenin of 1917 with not intending to permit the nascent power of the Soviets to continue beyond the revolution. That would be nonsensical; for did he not expressly say at the time, in his significant *Report on the Political Situation*, of the State that would arise when the Councils took the power into their own hands (a State that "would no longer be a State in the accepted sense"), that although such a Power had never yet maintained itself in the world for any length of time, "the whole Workers' Movement all over the world was going in that direction?" What I complain of in Lenin is rather his failure to understand that a fundamental centralism is incompatible with the existence of such a Power beyond the Revolution's immediate sphere of action. It is noteworthy that Lenin says in the same Report that the latter was a State-form "which represents the first steps towards Socialism and is unavoidable in the first phases of socialist society". These words indicate, I think, that it was conceived of as being only a stepping-stone to a higher, "socialist" centralism; and doubtless in the field of economics so vitally important for any final remodelling of society Lenin saw strict centralism as the goal. At that very meeting he emphasized that "the French Revolution passed through a period of municipal revolution when it settled down to local self-administration", and that the Russian revolution was going

through a similar phase. It is difficult not to think of the
extreme centralism that followed this period of the French
Revolution.

Viewed from yet another angle Lenin's doctrine of 1917 leads
us to the same result. "Private ownership of ground and of
land must be abolished," he says. "That is the task that stands
before us, because the majority of the people are for it. That
is why we need the Councils. This measure cannot possibly
be carried through with the old State officials." Such is the
substance of the answer which Lenin gives in his political
Report to the question: "Why do we want power to pass into
the hands of the Workers' and Soldiers' Deputy Councils?"
Here the Marxist respect for "circumstances" is carried to
doubtful lengths: private ownership of land is to be abolished
not to build up Socialism but simply and solely because the
majority of the people want it; and the Councils are necessary
not to serve as cells of the new society but to execute the
measures demanded by the majority. I would like to assume
that we would do well not to take this argument of Lenin's too
literally.

But only now does Lenin's theory of the Councils enter the
decisive phase. The months in which he was preparing, from
Finland, the Bolshevist "special action", "the Second Revolution", were at the same time those in which he based his thought
as to the function of the Councils primarily and in principle on
Marx's idea of the Commune (in his well-known *State and
Revolution*), and then expands it in practice, with reference to
the action he had prepared (in his most important political
essay *Will the Bolshevists Maintain Power?*). The bulk of the
former was written in September at the time of the attempted
counter-revolution and its suppression—an attempt whose only
effect was to rouse the fighting spirit of the masses and bring
them closer to the radical Party; the second in the middle of
October, when the majority of the St. Petersburg and Moscow
Soviets opted for this party and, as a direct result of this,
the call "All Power to the Soviets!", from being a revolutionary-political demand, became the slogan of the impending
attack.

Fired by these events, Lenin glorified in his essay the significance of the Councils for the development of the revolution as
never before. In connexion with the statement made by the
Menshevik leader Martov that the Councils had been "called

into being in the first days of the revolution by the mighty outburst of genuine creative folk-power", Lenin says: "Had the creative folk-power of the revolutionary classes [this latter term goes beyond Martov's words and gives them a Bolshevist twist] not produced the Councils, the proletarian revolution in Russia would have been a hopeless affair." Here the conception of the Councils as an instrument for "driving the revolution forwards" struck its most powerful historical note.

In this essay Lenin lists for the first time the various elements which in his view give the Councils their fundamental importance. The sequence in which he cites these elements is characteristic of his outlook.

Firstly, the "new State apparatus", by substituting the Red Guard for the standing Army, invests the people themselves with armed power.

Secondly, it establishes an indissolubly close and "easily controlled" bond between the leaders and the masses.

Thirdly, by means of the principle of eligibility and dismissibility, it puts an end to bureaucracy.

Fourthly, by the very fact that it establishes contact with the various professions [later Lenin puts it more precisely: professions and productive units] it facilitates the weightiest reforms.

Fifthly, it organizes the Avant-garde, which shall raise up and educate the masses.

Sixthly, by means of the tie between the Legislature and the Executive it unites the advantages of Parliamentarianism with those of non-parliamentary Democracy.

The first place is given to revolutionary power-politics; the second to the organization of reforms; the third to the form of the State. The question of the possible importance of the Councils for a reshaping of the social structure is not even asked.

In Lenin's view, however, it only became possible for the Councils to master the tasks set them because the Bolsheviks had seized control in and through the Councils and filled the new form with a concrete content of action, whereas formerly they had been "reduced by the Social Revolutionaries and the Mensheviks to chatter-boxes", more, to "a body rotting on its feet". "The Councils," Lenin continues, "can only really develop, only display their talents and capabilities to the full, after the seizure of supreme power, for otherwise they have nothing to do, otherwise they are either simple germ-cells (and one cannot be a germ-cell for too long) or a plaything." This sentence is remarkable for more than one reason. The simile of the germ-cells necessarily forces the question on us as to whether in Lenin's opinion the Councils might not, by growth and association, ripen sufficiently to become the cells of a renewed social organism; but evidently that is not Lenin's opinion. And then the expression "plaything" turns up again a few days later in a curious connection, in Lenin's theses for a Conference in St. Petersburg, where we read: "The whole experience of the two revolutions of 1905 and 1917 confirms that the Workers' and Soldiers' Deputy Councils are only real as organs of revolt, as organs of revolutionary force. Outside these tasks the Councils are a mere plaything." This makes it unmistakably plain what the important thing really is for Lenin. He had, to be sure, to lay stress on the question of the hour; but the exclusiveness with which he does so, brooking no thought whatever of the Councils eventually becoming independent and permanent entities, speaks a language that cannot be misunderstood. In addition those phrases of 1915 ("organs of revolt" and "only in connexion with the revolt") recur almost word for word; whatever Lenin may have learnt and thought about the Councils during those two years in which he became essentially the historical Lenin, they still remained for him the means to a revolutionary end. That the Councils might not merely exist for the sake of the revolution, but that—and this in a far more profound and primary sense—the revolution might exist for the sake of the Councils, was something that simply never occurred to him. From this point of view—by which I mean not Lenin as a person but the sort of mentality that found an arch-exemplar in him—it is easy to understand why the Councils petered out both as a reality and as an idea.

That Lenin's slogan "All power to the Soviets!" was meant in nothing but a revolutionary-political sense is forced upon us even more strikingly when we come to the following exclamation in that essay: "And yet the 240,000 members of the Bolshevik Party are supposed to be incapable of governing Russia in the interests of the poor and against those of the rich!" So that "All power to the Soviets!" means little more at bottom than "All power to the Party through the Soviets!"—and there is nothing that points beyond this revolutionary-political, indeed party-political aspect to something different, socialistic and structural. Soon afterwards Lenin asserts that the Bolsheviks are "centralists by conviction, by the nature of the programme and the whole tactics of their party"; hence centralism is expressly characterized as being not merely tactical but a matter of principle. The proletarian State, we are told, is to be centralist. The Councils, therefore, have to subordinate themselves to a "strong Government"—what remains then of their autonomous reality? It is true that they, too, are conceded a "special centralism": no Bolshevist has anything to say against their "concentration into branches of production", their centralization. But obviously Lenin had no inkling that such "concentrations" bear a socialist, socially formative character only when they arise spontaneously, from below upwards, when they are not concentrations at all but associations, not a centralist process but a federalist one.

In Lenin's summons "To the People" ten days after the seizure of power we read: "From now on your Councils are organs of State-power, fully authorized to make all decisions." The tasks that were assigned soon afterwards to the Councils referred essentially to control. This was due very largely to the situation itself, but the frame of reference was far too small; the positive counterbalance was missing. Such petty powers were not enough to enable the Councils "to display their talents and capabilities to the full". We hear Lenin repeating in March, 1918, at the Party Congress his ideas about the new type of State "without bureaucracy, without police, without a standing Army", but he adds: "In Russia hardly more than a beginning has been made, and a bad beginning at that." It would be a grave error to think that only the inadequate execution of an adequate design was to blame: the design itself lacked the substance of life. "In our Soviets," he says by way of explanation, "there is still much that is crude, incomplete"; but the really dire and disastrous thing about it was that the leaders, who were not merely political but spiritual leaders as well, never directed the Soviets towards development and completion. "The men who created the Commune," Lenin goes on, "did not understand it." This is reminiscent of his utterance the day after his arrival in Russia: "We have clung to the Councils, but have not grasped them." The truth is that he did not "understand" them even now for what they really were—and did not wish to understand them.

In the same speech Lenin declared in answer to Bukharin, who had demanded that an outline of the socialist order be included in the programme, that "We cannot outline Socialism. What Socialism will look like when it takes on its final forms we do not know and cannot say." No doubt this is the Marxist line of thought, but it shows up in the full light of history the limitations of the Marxist outlook in its relation to an emergent or would-be emergent reality: a failure to recognize potentialities which require, if they are to develop, the stimulus of the idea of social form. We may not "know" what Socialism will look like, but we can know what we want it to look like, and this knowing and willing, this conscious willing itself influences what is to be—and if one is a centralist one's centralism influences what is to be. Always in history there exist, even if in varying degrees of strength, centralist and decentralist trends of development side by side; and it is of vital importance in the long run *for which* of the two the conscious will, together with whatever power it may have acquired at the time, elects. What is more, there is scarcely anything harder, or more rare, than for a will invested with power to free itself from centralism. What more natural or more logical than that a centralist will should fail to recognize the decentralist potentialities in the forms it makes use of? "The bricks are not yet made," says Lenin, "with which Socialism will be built." Because of his centralism he could not know and acknowledge the Councils as such bricks, he could not help them to become so, nor did they become so.

Soon after the Party Congress Lenin stated in the first draft of the *Theses on the Immediate Tasks of Soviet Authority*, in a section not included in the final version: "We are for democratic centralism. . . . The opponents of centralism are always pointing to autonomy and federation as a means of combating the hazards of centralism. In reality democratic centralism in no way precludes autonomy, rather it postulates the need for it. In reality even federation [here Lenin only has political federation in mind] in no way contradicts democratic centralism. In a really democratic order, and all the more in a State built up on the Soviet principle, federation is only a step towards a really democratic centralism." It is clear that Lenin has no thought of limiting the centralist principle by the federalist principle; from his revolutionary-political point of view he only tolerates a federal reality so long as it resolves itself into centralism. The direction, the whole line of thought is thus unequivocally centralistic. Nor is there any essential difference when we come to local autonomy: it is expedient to permit this to a certain degree and to grant it its terms of action; only the line must be drawn at that point where the real decisions and consequently the central instructions begin. All these popular and social formations only have political, strategic, tactical and provisional validity; not one of them is endowed with a genuine *raison d'être*, an independent structural value; not one of them is to be preserved and fostered as a living limb of the community-to-be.

A month after Lenin had dictated his draft the "Left Communists" pointed out how injurious it was for the seeds of Socialism that the form which State administration was taking lay in the direction of bureaucratic centralization, elimination of the independence of the local Soviets and repudiation, in fact, of the type of "Commune-State" governing itself from below—the very type, therefore, of which Lenin said in his speech that the Soviet Authority actually was. There can be no more doubt to-day as to who was right in assessing the situation and the trends to come—Lenin or his critics. But Lenin himself knew it well enough towards the end of his life. References to the Paris Commune become fewer and fewer after that speech, until they cease altogether.

A year after the October Revolution, Lenin had stated that "the apparatus of officialdom in Russia was completely shattered", but at the end of 1920 he characterized the Soviet Republic as "a Work-State with bureaucratic excrescences", and that, he said, "was the truth about the transition". The fact that in the years to come the proportion of excrescences to the trunk from which they sprouted increased alarmingly, and the buddings of the state of affairs to which the transition was supposed to lead grew less and less, could not remain hidden from Lenin. At the end of 1922 in the report *Five Years of Russian Revolution and the World Revolution in Perspective* which Lenin made to the Fourth Congress of the Communist International, he says simply: "We have taken over the old State apparatus." He solaces himself with the assurance that in a few years they will succeed in modifying the apparatus from top to bottom. This hope was not fulfilled and could not be fulfilled given Lenin's assumptions: he was thinking in the main of training and attracting new forces, but

the problem was one of structure and not of personnel; a bureaucracy does not change when its names are changed, and even
the best-trained graduates of the Soviet schools and Workers'
Faculties succumb to its atmosphere.

Lenin's main disappointment was the continued existence of
the bureaucracy which, if not in its personnel, certainly in its
ruthless efficacy, once more proved stronger than the revolutionary principle. He does not seem to have touched the deeper
causes of this phenomenon, and that is understandable enough.
The October Revolution was a social revolution only in the
sense that it effected certain changes in the social order and its
stratification, in the social forms and institutions. But a true
social revolution must, over and above that, establish the rights
of society *vis-à-vis* the State. Although in respect of this task
Lenin pointed out that the withering away of the State would
be accomplished by way of a development whose duration
could not as yet be measured nor its manner imagined, yet,
to the extent that this development could be realized right
now, he acknowledged the task as determining the leaders'
immediate programme of action and called the new State-
form whose realization was to be tackled at once, the
"Commune State". But the "Commune State" had been
characterized clearly enough by Marx as freeing economic
society to the greatest possible extent from the shackles of the
political principle. "Once the communal order of things," he
wrote, "had been introduced in Paris and in the centres of
second rank, the old centralized government would have had
to give way in the provinces also to the producers' self-government." This shifting of the power of decision from the political
to the social principle—which had been worked out and given
its ideal basis in France by the social thinking from Saint-
Simon to Proudhon—was proclaimed by Lenin as the base-
line for the organizing activity of the leaders, but in point of
fact it did not become such a base-line. The political principle
established itself anew, in changed guise, all-powerful; and the
perils actually threatening the revolution gave him a broad
justification. Let it remain undisputed that the situation as it
was would not have allowed of a radical reduction of the
political principle; what, however, would at any rate have been
possible was the laying down of a base-line in accordance
with which, as changing circumstances allowed, the power-
frontiers of the social principle could have been extended.

Precisely the opposite happened. The representatives of the political principle, that is, mainly the "professional revolutionaries" who got to the top, jealously watched over the unrestrictedness of their sphere of action. It is true that they augmented their ranks with competent persons recruited from the people and that they filled up the gaps as they arose, but those who were admitted to the directorate bore the stamp of the political principle on their very souls; they became elements of the State substance and ceased to be elements of the social substance, and whoever resisted this change could not make himself heard at the top or soon ceased to want to. The power of the social principle could not and dared not grow. The beginnings of a "producers' self-government" to which the revolution spontaneously gave rise, above all the local Soviets, became, despite the apparent freedom of expression and decision, so enfeebled by the all-pervading Party domination with its innumerable ways visible and invisible of compelling people to conform to the doctrine and will of the Central Authority, that little was left of that "outburst of creative folk-power" which had produced them. The "dictatorship of the proletariat" is *de facto* a dictatorship of the State over society, one that is naturally acclaimed or tolerated by the overwhelming mass of people for the sake of the completed social revolution they still hope to see achieved by this means. The bureaucratism from which Lenin suffered, and suffered precisely because it had been his business to abolish it (the "Commune State" being, for him, nothing less than the debureaucratized State), is merely the necessary concomitant to the sovereignty of the political principle.

It is worth noting that within the Party itself attempts were made again and again to break this sovereignty. The most interesting of them, because it sprang from the industrial workers, seems to my mind to be the "Workers' Opposition" of March, 1921, which proposed that the Central Organs for the administration of the whole national economy of the Republic should be elected by the united trades-associations of producers. This was not a Producers' Government by any means but it was an important step towards it, although lacking any real decentralist character. Lenin rejected this "anarcho-syndicalist deviation" on the ground that a union of producers could be considered by a Marxist only in a classless society composed exclusively of workers as producers, but that in Russia at present there were, apart from remnants of the capitalist epoch, still two classes left—peasants and workers. So long, therefore, as Communism was still aiming at perfection and had not turned all peasants into workers a self-governing economy could not, in Lenin's opinion, be considered. In other words (since the completion of Communism coincides with the complete withering away of the State): a fundamental reduction of the State's internal sphere of power cannot be thought of before the State has breathed its last. This paradox has become the operative maxim for the directorate of the Soviet Régime.

Only from this point of view can Lenin's changing attitude to the Co-operative System be grasped as a whole.

There is no point, however, in picking on the contradictions in a critical spirit. Lenin himself emphasized in 1918, not without reason, that always when a new class enters the historical arena as the leader of society there comes unfailingly a period of experiment and vacillation over the choice of new methods to meet the new objective situation; three years later he even asserted that things had only proved, "as always in the history of revolutions, that the movement runs in a zigzag". He failed to notice that though all this may be true of political revolutions, yet when, for the first time in history on so large a scale, the element of social change is added, humanity as a whole (and this means the people to whom events happen as well as the witnesses of them) longs despite all the experiments and vacillations to be made aware of the one clear earnest of the future: the movement towards community in freedom. In the case of the Russian Revolution whatever else may have appeared to them in the way of portents nothing of this kind ever became visible, and Lenin's changing attitude to the Co-operative system is one proof the more that such a movement does not exist.

In the pre-revolutionary period Lenin regarded the Co-operatives existing in bourgeois society as "miserable palliatives" only and bulwarks of the petty bourgeois spirit. A month before the October Revolution, faced with the tremendous economic crisis that was sweeping Russia, he put forward among the "revolutionary-democratic" measures to be taken immediately, the compulsory unification of the whole nation into Consumer Co-operatives. The following January he wrote in the draft of a decree: "All citizens must belong to a local Consumer Co-operative" and "the existing Consumer Co-operatives will be nationalized". In some Party circles this demand was understood and approved as aiming at the elimination of the Co-operatives, for they saw, as a Bolshevist theoretician no doubt rightly expressed it, in the element of *voluntary* membership the essential hallmark of a Co-operative. Lenin did not intend it to be understood that way. True, the Co-operative as a small island in capitalist society was, so he said, only "a shop", but the Co-operative which, after the abolition of private capital, comprises the whole of society "is Socialism", and it is therefore the task of the Soviet authorities to change all citizens without exception into members of a general State Co-operative, "a single gigantic Co-opera-tive". He does not see that the Co-operative principle thereby loses all independent content, indeed its very existence as a principle, and that nothing remains but a necessarily centralist-bureaucratic State-institution under a name that has become meaningless. The realization of this programme was under-taken in the years immediately following: all Co-operatives were merged under the leadership of the Consumer Co-opera-tives, which were turned into what amounted to State goods-distribution centres. As to immediate nationalization pure and simple, even two years after he had formulated the "Tasks of the Soviet Authority" Lenin was still holding back. He denounced those who were outspoken enough to demand a single nexus of State organizations to replace the Co-operatives. "That would be all right, but it is impossible", he said, meaning "impossible at present". At the same time he held fast in principle to the idea of the Co-operative as such, which, he declared (recalling Marx and his own attitude at the Copen-hagen Congress of the International in 1910, where he had stressed the possible socializing influence of the Co-operative after the capitalists had been expropriated), might be a means of building the new economic order. It was therefore a question, he said, of finding new Co-operative forms "which correspond to the economic and political conditions of the proletarian dictatorship" and which "facilitate the transition to real socialist centralism". An institution the very essence of which is the germ and core of social decentralization was in con-sequence to be made the building element of a new close-meshed State centralism of "socialist" stamp. Obviously Lenin was not proceeding from theoretical assumptions but from the practical requirements of the hour which, as the world knows, were extremely grave and necessitated the most strenuous exertions. When Lenin, in a statement reminiscent of the postulates of the "Utopians" and "Anarchists"—but naturally twisting their meaning into its exact opposite—demanded the union of the Producer and Consumer Co-operatives, he did so because of the need to increase the supply of goods: the fitness of this measure being proved by the experience of the last two years. A year later we hear him polemicizing violently against the Co-operatives, which in their old and still unconquered form were a "bulwark of counter-revolutionary opinion". In his famous treatise on *Taxation in Kind* (spring, 1921) he points emphatically to the danger that lurks in the co-operation of small producers: it inevitably strengthens petty bourgeois capitalism. "The freedom and rights of the Co-operatives," he continues, "mean under present conditions in Russia, freedom and rights for capitalism. It would be a stupidity or a crime to close our eyes to this obvious truth." And further: "Under Soviet power Co-operative capitalism, as distinct from private capitalism, creates a variant of State capitalism and is as such advantageous and useful to us at present. . . . We must endeavour to guide the development of capitalism into the channels of Co-operative capitalism." This instructive warning only expressed what, in those years of falsely so-called "War Communism" (in October, 1921, Lenin himself spoke retrospectively of the mistake that had been made by "our having resolved to take in hand the immediate change-over to communist production and distribution") had been the guiding principle in practice.

But in the wake of the unfavourable outcome of extreme centralization and in connexion with the "New Economic policy" just beginning, a regressive tendency was already making itself felt. Shortly before that warning declaration of Lenin's a decree had been promulgated on the re-establishment of the various kinds of Co-operative—Consumer, Agricultural and Industrial—as an economic organization. Two months later there followed a decree with which a beginning was made for the wholesale cancellation of the previously arranged merging of all Co-operatives in the Association of Consumer Co-operatives, the "Zentrosoyus". Towards the end of the same year the president of this Association declared in a speech on the position and tasks of the Co-operatives that it was only natural that the State Co-operative apparatus, functioning in accordance with a fixed plan, should have become "bureau-cratic, inelastic and immovable", and he made mention of the voices "that spoke of the necessity of freeing the Co-operative from slavery to the State", indeed, he even admitted that there were times "when one had to speak of such a freeing". And true enough the people had often come to compare compulsory organization with bondage. Now the authorities "completely and unreservedly" abjured all official interference in the affairs of the Agricultural Co-operatives and contented themselves with the wide possibilities within the system of State Capital-ism for "influencing and regulating the Co-operatives by eco-nomic pressure", until those that "could not or would not adapt themselves" had been "rubbed out and liquidated". All the same, care was taken that reliable Party members should get into the directorate of the central as well as of the individual Societies and that the necessary "purges" were carried out under the representatives of the Co-operative.

Two years after the appearance of his *Taxation in Kind*, Lenin, in May, 1923, the peak period of the New Economic Development, provided the latter with its theoretical foundation in his great essay on the Co-operative System. "When we went over to the New Economics," he said, "we acted precipitately in one respect, namely, we forgot to think of the Co-operative System." But he no longer contents himself now with approving the Co-operative as a mere element to be built into the State economy of the transition period. All of a sudden the Co-opera-tive is jerked into the very centre of the social new order. Lenin now describes the Co-operative education of the people as "the only task that is left us". The "co-operativization" of Russia has acquired in his eyes a "colossal", a "gigantic", a "limitless" significance. "It is," he says, "not yet the actual building of the socialist society, but it contains everything necessary and sufficient for the building of this society." Yes, he goes even further: the Co-operative has become for him not merely the pre-condition of social building but the very core of it. "A social order of enlightened Co-operatives," he asserts, "with common ownership of the means of production, based on the class-victory of the proletariat over the bourgeoisie—that is a socialist order of society," and he concludes: "The simple growth of the Co-operative is as important for us as the growth of socialism," yes, "conditional to the complete co-operativiza-tion of Russia we would be already standing with both feet on socialist ground." In the planned, all-embracing State Co-operative he sees the fulfilment of the "dreams" of the old Co-operatives "begun with Robert Owen". Here the contradiction between idea and realization reaches its apogee. What those "Utopians", beginning with Robert Owen, were concerned about in their thoughts and plans for association was the voluntary combination of people into small independent units of communal life and work, and the voluntary combination of those into a community of communities. What Lenin describes as the fulfilment of these thoughts and plans is the diametrical opposite of them, is an immense, utterly centralized complex of State production-centres and State distribution-centres, a mechanism of bureaucratically run institutes for production and consumption, each locked into the other like cog-wheels: as for spontaneity, free association, there is no longer any room for them whatever, no longer the possibility of even dreaming of them—with the "fulfilment" of the dream the dream is gone. Such at any rate had been Lenin's conception of the dovetailing of the Co-operative system into the State, and in that otherwise very exhaustive essay of his written eight months before his death he did not deny it. He wanted to give the movement which had then reached its peak and which implied a reduction of centralism in all fields, a definitive theoretical basis; but he denied it— necessarily, given his train of thought—the basis of all bases: the element of freedom.

Some people have thought they could see in this marked turning of Lenin's towards the Co-operatives an approach to the theories of the Russian Populists, for whom such forms of communal association as persisted or renewed themselves within the body of the people were the core and bud of a future order of society, and whom Lenin had fought for so long. But the affinity is only apparent. Even now Lenin was not thinking for a moment of the Co-operative as a spontaneous, independent formation growing dynamically and a law unto itself. What he was now dreaming of, after all his grievous efforts to weld the people into a uniform whole that would follow him with utter devotion, after all his disappointments over "bureaucratic excrescences", with the mark of illness on him and near to death—was to unite two things which cannot be united, the all-overshadowing State and the full-blooded Co-operative, in other words: compulsion and freedom. At all periods of human history the Co-operative and its prototypes have been able really to develop only in the gaps left by the effective power of the State and its prototypes. A State with no gaps inevitably precludes the development of the Co-operative. Lenin's final idea was so to extend the Co-operative in scope and so to unify it in structure that it would only differ from the State functionally but coincide with it materially. That is the squaring of the circle.

Stalin has explained the change in Lenin's attitude to the Co-operatives from 1921 to 1923 by saying that State Capitalism had not gained foothold to the degree desired, and that the Co-operatives with their ten million members had begun to ally themselves very closely with the newly developing socialized industries. This certainly draws attention to Lenin's real motives, but it is not sufficient to explain his unexpected enthusiasm for Co-operatives. Rather, it is obvious that Lenin now perceived in the Co-operative principle a counterbalance to the bureaucracy he found so offensive. But the Co-operative could only have become such a counterbalance in its original free form, not in Lenin's compulsory form, which was dependent on a truly "gigantic" bureaucracy.

As we have said, Lenin's idea of compulsion was not carried out to the full. The regressive movement finally led, in May, 1924, to the restoration of voluntary membership, at first only for full citizens, that is, citizens entitled to vote, but later, early in 1928, in the rural Consumer Co-operatives for others as well, although with some limitation as to their rights. Towards the end of 1923 the Board of the Zentrosoyus stated: "We must confess that this change-over to free membership ought to have been made earlier. We could then have met this crisis on a surer foundation." All the same an indirect compulsion was henceforth exercised by means of preferential supplies to the Co-operatives. In 1925 we hear from the mouth of the then president of the Central Council of the Trades Unions that the Government, when issuing subsidies and loans, took account of a person's membership in a manner that came very near to compulsion. And ten years afterwards the urban Co-operatives, which had long suffered gravely under State interference, were abolished at a stroke in 654 cities.

What has been said will suffice to show how the Soviet régime continually oscillated in practice between immediate radical centralization and provisional tolerance of relatively decentralized areas, but never, even to the slightest degree, made the trend towards the goal of Socialism as formulated by Marx, namely, "the sloughing off of the political husk", the maxim of its conduct. One might amplify this by mentioning the changing attitude it adopted during the Five Year Plan of 1926 to 1931 to the collectivization of the peasantry. I shall content myself with listing a few characteristic proclamations and procedures in chronological sequence.

Towards the end of 1927, Molotov drew attention to the backwardness of agriculture and in order to overcome it demanded that the village Collectives—valuable despite their defects—should develop in conjunction with the general plan of industrialization. In June, 1928, Stalin declared it necessary to expand the existing Collectives as intensively as possible and establish new ones. In April, 1929, the slogan was given out at the Party Congress for the creation, still within the framework of the Five Year Plan, of a socialized area of production as a counterbalance to individual economy. The process of collectivization soon took on more or less obvious forms of compulsion and seemed so successful at first that Stalin stated at the end of the same year: "If collectivization goes on at this rate the contrast between town and village will be wiped out in accelerated tempo." At the beginning of 1930 the Central Committee of the Party estimated that the tempo envisaged in the Plan had been outstripped, and emphatically stressed the need for a concerted campaign against all attempts to slow the movement down. In three years' time complete collectivization would have been achieved with the techniques of persuasion, "aided by certain levers". The Executive Committees of the various districts vied with one another in the thoroughness of their administrative measures; a district was not infrequently declared an "area of complete collectivization" and where persuasion did not help threats were used. But it soon proved that the impression of smashing success, an impression fostered by the marked increase in the number of collective farm-economies, was a delusion. The peasants reacted in their own way, by anything from the slaughtering of cattle to actual uprisings, and the measures taken to liquidate the kulaks did little to remedy the evil; the small peasants often joined forces and the Red Army itself with its peasant sons reflected the prevailing dissatisfaction. Then Stalin, in his famous article "Dizzy with Success", performed the volte face that seemed necessary. The policy of collectivization, he declared, rested according to Lenin's doctrine on voluntary action. "You cannot create collective economies by force. That would be stupid and reactionary." Lenin had also taught, he said, that "it would be the greatest folly to try to introduce collective cultivation of the land by decree". The voluntary principle had suffered injury, the tempo of action had not corresponded to that of development, important intermediate stages on the way to the complete Village Commune had been by-passed. The Central Committee was therefore arranging, he said, for an end to be made of compulsory methods. In July the Party Congress proclaimed that collective economies could only be based on the principle of voluntary admission, all attempts to apply force or administrative coercion were "an offence against the Party line and an abuse of power". In the autumn the Commissar for Agriculture once more criticized "the crude and ultra-administrative methods which have been employed in respect of the collective economies and their members". But less than five months later, after a considerable number of peasants, as a result of the greater measure of freedom but in spite of the privileges newly offered, had left the Collectives, the same Commissar said in his Report to the Congress of the Soviets regarding the small and middling peasants who had not joined the Collective Movement: "Who are they for, for the kulaks or for the Collectives? ... Is it possible to remain neutral to-day?" In other words: he who is not for collectivization is against the Soviet régime. The Congress confirmed this view. During the next few years renewed measures of severity followed the alleviations necessitated by the famine crisis, until in 1936 nearly 90 per cent of the peasants had been collectivized, of which the Full Communes comprised only a diminishing fraction.

The old rustic Russia, as Maynard has rightly said, lasted up to 1929. That it was bundled out of the world with its traditional system of land-cultivation can, from the point of view of economic efficiency, only be approved. But, from the point of view of social structure, the question must be put very differently. From this angle there should be no talk of an Either-Or; the specific task was so to transform the existing structural units that they should be equal to the new conditions and demands, and at the same time retain their structural character and nature as self-activating cells. This task has not been fulfilled. It has been said, rightly enough, that Marxist thinking, geared as it is to the rationalized big-business form of farming, the industrialization and mechanization of agriculture, has been grafted onto the old Russian Village Community which had accustomed the peasants to the communal management of land. But the politically inspired tendency to turn agriculture into a department of industry and the peasants into the hired workers of this industry; the tendency to an all-embracing and all-regulating State economy; a tendency which regards the Agricultural Co-operative only as a stepping-stone to the Full Commune and this in its turn only as a stepping-stone to the local branch of the Agricultural Department of the Universal State Factory—such a tendency destroyed and was bound to destroy the whole structural value of the Village Community. One cannot treat either an individual or a social organism as a means to an end absolutely, without robbing it of its life-substance. "From the standpoint of Leninism," said Stalin in 1933, "the collective economies, and the Soviets as well, are, taken as a form of organization, a weapon and nothing but a weapon." One cannot in the nature of things expect a little tree that has been turned into a club to put forth leaves.

Far longer than with any other people the "medieval" tendency to associate in little bands for the purpose of common work has been preserved among the Russians. Of the most singular social formation to have sprung from this tendency, the *Artel*, Kropotkin could say some forty years ago that it constituted the proper substance of Russian peasant life—a loose, shifting association of fishermen and hunters, manual workers and traders, hauliers and returned Siberian convicts, peasants who travelled to the city to work as weavers or carpenters, and peasants who went in for communal corn-growing or cattle-raising in the village, with, however, divisions as between communal and individual property. Here an incomparable building element lay ready to hand for a great re-structural idea. The Bolshevist Revolution never used it. It had no use for independent small communities. Among the various types of "Kolkhoz" it favoured "for the present", as Stalin said, the agricultural *Artel* for economic reasons, but naturally the revolution saw in it nothing but a stepping-stone. One of Russia's best theoreticians of economics has defined the aim. Land cultivation, he said, would only be regarded as socialized when all the agricultural *Artels* had been replaced by State Collectives, when land, means of production and livestock belonged to the State. Then the peasants would live in community-houses as hired labourers of the State, in huge agrarian cities, themselves the nodes of areas blessed with more and more electrification. The fantastic picture to which this conception belongs is in very truth the picture of a society finally and utterly de-structured and destroyed. It is more—it is the picture of a State that has devoured society altogether.

The Soviet régime has achieved great things in the technology of economics and still greater things in the technology of war. Its citizens seem in the main to approve of it, for a variety of reasons, negative and positive, fictitious and real. In their attitude vague resignation appears mixed with practical confidence. It can be said in general that the individual submits to this régime, which grants him so little freedom of thought and action, perhaps because there is no going back and as regards technical achievements there is at least a going forward. Things look very different, at least to the impartial eye, when it comes to what has actually been achieved in the matter of Socialism: a mass of socialistic expostulations, no Socialist form at all. "What," asked the great sociologist Max Weber in 1918, "will that 'association' look like of which the Communist Manifesto speaks? What germ-cells of that kind of organization has Socialism in particular to offer if ever it gets a real chance to seize power and rule as it wills?" In the country where Socialism did get this chance there still existed such germ-cells, which no other country in our epoch could rival; but they were not brought to fruition. Nevertheless, there is still breathing-space for change and transformation—by which is meant not a change of tactics such as Lenin and his fellow-workers often effected, but a change of fundamentals. The change cannot go backwards, only forwards—but in a new direction. Whether forces as yet unnamed are stirring in the depths and will suddenly burst forth to bring about this change, on this question tremendous things depend.

Pierre Leroux, the man who appears to have used the word "Socialism" for the first time, knew what he was saying when he addressed the National Assembly in 1848 with these words: "If you have no will for human association I tell you that you are exposing civilization to the fate of dying in fearful agony."

X

IN THE MIDST OF CRISIS

FOR the last three decades we have felt that we were living in the initial phases of the greatest crisis humanity has ever known. It grows increasingly clear to us that the tremendous happenings of the past years, too, can be understood only as symptoms of this crisis. It is not merely the crisis of one economic and social system being superseded by another, more or less ready to take its place; rather all systems, old and new, are equally involved in the crisis. What is in question, therefore, is nothing less than man's whole existence in the world.

Ages ago, far beyond our calculation, this creature "Man" set out on his journey; from the point of view of Nature a well-nigh incomprehensible anomaly; from the point of view of the spirit an incarnation hardly less incomprehensible, perhaps unique; from the point of view of both a being whose very essence it was to be threatened with disaster every instant, both from within and without, exposed to deeper and deeper crises. During the ages of his earthly journey man has multiplied what he likes to call his "power over Nature" in increasingly rapid tempo, and he has borne what he likes to call the "creations of his spirit" from triumph to triumph. But at the same time he has felt more and more profoundly, as one crisis succeeded another, how fragile all his glories are; and in moments of clairvoyance he has come to realize that in spite of everything he likes to call "progress" he is not travelling along the high-road at all, but is picking his precarious way along a narrow ledge between two abysses. The graver the crisis becomes the more earnest and consciously responsible is the knowledge demanded of us; for although what is demanded is a deed, only that deed which is born of knowledge will help to overcome the crisis. In a time of great crisis it is not enough to look back to the immediate past in order to bring the enigma of the present nearer to solution: we have to bring the stage of the journey we have now reached face to face with its beginnings, so far as we can picture them.

The essential thing among all those things which once helped man to emerge from Nature and, notwithstanding his feebleness as a natural being, to assert himself—more essential even than the making of a "technical" world out of things expressly formed for the purpose—was this: that he banded together with his own kind for protection and hunting, food gathering and work; and did so in such a way that from the very beginning and thereafter to an increasing degree he faced the others as more or less independent entities and communicated with them as such, addressing and being addressed by them in that manner. This creation of a "social" world out of persons at once mutually dependent and independent differed in kind from all similar undertakings on the part of animals, just as the technical work of man differed in kind from all the animals' works. Apes, too, make use of some stick they happen to have found, as a lever, a digging-tool or a weapon; but that is an affair of chance only: they cannot conceive and produce a tool as an object constituted so and not otherwise and having an existence of its own. And again, many of the insects live in societies built up on a strict division of labour; but it is just this division of labour that governs absolutely their relations with one another; they are all as it were tools; only, their own society is the thing that makes use of them for its "instinctive" purposes; there is no improvisation, no degree, however modest, of mutual independence, no possibility of "free" regard for one another, and thus no person-to-person relationship. Just as the specific technical creations of man mean the conferring of independence on things, so his specific social creation means the conferring of independence on beings of his own kind. It is in the light of this specifically human idiosyncrasy that we have to interpret man's journey with all its ups and downs, and so also the point we have reached on this journey, our great and particular crisis.

In the evolution of mankind hitherto this, then, is the line that predominates: the forming and re-forming of communities on the basis of growing personal independence, their mutual recognition and collaboration on that basis. The two most important steps that the man of early times took on the road to human society can be established with some certainty. The first is that inside the individual clan each individual, through an extremely primitive form of division of labour, was recognized and utilized in his special capacity, so that the clan increasingly took on the character of an ever-renewed association of persons each the vehicle of a different function. The second is that different clans would, under certain conditions, band together in quest of food and for campaigns, and consolidated their mutual help as customs and laws that took firmer and firmer root; so that as once between individuals, so now between communities people discerned and acknowledged differences of nature and function. Wherever genuine human society has since developed it has always been on this same basis of functional autonomy, mutual recognition and mutual responsibility, whether individual or collective. Power-centres of various kinds have split off, organizing and guaranteeing the common order and security of all; but to the political sphere in the stricter sense, the State with its police-system and its bureaucracy, there was always opposed the organic, functionally organized society as such, a great society built up of various societies, the great society in which men lived and worked, competed with one another and helped one another; and in each of the big and little societies composing it, in each of these communes and communities the individual human being, despite all the difficulties and conflicts, felt himself at home as once in the clan, felt himself approved and affirmed in his functional independence and responsibility.

All this changed more and more as the centralistic political principle subordinated the de-centralistic social principle. The crucial thing here was not that the State, particularly in its more or less totalitarian forms, weakened and gradually displaced the free associations, but that the political principle with all its centralistic features percolated into the associations themselves, modifying their structure and their whole inner life, and thus politicized society to an ever-increasing extent. Society's assimilation in the State was accelerated by the fact that, as a result of modern industrial development and its ordered chaos, involving the struggle of all against all for access to raw materials and for a larger share of the world-market, there grew up, in place of the old struggles between States, struggles between whole societies. The individual society, feeling itself threatened not only by its neighbours' lust for

aggression but also by things in general, knew no way of
salvation save in complete submission to the principle of
centralized power; and, in the democratic forms of society no
less than in its totalitarian forms, it made this its guiding
principle. Everywhere the only thing of importance was the
minute organization of power, the unquestioning observance
of slogans, the saturation of the whole of society with the real
or supposed interests of the State. Concurrently with this there
is an internal development. In the monstrous confusion of
modern life, only thinly disguised by the reliable functioning
of the economic and State-apparatus, the individual clings
desperately to the collectivity. The little society in which he
was embedded cannot help him; only the great collectivities,
so he thinks, can do that, and he is all too willing to let himself
be deprived of personal responsibility: he only wants to obey.
And the most valuable of all goods—the life between man and
man—gets lost in the process; the autonomous relationships
become meaningless, personal relationships wither; and the
very spirit of man hires itself out as a functionary. The personal
human being ceases to be the living member of a social body
and becomes a cog in the "collective" machine. Just as his
degenerate technology is causing man to lose the feel of good
work and proportion, so the degrading social life he leads is
causing him to lose the feel of community—just when he is so
full of the illusion of living in perfect devotion to his
community.

A crisis of this kind cannot be overcome by struggling back
to an earlier stage of the journey, but only by trying to master
the problems as they are, without minimizing them. There
is no going back for us, we have to go through with it.
But we shall only get through if we know *where* we want to
go.

We must begin, obviously, with the establishment of a vital
peace which will deprive the political principle of its supremacy
over the social principle. And this primary objective cannot
in its turn be reached by any devices of political organization,
but only by the resolute will of all peoples to cultivate the
territories and raw materials of our planet and govern its
inhabitants, *together*. At this point, however, we are threatened
by a danger greater than all the previous ones: the danger of
a gigantic centralization of power covering the whole planet
and devouring all free community. Everything depends on

not handing the work of planetary management over to the political principle.

Common management is only possible as socialistic management. But if the fatal question for contemporary man is: Can he or can he not decide in favour of, and educate himself up to, a common socialistic economy? then the propriety of the question lies in an inquiry into Socialism itself: what sort of Socialism is it to be, under whose ægis the common economy of man is to come about, if at all?

The ambiguity of the terms we are employing is greater here than anywhere else. People say, for instance, that Socialism is the passing of the control of the means of production out of the hands of the entrepreneurs into the hands of the collectivity; but again, it all depends on what you mean by "collectivity". If it is what we generally call the "State", that is to say, an institution in which a virtually unorganized mass allows its affairs to be conducted by "representation", as they call it, then the chief change in a socialistic society will be this: that the workers will feel themselves represented by the holders of power. But what is representation? Does not the worst defect of modern society lie precisely in everybody letting himself be represented *ad libitum*? And in a "socialistic" society will there not, on top of this passive political representation, be added a passive economic representation, so that, with everybody letting himself be represented by everybody else, we reach a state of practically unlimited representation and hence, ultimately, the reign of practically unlimited centralist accumulation of power? But the more a human group lets itself be represented in the management of its common affairs, and the more it lets itself be represented from outside, the less communal life there is in it and the more impoverished it becomes as a community. For community—not the primitive sort, but the sort possible and appropriate to modern man—declares itself primarily in the common and active management of what it has in common, and without this it cannot exist.

The primary aspiration of all history is a genuine community of human beings—genuine because it is *community all through*. A community that failed to base itself on the actual and communal life of big and little groups living and working together, and on their mutual relationships, would be fictitious and counterfeit. Hence everything depends on whether the collectivity into whose hands the control of the means of pro-

duction passes will facilitate and promote in its very structure
and in all its institutions the genuine common life of the various
groups composing it—on whether, in fact, these groups themselves become proper foci of the productive process; therefore
on whether the masses are so organized in their separate
organizations (the various "communities") as to be as powerful
as the common economy of man permits; therefore on whether
centralist representation only goes as far as the new order of
things absolutely demands. The fatal question does not take
the form of a fundamental Either-Or: it is only a question of
the right line of demarcation that has to be drawn ever anew—
the thousandfold system of demarcation between the spheres
which must of necessity be centralized and those which can
operate in freedom; between the degree of government and the
degree of autonomy; between the law of unity and the claims
of community. The unwearying scrutiny of conditions in terms
of the claims of community, as something continually exposed
to the depredations of centralist power—the *custody of the true
boundaries*, ever changing in accordance with changing historical
circumstances: such would be the task of humanity's spiritual
conscience, a Supreme Court unexampled in kind, the right
true representation of a living idea. A new incarnation is
waiting here for Plato's "custodians".

Representation of an idea, I say: not of a rigid principle but
of a living form that wants to be shaped in the daily stuff of
this earth. Community should not be made into a principle;
it, too, should always satisfy a situation rather than an abstraction. The realization of community, like the realization of any
idea, cannot occur once and for all time: always it must be the
moment's answer to the moment's question, and nothing
more.

In the interests of its vital meaning, therefore, the idea of
community must be guarded against all contamination by
sentimentality or emotionalism. Community is never a mere
attitude of mind, and if it is *feeling* it is an inner disposition
that is felt. Community is the inner disposition or constitution
of a life in common, which knows and embraces in itself hard
"calculation", adverse "chance", the sudden access of
"anxiety". It is community of tribulation and only because of
that community of spirit; community of toil and only because
of that community of salvation. Even those communities which
call the spirit their master and salvation their Promised Land,

the "religious" communities, are community only if they serve
their lord and master in the midst of simple, unexalted,
unselected reality, a reality not so much chosen by them as
sent to them just as it is; they are community only if they
prepare the way to the Promised Land through the thickets of
this pathless hour. True, it is not "works" that count, but the
work of faith does. A community of faith truly exists only
when it is a community of work.

The real essence of community is to be found in the fact—
manifest or otherwise—that is has a centre. The real beginning
of a community is when its members have a common relation
to the centre overriding all other relations: the circle is described
by the radii, not by the points along its circumference. And the
originality of the centre cannot be discerned unless it is discerned as being transpicuous to the light of something divine.
All this is true; but the more earthly, the more creaturely, the
more attached the centre is, the truer and more transpicuous
it will be. This is where the "social" element comes in. Not as
something separate, but as the all-pervading realm where man
stands the test; and it is here that the truth of the centre is
proved. The early Christians were not content with the community that existed alongside or even above the world, and
they went into the desert so as to have no more community
save with God and no more disturbing world. But it was
shown them that God does not wish man to be alone with him;
and above the holy impotence of the hermit there rose the
Brotherhood. Finally, going beyond St. Benedict, St. Francis
entered into alliance with all creatures.

Yet a community need not be "founded". Wherever
historical destiny had brought a group of men together in a
common fold, there was room for the growth of a genuine
community; and there was no need of an altar to the city deity
in the midst when the citizens knew they were united round—
and by—the Nameless. A living togetherness, constantly renewing itself, was already there, and all that needed strengthening
was the immediacy of relationships. In the happiest instances common affairs were deliberated and decided not
through representatives but in gatherings in the market-place;
and the unity that was felt in public permeated all personal
contacts. The danger of seclusion might hang over the community, but the communal spirit banished it; for here this
spirit flourished as nowhere else and broke windows for itself

in the narrow walls, with a large view of people, mankind and the world.

All this, I may be told, has gone irrevocably and for ever. The modern city has no agora and the modern man has no time for negotiations of which his elected representatives can very well relieve him. The pressure of numbers and the forms of organization have destroyed any real togetherness. Work forges other personal links than does leisure, sport again others than politics, the day is cleanly divided and the soul too. These links are material ones; though we follow our common interests and tendencies together, we have no use for "immediacy". The collectivity is not a warm, friendly gathering but a great link-up of economic and political forces inimical to the play of romantic fancies, only understandable in terms of quantity, expressing itself in actions and effects—a thing which the individual has to belong to with no intimacies of any kind but all the time conscious of his energetic contribution. Any "unions" that resist the inevitable trend of events must disappear. There is still the family, of course, which, as a domestic community, seems to demand and guarantee a modicum of communal life; but it too will either emerge from the crisis in which it is involved, as an association for a common purpose, or else it will perish.

Faced with this medley of correct premises and absurd conclusions I declare in favour of a rebirth of the commune. A rebirth—not a bringing back. It cannot in fact be brought back, although I sometimes think that every touch of helpful neighbourliness in the apartment-house, every wave of warmer comradeship in the lulls and "knock-offs" that occur even in the most perfectly "rationalized" factory, means an addition to the world's community-content; and although a rightly constituted village commune sometimes strikes me as being a more real thing than a parliament; but it cannot be brought back. Yet whether a rebirth of the commune will ensue from the "water and spirit" of the social transformation that is imminent —on this, it seems to me, hangs the whole fate of the human race. An organic commonwealth—and only such commonwealths can join together to form a shapely and articulated race of men—will never build itself up out of individuals but only out of small and ever smaller communities: a nation is a community to the degree that it is a community of communities. If the family does not emerge from the crisis which to-day has all the appearance of a disintegration, purified and renewed, then the State will be nothing more than a machine stoked with the bodies of generations of men. The community that would be capable of such a renewal exists only as a residue. If I speak of its rebirth I am not thinking of a permanent world-situation but an altered one. By the new communes—they might equally well be called the new Co-operatives—I mean the subjects of a changed economy: the collectives into whose hands the control of the means of production is to pass. Once again, everything depends on whether they will be ready.

Just how much economic and political autonomy—for they will of necessity be economic and political units at once—will have to be conceded to them is a technical question that must be asked and answered over and over again; but asked and answered beyond the technical level, in the knowledge that the internal authority of a community hangs together with its external authority. The relationship between centralism and decentralization is a problem which, as we have seen, cannot be approached in principle, but, like everything to do with the relationship between idea and reality, only with great spiritual tact, with the constant and tireless weighing and measuring of the right proportion between them. Centralization—but only so much as is indispensable in the given conditions of time and place. And if the authorities responsible for the drawing and re-drawing of lines of demarcation keep an alert conscience, the relations between the base and the apex of the power-pyramid will be very different from what they are now, even in States that call themselves Communist, i.e. struggling for community. There will have to be a system of representation, too, in the sort of social pattern I have in mind; but it will not, as now, be composed of the pseudo-representatives of amorphous masses of electors but of representatives well tested in the life and work of the communes. The represented will not, as they are to-day, be bound to their representatives by some windy abstraction, by the mere phraseology of a party-programme, but concretely, through common action and common experience.

The essential thing, however, is that the process of community-building shall run all through the relations of the communes with one another. Only a community of communities merits the title of Commonwealth.

The picture I have hastily sketched will doubtless be laid among the documents of "Utopian Socialism" until the storm turns them up again. Just as I do not believe in Marx's "gestation" of the new form, so I do not believe either in Bakunin's virgin-birth from the womb of Revolution. But I do believe in the meeting of idea and fate in the creative hour.

EPILOGUE

AN EXPERIMENT
THAT DID NOT FAIL

THE era of advanced Capitalism has broken down the structure of society. The society which preceded it was composed of different societies; it was complex, and pluralistic in structure. This is what gave it its peculiar social vitality and enabled it to resist the totalitarian tendencies inherent in the pre-revolutionary centralistic State, though many elements were very much weakened in their autonomous life. This resistance was broken by the policy of the French Revolution, which was directed against the special rights of all free associations. Thereafter centralism in its new, capitalistic form succeeded where the old had failed: in atomizing society. Exercising control over the machines and, with their help, over the whole society, Capitalism wants to deal only with individuals; and the modern State aids and abets it by progressively dispossessing groups of their autonomy. The militant organizations which the proletariat erected against Capitalism—Trades Unions in the economic sphere and the Party in the political—are unable in the nature of things to counteract this process of dissolution, since they have no access to the life of society itself and its foundations: production and consumption. Even the transfer of capital to the State is powerless to modify the social structure, even when the State establishes a network of compulsory associations, which, having no autonomous life, are unfitted to become the cells of a new socialist society.

From this point of view the heart and soul of the Co-operative Movement is to be found in the trend of a society towards structural renewal, the re-acquisition, in new tectonic forms, of the internal social relationships, the establishment of a new *consociatio consociationum*. It is (as I have shown) a fundamental error to view this trend as romantic or utopian merely because in its early stages it had romantic reminiscences and utopian fantasies. At bottom it is thoroughly topical and constructive; that is to say, it aims at changes which, in the given circumstances and with the means at its disposal, are feasible. And, psychologically speaking, it is based on one of the eternal human needs, even though this need has often been forcibly suppressed or rendered insensible: the need of man to feel his own house as a room in some greater, all-embracing structure in which he is at home, to feel that the other inhabitants of it with whom he lives and works are all acknowledging and confirming his individual existence. An association based on community of views and aspirations alone cannot satisfy this need; the only thing that can do that is an association which makes for communal living. But here the co-operative organization of production or consumption proves, each in its own way, inadequate, because both touch the individual only at a certain point and do not mould his actual life. On account of their merely partial or functional character all such organizations are equally unfitted to act as cells of a new society. Both these partial forms have undergone vigorous development, but the Consumer Co-operatives only in highly bureaucratic forms and the Producer Co-operatives in highly specialized forms: they are less able to embrace the whole life of society to-day than ever. The consciousness of this fact is leading to the synthetic form: the Full Co-operative. By far the most powerful effort in this direction is the Village Commune, where communal living is based on the amalgamation of production and consumption, production being understood not exclusively as agriculture alone but as the organic union of agriculture with industry and with the handicrafts as well.

The repeated attempts that have been made during the last 150 years, both in Europe and America, to found village settlements of this kind, whether communistic or co-operative in the narrower sense, have mostly met with failure.[1] I would apply the word "failure" not merely to those settlements, or attempts at settlements, which after a more or less short-lived existence either disintegrated completely or took on a Capitalist complexion, thus going over to the enemy camp; I would also

[1] Of course, I am not dealing here with the otherwise successful "socio-economic organizations, used by governmental or semi-governmental agencies to improve rural conditions" (Infield, *Co-operative Communities at Work*, p. 63).

apply it to those that maintained themselves in isolation. For the real, the truly structural task of the new Village Communes begins with their *federation*, that is, their union under the same principle that operates in their internal structure. Hardly anywhere has it come to this. Even where, as with the Dukhobors in Canada, a sort of federative union exists, the federation itself continues to be isolated and exerts no attractive and educative influence on society as a whole, with the result that the task never gets beyond its beginnings and, consequently, there can be no talk of success in the socialist sense. It is remarkable that Kropotkin saw in these two elements—isolation of the settlements from one another and isolation from the rest of society—the efficient causes of their failure even as ordinarily understood.

The socialistic task can only be accomplished to the degree that the new Village Commune, combining the various forms of production and uniting production and consumption, exerts a structural influence on the amorphous urban society. The influence will only make itself felt to the full if, and to the extent that, further technological developments facilitate and actually require the decentralization of industry; but even now a pervasive force is latent in the modern communal village, and it may spread to the towns. It must be emphasized again that the tendency we are dealing with is constructive and topical: it would be romantic and utopian to want to destroy the towns, as once it was romantic and utopian to want to destroy the machines, but it is constructive and topical to try to transform the town organically in the closest possible alliance with technological developments and to turn it into an aggregate composed of smaller units. Indeed, many countries to-day show significant beginnings in this respect.

As I see history and the present, there is only one all-out effort to create a Full Co-operative which justifies our speaking of success in the socialistic sense, and that is the Jewish Village Commune in its various forms, as found in Palestine. No doubt it, too, is up against grave problems in the sphere of internal relationships, federation, and influence on society at large, but it alone has proved its vitality in all three spheres. Nowhere else in the history of communal settlements is there this tireless groping for the form of community-life best suited to this particular human group, nowhere else this continual trying and trying again, this going to it and getting down to it, this critical awareness, this sprouting of new branches from the same stem and out of the same formative impulse. And nowhere else is there this alertness to one's own problems, this constant facing up to them, this tough will to come to terms with them, and this indefatigable struggle—albeit seldom expressed in words—to overcome them. Here, and here alone, do we find in the emergent community organs of self-knowledge whose very sensitiveness has constantly reduced its members to despair—but this is a despair that destroys wishful thinking only to raise up in its stead a greater hope which is no longer emotionalism but sheer work. Thus on the soberest survey and on the soberest reflection one can say that, in this one spot in a world of partial failures, we can recognize a non-failure—and, such as it is, a signal non-failure.

What are the reasons for this? We could not get to know the peculiar character of this co-operative colonization better than by following up these reasons.

One element in these reasons has been repeatedly pointed out: that the Jewish Village Commune in Palestine owes its existence not to a doctrine but to a situation, to the needs, the stress, the demands of the situation. In establishing the "Kvuza" or Village Commune the primary thing was not ideology but work. This is certainly correct, but with one limitation. True, the point was to solve certain problems of work and construction which the Palestinian reality forced on the settlers, by collaborating; what a loose conglomeration of individuals could not, in the nature of things, hope to overcome, or even try to overcome, things being what they were, the collective could try to do and actually succeeded in doing. But what is called the "ideology"—I personally prefer the old but untarnished word "Ideal"—was not just something to be added afterwards, that would justify the accomplished facts. In the spirit of the members of the first Palestinian Communes ideal motives joined hands with the dictates of the hour; and in the motives there was a curious mixture of memories of the Russian *Artel*, impressions left over from reading the so-called "utopian" Socialists, and the half-unconscious after-effects of the Bible's teachings about social justice. The important thing is that this ideal motive remained loose and pliable in almost every respect. There were various dreams about the future: people saw before them a new, more comprehensive form of the family, they saw themselves as the advance guard of the

Workers' Movement, as the direct instrument for the realization of Socialism, as the prototype of the new society; they had as their goal the creation of a new man and a new world. But nothing of this ever hardened into a cut-and-dried programme. These men did not, as everywhere else in the history of co-operative settlements, bring a plan with them, a plan which the concrete situation could only fill out, not modify; the ideal gave an impetus but no dogma, it stimulated but did not dictate.

More important, however, is that, behind the Palestinian situation that set the tasks of work and reconstruction, there was the historical situation of a people visited by a great external crisis and responding to it with a great inner change. Further, this historical situation threw up an élite—the "Chaluzim" or pioneers—drawn from all classes of the people and thus beyond class. The form of life that befitted this élite was the Village Commune, by which I mean not a single note but the whole scale, ranging from the social structure of "mutual aid" to the Commune itself. This form was the best fitted to fulfil the tasks of the central Chaluzim, and at the same time the one in which the social ideal could materially influence the national idea. As the historical conditions have shown, it was impossible for this élite and the form of life it favoured, to become static or isolated; all its tasks, everything it did, its whole pioneering spirit made it the centre of attraction and a central influence. The Pioneer spirit ("Chaluziuth") is, in every part of it, related to the growth of a new and transformed national community; the moment it grew self-sufficient it would have lost its soul. The Village Commune, as the nucleus of the evolving society, had to exert a powerful pull on the people dedicated to this evolution, and it had not merely to educate its friends and associates for genuine communal living, but also to exercise a formative structural effect on the social periphery. The dynamics of history determined the dynamic character of the relations between Village Commune and society.

This character suffered a considerable setback when the tempo of the crisis in the outer world became so rapid, and its symptoms so drastic, that the inner change could not keep pace with them. To the extent that Palestine had been turned from the one and only land of the "Aliyah"—ascent—into a country of immigrants, a quasi-Chaluziuth came into being

alongside the genuine Chaluziuth. The pull exerted by the
Commune did not abate, but its educative powers were not
adapted to the influx of very different human material, and
this material sometimes succeeded in influencing the tone of
the community. At the same time the Commune's relations
with society at large underwent a change. As the structure of
the latter altered, it withdrew more and more from the
transforming influence of the focal cells, indeed, it began in
its turn to exert an influence on them—not always noticeable
at first, but unmistakable to-day—by seizing on certain
essential elements in them and assimilating them to
itself.

In the life of peoples, and particularly peoples who find
themselves in the midst of some historical crisis, it is of crucial
importance whether genuine élites (which means élites that do
not usurp but are called to their central function) arise, whether
these élites remain loyal to their duty to society, establishing
a relationship to it rather than to themselves, and finally,
whether they have the power to replenish and renew themselves in a manner conformable with their task. The historical
destiny of the Jewish settlements in Palestine brought the élite
of the Chaluzim to birth, and it found its social nuclear form in
the Village Commune. Another wave of this same destiny has
washed up, together with the quasi-Chaluzim, a problem for the
real Chaluzim élite. It has caused a problem that was always
latent to come to the surface. They have not yet succeeded in
mastering it and yet must master it before they can reach the next
stage of their task. The inner tension between those who take
the *whole* responsibility for the community on their shoulders
and those who somehow evade it, can be resolved only at a very
deep level.

The point where the problem emerges is neither the individual's relationship to the idea nor his relationship to the community nor yet to work; on all these points even the quasi-
Chaluzim gird up their loins and do by and large what is
expected of them. The point where the problem emerges,
where people are apt to slip, is in their relationship
to their fellows. By this I do not mean the question, much
discussed in its day, of the intimacy that exists in the small
and the loss of this intimacy in the big Kvuza; I mean
something that has nothing whatever to do with the size of the
Commune. It is not a matter of intimacy at all; this appears

when it must, and if it is lacking, that's all there is to it. The question is rather one of openness. A real community need not consist of people who are perpetually together; but it must consist of people who, precisely because they are comrades, have mutual access to one another and are ready for one another. A real community is one which in every point of its being possesses, potentially at least, the whole character of community. The internal questions of a community are thus in reality questions relating to its own genuineness, hence to its inner strength and stability. The men who created the Jewish Communes in Palestine instinctively knew this; but the instinct no longer seems to be as common and alert as it was. Yet it is in this most important field that we find that remorselessly clear-sighted collective self-observation and self-criticism to which I have already drawn attention. But to understand and value it aright we must see it together with the amazingly positive relationship—amounting to a regular faith—which these men have to the inmost being of their Commune. The two things are two sides of the same spiritual world and neither can be understood without the other.

In order to make the causes of the non-failure of these Jewish communal settlements sufficiently vivid, in Palestine, I began with the non-doctrinaire character of their origins. This character also determined their development in all essentials. New forms and new intermediate forms were constantly branching off—in complete freedom. Each one grew out of the particular social and spiritual needs as these came to light—in complete freedom, and each one acquired, even in the initial stages, its own ideology—in complete freedom, each struggling to propagate itself and spread and establish its proper sphere—all in complete freedom. The champions of the various forms each had his say, the pros and cons of each individual form were frankly and fiercely debated—always, however, on the plane which everybody accepted as obvious: the common cause and common task, where each form recognized the relative justice of all the other forms in their special functions. All this is unique in the history of co-operative settlements. What is more: nowhere, as far as I see, in the history of the Socialist movement were men so deeply involved in the process of differentiation and yet so intent on preserving the principle of integration.

The various forms and intermediate forms that arose in this

way at different times and in different situations represented different kinds of social structure. The people who built them were generally aware of this as also of the particular social and spiritual needs that actuated them. They were not aware to the same extent that the different forms corresponded to different human types and that just as new forms branched off from the original Kvuza, so new types branched off from the original Chaluz type, each with its special mode of being and each demanding its particular sort of realization. More often than not it was economic and suchlike external factors that led certain people to break away from one form and attach themselves to another. But in the main it happened that each type looked for the social realization of its peculiarities in this particular form and, on the whole, found it there. And not only was each form based on a definite type, it moulded and keeps on moulding this type. It was and is intent on developing it; the constitution, organization and educational system of each form are—no matter how consciously or unconsciously—dedicated to this end. Thus something has been produced which is essentially different from all the social experiments that have ever been made: not a laboratory where everybody works for himself, alone with his problems and plans, but an experimental station where, on common soil, different colonies or "cultures" are tested out according to different methods for a common purpose.

Yet here, too, a problem emerged, no longer within the individual group but in the relation of the groups to one another; nor did it come from without, it came from within—in fact, from the very heart of the principle of freedom.

Even in its first undifferentiated form a tendency towards federation was innate in the Kvuza, to merge the Kvuzoth in some higher social unit; and a very important tendency it was, since it showed that the Kvuza implicitly understood that it was the cell of a newly structured society. With the splitting off and proliferation of the various forms, from the semi-individualistic form which jealously guarded personal independence in its domestic economy, way of life, children's education, etc., to the pure Communistic form, the single unit was supplanted by a series of units in each of which a definite form of colony and a more or less definite human type constituted itself on a federal basis. The fundamental assumption was that the local groups would combine on the same principle of solidarity and mutual help as reigned within the individual group. But the trend towards a larger unit is far from having atrophied in the process. On the contrary, at least in the Kibbuz or Collectivist Movement, it asserts itself with great force and clarity; it recognizes the federative Kibbuzim—units where the local groups have pooled their various aspirations—as a provisional structure; indeed, a thoughtful leader of their movement calls them a substitute for a Commune of Communes. Apart from the fact, however, that individual forms, especially, for instance, the "Moshavim" or semi-individualistic Labour Settlements—though these do not fall short of any of the other forms in the matter of communal economic control and mutual help—are already too far removed from the basic form to be included in a unitary plan, in the Kibbuz Movement itself subsidiary organizations stand in the way of the trend towards unification which wants to embrace and absorb them. Each has developed its own special character and consolidated it in the unit, and it is natural that each should incline to view unification as an extension of its own influence. But something else has been added that has led to an enormous intensification of this attitude on the part of the single units: political development. Twenty years ago a leader of one of the big units could say emphatically: "We are a community and not a Party." This has radically changed in the meantime, and the conditions for unification have been aggravated accordingly. The lamentable fact has emerged that the all-important attitude of neighbourly relationship has not been adequately developed, although not a few cases are on record of a flourishing and rich village giving generous help to a young and poor neighbour which belonged to another unit. In these circumstances the great struggle that has broken out on the question of unification, particularly in the last decade, is the more remarkable. Nobody who is a Socialist at heart can read the great document of this struggle, the Hebrew compilation entitled *The Kibbuz and the Kvuza,* edited by the late labour leader Berl Kaznelson, without being lost in admiration of the high-minded passion with which these two camps battled with one another for genuine unity. The union will probably not be attained save as the outcome of a situation that makes it absolutely necessary. But that the men of the Jewish Communes have laboured so strenuously with one another and against one another for the emergence of a *communitas communi-*

tatum, that is to say, for a structurally new society—this will not be forgotten in the history of mankind's struggle for self-renewal.

I have said that I see in this bold Jewish undertaking a "signal non-failure". I cannot say: a signal success. To become that, much has still to be done. Yet it is in this way, in this kind of tempo, with such setbacks, disappointments, and new ventures, that the real changes are accomplished in this our mortal world.

But can one speak of this non-failure as "signal"? I have pointed out the peculiar nature of the premises and conditions that led to it. And what one of its own representatives has said of the Kvuza, that it is a typically Palestinian product, is true of all these forms.

Still, if an experiment conducted under certain conditions has proved successful up to a point, we can set about varying it under other, less favourable, conditions.

There can hardly be any doubt that we must regard the last war as the end of the prelude to a world crisis. This crisis will probably break out—after a sombre "interlude" that cannot last very long—first among some of the nations of the West, who will be able to restore their shattered economy in appearance only. They will see themselves faced with the immediate need for radical socialization, above all the expropriation of the land. It will then be of absolutely decisive importance *who* is the real subject of an economy so transformed, and who is the owner of the social means of production. Is it to be the central authority in a highly centralized State, or the social units of urban and rural workers, living and producing on a communal basis, and their representative bodies? In the latter case the remodelled organs of the State will discharge the functions of adjustment and administration only. On these issues will largely depend the growth of a new society and a new civilization. The essential point is to decide on the fundamentals: a re-structuring of society as a League of Leagues, and a reduction of the State to its proper function, which is to maintain unity; or a devouring of an amorphous society by the omnipotent State; Socialist Pluralism or so-called Socialist Unitarianism. The right proportion, tested anew every day according to changing conditions, between group-freedom and collective order; or absolute order imposed indefinitely for the sake of an era of freedom alleged to follow "of its own accord". So long as

Russia has not undergone an essential inner change—and to-day we have no means of knowing when and how that will come to pass—we must designate one of the two poles of Socialism between which our choice lies, by the formidable name of "Moscow". The other, I would make bold to call "Jerusalem".

INDEX

Acquisitive Society, The (Tawney), 41
"A.E.", 77
Anti-Dühring (Engels), 3, 4
Artel, the, 127–8, 142
Association of All Classes of All Nations, 22
Atelier, L', 67

Babeuf, 1, 31
Bakunin, 42, 44, 138
Bazard, 18, 19, 66
Bebel, August, 97
Benedict, St., 135
Berlin Party Congress (1892), 97
Bernstein, Eduard, 36, 94, 95
Blanc, Louis, 30, 35, 59, 67–9, 85
Buchez, 59, 60, 65–7, 69, 72, 89
Bukharin, 115

Cabet, 1, 59, 76
Caesarism and Christianity (Proudhon), 26
Capital (Marx), 90, 92, 93; Engels' reviews of, 4
Chaluzim, 143–4
Chaluziuth, 143–6
Chartists, 62
Christian Socialists, 70
Civil War in France, The (Marx), 86, 94, 102
Class War in France, The (Marx), 84
Communist Manifesto, 1–4, 19, 31, 84, 94, 102
Comte, Auguste, 26
Considérant, 19, 31
Co-operatives, 58 ff.; Marx and, 89; Lenin and, 119 ff.
Co-operator, The, 60–1
Copenhagen Congress (1910), 120
Critical Glosses (Marx), 82
Critique of Political Economy, A (Marx), 83, 88

De la Réorganisation de la Société Européenne (Saint-Simon), 21
"Dizzy with Success", 125
Dukhobors, 73, 141
Du Principe Fédératif (Proudhon), 25

Economic Contradictions or The Philosophy of Misery (Proudhon), 3, 4
Eighteenth Brumaire, The (Marx), 84
Enfantin, 26
Engels, 1–6, 9, 15, 23, 88–9, 94–7, 99–104

Erfurt Programme (1891), 97
Européen, L', 65
Evolution of Socialism from Utopia to Science (Engels), 3, 94

Fields, Factories and Workshops (Kropotkin), 45
Figgis, 40
Five Years of Russian Revolution (Lenin), 116
Fourier, 1–4, 6, 9, 11, 16, 18–21, 23, 26, 72
Fourierists, 1
Francis, St., 135

Geneva Congress (1866), 85
German Peasant War in 1850 (Engels), 6
Gide, Charles, 18, 65
Gierke, 14, 30, 39
Gotha Unification Programme, 89, 97
Guild Socialism, 78

Hanover Party Congress (1899), 98
Hegel, 10, 25
Heimann, Eduard, 11
Heppenheim Conference, 6, 15
History of the Co-operative Theories (Mladenatz), 63
Hobbes, 39–40
Holy Family, The (Marx and Engels), 4
Huber, Victor Aimé, 63
Hugo, Victor, 14

"Icaria", 59, 76
Inaugural Address to the International Workers' Association (Marx), 85
Infield, 140 n.

Kant, 25
Kaznelson, Berl, 147
Keller, Gottfried, 52
Kibbuz and the Kouza, The (Kaznelson), 147
Kibbuzim, 147
King, William, 59–62, 64, 66, 69, 72
Kireyewski, 38
Kropotkin, 13, 16–17, 38–46, 53, 55–6, 69, 73–4, 108, 127, 141
Kvuzoth, 142, 144, 146–8

Landauer, Gustav, 16–17, 40, 46–57, 108
Lassalle, 4, 30, 67, 85, 97
"League of Communists", 2

"League of the Just", 1, 2
Lenin, 94–5, 99 ff.
Leroux, Pierre, 128
Leviathan (Hobbes), 40
Liebknecht, Wilhelm, 96
List, Friedrich, 75

Magdeburg Party Congress (1910), 98
Maitland, 39
Manifeste des Égaux (Babeuf), 31
Manifesto of the Sixty, 31
Martov, 111
Marx, Karl, 1, 2, 4–5, 9–10, 12, 24, 31,
  44, 50, 81–104, 106–7, 110, 117, 125,
  138
Maynard, 126
Michelet, 35
Mladenatz, 63
Modern Science and Anarchy (Kropotkin),
  38, 74
Molotov, 125
More, Thomas, 9
Morgan, 92
Moshavim, 147
Mutual Aid (Kropotkin), 42

Naphtali, Fritz, 64
National Being, The ("A.E."), 77
New Harmony, 75
New View of Society, A (Owen), 21

On the Housing Question (Proudhon), 5
On the Jewish Question (Marx), 82
Oppenheimer, Franz, 71
Organization of Labour (Proudhon), 36
Owen, R., 1, 3, 6, 16, 19, 21–3, 26, 59,
  62, 72, 75, 123

Paris Commune, 86 ff., 102–4, 107–8
Pascal, 25
Philosophy of Progress (Proudhon), 26
Plato, 9
Political Capacity of the Working Classes
  (Proudhon), 31
Populists, 123
Proudhon, 1–5, 12–13, 16, 24–37, 41–4,
  48, 50, 52, 56, 63, 69, 86, 88, 117

Report on the Political Situation (Lenin),
  110
Report to the County of Lanark (Owen), 21

Revolution, The (Landauer), 51
Rochdale Pioneers, 59, 62 ff.
Rosenberg, Arthur, 108
Rosenzweig, Franz, 100
Russell, G. W., 77
Ryazanov, 90

Saint-Simon, 1, 3, 6, 16–18, 20, 21, 23,
  27, 32, 35, 65, 117
Schmitt, Karl, 40
Socialism from Faith, 6 n.
Socialist League (Landauer's), 55
Solon, 56 n.
Solution of the Social Problem, The
  (Proudhon), 28
Soviets, 106 ff.
Stalin, 100, 124, 125, 127
State and Revolution, The, 111
Stein, Lorenz von, 17
Stepuiak, 90
Stockjobbers' Handbook (Proudhon), 29
Système Industriel ((Saint-Simon), 20

Tawney, 41
Taxation in Kind (Lenin), 121
Théorie des Quatre Mouvements (Fourier),
  21
Theory of Taxation (Proudhon), 33
*Thesis on the Immediate Tasks of Soviet
  Authority* (Lenin), 115
Thompson, Wm., 69
Tillich, Paul, 11
Tönnies, 21, 65, 93
Traité d'Association Domestique Agricole
  (Fourier), 20
Trotsky, 106

Unamuno, 25
Union des associations fraternelles, 69

Webb, Beatrice, 70
Weber, Max, 41, 128
Weitling, 1
Whitman, Walt, 50
Will the Bolshevists Maintain Power?
  (Lenin), 111

Zasulitch, Vera, 90, 93–4
Zentrosoyus, 121, 124